Lecture Notes in Computer Science   10431

Commenced Publication in 1973
Founding and Former Series Editors:
Gerhard Goos, Juris Hartmanis, and Jan van Leeuwen

More information about this series at http://www.springer.com/series/7410

Christian Kraetzer · Yun-Qing Shi
Jana Dittmann · Hyoung Joong Kim (Eds.)

Digital Forensics
and Watermarking

16th International Workshop, IWDW 2017
Magdeburg, Germany, August 23–25, 2017
Proceedings

Editors
Christian Kraetzer
Department of Computer Science
Otto-von-Guericke University Magdeburg
Magdeburg
Germany

Yun-Qing Shi
Department of Electrical and Computer
  Engineering
New Jersey Institute of Technology
Newark, NJ
USA

Jana Dittmann
Department of Computer Science
Otto-von-Guericke University Magdeburg
Magdeburg
Germany

Hyoung Joong Kim
Graduate School Information Security
Korea University
Seoul
Korea

ISSN 0302-9743   ISSN 1611-3349   (electronic)
Lecture Notes in Computer Science
ISBN 978-3-319-64184-3   ISBN 978-3-319-64185-0   (eBook)
DOI 10.1007/978-3-319-64185-0

Library of Congress Control Number: 2017931057

LNCS Sublibrary: SL4 – Security and Cryptology

Printed on acid-free paper

This Springer imprint is published by Springer Nature
The registered company is Springer International Publishing AG
The registered company address is: Gewerbestrasse 11, 6330 Cham, Switzerland

Preface

The 16th International Workshop on Digital Forensics and Watermarking (IWDW 2017), hosted by the Advanced Multimedia and Security Lab (AMSL) of the Department of Computer Science, Otto von Guericke University Magdeburg, was held on the premises of the newly renovated "Haus des Handwerks" in Magdeburg, Germany, during August 23–25, 2017. The chosen venue is close to the place where Otto von Guericke first held his famous Magdeburg Hemispheres Experiment in the 17th century.

IWDW 2017, following the principles of the IWDW series, aimed at providing a technical program covering state-of-the-art theoretical and practical developments in the fields of digital watermarking, steganography and steganalysis, forensics and anti-forensics, visual cryptography, and other multimedia-related security issues. Among 48 submissions from Europe, Asia, and North America, the Technical Program Committee selected 30 papers for presentation and publication, including one paper for a best paper award. The selection was based on the reviews provided by 52 Program Committee members.

Besides the regular presentations, two special session were held: The first one ("Emerging threats of Criminal Use of Information Hiding: Usage Scenarios and Detection Approaches") was organized jointly with the Europol EC3 initiative CUING (Criminal Use of Information Hiding) and aimed to bring together academic and law-enforcement-related research on the application of steganography, covert channels, watermarking and other forms of information hiding in the context of cybercrime. The second special session ("Biometric Image-Tampering Detection") was co-organized by the German national research project ANANAS (Anomalie-Erkennung zur Verhinderung von Angriffen auf gesichtsbildbasierte Authentifikationssysteme: Anomaly Detection for the Prevention of Attacks Against Face Image-Based Authentication Systems), to address the challenging task of blind validation of biometric image authenticity. Here, detecting traces of illegitimate image editing and distinguishing them from traces of legitimate image editing was the major concern of this session, motivated by the fact that digital photographs have recently been actively used in machine-readable documents for the purpose of biometric identity verification, generating the risk of criminal intent to overcome automated recognition systems by image manipulation.

In addition to the paper presentations, the workshop featured two invited talks: One keynote "Applications of Natural Laws for Multimedia Security and Forensics," presented by Professor Anthony T.S. Ho (University of Surrey, UK) and an introductory talk for one of the special sessions, titled "Media Forensics and Trustworthiness of Biometric Images – An Industry Perspective" by Dr. Andreas Wolf (Principal Scientist Biometrics at Bundesdruckerei GmbH, Germany, and one of the German DIN experts delegated to the ISO/IEC JTC1 committees SC17, SC31, and SC37 as well as to the European Standards Committee CEN).

We wish to thank Springer for sponsoring a Best Paper Award for IWDW 2017. It was decided to be awarded to the paper with the title "Topological Data Analysis For Image Tampering Detection" by Aras Asaad and Sabah Jassim (The University of Buckingham, UK). As the reviewers pointed out for this paper, the application of Topological Data Analysis to media forensics done is still early stage work, but it opens a new and promising perspective in the field of media forensics. We feel that this novelty deserves to be awarded to encourage (especially young) researchers to step outside the well established routes.

We would like to thank all of the authors, reviewers, lecturers, and participants for their valuable contributions to IWDW 2017. Our sincere gratitude also goes to all the members of the Technical Program Committee, special session reviewers, and our local volunteers for their careful work and great efforts made in the wonderful organization of this workshop.

Finally, we hope that the readers will enjoy this volume and that it will provide inspiration and opportunities for future research.

August 2017

Christian Kraetzer
Yun-Qing Shi
Jana Dittmann
Hyoung Joong Kim

Organization

General Chairs

Jana Dittmann   Otto von Guericke University Magdeburg, Germany
Christian Kraetzer   Otto von Guericke University Magdeburg, Germany

Technical Program Chairs

Yun-Qing Shi   New Jersey Institute of Technology (NJIT), USA
Hyoung Joong Kim   Korea University, Korea

Organizing Chair

Silke Reifgerste   Otto von Guericke University Magdeburg, Germany

Technical Program Committee

Claude Delpha	Laboratoire des Signaux et Systèmes (L2S), CNRS – Centrale Supelec, Université Paris Sud, France
Yan Diqun	CKC Software Laboratory, Ningbo University, China
Jana Dittmann	Otto von Guericke University Magdeburg, Germany
Isao Echizen	National Institute of Informatics, Japan
Jiankun Hu	The University of New South Wales, Australia
Guang Hua	Huazhong University of Science and Technology, China
Fangjun Huang	Sun Yat-Sen University, China
Sabah Jassim	The University of Buckingham, UK
Xinghao Jiang	Shanghai Jiao Tong University, China
Ton Kalker	DTS, Inc., USA
Xiangui Kang	Sun Yat-Sen University, China
Mohan Kankanhalli	National University of Singapore, Singapore
Stefan Katzenbeisser	TU Darmstadt, Germany
Andrew Ker	University of Oxford, UK
Anja Keskinarkaus	University of Oulu, Finland
Hyoung Joong Kim	Korea University, Korea
Christian Kraetzer	Otto von Guericke University Magdeburg, Germany
Minoru Kuribayashi	Okayama University, Japan
Heung-Kyu Lee	Korea Advanced Institute of Science and Technology, Korea
Chang-Tsun Li	Charles Sturt University, Australia
Shenghong Li	Shanghai Jiaotong University, China
Feng Liu	Chinese Academy of Sciences, China

Zhe-Ming Lu	Zhejiang University, China
Bin Ma	Qilu University of Technology, Jinan, China
Wojciech Mazurczyk	Warsaw University of Technology, Institute of Telecommunications, Poland
Jiangqun Ni	Sun Yat-sen University, China
Rongrong Ni	Beijing Jiaotong University, China
Michiharu Niimi	Kyushu Institute of Technology, Japan
Akira Nishimura	Tokyo University of Information Sciences, Japan
Cecilia Pasquini	Universität Innsbruck, Austria
Tomas Pevny	Czech Technical University in Prague, Czech Republic
Alessandro Piva	University of Florence, Italy
Yong Man Ro	KAIST, Korea
Pascal Schoettle	Universität Innsbruck, Austria
Yun-Qing Shi	New Jersey Institute of Technology (NJIT), USA
Athanassios Skodras	University of Patras, Greece
Martin Steinebach	Fraunhofer Institute for Secure Information Technology, Germany
Krzysztof Szczypiorski	Warsaw University of Technology, Institute of Telecommunications, Poland
Claus Vielhauer	Brandenburg University of Applied Sciences, Germany
Sviatsolav Voloshynovskiy	University of Geneva, Switzerland
Steffen Wendzel	Worms University of Applied Sciences, Germany
Andreas Westfeld	University of Applied Sciences Dresden, Germany
Xiaotian Wu	Jinan University, China
James C.N. Yang	National Dong Hwa University, Taiwan
Xinpeng Zhang	Shanghai University, China
Xianfeng Zhao	Institute of Information Engineering, Chinese Academy of Sciences, China
Guopu Zhu	Shenzhen Institutes of Advanced Technology, Chinese Academy of Sciences, China

Special Session Reviewers for the CUING Special Session

Bernhard Fechner	FernUniversität Hagen, Germany
Sebastian Zander	Murdoch University, Australia
Jean-Francois Lalande	INSA Centre Val de Loire, France
Saffija Kasem-Madani	University of Bonn, Germany

International Publicity Liaisons

Ton Kalker	DTS, Inc., USA

Contents

Other Topics

Forensics

HEVC Double Compression Detection Based on SN-PUPM Feature

Qianyi Xu[1], Tanfeng Sun[1,2(✉)], Xinghao Jiang[1,2], and Yi Dong[1]

[1] School of Electronic Information and Electronic Engineering,
Shanghai Jiao Tong University, Shanghai, China
{qyxu.kristen, tfsun, xhjiang, aa44}@sjtu.edu.cn
[2] National Engineering Lab on Information Content Analysis Techniques,
GT036001, Shanghai, People's Republic of China

Abstract. During the process of video forgery detection, double compression is a significant evidence. A novel scheme based on the Sequence of Number of Prediction Unit of its Prediction Mode (SN-PUPM) is proposed to conduct double compression detection on videos under HEVC standard, together with estimation on GOP structures. Number of PU with three kinds of prediction mode (INTRA, INTER and SKIP) is firstly extracted from each frame inside a given video sequence. Then the SN-PUPM is calculated by Absolute Difference Values from adjacent three frames in original extracted features and filtered with Twice Averaging Filter to reduce noises induced by the process. Then, an initiative Abnormal Value Classifier is trained with SVM to label I-P frames and have a final sequence for double compression detection and GOP analysis. Nineteen original YUV sequences are adopted for dataset in experiments. Results have demonstrated better performance in HEVC double compression than previous method adapted to HEVC.

Keywords: HEVC · Double compression · First GOP detection · Sequence of number of PU of PM · Prediction mode

1 Introduction

For the time being, with rapid expansion of civil surveillance system, much attention has been drawn to video falsify and forgery detection. One of the most extraordinary distinctions of modified videos is double compression. Forgery of videos is commonly accomplished in non-compressed domain with binary code stream [1]. For video tampering process, decoder will first decompress the original videos that have been compressed from primitive YUV sequences, and then go through recompression procedure after alteration in frames [2].

Evident features could be extracted from double compressed videos to compare with one-compressed videos and that have been studied for years over several video encoding standard as MPEG and AVC. [3, 4] introduced parametric law for first digit distribution of Discrete Cosine Transform (DCT) coefficients in order to detect double compression in MPEG videos. Furthermore, Markov features constructed by

C. Kraetzer et al. (Eds.): IWDW 2017, LNCS 10431, pp. 3–17, 2017.
DOI: 10.1007/978-3-319-64185-0_1

computing abstracted quantized DCT coefficient into array is used for MPEG-4 recompression inspection [5] and Huber Markov Random Field (HMRF) is used to denote the compression noise characteristic [6]. In [7, 8], robust schemes for MPEG-4 and AVC detection are proposed by He et al. which combined block artifact and motion vector oriented mensuration with Variation of Prediction Footprint (VPF).

High Efficiency Video Coding (HEVC) is the newest video coding standard prepared by the Joint Collaborative Team on Video Coding [9]. After AVC has been fully developed, only a small number of studies have been found in HEVC double compression detection. In [10], number of 4*4 PU block are extracted from HEVC videos compressed with same Quantization Parameters for comparison. Based on researches of Wang [4], Huang et al. obtained statistical characteristics [11] and co-occurrence matrix [12] of DCT coefficients in videos with different QP to detect recompression. In order to enhance correctness of discrimination rates between first and double compression, second-order Markov matrix of transition probability is generated from DCT coefficients form samples [13]. However, some issues are not solved in this newly researched region. Prediction Modes in PU, together with residual coefficients have not been studied. Methods that show high efficiency in AVC are not tested in HEVC double compression.

In this paper, theory applied to AVC and MPEG detection presented by Vázquez-Padín et al. in [14] and analyzing method used by Chen et al. in [15] is partly adopted for double compression detection in HEVC. Due to the different coding scheme in HEVC and feature construction, performance of method proposed in [15] is evidently degraded. To overcome the limitation, a novel scheme is put forward in this paper based on distinction of the SN-PUPM (Sequence of Number of Prediction Unit on Prediction Mode) feature. The proposed scheme observes the abnormal and periodical peaks in the SN-PUPM in I-P frames (P-frame in double compressed videos after encoding I frame in first compression), compared with P-P frames (P-frames that are both P frames after first and second compression). This new feature can distinguish double compressed videos and can identify the first coding GOP size with high accuracies. Results of experiments have demonstrated that the proposed scheme for detection of HEVC double compression has better performance in detection on HEVC videos than method in [15].

The rest of this paper is organized as follows. Section 2 reviews unique features of I-P frames in double compression videos with diversified GOP size. The algorithm used in proposed scheme for detection is illustrated in Sect. 3, together with steps for feature construction and framework. In Sect. 4, results of experiments are shown and compared with former work to highlights the outstanding performance of the detection scheme. The conclusions and future work are summarized in Sect. 5.

2   Features Model of I-P Frames

Considering the video coding standard HEVC, three kinds of slices–Intra-coded frame (I-frame), Predictive-coded frame (P-frame) and B-frame (Bi-directionally predictive-coded frame) realize the integrity of the video. During the encoding procedure, frames will be grouped into GOPs, where GOP stands for group of pictures. Generally speaking, each GOP starts with an I-frame, followed by P-frames or B-frames or both. To simplify, B-frames are not included in testing videos by setting parameters in the HEVC codec to exclude B-frames. As can be concluded, the GOP size is referred as number of slices in a single GOP (one I-frame plus [(GOP size)-1] P frames). Let G1 and G2 denote the GOP size applied in first and second compression distinctively. In our scheme, G1 and G2 are different.

Difference of GOP size in two encoding process brings about the appearance of I-P frames. The procedure is demonstrated below in Fig. 1.

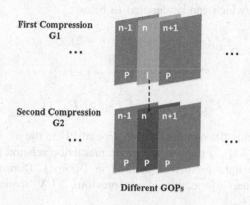

Fig. 1. Generation of I-P frames and P-P frames with different GOPs

There exist three main types of prediction mode in PU inside P-frames: intra-coded PU (I-PU), inter-coded PU (P-PU) skipped PU (S-PU). Number of each type of PU is extracted from the HEVC videos. Inside an I-P frame, a specific variation of the number of different PU coded as I-PU, P-PU and S-PU shows up compared to neighbor P-P frames. In videos that have gone through second encoding process with different GOP size, periodically low ebb in sequence of number of S-PU and P-PU, together with abrupt ascending in number of I-PU, is evidently visible in a cycle of the former GOP size in the place of novel I-P frames, which is later presented by graphs in Sect. 3.

This phenomenon could be explained as the differences in coding strategy in I-frames and P-frames, as Vázquez-Padín explained in [15]. Compared with fixed prediction macroblocks in AVC, size of PU could be changed during coding process with respect to its related I-frames in HEVC. Change of a P-PU or S-PU into an I-PU should be resulted from some blocks using INTRA coding that the motion vectors and bits inside blocks are intended for more information and better match with reference frames. Furthermore, change of a S-PU into a P-PU could be seen as follows: PU that skipped the prediction in the first compression uses neither the motion vector or residual coefficients to do the encoding process. Some slight changes would happen in PU when I-frames are compressed into P-frames and SKIP flags would be impossible to use, because of the requirements for references from other frames.

An original YUV sequence of length N could be denoted as:

$$YUV = \{D_1, D_2, \ldots, D_N\}, N \in \mathbb{Z}^+ \tag{1}$$

where D_n represents the coding source information included in the nth uncoded frame, $\mathbb{Z}^+$ represents the set of positive integers which could be used as the length of the sequence. Considered frames indexed from $(n - 1)$ to $(n + 1)$, number of S-PU, I-PU and P-PU in the nth frame is unified as $F_{PU}^i(n)$ (separately notified as $s(n)$, $i(n)$ and $p(n)$) for any type of the three. The nth frame is encoded as I-frame and others is encoded as P-frames, which can be denoted as below:

$$F_{PU}^i(n - 1) = \mathcal{M}(F_{PU}^i(n - 2), D_{n-1}) \tag{2}$$

$$F_{PU}^i(n) = \mathcal{I}(F_{PU}^i(n - 1), D_n) \tag{3}$$

$$F_{PU}^i(n + 1) = \mathcal{M}(F_{PU}^i(n), D_{n+1}) \tag{4}$$

where $F_{PU}^i(n)$ represents the number of each type of PU in the nth frame after the first compression $(i = 1)$; $\mathcal{M}(\cdot, \cdot)$ denotes the mode prediction scheme in P-frames, where $\mathcal{I}(\cdot, \cdot)$ represents the intra prediction method in I-frames. During the compression process of each frame, information inside previous YUV sequence is referred in operator $\mathcal{M}(\cdot, \cdot)$ or $\mathcal{I}(\cdot, \cdot)$.

The second compression need to be conducted based on the decompressed YUV sequence from first compressed videos. The nth frame (I-frame) would be encoded into P-frames and the others would be still compressed as P-frames and can be represented as:

$$F_{PU}^{i+1}(n - 1) = \mathcal{M}(F_{PU}^{i+1}(n - 2), D_{n-1}^i) \tag{5}$$

$$F_{PU}^{i+1}(n) = \mathcal{M}(F_{PU}^{i+1}(n - 1), D_n^i) \tag{6}$$

$$F_{PU}^{i+1}(n + 1) = \mathcal{M}(F_{PU}^i(n), D_{n+1}^i) \tag{7}$$

$$where \; D_j^i = \mathcal{T}(F_{PU}^i(j)), j \in [1, 2, \ldots, N] \tag{8}$$

where $F_{PU}^{i+1}(n)$ denotes the number of each type of PU in the nth frame after double compression; D_n^i represents the nth frame in the decoded YUV sequence, which is the transform of $F_{PU}^i(n)$ and can be represented by $\mathcal{T}(F_{PU}^i(n))$; $\mathcal{T}(\cdot, \cdot)$ represents the information transition function from HEVC to YUV.

Based on Eqs. (2)–(8), numbers of three types of PU in P-P frames of index $(n-1)$ and $(n + 1)$ can be described as follows:

$$F_{PU}^{i+1}(n - 1) = \mathcal{M}(F_{PU}^{i+1}(n - 2), \mathcal{T}(\mathcal{M}(F_{PU}^i(n - 2), D_{n-1}))) \tag{9}$$

$$F_{PU}^{i+1}(n + 1) = \mathcal{M}(F_{PU}^{i+1}(n), \mathcal{T}(\mathcal{M}(F_{PU}^i(n), D_{n+1}))) \tag{10}$$

and the nth frame, which has been encoded as I-P frame could seen its feature in second compression as below:

$$F_{PU}^{i+1}(n) = \mathcal{M}(F_{PU}^{i+1}(n-1), \mathcal{T}(\mathcal{J}(F_{PU}^i(n-1), D_n)))$$ (11)

SN-PUPM is thus generated by applying Eqs. (9)–(11) to all video frames.

$$F_{SU-PUPM} = \left\{\ldots, F_{PU}^{i+1}(n-1), F_{PU}^{i+1}(n), F_{PU}^{i+1}(n+1), \ldots\right\}$$ (12)

In Eq. (12), different patterns between the nth and its neighbor $(n-1)^{th}$ and $(n+1)^{th}$ frames could be obtained due to the mode prediction scheme used in first coding process. This model can be used to the detection of double compression in videos with coding standard.

3 Framework of Proposed Scheme

The framework of the proposed scheme in this paper is given in Fig. 2. For a given video, there are four steps to complete the whole detection process.

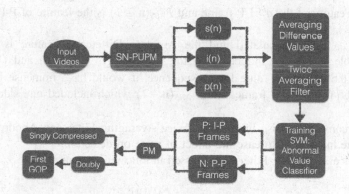

Fig. 2. Framework of proposed scheme

Step 1. Extraction of $F_{SU-PUPM}$
In the first step, $F_{SU-PUPM}$ is extracted from bitstream files directly during the video decompression procedure, which consists of number of S-PU $s(n)$, I-PU $i(n)$ and P-PU $p(n)$ (unified as f(n) in equations).

Step 2. Sequence Generation and De-noising
The original sequence extracted from N-length videos can not be used as direct detection feature because of noises and unusual values. Considered one more P-P frame

in the video sequences with index $(n - 2)$, it will have the following Eqs. (13)–(14) deducted from Eqs. (2)–(11), and thus having Eq. (15).

$$F_{PU}^i(n - 2) = \mathcal{M}(F_{PU}^i(n - 3), D_{n-2}) \tag{13}$$

$$F_{PU}^{i+1}(n - 2) = \mathcal{M}(F_{PU}^{i+1}(n - 3), D_{n-2}^i) \tag{14}$$

$$F_{PU}^{i+1}(n - 2) = \mathcal{M}(F_{PU}^{i+1}(n - 3), \mathcal{T}(\mathcal{M}(F_{PU}^i(n - 3), D_{n-2}))) \tag{15}$$

To demonstrate the differences between I-P frame and adjacent two P-P frames and make the feature more clearly to see, Absolute Difference Value is introduced between 3 adjacent frames, which can be calculated from Eqs. (2)–(15) as follows:

$$F_{ABS}(n - 1) = \Delta F_{PU}(n - 1)$$
$$= abs\left(F_{PU}^{i+1}(n - 1) - F_{PU}^{i+1}(n - 2)\right) + abs\left(F_{PU}^{i+1}(n - 1) - F_{PU}^{i+1}(n)\right) \tag{16}$$
$$F_{ABS}(n) = \Delta(n)$$

$$= abs\left(F_{PU}^{i+1}(n) - F_{PU}^{i+1}(n - 1)\right) + abs\left(F_{PU}^{i+1}(n) - F_{PU}^{i+1}(n + 1)\right) \tag{17}$$

where $abs(\cdot, \cdot)$ denotes the Absolute Value Function and $F_{ABS}(n)$ is the Absolute Difference Feature of the nth I-P frame and $F_{ABS}(n - 1)$ is the feature of P-P frame of index $(n - 1)$.

After $F_{ABS}(n)$ is calculated and the Absolute Difference Feature is obtained, non-negligible noises are induced into the sequence. In Eqs. (16) and (17), since $F_{PU}^{i+1}(n)$ is the abnormal value in the sequence, it would have immense impact on feature of the nearest P-P frames like $F_{ABS}(n - 1)$ which included one side effect of $F_{PU}^{i+1}(n)$.

To overcome this noise limitation, Twice Averaging Filter and Abnormal Value Classifier are introduced to ease the effect of noise on detection.

The Twice Averaging Filter is expressed in following equation:

$$F_{AF1}(n) = \frac{F_{ABS}(n)}{Q},$$

if $max(F_{ABS}(n), average(F_{ABS}(n - 1), F_{ABS}(n), F_{ABS}(n + 1))) = ave.$ (18)

$$F_{AF2}(n) = \frac{F_{AF1}(n)}{Q},$$

if $max(F_{AF1}(n), average(from\, F_{AF1}(n - 2)\, to\, F_{AF1}(n + 2))) = ave.$ (19)

where Q is the scaling parameter which is set to 10 after several optimal testing, $F_{AF2}(n)$ denotes the result of the Twice Averaging Filter.

Step 3. Classifier Training using SVM

After noise is almost eliminated from the feature sequence except some tiny peaks between intervals of general peaks, an Abnormal Value Classifier based on SVM is trained to classify the general peaks and remembered their indexes in the sequence. Kernel function used in SVM is Radial Basis Function (RBF), with maximum iterations of 20000. The classifier and indexes of I-P frames is denoted as:

$$Classifier\_AB = SVM(positive: P \ in \ 1^{st} \ \& \ PP \ in \ 2^{nd}, negative: IP) \qquad (20)$$

$$ID(sequence) = locate(sample \ labeled \ 1 \ in \ Classifier\_AB) \qquad (21)$$

Thus, according to the indexes, peak values without any noises are drawn from the filtered feature for double compression and further GOP detection.

$$F_{SEQ}(s(n), i(n), p(n)) = F_{AF2}(ID(sequence)) \qquad (22)$$

At this point, the final feature sequence $F_{SEQ}(n)$ has been obtained. This feature has three dimensions, for each single frame with 3 feature: $s(n), i(n), p(n)$. Figure 3(a1)–(a3) illustrate the multiple peaks in $F_{ABS}(n)$ at frames near I-P frames before filtering, while (b1)–(b3) and (c1)–(c3) show the effectiveness of de-noising and SVM classification. In Fig. 3(c1)–(c3), the periodic pattern could clearly be seen in the $F_{SEQ}(n)$, with period of the first encoding GOP size 15. The peaks appear every 15 frames inside the sequence and is exactly the period of the sequence without any noise. Considering the fact that the video is re-compressed with GOP size 33, the peak has its absence at frame numbered 165, which is the common multiple of 33 and 15, because frame 165 is encoded as I-frame in the second compression.

Step 4. Periodic Measurements

Based on the periodic analysis method used in [15], the PM method is introduced in this step to decide whether $F_{SEQ}(n)$ is from a doubly compressed video, and analyzes the first GOP size of the video. The possible GOP candidate set is derived from matching intervals between peaks in F_{SEQ} as follows:

$$.\mathbb{P}_{SEQ} = \{p \in \{2, \dots, N\}, \exists n_1, n_2 \in [1, N], GCD(n_1, n_2) = p, p < \frac{N}{5}\} \qquad (23)$$

where GCD is the Greatest Common Divisor utilized to generate candidate p and p should not be greater than one fifth of number of frames. The estimated GOP in first coding process could be calculated from the fitness value ϕ with possible GOP candidate set $\mathbb{P}_{SEQ}$:

$$\phi(p) = \sum_{n=kp} F_{SEQ}(n) - \sum_{m=kp} 0.3\max\{F_{SEQ}(n)\} - \max\{\sum_{k=0}^{N/v} F_{SEQ}(n)\} \qquad (24)$$

$$with \ k \in \left[0, \frac{N}{p}\right], n \in \mathbb{P}_{SEQ}, m \ not \ in \ \mathbb{P}_{SEQ}, v \in [1, p-1] \qquad (25)$$

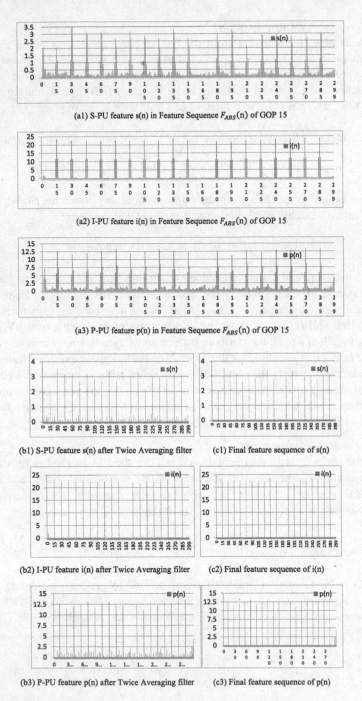

(a1) S-PU feature s(n) in Feature Sequence F_{ABS}(n) of GOP 15

(a2) I-PU feature i(n) in Feature Sequence F_{ABS}(n) of GOP 15

(a3) P-PU feature p(n) in Feature Sequence F_{ABS}(n) of GOP 15

(b1) S-PU feature s(n) after Twice Averaging filter

(c1) Final feature sequence of s(n)

(b2) I-PU feature i(n) after Twice Averaging filter

(c2) Final feature sequence of i(n)

(b3) P-PU feature p(n) after Twice Averaging filter

(c3) Final feature sequence of p(n)

Fig. 3. Feature sequences obtained through 4 steps.

Then a threshold with $\phi(p)$ should be generated to compare and classify whether the sequence is from doubly compressed video. The feature sequence $F_{SEQ}(n)$ is determined from re-compressed video as $\phi(p)$ is greater than the threshold. The estimated GOP size of first coding process is thus:

$$\hat{G}_1 = \arg max\phi(p) \tag{26}$$

4 Experiments and Analysis

4.1 Data Setup

The dataset for the experiment is built with 19 original YUV sequences (*aspen, controlled burn, crowd run, ducks take off, in to tree, old town cross, park joy, pedestrian area, red kayak, rush field cuts, rush hour, snow mnt, speed bag, station2, sunflower, touchdown pass, tractor (2), west wind easy*). All the videos are shot with natural scenes, as some animations YUV are erased because they may have different situations from natural scenes. All the sequences above are used for dissection of 300 frames for one YUV sequence. Furthermore, the pixel format for 19 sequences is set as YUV420P. During the first compression by codec X265.exe, 4 different types of GOP size and bitrates are involved. After decompression, 304 one-compression YUV sequences have been obtained and GOP size will be changed during second encoding process, thus 4864 double compression videos are produced. Numbers of INTRA or INTER PRED mode are extracted during the first and second decompression with HM16.15 TAppDecoder.exe. Since some YUV sequences contains shot cuts from one scene to another, which leads to unexpected data rise or drop in $F_{SU-PUPM}$ and impact the feature de-noising, videos are separated into video groups without scene cuts and groups with scene cuts.

Details of parameters in sequences and videos, together with parameters in experiments could be seen in Table 1.

4.2 Comparison Experiment

AUC (area under the Receiver Operating Characteristic (ROC) curves) is used to illustrate the performance of a binary classifier system as the discrimination threshold is varied. $F_{SU-PUPM}$ is of three dimensions and experiments are conducted 40 times, thus average AUC can be seen in Table 2. Also, with re-encoded videos, GOP precision of *3584 videos without scene cuts* is demonstrated in Table 2.

In Table 2, considering the average AUC, proposed method is 0.0219 higher than Chen's method and 0.0397 higher than Vázquez-Padín's method. In AVC double compression detection of [15], Chen's method achieves AUC of 0.9306 regarding double AVC compression, which is degraded by 0.0199 in HEVC detection. This could be explained as below:

Table 1. Parameters description for the dataset of double compressed videos

Parameters	First encoding	Second encoding
Encoder	X265	X265
Decoder	HM16.15	HM16.15
YUV sequence number	14 (no scene cuts); 5 (with scene cuts)	224 (no scene cuts); 5 (with scene cuts)
Resolution of sequence	1920 × 1080	1920 × 1080
Bitrate (Mb/s)	{8, 10, 20, 50}	{8, 10, 20, 50}
GOP size	{10, 15, 30, 50}	{9, 17, 33, 50}
HEVC sequence number	224 (no scene cuts); 80 (with scene cuts)	3584(no scene cuts); 1280(with scene cuts)
Number in AUC	224	224
SVM classifier	Positive: I-P frames; Number: 7908 random selected from 3584 videos Negative: P-P frames; Number: 7908 random selected from 3584 videos	
SVM kernel function SVM maximum iteration	Radial Basis Function (RBF) 15000	

Table 2. Performance comparison in double compression detection

Transcoding process	Proposed	Chen's method	Vázquez's method
Averaging AUC	**0.9226**	0.9107	0.8829
GOP precision	**89.82%**	85.65%	77.83%

1. HEVC has different coding strategy in PU with varied number of PU in each frame compared to fixed number in AVC. In V's method, the feature energy uses information in I-MB and S-MB to construct the feature not including P-MB, as sum of these three types of macroblock in frames are fixed, which result in changes in P-MB not as evident as $p(n)$ in our feature does.
2. In Chen's method, JSD of residual coefficients are proposed. This feature has great performance in AUC with 0.9107, as residual in frames is not linked to macroblocks, which is the advantage of it compared to V's method. However, it does not have the same efficiency under HEVC as AVC, since the coding strategy used in HEVC is more complex and make difference in distribution of residual not as evident as before. What's more, feature proposed has three dimensions and is more solid than feature in Chen's method.

In GOP precision, method proposed in this paper is 4.17% higher than method in [15], while method in [14] has worse performance of 11.99% than proposed method. It is proved that the feature with 3 dimensions is more effective than 1 dimension feature constructed with JSD of DCT residual coefficients in [15].

4.3 Performance Evaluation on Classification on I-P Frames and P-P Frames

As Eq. (20) demonstrating training process of the classifier explained in Sect. 3, details of SVM is shown in Table 1. Accuracies of classify (TP: True Positive; TN: True Negative; AR: Accuracy Rate) of I-P and P-P frames in 4864 videos on different GOP size is analyzed in Table 3.

Table 3. Classification accuracies of I-P frames and P-P frames on different GOP size

$G1$		9		17		33		50	
$/G2$	Frame	TP	AR	TP	AR	TP	AR	TP	AR
		TN	(%)	TN	(%)	TN	(%)	TN	(%)
10	I-P	**23/26**	92.59	**24/28**	93.98	**26/29**	95.00	**21/24**	96.27
	P-P	252/271		257/271		259/271		263/271	
15	I-P	**11/13**	93.53	**15/18**	93.20	**16/19**	94.67	**15/18**	94.31
	P-P	264/281		264/281		268/281		267/281	
30	I-P	**5/7**	94.30	**7/9**	94.67	**8/9**	96.00	**7/8**	93.98
	P-P	276/291		277/291		280/291		274/291	
40	I-P	**6/7**	94.33	**5/7**	93.00	**6/7**	95.33	**5/6**	95.32
	P-P	276/293		274/293		280/293		280/293	

In exact I-P frame location detection, it demonstrates TP accuracy of 25.54/29 (2 miss pred.) of GOP 10, 15.64/19 (3 miss pred.) of GOP 15, 7.22/9 (1 miss pred.) of GOP 30 and 5.78/7 (1 miss pred.) of GOP 40. It is because some P-P frames with abnormal values in videos with scene cuts are mistakenly predicted in SMV. The accuracy of I-P prediction still needs to be enhanced, but it is enough for GOP estimation. Prediction accuracy of P-P frames is in average 94.87%.

Averaging AR is 94.405%. When GOP combination is 10/9, the AR demonstrates the lowest rate of 92.59% because the I-P frame is close to the I frame of doubly compressed video and could be interfered by the averaging process done to I-frame. It has the highest accuracy of 96.00% in GOP 30/33 when there is no absence of I-P frames as the GCD(30,33) = 330 beyond the sequence length.

In conclusion, this method is of high accuracy in locating the I-P frames in double compression videos. It relies on the proposed feature $F_{SU-PUPM}$ with high distinction between I-P frame and P-P frame. $s(n)$ together with $i(n)$ and $p(n)$ provide the precision in this experiment.

4.4 Analyze on GOP Estimation with Video Scene Cuts

Scene cuts in videos could make motions have sudden variation, thus cause unusual peaks in $F_{SU-PUPM}$ and have impact on double compression detection. Performances of GOP estimation of 3584 doubly coded videos from 14 YUV that have no scene cuts and 1280 videos from 5 YUV that have scene cuts are illustrated separately in Tables 4 and 5.

14   Q. Xu et al.

Table 4. GOP estimation accuracy (bitrate combination) of 3584 videos with no scene cuts

B_1/B_2	Videos	8	10	20	50
8	Proposed	**94.67%**	**100%**	**100%**	**100%**
	[15]C's method	92.20%	99.55%	100%	100%
10	Proposed	**86.72%**	**93.75%**	**100%**	**100%**
	[15]C's method	80.14%	88.63%	99.55%	100%
20	Proposed	**80.48%**	85.50%	**92.41%**	**100%**
	[15]C's method	63.82%	**87.50%**	85.61%	100%
50	Proposed	**66.09%**	**72.02%**	**80.59%**	**79.91%**
	[15]C's method	54.01%	65.17%	79.66%	74.30%

Table 5. GOP estimation accuracy (bitrate combination) of 1280 videos with scene cuts

B_1/B_2	Videos	8	10	20	50
8	Proposed	**88.75%**	**97.50%**	**100%**	**100%**
	[15]C's method	76.25%	86.25%	98.75%	98.75%
10	Proposed	**75.00%**	**95.00%**	**98.75%**	**100%**
	[15]C's method	56.25%	77.50%	97.50%	98.75%
20	Proposed	**67.90%**	**73.75%**	**90.41%**	**98.75%**
	[15]C's method	51.25%	68.75%	81.25%	98.75%
50	Proposed	33.75%	43.75%	50. 00%	**61.25%**
	[15]C's method	**38.75%**	**47.50%**	**58.50%**	56.50%

For videos with no scene cuts, proposed method achieves accuracy of 89.50%, which is 3.87% higher than method in [15] (85.63%), almost consistent with result in Table 2. In proposed method, 100% accuracy could be obtained when bitrate of the second encoding process B_2 is higher than bitrate B_1 used in the first video compression. At bitrate combination of 50/8 Mb/s, Chen's method is almost noneffective with accuracy of only 54.01%, but proposed method has more valid accuracy of 66.09%.

In videos with scene cuts, proposed method shows accuracy of 79.66%, 5.60% higher than method from [15]. Data marked in red is the invalid prediction rate. When the second bitrate is smaller than first one, Chen's method has comparatively much worse performance with average of 53.13% (proposed 57.39%), with both methods lost their efficiency. This situation should have its origin in the hiding coding traces of first compression when there is lower second compression bitrates. Features extracted from videos with above bitrate combinations have more inconspicuous peaks due to the hiding traces, which will in turn harm the PM detection of GOP Size.

By compare Table 5 with Table 4, it is analyzed that scene cuts within videos could result in some unusual values and sudden rise in sequence, and thus degrade the performances of GOP estimation.

The overall average accuracies of two types of videos are 86.39% in proposed method and 82.38% in method of [15]. It is due to the fact that the method of Chen is designed for AVC and MPEG and has just one feature for each frame. When residual feature in frames becomes weaker in HEVC, residual feature become ineffective, especially when $B_1 > B_2$.

To sum up, proposed method demonstrates higher accuracies than method in [15]. Especially in videos with scene cuts, features in proposed method show more university and robustness in GOP estimation.

4.5 Analyze on Performance of Different Video Contents

The results of detection accuracy with 18 different video contents are shown in Fig. 4. Researches on different video contents are of great importance because movements in videos, together with speed the scene grows can substantially affect the performance of proposed scheme.

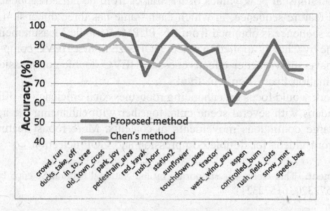

Fig. 4. GOP estimation accuracy with different video contents

In Fig. 4, the first 13 are without scene cuts while the last 5 have scene cuts. Comparatively, better performance of 4.30% can be seen for most videos with our proposed method with average of 86.28% than Chen's method with average of 81.98%, except for *red_kayak* (8.06% lower than Chen's) and *west_wind_easy* (10.17% lower than Chen's). Both methods show low efficiency in videos of *red_kayak* and *west_-wind_easy*, as they have rich texture and undergo severe variations in the videos. Large prediction could be introduced and P-frames rely heavily on reference frames, which make feature sequences have unpredictable and irregular peaks. But this would not influence the residual based method in [15]. Hence, future work could be focused on combined the residual coefficients in feature to enhance accuracies in videos above.

Notice that for videos *pedestrian_area* and *tractor*, performances of proposed method improve about 11% and 15% separately compared with Chen's method. The method is steady when the video shot is slow in motion.

In videos with shot cuts, method proposed achieves accuracy of 79.48% and is 5.63% higher than method in [15], especially in *aspen* (5.19% higher than Chen's), because *aspen* have 6 switches of scenes during the sequence and this contributes to the low efficiency rate of GOP detection in Chen's method.

In conclusion, in comparison of the two schemes, as the unique coding pattern in HEVC, the GOP estimation performance of proposed scheme performs better accuracies of 4.02% higher than Chen's method.

5 Conclusions

In this paper, a novel scheme for detection of double compression videos encoded under HEVC standard is proposed. The proposed feature SN-PUPM regarding each type of PU (S-PU, I-PU, P-PU) has the capability in differentiating the special features in P-P frames and I-P frames. Absolute Difference Values of SN-PUPM are analyzed to make distinction clearer, while Twice Averaging Filter is utilized to reduce noises imported by former operations. This method also uses SVM to train a special classifier, which can label unusual peak values of I-P frames from de-noised sequences and thus have the final feature sequence, in which each frame has three dimension of features. As the feature sequence is obtained from SN-PUPM, Periodic Measurements based on general scheme by Chen is applied to detect GOP Size in first HEVC compression. The experiments have shown better effectiveness in HEVC double compression detection and GOP estimation than Chen's method.

Further work would focus on enhancing robustness and efficiency in different video contents or videos with several scene cuts, together with enhancing the accuracies of videos with large continuous movements in contents. More robust feature could be constructed from videos for double compression and GOP detection.

Acknowledgement. This work was supported by the National Natural Science Foundation of China (No. 61572320, 61572321).

References

1. Al-Sanjary, O., Sulong, G.: Detection of video forgery: a review of literature. J. Theor. Appl. Inf. Techn. **74**(2), 207–220 (2015)
2. Milani, S., Fontani, M., et al.: An overview on video forensics. In: Asian-Pacific Signal and Information Processing Association, APSIPA 2012, Hollywood, CA, USA, vol. 1(1), pp. 1229–1233, 3–6 December 2012
3. Chen, W., Shi, Y.Q.: Detection of double MPEG compression based on first digit statistics. In: International Workshop on Digital Watermarking, IWDW 2008, Busan, Korea, Selected Papers. DBLP, pp. 16–30, 10–12 November 2008
4. Sun, T.F., Wang, W., Jiang, X.H.: Exposing video forgeries by detecting MPEG double compression. In: 2012 IEEE International Conference on Acoustics, Speech and Signal Processing, ICASSP 2012, Kyoto, Japan, pp. 1389–1392. IEEE, 25–30 March 2012
5. Jiang, X.H., Wang, W., Sun, T.F., Shi, Y.Q., Wang, S.: Detection of double compression in MPEG-4 videos based on Markov statistics. IEEE Signal Process. Lett. **20**(5), 447–450 (2013)
6. Ravi, H., Subramanyam, A., Gupta G., Kumar, B.A.: Compression noise based video forgery detection. In: 2014 IEEE International Conference on Image Processing, ICIP 2014, Paris, France, pp. 5352–5356. IEEE, 27–30 October 2014

7. He, P., Sun, T., Jiang, X., Wang, S.: Double compression detection in mpeg-4 videos based on block artifact measurement with variation of prediction footprint. In: Huang, D.-S., Han, K. (eds.) ICIC 2015, Part III. LNCS, vol. 9227, pp. 787–793. Springer, Cham (2015). doi:10.1007/978-3-319-22053-6_84

8. He, P.S., Jiang, X.H., Sun, T.F., Wang, S.: Double compression detection based on local motion vector field in staticbackground videos. J. Vis. Commun. Image Represent. **35**, 55–66 (2016)

9. Sullivan, G., Ohm, J., Han, W., et al.: Overview of the high efficiency video coding (HEVC) standard. IEEE Trans. Circ. Syst. Video Technol. **22**(12), 1649–1668 (2012)

10. Jia, R.S., Li, Z.H., Zhang, Z.Z., Li, D.D.: Double HEVC compression detection with the same QPs based on the PU numbers. In: ITM Web of Conferences, ITA 2016, vol. 7, p. 02010 (2016)

11. Huang, M.L., Wang, R.D., Xu, J., et al.: Detection of double compression in HEVC videos based on the statistical characteristic of DCT coefficient. Guangdianzi Jiguang/J. Optoelectron. Laser **26**(4), 733–739 (2015)

12. Huang, M., Wang, R., Xu, J., Xu, D., Li, Q.: Detection of double compression for hevc videos based on the co-occurrence matrix of DCT coefficients. In: Shi, Y.-Q., Kim, H.J., Pérez-González, F., Echizen, I. (eds.) IWDW 2015. LNCS, vol. 9569, pp. 61–71. Springer, Cham (2016). doi:10.1007/978-3-319-31960-5_6

13. Huang, M.L., Wang, R.D., Xu, J., Xu, D.W., Li, Q.: Detection of double compression based on optimization of Markov features for HEVC videos. In: Proceeding of 12th China Information Hiding Workshop, CIHW 2015, Wuhan, China, pp. 475–481, 28–29 March 2015

14. Vazquez-Padin, D., Fontani, M., Bianchi, T., Comesana, P., Piva, A., Barni, M.: Detection of video double encoding with GOP size estimation. In: IEEE International Workshop on Information Forensics and Security, WIFS 2013, Guangzhou, China, vol. 2, pp. 151–156. IEEE, 18–21 November 2013

15. Chen, S., Sun, T.F., Jiang, X.H., He, P.S., Wang, S.L., Shi, Y.Q.: Detecting double H.264 compression based on analyzing prediction residual distribution. In: Shi, Y.Q., Kim, H.J., Perez-Gonzalez, F., Liu, F. (eds.) IWDW 2016. LNCS, vol. 10082, pp. 61–74. Springer, Cham (2017). doi:10.1007/978-3-319-53465-7_5

Towards Automated Forensic Pen Ink Verification by Spectral Analysis

Michael Kalbitz[1,2]($\boxtimes$), Tobias Scheidat[1,2], Benjamin Yüksel[1],
and Claus Vielhauer[1,2]

[1] Department of Informatics and Media,
University of Applied Sciences Brandenburg,
Magdeburger Str. 50, 14770 Brandenburg an der Havel, Germany
`michael.kalbitz@th-brandenburg.de`
[2] Faculty of Computer Science, Otto-von-Guericke-University Magdeburg,
Universitätsplatz 2, 39106 Magdeburg, Germany

Abstract. Handwriting analysis plays an important role in crime scene forensics. Tasks of handwriting examination experts are for example identification of the originator of a given document, decision whether a signature is genuine or not, or to find strokes added to an existing writing in hindsight. In this paper we introduce the application of an UV–VIS–NIR spectroscope to digitize the reflection behavior of handwriting traces in the wavelength range from 163 nm to 844 nm (from ultraviolet over visible to near infrared). Further we suggest a method to distinguish ink of different pens from each other. The test set is build by 36 pens (nine different types in four colors each). From the individual strokes feature vectors are extracted which allows for a balanced classification accuracy of 96.12% using L1-norm and 95.26% for L2-norm.

Keywords: Handwriting forensics · Spectral analysis · Ink determination

1 Introduction

Handwriting still plays an important role in criminal forensics. Besides the question of who wrote a given document, there is also the question of whether some text or strokes were subsequently added with a different pen or ink. In forensic cases, such alterations are typically found in fabricated testaments or bank transfer forms.

Non-destructive examination is important for forensic work, since multiple investigations, of the same relevant substrate material, are often needed. In some cases, for example, a document must be examined for fingerprints after the handwriting analysis has been completed. Some conventional investigations, however, modify the evidence by physical or chemical treatment. That means that the investigation is partly destructive in nature. To address this drawback, there has been increasing interest in using surface scanning for forensic analysis in the digital domain.

© Springer International Publishing AG 2017
C. Kraetzer et al. (Eds.): IWDW 2017, LNCS 10431, pp. 18–30, 2017.
DOI: 10.1007/978-3-319-64185-0_2

While much research in forensics deals with the integrity and authenticity of digital media, there is also the question of whether digital representation might actually improve forensic investigation. Hildebrandt et al. [4], for example, show that a spectroscopic scan can make latent fingerprints visible. Another benefit of this approach is that it is possible to do both fingerprint and handwriting investigations with one scan.

In this paper, we propose a new method for ink verification in forensic documents by means of automated spectral analysis and classification. We introduce a new method based on the gradients of the spectral power histogram, present our first results of intra-class as well as inter-class feature distribution, and threshold-based classification.

This paper is structured as follows: Sect. 2 provides an overview of related work. The proposed process pipeline is described in Sect. 3. Detailed descriptions of the test set and the evaluation are presented in Sect. 4. Section 5 includes a short conclusion and the prospects for future work.

2 Related Work

To decide whether a handwritten document has been modified, it is important to be able to classify the writing instrument used, and identify handwriting strokes that have been added at a later date to an existing writing trace. In [7] Silva et al. present a method based on linear discriminant analysis to classify different types and brands of pens (five brands of ballpoint, two brands of roller ball, and three brands of gel). Here, data is acquired by an infrared spectroscope. The authors report correct recognition of type and brand in 99.5% and 100% of the test cases, respectively. These are good results, but at the described approach, the forensic expert has to define the measure points manually. In [3], Denman et al. use Time-of-Flight Secondary Ion Mass Spectroscopy for non-destructive analysis of organic and inorganic ink components. Their recognition rates for organic components and inorganic components were 84.4% and 91.1%, respectively.

An overview of typical components found in pen inks is given in [6]. Here, the author explains that pastes for ballpoint pens are still the most commonly used inks, but that there are some interesting alternatives, such as those used for roller handle or gel pens. In [5], the authors classify black gel pens and propose methods for estimating the age of a written document. In [2], Adam et al. investigate 25 black ballpoint pens from the UK market. They propose a principal component analysis to identify specific inks. Most of these approaches, however, are based on chemical investigations of the ink in question, and some are invasive in nature. Our question remains: is chemical knowledge of an ink really needed to verify or identify it?

The handwriting probes for our experimental evaluation were acquired using a UV–VIS–NIR spectroscope [1] (hereafter *UV–VIS–NIR*). Here, UV stands for ultra–violet radiation, VIS stands for visible light, and NIR stands for near infrared radiation. This industrial surface examination sensor can capture luminance values at 2048 discrete levels for wavelengths between 163 nm and 844 nm, that is, for wavelengths in the ultraviolet, visible, and near infrared ranges. The measurement of each single point results in 2048 values, one for each discrete level within the wavelength range provided by UV–VIS–NIR. The results between 163 nm and 200 nm, however, are quite noisy, due to oxygen absorption of the ultraviolet radiation.

3   Methodology

The Methodology is based on a four-step processing pipeline introduced by Vielhauer in [8]. The processing pipeline is shown in Fig. 1, and described in the following subsections in context of the suggested methodology.

Fig. 1. Processing pipeline

3.1   Data Acquisition

With best knowledge of the authors, there is no public test database available, containing spectral information of different inks. By this reason, an appropriate testset was created. For preparation of handwriting traces we use 9 types of pens with four color instances each (blue, black, red, green). A list of all 36 pens is given in Table 1. Since we do not need complete handwriting traces to determine the used ink, the probes are simplified to a single stroke of approximately 5 mm per pen on white copy paper ($80\,g/m^2$).

Table 1. List of inks in our test set

Pen id	Brand id	Type	Color
1	1	Ballpoint pen	Blue, black, red, green
2	2	Four color ballpoint pen	
3	3	Ballpoint pen	
4	4	Gel rollerball	
5	4	Liquid ink rollerball	
6	4	Fineliner	
7	4	Fibre tip-pen	
8	5	Liquid gel pen	
9	6	Four color ballpoint pen	

During acquisition, each stroke is measured by the UV–VIS–NIR. We use a scan area of $2.8 \times 1.6\,\text{mm}^2$ with a dot distance of $100\,\mu\text{m}$ and an integration time of $300\,\text{ms}$. This means, in total we obtain $28 \times 16 = 448$ measure points per stroke. For each measure point the sensor provides a vector of 2048 entries, each of them represents the reflection power in one of 2048 wavelength bins $w0, \ldots, w2047$. The structure of the UV–VIS–NIR data is shown in Fig. 2.

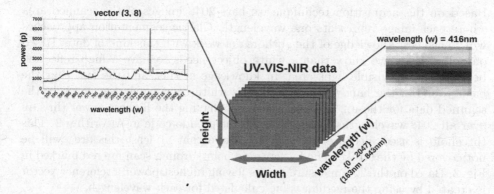

Fig. 2. Structure of the sensor data: for each of the stroke samples (right), 28/16 measurement points in width/height respectively (middle) are taken. For each point, the wavelength response is provided as a power histogram of 2048 wavelength bands (left).

3.2 Pre-processing

The aim of the pre-processing is to extract measure points which contain parts of the stroke. Figure 3 show the suggested pre-processing chain. We identified five steps for our pre-processing:

1. remove measurement drop-outs
2. built a reference vector
3. normalize the wavelength
4. extract writing trace
5. export data

The measurement drop-outs addressed in the first step occur, if the reflected energy is considered insufficiently low by the sensor. In Fig. 3 such errors are the black pixels in the image on top. If drop-out occur, this values are replaced by the median for each wavelength (of the 2048) from the neighbors of this measure point. The pseudo code for this step is given in Algorithm 1.

The second step is to built a reference vector. Therefore it is needed to determine which measure points are background (white paper) and which are foreground (ink of stroke). The reference vector represents for each wavelength the reflection behavior of the used lamp and the carrier material.

Algorithm 1. Remove measure errors

---

  for all mp in measure–points **do**
    if norm(mp) == 0 **then**
      $mp \leftarrow$ median–from–neighbors(mp)
    end if
  end for

Based on this acquisition technique we have 2048 images of the scanned area where each image represents one wavelength. Classic segmentation approaches will to the best knowledge of the authors not work with this kind of data. Based on color theory we know that a white object needs to have a high reflection behavior in the visible light area. In knowledge of this, and the fact that the background of the handwriting samples is white copy paper we search in the scanned data for those 20% measured points having the highest power (in sum over all 2048 wavelengths) as shown with the pseudo-code in Algorithm 2. This threshold is used, because we want to ensure that at least this area will be not covered by the stroke. The background points from a scan are red marked in Fig. 3. Based on the 20% measure points having highest power a reference vector is created by using the median value calculated for each wavelength.

Algorithm 2. Background detection

---

  smp $\leftarrow$ sort–by–max–norm(measure–points)
  smp20 $\leftarrow$ get–first–20–percent–entries(smp)
  for i = 0; i < count–wavelength; i++ **do**
    reference–vector(i) $\leftarrow$ get–median–over–all–entries(smp20, i)
  end forreturn reference–vector

The third step is to normalize the wavelengths for each measure point, based on the reference wavelengths. This will be done by division of each measure point by the reference background value at the same wavelength. After normalisation, we observe normalized wavelength response values in the range of 0.18 to 1.16, former they are in a range of 642 to 7806. An example for a normalised measure point is shown in the middle of Fig. 3. Tests with different normalization methods such as min max mapped to $[0\ldots1]$ does not show significant changes of the contribution of the latter computed distances.

The fourth step extract the relevant measure points from the handwriting strokes. With the knowledge that our acquired stroke has 28 columns (as shown in Fig. 2) an iteration from left to right combined with a search for the measure point having the highest power is carried out. The selected measure points from the stroke are also red marked in the lower portion of Fig. 3.

In the fifth step the relevant measure points are exported to a csv–file. This was done to decrease the processing time of the feature extraction. Thus, there are 28 vectors for each of the 36 strokes. An exemplary file is shown in the bottom of Fig. 3. In the first column is a index, the second column contains the

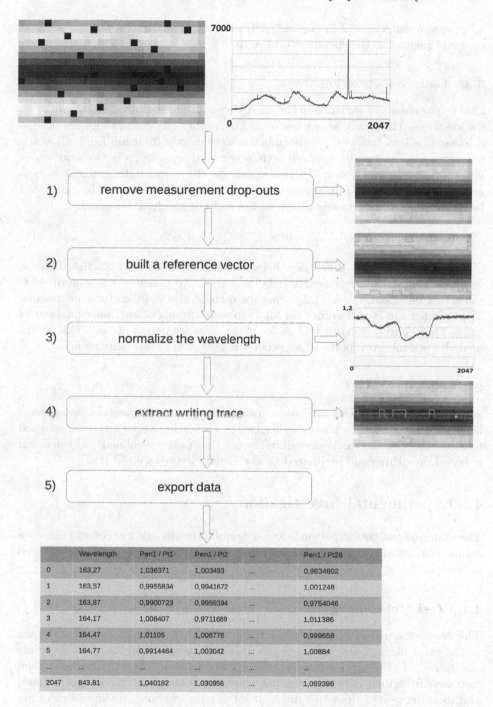

Fig. 3. Pre-Processing approach on the example of pen 1. From top to bottom: raw data, pre-processing steps with interim results, pre-processing result. Measure points, which are detected in the single steps, are marked with a red border. (Color figure online)

specific wavelength, and in the last (28) columns are the values of the selected measure points for the specific wavelength.

3.3 Feature Extraction

Due to the observed variance in the energy response of the wavelength bands, we decide to use the gradients as features. To simplify the calculation, we assume a linear gradient between two neighbored wavelengths by using Eq. 1. In which w_{i-1}/p_{i-1} is the previous wavelength/power and w_{i+1}/p_{i+1} is the next wavelength/power in the vector. In this approach, the wavelength gradient is estimated by a numerical differentiation. The exact gradient can not be calculated because we have only values of a function and not the function itself.

$$m = \frac{p_{i-1} - p_{i+1}}{w_{i-1} - w_{i+1}} \tag{1}$$

To determine the difference between two measure points, the distance between this vectors is calculated by means of the absolute value norm (*L1-norm*) or euclidean-norm (*L2-norm*) for each of the 2048 vector components. This comparison is carried out for all 28 measure points of any individual stroke (intra class comparison) as well as for all 28 measure points of one single stroke against each measure point of all other strokes (inter class comparison).

3.4 Classification

The classification of the suggested methodology is a verification based on a binary decision that decides whether two given feature vectors can be assigned to the same class (intra class, verified) or not (inter class, declined). The decision is based on a threshold estimated by the Equal Error Rate (EER).

4 Experimental Investigation

The experimental investigation is focused on the classification accuracy. The data acquisition, pre-processing, and feature extraction are carried out as described in Sect. 3.

4.1 Test Methodology

The test set consists of 36 strokes written using 9 different pen types (each in the color black, blue, red, and green). From every stroke 28 measure points are extracted. This procedure results in 1008 measure points. For the evaluation we distinguish between measure points from the same stroke (intra class) and measure points from two different strokes (inter class). Since distances are determined, we treat the comparisons symmetrically, i.e. when measure point 1 has been compared to point 2, we do not need to compare 2 to 1 again. The comparisons are based on L1-norm, and L2-norm. The procedure of intra class

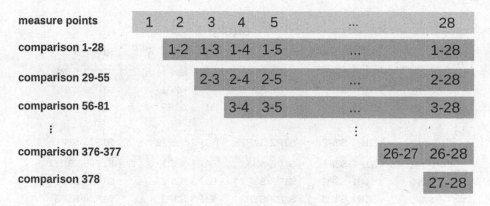

Fig. 4. Intra test method for one stroke

comparisons is shown in Fig. 4. We compare each measure point from a stroke which each other measure point from the same stroke. The number of resulting comparisons (c) for the complete intra test can be calculated by Eq. 2 where p is the number of used pens (36), and n is the number of extracted measure points (28).

$$c = p * \frac{n * (n - 1)}{2} \tag{2}$$

For the intra test 378 comparisons are made per stroke or a total of 13 608 comparisons. The method for the inter class comparison is illustrated in Fig. 5. Here, we compare each measure point of each stroke with each measure point of all other strokes. That means 980 comparisons for each measure point (28 measure points $*$ 35 pens). Overall the amount on comparisons for the inter class test can be calculated with the formula 3 where p is the number of used pens (36), n is the number of extracted measure points (28), and *intra* is the number of intra test comparisons. This means over all we made 493 920 inter class comparisons.

$$c = \frac{p * n * (p * n - 1)}{2} - intra \tag{3}$$

The distribution (over all comparisons) for L1-norm and L2-norm are shown in Figs. 6 and 7.

4.2   Evaluation

Based on the distribution of the distances for intra and inter classes we calculate FMR and FNMR for different threshold which map all occurring distances. The plots are shown in Fig. 8 for L1-norm and Fig. 9 for L2-norm. FMR means False Match Rate that happen if the distance is less than the selected threshold but it is not in the same class. FNMR means False None Match Rate that happens if the distance is greater than the threshold but is in the same class. The intersection

stroke 1

	S1P1	S1P2	S1P3	...	S1P28
S2P1	S1P1-S2P1	S1P2-S2P1	S1P3-S2P1	...	S1P28-S2P1
S2P2	S1P1-S2P2	S1P2-S2P2	S1P3-S2P2	...	S1P28-S2P2
S2P3	S1P1-S2P3	S1P2-S2P3	S1P3-S2P3	...	S1P28-S2P3
...	...	...	...	...	...
S2P28	S1P1-S2P28	S1P2-S2P28	S1P3-S2P28	...	S1P28-S2P28
S3P1	S1P1-S3P1	S1P2-S3P1	S1P3-S3P1	...	S1P28-S3P1
S3P2	S1P1-S3P2	S1P2-S3P2	S1P3-S3P2	...	S1P28-S3P2
S3P3	S1P1-S3P3	S1P2-S3P3	S1P3-S3P3	...	S1P28-S3P3
...	...	...	...	...	...
S3P28	S1P1-S3P28	S1P2-S3P28	S1P3-S3P28	...	S1P28-S3P28
⋮	⋮	⋮	⋮	⋮	⋮
S36P1	S1P1-S36P1	S1P2-S36P1	S1P3-S36P1	...	S1P28-S36P1
S36P2	S1P1-S36P2	S1P2-S36P2	S1P3-S36P2	...	S1P28-S36P2
S36P3	S1P1-S36P3	S1P2-S36P3	S1P3-S36P3	...	S1P28-S36P3
...	...	...	...	...	...
S36P28	S1P1-S36P28	S1P2-S36P28	S1P3-S36P28	...	S1P28-S36P28

(row groups labelled at left: stroke 2, stroke 3, stroke 36)

Fig. 5. Inter test method on the example of stroke 1.

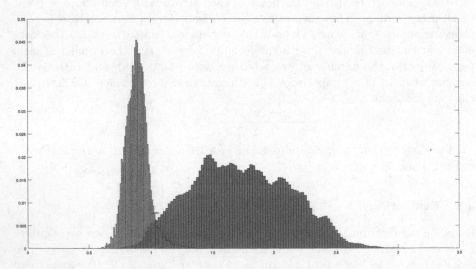

Fig. 6. Distribution of L1-norm (orange = intra class, blue = inter class). The distributions are relative represent, that means it show the percentage frequency for each distance (Color figure online)

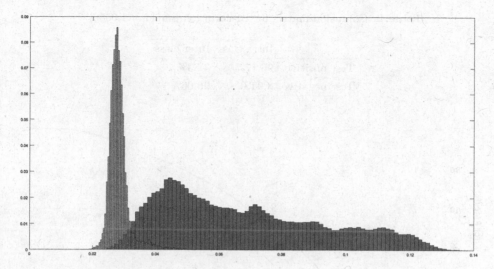

Fig. 7. Distribution of L2-norm (orange = intra class, blue = inter class). The distributions are relative represent, that means it show the percentage frequency for each distance (Color figure online)

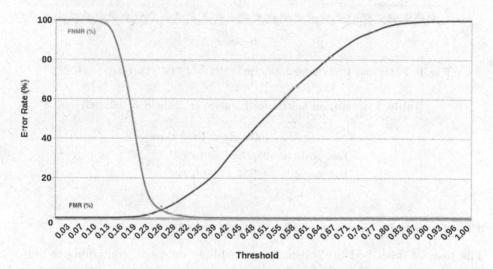

Fig. 8. FMR and FNMR for L1-norm, EER = 3.88%, Threshold = 0.256

of the both curve is the EER. Based on the EER we got a balanced classification accuracy of 96.12% for L1-norm, and 95.26% for the L2-norm.

Relative confusion matrices for L1/L2-norm are shown in Tables 2 and 3 determined on the base of the threshold of the EER for the intra and inter classification accuracy.

Table 2. Confusion matrix for L1-norm (threshold = 1.0656)

	Intra class	Inter class
Test positive	96.17%	3.83%
Test negative	3.94%	96.06%

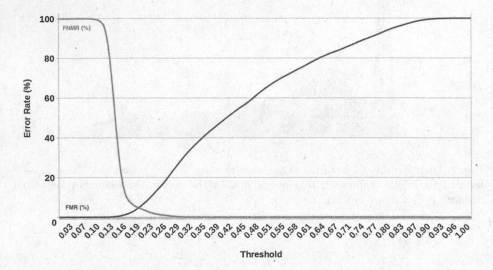

Fig. 9. FMR and FNMR for L2-norm, EER = 4.74%, Threshold = 0.192

Table 3. Confusion matrix for L2-norm (threshold = 0.03496)

	Intra class	Inter class
Test positive	95.27%	4.73%
Test negative	4.76%	95.24%

4.3   Results in Context of the State of the Art

The test set described in [7] consists of 100 blue ink pens, containing ten different instances per brand of ballpoint pens (five brands), roller ball pens (two brands) and gel pens (three brands). Best result determined for the identification of pen type described in [7] amounts 99.5%. Compared to the highest classification accuracy of 96.12% calculated in this paper there is a marginal difference. In contrast to our automatic approach, the measure points are preselected by hand. Keeping in mind, since the values are based on varying test sets containing different compilations of pen types, colors, and brands, the results are not comparable to each other directly. However, the evaluation shows feasible methodology and test setup for ink investigation within handwriting forensic context. Further, the results of our initial research are based on a simple approach by using the linear gradients between neighbored frequencies as features. On the other side, data acquired by the UV–VIS–NIR provides comprehensive information to develop additional features in future work to increase classification accuracy further more.

5   Conclusion and Future Work

Ink verification by spectral analysis seems to be promising. Even based on one simple feature we observe first quite good results for both intra and inter class determination. Based on our results, it is possible to verify different inks automatically in a scan with an EER of 3.88% (L1-norm). To do an identification of the ink there is the need to establish a database with reference scans for as many as possible inks.

The challenge for the intra class determination is that the amount of tests is just a fraction of the inter tests (nearly 3%). A false positive ratio of 3.83% represent absolute more measure point recognize as false positive as true positive. To decrease the number of false positive, it should be investigated, if it would useful to classify on a vote from several measure points instead of a single measure point. Another possibility could be to add more features to get a higher sensitivity.

Future work could be include investigations on overlapped strokes as well as on the influence of different writing conditions, such as black permanent marker, text marker or colored paper. Further, additional features will be designed and implemented in future. Based on those, possibilities of machine learning methods can be studied for ink identification. Another future topic is the research on effects of inks aging (duration between writing time and acquisition time) on recognition behavior. Furthermore, methods should be investigated to identify the ink type and/or brand based on a scan of the whole document.

Acknowledgments. This work has been funded by the German Federal Ministry of Education and Research (BMBF, contract no. FKZ 03FH028IX5). Authors would like to thank the staff of the FRT GmbH for their support and fruitful discussions on relevant features for ink identification. Further, we thank all colleagues of the two research groups at both universities for their advices.

References

1. FRT GmbH - The Art of Metrology (2016). https://frtmetrology.com/en. Accessed 16 May 2017
2. Adam, C.D., Sherratt, S.L., Zholobenko, V.L.: Classification and individualisation of black ballpoint pen inks using principal component analysis of uv-vis absorption spectra. Forensic Sci. Int. **174**(1), 16–25 (2008). http://www.sciencedirect.com/science/article/pii/S0379073807001326
3. Denman, J.A., Skinner, W.M., Kirkbride, K.P., Kempson, I.M.: Organic and inorganic discrimination of ballpoint pen inks by ToF-SIMS and multivariate statistics. Appl. Surf. Sci. **256**, 2155–2163 (2010)

4. Hildebrandt, M., Makrushin, A., Qian, K., Dittmann, J.: Visibility assessment of latent fingerprints on challenging substrates in spectroscopic scans. In: Decker, B., Dittmann, J., Kraetzer, C., Vielhauer, C. (eds.) CMS 2013. LNCS, vol. 8099, pp. 200–203. Springer, Heidelberg (2013). doi:10.1007/978-3-642-40779-6_18

5. Liu, Y.Z., Yu, J., Xie, M.X., Liu, Y., Han, J., Jing, T.T.: Classification and dating of black gel pen ink by ion-pairing high-performance liquid chromatography. J. Chromatogr. A **1135**(1), 57–64 (2006). http://www.sciencedirect.com/science/article/pii/S0021967306017808

6. Petrov, P.: Classification Pen by Type of Ink (2017). http://blogadney.eu/classification-pen-by-type-of-ink/. Accessed 17 May 2017

7. Silva, C.S., de Borba, F.S.L., Pimentel, M.F., Pontes, M.J.C., Honorato, R.S., Pasquini, C.: Classification of blue pen ink using infrared spectroscopy and linear discriminant analysis. Microchem. J. **109**, 122–127 (2013)

8. Vielhauer, C.: Biometric User Authentication for IT Security: From Fundamentals to Handwriting. Springer, New York (2006)

Recaptured Image Forensics Based on Quality Aware and Histogram Feature

Pengpeng Yang, Ruihan Li, Rongrong Ni[✉], and Yao Zhao

Beijing Key Laboratory of Advanced Information Science and Network Technology,
Institute of Information Science, Beijing Jiaotong University, Beijing 100044, China
{rrni,yzhao}@bjtu.edu.cn

Abstract. The recaptured images forensics has drawn much attention in forensics community. The technology can provide some evidences for copyright protection and protect the face spoofing system to a certain degree. In this paper, we propose an algorithm to detect the images recaptured from LCD screen. On the one hand, the quality of the recaptured images would be affect in general. The generalized Gaussian distribution (GGD) and zero mode asymmetric generalized Gaussian distribution (AGGD) effectively capture the behavior of the coefficients of natural and distorted versions of them. So the parameters of GGD with zero mean and zero mode AGGD are estimated as the quality aware feature. On the other hand, the correlation of DCT coefficients between two adjacent positions would be changed. The histogram feature of difference matrix of DCT coefficients is used to measure it. The experimental results show that the proposed method obtains a outstanding detection accuracy.

Keywords: Recaptured image forensics · Quality aware features · DCT coefficient

1 Introduction

Image forensics is an important technology to distinguish the authenticity and the acquisition source of the query image, which can provide some evidents for copyright protection and other cases in court. Many researchers in forensic community have proposed some effective algorithms for different topics on image forensics [1], such as double JPEG compression, median filter, copy-move and splicing detection.

Recaptured image forensics has drawn much attention in recent year. The acquisition process of the recapture images is shown in Fig. 1. The original image, at first, is projected on some media, such as paper, LCD screen, and then shot again using a camera. The detection of the recaptured images play an important role in image forensics community. In one cases, the attacks try to recapture the forgery image, in order to eliminate the traces left during the image editing, which make some algorithms for tamper detection unuseful. Besides, face spoofing attacks can be achieved by photo attacks. The spoofing artefact is a

C. Kraetzer et al. (Eds.): IWDW 2017, LNCS 10431, pp. 31–41, 2017.
DOI: 10.1007/978-3-319-64185-0_3

photograph of the genuine client which can be presented to the sensor on a paper or the screen of a digital device. In both of these cases, the detection of recaptured images is needed. To a certain degree, recaptured image forensics can provide an effective way to verify the authenticity of the query image and pretect the face spoofing system.

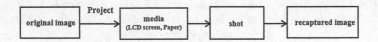

Fig. 1. The acquisition process of the recaptured images

Some algorithms for detecting the recaptured images have been proposed. According to the media projected during recapture operation, the algorithms can be divided into three categories: image forensics for recaptured images projected on LCD screens, on papers, or on both of these cases. Farid et al. [2] proposed the method based on higher-order wavelet statistics: mean, var, skewness, and kurtosis. In the work [3], Cao Hong et al. provided a way to capture the high-quality recaptured images by setting the appropriate shooting environments and extracted three kind of features to detect the recaptured images: texture features based on LBP, loss-of-detail features based on multi-scale wavelet statistics, and color features, respectively. According to the reported results in this work, the texture features based on LBP have better performance than the others. Tian-Tsong Ng et al. built a dichromatic reflectance model [4] and a general image recapturing model [5]. The ratio between the specular and input images were calculated as features and the authors pointed out that the histogram of the specular ratio's gradient generally follows a Laplacian-like distribution while that of the corresponding recaptured images follows a Rayleigh-like distribution. In the work, the authors proposed seven kind of physics-based features: background contextual information, spatial distribution of specularity, surface gradient, color histogram, contrast, chromaticity, and blurriness, respectively. Xiaobo Zhai et al. [6,7] proposed the features based on color moments, DCT coefficients, and texture features. The color moments were counted by computing the means, variance, and skewness of three color channels. The distribution of first digit of DCT coefficients were calculated as the features based on DCT coefficients. For the texture features, LBPV and GLCM were used. Ruihan Li et al. [8] analyzed the physical traits of recaptured images on LCD screens and proposed two kind of effective features. One of the features is the block effect and blurriness effect caused by JPEG compression. Another is the screen effect described by wavelet decomposition with aliasing-enhancement preprocessing.

These algorithms mentioned above belong to the traditional scheme. The feature extraction and feature classification are executed separately and the design of features is of great concern. In the recent study, the data-driven, end-to-end algorithms based on deep learning has more and more attention. Pengpeng Yang et al. [9] has proposed the Laplacian convolutional neural networks to detect the recaptured images. Then, Haoliang Li et al. [10] used the convolutional neural networks to extract the feature based on image patches and then applied recurrent neural networks for learning and classifying these features. As stated in these work, the methods based on deep learning have better performance than the traditional schemes, especially, in the case of detecting the small-size recaptured images. Although the high detection accuracy of these methods, they need to be supposed by the hardware capacities. The simple and effective algorithms still is worthy for recaptured image forensics.

In this work, we propose an algorithm to detect the images recaptured from LCD screen based on quality aware feature and histogram feature. Firstly, considering the situation that the quality of the recaptured images could be affected by the recapture operation, the difference of image quality between the original and recaptured images would be generated. The generalized Gaussian distribution (GGD) and zero mode asymmetric generalized Gaussian distribution (AGGD) effectively capture the behavior of the coefficients of natural and distorted versions of them. And the parameters of GGD with zero mean and zero mode AGGD are estimated as the quality aware feature. Secondly, the correlation of DCT coefficients between two adjacent positions would be changed. Because that the recaptured images suffer double JPEG compression due to the second camera shooting. The histogram feature of difference matrix of DCT coefficients is used to measure these changes. The experimental results show that the proposed method obtains a outstanding detection accuracy.

The remainder of this paper is organized as follows. Section 2 our scheme is detailed. Experiment results and discussion are provided in Sect. 3, and we draw some conclusions in Sect. 4.

2   Proposed Method

The statistical properties of the natural images would be changed by the recapture operation as the reported results in some works mentioned above. It is an common and effective way for recaptured image detection to find distinguished features between the original and recaptured images. In this work, we extract two kind of features from the original and recaptured images. Firstly, from the point of image quality, as shown in Fig. 2, it is easy to find that the image quality will be changed after projecting the media and shotting again. The recapture operation will lead to the distortions of the images. The generalized Gaussian distribution (GGD) and zero mode asymmetric generalized Gaussian distribution (AGGD) effectively capture the behavior of the coefficients of natural and distorted versions of them. So the parameters of GGD with zero mean and zero mode AGGD are estimated as the quality aware feature. Secondly, for image storage, JPEG is a popular image format which is applied automatically during photography. The recaptured images suffer double JPEG compression due to the second camera shooting, which will change the DCT coefficients. The histogram feature of difference matrix of DCT coefficients is used to measure it. At the training stage, the quality aware feature and histogram feature are extracted from the dataset. Then these features are fed into SVM to train a good classifier. At the testing stage, the features of the query image are calculated and given into classifier to get the result.

2.1   The Quality Aware Features

The recaptured image is the reproduction of original image shown on LCD screens and the recaptured image quality would be changed. As reported in the work [8], the texture of the preprocessed recaptured images presents the property of aliasing, on the contrary, texture of the preprocessed original images is relatively clear with keeping the outline of the original content. It means that the recapture operation would lead to the distortion and has the bad effect on the image quality. The quality aware feature, has proposed in the work [11], is used in this work to find the differences between the original and recaptured images. The quality aware feature was allowed to make a 'completely blind' image quality analysis, which is suitable for recaptured image forensics.

As stated in the work [11], the quality aware features are derived from simple but highly regular natural scene statistic (NSS) model. The quality of a given test images is then expressed as the distance between a multivariate Gaussian (MVG) fit of the NSS features extracted from the test image. There are three steps for extracting the quality features as following.

Firstly, The images are processed by formula (1), it is a normalization.

$$\hat{I} = \frac{I(i,j) - I'(i,j)}{I''(i,j) + 1} \tag{1}$$

$$I'(i,j) = \sum_{a=-A}^{A} \sum_{b=-B}^{B} W_{a,b} I(i+a, j+b) \tag{2}$$

$$I''(i,j) = \sqrt{\sum_{a=-A}^{A} \sum_{b=-B}^{B} W_{a,b} (I(i+a, j+b) - I'(i,j))^2} \tag{3}$$

where, $i \in 1, 2......M, j \in 1, 2......N$ are spatial indices, M and N are the image sizes, $\omega = \{W_{a,b} | a = -A, ..., A, b = -B, ...B\}$ is a 2D circularly-symtetric Gaussian weighting function sampled out to 3 standard deviations ($A = B = 3$) The coefficients in formula (1) have been observed to reliable follow a Guassian distribution when computed from natural images that suffered little or no apparent distortion.

Secondly, the patch selection is applied. The image areas have the different distortion. In general, the sharp image regions would have been more attention for human's judgments for image quality. So more salient quality measurements can be made from sharp patches. Letting the P × P sized patches be indexed $c = 1, 2, ...C$, a direct approach is to compute the average local deviation field of each patch indexed:

$$\delta(c) = \sum_{(i,j) \in patch(c)} I''(i,j) \tag{4}$$

Fig. 2. Images samples. The left column represent the original images and the right column denote the recaptured images

where, δ denotes local activity sharpness. Once the sharpness of each patch is found, those having a suprathreshold sharpness $\delta > T$ are selected. In our experiments, we used the nominal value $T = 0.75$ and $P = 96$.

Lastly, given a collection of natual image patches selected as above, their statistics are characterized by "quality aware" NSS features computed from each selected patch. Prior studies of NSS based image quality have shown that the generalized Gaussian distribution effectively captures the behavior of the coefficients of natual and distorted version of them. The generalized Gaussian distribution (GGD) with zero mean is given by:

$$f(x; \alpha, \beta) = \frac{\alpha}{2\beta\Gamma(1/\alpha))} exp(-(\frac{|x|}{\beta})^\alpha)))$$ (5)

where, $\Gamma(.)$ is the gamma function:

$$\Gamma(a) = \int_0^\infty t^{a-1} e^{-t} dt, a > 0$$ (6)

The parameters of the GGD (α, β), can be reliably estimated using the moment-matching based approach proposed. The signs of the transformed image coefficients have been observed to follow a fairly regular structure. However, distortions disturb this correlation structure. This deviation can be captured by analysis the sample distribution of the products of pairs of adjacent coefficients computed along horizontal, vertical and diagonal orientations: $\hat{I}(i,j)\hat{I}(i, j+1)$, $\hat{I}(i,j)\hat{I}(i+1,j)$, $\hat{I}(i,j)\hat{I}(i+1,j+1)$ and $\hat{I}(i,j)\hat{I}(i+1,j-1)$ for $i\epsilon\{1, 2, ...M\}$ and $j\epsilon\{1, 2, ...N\}$. The products of neighboring coefficients are well-modeled as following a zero mode asymmetric generalized Gaussian distribution (AGGD):

$$f(x, \gamma, \beta_l, \beta_r) = \frac{\gamma}{(\beta_l + \beta_r)\Gamma(\frac{1}{\gamma})} exp(-(\frac{-x}{\beta_l})^\gamma), \forall x \leq 0$$ (7)

$$f(x, \gamma, \beta_l, \beta_r) = \frac{\gamma}{(\beta_l + \beta_r)\Gamma(\frac{1}{\gamma})} exp(-(\frac{-x}{\beta_r})^\gamma), \forall x \geq 0$$ (8)

The parameters of the AGGD $(\gamma, \beta_l, \beta_r)$ can be efficiently estimated using the moment-matching based approach. The mean of the distribution is useful:

$$\eta = (\beta_r - \beta_l)\frac{\Gamma(\frac{2}{\gamma}))}{\Gamma(\frac{1}{\gamma}))}$$ (9)

By extracting estimates along the four orientations, we can get 18 parameters. All features are computed at two scales to capture multiscale behavior, by low pass filtering and downsampling by a factor of 2, yield a set of 36 features. Considering the effect of feature dimensions, the features extracting from each image patches are averaged to generate the new features:

$$Fea_1 = \{\bar{\alpha}, \bar{\beta}, \bar{\gamma}_{\{h,v,d1,d2\}}, \bar{\beta}_{l_{\{h,v,d1,d2\}}}, \bar{\beta}_{r_{\{h,v,d1,d2\}}}, \bar{\eta}_{\{h,v,d1,d2\}}\}$$ (10)

where, $h, v, d1, d2$ denote the four different orientations. In Fig. 3, several pairs of images and their values of the quality aware features in the case of low pass filtering are shown. The figures manifest the differences of the quality aware features between the original and recaptured images.

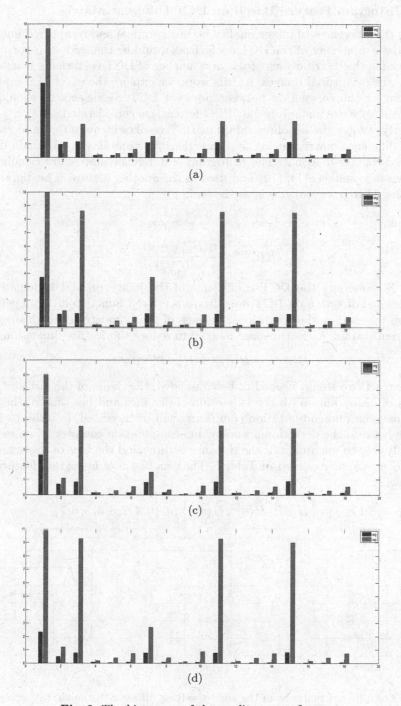

Fig. 3. The histogram of the quality aware features.

2.2   Histogram Feature Based on DCT Different Matrix

Besides the differences of image quality between original and recaptured images, the statistic properties of the DCT coefficients would be changed, as reported in the work [8], the distributions of the first number of DCT coefficients is used to identify the recaptured images. In this work, we explore the effect of recapture operation for the correlation between adjacent DCT coefficients. It should be noted that only the images in the JPEG format are considerated.

Firstly, we get the absolute values of DCT coefficient quantized and calculate its difference matrix among four directions: horizontal, vertical, main diagonal, and counter-diagonal. The histogram of difference matrix are calculated, as shown in formulas (11), (12) and used as the another feature. The digram of extracting histogram features is as shown in Fig. 4.

$$D_{i,j,k}^m = X_{p,q}^m - X_{i,j} \tag{11}$$

$$H(d)^m = \frac{n(D_{i,j,k}^m = d)}{n(D_{i,j,k}^m)} \tag{12}$$

where, X represents the DCT coefficients of the image, m and k denote the distances and direction on DCT domain, respectively. Function n(.) can get the numbers that satisfy the conditions. Because of the symmetry of the histogram of different matrix, its features are merged to reduce the feature dimensions:

$$\hat{H}(d)^m = H(d)^m + H(-d)^m, d \neq 0 \tag{13}$$

There are two things needed to be considered, the choise of the distance and the bin of histogram. With the expansion of distance and bin chosen, the feature dimension and computation complexity will be increased. In order to keep balance between the detection accuracy and computation complexity, we experimentally set the maximum of the distance is three and the bins of histogram is equal to serven, as reported in Table 1. The denotation of histogram features is as following:

$$Fea_2 = \left\{ \hat{H}(d)^1, \hat{H}(d)^2, \hat{H}(d)^3 \right\}, d\epsilon\{0, 1, 2, 3, 4, 5, 6, 7\} \tag{14}$$

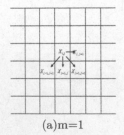 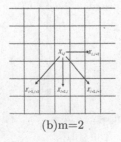 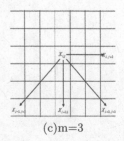

(a)m=1   (b)m=2   (c)m=3

Fig. 4. The different matrices in the case of setting different distances. (a) represents the positions need to calculate when setting $m = 1$, (b) and (c) show the positions by setting $m = 2$ and $m = 3$, respectively

3   Experimental Results

To evaluate the effectiveness of the proposed algorithms for high resolution images, the image database in the work [8] is applied into our experiments, consisting of 636 original and 636 recaptured images, token by Nikon D600 and Cannon EOS 500D. The images includes different scenes, such as buildings, persons, materials, scenery, etc.

The extracted features are feed into SVM classifier with the help of toolbox of LIBSVM and the selected kernel function is radial basis kernel function (RBF). Here, 636 original images are selected as negative samples and 636 recaptured images are selected as positive samples in the experiment. The proportion between the training and the testing is 5:1, that is, the 5/6 of all images are used training model and the remainder 1/6 is used as testing. To ensure the objectivity of distinguishing result, the quantities of training and testing images are always consistent. Then, the cross-validations are carried out ten times to get the average value.

The detection performance indexs are as following. TP represents the recaptured images are classified as the recaptured ones. TN means the original images are identified as the original ones. FP represents the original images are classified as the recaptured images. FN represents the recaptured images are identified as the original ones.

$$Accuracy = \frac{TP + TN}{TP + TN + FP + FN} \tag{15}$$

$$Recall = \frac{TP}{TP + FN} \tag{16}$$

$$Precision = \frac{TP}{TP + FP} \tag{17}$$

3.1   Experiment 1

In order to find the best parameters for histogram features, we test all possible parameters, $[m, d]$ to detect the recaptured images in this experiments. The results are shown in Fig. 5. In the case of setting the parameters, $m = 3, d = 7$, the best detection accuracy is achieved. So in the follow-up experiments, the same setting for parameters is used.

3.2   Experiment 2

The second experiment is conducted to prove that the proposed method has the better detection performance. The results is shown in Table 1. Compared with three algorithms, LBP method proposed in the work [3] that is common baseline method, the methods based on physical traits [8], color moments, and DCT coefficients features [7]. The proposed method in this work has the best detection performance.

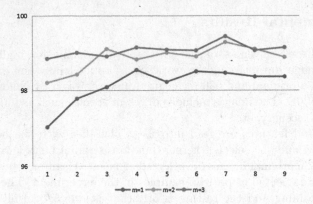

Fig. 5. The detect accuracies in the case of different setting parameters.

Table 1. The detection accuracy (%). The best results are highlighten in bold.

Method	ACC	Recall	Precision
LBP [3]	98.11	98.39	97.83
Block_Blur_YCbCr [8]	95.20	97.40	93.38
Pre_Wavlet [8]	96.38	96.46	96.32
Block_Blur_YCbCr+Pre_Wavlet [8]	98.23	98.50	97.97
CM+MBFDF_Y +MBFDF_Cr [7]	98.27	98.58	97.97
Proposed method	**98.74**	**99.29**	**98.21**

4   Conclusions

we proposed an algorithm to detect the images recaptured from LCD screen based on quality aware feature and histogram feature. Firstly, considering the situation that the quality of the recaptured images could be affected by the recapture operation, the difference of image quality between the original and recaptured images would be generated. And the parameters of GGD with zero mean and zero mode AGGD are estimated as the quality aware feature. Secondly, The histogram feature of difference matrix of DCT coefficients is used to measure these changes. The experimental results show that the proposed method obtains a outstanding detection accuracy.

Acknowledgments. This work was supported in part by National NSF of China (61672090, 61332012), the National key research and development program of China (2016YFB0800404), Fundamental Research Funds for the Central Universities (2015JBZ002).

References

1. Piva, A.: An overview on image forensics. ISRN Sig. Process. **2013**, 22 (2013)
2. Lyu, S., Farid, H.: How realistic is photorealistic? IEEE Trans. Sig. Process. **53**(2), 845–850 (2005)
3. Cao, H., Kot, A.C.: Identification of recaptured photographs on LCD screens. In: 2010 IEEE International Conference on Acoustics, Speech and Signal Processing. IEEE (2010)
4. Yu, H., Ng, T.-T., Sun, Q.: Recaptured photo detection using specularity distribution. In: 2008 15th IEEE International Conference on Image Processing. IEEE (2008)
5. Gao, X., et al.: Single-view recaptured image detection based on physics-based features. In: 2010 IEEE International Conference on Multimedia and Expo (ICME). IEEE (2010)
6. Zhai, X., Ni, R., Zhao, Y.: Recaptured image detection based on texture features. In: 2013 Ninth International Conference on Intelligent Information Hiding and Multimedia Signal Processing. IEEE (2013)
7. Ni, R., Zhao, Y., Zhai, X.: Recaptured images forensics based on color moments and DCT coefficients features (2015)
8. Li, R., Ni, R., Zhao, Y.: An effective detection method based on physical traits of recaptured images on LCD screens. In: Shi, Y.-Q., Kim, H.J., Pérez-González, F., Echizen, I. (eds.) IWDW 2015. LNCS, vol. 9569, pp. 107–116. Springer, Cham (2016). doi:10.1007/978-3-319-31960-5_10
9. Yang, P., Ni, R., Zhao, Y.: Recapture image forensics based on Laplacian convolutional neural networks. In: Shi, Y.Q., Kim, H.J., Perez-Gonzalez, F., Liu, F. (eds.) IWDW 2016. LNCS, vol. 10082, pp. 119–128. Springer, Cham (2017). doi:10.1007/978-3-319-53465-7_9
10. Li, H., Wang, S., Kot, A.C.: Image recapturing detection with convolutional and recurrent neural network. In: Proceedings of IS&T, Electronic Imaging, Media Watermarking, Security, and Forensics (2017)
11. Mittal, A., Soundararajan, R., Bovik, A.C.: Making a completely blind image quality analyzer. IEEE Sig. Process. Lett. **20**(3), 209–212 (2013)

Website Fingerprinting Attack on Psiphon and Its Forensic Analysis

Tekachew Gobena Ejeta[1] and Hyoung Joong Kim[2(✉)]

[1] Department of Cyber Defense, Korea University, Seoul, South Korea
totekish@gmail.com
[2] Graduate School of Information Security,
Korea University, Seoul, South Korea
khj-@korea.ac.kr

Abstract. Internet circumvention applications – such as *Psiphon* – are widely used to bypass control mechanisms, and each of such anti-censorship application uses a unique mechanism to bypass internet censorship. Although anti-censorship applications provide a unique means to ensure internet freedom, some applications severely degrade network performance and possibly open the door for network security breaches. Anti-censorship applications such as *Psiphon* can be used as cover for hacking attempts and can assist in many criminal activities. In this paper, we analyze the *Psiphon* service and perform a passive traffic analysis to detect Psiphon traffic. Moreover, we profile the top 100 websites based on their Alexa rankings according to five different categories under *Psiphon* and perform an effective website fingerprinting attack. Our analysis uses the well-known k-nearest neighbors for website fingerprinting and support vector machine classifier to detect Psiphon traffic.

Keywords: Psiphon · Fingerprinting attack · Digital forensics · Internet censorship

1 Introduction

Psiphon [1] is developed and maintained by Psiphon Inc. as a powerful tool to evade internet censorship. In this paper, we conduct a passive traffic analysis attack to detect *Psiphon* traffic and a website fingerprinting (WFP) attack on Psiphon to infer a user's web activity. Although most WFP attack research is done on the Tor network, anti-censorship technologies like *Psiphon* that use security settings such IPSec tunnels and SSH tunnels that are vulnerable to a WFP attack [2–5]. To the best of our knowledge, this is the first work to analyze and perform passive traffic analysis and WFP attack on *Psiphon* anti-censorship service.

The remainder of this paper is organized as follows. Section 2 provides background information on *Psiphon* and a WFP attack. Section 3 reviews passive traffic analysis and WFP with various privacy enhancing and anti-censorship technologies. Section 4 presents our data collection methodology and testing environment. Section 5 discusses the passive traffic analysis attack for *Psiphon* traffic detection and WFP attack on *Psiphon*.

© Springer International Publishing AG 2017
C. Kraetzer et al. (Eds.): IWDW 2017, LNCS 10431, pp. 42–51, 2017.
DOI: 10.1007/978-3-319-64185-0_4

Section 6 describes the performance of our attack. Section 7 provides the conclusion and discusses future work.

2 Background

Psiphon uses a combination of a virtual private network (VPN), SSH, and secure HTTP Proxy communications and obfuscation technologies to bypass internet filtering (i.e., censorship) systems that are commonly used by government agencies. Psiphon Inc. operates servers to which a client connects via VPN or a secure SSH connection. Each client has a list of servers that are added over time to ensure new backup new servers are available as older servers are blocked. System integrity is maintained with each client digitally signed to certify authenticity, and each server possesses embedded certificates to ensure authenticity. *Psiphon* limits the number of servers it reveals to its client application to avoid attackers listing all its server addresses and blocking them. As a result, *Psiphon* services cannot be blocked via IP and DNS filtering. Although *Psiphon* applications cannot be blocked using IP and DNS information, they are vulnerable to traffic analysis attacks, including WFP attacks.

In a WFP attack, an attacker first retrieves a certain number of relevant web pages as training data for fingerprinting using the *Psiphon* application, assuming the victim uses these as well. The attacker records the transferred packets with a traffic analyzer tool such as *Wireshark*, which provides information regarding the IP layer packets, e.g., the length of the packet, the time the packet was sent or received, the order in which the packets were sent and received, etc. The attacker can make use of various information contained in the packets that are collected to create a profile of each web page, which is the website fingerprint. Later, wiretapping the victim's traffic, the attacker similarly collects data, which we call test data. The test data resembles fingerprints, but it usually differs from training data due to various reasons, e.g., deterministic packet fragmentation, updates in web pages, etc. Hence, the attacker needs to apply machine-learning methods to compare the information that is recorded to the fingerprints in order to match these to a certain web page.

A WFP attack is commonly evaluated in a closed and open world scenario. In the closed word scenario, the number of websites a user may visit is limited to a fixed number, which is not realistic but is suitable for a comparison and analysis of the classification performance under various approaches. In the more realistic open-world scenario, the adversary tries to identify whether a visited website belongs to a given set of monitored websites even though the user may also visit sites unknown to the adversary. The closed world scenario is also suitable for attack on anti-censorship applications such as *Psiphon*. The primary goal in attacking an anti-censorship application is to stop the monitored service or website. In most cases, censored services or websites are limited in number. Hence, performing a WFP attack on *Psiphon* on a closed world scenario is more practical.

3   Related Works

In this section, we review prior literature on passive traffic analysis, WFP and related technologies for network traffic classification.

Herrmann et al. [2] conducted a WFP attack on *Tor* for the first time. They used a classical text mining classifier called *multinomial naïve-Bayes classifier* on a closed world setting of 775 web pages. They used the frequency distribution of the IP packet sizes as the main feature for classification. Information such as the packet order and timing information was not considered. Although the authors achieved only 2.95% accuracy for *Tor*, they achieved a much higher accuracy for other privacy enhancing technologies.

Hayes and Danezis [6] used a novel feature extraction and selection method. They used *random forest* to extract robust fingerprints from web pages, and they conducted a systematic analysis of every single feature extracted from the *random forest* and measured its relevance for the classification problem. This analysis allowed them to increase the accuracy to 91%. They also reduced the time needed for training and concluded that simple features tend to be more distinctive than complex features.

Rimmer [7] applied a deep learning technique to extract and select WFP features and performed de-anonymization attacks on anonymized *Tor* traffic. His classifier works in three stages. First, it performs unsupervised feature extraction and selection for the building component, auto encoders, by learning the underlying patterns in traffic traces and deriving the most distinctive characteristics of the input data. The next step of training is supervised fine-tuning of the whole deep neural network. During this stage, the model learns to classify traffic into a set of web pages based on derived traffic features. After training, the adversary evaluates their model on the test set based on the accuracy of the website identification and other performance metrics.

Panchenko and Niessen [8] improved the accuracy in *Tor* from 3% to 55% and in *Java Anon Proxy* (*JAP*) from 20% to 80%. They first defined features for WFP solely based on volume, time, and direction of the traffic, then applied *support vector machine* (*SVM*) with the introduced features to achieve those results. This study was also the first to evaluate an open-world scenario, i.e., the identification of certain websites in a large set of unknown websites. They performed the first successful attack in the open-world, which is a more complex and realistic setting of the attack than a closed-world of a fixed number of websites.

Cai et al. [5] proposed a new attack based on a new representation of the classification instances and *SVM classifier*. Each traffic trace was a string of 1 and −1, representing a cell in one or another direction. Their *SVM* used the Damerau-Levenshtein edit distance and used the *SVM kernel trick* to pre-compute the distances between the traces. This classifier achieved 88% accuracy in a closed-world of 100 web pages.

Al-Qura'n et al. [9] proposed a behavioral-based solution to detect and block ultrasurf traffic, which is a program using encryption in a single hop proxy architecture to evade censorship. The results of their evaluation showed that the proposed solution was capable of achieving successful detection.

4   Data Collection

In this study, we profiled 100 websites from 5 categories. We selected the top 20 websites in the world based on Alexa [10] ranking from news, shopping, sport, games and science website categories. We used *iMacros* to automate a user visit to the top 100 websites that were selected. *iMacros* is designed to automate repetitive tasks on the web [11]. We used the *iMacros 9.0.3* plugin for *Mozilla 52* to automate a user visit to the top 100 websites and *Wireshark* to capture the traffic trace. We collected all traffic traces while running *Psiphon 3*. All Firefox plugins were disabled during data collection. We used a Windows 10 PC with an Intel(R) Core(TM) i7 3.40 GHz processor and 16 GB of RAM. We prepared two data sets. In the first data set, we run the *Psiphon* application and used *iMacros* to automate a visit to the websites and capture the data, and we named this data set top100PS. For the second data set, we conducted the same capture without running the *Psiphon* application, and we named this data set top100. The difference between 100PS and 100 is simple: running *Psiphon* during data collection or not, respectively.

5   Passive Traffic Analysis Attack on Psiphon

5.1   Attack Model

We assume that the attacker is a passive observer who does not modify transmissions and is not able to decrypt packets. The attacker is able to monitor traffic between the users who use the *Psiphon* application to browse the internet. Furthermore, we assume that the attacker possess sufficient computational resources to train the fingerprinting technique on large training datasets.

In general, the attacker's strategy is as follows. The attacker collects packet traces from several web pages which he is interested in monitoring. Then, the attacker observes packet traces that are generated by the client during web browsing and compares these traces with those collected by conducting supervised classification. We note two assumptions that all previous works on WFP have made of an attacker.

- **Well-defined packet traces.** The attacker is assumed to know where the packet trace of a single page load starts and ends. If the client takes much longer to load the next page after the current one is loaded, this assumption can be justified.
- **No other activity.** We assume the client does not perform any other activity that could be confused for page-loading behavior, such as downloading a file.

In this section, we describe our attack, which is designed to break *Psiphon* services. We perform our attack in two phases. First, we classify *Psiphon* traffic. Second, we perform the WFP attack. Our attacks are based on the well-known *k-nearest neighbors* (*k-NN*) for a WFP attack and *SVM classifier* for *Psiphon* traffic detection. We tackle two problem scenarios: multiclass classification for WFP and binary classification to detect *Psiphon* traffic. In both scenarios, a set of top100 websites are profiled, and the traffic trace of the top100 websites is prepared as described in detail in Sect. 4.

- **Multi-level Classification (WFP attack on *Psiphon*).** Given a test traffic trace, which is known to be a visit to a website in top100PS, identify the website.
- **Binary Classification (*Psiphon* traffic detection).** Given a test stream, determine whether it is a visit to a website in top100PS or top100. We examine the false positive rate (FPR) and false negative rate (FNR) for identification.

5.2   Feature Extraction

We used passive traffic analysis to fingerprint website usage under *Psiphon* services. Two important observations enabled us to adopt this model. First, a web page download via HTTP is highly structured. Second, encryption and tunneling through *Psiphon* alter neither the packet size severely nor the packet ordering information in the traffic trace. All robust features of the HTTP protocol, such as a parallel TCP connection request, pipelining and TCP connection re-usage to download multiple object or resources from the website are considered to exist in our traffic traces. Moreover, all sessions are multiplexed into one session when they tunnel through *Psiphon*. Empty TCP payload packets are filtered out from the traffic traces since this only indicates transport layer signaling of the TCP connection and does not contain relevant information regarding the websites.

The features we used for fingerprinting are based on the packet size, direction, and ordering, and the construction of our feature set is based on how WFP works in various studies. We generally categorized the feature set into direct feature and synthesized features.

Direct Features
- **Packet Length Uniqueness.** These features are very useful since no packet padding is applied while traffic is tunneled through *Psiphon*. Here, "1" represents the packet length uniqueness and "0" otherwise. This is similar to the algorithm used by Liberatore and Levine [12] and Herrmann et al. [2].
- **Total Transmission.** We add the total incoming and outgoing packet count and total connection time as features.
- **Lengths of the Initial Packets.** We add the first 20 packets' length.

Synthesized Features
- **Packet Order Information.** For each outgoing packet, we add, in order, a feature indicating the total number of packets before it in the sequence. We also add a feature that indicates the total number of incoming packets between this outgoing packet and the previous one. This captures the burst patterns that helped Cai et al. [5] achieve high accuracy rates, and this feature is also adopted by Wang et al. [13].
- **Concentration of Outgoing Packets.** We add a number of outgoing packets in non-overlapping spans of 30 packets as a feature. This is the same as what Wang et al. [13] used to capture the concentration of outgoing packets.

- **Bursts.** We used the definition of a burst of outgoing packets as a sequence of outgoing packets, as in Wang et al. [13], where there are no two adjacent incoming packets. We add the maximum and mean burst length as well as the number of bursts as features.

6 Attack Evaluation

6.1 Psiphon Traffic Classification

In traffic classification, two metrics are typically used to quantify the performance of the classifier: Detection Rate (DR) and False Positive Rate (FP). A high DR rate and a low FP rate would be the desired outcomes, and these are calculated as follows:

$$DR = 1 - \frac{\# \, FN \, Classifications}{Total \, Number \, Psiphon \, Classifications}$$

$$FP = \frac{\# \, FP \, Classifications}{Total \, Number \, Non\text{-}Psiphon \, Classifications}$$

Where False Negative (FN) means *Psiphon* traffic classified as non-*Psiphon* traffic and False Positive (FP) means non-*Psiphon* traffic classified as *Psiphon* traffic. Once the aforementioned features are extracted from the traffic traces, then *SVM classifiers* are trained on the data using 5-fold cross-validation. To this end, we used the *MATLAB classification learner* [14] application, which is makes it easy to experiment with various algorithms. The *MATLAB classification learner* application provides an easy-to-use interface for different machine learning algorithms that we used.

Table 1 shows the performance of the algorithms on the top100PS and top100 data set. In this case, the SVM algorithm can correctly classify 90% (overall accuracy) of the instances. Moreover, SVM can identify Psiphon traffic with a high DR and a low FP rate. Table 2 shows the confusion matrix, and it is now apparent that the SVM can classify 99% of the Psiphon traces correctly, whereas less than 1% Psiphon flows are misclassified as non-Psiphon.

Table 1. Psiphon traffic classification

Psiphon traffic classification 3,763 features 5,062 observations	
Algorithm	Accuracy
Linear discriminant analysis	89.4%
k-NN	89.9%
SVM	90.2%

Table 2. Confusion matrix for Psiphon traffic classification

True class	Non-Psiphon	62%	38%	62%	38%
	Psiphon	<1%	>99%	>99%	<1%
				True positive rate	

Table 3. Confusion matrix for WFP attack of 20 websites

	Accuweather.com	Amazon.com	Autodesk.com	Cnn.com	Ea.com	Flashscore.com	Foxnews.com	Huffingtonpost.com	Nationalgeographic.com	News.yahoo.com	Nhl.com	Nytimes.com	Store.steampowered.com	Theguardian.com	Walmart.com	Wowhead.com	Xbox.com	Howstuffworks.com	www.ieee.org	www.usatoday.com
Accuweather.com	26	5	1		12	1	18	24	3			1	3		5	3	2		1	17
Amazon.com	7	39	7	6	3		3	7	7	4		2	7		5	1	3		5	
Autodesk.com		5	36	1	9	2	18	11	6	5	1				1	1	3		5	
Cnn.com	2	5	3	32	4	3	18	9	10	1		7	3	1	1		4		3	
Ea.com	1	2	5		31	9	10	8	8	6	3		3		2	8	3		7	1
Flashscore.com	1	3	3	2	14	12	14	18	15	2	1	3	3			3	3		2	1
Foxnews.com		2	7	5	3	3	41	12	3	10	2	1		1		3	5		8	1
Huffingtonpost.com	1	7	3	7	5	3	14	34	5	9	1	3	8		1	3			1	3
Nationalgeographic.com	2	1	7	9	10	7	12	11	24	1	9				4	2	3		3	
News.yahoo.com	1	1	1	1	12	1	28	14	5	31	1	2			1	2	1		5	
Nhl.com	2		10		11	5	10	6	11	4	28	1	4		1	5	4		3	
Nytimes.com	1		9	13	1		12	5	8	2		45	1		1	1	4		5	
Store.steampowered.com	4	2	3		8	3	10	9	10	1	8	1	27		13	1	2		3	1
Theguardian.com		1	1	2			2													
Walmart.com	3	5	8	6	5	4	4	3	9	5	3	1	10		23	2	5		9	
Wowhead.com	7	3	2	1	11	3	7	7	2	1	4	1	4		2	36	8		6	
Xbox.com	3	2	4	2	6	5	8	9	5	1	2	1	5			6	31		13	1
Howstuffworks.com		5			19	36	37											3		
www.ieee.org	1	1	7	3	9	2	10	6	8		1				8	2	6		41	
www.usatoday.com																				100

6.2 Website Fingerprinting Attack on Psiphon

We investigated the simplest scenario to gain intuition about the complexity of the problem in relation to a web page classifier under an anti-censorship application. To do this, we conducted the following experiment. Note that we used the same feature set for WFP given the features we used for *Psiphon* traffic detection. Note that the main aim of an attack on an anti-censorship application is to stop the service or website that is being accessed by using such an anti-censorship application. For an effective attack on an anti-censorship application, the website or service should be identified in time to stop it. Hence, attacks on an anti-censorship application should be fast relative to those in anonymized networks.

In a closed-world setting, we aimed to differentiate between 20 websites in our top100PS data set. We selected those 20 sites from a top100PS data set based on the number of instances we have on them. Websites with a higher number of instances or observations are selected for our fingerprinting experiment. We used all aforementioned features from the traffic trace, such as the packet size, packet order, and direction and concentration. The total number of features is 3,763, and the overall number of observations is 2,000 for 20 sites. Each website has 100 instances (Table 4).

Table 4. WFP attack accuracy for 20 websites

20 websites, 100 instances each 3,763 features 2,000 observations	
Algorithm	Accuracy
k-NN with Jaccard distance metric	33.1%

Table 5. Accuracy, dataset, algorithm of various works

Author	Anonymizer/Anti-censorship	Dataset/websites	Algorithm	Accuracy
Herrmann et al. [2]	Tor	755	Multinomial Naïve-Bayes	2.95%
Panchenko et al. [8]	JAP	755	SVM	20.00%
Panchenko et al. [8]	Tor	755	SVM	55.00%
Cai et al. [5]	Tor	100	SVM	88.00%
Ours	Psiphon	20	k-NN	33.10%

We used the *MATLAB classification learner* application to perform the website classification. We employed the *k-NN algorithm* with Jaccard distance metric with 5-fold cross-validation. The advantages of choosing the *k-NN classifier* are that it requires less testing time and is capable of capturing the multi-modal nature of the website traffic trace data. Table 3 shows the confusion matrix for the 20 websites using the *MATLAB classification learner* application. In this closed world experiment of 20 websites, the identification performance reached a 33% accuracy. The Jaccard distance metric produced a good accuracy compared to the rest of the distant metric, such as the Euclidian distance.

In summary, the website classification in a closed-world scenario is significantly more difficult compared to the *Psiphon* traffic classification. In reality, it is expected that for certain websites, an adversary is not able to train all sub-pages due to their number, similar to the case in which he cannot train a web page classifier on the whole universe. We reduced the number of pages available for training to 20 websites, with a good observation from our top100PS data set. Therefore, we demonstrated a WFP attack on *Psiphon* anti-censorship services. In the WFP attack, a relatively higher accuracy can be achieved depending on the data set used, distance function, and the training time as shown in Table 5. Those attacks are effective for an anonymization network as the final goal of the attack is only to identify the website. Since the purpose of the anti-censorship application is mainly to bypass censorship and not to hide the users' or website's identity, the attack should finally aim at stopping access to the website. Therefore, a high accuracy should be accompanied with high prediction speed for an effective WFP attack against anti-censorship tools.

7 Conclusion and Future Work

In this work, we employed a passive traffic analysis attack on *Psiphon* anti-censorship services. We used *SVM* and *k-NN supervised learning algorithms* to classify the *Psiphon* traffic traces and website classification, respectively. To do so, we prepared a data set of top100 websites from five categories including news, shopping, gaming, sports and science. We used the *iMacros* plug-in for *Mozilla* to automate a user visit to those websites and prepared two data sets, top100PS and top100 each collected under *Psiphon* and without *Psiphon*, respectively. We extracted features including the packet count for incoming and outgoing connections, packet order and connection time as a general feature.

In *Psiphon* traffic classification, the *SVM algorithm* can correctly classify 90% (overall accuracy) of the instances. Moreover, SVM can identify *Psiphon* traffic with a high DR and a low FP rate. The SVM classifier can classify 99% of the *Psiphon* traces correctly whereas less than 1% of the *Psiphon* flows are misclassified as non-*Psiphon*.

Next, we selected 20 websites from top100PS data set with a high number of instances. We employed a *k-NN classifier* with the Jaccard distance metric to identify the websites. We demonstrated an effective WFP attack on *Psiphon* anti-censorship services with an accuracy that grows as the traffic trace is collected.

Finally, in this work, we have shown that it is possible to identify *Psiphon* traffic from a given traffic trace as well as classifying website browsing over *Psiphon* without using features such as payload, IP addresses and source/destination ports. Future work will follow similar methods to generate more realistic and larger data sets to test the robustness of the classifier for website classification and different applications running over *Psiphon*.

References

1. Psiphon, Privacy Policy. https://psiphon.ca/en/privacy.html. Accessed 24 Apr 2017
2. Herrmann, D., Wendolsky, R., Federrath, H.: Website fingerprinting: attacking popular privacy enhancing technologies with the multinomial Naïve Bayes classifier. In: Proceedings of the 2009 ACM workshop on Cloud Computing Security, pp. 31–42 (2009)
3. Wang, T.: Website fingerprinting: attacks and defenses, Ph.D. Dissertation, University of Waterloo (2016)
4. Dyer, K.P., Coull, S.E., Ristenpart, T., Shrimpton, T.: Peek-a-boo, I still see you: why efficient traffic analysis countermeasures fail. In: Proceedings of the IEEE Symposium on Security and Privacy, pp. 332–346 (2012)
5. Cai, X., Zhang, X., Joshi, B., Johnson, R.: Touching from a distance: website fingerprinting attacks and defenses. In: Proceedings of the ACM Conference on Computer and Communications Security, pp. 605–616 (2012)
6. Hayes, J., Danezis, G.: Website fingerprinting at scale (2016). arXiv:1509.00789v2
7. Rimmer, V.: Deep Learning Website Fingerprinting Features, MS thesis, KU Leuven (2017)
8. Panchenko, A., Niessen, L.: Website fingerprinting in onion routing based anonymization networks. In: Proceedings of the Annual ACM Workshop on Privacy in the Electronic Society, pp. 103–114 (2011)
9. Al-Qura'n, R., Hadi, A., Atoum, J., Al-Zewairi, M.: Ultrasurf traffic classification: detection and prevention. Int. J. Commun. Netw. Syst. Sci. **8**(8), 304–311 (2015)
10. Alexa Top 500 Global Sites. http://www.alexa.com/topsites. Accessed 8 Jun 2017
11. The #1 Browser Automation, Data Extraction, and Web Testing Tool, iMacros Software. http://imacros.net/overview. Accessed 24 Mar 2017
12. Liberatore, M., Levine, B.N.: Inferring the source of encrypted HTTP connections. In: Proceedings of the ACM conference on Computer and Communications Security, pp. 255–263 (2006)
13. Wang, T., Cai, X., Nithyanand, R., Johnson, R., Goldberg, I.: Effective attacks and provable defenses for website fingerprinting. In: Proceedings of the USENIX Security Symposium, pp. 143–157 (2014)
14. Train models to classify data using supervised machine learning - MATLAB. https://www.mathworks.com/help/stats/classificationlearner-app.html?s_tid=gn_loc_drop. Accessed 14 Apr 2017

Deep Learning Based Counter–Forensic Image Classification for Camera Model Identification

Venkata Udaya Sameer$^{(\boxtimes)}$, Ruchira Naskar, Nikhita Musthyala, and Kalyan Kokkalla

Department of Computer Science and Engineering,
National Institute of Technology, Rourkela 769008, Odisha, India
{515CS1003,naskarr,714cs2045,114cs0359}@nitrkl.ac.in

Abstract. *Camera Model Identification* is the digital forensic problem of identifying the source of an image under question, i.e., to map the image to its source device. This assists forensic analysts to map a suspect's camera with a possibly illegal image repository, or to attribute an image under question to its legitimate source. Counter–forensic attacks to Camera Model Identification techniques, primarily comprise of image anonymization. *Image Anonymization* is a technique adopted by an intelligent adversary for modifying an image illegitimately, so as to disable attribution of the image to its source; hence to fool a forensic analyst and prevent image source identification. In the recent years, there has been a rapid growth of research interest in the domain of counter–forensics. In this paper, we develop a deep learning based Convolutional Neural Network (CNN) to detect whether an image under question has undergone any form of counter–forensic source anonymization attack. This will enable a forensic analyst to find out whether an image, whose source is being investigated, is authentic, or has it been tampered so as to prevent correct source identification. We deal with three major classes of source anonymization attacks in this paper, viz., *Seam Carving, Fingerprint Copying*, and *Adaptive PRNU Denoising*. If an image is detected to have indeed undergone a counter–forensic attack, the proposed model additionally enables detection of the specific class of attack, through multiclass classification. Our experimental results prove that the detection accuracy of the proposed system is considerably high, and it passes the overfitting test too.

Keywords: Classification · Convolutional neural network · Counter–forensics · Deep learning · Digital forensics · Source camera identification

1 Introduction

Digital Forensics is a branch of science which helps law enforcement agencies in providing legal evidences to digital crimes. In today's digital era, digital crime rate is on a high rise. *Digital image forensics* [1] is a sub–area of digital forensics that deals with images involved in the digital crime scenarios.

© Springer International Publishing AG 2017
C. Kraetzer et al. (Eds.): IWDW 2017, LNCS 10431, pp. 52–64, 2017.
DOI: 10.1007/978-3-319-64185-0_5

Camera Model Identification [2–13], is the problem of identifying the legitimate source of an image under question, through forensic investigations. This is primarily done by attributing an image to its source using camera fingerprints such as Photo Response Non Uniformity (PRNU) or through a machine learning classification using feature such as Image Quality Metrics (IQM), High Order Wavelet Statistics (HOWS) etc.

Counter-forensics with respect to camera model identification [14–18] are aimed towards defeating state–of–the–art camera model identification techniques by fooling the forensic analysis process. Counter–forensic attacks against camera model identification are majorly comprised of *source anonymization* techniques. *Source anonymization* is a form of intelligent adversarial attack, which hinders source attribution of images through illegitimate image modifications. Such attacks are motivated by image anonymization works [14] that aim at user anonymity, which are of relevance in protecting the privacy of on–line users. However, image anonymity acts as a hindrance to forensic image source identification.

Recent counter–forensic techniques [14–18] have proved to be quite effective in battling state–of–the–art camera model identification. Hence, it is imperative that the state–of–the–art camera model identification techniques be made capable enough to resist counter–forensic attacks. In this context, here we propose a deep learning based classification model using Convolutional Neural Networks (CNN) to detect whether an image (to be analyzed forensically) is authentic, or it has undergone counter–forensic modifications which would result in invalidation of the forensic analysis results.

Our major contribution in this paper is the development of a deep learning based CNN model for classification between authentic and counter–forensically modified images. In addition, the proposed model performs a second level of (multi–class) classification to identify the specific class of counter–forensic attack the (tampered) image has undergone. The performance of a machine learning system largely depends on how effectively features of the concerned dataset are identified and extracted. Many artificial intelligence problems are solved through machine learning, only when the appropriate features are successfully identified and extracted. It is this dependency of machine learning based models on the representation (features) of the data, that many times makes such systems ineffective; specifically, when the features are difficult to be identified. *Deep Learning* is a fast emerging trend, where feature identification and extraction is taken care of by the underlying neural network, i.e., the deep learning network does a representation learning for the given data. We utilize this ability of a deep neural network to perform a representation learning of counter–forensic images and hence to develop a classification model for those. A *Convolutional Neural Network* (CNN), used to build the proposed model in this work, is a special type of deep neural network which is based on linear mathematical convolution.

In Fig. 1, we present the operational flowchart of the proposed two–level classification system. Figure 1 shows that proposed model primarily consists of a *counter–forensic detection module*, which is a deep learning network (CNN), that detects whether the image is authentic or counter–forensically modified.

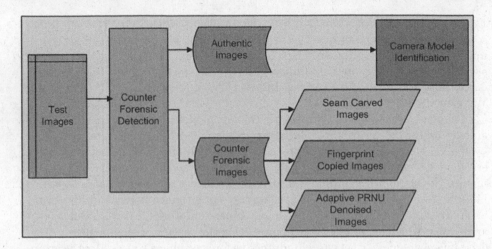

Fig. 1. Operational flowchart of the proposed model for classification of counter-forensic images with respect to camera model identification.

If an image is detected to be authentic, it is taken up for forensic investigations. Else, if the image is detected to be counter–forensically modified, the proposed model tries to identify the class of source anonymization performed on it, so as to assist the forensic analyst to adopt possible measures for retrieving the image back to its original form. This is done by a multi–class classification among the major classes of state–of–the–art source anonymization techniques, using deep learning.

In this paper, we deal with the three broad classes constituting the state–of–the–art in source anonymization, viz., *Seam Carving* [14,15], *Fingerprint Copying* [16], and *Adaptive PRNU Denoising* [17]. Our experimental results prove that the classification accuracy of the proposed model is considerably high.

The rest of the paper is organized as follows. In Sect. 2, we present the relevant background on camera model identification and related source anonymization techniques. In Sect. 3, we present the proposed deep learning Convolutional Neural Network model for classification of source anonymized images. Our experimental results are presented in Sect. 4. Finally, we conclude with future research directions in Sect. 5.

2   Background

In the existing state–of–the–art, there are mainly two approaches to image source identification, viz., fingerprint based approach [5,7,19] and feature based machine learning approach [2–4,8–11,21]. We discuss the basic operation of both the approaches in Sect. 2.1. In Sect. 2.2 we present relevant background on existing counter–forensic (source anonymization) attacks on camera model identification.

2.1   Camera Model Identification

Kharrazi et al. [2] proposed a feature based image source iedntification technique, by representing an image as a set of numerical features. The features are computed in both spatial domain (Image Quality Metrics (IQM)) and wavelet domain (High Order Wavelet Statistics (HOWS)). Ever since, several researchers have used different image feature sets to perform camera model identification. Those include Binary Similarity Metrics (BSM) used by Celiktutan et al. [3], features based on Color Filter Array (CFA) interpolation used by Bayram et al. [4], extended color feature set used by Gloe et al. [21], image texture features like Local Binary Pattern (LBP) and Local Phase Quantization (LPQ) features used by Bing et al. [9], ensemble of demosaicing features used by Chen et al. [11], among others. Supervised machine learning based classification techniques (such as Support Vector Machine (SVM)) are used in the above researches to perform classification among different camera models.

In fingerprint based techniques for image source identification, Photo Response Non–Uniformity (PRNU) noise has been used as unique camera fingerprint to map an image to its source [5,7,19]. PRNU of a test image, and Sensor Pattern Noises (SPN) of possible camera models are computed, and a correlation mechanism between those is employed to correlate an image to its source. Correlation mechanisms used in the literature include Normalised Cross Correlation (NCC) [5] and Peak to Correlation Energy (PCE) [6].

Very recently, a number of researchers have started using deep learning techniques in camera model identification [12,13]. In these works, different deep learning architectures are studied and the deep neural networks are tuned to perform efficient camera model identification. In [12] a simple CNN is trained for camera model identification and in [13], a CNN followed by a transfer learning using SVM is proposed. Both these techniques offer a new perspective to camera model identification as there is no pre–processing step involved. In case of a feature based techniques, the pre–processing involved consists of feature engineering; and in case of fingerprint based techniques, sensor patter noise and PRNU computations.

2.2   Counter–Forensics for Image Source Identification

As stated previously, image source anonymization is the major form of counter–forensic attack against camera model identification. Next, we discuss the basic operating principles of the three major classes of source anonymization algorithms, viz., *Seam Carving* [14,15], *Fingerprint Copying* [16], and *Adaptive PRNU Denoising* [17].

Seam Carving. *Seam Carving* [22] is a content aware resizing approach which finds wide use in counter–forensics [14,15]. Seam carving technique is used to disturb an image's reference noise pattern, so as to defeat PRNU based image source attribution, which operates by correlating image noise pattern with (possible) camera reference patterns.

Specifically, seam carving disturbs the PRNU content of an image through image resizing, thus removes *seams* (connected paths of pixels with least variation from surrounding pixels) [22] of an image. For an image with m rows and n columns, a vertical seam s is nothing but a path connecting pixels from top to bottom with horizontal offsets (between adjacent rows) not more than one pixel, and is represented mathematically as,

$$s = \{s_i\}_{i=1}^{n-1} = \{(col(i), i)\}_{i=1}^{n-1}, \text{ where } |col(i+1) - col(i)| \le 1 \tag{1}$$

where i represents an image column and $col(i)$ is a mapping from $[1 \cdots n]$ to $[1 \cdots m]$. The seam is a 8–connected path from top to bottom, with exactly one pixel per row. Finally, the pixels forming the seam s would be $I(s_i)_{i=1}^{n-1} = I(col(i), i)_{i=1}^{n-1}$.

An optimal seam (s^*) is the seam with the lowest sum of energy [22], where the energy function is given by,

$$e(I) = \left|\frac{\partial I}{\partial x}\right| + \left|\frac{\partial I}{\partial y}\right| \tag{2}$$

and, an optimal seam (s^*) is computed as,

$$s^* = \min_s \sum_{i=1}^{n} e(I(s_i)) \tag{3}$$

It is evident from the above equation that the optimal seam is computed using the cumulative minimum energy, for all possible connected seams, from the first to the last column. Such optimal seams are removed from the original image to get a seam carved image.

What makes a seam carved image difficult to analyse, is the lack of information about the location or number of its seams removed. This is because the process of seam carving is irreversible, and the PRNU pattern of the seam carved image, will correlate very poorly with noise reference pattern of its source.

Fingerprint Copy Attack. *Fingerprint copy* [16,23], as the name suggests, is the technique of masking one camera reference pattern with another. The adversary masks his own camera pattern with another innocent's camera pattern, thus resulting into high rate of false positives in camera model identification. In a sensitive forensic application as camera model identification, it is of paramount importance to keep the false positive alarms minimal. Hence, the fingerprint copy attack poses as an imminent threat to the credibility of the forensic source identification systems, by leading an innocent to be detected wrongly as culprit.

Fingerprint copy attack is delivered as follows. Let image I be originating from camera A, possessed by an adversary. Let us assume that the adversary additionally gets access to some images captured by some other person's camera B, and estimates the noise residuals of both cameras A and B, NR_A and NR_B

respectively, from the available images. Now, he removes his camera's fingerprint from I, and adds the fingerprint of B to I, by the following:

$$\tilde{I} = I - \alpha \times NR_A + \beta \times NR_B \tag{4}$$

where NR_A and NR_B are the noise residuals of cameras A and B respectively, and α and β are the camera substitution parameters that determine the strength of the fingerprint copy.

As a result, the forénsic analyst is fooled to believe that image I originated from camera B, and not from A, as a result of his investigations. This renders the owner of camera B to be the culprit, instead of that of camera A.

Adaptive PRNU Denoising (APD). Image PRNU is resilient to various geometric and compression manipulations [5]. Hence to make an image untraceable to its source camera, different attacks started targeting the PRNU content of an image, a major identifier of the underlying sensor. *Adaptive PRNU Denoising (APD)* [17] is one such counter–forensic attack which denoises an image, repetitively, until it has sufficiently suppressed the image PRNU to prevent its source identification. In the following Eq. 5, a Denoising Filter (DF) is applied m times to suppress the noise residual of an image I.

$$\hat{I} = DF(DF(DF \cdots m \ times \ (I))) = DF^m(I) \tag{5}$$

The objective is to obtain an image which would correlate very poorly with its own PRNU noise pattern. In order to achieve this, the PRNU estimate of the image I (NR_I) is computed as in [5], and a magnitude adjustment factor β is estimated according to Eq. 6 below.

$$Corr((I - \beta \times NR_I), NR_I) \approx 0 \tag{6}$$

APD lowers the correlation of an image to its source efficiently, without affecting any visual artifact. Since no additional artifacts are introduced due to repeated denoising, to detect whether an image has undergone this process, is difficult.

The existing counter–forensic techniques presented above, are extremely efficient in defeating state–of–the–art camera model identification methods. Hence it would be helpful to distinguish between authentic and counter–forensic images, so as not to fool the forensic investigations. As of yet no suitable feature or common artifacts have been identified, which are capable enough to distinguish counter–forensic images. Hence we adopt a deep learning architecture in this work, for the task of counter–forensic image classification, whereby the feature learning happens through deep neural network.

3 Proposed Deep Learning Based Convolutional Neural Network (CNN) Model for Counter–Forensic Image Classification

In a machine learning based classification system, the feature representations have to be accurately defined. However, in scenarios where it is impossible or difficult to pre–define a feature representation of given dataset, machine learning techniques are bound to fail. Deep learning techniques, having the ability to acquire knowledge through the inherent characteristics of training data where the knowledge acquired is stored as the weights of the network, overcomes this limitation of machine learning models. Regular neural networks do perform well in image classification, but due to high computational complexity and as the weights in successive layers keep on increasing, having a full connectivity in every layer, would involve huge number of parameters, and quickly lead to overfitting. Convolutional Neural Networks (CNN) [27] constitute a type of deep learning neural networks, which perform well with images. They have been found to be useful in various computer vision and image processing applications, such as object recognition [26], number recognition from hand written text etc. [27].

In this paper, we use convolutional neural networks to perform a two stage classification for counter–forensic images. First, a binary classification to separate counter–forensic images from authentic ones, and second, a multi–class classification to identify the type of counter–forensic image. The proposed CNN architecture is shown as a block diagram in Fig. 2, which includes the followings:

- The first convolution layer (Conv1) with a 3×3 kernel and 32 filters, followed by a Rectifier Linera Unit (ReLU).
- The second convolution layer (Conv2) with a 3×3 kernel and 32 filters, followed by another ReLU.
- Max Pooling with a 2×2 window, followed by the first dropout layer (DropOut1) with drop out parameter 0.2.
- A fully connected layer, followed by a ReLU activation, which is subsequently followed by the second dropout layer (DropOut2) with drop out parameter of 0.5.
- A fully connected layer, followed by a softmax layer for loss computation.

Next, we describe in detail, the structure of different layers (specified above) used in this architecture, along with the importance of each.

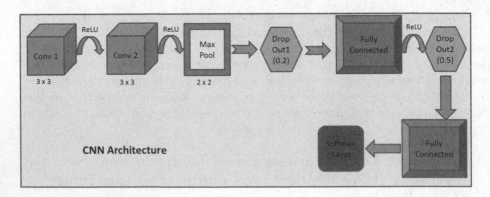

Fig. 2. Proposed CNN architecture for counter–forensic image classification.

3.1   Convolution

The major operation performed in a CNN is *convolution*. Convolutional networks are simply neural networks, that use convolution in place of general matrix multiplication in at least one of their layers [24]. The convolution operation [25] on a signal S, using a window W, is defined as follows:

$$C(t) = \int S(x)W(t-x)dx \qquad (7)$$

In CNN terminology, the first argument to a convolution operation ($S(x)$ in Eq. 7) is called the *input* and the second argument ($W(t-x)$ in Eq. 7) is called the *kernel*. The output of the convolution operation is a *feature map* ($C(t)$ in Eq. 7).

On a two dimensional signal, such as an image I, of dimension $m \times n$, using a kernel K, the convolution operation is carried out as follows:

$$C(i,j) = \sum_m \sum_n I(m,n)K(i-m, j-n) \qquad (8)$$

From each test image I (authentic or counter–forensic), we crop out a central portion (of size 32×32, 64×64 or 128×128), which are fed as input to the proposed CNN in batches of sizes 64, 128 and 256. Here, we use two convolution layers with 32 filters and kernel of size 3×3 each. In the next section, we describe the activation and pooling types used in this work.

3.2   Activation and Pooling

A CNN performs three primitive operational steps while doing a classification. It starts with a convolution operation using a specific kernel, then uses an activation function in the *detector stage* for feature extraction, and finally enhances the output further, through a *pooling* layer. An activation function takes the output of the previous layer which is nothing but a weighted data and produces a non–linear transformation of the data. Most used activation functions include sigmoid ($\frac{1}{1+e^{-x}}$) and tanh ($f(x) = tanh(x)$), (x being the input signal) [24]. Rectified Linear Units (ReLU) are used extensively in deep learning to achieve *non–linearity*. In a ReLU, $f(x) \approx log(1 + e^x)$, where x is the input signal.

In this paper, we use three ReLU activations to introduce non–linearity in the layers. The advantage of a ReLU over a Sigmoid function is that the gradient of sigmoid function reaches approximately zero when we increase or decrease x; but in case of a ReLU, the gradient does not vanish when x is varied.

In the pooling layer, the output of the previous layer at a particular position is replaced with the summary statistics of its neighborhood. The popular pooling mechanisms adopted are, max pooling (which replaces the value with the maximum element in the pre–defined neighborhood), average pooling (which replaces the average value of the pre–defined neighborhood), L^2 norm of neighborhood (which replaces the value with square root of sum of squares of the activations in the neighborhood). In this paper, we use a max pooling layer with a 2×2 window. Next, we describe the type of optimizer used in our CNN.

3.3 Optimizer

The most important module involved in a neural network is the performance evaluation of the learning task at hand, to measure how well the network is able to optimize the cost function $J(\theta)$ (where θ is the parameter space of the architecture). The cost function in this paper is considered to be the 'classification error'. Hence, in this work, the objective is to minimize the classification error, i.e., to minimize the cost function.

The function of the *optimizer* in a CNN is to find the optimal set of θ values, i.e., the set which would optimize cost function $J(\theta)$. The types of optimizers used commonly in deep learning are, *Stochastic Gradient Descent, RMS Prop, Adam, AdaDelta* [24] etc.

In this paper, we use Stochastic Gradient Descent optimizer, with a learning rate of 0.01, and momentum fixed at 0.9. Additionally, dropout layers are used in the proposed CNN to overcome overfitting. In a dropout layer, the updation of weights of random nodes is stopped, so that the network is forced to learn independent representations of the data, and hence to prevent overfitting.

4   Experimental Results

In this section we provide our experimental results to measure the accuracy of the proposed deep learning model in classifying counter–forensic images.

4.1   Experimental Setup

We conducted our experiments on the Dresden Image Database [20], which is a benchmark dataset, available publicly for image forensic research. In this work, we have used a total of 12,500 natural images of the Dresden database, for our experiments, out of which 5,000 are authentic and the rest 7,500 are counter–forensically modified. The 7,500 counter–forensic images, consist of three sets of 2,500 images, modified manually through seam carving, fingerprint copy attack and Adaptive PRNU Denoising, respectively, following the procedure discussed in Sect. 2.2.

The proposed CNN takes input on varied batches as 64, 128 and 256 for 32×32, 64×64 and 128×128 image blocks. The proposed network architecture is presented in Fig. 2. A 3×3 kernel is used in convolution and a 2×2 window in max pooling layer. The convolution layers are followed by a ReLU activation to introduce non–linearity. All the different batches are trained using Stochastic Gradient Descent (SGD) with a momentum fixed at 0.9, learning rate of 0.01 and decay of 0.005. Two drop–out layers are used to fight overfitting with dropout probabilities 0.2 and 0.5 respectively. The last layer is a softmax layer that computes the loss function.

In our work, the CNN training is carried out using the keras [28] framework developed for deep learning. We have used a workstation with an Intel Xeon CPU (E3-1225 v5, 3.3 GHz), 16 GB RAM and a GPU (Geforce GTX 970) with 1664 CUDA cores.

4.2   Performance of the Proposed Model

Experiment 1. The first step in our proposed methodology is to perform a binary classification between authentic and counter–forensic images. The training samples are labelled with two classes: authentic (5000 samples) or counter–forensic (7500 samples). The confusion matrix representing the binary classification results, is shown in Table 1. The overall classification accuracy achieved is 93.4%.

Table 1. Classification accuracy results for binary classification between authentic and counter–forensic images. (Overall accuracy 93.4%)

Actual	Predicted	
	Authentic	Counter–Forensic
Authentic	94.72%	5.28%
Counter–Forensic	7.48%	92.52%

Experiment 2. In the second step, the counter–forensic images are further classified according to the class of source anonymization attack that they have undergone (seam carved, fingerprint copied, or APD). We used 2500 labelled training samples from each type of counter–forensic class. In Table 2, we present the second level classification accuracy results between seam carved, fingerprint copied, and PRNU denoised images, with varied image sizes (32×32, 64×64 and 128×128) and batch sizes ($64, 128, 256$).

In our experiments, we achieve the maximum classification accuracy of 85.7% for image size 64×64, and batch size 128, using a stochastic gradient descent optimizer with learning rate of 0.01 and momentum of 0.9.

As evident from Table 2, the classification accuracy varies with image (crop–out) size. We observe the the best performance with 64×64 sized images. This result is in compliance with the findings made in [13], where 64×64 sized image patches proved to give best performance in source camera identification.

Table 2. Classification accuracy (%) among seam carved, fingerprint copied, and PRNU denoised images.

Image size	32×32			64×64			128×128		
Batch size	64	128	256	64	128	256	64	128	256
100 epochs	33.3	48.7	48.4	73.1	72.6	75.1	36.7	34.3	33.3
200 epochs	42.7	50.1	53.6	76.4	78.1	76.2	42.2	40.2	38.3
300 epochs	48.1	52.6	56.2	77.3	81.2	77.9	50.4	52.6	42.4
500 epochs	52.3	59.3	59.1	81.5	84.2	82.6	55.2	57.3	51.3
1000 epochs	55.7	61.2	60.2	84.6	**85.7**	84.1	59.2	61.2	56.4

Discussion. An epoch represents the time taken for one forward pass and one backward pass of all the training examples. That is, when there are N training samples and batches are of size b, then it takes $\frac{N}{b}$ iterations to complete one epoch. In our experiments, we varied the number of epochs until the performance of the proposed system stabilizes, and does not significantly change from one epoch to the next.

The image batch size also plays a crucial role in representation learning. It represents the number of samples that are going to be propagated through the deep learning model. Larger batch size implies higher memory requirement. For instance, if there are N training samples, and the batch size is fixed to be b, then sequential batches of $\frac{N}{b}$ samples are used iteratively for training the network. The advantage of using the concept of batches is that the entire dataset need not be loaded into memory at once. Also it makes the learning of the model faster, as the network weights are updated at every iteration.

In order to avoid overfitting, two dropout layers are used with values 0.2 and 0.5 respectively and we used a validation dataset to evaluate our performance (which is completely hidden from training) with 20% of total images. The classification accuracies presented in Tables 1 and 2 are for the validation dataset. This proves that the proposed CNN architecture is capable of distinguishing between authentic and counter–forensic images with a considerably high efficiency; and it further detects the type of counter–forensic attack efficiently (with 64×64 images).

All the above mentioned parameters, viz., image size, batch size, number of epochs, kind of optimizer used (SGD in our case), hyperparameters like learning rate, momentum etc., decide the performance of a deep neural network.

5   Conclusion

In image source identification, the presence of counter–forensic images poses a serious threat to a forensic analyst, with respect to the credibility of the investigation results. Thus it is of paramount importance to identify whether an image is counter–forensically modified, and hence to remove those from the source identification module. In this paper, we perform a counter–forensic image classification, by adopting a two–level classification mechanism. At level one the proposed system distinguishes between authentic and counter–forensically modified images. At level two, the counter–forensic images are further classified according to the source anonymization attack that they have undergone.

Future research in this direction would involve formulation of anti counter–forensic measures to combat the existing counter–forensic attacks, and hence to achieve highly accurate source identification, even with counter–forensic images.

References

1. Fridrich, J.: Digital Image Forensics: There is More to a Picture than Meets the Eye. Springer, New York (2012)
2. Kharrazi, M., Sencar, H.T., Memon, N.: Blind source camera identification. In: International Conference on Image Processing (ICIP) (2004)
3. Celiktutan, O., Sankur, B., Avcibas, I.: Blind identification of source cell-phone model. IEEE Trans. Inf. Forensics Secur. **3**(3), 553–566 (2008)
4. Bayram, S., Sencar, H.T., Memon, N.: Improvements on source camera-model identification based on CFA interpolation. In: Proceedings of the WG (2006)
5. Lukas, J.: Digital camera identification from sensor pattern noise. IEEE Trans. Inf. Forensics Secur. **1**(2), 205–214 (2006)
6. Goljan, M., Fridrich, J., Filler, T.: Large scale test of sensor fingerprint camera identification. In: IS&T/SPIE Electronic Imaging, p. 72540I–72540I (2009)
7. Li, C.-T.: Digital camera identification from sensor pattern noise. IEEE Trans. Inf. Forensics Secur. **5**(2), 280–287 (2010)
8. Akshatha, K.R., Karunakar, A.K., Anitha, H., Raghavendra, U., Shetty, D.: Digital camera identification using PRNU: a feature based approach. Digit. Invest. **19**, 69–77 (2016). Elsevier
9. Bingchao, X., XiaofengWang, X., JianghuanXi, S.: Source camera identification from image texture features. Neurocomputing **207**, 131–140 (2016). Elsevier
10. Deng, L., Gen, L., Shao, Y., Fei, M., Huosheng, H.: A novel camera calibration technique based on differential evolution particle swarm optimization algorithm. Neurocomputing **174**, 456–465 (2016). Elsevier
11. Chen, C., Stamm, M.C.: Camera model identification framework using an ensemble of demosaicing features. In: IEEE International Workshop on Information Forensics and Security (WIFS) (2015)
12. Tuama, A., Comby, F., Chaumont, M.: Camera model identification with the use of deep convolutional neural networks. In: IEEE International Workshop on Information Forensics and Security (WIFS) (2016)
13. Bondi, L., Baroffio, L., Guera, D., Bestagini, P., Delp, E.J., Tubaro, S.: First steps towards camera model identification with convolutional neural networks. IEEE Sig. Process. Lett. **24**(3), 259–263 (2017)
14. Bayram, S., Sencar, H.T., Memon, N.D.: Seam-carving based anonymization against image and video source attribution. In: Proceedings of the IEEE 15th International Workshop Multimedia Signal Processing (MMSP) (2013)
15. Dirik, A.E., Sencar, H.T., Memon, N.: Analysis of seam-carving-based anonymization of images against PRNU noise pattern-based source attribution. IEEE Trans. Inf. Forensics Secur. **9**(12), 2277–2290 (2014)
16. Quirring, E., Krichner, M.: Fragile sensor fingerprint camera identification. In: IEEE International Workshop on Information Forensics and Security (WIFS) (2015)
17. Karakk, A., Dirik, A.E.: Adaptive photo-response non-uniformity noise removal against image source attribution. Digit. Invest. **12**, 66–76 (2015). Elsevier
18. Karakuuk, A., Dirik, A.E., Sencar, H.T., Memon, N.D.: Recent advances in counter PRNU based source attribution and beyond. In: Proceedings of the SPIE 9409, Media Watermarking, Security, and Forensics (2015)
19. Lawgaly, A., Khelifi, F.: Sensor pattern noise estimation based on improved locally adaptive DCT filtering and weighted averaging for source camera identification and verification. IEEE Trans. Inf. Forensics Secur. **12**(2), 392–404 (2017)

20. Gloe, T., Bhme, R.: Dresden image database for benchmarking digital image forensics. In: IEEE International Conference on Acoustics, Speech and Signal Processing (2010)

21. Gloe, T.: Feature-based forensic camera model identification. In: Shi, Y.Q., Katzenbeisser, S. (eds.) Transactions on Data Hiding and Multimedia Security VIII. LNCS, vol. 7228, pp. 42–62. Springer, Heidelberg (2012). doi:10.1007/978-3-642-31971-6_3

22. Avidan, S., Shamir, A.: Seam carving for content-aware image resizing. ACM Trans. Graph. (TOG) **26**(3) (2007). No. 10

23. Zeng, H.: Rebuilding the credibility of sensor-based camera source identification. Multimedia Tools Appl. **75**(21), 13871–13882 (2016). Springer

24. Goodfellow, I., Bengio, Y., Courville, A.: Deep Learning. MIT Press (2016). http://www.deeplearningbook.org

25. Gonzalez, R.C., Woods, R.E.: Image processing. In: Digital Image Processing, vol. 2 (2007)

26. Zhou, B., Lapedriza, A., Xiao, J., Torralba, A., Oliva, A.: Learning deep features for scene recognition using places database. In: Advances in Neural Information Processing Systems, pp. 487–495 (2014)

27. Krizhevsky, A.A., Sutskever, I., Hinton, G.: Imagenet classification with deep convolutional neural networks. In: Advances in Neural Information Processing Systems, pp. 1097–1105 (2012)

28. Chollet, F.: Keras (2015). https://github.com/fchollet/keras

Block-Based Convolutional Neural Network for Image Forgery Detection

Jianghong Zhou, Jiangqun Ni[✉], and Yuan Rao

Sun Yat-sen University, Da-Xue-Cheng, Guangzhou, China
issjqni@mail.sysu.edu.cn

Abstract. With the development of a variety of image editing tools, performing digital image forgery and concealing the forgery edge is easier. On the other hand, these visually convincing tampering operations also make authentication of digital images difficult. Therefore, developing a precise and robust method to detect these splicing images is urgently required. In the past, some researchers proposed some methods, which achieves an accuracy of over 97%, but robustness of these methods remains unknown. In this paper, a novel image forgery detection method based on a special blocking strategy is proposed, in which the processing unit for each block is a rich model convolutional neural network (rCNN). The proposed method is not only able to detect the splicing image but also reserves its effectiveness under circumstances of JPG compression. Extensive experiments with CASIA v1.0, CASIO v2.0 and Columbia image forgery evaluation databases were carried out, which demonstrates the effectiveness and strong robustness of the proposed method.

Keywords: Splicing image detection · Rich model · Convolutional neural network · Blocking strategy

1 Introduction

With the development of a variety of image editing tools, editing digital images is easier, among which image forgery is one of the most common techniques. Image forgery is commonly considered as a process of cropping and pasting regions on the same or separate sources [1]. Therefore, in accordance with the sources of the pasting regions, the problems can be classified into image splicing and copy-move forgery [2]. If the pasting region are from the images other than pasted one, the process is considered as image splicing, otherwise it is copy-move forgery. Generally, the detection of these image forgery is based on the inevitable alternative of the underlying statistical characteristic of an image during the process of image forgery [2].

There exist numerous methods for image forgery detection. Many of them consider the statistical characteristic in different domains. Shi *et al.* [3] propose a natural image model for image splicing detection, in which they apply discrete cosine transformation (DCT) and extract features from DCT domain.

© Springer International Publishing AG 2017
C. Kraetzer et al. (Eds.): IWDW 2017, LNCS 10431, pp. 65–76, 2017.
DOI: 10.1007/978-3-319-64185-0_6

Zhou *et al.* proposed a Markov-based method to extract features from DCT and DWT domain [2]. Different from aforementioned methods, the approach of Lyu *et al.* directly focus on the inconsistence of noise surrounding to the forgery edge, because they assume the noises are different if the image is from different camera sensors [4]. Except for noises inconsistency, some researchers discover that the texture micro-patterns are different between two sides of forgery edge. Inspired by this, G. Muhammad *et al.* extract local binary pattern from the image, and apply steerable pyramid transformation to it. The features effectively represent the distortions of the texture patterns of the tampered image, and achieve so far the best detection performance on CASIA dataset [5,6].

In contrast to the aforementioned methods, we do not focus on any specific feature or any domain, but concentrate on constructing a model to extract useful features automatically. Our model is based on deep neural network. The models of deep neural network are diverse, such as Deep Belief Network [7], Deep Auto Encoder [8] and Convolutional Neural Network(CNN) [9]. Among which, CNN is one of the widely-used deep neural network models for computer vision tasks, and is also adopted in our work [10,11,13]. It applies trainable filters and local neighborhood pooling operations on the raw input image, resulting in a hierarchy of increasingly abstract features. CNN can achieve superior performance on visual object recognition [10], due to its structure and working principle are highly similar to visual system [14]. The basic operations and structures of CNNs contain initializers, activator, pooling layer, filter-training layers and classifiers [15]. The combinations of these structures and operations can result in different models, like VGG [17], LeNet [19] and AlexNet [18]. Their performances in a certain field of applications can be different. Therefore, the structures can be various for the applications. Besides, deep learning is also called the art of tuning, because the model has a large amount of parameters and a fine tuning may affect whether the network can achieve the expected performance for the task [19]. In our proposed CNN, we apply rich model to initialize the first layer of the neural network, which we proposed in [20] and has been certified that can help the model achieve high performance in forgery image detection. Figure 1 shows the features from different layers, from forgery image and authenticated image respectively. The feature maps from the first layer are very different around the forgery part. These highlighted features maybe significant in our task. However, directly applying stretching transformation to the image does deteriorate the performance of the CNN-based method, because the features of the forgery edge are very sensitive to stretching transformation. To avoid stretching transformation, we apply some special methods. In [20], we apply Max-pooling to the feature maps. The feature maps from Max-pooling can achieve 98.02% through support vector machine(SVM) (When we use Contrastive Loss Function). Notwithstanding, Max-pooling's robustness to JPEG compression is not strong enough. Therefore, we design a novel strategy to strengthen the ability.

In this paper, we propose a new blocking strategy. In our proposed method, we firstly split the big image into small blocks. If an image block contains the forgery block, it is labeled as a forgery one, otherwise, it is labeled an authenticated block.

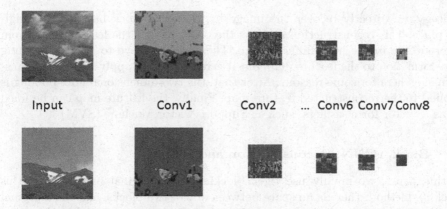

Fig. 1. The feature maps of a forgery image and an authenticated image from different layers. The forgery part is highlighted

Then, we use these data to train rCNN. The trained rCNN serves as the block descriptor for image forgery detection. After that, we apply split-and-reconstruct method to process the original image. The new expression is resized and pooled. Finally, we have the features for SVM and classify the images. Compared to Max-pooling, the advantage of our method is obvious. First of all, it contains more image information. The max-pooling only extract the activated information. Not only does the proposed method extract the activated information, but also it contains the distributions of these activated area. Besides, max-pooling is very sensitive to the maximum value. If the area is not correctly activated, it can cover other error-correcting information and lead to wrong classification.

The rest of the paper is organized as follows: In Sect. 2, we delineate the process of the blocking strategies. In Sect. 3, we represent the experimental results of the proposed method in different database. And finally, the conclusion of this paper is drawn in Sect. 4.

2   The Proposed Block-Based CNN

For CNN based CV tasks, e.g., image processing applications, the computation complexity for CNN training is generally proportional to the image dimensions (in between linear and exponential). To accelerate the computation, we adopt the strategy of block based CNN in our implementation. On the other hand, CNN is a kind of data-driven approach. The blocking strategy helps to greatly expand the training set for effective feature learning. After the processing of CNN, the features of each block or the solutions of local parts are required to be combined to obtain the solution of the whole problem. In past, we apply one-dimensional max-pooling to avoid the stretching transformation, because stretching transformation may damage the forgery edge with interpolation and sampling. However, this method largely ignores the geometry and error-correcting information. It is very sensitive to the large value activated by CNN. Therefore, in our blocking strategy, we directly recover the image by place the block back to the original place. This reconstruction remains the problem that the feature maps from different size image have different size. Therefore, we have to apply stretching transformation to the feature map, but it is reasonable to apply stretching transformation here for some reasons. After that, the two-dimensional max-pooling is applied to the reconstructed feature map. Finally, the feature map can be lined up as a vector for classifiers, such as Support Vector Machine (SVM).

2.1   Block, rCNN, Reconstruction and Resize

In this paper, we mainly use tight blocking and marginal blocking. By this blocking method, there is no space between any of two blocks, and the marginal part is directly taken from inverse direction. In fact, marginal blocking may cause an important problem. The proposed method eventually reconstructs the blocks. The process of reconstruction causes some repeated areas (Fig. 1).

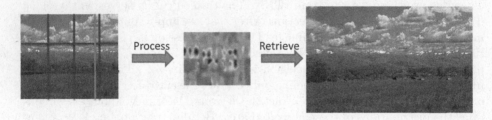

Fig. 2. Considering the right side of the recovery image, it is easy to find that part of the image is repeated.

However, it does not affect the classification. Since the final result is determined by features from each block. In the proposed method, the most important feature descriptor is rCNN. rCNN process the blocks, so the description is local. If each block is not labeled as forgery image, the combination of these blocks is also not forgery (Fig. 2).

After the blocking, take our experiments as an example. The block's size is 128×128. After processing them with the CNN in Table 1. The features are extracted from the Convolution layer 8, whose size is $5 \times 5 \times 16$.

After blocking and the CNN processing, the blocks should be reconstructed as a feature of the original image. The reconstruction is placing the blocks back to the original position so that the features in the feature map are reflections of original image. However, before this operation, the feature maps should be processed centrosymmetry, because while extracting the features with CNN, the image is in fact processed centrosymmetry. Therefore, this operation can erase the direction influence of CNN.

Notwithstanding, the reconstruction cannot promise the reconstructed features are the same size and thus a resize process is required. The resize process

Table 1. The structure and the setting of rCNN in this paper.

Layer	Operations	Input size	Output size	Filter size	Parameters
Convolution layer 1	Rich Model	$128 \times 128 \times 3$ (crop to $127 \times 127 \times 3$)	30	5×5	2 and no pad
ReLU	-	$123 \times 123 \times 30$	-	-	-
Convolution layer 2	Xavier	$123 \times 123 \times 30$	30	5×5	2 and no pad
ReLU	-	$60 \times 60 \times 30$	-	-	-
Pool	Max	$60 \times 60 \times 30$	-	2×2	2 no pad
LRN	-	$30 \times 30 \times 30$	-	Local size: 5	Alpha: 0.0001 Beta: 0.75
Convolution layer 3	Xaiver	$30 \times 30 \times 30$	16	3×3	1 no pad
ReLU	-	$28 \times 28 \times 16$	-	-	-
Convolution layer 4	Xavier	$28 \times 2n8 \times 16$	16	3×3	1 no pad
ReLU	-	$26 \times 26 \times 16$	-	-	-
Pool	MAX	$26 \times 26 \times 16$	2×2	2	no pad
LRN	-	$3 \times 13 \times 16$	-	5×5	Alpha: 0.0001 Beta: 0.75
Convolution layer 5	Xavier	$13 \times 13 \times 16$	16	3×3	1 no pad
ReLU	-	$11 \times 11 \times 16$	-	-	-
Convolution layer 6	Xavier	$11 \times 11 \times 16$	16	3×3	1 no pad
ReLU	-	$9 \times 9 \times 16$	-	-	-
Convolution layer 6	-	$9 \times 9 \times 16$	16	3×3	1 no pad
ReLU	-	$7 \times 7 \times 16$	-	-	-
Convolution layer 7	Xavier	$7 \times 7 \times 16$	16	3×3	1 no pad
ReLU	-	$5 \times 5 \times 16$	-	-	-
Dropout		$5 \times 5 \times 16$	-	-	- Ration: 0.5
Ip1	- $5 \times 5 \times 16$	- 2	-		
Softmax with loss	-	2			

is actually a stretching transformation of the big feature map, resulting a same size of feature to perform pooling and finally the classifiers can classify input image based on a fixed-sized feature vector. Stretching transformation is not preferable in the forgery image detection because statistical information of the forgery edge is sensitive to such transformation. However, compared to the original image, feature is sparse. CNN in fact applies many times activating and pooling operations to original image and each layer enlarges the activated value while reduces the redundancy. Because of sparsity, the feature is supposed to be more robust to stretching transformation. The experimental result also supports the conjecture. The stretching transformation of feature is useful and better than stretching transformation of original feature (Table 2).

In Table 2, applying stretching transformation to the original image deteriorates the performance of the classification badly. On the contrary, applying stretching transformation to the feature achieves a better performance. Consequently, applying stretching transformation to the feature is more suitable.

Table 2. Operation 1 is applying stretching transformation to the original image and use the classifying method in this paper. Operation 2 is Softmax Classifier, which is the direct result of rCNN. Operation 3 is applying stretching transformation to the feature and using the classifying method in this paper.

Operation	CASIA2	CASIA1	Columbia
Operation 1	74.24%	72.23%	74.32%
Operation 2	93.21%	94.36%	95.52%
Operation 3	97.97%	97.86%	97.04%

2.2 Two-dimensional Pooling

Pooling is a common operation in neural network, which is useful to reduce redundancy and extract the important information. In fact, the principle of pooling is similar to visual systems. Mammals visual system is very sensitive to a specific value in a small area. This working process is very useful in digital image processing. In this way, the storage requirement can be significantly alleviated. Generally speaking, pooling is a process of a specific window function. The window function can be mean function, maximum function, minimum function and etc. The window slide with specific steps and the windows processed area can be overlapped or loosen. The window function gives a value from the processed area. Besides, pooling operation can be multi-dimensional. Figure 3 respectively represents the process of one-dimensional max pooling and two-dimensional pooling.

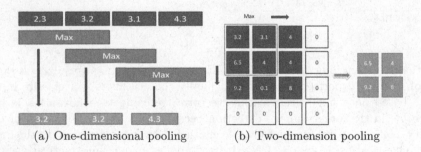

(a) One-dimensional pooling   (b) Two-dimension pooling

Fig. 3. (a) is a one-dimension maximum pooling. The window function is maximum function and the slide step is one. (b) is a two-dimension pooling. The window function is also maximum function. However, this poolings slide step is two and it also contains a zero padding to resolve the remain-part problem.

The pooling methods are various, because the setting of slide step, window function and padding are different. In this paper, our pooling does not apply padding. Therefore, the setting of step, window functions size and size of object should satisfy the Eq. (1).

$$T = \begin{cases} \frac{S}{p} - \frac{W+1}{2p} & W \ is \ odd \\ \frac{S}{p} - \frac{W+2}{2p} & W \ is \ even \end{cases} \tag{1}$$

where, T is the moving times of the window function. S is the length of the pooling process, and p is the sliding step. Obviously, all of them are positive integer or zero. In fact, the setting of the pooling greatly influences the performance of the result. A great setting of the pooling parameters requires a lot of tests.

2.3   The Proposed Detection Method

In the past, a one-dimension max pooling has been applied to process the features of rCNN. In this paper, a blocking method is proposed (Figure 4).

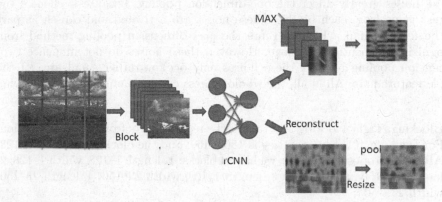

Fig. 4. The process of one-dimension pooling method and two dimension pooling method.

The one-dimension pooling feature is not related to the original image in geometry at all. However, from two-dimension pooling feature, it is easy to figure out the position of forgery area, though it may not very accurate. In fact, if one of the blocks is classified as a forgery image, the one-dimension pooling feature is easily classified as forgery image, because all the big values of the block are reserved during pooling. Commonly, many blocks are classified as forgery ones at the same time if the original image is forgery. Therefore, one-dimension pooling is very strong to find out forgery images. However, sometimes one of blocks of the authenticated image can be classified as forgery image improperly, which overwhelms other blocks. On the other hand, two-dimension pooling method is robust. A few mistaken blocks do not affect whole feature greatly. However, this method may be badly influenced by very special forgery edge. For example, if the forgery part is very small, it can be considered as noise. The experiment shows that two-dimension pooling method is very strong to classify authenticated image. Table 3 supports the aforementioned discussion.

Table 3. Performance comparison of two different pooling methods.

Methods	TP	TN	Accuracy
One-dimension pooling	99.96%	96.08%	98.02%
Two dimension pooling	95.74%	100%	97.87%

The result also shows that performance of two-dimension pooling method is weaker than one dimension pooling method. However, two-dimension pooling method is more robust to JPEG compression than one-dimension pooling, which is shown in Sect. 3, experiment part. In fact, JPEG compression is easy to cause small color blocks, whose edges are very similar to forgery edge. In the process of rCNN, JPEG compression causes a lot of noises because of these color blocks. These noises greatly affect the one-dimension pooling, because it chooses the largest value from each blocks. These noises are activated and chosen as part of the feature map, which prevents the one -dimension pooling method from recognizing authenticated image. However, these noises do not influence two-dimension pooling because these noises only occupy rather small area of the whole feature map. All in all, the whole process can be summarized as following steps:

1. Blocking: Tight blocking and taking the remain parts from inverse direction. For example, if the image's size is 150×150, and the block's size is 128×128. After the proposed blocking, we have 4 blocks: 1. length 1–128, width 1–128; 2. length 23–150, width 1:128; 3. length 1–128, width 23–150; 4. length 23–150, width 23–150.
2. rCNN processing: The blocks are processed by rCNN. The structure of rCNN can be seen in Table 1 and the details of rCNN can check in [20]. For instance, if we extract features from convolution layer 8, we have 4 features, whose size is $5 \times 5 \times 16$.
3. Reconstruction: Placing centrosymmetry of the feature map of the block back to the taken position of the original image. After the reconstruction, a $10 \times 10 \times 16$ big feature is given.
4. Resize: Stretching transformation. For example, we apply stretching transformation to resize a $10 \times 10 \times 16$ feature into a $20 \times 20 \times 16$ feature.
5. Pooling: two dimensional maximum pooling without padding. In this paper, we apply a size 5×5, moving steps 3 pooling. According to Sect. 2.2, we have a $6 \times 6 \times 16$ feature after pooling the $20 \times 20 \times 6$ feature.
6. SVM: Using SVM to classified the vectors lining up from the pooling feature. We line up $6 \times 6 \times 16$ feature and then have a vector, whose length is 576. We in fact line up the feature layer by layer. We line up the first layer and have a length 36 vector, and then connect it to the length 36 vector from the next layer. One by one, we finally have a length 576 vector. We use it as the input of SVM.

3 Experimental Results and Analysis

In this Section, we compare the detection accuracy and robustness to the JPEG compression of the proposed method with other state-of-the-art methods. The involved competing methods include: the SPT & LBP method [5] which achieves the state-of-the-art detection performance so far, and the DWT & DCT method by He [5]. We choose He's method, because it is based on domain transformation. Three common datasets, i.e., CASIA1, CASIA2 and Columbia forgery image database, are used as the benchmarks for training and testingre [6, 22]. The CASIA v1.0 dataset consists of 1725 color images of size 384×256 pixels in JPEG format, among which 925 images are forged image. The forgery part may be processed resizing, rotation or deformation. The CASIA v2.0 database is more difficult, because the producers of the data set applies other post-processing to the tampered area. It has 7491 authenticated images and 5132 forgery ones. The sizes of these images are various from 240×160 to 900×600. Their storage formats are also of diversity, including JPEG, BMP and TIFF. Both of CASIA v1.0 and v2.0 contain splicing and copy-move forgery images. The Columbia dataset, also called DVMM, has 933 authenticated images and 912 spliced images, whose size is 128×128. Those images are not processed by any other processing but splicing or copy-move operation. Additionally, all of them are gray images. Except from the details about the dataset, the structure of the rCNN is introduced in Table 1. First of all, for convenience, we cut all the training images into 128×128 images to train. This operation is helpful for us to have a large training set. By changing the directions and applying symmetry operations, the data set is further expanded. While testing, all the images are strictly not changed. They are processed by the aforementioned methods or the compared methods. Besides, the experiment is ten-fold, which means that the dataset is divided into ten parts and for one experiment, nine of the parts are training sets and the other one part is the testing set. After ten times experiments, the mean of all of the results is the final result. Moreover, for convenience, in this test, we mainly use CAFFE framework and mainly apply the functions of DIP package in Matlab [23, 24]. Those tools are very useful to make the experiment easily. What is more, all the SVM uses functions from LIBSVM 3.2 [25]. All the important parameters (C, G) is automatically set by easy.py in LIBSVM. Therefore, except using method, all the other setting is the same. In this experiment, all the images are strictly the same as the ones of the datasets. Table 4 shows the result of the accuracy of different methods in different datasets. In terms of the important setting, the blocks' size is 128×128, and CNN features are extracted from convolution 8 layer. Besides, the reconstructed feature is resized to 20×20. Then, a size 5×5, step 3 max pooling is applied to the feature so that a $6 \times 6 \times 16$ feature is given. Eventually, we line up them as a 576 vector and use a SVM to finish the classification, and the C and G are commonly 1024 and 1 respectively.

It is observed in Table 4 that our CNN-based methods achieve the better detection performance than other competing methods on all 3 datasets.

Table 4. The performance comparison of our proposed method with other competing methods

Data set (%)	LBP & SPT	DWT & DCT	Proposed	Max-pooling
CASIA v1.0	94.89	-	97.62	98.04
CASIA v2.0	97.33	89.76	97.87	98.02
DVMM	95.48	93.55	96.41	96.38

We then compare the robustness performance of the involved methods, which is summarized in Fig. 5. The JPEG compression is implemented by imwrite function in Matlab DIP package. The images' format is set by '.jpg' and the factors are various. We respectively set JPEG compression's factor 95, 85, 75, 65, 55, 45, 35, 25, 15, 5. Figure 5 shows that our method is the most robust one among all the involved methods. Besides, from the curve, we find out the proposed method is robust to the compression factor. Although its performance worsen immediately when the compression is applied, the performance is very stable even the factor drops to 0.05. It is possible that the proposed method is able to learn the important stable features in the process of JPEG compression. On the other hand, LBP & SPT is very sensitive to JPEG compression. The accuracy drops to 50% very soon. The experimental results show that the proposed block-based CNN approach and the pooling strategy are very effective to detect the forgery image and robust to the JPEG compression.

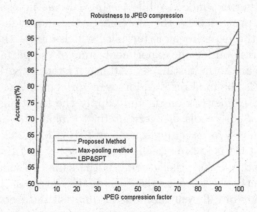

Fig. 5. The result about different methods's robustness to JPEG compression.

4   Conclusion

In this paper, we propose a novel block based CNN method for image forgery detection. This paper shows that our method is one of the best methods to detect forgery images. Not only it is able to achieve the performance close to the state of art, but also it is highly robust to a very common operation: JPEG compression. As we mention before, detecting forgery image is significant in information security but also has special meaning for digital image processing and object recognition, because edge information is very important in digital image processing and edge is also a very special object in object recognition.

In fact, there are many other operations post processing forgery edge. In this paper, we only show the robustness to JPEG compression. Apparently, rCNN has strong learning ability to cope with a variety of operations. Therefore, further research about the proposed method is required, which can find out all of its potential. Additionally, computing is another key issue in CNN based image forgery detection. In fact, although we train the CNN model with the up-to-date GPU, it is still quite time-consuming. Therefore, it is critical to find way to accelerate the computation, e.g., the cluster GPU computing, which is the direction of our future research effort.

References

1. Jing, W., Hongbin, Z.: Exposing digital forgeries by detecting traces of image splicing. In: 2006 8th International Conference on Signal Processing, vol. 2. IEEE (2006)
2. He, Z., Lu, W., Sun, W., Huang, J.: Digital image splicing detection based on Markov features in DCT and DWT domain. Pattern Recogn. 45(12), 4292–4299 (2012)
3. Shi, Y.Q., Chen, C., Chen, W.: A natural image model approach to splicing detection. In: Proceedings of the 9th Workshop on Multimedia & Security. ACM (2007)
4. Pan, X., Zhang, X., Lyu, S.: Exposing image splicing with inconsistent local noise variances. In: 2012 IEEE International Conference on Computational Photography (ICCP). IEEE (2012)
5. Muhammad, G., et al.: Image forgery detection using steerable pyramid transform and local binary pattern. Mach. Vis. Appl. 25(4), 985–995 (2015)
6. Dong, J., Wang, W.: CASIA tampered image detection evaluation (TIDE) database, v1.0 and v2.0. (2011). http://forensics.idealtest.org/
7. Lee, H., Ekanadham, C., Ng, A.Y.: Sparse deep belief net model for visual area V2. In: Advances in Neural Information Processing Systems 20 (NIPS) (2008)
8. Larochelle, H., et al.: Exploring strategies for training deep neural networks. J. Mach. Learn. Res. 10(10), 1–40 (2009)
9. LeCun, Y., Bottou, L., Bengio, Y., Haffner, P.: Gradient-based learning applied to document recognition. Proc. IEEE 86(11), 2278–2324 (1998)
10. Giacinto, G., Roli, F.: Design of effective neural network ensembles for image classification purposes. Image Vis. Comput. 19(9), 699–707 (2001)
11. Hinton, G., et al.: Deep neural networks for acoustic modeling in speech recognition: the shared views of four research groups. IEEE Signal Process. Mag. 29(6), 82–97 (2012)
12. Ji, S., et al.: 3D convolutional neural networks for human action recognition. IEEE Trans. Pattern Anal. Mach. Intell. 35(1), 221–231 (2013)
13. Collobert, R., Weston, J.: A unified architecture for natural language processing: deep neural networks with multitask learning. In: Proceedings of the 25th International Conference on Machine Learning. ACM (2008)

14. Fukushima, K., Miyake, S., Ito, T.: Neocognitron: a neural network model for a mechanism of visual pattern recognition. IEEE Trans. Syst. Man Cybern. **5**, 826–834 (1983)
15. LeCun, Y., Bengio, Y., Hinton, G.: Deep learning. Nature **521**(7553), 436–444 (2015)
16. Srivastava, N., et al.: Dropout: a simple way to prevent neural networks from overfitting. J. Mach. Learn. Res. **15**(1), 1929–1958 (2014)
17. Simonyan, K., Zisserman, A.: Very deep convolutional networks for large-scale image recognition. arXiv preprint arXiv:1409.1556 (2014)
18. LeCun, Y.: LeNet-5, convolutional neural networks (2015). http://yann.lecun.com/exdb/lenet
19. Hinton, G.E., Salakhutdinov, R.R.: Reducing the dimensionality of data with neural networks. Science **313**(5786), 504–507 (2006)
20. Rao, Y., Ni, J.: A deep learning approach to detection of splicing and copy-move forgeries in images. In: 2016 IEEE International Workshop on Information Forensics and Security (WIFS). IEEE (2016)
21. Gonzalez, R.C., Woods, R.E.: Image Processing. Digital Image Processing, vol. 2 (2007)
22. Columbia, D.: Research Lab: Columbia Image Splicing Detection Evaluation Dataset (2012). http://www.ee.columbia.edu/ln/dvmm/downloads/AuthSplicedDataSet/dlform.html
23. Jia, Y., et al.: Caffe: convolutional architecture for fast feature embedding. In: Proceedings of the 22nd ACM International Conference on Multimedia ACM (2014)
24. Kovesi, P.D.: MATLAB and Octave functions for computer vision and image processing (2000). http://www.csse.uwa.edu.au/~pk/Research/MatlabFns/#match
25. Chang, C.-C., Lin, C.-J.: LIBSVM: a library for support vector machines. ACM Trans. Intell. Syst. Technol. (TIST) **2**(3), 27 (2011)

A Hybrid Feature Model for Seam Carving Detection

Jingyu Ye[✉] and Yun-Qing Shi

Department of Electrical and Computer Engineering,
New Jersey Institute of Technology, Newark, NJ 07102, USA
{jy58, shi}@njit.edu

Abstract. Seam carving, as a content-aware image resizing algorithm, is widely used nowadays. In this paper, an advanced hybrid feature model is presented to reveal the trace of seam carving, especially seam carving at a low carving rate, applied to uncompressed digital images. Two groups of features are designed to capture energy variation and pixel variation caused by scam carving, respectively. As indicated by the experimental works, the state of the art performance on detecting 5% and 10% carving rate cases has been improved from 81.13% and 90.26% to 85.75% and 94.87%, respectively.

Keywords: Seam carving detection · Image forensics · Local derivative pattern · Markov transition probability · Support vector machine

1 Introduction

Due to the efficiency of preserving and exchanging information, digital images have become the most important and influential medium nowadays, thus the authenticity of digital images is crucial to the information security. However, with the tremendous development in digital image editing technology, the integrity of a digital image can no longer be guaranteed because the content of a digital image can be easily manipulated by any individual. To fight against the counterfeiting and reveal the truth, digital image forensics [1] has increasingly attracted wide attention. In this paper, an advanced hybrid feature model is presented to detect seam carving applied to digital images, particularly uncompressed images.

Seam carving [2] is designed by Avidan and Shamir for content-aware image resizing. By recursively removing an optimal seam, which consists of 8-connected pixels and has the lowest cumulative energy, from the target image, image size is to be manipulated and the important image content is assumed to be well preserved. Because of its content awareness, seam carving has become one of the most popular image resizing algorithm widely in used nowadays, and it has been included as a feature in many popular image processing software, such as PhotoShop CS4, GIMP, and ImageMagick.

In the past decade, a few forensic works have been presented for seam carving detection. Sharker et al. [3] presented the first solution for blind seam carving detection. By modelling the difference JPEG 2-D array with Markov random process, the transition probabilities, called Markov features, are utilized to reveal the trace in block-based frequency domain left by the process of seam carving so as to differentiate

C. Kraetzer et al. (Eds.): IWDW 2017, LNCS 10431, pp. 77–89, 2017.
DOI: 10.1007/978-3-319-64185-0_7

seam carved JPEG images from un-seam carved ones. Later, Fillion and Sharma [4] proposed a new model comprised of energy bias based features, seam behavior based features and wavelet absolute moments to identify seam carving in uncompressed images. In [5–9], the forensic research of detecting seam carving applied to JPEG images is kept pushing forward. In [10], Wei et al. presented a patch based method to detect seam carving in uncompressed images. Ryu et al. [11] reported an energy based forensic technique for seam carving detection in uncompressed domain, and the work is later extended by Yin et al. [12]. In [13], Lu and Wu proposed to detect seam carving by authenticating pre-embedded SIFT features.

In our previous works [14, 15], two methods have been presented to reveal the trace of seam carving applied to uncompressed images from the perspectives of energy variation and pixel variation, respectively. Both of the methods outperform the prior state-of-the-art significantly on detecting low carving rate cases. In order to further improve the current detection accuracy of seam carved images at a low carving rate, we propose a more advanced hybrid feature model, which consists of two groups of features, in this paper. The first group of features is designed to capture energy distribution variation caused by seam carving, while the second group of feature is utilized to monitor relationship change among neighboring pixels. As illustrated in the conducted experimental works, the state-of-the-art performance is achieved, especially the performance of detecting low carving rate seam carving is further improved. The construction of rest paper is as follows. The algorithm of seam carving is briefly introduced in Sect. 2. In Sect. 3, the proposed method is presented in detail. The experimental results are reported in Sect. 4, and the paper is concluded in Sect. 5.

2 Algorithm of Seam Carving

As previously introduced, Seam carving is a content-aware image resizing algorithm which aims at reducing the image without destroying the important image content. For a given image I with the size of $m \times n$, the importance of each pixel can be evaluated by an energy function, such as gradient calculated as follows,

$$e(I(x,y)) = \left| \frac{\partial}{\partial x} I(x,y) \right| + \left| \frac{\partial}{\partial y} I(x,y) \right|. \tag{1}$$

In order to keep the rectangular shape of the image, a horizontal seam, which is a path across the image from left to right, is defined as,

$$s^H = \left\{ s_i^H \right\}_{i=1}^n = \left\{ (x(i), i) \right\}_{i=1}^n, s.t. \forall i, |x(i) - x(i-1)| \le 1, \tag{2}$$

where s_i^H is the coordinates of each pixel in the horizontal seam and $x(i)$ is the row coordinate corresponding to the pixel in column i. Therefore, pixels in each seam are 8-connected, and only one pixel in each column is to be involved in a horizontal seam. Similarly, a vertical seam can be defined as a path of 8-connected pixels through the image from top to bottom.

Denote $E(s)$ as the cumulative energy of seam s, the optimal seam s^* which has the minimum energy is defined as,

$$s^* = \min_s E(s) = \min_s \sum_{i=1}^{n} e(I(s_i^H)). \tag{3}$$

Therefore, image size can be reduced by recursively removing such optimal seams from the target image, and the important image content is assumed to be preserved.

3 Proposed Method

By reviewing the algorithm of seam carving as previously introduced, the trace of seam carving could be exposed from two different angles. Firstly, deletion of seams with low cumulative energy is to change energy distribution of entire image, and the cumulative energy of possible seams could be distinguishing between an un-seam carved image and its seam carved copies. Therefore, features captured such energy variation are considered to be effective on revealing the process of seam carving applied to digital images. Secondly, local region is to be altered once pixels are removed by seam carving, and the relationship among neighboring pixels is changed as well. For this reason, investigating pixel variation could be another possible way to determine whether a digital image has been seam carved or not.

In [14, 15], two different methods have been proposed to solve this forensic problem from one of the two distinct angles discussed above, and both of them outperform the state-of-the-art in the experimental works. However, for seam carved images at low carving rate, such as 5% and 10%, which is more difficult to be detected and more practical in real life, the state-of-the-art detection accuracy is still far from perfect. Therefore, in this paper, we merge the ideas of [14, 15], and propose a more advanced hybrid feature model to unveil seam carving applied to digital images. In the proposed model, differ from the existing works, two groups of features are adopted to monitor energy distribution change and neighboring pixels relationship change respectively. It is believed that such hybrid model could be more effective on detecting seam carving when carving rate is relatively small. In the following, the proposed model is described in detail.

3.1 Features Captured Energy Variation

Inspired by prior arts [11, 12], three types of energy features are utilized to capture energy variation caused by seam carving in our previous work [14]. In this paper, we introduce another twelve energy based features to investigate the energy change of possible seams in quarter and three-quarter image to further enhance the performance.

Similar with [14], the proposed energy variation based feature set consists of three types of features. The first kind of features are utilized to measure the global energy distribution. As an optimal seam, which has the lowest cumulative energy, normally includes more low energy pixels than high energy pixels, it is more likely that the average pixel energy in an un-seam carved image should differ from its seam carved copy due to the deletion of multiple optimal seams. Therefore, four average energy based features are adopted to capture the global energy variation.

Furthermore, as the optimal seam which has the lowest cumulative energy is removed by seam carving, the energy of possible seams in an un-seam carved image could be different from that of possible seams in the image after seam carving. For this reason, ten features are adopted to measure the energy of possible seams in an image, and another eighteen features are utilized to measure the energy of possible seams throughout half image, quarter image, and three-quarter image, respectively. At last, four statistics, i.e., mean, standard deviation, skewness and kurtosis, are applied as features because seam carving could change the noise level of an image. Consequently, thirty-six features, as shown in Table 1, are utilized to monitor energy variation caused by seam carving.

3.2   Local Derivative Pattern Images Based Energy Feature Set

Local derivative pattern (LDP) [16] is a high order local descriptor which encodes directional derivatives of local neighboring pixels into an 8-bit binary code. By choosing various sampling radii and directions of derivatives, different LDPs of a given pixel can be obtained so as to capture information of different local regions centered at the given pixel. For a 5×5 local region in image I as shown in Fig. 1, the 1st order derivatives of the central pixel Z_0 along $0°$, $45°$, $90°$, and $135°$ are derived as follows,

$$
\begin{aligned}
I'_{\alpha=0°}(Z_0) &= I(Z_0) - I(Z_1) \\
I'_{\alpha=45°}(Z_0) &= I(Z_0) - I(Z_2) \\
I'_{\alpha=90°}(Z_0) &= I(Z_0) - I(Z_3) \\
I'_{\alpha=135°}(Z_0) &= I(Z_0) - I(Z_4)
\end{aligned}
\tag{4}
$$

where $I(Z)$ denotes the intensity of pixel Z, and α is the direction of derivatives. Then, the 2nd order LDP, denoted as LDP^2_α, of Z_0 is,

$$
LDP^2_\alpha(Z_0) = \{f(I'_\alpha(Z_0), I'_\alpha(Z_1)), \ldots, f(I'_\alpha(Z_0), I'_\alpha(Z_8))\},
\tag{5}
$$

where $\{Z_i \mid i = 1,\ldots,8\}$ are the eight neighbors when radius equals to 1, and f$(\cdot,\cdot)$ is a binary encoding function with the following rule,

$$
f(I'_\alpha(Z_0), I'_\alpha(Z_i)) = \begin{cases} 0, & if\ I'_\alpha(Z_0) \cdot I'_\alpha(Z_i) > 0 \\ 1, & otherwise \end{cases}, i = 1\ldots8
\tag{6}
$$

With the fixed α and radius, the corresponding LDP^2_α can be calculated for each pixel, thus the LDP 2-D array is generated. As each LDP^2_α is an 8-bit binary code, the value of a decimalized LDP, denoted as $DLDP^2_\alpha$, is within [0, 255] which is similar to the 8-bit intensity of a pixel. Therefore, the $DLDP^2_\alpha$ 2-D array is also called LDP image

Table 1. Description of 36-D features

Feature	Description
1. Average Horizontal Energy	$\frac{1}{m \times n} \sum_{i=1}^{m} \sum_{j=1}^{n} \left| \frac{\partial}{\partial x} I(i,j) \right|$
2. Average Vertical Energy	$\frac{1}{m \times n} \sum_{i=1}^{m} \sum_{j=1}^{n} \left| \frac{\partial}{\partial y} I(i,j) \right|$
3. Sum of Feature #1 and #2	$\frac{1}{m \times n} \sum_{i=1}^{m} \sum_{j=1}^{n} \left(\left| \frac{\partial}{\partial x} I(i,j) \right| + \left| \frac{\partial}{\partial y} I(i,j) \right| \right)$
4. Difference of Feature #1 and #2	$\frac{1}{m \times n} \sum_{i=1}^{m} \sum_{j=1}^{n} \left(\left| \frac{\partial}{\partial x} I(i,j) \right| - \left| \frac{\partial}{\partial y} I(i,j) \right| \right)$
5. Horizontal Seam$_{max}$	$max_{i=1}^{m} M(i,n)$
6. Horizontal Seam$_{min}$	$min_{i=1}^{m} M(i,n)$
7. Horizontal Seam$_{mean}$	$\frac{1}{m} \sum_{i=1}^{m} M(i,n)$
8. Horizontal Seam$_{std}$	$\sqrt{\frac{1}{m} \sum_{i=1}^{m} (Horizontal\ Seam_{mean} - M(i,n))^2}$
9. Horizontal Seam$_{diff}$	$Horizontal\ Seam_{max} - Horizontal\ Seam_{min}$
10. Vertical Seam$_{max}$	$max_{i=1}^{n} M(m,i)$
11. Vertical Seam$_{min}$	$min_{i=1}^{n} M(m,i)$
12. Vertical Seam$_{mean}$	$\frac{1}{n} \sum_{i=1}^{n} M(m,i)$
13. Vertical Seam$_{std}$	$\sqrt{\frac{1}{n} \sum_{i=1}^{n} (Vertical\ Seam_{mean} - M(m,i))^2}$
14. Vertical Seam$_{diff}$	$Vertical\ Seam_{max} - Vertical\ Seam_{min}$
15. Half-Horizontal Seam$_{max}$	$max_{i=1}^{m} M(i,\frac{n}{2})$
16. Half-Horizontal Seam$_{min}$	$min_{i=1}^{m} M(i,\frac{n}{2})$
17. Half-Horizontal Seam$_{mean}$	$\frac{1}{m} \sum_{i=1}^{m} M(i,\frac{n}{2})$
18. Half-Vertical Seam$_{max}$	$max_{i=1}^{n} M(\frac{m}{2},i)$
19. Half-Vertical Seam$_{min}$	$min_{i=1}^{n} M(\frac{m}{2},i)$
20. Half-Vertical Seam$_{mean}$	$\frac{1}{n} \sum_{i=1}^{n} M(\frac{m}{2},i)$
21. Quarter Horizontal Seam$_{max}$	..
22. Quarter Horizontal Seam$_{min}$	$min_{i=1}^{m} M(i,\frac{n}{4})$
23. Quarter Horizontal Seam$_{mean}$	$\frac{1}{m} \sum_{i=1}^{m} M(i,\frac{n}{4})$
24. Quarter Vertical Seam$_{max}$	$max_{i=1}^{n} M(\frac{m}{4},i)$
25. Quarter Vertical Seam$_{min}$	$min_{i=1}^{n} M(\frac{m}{4},i)$
26. Quarter Vertical Seam$_{mean}$	$\frac{1}{n} \sum_{i=1}^{n} M(\frac{m}{4},i)$
27. Three-Quarter Horizontal Seam$_{max}$	$max_{i=1}^{m} M(i,\frac{3n}{4})$

(continued)

Table 1. (*continued*)

Feature	Description
28. Three-Quarter Horizontal Seam$_{min}$	$min_{i=1}^{m} M(i, \frac{3n}{4})$
29. Three-Quarter Horizontal Seam$_{mean}$	$\frac{1}{m}\sum_{i=1}^{m} M(i, \frac{3n}{4})$
30. Three-Quarter Vertical Seam$_{max}$	$max_{i=1}^{n} M(\frac{3m}{4}, i)$
31. Three-Quarter Vertical Seam$_{min}$	$min_{i=1}^{n} M(\frac{3m}{4}, i)$
32. Three-Quarter Vertical Seam$_{mean}$	$\frac{1}{n}\sum_{i=1}^{n} M(\frac{3m}{4}, i)$
33. Noise$_{mean}$	$\frac{1}{m\times n}\sum_{i=1}^{m}\sum_{j=1}^{n} N(i,j)$
34. Noise$_{std}$	$\sqrt{\frac{1}{m\times n}\sum_{i=1}^{m}\sum_{j=1}^{n}(N(i,j) - Noise_{mean})^2}$
35. Noise$_{skewness}$	$\frac{1}{m\times n}\sum_{i=1}^{m}\sum_{j=1}^{n}(\frac{N(i,j)-Noise_{mean}}{Noise_{std}})^3$
36. Noise$_{kurtosis}$	$\frac{1}{m\times n}\sum_{i=1}^{m}\sum_{j=1}^{n}(\frac{N(i,j)-Noise_{mean}}{Noise_{std}})^4$

$I(Z_{15})$	$I(Z_{14})$	$I(Z_{13})$	$I(Z_{12})$	$I(Z_{11})$
$I(Z_{16})$	$I(Z_4)$	$I(Z_3)$	$I(Z_2)$	$I(Z_{10})$
$I(Z_{17})$	$I(Z_5)$	$I(Z_0)$	$I(Z_1)$	$I(Z_9)$
$I(Z_{18})$	$I(Z_6)$	$I(Z_7)$	$I(Z_8)$	$I(Z_{24})$
$I(Z_{19})$	$I(Z_{20})$	$I(Z_{21})$	$I(Z_{22})$	$I(Z_{23})$

Fig. 1. Local 5×5 block with central pixel at Z_0 in image I.

in this paper. As illustrated in Fig. 2, $LDP_{0°}^2$ of the central pixel $I(Z_0) = 40$ in a selected 5×5 region is {00001100}, and the corresponding $DLDP_{0°}^2(Z_0)$ is calculated as 48. The generated LDP image is visualized as shown in Fig. 2. Because LDP is sensitive to the texture manipulation, it is believed that the trace of seam carving could be amplified by LDP images. In this paper, we adopt horizontal and vertical LDP images in this work. We also applied multi-resolution [17] generate different types of LDPs, and utilized circular sampling instead of rectangular sampling to preserve more information.

The construction of the first group of features is demonstrated in Fig. 3. Four types of LDP encoder are selected in order to generate four different LDP images, and the energy features presented before are extracted from each of the LDP images, and the original image as well. Consequently, a 180-D feature vector is formed to monitor the energy variation caused by seam carving.

$I(Z_0) = 40$

$LDP_{0°}^2(Z_0) = \{ f(40-48, 48-54),$
$..., f(40-48, 45-52) \}$
$= \{0, 0, 0, 0, 1, 1, 0, 0\}$

$DLDP_{0°}^2(Z_0) = \underline{48}$

Fig. 2. Example of the calculation of $DLDP_{0°}^2$ for central pixel at Z_0 in a local 5×5 block of image I.

3.3 Features Captured Pixel Variation

Differ from the energy features introduced above, the second group of features is designed to capture the pixel variation caused by seam carving. As seam carving is to resize an image by deleting pixels, the relationship among neighboring pixels is changed consequently. Based on our previous experience [14], this change of pixels relation can be effectively reflected by the combination of LDP features, Markov features and subtractive pixel adjacency model (SPAM) features. Therefore, these three types of statistical features are adopted to form the second group of features in the proposed model.

As introduced before, LDP is sensitive to the change of local texture. However, straightforwardly applying each LDP as a feature could be insufficiently reflect the

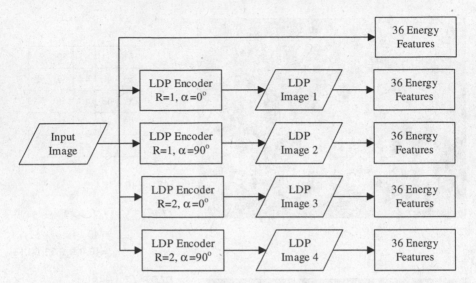

Fig. 3. Feature formation procedure of proposed first group of features to capture energy variation, and the feature dimensionality is 180. R is the sampling radius.

difference between un-seam carved images and seam carved images. Therefore, the global LDP features, i.e., histogram of LDPs, is suggested to be utilized. Since each LDP is an 8-bit binary code, the dimension of each type of global LDP features is $2^8 = 256$. In addition to the 2nd order LDP, the 3rd order LDP is also considered in this paper. By calculating the 2nd order directional derivatives as follows,

$$I''_\alpha(Z_0) = I'_\alpha(Z_0) - I'_\alpha(Z_i), i = 1, \ldots, 8, \tag{7}$$

where Z_0 is any pixel in the image and each of Z_i is the neighboring pixel, the 3rd order LDP can be generated similar to Eq. 5. Besides, LDPs with $\alpha = 0^\circ$ or 90° are considered, while radius is set to 1 or 2. Consequently, eight types of LDP features are included, and the feature dimensionality is 2048.

Besides LDP features, the 1st order Markov features, also called Markov features, and subtractive pixel adjacency model (SPAM) features are also adopted because both types of features are transition probability based which could be changed due to the seam removal. Denote the first order horizontal difference matrix by $D_{\alpha=0^\circ}$, it is derived as,

$$D_{\alpha=0^\circ}(x, y) = I(x, y) - I(x, y+1), \tag{8}$$

where $I(x, y)$ is the pixel intensity, and α is the direction. Therefore, the Markov feature $M_{a,b|\alpha=0^\circ}$ can be calculated as follows,

$$M_{a,b|\alpha=0^\circ} = p_{\alpha=0^\circ}\{D_{\alpha=0^\circ}(x,y+1) = a | D_{\alpha=0^\circ}(x,y) = b\}$$

$$= \frac{\sum_{x,y} \delta(D_{\alpha=0^\circ}(x,y) = b, D_{\alpha=0^\circ}(x,y+1) = a)}{\sum_{x,y} \delta(D_{\alpha=0^\circ}(x,y) = b)},$$

$$\delta(D_1 = a, D_2 = b) = \begin{cases} 1, & if\ D_1 = a, D_2 = b \\ 0, & otherwise \end{cases}, \tag{9}$$

where a and b are any integers within the range of $[-T_1, T_1]$, T_1 is the threshold in order to reduce the dimension of resulted Markov features. As a result, $(2T_1 + 1)^2$ Markov features can be obtained for each direction α. In this paper, we consider Markov features along four directions, i.e., horizontal, vertical, diagonal, and minor diagonal, while T_1 is fixed as 4. Therefore, $4 \times 81 = 324$ Markov features are utilized in the proposed model.

The difference between SPAM feature and Markov feature is that SPAM feature depicts the relationship between three adjacent pixels while Markov feature depicts that of two adjacent pixels. Therefore, SPAM feature is similar to the 2nd order Markov feature. By calculating the 2nd order Markov feature $M_{a,b,c|\alpha}$ on direction α,

$$M_{a,b,c|\alpha} = p_\alpha\{D(x_1,y_1) = a | D(x_2,y_2) = b, D(x_3,y_3) = c\}, \tag{10}$$

where (x_1, y_1), (x_2, y_2) and (x_3, y_3) are the coordinates of three adjacent pixels along direction α, respectively. a, b and c are integers within the range of $[-T_2, T_2]$, while T_2 is the threshold similar to T_1 for Markov features. After computing the 2nd order Markov features along eight directions, i.e., $M_{a|\alpha = 0^\circ, 45^\circ, 90^\circ, 135^\circ, 180^\circ, 225^\circ, 270^\circ, 315^\circ}$, the SPAM features is formed by averaging $M_{a|\alpha = 0^\circ, 90^\circ, 180^\circ, 270^\circ}$ and $M_{a|\alpha = 45^\circ, 135^\circ, 225^\circ, 315^\circ}$, separately. Therefore, the dimension of SPAM features is $2 \times (2T_2 + 1)^3$. In this paper, we set T2 as 3 not only to prevent a huge feature size but also obtain satisfactory performance.

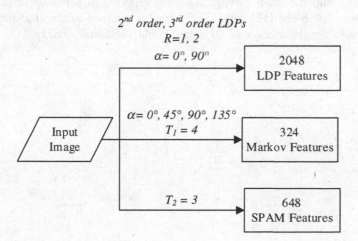

Fig. 4. Feature formation procedure of proposed features to capture pixel variation, and the feature dimensionality is 3058.

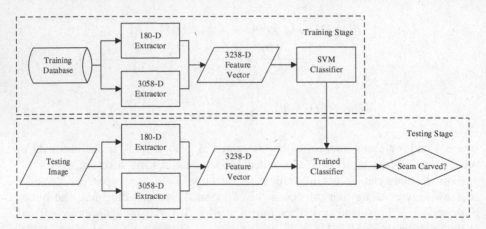

Fig. 5. Forensic framework by utilizing the proposed hybrid feature model.

Consequently, the second group of features is constructed as shown in Fig. 4, and the whole forensic framework is illustrated in Fig. 5.

4   Experimental Results

To evaluate the performance of proposed hybrid feature model, we compared the performance of proposed method and the state-of-the-art [11, 12, 14, 15] on 12 different seam carving scenarios, i.e., '5%H', '5%V', '10%H', '10%V', '20%H', '20%V', '30%H', '30%V', '40%H', '40%V', '50%H', and '50%V'. '5%H' means 5% of the image content is removed by horizontal seam carving, and '5%V' stands for 5% of the image content is deleted by vertical seam carving, and so on so forth. For each seam carving scenario, 1338 seam carved images are generated on the basis of UCID database [18], and the seam carving algorithm reported in [2] is implemented and applied. Then, Lib-SVM [19] with linear kernel is adopted as the classifier, and all reported results are the average of 10 times' 6-fold validation strategy.

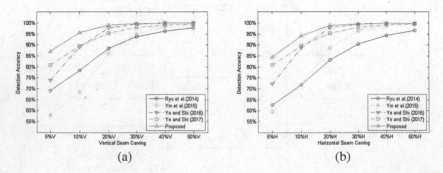

(a)   (b)

Fig. 6. Performance of proposed hybrid feature model versus the state-of-the-art on detecting 12 different seam carving scenarios.

As illustrated in Fig. 6, it is observed that the proposed hybrid model is much more effective versus the state-of-the-art on detecting seam carving images with a carving rate lower than 30%. In particular, as reported in Table 2, our previous works [14, 15] can only achieve 73.03% and 81.13% average detection accuracies on detecting seam carving at a carving rate as 5%, respectively, while the performance has been boosted to 85.75% by the proposed model. Similarly, the average detection accuracy achieved by proposed feature model is almost 5% higher than the best of [14, 15] on detecting cases at a carving rate equal to 10%. The ROC curves shown in Figs. 6 and 7 also

Table 2. Average detection accuracy of proposed feature model versus the state-of-the-art.

	5%	10%	20%	30%	40%	50%
Ryu et al. [11]	65.89%	75.15%	85.79%	92.11%	95.26%	97.25%
Yin et al. [12]	58.72%	70.22%	87.37%	95.63%	98.58%	99.51%
Ye and Shi [14]	73.03%	88.88%	97.78%	99.44%	**99.91%**	**99.96%**
Ye and Shi [15]	81.13%	90.26%	96.04%	98.38%	99.26%	99.62%
Proposed	**85.75%**	**94.87%**	**98.91%**	**99.65%**	99.89%	99.94%

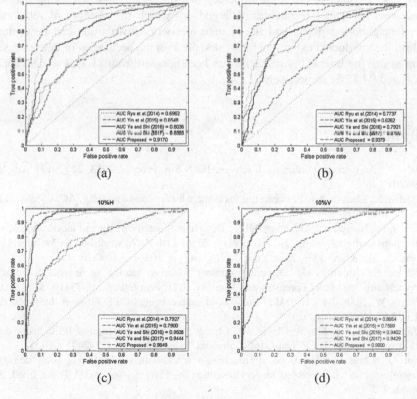

(a)   (b)

(c)   (d)

Fig. 7. ROCs of proposed hybrid feature model versus the state-of-the-art on detecting seam carving with carving rate as 5% and 10%, respectively.

indicated that the proposed hybrid feature model is more reliable and effective on revealing seam carving at low carving rate versus the other compared methods.

It is also noted, although the proposed model has been dominated on discriminating seam carved images at low carving rate from un-carved images, [14] achieves almost equivalent performance as that achieved by 3238-D on detecting high carving rate cases, particularly cases at a carving rate as 40% and 50%. To reveal the reason behind such observation, the training performance has been investigated. It is observed that the proposed model achieves the best performance on all cases in the training, particularly the proposed model achieves 100% detection accuracy when the carving rate is higher than 20%. Even though such overfitting is observed in the conducted experiments, the proposed model still outperforms other existing methods on most of designed seam carving scenarios, especially when the carving rate is as low as 5% or 10% which are considered more general in real life and more difficult to be detected.

5   Conclusion

In this paper, an advanced hybrid model is designed to further improve the performance of the state-of-the-art on detecting seam carving applied to digital images at low carving rate. In order to catch the imperceptible traces left by low carving rate seam carving, two groups of features are merged, by which the changes of relationship between neighboring pixels and the change of energy distribution can be captured. Based on the conducted experimental works, the average accuracies of detecting seam carving at carving rate as 5% and 10% has been boosted from 81.13% and 90.26% to 85.75% and 94.87%, respectively.

References

1. Piva, A.: An overview on image forensics. ISRN Sig. Process. **2013**, 22 (2013). Article ID 496701
2. Avidan, S., Shamir, A.: Seam carving for content-aware image resizing. ACM Trans. Graph. **26**(3), 10 (2007)
3. Sarkar, A., Nataraj, L., Manjunath, B.S.: Detection of seam carving and localization of seam insertions in digital images. In: Proceedings of the 11th ACM workshop on Multimedia and security, MM&Sec 2009, New York, NY, USA, pp. 107–116 (2009)
4. Fillion, C., Sharma, G.: Detecting content adaptive scaling of images for forensic applications. In: Media Forensics and Security. SPIE Proceedings, p. 75410. SPIE (2010)
5. Chang, W., Shih, T.K., Hsu, H.: Detection of seam carving in JPEG images. In: Proceedings of iCAST-UMEDIA (2013)
6. Wattanachote, K., Shih, T., Chang, W., Chang, H.: Tamper detection of JPEG image due to seam modification. IEEE Trans. Inf. Forensics Secur. **10**(12), 2477–2491 (2015)
7. Liu, Q., Chen, Z.: Improved approaches with calibrated neighboring joint density to steganalysis and seam-carved forgery detection in JPEG images. ACM Trans. Intell. Syst. Technol. **5**(4), 63 (2014)

8. Liu, Q.: Exposing seam carving forgery under recompression attacks by hybrid large feature mining. In: 23rd International Conference on Pattern Recognition (ICPR), pp. 1036–1041 (2016)
9. Liu, Q.: An approach to detecting JPEG down-recompression and seam carving forgery under recompression anti-forensics. Pattern Recogn. **65**, 35–46 (2016)
10. Wei, J., Lin, Y., Wu, Y.: A patch analysis method to detect seam carved images. Pattern Recogn. Lett. **36**, 100–106 (2014)
11. Ryu, S., Lee, H., Lee, H.: Detecting trace of seam carving for forensic analysis. IEICE Trans. Inf. Syst. **E97-D**(5), 1304–1311 (2014)
12. Yin, T., Yang, G., Li, L., Zhang, D., Sun, X.: Detecting seam carving based image resizing using local binary patterns. Comput. Secur. **55**, 130–141 (2015)
13. Lu, W., Wu, M.: Seam carving estimation using forensic hash. In: Proceedings of the Thirteenth ACM Multimedia Workshop on Multimedia and Security, MM&Sec 2011, New York, NY, USA, pp. 9–14 (2011)
14. Ye, J., Shi, Y.-Q.: A local derivative pattern based image forensic framework for seam carving detection. In: Shi, Y.Q., Kim, H.J., Perez-Gonzalez, F., Liu, F. (eds.) IWDW 2016. LNCS, vol. 10082, pp. 172–184. Springer, Cham (2016). doi:10.1007/978-3-319-53465-7_13
15. Ye, J., Shi, Y.Q.: An effective method for seam carving detection. J. Inf. Secur. Appl. **35**, 13–22 (2017). doi:10.1016/j.jisa.2017.04.003
16. Zhang, B., Gao, Y., Zhao, S., Liu, J.: Local derivative pattern versus local binary pattern: face recognition with high-order local pattern descriptor. IEEE Trans. Image Process. **19**(2), 533–544 (2010)
17. Ojala, T., Pietikäinen, M., Mäenpää, T.: Multiresolution gray-scale and rotation invariant texture classification with local binary patterns. IEEE Trans. Pattern Anal. Mach. Intell. **24** (7), 971–987 (2002)
18. Schaefer, G., Stich, M.: UCID - an uncompressed colour image database. In: Storage and Retrieval Methods and Applications for Multimedia 2004. Proceedings of SPIE, vol. 5307, pp. 472–480 (2004)
19. Chang, C.C., Lin, C.J.: LIBSVM: a library for support vector machines. ACM Trans. Intell. Syst. Technol. **2**, 27:1–27:27 (2011). http://www.csie.ntu.edu.tw/~cjlin/libsvm/

Biometric Image Tampering Detection

Face Morphing Detection: An Approach Based on Image Degradation Analysis

Tom Neubert[✉]

Research Group Multimedia and Security, Otto-von-Guericke-University Magdeburg,
P.O. Box 4120, 39016 Magdeburg, Germany
tom.neubert@iti.cs.uni-magdeburg.de

Abstract. In 2014 a novel identity theft scheme targeting specific application scenarios in face biometrics was introduced. In this scheme, a so called face morph melts two or more face images of different persons into one image, which is visually similar to multiple real world persons. Based on this non authentic image, it is possible to apply for an image based identity document to be issued by a corresponding authority. Thus, multiple persons can use such a document to pass image based person verification scenarios with a single document containing an artificially weakened template. Currently there is no reliable existing security mechanism to detect this attack.

This paper introduces a novel detection approach for face morphing forgeries based on a continuous image degradation. This is considered relevant because the degradation approach creates multiple artificial self-references and measures the "distance" from these references to the input. A small distance (significantly smaller than the one to be expected from a pristine image) could be considered as an anomaly here, indicating media manipulations (e.g. caused by morphing). Our degradation process is based on JPEG compression with different compression values. The evaluation results of our detection approach are classification accuracies of 90.1% under laboratory conditions and 84.3% under real world conditions.

Keywords: Digital image forensics · Detection of face morphing attacks

1   Introduction

The face is a widespread and well accepted biometric modality for many authentification scenarios. The identity verification of a person in such scenarios is often performed by using a face image in an identification document. Due to the wide spread usage of face image based authentification scenarios, they are in the focus of various identity theft schemes.

Ferrera et al. present in their paper "The magic passport" [1] a novel identity theft scheme for face biometrics, which describes an approach allowing two or more persons pass an identity verification scenario with only one artificially weakened template in form of a "magic" passport. For this attack they create a

© Springer International Publishing AG 2017
C. Kraetzer et al. (Eds.): IWDW 2017, LNCS 10431, pp. 93–106, 2017.
DOI: 10.1007/978-3-319-64185-0_8

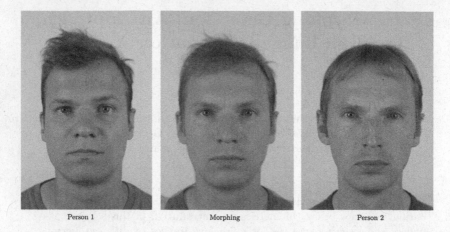

Person 1   Morphing   Person 2

Fig. 1. Example of a manually created face morphing forgery of two different persons

so called face morph which melts two or more face images of different persons, so that it is similar to multiple real persons (see Fig. 1 for example). If this morphed image is used for the creation of an identification document, the document could successfully be used by multiple persons, whose faces are morphed in the face image integrated in the document.

Ferrera et al. figure out in [1] that the document successfully passes all optical and electronic authenticity and integrity checks. This reveals a weakness in official authentification checks, because currently there is no reliable existing security mechanism to detect this kind of attack.

In this paper, we introduce a novel detection approach for face morphing forgeries based on a continuous image degradation analysis, which can be seen as the main scientific contribution of our paper. For the image degradation process we perform a JPEG compression, with different compression values on a decompressed input file. To analyze the degradation process, we use a feature set derived from existing OpenCV (http://opencv.org) edge detecting methods. Afterwards, we compare the extracted feature values from the degraded images with the reference image (input) to describe the degradation. For genuine face images, we should observe a significant loss of edge-information in the face region because of the degradation. We assume that morphings create an anomaly here, because the loss of information through the degradation process should be significantly lower as a result of the blending operations in the morphing pipeline. These operations causes a loss of face details in the input image and the additional degradation should have a "smaller" influence on morphings than on genuine images.

Our work is structured as follows: Sect. 2 describes related work in forensics on face morphing attacks. In Sect. 3 we describe the concept for our degradation detection approach, including the feature space for our pattern recognition based detection. The next section gives an overview of our experimental dataset and introduces the testing goals for our morphing detection experiment. Section 5 shows the results of our experiment and Sect. 6 concludes the paper with a summary and future work.

2 Related Work

In 2014 Ferrera et al. introduce in [1] a novel approach to attack face image based person verification systems with a so called face morphing attack. In their work they present a "magic passport" with a face morphed image on the photo ID document, which is created by a official authority and looks similar to multiple real world persons.

The vulnerability exploited in this attack is the fact, that in many countries self acquired photos are allowed to be submitted while document generation. So this passport could for example be successfully used by those multiple person on a border control because the document is absolutely authentic and will pass all optical and electronic authenticity and integrity checks. Ferrera et al. present no security mechanism to detect this attack and because of that it is important to find a detection mechanism for this easy to realize attack.

In [4] the relevance of the attack from [1] is confirmed. In this work Ferrera et al. analyze the performance of three automatic face recognition (AFR) systems to reject face morphed images. The results are frightening, the evaluated AFR systems are not able to distinguish between morphed and genuine faces.

The morphing attack from [1] uses manual generated morphed faces with GIMP/GAP (www.gimp.org), which makes the morphing process time consuming and allows only a small number of generated morphings. Therefore, they create an automated process for the generation of visually faultless facial morphings in [2]. This allows the generation of big experimental data, which is essential for the training of forensic detectors. The quality of these morphings is verified with an AFR (Luxand FaceSDK 6.1 [19]) system. The AFR system accepts "11.78% of morphings against any of genuine images at the decision threshold of 1% false acceptance rate". In addition we present a subjective experiment which demonstrates that humans ability to differ between these automatic generated morphings and genuine faces is close to random guessing. These results confirm that morphings are a serious issue for document security. This automated process is used in this work for the creation of morphings for training and test data sets. We also proposed a detection approach to automatically detect morphings making use of Benford features derived from quantized DCT coefficients of JPEG images. The evaluation reveals that the distribution of the coefficients shows an anomaly with morphed images, resulting from the image pre-processing steps.

In [3] the authors benchmark the robustness of the detection approach from [2] with different post-processing techniques and anti-forensic methods. Therefore, they have generated 86614 samples based on the Utrecht Face DB [18] to analyze the influence of the applied image processing to the AFR system and the forensic detector from [2]. The evaluation shows, that the performance of the forensic detector is very critical for some kind of processing techniques. For the biometric AFR system the processing has nearly no influence.

The authors of [7] focus on masking the gender information in a face image with respect to an automated gender estimation scheme, while retaining its ability to be used by a face matcher in their work. To do so they use a morphing scheme to create a mixed image of two facial inputs. The morphing process "can be used to progressively modify the input image, such that its gender information is progressively suppressed".

Schetinger et al. assert in [5] that CFA and double JPEG compression artifacts are plausible as traces for morphing detection.

Furthermore, Raghavendra et al. introduce in [6] a morph detection approach. The approach is based on binarized statistical image features used in conjunction with a linear SVM.

In [8] the authors have evaluated the vulnerability of two different face recognition system with respect to scanned morph face images. Additionally a comparative study on different currently proposed face morph detectors is introduced.

Gomez-Barrero et al. present in their paper [9] a new framework for the evaluation of the vulnerability of biometric system to morphing attacks. The analysis implies that biometric systems are vulnerable to different kind of attacks, depending on the verification threshold and the shape of the mated and non-mated score distributions.

Despite to the research released in this field, there exists, to the best of our knowledge, no absolutely reliable detection approach for face morphing forgeries and it is a novel and promising idea to use a degradation process for the detection of face morphing forgeries.

3   Concept of Our Morphing Detection Approach Based on Image Degradation

In this section, we introduce our detection approach based on a continuous image degradation. Basically, the approach is not a native morphing detection approach, but rather an anomaly detection approach which detects anomalies resulting from the face morphing process. The approach is based on the idea that our proposed features react sensibly to the degradation of authentic images and not so sensibly to the degradation of morphed images. We use three different corner feature detectors in the face region. Due to the degradation, the number of detected corner features should decrease significantly for authentic images. We assume that morphings have an anomaly here, as a result of blending operations in the morphing pipeline. So, the degradation should not have such a significant impact on morphed images as on authentic images. The degradation process has 3 basic steps (Step I: Pre-Processing, Step II: Feature Extraction, Step III: Normalization of the Feature Vector) and is visualized in Fig. 2.

Before we start the process with the pre-processing, we decompress and store all used images in PNG image file format to have a homogeneous base for each used input file. We recommend this format because it is lossless and well known. As pre-processing (step I), prior to feature extraction (step II), the facial landmarks are extracted from *Img* by using the *dlib* programming library version

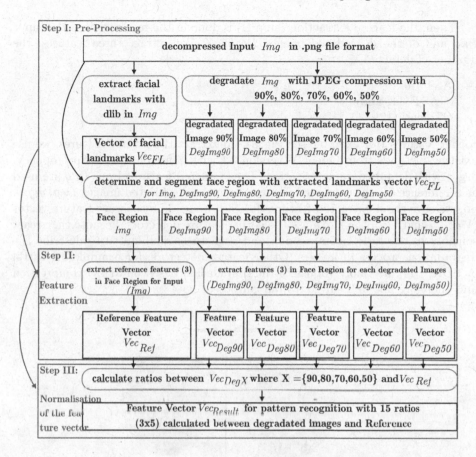

Fig. 2. Image degradation process of a single image

19.2 (http://dlib.net/). The coordinates of the facial landmarks are saved in a Vector Vec_{FL}. In parallel, we build five degradated images $DegImgX$ from Img with the following JPEG quality levels $X = \{90\%, 80\%, 70\%, 60\%, 50\%\}$.

In general, it is possible to degradate an image with other methods, for example different filtering methods, but we use the JPEG compression, because it is a standard and widespread method to degradate or compress images. Additionally, more JPEG quality parameters could be used to describe the degradation process more accurately, but we suppose that it leads to similar results. Afterwards, we use Vec_{FL} to determine and segment the convex hull of the facial landmarks for Img and $DegImgX$. Subsequently, we remove any image information outside of the determined convex hull of the face region for all used images (Img and $DegImgX$). Thus, the pre-processing results in 6 images (input Img and 5 degradated images $DegImgX$) containing only the face region of a person.

Then, the feature extraction (step II) is done in the face region of the input *Img* and of the degraded images *DegImgX*. We extract three features, the number of detected

- FAST [10],
- AGAST [11] and
- shiTomasi [12]

corner features (for example see Fig. 3). To extract these three features, we use existing methods from OpenCV version 3.1 with contributions (http://opencv.org/) with default parameterization. The extracted features from *Img* are used as a reference for the extracted features from the degradated images *DegImgX*. So, we save the 3 extracted features for each image in a separate feature vector (Vec_{Ref} and Vec_{DegX}). We use the corner feature detectors, because they react sensibly to the JPEG compression and seem to be well suited to describe the degradation process in images. Other feature detectors, for example SIFT [13] or SURF [14], are more robust to the degradation based on JPEG compression and therefore not well suited for our purpose.

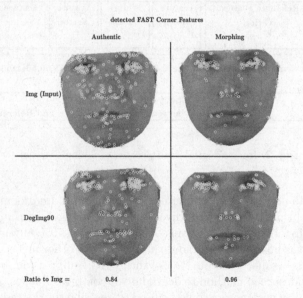

Fig. 3. Example of detected FAST corner features for an authentic sample and a morphed sample for *Img* and *DegImg*90

After feature extraction, the normalization of the feature vector follows in step III. Therefore, we use the absolute number of detected corner features for each of the 3 features. Basically, we calculate only the ratios between the feature vectors of the degradated images Vec_{DegX} and the reference feature vector Vec_{Ref} from the input ($\frac{Vec_{Deg90}.at(0)}{Vec_{Ref}.at(0)}, \ldots, \frac{Vec_{Deg50}.at(2)}{Vec_{Ref}.at(2)}$). In the end, we get 15 features (3 ratios for each of the 5 degradated images) for Img, which describe the degradation process. We intentionally get rid of further normalization steps (for example: normalization of the image resolution by dividing the number of detected corner features by the number of face pixels) in order to not distort the degradation process. The features are saved in a labeled ("Morphing" or "Authentic") feature vector Vec_{Result} for our pattern recognition based approach to detect morphed images. For the detection approach we train a two-class classification model Mod, by applying the described degradation process to all images in both classes. One class is for authentic face images and the other class for morphed face images. The experimental set up is described in Sect. 4.

4   Evaluation Goals and Setup

This section describes our pattern recognition based detection approach and gives an overview of our training and test data. Furthermore we define our evaluation goals.

4.1   Evaluation Goals

In order to evaluate our degradation process as a valid possibility to detect anomalies in morphed images, we define three evaluation goals:

- G_1 : Determine a reference accuracy of our classification model Mod for two exemplary attack realizations by a 10-fold cross validation to evaluate our designed feature space.
- G_2 : Analyze the impact of the degradation process to the feature space of Mod for authentic and morphed images.
- G_3 : Determine the detection accuracy of Mod for different test data sets, which have not been involved into training.

The three goals are addressed in three separate evaluation tests (T_1, T_2, T_3) described in the following subsection. The cross-validation in G_1 reproduces a laboratory test. Here the detector is tested under idealized conditions. We choose a 10-fold cross validation, because here the complete data of Mod is used for training and test data and it delivers more accurate results (especially with regards to outliers) than a single percentage split of the data. A higher number of folds during the cross validation is not suitable because it is more time consuming and delivers comparable results. G_2 checks the descriminatory power of the features of Mod to validate the feature space and G_3 aims at generalizing the detection accuracies of Mod under more realistic conditions with separate test sets, which are described in Subsect. 4.2.

4.2   Evaluation Setup

We use a pattern recognition based approach to analyze the degradation process and to detect morphed face images. Due to this, we train a classification model Mod with two classes

– class 1: *"Authentic"* (600 Samples) and
– class 2: *"Morphing"* (600 Samples),

and apply the introduced degradation process (see Fig. 2) to each sample, as mentioned in Sect. 3. The class *Authentic* contains self acquired non-modified face images, which represents our ground-truth, see Fig. 1 (Person 1 and Person 2). All these training images follow the ICAO standard [15] for images used in international passport documents to create a realistic passport setup. The class "Authentic" includes 600 samples of 50 different persons, so we use 12 face images for each person, which are acquired with 2 different cameras and different parameters. Additionally we use two different instances of both cameras. With that we try to create a diverse dataset for the training class *Authentic*. We assume that this could lead to more accurate results under realistic test conditions. The parameters and the used cameras are shown in Table 1.

Table 1. Used cameras and acquisition parameters for the training data in *Mod*

Camera	Resolution	ISO-value
2 * Canon EOS 1200D	2304×3456	100,400
Lens: EF28-1005 f/4-5.6	1728×2592	100
2 * Nikon Coolpix A100	1704×2272	100,400
	1200×1600	100

The second class *Morphing* of our classification model is trained with two different attack types of automatically generated face morphing images. These two morphing approaches are described in [2], see Sect. 2. The first attack type $Morph_{complete}$ could be seen as a result of warping and blending of complete facial images including hair, torso and background. The second attack type $Morph_{splicing}$ achieves a more realistic appearance by cutting facial regions, warp them and blend them to a mutual face and seamlessly stitch it back into one of the input images. An example to visualize these two attack types is given in Fig. 4. The clearly recognizable ghosting artefacts for $Morph_{complete}$ are negligible, because we are only using the convex hull of the face region for our approach and we are aware that an attacker would probably remove such clearly visible artefacts. Both attack types are thus well suited as training and test data, as they represent realistic faces almost entirely devoid of visual artefacts. The morphings are randomly created and selected from the 50 subject of the class *Authentic*. In order to train an unbiased classification model, we select 600 morphing samples for an equal distribution of both classes. For $Morph_{complete}$ we got 200 samples and for $Morph_{splicing}$ 400 samples, the higher number of samples for the latter attack type is intended to reflect the two morph targets (see Fig. 4).

Hence, *Mod* includes 1200 training samples to analyze our evaluation goals $(G_1 - G_3)$. In order to achieve these goals we perform three tests (T_1, T_2, T_3).

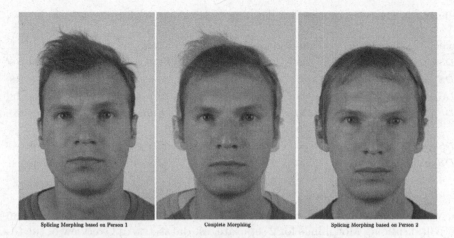

Splicing Morphing based on Person 1   Complete Morphing   Splicing Morphing based on Person 2

Fig. 4. Example of automatically created face morphing images ($Morph_{splicing}$ and $Morph_{complete}$)

- T_1 : To achieve G_1 we perform a 10-fold cross-validation to evaluate the reference accuracy of Mod, because the test is performed under optimized conditions. We use the open source data mining suite WEKA [16] version 3.8.0 with a Logistic Model Tree [17] (LMT) classifier with default parameterization. The LMT is a decision tree with logistic regression functions at the leaves. We have tested different alternative classifiers (for example: a pruned C4.5 decision tree, naive bayes, bagging predictors), but the LMT decision tree delivers the most accurate results for our performed tests.
- T_2 : For G_2 we investigate all extracted features of our feature space from both classes Mod. Therefore we build the mean value from each features for all 600 samples per class. With this data we are able to visualize to degradation process for the 3 extracted corner features (FAST, AGAST, shiTomasi) for morphed and authentic face images.
- T_3 : For G_3, we evaluate the classification accuracy of Mod under more realistic conditions with independent test sets. For the classification of the test datasets, we use also the LMT decision tree, to make the results comparable to T_1. With this test, we get an idea, how well our detection approach could work under real world conditions.

In order to perform T_3, we determine the classification accuracy of Mod for images from different origin. Therefore we create six separate and independent test datasets. Three of them are generated based on Utrecht ECVP [18], a publicly available face reference database. We use the non-smiling Utrecht genuine face images, to build $Morph_{complete}$ (1326 samples) and $Morph_{splicing}$ (2614 samples). Furthermore, we use 400 self-acquired genuine face images of the same 50 subjects as in the training data, but for this data we use two different cameras (2x Nikon D3300, Lens: Nikkor Lens: AF-S50mmf/1.8G) with different parameters (resolution: 2000 × 2992, 3000 × 4496 and ISO-values: 100, 400).

Table 2. Overview of used test datasets (independent from training data) in T_3

Name	Resolution	Type	Class	Samples	Base
$TDS_{Authentic-Utrecht}$	900×1200	Genuine	*Authentic*	73	Utrecht [18]
$TDS_{MorphSplicing-Utrecht}$	900×1200	$Morph_{splicing}$	*Morphing*	2614	Utrecht [18]
$TDS_{MorphComplete-Utrecht}$	900×1200	$Morph_{complete}$	*Morphing*	1326	Utrecht [18]
$TDS_{Authentic-AMSL}$	2000×2992	Genuine	*Authentic*	400	self-aquired
	3000×4496				
$TDS_{MorphSplicing-AMSL}$	2000×2992	$Morph_{splicing}$	*Morphing*	300	self-aquired
$TDS_{MorphComplete-AMSL}$	2000×2992	$Morph_{complete}$	*Morphing*	100	self-aquired

So, we acquire 8 images of each person. Based on this data, we generate complete und splicing Morphings for 2 separate test datasets. An Overview of the test datasets gives Table 2. We observe that the three self acquired test datasets are not completely independent from the training data because the 50 test persons are the same. But we assume, that the different acquisition parameters (Camera, Lens and Resolution) should make the test data unbiased to the training data. The evaluation results of the described three tests (T_1, T_2, T_3) are presented in the next section.

5   Evaluation Results

This section specifies the results of our three tests (Sect. 4.2). In addition we discuss, whether we could achieve our evaluation goals (Sect. 4.1).

In T_1 we evaluate the accuracy of our classification model Mod. This test determines a reference detection accuracy (G_1) under optimized conditions for our exemplary two morphing attack types ($Morph_{splicing}$ and $Morph_{complete}$). The results for T_1 are shown in Table 3.

Table 3. Results of the 10-fold cross validation for Mod with LMT classifier (T_1)

Authentic	Morphing	<− classified as
89.0%	11.0%	Authentic (Ground-Truth)
8.7%	**91.3%**	Morphing (Ground-Truth)

The reference classification accuracy of Mod is 90.2% (G_1). So, the degradation process does not have such a big impact on any authentic face image as we assumed. For example, the detection accuracy for "smooth" genuine faces is not as good as assumed, because the reduction of edge keypoints through the degradation process, is similarly low as for morphed face images.

To analyze the impact of the degradation process on morphed and authentic face images (G_2), we perform our second test T_2. For this, we compare the mean

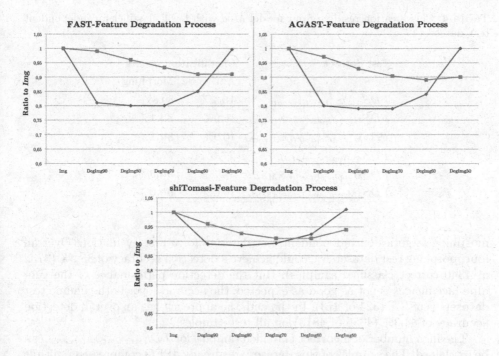

Fig. 5. Impact of the image degradation process on morphed and authentic face images (T_2) for three corner feature detectors (determined by the mean values of the features from each class of the training data). Blue Class: *Authentic*, Red Class: *Morphing* (Color figure online)

values of all extracted features (based on the training samples of Mod) for each corner detector (FAST, AGAST, shiTomasi). Figure 5 shows that the impact of the degradation process is very different on authentic and morphed face images.

The influence of the process results in a higher quality loss for authentic face images than for morphed face images on all three corner features. The number of detected corner features for morphings for all 3 features on the lossy degradated images ($DegImg60$ and $DegImg50$) increases due to detected JPEG compression artifacts. But we also see that the shiTomasi corner detector is more robust to the degradation than the 2 other detectors. So, the shiTomasi features do not have such a descriminatory power as the features from the FAST and AGAST corner detectors. In the end we can assert, that the degradation process got a significant impact on genuine face images with the FAST and AGAST corner features, compared to the influence on morphed face images. So T_2 validates and justifies the selection of our feature space, but it also encourages to find more suitable features to describe the degradation process.

In T_3 we want to evaluate our classification model Mod under more realistic conditions. To do so, we determine the detection accuracies for Mod on 6 separate and independent test datasets (G_3), summarized in Table 2. The results for T_3 are shown in Table 4. T_3 shows acceptable detection accuracies for face

Table 4. Classification results of our model Mod with LMT classifier for independent test datasets (T_3)

Test dataset	Classification results	
	Authentic	Morphing
$TDS_{Authentic-Utrecht}$	**19.2%**	80.8%
$TDS_{MorphSplicing-Utrecht}$	16.9%	**83.1%**
$TDS_{MorphComplete-Utrecht}$	10.9%	**89.1%**
$TDS_{Authentic-AMSL}$	**77.5%**	22.5%
$TDS_{MorphSplicing-AMSL}$	3.7%	**96.3%**
$TDS_{MorphComplete-AMSL}$	10.0%	**90.0%**

morphing forgeries on independent test datasets for a first evaluation. Over all four morphing test datasets we could achieve a detection accuracy of 85.9% (3732 of 4340 correct classified samples). But the detection performance of the genuine face images is not as good as expected, the accuracy over both genuine test datasets is 68.4% (324 of 473). In the end, the approach has an overall detection accuracy of 84.3% (4056 of 4813) on all test samples.

The high number of incorrect classified samples for $TDS_{Authentic-Utrecht}$ can be explained. The samples of this dataset are already JPEG compressed multiple times. Because of that, the degradation has an influence on samples, that is more similar to the morphed images than to images taken directly from a camera. So, we recommend a strict compression policy for images used in international passport documents. Besides, the false alarm rate for $TDS_{Authentic-AMSL}$ is still high (22.5%), due to the reasons mentioned for T_1. We hope, the false alarm rate could be oppressed by other mechanisms that may support this approach in the future as a part of a security system. In the end, the results of the three tests (T_1, T_2, T_3) show that our degradation process is promising for the detection of face morphing forgeries. The results are acceptable for a first evaluation and with more training data and a process with more particular degradation steps, the approach should lead to even better results.

6   Conclusion and Future Work

Our paper introduces a novel detection approach for face morphing forgeries based on image degradation. It is a promising blind anomaly detection approach working on self-created artificial references. We present the design of our degradation process and perform a pattern recognition based detection approach. We implement a first test setup to evaluate the performance of our approach. Our experimental setup shows that the process works quite well under laboratory conditions. Here, we achieve an overall detection accuracy of 91.3% for face morphing forgeries with our classification model. Additionally the impact of the created degradation process is visualized and compared for morphed and for genuine face images. This comparison shows a significant difference of both types of images, which validates our feature space. After this, we evaluate the accuracy of our classification model under more realistic conditions with six different test datasets. This evaluation shows detection accuracies for face morphings (85.9%), but struggles to classify authentic images correctly (68.4%). So, the false alarm rate is not acceptable for real world applications and has to be improved if the process should be a part of a real world application. All in all the degradation process is promissing to detect face morphings and encourages further research on this approach.

In future work, a bigger ground truth training dataset would be meaningful to train a more detailed classification model, which hopefully delivers more accurate evaluation results. Furthermore the granularity of the degradation process should be increased, to see whether it could lead to better classification results. Moreover the degradation process can be performed with other degradating procedures for example median filtering. Currently, our approach is based on three corner detectors which describe the degradation. It would be meaningful to expand the feature space by more degradation sensitive features.

Acknowledgments. The work in this paper has been funded in part by the German Federal Ministry of Education and Research (BMBF) through the research programme ANANAS under the contract no. FKZ: 16KIS0509K. The author would like to thank Jana Dittmann and Andrey Makrushin for the initial ideas as well as the joint work with both of them and Christian Kraetzer for discussions on the approach evaluated in this paper.

References

1. Ferrera, M., Franco, A., Maltoni, D.: The magic passport. In: Proceedings of the IEEE IEEE International Conference on Biometrics, Clearwater, Florida, pp. 1–7 (2014)
2. Makrushin, A., Neubert, T., Dittmann, J.: Automatic generation and detection of visually faultless facial morphs. In: Proceedings of the 12th International Joint Conference on Computer Vision, Imaging and Computer Graphics Theory and Applications (VISIGRAPP 2017). VISAPP, vol. 6, pp. 39–50 (2017). ISBN: 978-989-758-227-1
3. Hildebrandt, M., Neubert, T., Makrushin, A., Dittmann, J.: Benchmarking face morphing forgery detection: application of StirTrace for impact simulation of different processing steps. In: Li, C.-T. (ed.) Proceedings of the International Workshop on Biometrics and Forensics (IWBF 2017), Coventry, UK, University of Warwick, 4–5 April 2017
4. Ferrara, M., Franco, A., Maltoni, D.: On the effects of image alterations on face recognition accuracy. In: Bourlai, T. (ed.) Face Recognition Across the Imaging Spectrum, pp. 195–222. Springer, Cham (2016). doi:10.1007/978-3-319-28501-6_9
5. Schetinger, V., Iuliani, M., Piva, A., Oliveira, M.: Digital Image Forensics vs. Image Composition: An Indirect Arms Race. CoRR abs/1601.03239 (2016)
6. Raghavendra, R., Raja, K., Busch, C.: Detecting morphed facial images. In: Proceedings of 8th IEEE International Conference on Biometrics: Theory, Applications and Systems (BTAS 2016), Niagra Falls, USA, 6–9 September 2016

7. Othman, A., Ross, A.: Privacy of facial soft biometrics: suppressing gender but retaining identity. In: Agapito, L., Bronstein, M.M., Rother, C. (eds.) ECCV 2014. LNCS, vol. 8926, pp. 682–696. Springer, Cham (2015). doi:10.1007/978-3-319-16181-5_52

8. Scherhag, U., Raghavendra, R., Raja, K.B., Gomez-Barrero, M., Rathgeb, C., Busch, C.: On the vulnerability of face recognition systems towards morphed face attacks. In: Li, C.-T.(ed.) Proceedings of the International Workshop on Biometrics and Forensics (IWBF 2017), Coventry, UK, University of Warwick, 4–5 April 2017

9. Gomez-Barrero, M., Rathgeb, C., Scherhag, U., Busch, C.: Is your biometric system robust to morphing attacks? In: Li, C.-T. (ed.) Proceedings of the International Workshop on Biometrics and Forensics (IWBF 2017), Coventry, UK, University of Warwick, 4–5 April 2017

10. Rosten, E., Drummond, T.: Fusing points and lines for high performance tracking. In: IEEE International Conference on Computer Vision, vol. 2, pp. 1508–1511 (2005). doi:10.1109/ICCV.2005.104

11. Mair, E., Hager, G., Burschka, D., Suppa, M., Hirzinger, G.: Adaptive and Generic Corner Detection Based on the Accelerated Segment Test (2010). http://www6.in.tum.de/Main/Publications/Mair2010c.pdf. Access 7 Feb 2017

12. Shi, J., Tomasi, C.: Good features to track. In: Proceedings of the IEEE Conference on Computer Vision and Pattern Recognition, pp. 593–600 (1994)

13. Low, D.: Object recognition from local scale-invariant features. In: Proceedings of the International Conference on Computer Vision (1999)

14. Bay, H., Tuytelaars, T., Gool, L.: SURF: speeded up robust features. In: Leonardis, A., Bischof, H., Pinz, A. (eds.) ECCV 2006, Part I. LNCS, vol. 3951, pp. 404–417. Springer, Heidelberg (2006). doi:10.1007/11744023_32

15. Wolf, A.: Portrait Quality (Reference Facial Images for MRTD). Version: 0.08 ICAO, Published by authority of the Secretary General (2017)

16. Hall, M., et al.: The WEKA data mining software: an update. SIGKDD Explor. **11**(1), 10–18 (2009)

17. Landwehr, N., Hall, M., Frank, E.: Logistic model trees. In: Proceedings in Machine Learning, pp. 161–205 (2005)

18. Hancock, P.: Psychological image collection at stirling (pics) - 2d face sets - Utrecht ECVP. http://pics.psych.stir.ac.uk/. Accessed 21 Apr 2017

19. Luxand, Inc.: Luxand - detect and recognize faces and facial features with luxand facesdk (2016). https://www.luxand.com/facesdk/. Accessed 6 June 2017

Detection of Face Morphing Attacks
by Deep Learning

Clemens Seibold[1(✉)], Wojciech Samek[1], Anna Hilsmann[1], and Peter Eisert[1,2]

[1] Fraunhofer HHI, Einsteinufer 37, 10587 Berlin, Germany
clemens.seibold@hhi.fraunhofer.de
[2] Humboldt University Berlin, Unter den Linden 6, 10099 Berlin, Germany

Abstract. Identification by biometric features has become more popular in the last decade. High quality video and fingerprint sensors have
become less expensive and are nowadays standard components in many
mobile devices. Thus, many devices can be unlocked via fingerprint or
face verification. The state of the art accuracy of biometric facial recognition systems prompted even systems that need high security standards
like border control at airports to rely on biometric systems. While most
biometric facial recognition systems perform quite accurate under a controlled environment, they can easily be tricked by morphing attacks.
The concept of a morphing attack is to create a synthetic face image
that contains characteristics of two different individuals and to use this
image on a document or as reference image in a database. Using this
image for authentication, a biometric facial recognition system accepts
both individuals. In this paper, we propose a morphing attack detection approach based on convolutional neural networks. We present an
automatic morphing pipeline to generate morphing attacks, train neural
networks based on this data and analyze their accuracy. The accuracy of
different well-known network architectures are compared and the advantage of using pretrained networks compared to networks learned from
scratch is studied.

Keywords: Automatic face morphing · Face image forgery detection ·
Convolutional neural networks · Morphing attack

1 Introduction

Biometric facial recognition systems are nowadays present in many areas of daily
life. They are used to identify people, find pictures of the same person in your
digital image collection, to make suggestions for tagging people in social media
or for verification tasks like unlocking a phone or a computer. Apart from these
consumer market applications, biometric facial recognition systems found also
their way into sovereign tasks like automatic border control at airports. In particular, for these tasks the verification system has to be reliable and secure.

Even though biometric facial recognition systems achieve false rejection rates
below 1% at a false acceptance rate of 0.1% in a controlled environment [1],

© Springer International Publishing AG 2017
C. Kraetzer et al. (Eds.): IWDW 2017, LNCS 10431, pp. 107–120, 2017.
DOI: 10.1007/978-3-319-64185-0_9

Fig. 1. Morphing attack (left, right: original images, center: morphing attack)

they can easily be tricked by a specific attack, known as morphing attack [2]. The concept of this attack is to create a synthetic face image that is, in the eye of the recognition system, similar to the faces of two different individuals (Fig. 1). Thus, both can use the same synthetic face image for authentication. This attack is usually performed by creating a face image that contains characteristics of both faces, for example by face morphing. Since such an attack has a drastic impact on the authenticity of its underlying system, its automatic detection is of outmost importance.

The detection of attacks by image manipulation has been studied for various tasks. Several publications deal with the detection of resampling artifacts [3,4], the use of specific filters, e.g. median filters [5], or JPEG-double compression [6,7]. Beside these analyses based on signal theory, several authors proposed image forgery detection methods based on semantic image content by analyzing reflections and shadows [8,9]. Recently, the detection and analysis of forged face images with the purpose of tricking a facial recognition system became interesting to many researchers, which were certainly influenced by the publication of a manual for morphing attacks from Ferrara et al. [2]. Makrushin et al. [10] proposed an approach for automatic generation of facial morphs and their detection based on the distribution of Benford features extracted from quantized DCT coefficients of JPEG-compressed morphs. Raghavendra et al. [11] presented a morphing detection method based on binary statistical images features and evaluated its accuracy on manually created morphed face images.

In this work, we analyze the practical usability of deep neural networks (DNNs) for detection of morphed face images (morphing attacks). DNNs are state of the art image classification methods, since the DNN AlexNet [12] broke in 2012 the record error rate of 25.7% in the object recognition challenge (ILSVRC2012) and reduced it to 16.4%. This DNN architecture has five convolutional layers and ends with three fully connected layers. Pursuing the concept of "simple but deep", Simonyan and Zisserman [13] showed in 2015 that a simple architecture concept (VGG19) with only 3×3 convolutional filters, but with a depth of 16 convolutional layers also performs as well as state of the art architectures with error rates for object classification of about 7%. Szegedy et al. [14] moved away from the concept of a simple architecture and introduced the GoogLeNet with a complex structure containing inception layers. An inception layer consists of several convolutional filters that operate in parallel and whose outputs are concatenated. On one hand, the GoogLeNet needs, due to this structure, less parameters to describe even complex features and is thus less prone to overfitting, but on the other hand, the learned features are more difficult to interpret.

We focus on the accuracy analysis of the three architectures named above, since all of these architectures have successfully been used for the task of image classification and pretrained models are publicly available. Similar to the task of object classification, we do not want to detect low-level artifacts, e.g. resampling, median filtering or blurring artifacts like Bayar and Stamm [15] did using a different CNN architecture for image forgery detection. Instead, we want our DNNs to decide based on semantic features like unrealistic eyes forms, specular highlights or other semantic artifacts caused by the morphing process.

Since a huge amount of data is needed for the training of DNNs, we designed a fully automatic morphing algorithm that takes two 2D face images, aligns the facial features, such that they are at the same position, blends the whole aligned images and gets rid of ghosting artifacts due to different hairstyles, ear geometry etc. in a post-processing step that fits the blended face into a warped source image. Some components, like the face alignment, are exchangeable due to the pipeline structure of our morphing algorithm. To overcome the problem of learning low-level features, like resampling artifacts, all images - original face images and morphing attacks - are preprocessed in several ways.

In Sect. 2, we describe our fully automatic morphing algorithm with exchangeable components which is used to create a database of morphed images. The preprocessing steps, which are independent of the morphing process, and our database of original face images and morphing attacks are presented in Sect. 3. Our morphing attack detection experiments are shown in Sect. 4. Finally, the results are presented and discussed.

2 Morphing Pipeline

In this section, we introduce our fully automatic morphing algorithm. We start by introducing the general steps of morphing algorithms and finally describe our specific algorithm.

2.1 Overview on a General Morphing Pipeline

To trick a facial recognition system to match two different persons with one synthetic reference image, the synthetic image has to contain characteristics from both faces. If the feature space of the recognition system is known, the characteristics can be directly combined in that space. Since commercial face recognition system are often a black box and an attacker would not rely on the presence of a specific system, we adapt the facial characteristics in image space. The usual process of face image morphing is divided into four steps:

1. Locate facial landmarks
2. Align images by image warping such that the detected facial landmarks are at nearly the same position
3. Blend the images, e.g. additive blending with a blending factor of 0.5
4. Replace the inner part of a warped original image by the corresponding part of the blended image. To reduce artifacts, an optimal cutting path is computed.

Some morphing algorithms cut the inner part of the face and insert it into one original not warped face image. They apply an inverse morphing on the blended image and also need to handle the border between blended and original image.

2.2   Morphing Pipeline Implementation

Figure 2 illustrates our face image morphing pipeline. In the following we describe our implementation of the single steps in detail.

Landmark Detection. Sixty-eight facial landmarks are located using the dLib's [16] implementation of [17]. These landmarks are located around mouth, eyes, nose, eyebrows and the lower half of the head's silhouette, see also Figs. 2a,d.

Image Alignment. We implemented two different warping methods to align the images. One is based on a transformation of a triangle mesh and the other one uses the Beier-Neely morphing algorithm [18]. In both cases, the transformation is performed such that both faces are warped to an average geometry of both faces. The exact definition of the average geometry depends on the warping method, but both methods rely on average positions of the facial landmarks. These are calculated by averaging pairwise the location of the facial landmarks in the original images.

a. *Triangle warping:* We first add eight additional control points to the detected 68 facial landmark locations in each image to be able to morph also the region outside of the convex hull of the detected points. They are located in the four corners and on the middle of the four lines of a bounding box around the head. These eight control points are also subject to the averaging of facial landmark positions as described above. Following, the average positions are used to create a triangle mesh using the Delaunay [19] triangulation, see also Fig. 3a. To create the piecewise affine warped version of the first source image, for each pixel in the target image, we calculate the barycentric coordinates for the triangle enclosing the point and use them to calculate the color by bilinear interpolation in the source image. This corresponds to rendering the

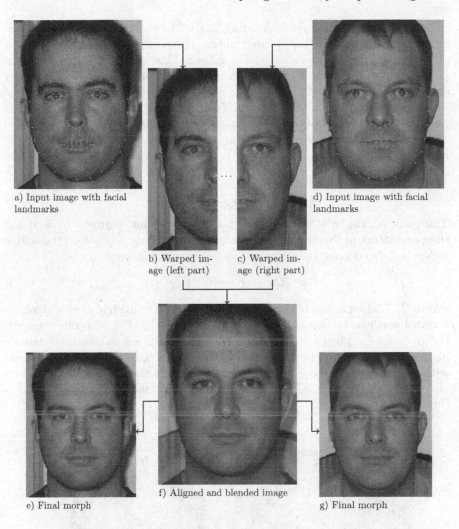

a) Input image with facial landmarks

d) Input image with facial landmarks

b) Warped image (left part)

c) Warped image (right part)

f) Aligned and blended image

e) Final morph

g) Final morph

Fig. 2. Morphing pipeline

triangle mesh using the common rendering pipeline with the average positions of the landmarks as coordinates, the landmark's positions of a source image as texture coordinates and the source image as texture map. The other image is warped accordingly.

b. *Field morphing:* In contrast to the triangle warping, the field morphing [18] needs no corresponding feature points, but corresponding feature line segments. To get corresponding feature line segments, we use the estimated landmark positions and connect them according to a predefined pattern, see Fig. 3b. The basic idea of the field morphing is to move every pixel according to the movement of each line segment weighted by the distance to them. Assuming there is only one line segment Q in the source image with end points Q_s and Q_e, one corresponding line Q' in the destination image and a given position p_w in the warped image, the corresponding position p_s in the source image can be calculated as follows. First, the position of the point p_w is calculated relative to the line in the destination image. This is done by calculating the distance d from p_w to a line that is defined by extending the line segment Q' to an infinite length. The distance d is signed, such that it is positive, if the normal of the line segment Q' points towards p_w and otherwise negative. Given the closest point s on this line to p_w, we parameterize the position of this intersection point by p_w using the start and end point of the line segment:

$$u = \frac{s - Q'_s}{\|Q'_e - Q'_s\|} \tag{1}$$

The point p_w can now be described relative to the line segment by u, d and the parameters of the line segment. The corresponding position in the source image is defined relative to the line in the source image as

$$u \cdot \|Q_e - Q_s\| + Q_s + Q_n \cdot d, \tag{2}$$

where Q_n is the normal of the line segment Q. The multi-line case is straightforward and can be done for every pixel individually: For each line segment, the motion of a pixel is calculated as described above and weighted according to its distance to the line segment with the weight decreasing nonlinear with the distance to a line segment. These motions and weights are added up and finally the motion is divided by the sum of all weights at this pixel. For further details see [18].

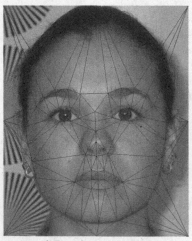
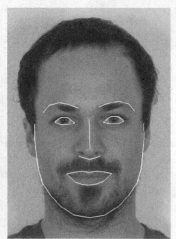

a) Triangle mesh warping   b) Feature lines for the field morphing

Fig. 3. Initialization for face warping

Image Blending. Our blending is performed by an additive alpha blending with a blending factor of 0.5 for both warped images. More complex blending methods, like spatially invariant blending factors based of the spatial frequencies or selected features might be useful to retain facial characteristics, e.g. moles and freckles, and will be part of our future work.

Warped/Blended Image Fusion. The warped and blended images are already usable for tricking a biometric facial recognition system but would be rejected by every human due to the ghosting artifacts around the borders of the heads, see also Fig. 2f. To get rid of these artifacts, we use the blended image only for the inner part of the synthetic face image, the rest of the image is taken from one of the warped source images. As a consequence of combining these two images, we have to deal with the border between the blended part of the face and the background. In order to hide this border to the human eye and morphing detection systems, we calculate a subtle transition between foreground and background. Two ellipses define a transition zone between foreground and background. They are located such that the outer ellipse is barely on the chin and underneath the hairline and the inner ellipse surrounds all detected facial landmarks. Figure 4a shows the ellipses in one blended image. The cyan point denotes the center of the ellipse and is defined relative to the two red marked facial landmaks on the nose. The width is defined relative to the X-distance from the center to the position of the red marked facial landmarks next to the ears and the height relative to the Y distance from the center to the red marked facial landmarks below the mouth and at the chin. The border/transition in this area is calculated separately for high and low spatial frequencies. The transition for low frequencies is calculated using Poisson Image Editing [20], while an optimal cutting path through the transition zone is searched for the high frequency details. For that purpose, the area defined by the two ellipses is unrolled from Cartesian to polar coordinates [21]. Thus, the column in the converted image defines the angle and the row defines the radius, see also Fig. 4a,b.

On these images, we calculate an optimal path using the graph cut algorithm for image segmentation. The top row and the bottom row are defined as foreground and background, and the rest as unknown component. In contrast to classical segmentation approaches, we want to find transitions with a minimal color difference as in [22]. However, in contrast to [22], we use a different objective function that uses a normalized color difference instead of the sum of absolute color differences. Thereby, we encourage cuts through similar regions, volatile or smooth, in both images and avoid artifacts along the cut. The cost function for two neighboring pixels $(x, y), (x + 1, y)$ or $(x, y), (x, y + 1)$ being not in the same class, in our case taken from different images, is thus defined as the weighted intensity difference between both images at these pixels:

$$C(x, y, x + 1, y) = \sqrt{\frac{(I_b(x, y) - I_s(x, y))^2 + (I_b(x + 1, y) - I_s(x + 1, y))^2}{n_x(x, y)}} \quad (3)$$

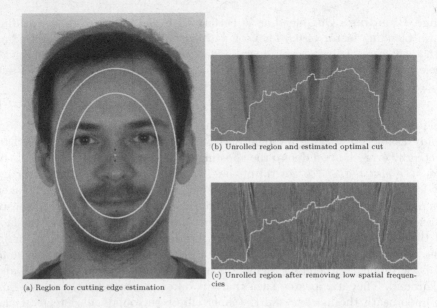

(a) Region for cutting edge estimation

(b) Unrolled region and estimated optimal cut

(c) Unrolled region after removing low spatial frequencies

Fig. 4. Estimation of cutting edge for the high spatial frequencies

$$C(x,y,x,y+1) = \sqrt{\frac{(I_b(x,y) - I_s(x,y))^2 + (I_b(x,y+1) - I_s(x,y+1))^2}{n_y(x,y)}}, \quad (4)$$

where $I_b(x,y)$ is the intensity at pixel (x,y) in the unrolled blended image after removing the low spatial frequencies, $I_s(x,y)$ in the corresponding unrolled background and

$$n_x(x,y) = (I_b(x-1,y) - I_b(x+1,y))^2 + (I_b(x,y) - I_b(x+2,y))^2 \quad (5)$$
$$+ (I_s(x-1,y) - I_s(x+1,y))^2 + (I_s(x,y) - I_s(x+2,y))^2$$

$$n_y(x,y) = (I_b(x,y-1) - I_b(x,y+1))^2 + (I_b(x,y) - I_b(x,y+2))^2 \quad (6)$$
$$+ (I_s(x,y-1) - I_s(x,y+1))^2 + (I_s(x,y) - I_s(x,y+2))^2$$

the normalization function. Put simply, cuts through regions that differ in both images are penalized. Figures 4b–c show the estimated cutting edge on an unrolled face image.

By separating high spatial frequencies and low spatial frequencies, we can obtain a border that provides a smooth transition and does not cut through high spatial frequency biometric characteristics. The estimation of the transition in the lower frequencies part allows a smoothly and subtly adjustment of different colors or different brightness on the skin due to both, differences in skin color and illumination. The estimation of a sharp border for the high frequencies provides a cutting path through the image along similar regions, thus visible borders or cuts through individual biometric characteristics like freckles, moles or scares are avoided.

3 Database and Preprocessing

In this section, we describe our face image database and the preprocessing steps that are applied to both types of images, original face images and morphing attacks. The preprocessing is applied to increase the variety of the data and prevent the neural networks from learning low-level artifacts like gradient distributions. Finally, we introduce a modified cross-validation method. It considers the dependency between our original face images and morphing attacks, caused by the morphing process itself, since it fuses two original images to one forged synthetic image containing characteristics of both original images.

3.1 Database

Our face image database contains about 1250 face images of different individuals. The database can be divided into 9 different groups of images, with nearly each group having similar capture conditions regarding illumination and camera type and properties. One group contains face images captured under varying conditions and with different cameras. All images show a face in a frontal pose. The captured person has open eyes, their mouth closed and a neutral expression, as demanded for passport images. Morphing attacks are only created using images from the same group. In this way, we can acquire morphing attacks of high quality, since difficult alignments due to different focal length, distortions or other camera parameters are avoided.

To ensure that our automatically created morphing attacks can be used successfully to trick biometric facial recognition systems, we tested our attack on a commercial biometric facial recognition software [23]. We used the system to check whether the morphing attack and the two genuine face images that were used to generate this attack show the same person. In about 95% of cases, both people were recognized when we set the false acceptance rate of the recognition system to 0.1% as recommended by FRONTEX for automated border control gates [24]. Since we select the source images for a morphing attack randomly, this rate might be increased by morphing only faces that do not differ heavily.

3.2 Preprocessing

To increase the variety in the data, we artificially add two types of noise and two types of blur to both, original images and morphed images. The parameters for artificially noise and blur were chosen randomly for each image, but with an upper limit as described in Table 1.

Beside adding more variety, this kind of preprocessing is also intended to prevent our networks from learning low-level artifacts caused by resampling or JPEG-compression. In summary, our dataset contains about 9000 fake images that are randomly processed by adding salt and pepper noise, Gaussian noise, motion blur, Gaussian Blur or none of them. The original face images are processed in the same way.

Table 1. Preprocessing parameters

Kind of noise/blur	Upper limit
Salt-and-pepper noise	1% of all pixels
Gaussian noise	Standard deviation up to 0.05
Gaussian blur	Standard deviation up to 0.5% of image width
motion blur	Angle randomly, length up to 1.2% of image width

Fig. 5. Morphing attacks after (left half) and before (right half) preprocessing: Gaussian blur, Gaussian noise, motion blur, Salt-and-pepper noise (from left to right)

3.3   Test Set Selection

We use 4-fold cross-validation to evaluate the robustness of our trained neural networks. Since the samples in our data are not independent due to the fact that a morphing attack is performed by averaging two samples (original face images), the separation of the datasets for the 4-fold cross-validation has to consider this dependency. Hence, we separate the dataset of morphed and original face images slightly different to the classical 4-fold cross-validation. The test and training sets are created as follow:

1. We separate the individuals into four disjunctive sets $\mathbf{I}_{1,2,3,4}$ of the same size.
2. We create the test sets $\mathbf{T}_{1,2,3,4}$, with $\mathbf{T}_i$ containing all images showing individuals in $\mathbf{I}_i$ and morphing attacks based on individuals in $\mathbf{I}_i$.
3. A training set $\bar{\mathbf{T}}_i$ contains all images that are not in $\mathbf{T}_i$.

By separating the images that way, some morphing attacks will appear in two test data sets, but we removed correlation between test and training data.

4   Experiments

In this section, we describe our experimental setup, in particular the preprocessing of the data to fit the requirements of the networks, e.g. the input size, outline the network architectures we use for the image forgery detection and present the accuracy of the networks for the task of forgery detection. For each network architecture, we analyze the morphing detection accuracy for the network trained from scratch and starting the training with pretrained models, which were trained for the task of object classification on the ILSVRC dataset.

4.1   Network Architectures

We analyze three different deep convolutional network architectures, AlexNet, GoogLeNet and VGG19, which are all well known for object classification tasks. All three networks have nearly the same input image size that is 224×224 pixels for the VGG19 and GoogLeNet architecture and 227×227 pixels for the AlexNet. While the AlexNet was the first DNN that revolutionized the area of object classification and its design focuses on performance on two graphics cards, the architecture of VGG19 was designed to be simple but powerful and all of its convolutional layers have kernels of size 3×3 and exactly one predecessor and one successor layer. In contrast to the AlexNet and the VGG19 architecture, the GoogLeNet has a quite complex structure. Its key components are inception modules [14]. These modules consist of multiple different sized convolution filters that process the same input and concatenate the results. Using this type of modules, the GoogLetNet achieves a similar accuracy for object classification tasks as the VGG19, but needs less than one-tenth of the parameters the VGG19 needs.

4.2   Preprocessing on Network Input

To reduce unnecessary variety, that can be removed in a trivial preprocessing step, we rotate the image on the image plane, such that the eyes are at the same height. All networks were fed with a complete facial image that contain only the inner part of the face that is between the eyebrows and the mouth and between the outer parts of the eyes. Since neural networks need images of fixed size as input, the images are rescaled such that this region fits the input size of the network. In order to get more variety in the data, the region extracted from the rotated and scaled image is randomly moved for up to 2 pixels in any direction. This process does not harm the correctness of this data since the features in the face are not aligned, e.g. the position and size of the eyebrows, nose, pupils varies from human to human, moreover the detected borders of the region are subject to small inaccuracies.

4.3   Training

We trained all three network architectures from scratch as well as starting with pretrained models, which were trained for the task of object classification on the ILSVRC dataset, using the deep learning framework caffe [25]. The average color, that is recommended to subtract before feeding the network, was set for all experiments to the average color of the ILSVRC dataset, since the pretrained networks use this average color - except for the AlexNet, which used an average image, which has the same average color. The training samples for one epoch of the network were shuffled and some original images duplicated, such that the probability of selecting a morphing attack is equal to the probability of selecting an original face image. The networks that were trained from scratch were initialized randomly, except for the VGG19, which was initialized using the random initialization procedure of [26]. In both cases, pretrained and training from scratch, the training was terminated after the loss function was not improved for several epochs.

4.4 Results

The training of all networks converged and the average loss on images of the training set was below $5 \cdot 10^{-5}$ for all networks. The accuracy in terms of False Acceptance Rate (FAR) and False Rejection Rate (FRR) is shown in Table 2. The FAR is defined as relative amount of morphing attacks classified as genuine images and the FRR as the relative amount of genuine images classified as morphing attacks. The FRR of VGG19 (pretrained) is only about a third of the FRR of the AlexNet (pretrained) and 2.1% points lower than the FRR of the GoogLeNet (pretrained). All network architectures performed better, when starting the training with pretrained networks instead of learning all weights from scratch. The FRR of the network architectures GoogLeNet and VGG19 outperformed the AlexNet in both cases, while the FAR is for all architectures nearly the same, but depends of the initialization of the weights.

Table 2. Accuracy of the trained networks in terms of False Acceptance Rate and False Rejection Rate

	AlexNet		GoogLeNet		VGG19	
	FRR	FAR	FRR	FAR	FRR	FAR
From scratch	16.2%	1.9%	10.0%	1.8%	10.9%	2.2%
Pretrained	11.4%	0.9%	5.6%	1.2%	3.5%	0.8%

5 Conclusion

In this paper, we proposed a morphing attack detection method based on deep convolution neural networks. A fully automatic face image morphing pipeline with exchangeable components was presented that was used to create training and test samples for the networks. Instead of detecting classical traces of tampering, e.g. caused by resampling or JPEG double compression, and their anti-forensic methods [27–29] we focused on semantic artifacts. To avoid learning a detector for these classical tampering traces, all images were preprocessed by scaling, rotating and cropping, before feeding them to the network. In addition, we added different kinds of noise and blur to the training and test data.

We trained three different convolutional neural network architectures from scratch and starting with pretrained networks. The FRR of our trained networks differ between 3.5% and 16.2% and the FAR between 0.8% and 2.2%. The VGG19 (pretrained) achieved for both rates the best result with a FRR of 3.5% and a FAR of 0.8%. The pretrained networks outperformed the networks trained from scratch for every architecture. This suggests that the features learned for object classification are also useful for detection of morphing attacks.

In future work, we plan to analyze the decisions made by our networks. In particular, we plan to study the regions that contribute to the decision of a network and analyze the differences between different architectures and pretrained networks using the LRP toolbox [30].

Acknowledgments. The work in this paper has been funded in part by the German Federal Ministry of Education and Research (BMBF) through the Research Program ANANAS under Contract No. FKZ: 16KIS0511.

References

1. Spreeuwers, L.J., Hendrikse, A.J., Gerritsen, K.J.: Evaluation of automatic face recognition for automatic border control on actual data recorded of travellers at schiphol airport. In: Proceedings of the International Conference of Biometrics Special Interest Group (BIOSIG), 1–6 September 2012
2. Ferrara, M., Franco, A., Maltoni, D.: The magic passport. In: IEEE International Joint Conference on Biometrics, 1–7 September 2014
3. Popescu, A.C., Farid, H.: Exposing digital forgeries by detecting traces of resampling. IEEE Trans. Sig. Process. **53**(2), 758–767 (2005)
4. Kirchner, M., Gloe, T.: On resampling detection in re-compressed images. In: 2009 First IEEE International Workshop on Information Forensics and Security (WIFS), 21–25 December 2009
5. Kirchner, M., Fridrich, J.: On detection of median filtering in digital images. Proc. SPIE **7541**, 754110–754110–12 (2010)
6. Lukáš, J., Fridrich, J.: Estimation of primary quantization matrix in double compressed JPEG images. In: Proceedings of DFRWS (2003)
7. Farid, H.: Exposing digital forgeries from JPEG ghosts. IEEE Trans. Inf. Forensics Secur. **4**(1), 154–160 (2009)
8. Johnson, M.K., Farid, H.: Exposing digital forgeries through specular highlights on the eye. In: Furon, T., Cayre, F., Doërr, G., Bas, P. (eds.) IH 2007. LNCS, vol. 4567, pp. 311–325. Springer, Heidelberg (2007). doi:10.1007/978-3-540-77370-2_21
9. Kee, E., O'brien, J.F., Farid, H.: Exposing photo manipulation from shading and shadows. ACM Trans. Graph. **33**(5), 165:1–165:21 (2014)
10. Makrushin, A., Neubert, T., Dittmann, J.: Automatic generation and detection of visually faultless facial morphs. In: Proceedings of the 12th International Joint Conference on Computer Vision, Imaging and Computer Graphics Theory and Applications (VISIGRAPP 2017), pp. 39–50 (2017)
11. Raghavendra, R., Raja, K.B., Busch, C.: Detecting morphed face images. In: 8th IEEE International Conference on Biometrics Theory, Applications and Systems, BTAS 2016, Niagara Falls, NY, USA, pp. 1–7, 6–9 September 2016
12. Krizhevsky, A., Sutskever, I., Hinton, G.E.: Imagenet classification with deep convolutional neural networks. In: Advances in Neural Information Processing Systems 25. Curran Associates, Inc., pp. 1097–1105 (2012)
13. Simonyan, K., Zisserman, A.: Very deep convolutional networks for large-scale image recognition. CoRR abs/1409.1556 (2014)
14. Szegedy, C., Liu, W., Jia, Y., Sermanet, P., Reed, S., Anguelov, D., Erhan, D., Vanhoucke, V., Rabinovich, A.: Going deeper with convolutions. In: Computer Vision and Pattern Recognition (CVPR) (2015)

15. Bayar, B., Stamm, M.C.: A deep learning approach to universal image manipulation detection using a new convolutional layer. In: Proceedings of the 4th ACM Workshop on Information Hiding and Multimedia Security, New York, NY, USA, pp. 5–10. ACM (2016)
16. King, D.E.: Dlib-ml: a machine learning toolkit. J. Mach. Learn. Res. **10**, 1755–1758 (2009)
17. Kazemi, V., Sullivan, J.: One millisecond face alignment with an ensemble of regression trees. In: Proceedings of the 2014 IEEE Conference on Computer Vision and Pattern Recognition. CVPR 2014, Computer Society, pp. 1867–1874. IEEE, Washington, DC (2014)
18. Beier, T., Neely, S.: Feature-based image metamorphosis. In: Proceedings of the 19th Annual Conference on Computer Graphics and Interactive Techniques, SIG-GRAPH 1992, pp. 35–42. ACM, New York (1992)
19. Delaunay, B.: Sur la sphere vide. Izv. Akad. Nauk SSSR, Otdelenie Matematicheskii i Estestvennyka Nauk **7**, 793–800 (1934)
20. Pérez, P., Gangnet, M., Blake, A.: Poisson image editing. In: ACM SIGGRAPH 2003 Papers, SIGGRAPH 2003, pp. 313–318. ACM, New York (2003)
21. Prestele, B., Schneider, D.C., Eisert, P.: System for the automated segmentation of heads from arbitrary background. In: ICIP, pp. 3257–3260. IEEE (2011)
22. Paier, W., Kettern, M., Hilsmann, A., Eisert, P.: Video-based facial re-animation. In: Proceedings of the 12th European Conference on Visual Media Production, London, United Kingdom, pp. 4:1–4:10, 24–25 November 2015
23. Neurotechnology Inc.: Verilook 9.0/megamatcher 9.0 faces identification technology (2017). http://www.neurotechnology.com/
24. FRONTEX - Research and Development Unit: Best practice technical guidelines for automated border control (abc) systems - v2.0 (2012)
25. Jia, Y., Shelhamer, E., Donahue, J., Karayev, S., Long, J., Girshick, R., Guadarrama, S., Darrell, T.: Caffe: convolutional architecture for fast feature embedding. arXiv preprint (2014). arXiv:1408.5093
26. Glorot, X., Bengio, Y.: Understanding the difficulty of training deep feedforward neural networks. In: Proceedings of the International Conference on Artificial Intelligence and Statistics (AISTATS10). Society for Artificial Intelligence and Statistics (2010)
27. Stamm, M.C., Liu, K.J.R.: Anti-forensics of digital image compression. IEEE Trans. Inf. Forensics Secur. **6**(3), 1050–1065 (2011)
28. Yu, J., Zhan, Y., Yang, J., Kang, X.: A multi-purpose image counter-anti-forensic method using convolutional neural networks. In: Shi, Y.Q., Kim, H.J., Perez-Gonzalez, F., Liu, F. (eds.) IWDW 2016. LNCS, vol. 10082, pp. 3–15. Springer, Cham (2017). doi:10.1007/978-3-319-53465-7_1
29. Kirchner, M., Bohme, R.: Hiding traces of resampling in digital images. IEEE Trans. Inf. Forensics Secur. **3**(4), 582–592 (2008)
30. Lapuschkin, S., Binder, A., Montavon, G., Müller, K.R., Samek, W.: Analyzing classifiers: fisher vectors and deep neural networks. In: Proceedings of the IEEE Conference on Computer Vision and Pattern Recognition (CVPR), pp. 2912–2920 (2016)

CNNs Under Attack: On the Vulnerability of Deep Neural Networks Based Face Recognition to Image Morphing

Lukasz Wandzik[✉], Raul Vicente Garcia, Gerald Kaeding, and Xi Chen

Fraunhofer Institute for Production Systems and Design Technology IPK,
Pascalstraße 8 – 9, 10587 Berlin, Germany
{lukasz.wandzik,raul.vicente,gerald.kaeding,xi.chen}@ipk.fraunhofer.de

Abstract. Facial recognition has become a critical constituent of common automatic border control gates. Despite many advances in recent years, face recognition systems remain susceptible to an ever evolving diversity of spoofing attacks. It has recently been shown that high-quality face morphing or splicing can be employed to deceive facial recognition systems in a border control scenario. Moreover, facial morphs can easily be produced by means of open source software and with minimal technical knowledge. The purpose of this work is to quantify the severeness of the problem using a large dataset of morphed face images. We employ a state-of-the-art face recognition algorithm based on deep convolutional neural networks and measure its performance on a dataset of 7260 high-quality facial morphs with varying blending factor. Using the *Inception-ResNet-v1* architecture we train a deep neural model on 4 million images to obtain a validation rate of 99.96% at 0.04% false acceptance rate (FAR) on the original, unmodified images. The same model fails to repel 1.13% of all morphing attacks, accepting both the impostor and the document owner. Based on these results, we discuss the observed weaknesses and possible remedies.

Keywords: Face recognition · Biometric spoofing · Face morphing · Deep learning

1 Introduction

The detection of biometric counterfeits, commonly known as anti-spoofing, is a very active field of research. A diversity of techniques has been proposed in literature for protecting face recognition systems in real authentication scenarios like border control. However, as shown in recent surveys [4,6], most works have only considered presentation attacks, neglecting the often fragile face biometrics enrollment process. In particular, a simple face morphing trick can be applied so that two different persons can potentially pass through an automated border control gate with the same electronic machine readable travel document (eMRTD). This attack simply consists in submitting for enrollment a facial image that is

© Springer International Publishing AG 2017
C. Kraetzer et al. (Eds.): IWDW 2017, LNCS 10431, pp. 121–135, 2017.
DOI: 10.1007/978-3-319-64185-0_10

obtained from morphing the face of the legitimate document owner (accomplice) and the face of a reasonably similar looking impostor. In a successful attack, the face recognition system positively matches the tampered template stored in the eMRTD to the live image of the impostor. The authors of [3] originally presented the possibility of such an attack. However, in that work only commercial, closed source face recognition systems and a very limited set of test images were employed. In contrast hereto, the main contribution of this work is a quantitative estimate of the severeness of the so-called *morphing attack* (see Fig. 1 for an example illustration) based on extensive experimental results, using a large test dataset and an exemplar face recognition method that is both state-of-the-art and publicly accessible. The employed exemplary methods and datasets are selected in order to model a sufficiently realistic, yet optimistic scenario. Herewith, we aim to estimate the lower bounds of the success rate of morphing attacks against current face recognition methods.

2   Related Work

Intentional manipulation of images and its impact on modern generic image recognition systems has been addressed in the case of image classification. The authors of [12,20] show how to perform image modifications that are imperceptible to the human eye, and yet drastically change the outputs of the attacked recognition system. Also unintentional effects produced by the image acquisition system, like perspective distortion, can pose a problem for face recognition. This has been addressed in [21] through image de-warping models. The dependency of recognition performance on image quality in a broader sense has been the subject of research in several works [1,8]. The threat of a morphing attack in a eMRTD scenario using commercial face recognition software was first identified in [3]. More recent publications [11,15] have addressed this specific problem and propose methods for both the generation of morphs and for the detection of manipulation traces in the image.

3   Methods

In this section, we introduce the methods employed for generating our face morphing dataset and describe the face recognition pipeline.

3.1   Face Morphing

Face morphing is usually done by projecting and blending the coordinates and texture informations of many corresponding image regions [23] from two source images S_1 and S_2 into a new synthesized destination image D. These regions can be generated by an automatic landmark detection followed by a Delaunay triangulation. One problem with this approach is the occurrence of blending artifacts, especially in non related regions. Since we only have reliable landmarks

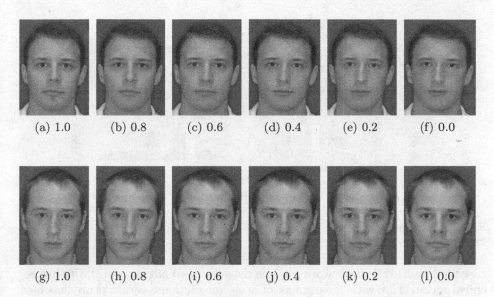

Fig. 1. Visualization of the morphing process with respect to blending factors. The images were generated using two identities 191 (top) and 217 (bottom) from the *MultiPIE* dataset [16]. A blending factor of 1.0 corresponds to the original, unmanipulated image, whereas 0.0 represents the case where the image information of the destination image was entirely replaced by the image data of the source image. All other images show a linear transformation between these two extremes.

for the facial regions, such unrelated assignments will occur outside the convex hull of these landmarks. A way to suppress such artifacts could be the manual retouch of the synthesized image, but this is infeasible for generating a large amount of examples. To address this problem, we only blend the facial regions $\hat{S}_1$ and $\hat{S}_2$ that lie within the convex hulls of our landmarks. To obtain these regions we first detect 68 landmarks [9] using the Dlib library [10] within S_1 and S_2, followed by a Delaunay triangulation. We next determine corresponding triangles to compute the projections. To obtain our morphing image we first set $D = S_2$. We next blend the geometry and texture informations of eyes, nose, and mouth of $\hat{S}_1$ and $\hat{S}_2$. By adopting the outer shape of $\hat{S}_2$ we obtain the destination image $\hat{D}$. At this moment $\hat{D}$ consists only of the morphed facial region. Finally, we blend $\hat{D}$ with D using the Poisson blending of [14]. An exemplary face morphing is depicted in Fig. 1. One can see that the outer shape of S_2 will be preserved, while the geometry and texture information of the relevant facial regions of both input images will be blended.

3.2   Face Recognition Methods

Face Registration. In order to improve performance of facial recognition systems a number of preprocessing steps are applied to the input images, including face detection and alignment. In our work, we use the recently proposed deep

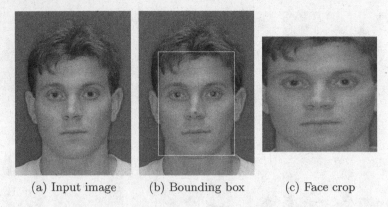

| (a) Input image | (b) Bounding box | (c) Face crop |

Fig. 2. Input image preprocessing using the deep cascaded multi-task framework [24].

cascaded multi-task framework for face detection and alignment [24]. Its hierarchical architecture with three stages of deep convolutional networks predicts face and landmark location in a coarse-to-fine manner. The resulting face bounding box is padded by a margin of 16 pixels on each side and finally resized to a 160×160 pixel square in order to fit the input of our neural network (Fig. 2). The input image size translates to about 90 pixels interpupillary distance, which complies with the ICAO recommendations[1] for eMRTDs and corresponds to the actual conditions of a real morphing attack.

Feature Extraction. We have tested several network architectures for face verification including the works of Parkhi et al. [13] and Schroff et al. [18]. The best performing network is based on the recently purposed *Inception-ResNet-v1* architecture [19]. Its topology includes inception modules as well as residual connections and achieves a state-of-the-art accuracy of $99.3\% \pm 0.04$ on the challenging LFW benchmark dataset [7]. We compute the face embeddings using a tensorflow implementation [17] of the *FaceNet* architecture introduced by Schroff et al. [18]. Instead of a pure inception model, as described in the original paper, [17] employs the *Inception-ResNet-v1* network architecture. Furthermore, the network is trained as a classifier using the Center Loss approach [22] instead of Triplet Loss. We extract the feature vectors by tapping the last fully connected layer before the softmax. The output of this layer is a 1792-dimensional L2-normalized vector. For decision making, we threshold the Euclidean distance between pairs of feature vectors computed by the neural network.

---

[1] ICAO, Machine Readable Travel Documents, Seventh Edition 2015, Part 9: Deployment of Biometric Identification and Electronic Storage of Data in eMRTDs.

4 Experiments

4.1 Datasets

Training. In order to train the deep neural network from scratch, we use the MS-Celeb-1M dataset which contains the top $100\,k$ subjects from the $1\,M$ most popular celebrities list [5]. There are approximately 100 images of each celebrity, resulting in about $10\,M$ images in total. Due to the vast number of automatically acquired data some images suffer from mislabeling. Therefore, only a subset of them was used for training. The dataset was cleaned up by computing the distance between a given image embedding and its class center. Keeping only 75% of the images that are closest to its class center reduces the dataset size to about $4\,M$ images divided into $51\,k$ classes.

Morphing. The face images used for investigating the impact of a morphing attack on our system come from the well known *MultiPIE* [16] dataset. The image data was collected under controlled conditions, similar to those prescribed for eMRTDs. *MultiPIE* contains images of 337 subjects from four different photo sessions, including variations in viewpoint, illumination and expression. In this work, we consider only frontal views and discard coarse illumination changes. To create our morphing dataset we only use images from session one and restrict ourselves to subjects that occur in at least one more session. Furthermore, we only consider subjects not wearing glasses and those belonging to the same gender, in order to avoid unnatural image artifacts. In total, we create 3630 pairs with 22 morphed images each. These images are used for enrollment purposes only, whereas images of session two to four are used for verification.

4.2 Data Preparation

We subdivide the dataset into *positive* and *negative* pairs of identities and use this structure for all experiments throughout the study. The positive pairs consist of the morphed image and the accomplice image whereas the negative pairs contain the impostor and the morphed image. Given subjects from session one of the *MultiPIE* dataset, we select two images I_a and I_b such that

$$\|\phi(I_a) - \phi(I_b)\|_2 > t \tag{1}$$

where ϕ is an embedding of facial features. By this constraint, we make sure that the recognition algorithm is able to discern the individuals. Next, we merge those two images using the method described in the previous section and obtain a morphed image I_{ab}

$$\mathrm{morph}(I_a, I_b) \rightarrow I_{ab} \tag{2}$$

During the evaluation process, the generated image I_{ab} is matched against images from session two to four, provided that the respective individual is available in that session

$$\|\phi(I_{ab}) - \phi(I_x)\|_2 < t, \text{ where } x \neq a \wedge x \neq b \tag{3}$$

so that the images used for producing the morphs are not being used in the evaluation process. For any given identity pair, we generate two kinds of morphing images I_{ab} and I_{ba} by swapping the source and destination identities. Following the described procedure, we generate 17992 image pairs for both positive and negative class, resulting in a total number of 35984 pairs.

4.3   Evaluation Procedure

The evaluation procedure starts by combining identity pairs that share a common morphed image into a triplet. We generate a total number of 44546 triplets using positive and negative identity pairs. The morphed image acts as reference and the accomplice or impostor image as query. For the purpose of this study we define the morphing attack as follows:

Definition 1. *Let I_a be the accomplice image and I_b the impostor image. Let t be some optimal threshold and ϕ an embedding of facial features. A morphing attack using a tempered template I_{ab} is successful if and only if*

$$\|\phi(I_{ab}) - \phi(I_b)\|_2 < t \ \wedge \ \|\phi(I_{ab}) - \phi(I_a)\|_2 < t \qquad (4)$$

We only consider triplets of images consisting of the morphed image I_{ab}, the impostor image I_a, and the accomplice image I_b. From that, we derive four possible outcome cases, as shown in Fig. 3.

Case 1. The first case represents a successful morphing attack where both the accomplice and the impostor succeed and get accepted by the system. We also consider cases where only one of the individuals gets accepted, either the accomplice or the impostor.

Case 2. The second case reflects a correct operation mode of a face recognition system where the accomplice gets accepted and the impostor is rejected.

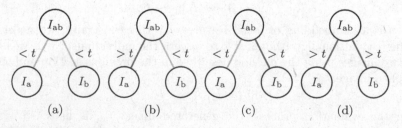

Fig. 3. Four possible outcome cases: (a) Successful morphing attack. (b) Correct verification. (c) Accomplice rejection. (d) Accomplice and impostor rejected.

Case 3. Case three represents the reverse situation where the impostor gets accepted and the accomplice is rejected. This case could also be seen as a successful morphing attack, but in this work we restrict ourselves only to Case 1 as defined in 1.

Case 4. In the last, fourth case, both the accomplice and impostor are rejected. In this situation, a total failure of an morphing attack is simulated.

4.4   Analysis of Variance

The success of a morphing attack is closely related to the discriminatory abilities of the employed classifier. By this token, a successful attack could be regarded as a misclassification error related to poor class separability in the feature space. In our case, the discriminant function was learned by the feature extracting neural network which encodes facial features and maps them to a new data distribution. We perform an analysis of variance in order to test for discriminatory power of features computed by our neural network. The goal is to determine at which blending factor a misclassification is most likely to occur. The analysis of variance (ANOVA) within and between the identity groups was conducted for positive as well as negative pairs of images by computing a test statistic. With this criterion, the quality of separability of classes in the feature space is measured. We perform a one-way ANOVA on the original images by using the Euclidean distance as a factor.

5   Results

5.1   Threshold Selection

Using the original images from the *MultiPIE* dataset, we compute the Euclidean distances between mated and unmated pairs of facial features and select a threshold at 0.1% FAR, as commonly prescribed for border control applications [2]. The optimal baseline threshold of 0.78 was selected using a 8-fold cross-validation procedure with a verification rate of 99.96% at 0.04% FAR.

5.2   Evaluation of Cases

Case 1: Successful Morphing Attack. As shown in Fig. 4 the *optimal* blending factor from the perspective of a potential impostor is 0.4 for our setup. The plot also shows the maximum percentage of successful attacks on our system which amounts to 1.13% (Table 1). The low success rate is due to an *early* rejection of the accomplice while the blending factor increases and not due to rejection of the impostor.

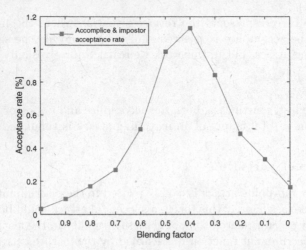

Fig. 4. Case 1: Successful morphing attack. The peak of 1.13% is reached at a blending factor of 0.4.

Table 1. Case 1: Successful attack rates for different blending factors. A factor of 1.0 corresponds to the original image and a factor of 0.0 to a complete replacement of the original face region. In this case both the accomplice and the impostor are accepted by the system.

Blending factor	Acceptance rate [%]	Threshold
1.0	0.03%	0.78
0.9	0.09%	0.78
0.8	0.17%	0.78
0.7	0.27%	0.78
0.6	0.51%	0.78
0.5	0.98%	0.78
0.4	**1.13%**	**0.78**
0.3	0.84%	0.78
0.2	0.49%	0.78
0.1	0.33%	0.78
0.0	0.16%	0.78

Case 2: Correct Verification. This case reflects the correct operation mode of a face recognition system. The performance of the system drops drastically for blending factors less than 0.7 (Fig. 5). The impostor rejection rate reaches its maximum of 29.86% at a blending factor of 0.0 (Table 2). This discrepancy is due to the fact that the accomplice fails to pass the verification process as we already stated in the previous paragraph. This is also the main reason for the low verification rate which, at a blending factor of 0.5, amounts to only 34.66%.

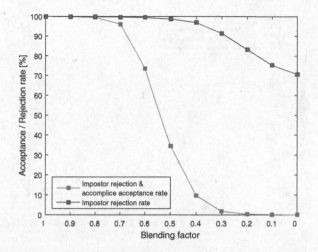

Fig. 5. Case 2: Correct verification rates for different blending factors. A factor of 1.0 corresponds to the original image and a factor of 0.0 to a complete replacement of the original face region. The main (blue) curve represents the correct verification case where the impostor gets rejected and the accomplice gets accepted. The impostor rejection rate was plotted for comparison. (Color figure online)

Table 2. Case 2: The table shows accomplice acceptance rates with respect to the blending factor. A factor of 1.0 corresponds to the original image and a factor of 0.0 to a complete replacement of the original face region. Here the accomplice is accepted and the impostor is rejected.

Blending factor	Acceptance/Rejection rate [%]	Threshold
1.0	**99.97%**	**0.78**
0.9	99.89%	0.78
0.8	99.49%	0.78
0.7	96.14%	0.78
0.6	73.50%	0.78
0.5	34.66%	0.78
0.4	9.76%	0.78
0.3	1.85%	0.78
0.2	0.41%	0.78
0.1	0.12%	0.78
0.0	0.03%	0.78

Case 3: Accomplice Rejection. In this case the accomplice gets rejected by the recognition system while the impostor gets accepted. There is almost no rejection of the accomplice down to a blending factor of 0.7 (Fig. 6). However, the system fails to accept most of the accomplices at a blending factor of 0.5.

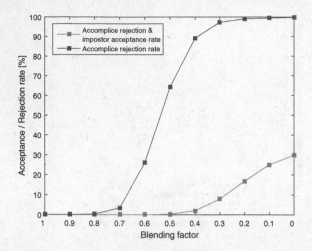

Fig. 6. Case 3: Accomplice rejection rates for different blending factors. A factor of 1.0 corresponds to the original image and a factor of 0.0 to a complete replacement of the original face region. The impostor is accepted and the accomplice is rejected in this case. The main curve corresponding to Case 3 is depicted in blue. (Color figure online)

Table 3. Case 3: The table shows impostor acceptance rates with respect to the blending factor. A factor of 1.0 corresponds to the original image and a factor of 0.0 to a complete replacement of the original face region. In this case the impostor is accepted and the accomplice is rejected.

Blending factor	Acceptance/Rejection rate [%]	Threshold
1.0	0.0%	0.78
0.9	0.0%	0.78
0.8	0.0%	0.78
0.7	0.0%	0.78
0.6	0.0%	0.78
0.5	0.27%	0.78
0.4	2.03%	0.78
0.3	7.90%	0.78
0.2	16.84%	0.78
0.1	25.05%	0.78
0.0	**29.86%**	**0.78**

This is due to manipulations introduced by our morphing tool which was to strong for the accomplice to get accepted. Up to this point there were also no impostor images that got accepted by the system (Table 3).

Table 4. Case 4: The table shows rejection rates with respect to the blending factor. A factor of 1.0 corresponds to the original image and a factor of 0.0 to a complete replacement of the original face region. In this case both the impostor and the accomplice are rejected.

Blending factor	Rejection rate [%]	Threshold
1.0	0.0%	0.78
0.9	0.02%	0.78
0.8	0.34%	0.78
0.7	3.59%	0.78
0.6	25.99%	0.78
0.5	64.08%	0.78
0.4	87.08%	0.78
0.3	**89.40%**	**0.78**
0.2	82.27%	0.78
0.1	74.50%	0.78
0.0	69.95%	0.78

Case 4: Complete Rejection. This case represents the complete opposite to the morphing attack, where both the accomplice and the impostor get rejected. The maximum rejection rate has its peak of about 90% at a blending factor of 0.3 (Table 4). After that, it drops to about 70% at 0.0. The drop is due to the increasing impostor acceptance rate, which is also shown in Fig. 7.

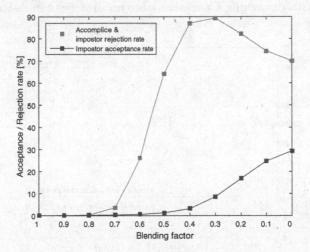

Fig. 7. Case 4: Complete rejection rates for different blending factors. A factor of 1.0 corresponds to the original image and a factor of 0.0 to a complete replacement of the original face region. Both the accomplice and the impostor are rejected in this case. The drop in the main curve (blue) is attributed to the increasing impostor acceptance rates depicted in orange. (Color figure online)

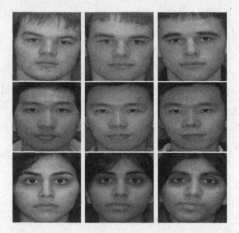

Fig. 8. Face images from three successful morphing attacks with a blending factor of 0.5. Accomplice image (left), morphed image (middle), impostor image (right).

5.3   Examples of Successful Attacks

In Fig. 8 three successful morphing attacks are shown. We only consider face morphs with a blending factor of 0.5 for this illustration and select individuals from three different ethnic groups. Our experiments revealed that about 75% of successful attacks were attributed to individuals of Asian descent. The reason for this situation may lay in our training dataset that contains mainly people of Caucasian descent. As a consequence, the model used for face recognition might be biased towards discerning Caucasian more accurately than Asians.

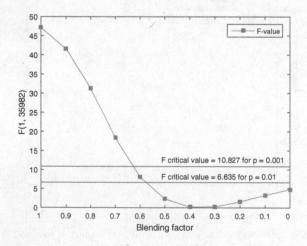

Fig. 9. F-values for increasing blending factors and critical F-values for two different significance levels. For values above 6.635, the null hypothesis that all group means are equal can be rejected with a significance level of 0.01.

5.4   Analysis of Variance

The null hypothesis is rejected if the F-value calculated from the data is greater than the critical value of the F-distribution for some desired false-rejection probability. The F-test reveals that for a blending factor of 1.0, the variance within positive and negative identity pairs is much lower than between the pairs. However, the situation changes with increasing blending factors. For a factor of 0.5, we fail to reject the null hypothesis with a significance level of 0.01 (Fig. 9). This means that starting from a blending factor of 0.5, the two groups containing positive and negative identity pairs cannot be separated anymore. A misclassification is most likely to occur at a blending factor of 0.4. The results are consistent with the evaluation presented in Sect. 5.1 (Table 5).

Table 5. ANOVA test for an increasing blending factor. The lowest value is measured at a blending factor of 0.4. This is consistent with the result obtained for case 1 (Fig. 4).

Blending factor											
	1.0	0.9	0.8	0.7	0.6	0.5	**0.4**	0.3	0.2	0.1	0.0
$F(1, \infty)$	47.1	41.6	31.2	18.4	8.1	2.3	**0.2**	0.3	1.6	3.3	4.9

6   Conclusions

We present the results of a simulated morphing attack on a state-of-the-art face recognition system using a large dataset with varying blending factor. By defining a successful morphing attack as a situation where both accomplice and impostor get accepted, we state that the main reason for the low success rate of the attack is the rejection of the accomplice. This is a direct consequence of the compactness of identity clusters which could be attributed to good feature representation delivered by the convolutional neural network. CNNs account for less variability within the identity groups than previous methods, thus allowing for tighter thresholds and making the morphing attack less significant. However, poor image quality and low resolution can have a negative impact on cluster compactness. This may open the door for potential morphing attacks, as less compact identity groups require wider baseline thresholds.

In order to improve the robustness against morphing attacks, we plan to analyze facial features in more detail using soft biometrics and face symmetry. This includes the analysis of regions affected by the blending operation, e.g. eyes and mouth as well as regions that were not manipulated, e.g. hair, ears and forehead. Face shape analysis is another factor that could help to reduce the number of successful attacks. The currently used registration method normalizes the original face shape, thus suppressing discriminative information that could help to repel the attack. We would like to investigate these presumptions in future work.

Acknowledgment. This work has been partially funded by the German Federal Ministry of Education and Research (BMBF) under contract number FKZ: 16KIS 0512.

References

1. Dutta, A.: Predicting Performance of a Face Recognition System Based on Image Quality. Ph.D. thesis, University of Twente (2015). http://arxiv.org/pdf/1510.07112v1
2. European Union, E.A.f.t.M.o.O.C.a.t.E.B.: Best Practice Technical Guidelines for Automated Border Control (ABC) Systems. FRONTEX (2015)
3. Ferrara, M., Franco, A., Maltoni, D.: The magic passport. In: 2014 IEEE International Joint Conference on Biometrics (IJCB), pp. 1–7 (2014)
4. Galbally, J., Marcel, S., Fierrez, J.: Biometric antispoofing methods: a survey in face recognition. IEEE Access **2**, 1530–1552 (2014)
5. Guo, Y., Zhang, L., Hu, Y., He, X., Gao, J.: MS-Celeb-1M: a dataset and benchmark for large-scale face recognition. In: Leibe, B., Matas, J., Sebe, N., Welling, M. (eds.) ECCV 2016. LNCS, vol. 9907, pp. 87–102. Springer, Cham (2016). doi:10.1007/978-3-319-46487-9_6
6. Hadid, A., Evans, N., Marcel, S., Fierrez, J.: Biometrics systems under spoofing attack: an evaluation methodology and lessons learned. IEEE Signal Process. Mag. **32**(5), 20–30 (2015)
7. Huang, G.B., Ramesh, M., Berg, T., Learned-Miller, E.: Labeled faces in the wild: a database for studying face recognition in unconstrained environments. Technical report, 07–49, University of Massachusetts, Amherst., October 2007
8. Zuo, J., Wechsler, H., et al.: Adaptive biometric authentication using nonlinear mappings on quality measures and verification scores. In: 2010 17th IEEE International Conference on Image Processing (ICIP), IEEE, Piscataway (2010). http://ieeexplore.ieee.org/servlet/opac?punumber=5641636
9. Kazemi, V., Sullivan, J.: One millisecond face alignment with an ensemble of regression trees. In: Proceedings of the IEEE Conference on Computer Vision and Pattern Recognition, pp. 1867–1874 (2014)
10. King, D.E.: Dlib-ml: a machine learning toolkit. J. Mach. Learn. Res. **10**, 1755–1758 (2009)
11. Makrushin, A., Neubert, T., Dittmann, J.: Automatic generation and detection of visually faultless facial morphs. In: Proceedings of the 12th International Joint Conference on Computer Vision, Imaging and Computer Graphics Theory and Applications, VISAPP, (VISIGRAPP 2017), vol. 6, pp. 39–50. INSTICC, ScitePress (2017)
12. Nguyen, A., Yosinski, J., Clune, J.: Deep neural networks are easily fooled: high confidence predictions for unrecognizable images. In: 2015 IEEE Conference on Computer Vision and Pattern Recognition (CVPR), pp. 427–436 (2015)
13. Parkhi, O.M., Vedaldi, A., Zisserman, A.: Deep face recognition. In: British Machine Vision Conference (2015)
14. Pérez, P., Gangnet, M., Blake, A.: Poisson image editing. ACM Trans. Graph. (TOG) **22**, 313–318 (2003). ACM
15. Raghavendra, R., Raja, K., Busch, C.: Detecting morphed facial images. In: Proceedings of 8th IEEE International Conference on Biometrics: Theory, Applications and Systems (BTAS-2016) 6–9 September, Niagra Falls, USA (2016)

16. Gross, R., Matthews, I., Cohn, J., Kanade, T., Baker, S.: Multi-pie. In: Proceedings of the IEEE International Conference on Automatic Face and Gesture Recognition. IEEE Computer Society (2008). https://www.microsoft.com/en-us/research/publication/multi-pie/
17. Sandberg, D.: Tensorflow implementation of the facenet face recognizer (2016). https://github.com/davidsandberg/facenet
18. Schroff, F., Kalenichenko, D., Philbin, J.: Facenet: a unified embedding for face recognition and clustering. CoRR abs/1503.03832 (2015). http://arxiv.org/abs/1503.03832
19. Szegedy, C., Ioffe, S., Vanhoucke, V., Alemi, A.: Inception-v4, inception-resnet and the impact of residual connections on learning (2016). http://arxiv.org/pdf/1602.07261v2
20. Szegedy, C., Zaremba, W., Sutskever, I., Bruna, J., Erhan, D., Goodfellow, I., Fergus, R.: Intriguing properties of neural networks (2013). http://arxiv.org/pdf/1312.6199v4
21. Valente, J., Soatto, S.: Perspective distortion modeling, learning and compensation. In: 2015 IEEE Conference on Computer Vision and Pattern Recognition Workshops (CVPRW), pp. 9–16 (2015)
22. Wen, Y., Zhang, K., Li, Z., Qiao, Y.: A discriminative feature learning approach for deep face recognition. In: Leibe, B., Matas, J., Sebe, N., Welling, M. (eds.) ECCV 2016. LNCS, vol. 9911, pp. 499–515. Springer, Cham (2016). doi:10.1007/978-3-319-46478-7_31
23. Wolberg, G.: Digital Image Warping, vol. 10662. IEEE Computer Society Press, Los Alamitos (1990)
24. Zhang, K., Zhang, Z., Li, Z., Qiao, Y.: Joint face detection and alignment using multitask cascaded convolutional networks. IEEE Sig. Process. Lett. 23(10), 1499–1503 (2016)

Topological Data Analysis for Image Tampering Detection

Aras Asaad[(✉)] and Sabah Jassim[(✉)]

Applied Computing Department,
The University of Buckingham, Buckingham, UK
{aras.asaad,sabah.jassim}@buckingham.ac.uk

Abstract. This paper introduces a topological approach to detection of image tampering for forensics purposes. This is based on the emerging Topological Data Analysis (TDA) concept of persistent homological invariants associated with certain image features. Image features of interest are pixels that have a uniform Local Binary pattern (LBP) code representing texture feature descriptors. We construct the sequence of simplicial complexes for increasing sequence of distance thresholds whose vertices are the selected set of pixels, and calculate the corresponding non-increasing sequence of homology invariants (number of connected components). The persistent homology of this construction describes the speed with which the sequence terminates, and our tamper detection scheme exploit its sensitivity to image tampering/degradation. We test the performance of this approach on a sufficiently large image dataset from a benchmark dataset of passport photos, and show that the persistent homology sequence defines a discriminating criterion for the morphing attacks (i.e. distinguishing morphed images from genuine ones).

Keywords: Topological Data Analysis · Persistent homology · Image tampering · Image morphing

1 Introduction

Digital image morphing is an image tampering attack that form a serious threat to the security of ID token based verification when applied to face photos. Morphing is the process of transforming one digital image into another digital image. Several powerful hardware and software tools are available for creating and manipulating images easily without leaving any noticeable noises on the digital image and thereby undermining the authenticity and integrity of digital images. When face images are used as evidence of person proofs then one can no longer take the authenticity of the face images for granted. Morphing can also be used to attack face biometric systems with adverse influence on recognition accuracy as a result of allowing non-authorized persons to access or pass the recognition system. This presents a serious challenge to the digital forensics community: how to distinguish a genuine source face image from a morphed image and prevent subsequent security breaches.

Ferrara et al. in [1] introduced morphing attack as a major security concern which can bypass all integrity checks (optical and electronic). The study illustrated that,

C. Kraetzer et al. (Eds.): IWDW 2017, LNCS 10431, pp. 136–146, 2017.
DOI: 10.1007/978-3-319-64185-0_11

Automatic Border Control (ABC) systems as well as human experts can be deceived by presenting a passport with a morphed face photo on it whereby they concluded that two persons can share one passport. Morphed images in [1] have been created by the freely available GNU Image manipulation software v2.8 (GIMP) [2] and the GIMP animation Package v2.6 (GAP) [3]. To evaluate the recognition systems, they tested the quality of morph images by two commercial tools: Neurotechnology VeryLook SDK 5.4 and Luxand Face SDK 4.0.

The morphing described in [1, 4] are time consuming because it requires a manual retouch for more realistic appearance. To overcome this issue, Makrushin et al. in [5] proposed an automatic splicing-based morphing algorithm to generate thousands of visually faultless facial morphs. In general, the quality of morphed images is 2-fold; (i) morphed images need to be visually faultless to human eyes (i.e. no visible artefacts) and (ii) morphs should be successfully verified against both source images by automatic face recognition systems. The splicing morph technique is a result of warping and alpha-blending of segmented facial regions and seamlessly stitching it back into one of the input (source) images. This approach is different from the complete morphing technique which takes the complete facial image to warp and blend including hair and background. Splicing morph result in a more natural looking image than the complete morph technique which cause the appearance of spurious shadows. Nonetheless, the geometry of splicing morphs is taken completely from one source image and it has minor ghosting artefacts which caused by inaccurate localization of facial landmarks. Also, if the skin color is different for both source images, a splice morph does not look realistic. These properties make splicing technique to pass the first morph quality measure, provided that both source images have similar skin color, but miserable regarding the second quality measure because splicing adopts geometry from one source image only and it may not look very similar to the other image. A combined morph technique was also proposed by [5] to overcome the limitations in the two previous algorithms. It warps the images into an average position first, then it cuts the facial regions, blending and finally stitching them back on to the warped image. Poison image editing will be applied as a final stage to obtain seamless transmission between the facial region and the rest of the image. Combined morph images have an average geometry and texture from both source images but has no major ghosting artefacts and skin color has no influence.

Different morphing techniques are expected to produce different changes on image features, and potential digital forensic schemes to detect morphing must identify the appropriate sensitive features and the nature of resulting changes in order to select appropriate classifiers. Makrushin et al. in [5] proposed an automatic morph detector based on Benford features computed from quantized Discrete Cosine Transformation (DCT) coefficients of JPEG-Compressed images. Frank Benford's law, roughly, states that the frequency distribution of leading digits of a set of (natural) numbers is logarithmic. The morphing detector adopted in [5] is based on the hypothesis that unlike naturally generated data, manipulated data do not obey the Benford's law. Although high accuracy in detection of morphed random face images obtained using Benford's law, however, they note that using legitimate image processing techniques, one can create face images with similar Benford feature distribution [5, 6].

In this work, we shall investigate the use of Topological Data Analysis based schemes that systematically construct the topological shapes associated with a given set of specific texture pixels distributed spatially in an image. We shall test the possibility of using the well-known persistent homology invariant relating to the number of connected components in the incrementally constructed sequences of shapes as a morphing predictor. We shall focus on using face images produced by three different types of morphing schemes (splicing, combined and complete morphing methods). Our proposed approach is based on the topology of texture descriptors, known as local binary patterns, of face images.

The rest of the paper organized as follows. Section 2 encompasses the topological data (image) analysis including recent applications of this emerging scheme. Local binary patterns are introduced in Sect. 3 as an image texture descriptor to build Rips complexes. In Sect. 4, our proposed method to detect image tampering introduced together with experimental results. Finally, Sect. 5 reports the conclusion and future directions.

2 Topological Data/Image Analysis

Topology is a field of mathematics that is concerned with the classification of shapes (objects) according to their closeness and connectivity properties. In recent years, the emergence of machine learning for the analysis of Bigdata has energized interest in utilizing shape and topology of data in complex classification applications. Understanding and classifying shape relies on expressing complex shapes in terms of simple shape building blocks using easy to implement combinatorial construction methods. Topological Data Analysis is concerned with such challenges [7, 8, 14]. Topologists have long developed a finite combinatorial process known as simplicial complex, which can be used to construct the topological shape of datasets of points in any metric space. Roughly speaking, simplicial complex takes a set of points (0-dimensional simplices), edges (1-dimensional simplices), triangles (2-dimensional simplices) and hyper-dimensional triangles and glue them together along their edges and faces to make complex patterns conveying connectivity and closeness properties. The fundamental idea behind using topology for data analysis is that via topology, one can extract shapes, or patterns, from complex high dimensional data sets and then obtaining deep intuitive understanding about them. Topology has three key properties which enables extracting patterns, or shapes, possible form high-dimensional data sets. These properties are; coordinate free, invariant under (small) deformation and compressed representation [8]. These three important properties of topology have been discussed in detail in [7, 8]. Recent application scope of topological data/image analysis includes, but is not limited to, gait recognition [9, 10, 22], brain artery [20], hurricane and galaxies analysis [11], dimensionality reduction schemes evaluation [12], classification of hepatic lesions [21], shape classification using LBP and persistent [13] and many more.

Topological properties of objects/shapes can be characterized by their homology. In general, to distinguish distinct objects from one another, one needs to use homology to measure the number of connected components, loops, and voids of those objects. The focus of this paper is mainly about computing the number of connected components of specific uniform LBP patterns from constructed simplicial complexes of face images. Mathematically, zero homology groups associated with simplicial complexes are basically equals to number of connected components. Persistent refers to constructing more than one simplicial complex from specific LBP patterns using different distance thresholds. The properties (features) of face images that persist (survive) after changing these thresholds, which will result in different simplicial complex structures, will be treated as a true property of that image. In this work, we will focus on computing persistent homology of Rips complexes as a morph detector constructed from a selected group of uniform LBP pattern which is the case of having two ones in the LBP code. In particular, the type of simplicial complex which will be built is known as Vietoris-Rips simplicial complex (or Rips complex). In order to construct and calculate the corresponding non-increasing sequence of homology invariants of Rips complex one needs to select a distance threshold (parameter) T as a first step of the construction.

Then gradually increasing T, higher dimensional simplices will be constructed. For sufficiently small T, only zero dimensional simplices will be obtained and for sufficiently large T, a single high dimensional simplex (object) will be constructed. The features that are surviving after changing the threshold are considered to be true features conveying information about morphing face images. The features that are not persistent by gradually increasing the threshold considered to be noise [7, 19]. This approach is known as persistent homology where at each distance threshold, homology invariants will be computed for the image of interest to make decision about being a morph or a genuine photo image.

3 Local Binary Patterns (LBP)

Local Binary pattern is an image texture descriptor which has been first introduced by Ojala et al. [15], but since then a variety of versions have been investigated and used in pattern recognition with considerable success. Given any image I, the original LBP generates a new image by associating with each pixel an 8 bit binary code determined by comparing its value with that of its 8 neighbors in a 3×3 window surrounding it in a clockwise order as illustrated in Fig. 1. The process works by first subtracting the central pixel value from the 8 neighboring pixels, and starting from the top left corner neighbor each cell is assigned 0 or 1 depending whether the subtraction outcome is negative or not. The LBP codes can be converted back to their decimal values representing the central pixel (x_c, y_c) using Eqs. (1) and (2), below:

$$LBP(x_c, y_c) = \sum_{i=0}^{i=7} \alpha(P_i - P_c)2^i \tag{1}$$

where P_i is the neighbouring grey value pixels, P_c is the centre grey value pixel and the function $\alpha(x)$ is as follow:

$$\alpha(x) = \begin{cases} 1 & if x \geq 0 \\ 0 & if x < 0 \end{cases} \tag{2}$$

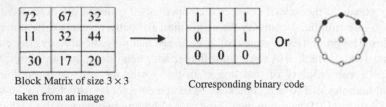

Block Matrix of size 3 × 3
taken from an image

Corresponding binary code

Fig. 1. Local binary operator

Applying above procedure on the block matrix will result in getting the binary string 11110000 (decimal = 15), see Fig. 1.

Local texture information, such as edges, lines, spots and flat regions are associated with certain types of LBP codes named, by Ojala et al. as uniform patterns referring to 8-bit circular bytes that contain either 0 or 2 bitwise transitions from 1 to 0 and from 0 to 1. For example, 11111111 (0-transition) and 00111111 (2-transitions) are uniform codes while 10111010 is non-uniform as it has 6 transitions. A circular 8-bit string are uniform if it contains a single run of 1's of a fixed length k, with k = 0, 1, 2, … 8. It is not difficult to show that the LBP of any monochrome image consists of 58 distinct uniform patterns. Ojala et al. [15], experimentally demonstrated that 90.6% of all LBP patterns in texture images are uniform and postulated that the histogram of the uniform LBP patterns is useful as a discriminating feature in image classification applications. Ahonen et al. [16], Shan et al. [17], and Meng et al. [18] have used the histogram of the uniform LBP bins as discriminating features for face recognition and facial expression recognition. Indeed, currently variations of this LBP-based scheme is adopted widely in a variety of pattern recognition schemes whenever image texture is an important image feature for the relevant application.

In this paper, we investigate the use of topological invariants of Rips simplicial complexes associated with uniform LBP pixels at different distance thresholds for the detection of morphing attacks on passport photos. Image tampering and morphing in particular is expected to result in a variety of changes to the position of the different uniform LBP codes which in return result in changing the corresponding simplicial complexes. The fact that over 90% of the LBP codes of a face image are expected to be uniform, constructing and quantifying the homological invariants of their Rips complexes is a rather daunting task. Instead, investigating the complexes constructed from specific and closely related groups of uniform codes is a more tractable task. Excluding, the two rather trivial uniform LBP codes of 0000000 and 11111111, the remaining 56 uniform codes can be divided into 7 groups of uniform codes where each group consists of codes with the same number of 1's. Each of the 7 groups consists of 8 LBP codes that can all be generated from a single one by rotation. By examining several images we noted some interesting statistical relations between uniform codes across the 7 groups, which may be exploited to determine the sensitivity of their topological invariants to image tampering. Figure 2, below illustrates this idea by showing the

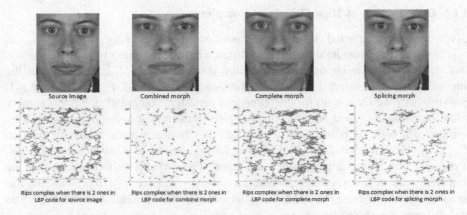

Fig. 2. Sensitivity of topological invariants to morphing

simplicial complexes constructed from the positions of a single uniform LBP code for an original image and its 3 different morphs with another face image.

We initialized our TDA based investigations by focusing first on homological invariants of the sequence of simplicial complexes associated with the group of 2-ones uniform LBP codes depicted in Fig. 3. This group is known to be associated with the geometric structure of an end of a line, and hence it is expected to play a significant role as image discriminating feature. In the rest of the paper, we shall investigate the

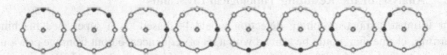

Fig. 3. Uniform LBP group of 2-Ones where dark nodes indicate the position of 1.

sensitivity to morphing attacks of the threshold-dependent simplicial complexes constructed from this group of uniform LBP codes.

4 Proposed Method

In this section, we describe the two main components of our topological proposal to detect image tampering. The first component is the procedure for constructing the threshold-dependent sequence of simplicial complexes associated with any input set of pixel points in an image. The second component describes our simplified analyses of the corresponding sequence of a chosen topological invariants for detecting image tampering. And we present the results of our experiments on relevant database of face images, where we chose each of the uniform 2-ones LBP pixel points, and the number of connected components as the topological invariant.

4.1   Construction of Rips Simplicial Complexes

Given a set of selected image pixel positions $P = \{p_1(x_1, y_1), p_2(x_2, y_2), \ldots, p_n(x_n, y_n)\}$. First compute the Euclidian distance between all pairs of points in the set, and determine the minimum and maximum distance values T_{min} and T_{max}. In the interval $[T_{min}, T_{max}]$ select k equidistant thresholds $\{T_1 = T_{min}, T_2, \ldots, T_k = T_{max}\}$. For simplicity we fix $k = 30$ for the purpose of persistent computation, but this number could be changed if need be. Start by iteratively constructing a simplicial complex by joining each pairs of points in P if the distance t between them satisfy the relation $T_{i-1} < t \leq T_i$ where i = 2, ..., k. Compute the number cc_i of connected components. If $cc_i = 1$ then stop else increment I and repeat. The output from this procedure is the sequence $(cc_0, cc_1, cc_2, \ldots cc_k)$, where $cc_i = \#(P)$ and $cc_k = 1$ represents the terminating threshold. Note that, different point sets may have different threshold intervals and different length sequences.

This procedure yields a sequence of graphs consisting of the 0-simplicies represented by the set P and the 1-simplices representing the added edges. At each step, this construction only generates 1-skeleton of the full Rips simplicial complex which is sufficient for the current purpose, but the full complex requires the addition of all possible higher dimensional simplices. For example, every 3 points form a 2-simplex if they are connected to each other by edges of length less than or equal to the given threshold. Note that, when the full complex is constructed, it is possible to use homology based tools to compute the number of distinct shape features within the complex.

4.2   Analysis of the Resulting Topological Invariants

Our ultimate tamper/morphing detection would be based on a supervised machine learning scheme that would be trained with a set of sequences, output from the previous step, computed for the Rips simplicial complexes of uniform 2-ones LBP point sets extracted from a set of original and morphed images. Note that, for each image there would be 8-sequences of invariants each representing one of 2-ones LBP rotations. For our proof of concept experiments, we adopted a simplified classification model by confining our analysis to the second entry (i.e. cc_2) of the sequences rather than all the entries. This will allow us to build a simple similarity function and a naive classifier for each of the 8 rotation and then use majority rule at the testing stage. The simple classifier is based on the distributions of the cc_2 values for a training set of original and morphed images.

We trained and tested performance of the classifier(s) using morphed images from the Utrecht face photo database which have been created by [5]. The training was based on, 28 images (14 original and 14 morphed) for each morphing schemes, and calculated the averages and standard deviations of the cc_2 values in each class for each of the 8 rotations of the uniform 2-ones LBP point set. Table 1, below, displays the results obtained for the original images and the 3 morphing schemes.

Table 1. Statistics of connected components (14 original and 14 morphed) images for 2-ones LBP at T_2

LBP code	Original		Splicing morphed		Combined morph		Complete morph	
	Mean	Std.	Mean	Std.	Mean	Std.	Mean	Std.
00000011	16.23	14.19	60.13	13.33	66.83	5.91	31.58	8.94
00000110	20.31	14.62	57.73	14.47	61.83	6.48	36.83	10.58
00001100	21.92	16.63	64.27	13.07	68	4.67	38.75	8.87
00011000	22.31	13.18	65.87	12.68	69	7.32	41.08	8.66
00110000	24	15.80	60.4	10.50	69.58	4.50	37.92	11.60
01100000	22.86	17.90	60.6	11.91	73.58	7.43	37.08	9.01
11000000	18.66	13.97	61.8	10.77	64.42	6.84	35.58	5.93
10000001	22.46	16.87	62.67	11.62	69.42	6.39	38.08	10

The results in this table, show that across all rotations the average cc_2 values for the original images are well below those calculated for the morphed images. Taking into account the corresponding standard deviations, we see that the best separation gap is achieved by the combined morphing scheme followed by those achieved by the splicing morphing, and the complete morphing resulted in significantly lower gaps. The positions of the considered texture features of 2-ones LBP pixels in human face images do not vary significantly, for a proof of concept it is reasonable to suppose that the cc_2 values are normally distributed. At later stages of this research work more sophisticated statistical measures will be used and larger number of images needs to be tested to determine the actual distribution of the cc_2 values.

The above assumption, although not completely necessary, allows us to use known facts about normal distributions to determine with good accuracy the probability that an input image belongs to either class (genuine or morphed). In fact, for each rotation we can classify an input image we simply need to find the position of its cc_2 value in relation to the overlap regions between the two distributions as depicted in Fig. 4.

When classifying any input image, we use all eight rotations and use majority voting to make the final decision on the class of image. Whenever the result of voting was a draw of 4 then it is an 'undecided' case.

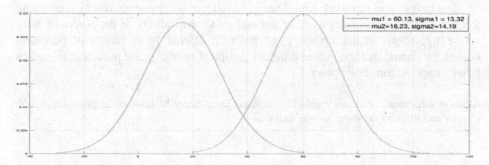

Fig. 4. Distributions of cc_2 values for and the training set of morphed and genuine images

4.3   Testing Experiments

We tested our hypothesis on a large number of face images from the Utrecht face database, excluding the 28 images in the training set. Morphed images in our experiment have been created by Makrushin et al. [5]. We randomly selected 100 images (38 original and 62 morphed) and calculated the cc_2 values for the 8 rotations of the 2-ones LBP pixels and classified them as describe above. For splicing morphing scheme, our method correctly classified 98% of the images. Incorrectly classified images were original images in this case. In the case of combined morph approach, 99% of the input testing images were correctly classified and unlike the splicing technique, misclassified images were morphed images. Unfortunately, around 60% accuracy was achieved with the complete morphing scheme and most misclassified images are morph images.

These testing results, demonstrates the viability of using TDA based classification to automatically detect morphing attacks. More testing are needed to confirm these results and other invariants might have to be incorporated to get high accuracy rates for all existing morphing schemes.

5   Conclusion

We introduced a new topological data analysis based approach to investigate image tampering and in particular to detect known morphing attacks on passport face photo images. The idea was conceived as a result of observations made on a variety of changes in image texture as a result of morphing two original images, and the growing evidence of success of the TDA concept of persistent homology on classification and clustering of textured geometric shapes. We noted a variety of changes of topological invariants of threshold dependent simplicial complexes constructed for uniform LBP image pixel points as a result of morphing. We conducted a proof of concept experiment to test the viability of using TDA for detecting image tampering, and we conclude that the noted changes on the various topological invariants is rich potential of using TDA for the detection of image tampering and to build digital forensics tools. The significantly high accuracy, albeit of limited experimental work, of a morphing detection scheme that uses only the invariance of connected components, as a face related texture descriptor, has shown the potential for success of TDA based approach beyond any doubts.

The next step in this work would be to consolidate our investigations by conducting a much wider experimental work to test and prove the validity of the proposed innovative hypothesis exploiting the huge potential offered by a variety of persistent homology invariants for a mix of different groups of uniform LBP point sets as well as other image texture descriptors.

Acknowledgement. Authors would like to thank Dr. Andrey Makrushin for providing morph images and discussions about morph techniques.

References

1. Ferrara, M., Franco, A., Maltoni, D.: The magic passport. In: IEEE Joint International Conference on Biometrics, Florida (2014)
2. GIMP, GNU Image Manipulation Program. https://www.gimp.org/. Accessed 8 May 2017
3. GIMP, GIMP Animation Package. https://www.gimp.org/tutorials/Using_GAP/. Accessed 8 May 2017
4. Ferrara, M., Franco, A., Maltoni, D.: On the effects of image alterations on face recognition accuracy. In: Bourlai, T. (ed.) Face Recognition Across the Imaging Spectrum, pp. 195–222. Springer, Cham (2016). doi:10.1007/978-3-319-28501-6_9
5. Makrushin, A., Neubert, T., Dittmann, J.: Automatic generation and detection of visually faultless facial morphs. In: Proceedings of the 12th International Joint Conference on Computer Vision, Imaging and Computer Graphics Theory and Applications, Porto (2017)
6. Wang, J., Cha, B., Cho, S., Jay Kuo, C.-C.: Understanding Benford's Law and its vulnerability in image forensics. In: IEEE International Conference on Multimedia and Expo, New York, USA (2009)
7. Gunnar, C.: Topology and data. Bull. Am. Math. Soc. **46**(2), 255–308 (2009)
8. Lum, P., Singh, G., Lehman, A., Ishkanov, T., Vejdemo-Johansson, M., Alagappan, M., Carlsson, J., Carlsson, G.: Extracting insights from the shape of complex data using topology. Nature scientific reports, no. 1236 (2013)
9. Lamar-León, J., García-Reyes, E.B., Gonzalez-Diaz, R.: Human gait identification using persistent homology. In: Alvarez, L., Mejail, M., Gomez, L., Jacobo, J. (eds.) CIARP 2012. LNCS, vol. 7441, pp. 244–251. Springer, Heidelberg (2012). doi:10.1007/978-3-642-33275-3_30
10. Leon, J.L., Alonso, R., Reyes, E.G., Diaz, R.G.: Topological features for monitoring human activities at distance. In: Mazzeo, P.L., Spagnolo, P., Moeslund, T.B. (eds.) AMMDS 2014. LNCS, vol. 8703, pp. 40–51. Springer, Cham (2014). doi:10.1007/978-3-319-13323-2_4
11. Sreeparna, B.: Size functions in galaxy morphology classification. Int. J. Comput. Appl. **100**(3), 1–4 (2014)
12. Rieck, B., Leitte, H.: Persistent homology for the evaluation of dimensionality reduction schemes. In: Eurographics Conference on Visualization (EuroVis) (2015)
13. Janusch, I., Kropatsch, W.: Shape classification using LBP and persistent of critical points. In: International Conference on Discrete Geometry for Computer Imagery, Heidelberg (2016)
14. Edelsbrunner, H., Morozov, D.: Persistent homology: theory and practice. In: European Congress of Mathematics, Kraków, 2–7 July 2012
15. Ojala, T., Pietikainen, M., Harwood, D.: A comparative study of texture measures with classification based on featured distributions. Pattern Recogn. **29**(1), 51–59 (1996)
16. Ahonen, T., Hadid, A., Peitikainen, M.: Face description with local binary patterns: application to face recognition. IEEE Trans. Pattern Anal. Mach. Intell. **28**(12), 2037–2041 (2006)
17. Shan, C., Gong, S., McOwan, P.: Facial expression recognition based on local binary patterns: a comprehensive study. Image Vis. Comput. **27**, 803–816 (2009)
18. Meng, J., Gao, Y., Wang, X., Lin, T., Zhang, J.: Face recognition based on local binary patterns with threshold. In: IEEE International Conference on Granular Computing, pp. 352–356 (2010)
19. Ghrist, R.: Barcodes: the persistent topology of data. Bull. Am. Math. Soc. (New Ser.) **45**(1), 61–75 (2008)

20. Bendich, P., Marron, J., Miller, E., Pieloch, A., Skwerer, S.: Persistent homology analysis of brain artery trees. Ann. Appl. Stat. **10**(1), 198–218 (2016)
21. Rubin, A., Carlsson, G.: Classification of hepatic lesions using the matching metric. Comput. Vis. Image Underst. **121**, 36–42 (2014)
22. Leon, J.L., Cerri, A., Reyes, E.G., Diaz, R.G.: Gait-based gender classification using persistent homology. In: Ruiz-Shulcloper, J., Sanniti di Baja, G. (eds.) CIARP 2013, Part II. LNCS, vol. 8259, pp. 366–373. Springer, Heidelberg (2013). doi:10.1007/978-3-642-41827-3_46

Steganography and Steganalysis

Coding Efficiency Preserving Steganography Based on HEVC Steganographic Channel Model

Yi Dong[1], Xinghao Jiang[1,2(✉)], Tanfeng Sun[1,2], and Dawen Xu[3]

[1] School of Electronic Information and Electrical Engineering,
Shanghai Jiao Tong University, Shanghai, China
{aa44,xhjiang,tfsun}@sjtu.edu.cn
[2] National Engineering Lab on Information Content Analysis Techniques,
GT036001, Shanghai, China
[3] School of Electronics and Information Engineering,
Ningbo University of Technology, Ningbo, People's Republic of China
xdw@nbut.edu.cn

Abstract. Steganographic Channel Model (SCM) is hard to build for different steganography algorithms in different embedding domains. Thus, theoretical analysis for some important factors in steganography, such as capacity, distortion, is hard to obtain. In this paper, to avoid introducing significant distortion into HEVC video file, a novel HEVC SCM is presented and analyzed. It is firstly proposed that the distortion optimization method in this SCM should be applied on coding efficiency instead of visual quality. According to this conclusion, a novel coding efficiency preserving steganography algorithm based on Prediction Units (PUs) is proposed for HEVC videos. The intra prediction modes of candidate PUs are taken as cover. This algorithm was tested on the dataset consisting of 17,136 HD sequences. The Experimental results prove the correctness of the previous conclusion and the practicability of the proposed channel model, and show that our algorithm outperforms the existing HEVC steganography algorithm in capacity and perceptibility.

Keywords: Steganography channel model · Coding efficiency · HEVC · Prediction Units

1 Introduction

The internet is one of the most important ways for people to access all kinds of information. Government and companies have need for secret transmission of a variety of complex data and multimedia objects. Securing the sensitive content of through open networks while ensuring the privacy of information has become essential but increasingly challenging. Encrypting a secret message transforms it to a noise-like data which is observable but meaningless. Modern steganography techniques are new research areas for these problems [1]. Compared with other kinds of steganography, video steganography has the advantage of higher capacity and lower distortion.

© Springer International Publishing AG 2017
C. Kraetzer et al. (Eds.): IWDW 2017, LNCS 10431, pp. 149–162, 2017.
DOI: 10.1007/978-3-319-64185-0_12

In general, there are two commonly used steganographic domains for videos: compression domain and pixel domain. In pixel domain, LSB is the most commonly used method [2] with high capacity, but it is fragile and easy to detect compared with compression domain methods [3–9]. In compression domain, steganography techniques are well researched for H.264/AVC. Hu et al. [3] have proposed a steganography algorithm based on intra prediction mode in H.264/AVC. Yang et al. [4] have improved Hu's method by matrix coding. Bouchama et al. [5] divided the intra prediction modes in H.264/AVC into four groups according to their prediction direction, the result shows a better video quality while ensuring high capacity. Zhang et al. [6] analyzes the texture of the video, and propose a high security adaptive embedding algorithm using STC.

Many works have been done in H.264/AVC, but only a few were researched in HEVC. Chang et al. [7] proposed an error propagation free method based on DST/DCT modulation. Tew et al. [8] presented an approach manipulating the CB (coding block) size decision on every coding tree unit to embed information based on the predefined mapping rules. Wang et al. [9] proposed intra prediction mode based method for HEVC, a mapping between angle difference and secret message was established to embed the data. Generally speaking, there are some limitations in steganography. First, SCM is hard to build for different steganography algorithms in different embedding domains. Thus, theoretical analysis for some important factors of steganography, such as capacity, distortion in different channels, are hard to obtain. Second, there is a tradeoff between capacity and perceptibility for many steganography algorithms. Third, because of lacking high quality evaluation indicator, the performance of steganography is hard to measure. In summary, practical steganography still needs a lot of researches.

In this paper, according to intra coding process of HEVC and distortion introduced by modifying PUs, a HEVC SCM is built. It is firstly proposed that the distortion optimization method in this SCM should be applied on coding efficiency instead of visual quality and the degradation of visual quality is mainly caused by the increment of QP, not increment of embedded bits. According to this SCM, a novel coding efficiency preserving steganography algorithm is proposed for HEVC videos. It outperforms the existing algorithm, and can provide high capacity while maintaining excellent perceptibility.

The rest of paper is organized as follows. In Sect. 2, the proposed HEVC SCM is introduced. Based on this model, Sect. 3 describes the HEVC steganography algorithm. In Sect. 4, experiments and analysis are presented. Finally, conclusion is drawn in Sect. 5.

2   SCM in HEVC

In this section, a novel HEVC SCM is built. In steganography, different covers have different properties. For example, coding process of DCT coefficients is different from motion vectors (MV). Steganography based on these two covers has many different characteristics, for instance, error propagation free method should be considered in DCT-based steganography, but it is not essential in MV-based steganography. Modifying DCT coefficients and modifying motion vectors will cause different distortion, and lead to different capacity. SCM can represent features for steganography in the same embedding domain. Thus, specific SCM should be studied for HEVC.

2.1 The Process and Characteristics of HEVC Intra Coding

Analyzing the process and characteristics of HEVC intra coding is necessary for the modeling process. Table 1 shows the main features of HEVC intra coding process.

Table 1. Main features of intra coding in HEVC

Functionality	HEVC
Prediction block size	4×4, 8×8, 16×16 and 32×32
Intra prediction mode	35
Most probable mode	3
Block partition	Recursive quadtree partition

HEVC is a block based video coding standard. It gives up the concept of macro block, and introduces three new structures: coding unit (CU), PU and transform unit (TU). In intra coding process, HEVC will first split the intra frames into non-overlapping coding tree units (CTU), each of which is further split into smaller CUs with a recursive quadtree decomposition. For one $N \times N$ intra CU with $N \in \{32, 16, 8\}$, two PU partition mode is available: $N \times N$ and $N/2 \times N/2$. For intra CU with the size of 64×64, only the latter is available. Thus, the size of one intra PU is range from 4×4 to 32×32. The HEVC encoder generates 35 prediction directions from corresponding neighboring pixels and intra prediction modes. Rate distortion optimization (RDO) technique is used to achieve the best prediction direction:

$$J = D + \lambda R \qquad (1)$$

Where J denotes the RD cost, λ denotes the Lagrangian multiplier which depends on quantization parameter QP, D and R represent the distortion and the estimated bitrate of the current PU respectively. The intra prediction mode that yields the minimum RD cost is selected as the optimal one to predict and encode the current PU.

The intro coding process will cause a regular statistical character in the histogram of PU prediction modes. The regular statistical character is showed in Fig. 1.

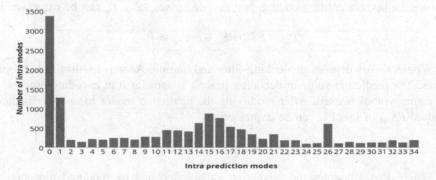

Fig. 1. Histogram of prediction modes in an I frame from an original video

From Fig. 1, it shows that the histogram has these patterns: the bar 0 and bar 1 have the higher frequency than others, and adjacent bars have a similar frequency. This phenomenon is mainly caused by the most probable modes (MPM) selection rule in HEVC. In the process of recursive mode decision, only three MPMs and several candidate modes are calculated. According to the selection rule, the first two MPMs are selected from upper and left neighboring PUs' prediction modes. If either of them is not available, prediction mode 1 was selected as the MPM, and prediction mode 0 (Planar) is the most commonly used mode for the third MPM. During the embedding process, these patterns shouldn't be broken.

2.2 Analysis of Dominant Distortion

In this section, dominant distortion caused by HEVC steganography will be analyzed to help building the SCM. When the prediction mode m_1 of one PU is modified to m_2. The original residual of this PU, denoted as RS_o, can be expressed as:

$$RS_o = P_o - Pre_o \tag{2}$$

Where P_o denotes the original pixel value, and Pre_o denotes the prediction value calculated by original mode m_1. After obtaining the RS_o, the bits B_O used to encode this PU can be expressed as follows:

$$B_o = Ent(RT(\frac{DCT(RS_o)}{Q \times QS})) \tag{3}$$

Where $DCT(.)$ denotes the integer discrete cosine transform, $RT(.)$ denotes the rounding and truncating operations, $Ent(.)$ denotes entropy coding, Q denotes the fixed quantization matrix, QS denotes the quantiser scale. At the decoding process, the reconstruction residual RS_o^r can be calculated as:

$$RS_o^r = IDCT(IEnt(B_o) \times Q \times QS) \tag{4}$$

Where $IDCT(.)$ denotes the inverse integer discrete cosine transform, $IEnt(.)$ denotes the inverse entropy coding, and decoded pixel value P_o^r can be expressed as:

$$P_o^r = FTR(RS_o^r + Pre_o) \approx P_o \tag{5}$$

Where $FTR(.)$ denotes deblocking filter and Sample Adaptive Offset (SAO) operations. The prediction value in decoding process is same as it in encoding process, so the same symbol is used. After modifying the prediction modes to m_2, the modified residual RS_{md} of this PU can be expressed as:

$$RS_{md} = P_o - Pre_{md} \tag{6}$$

Where Pre_{md} denotes the prediction value calculated by modified mode m_2. It shows that sum of modified prediction value and its residual is still equal to the true pixel value. So, after processing the modified residual value with same parameters as the original, following equation can be obtained:

$$P_{md}^r = FTR(RS_{md}^r + Pre_{md}) \approx P_o \tag{7}$$

Where P_{md}^r denotes the modified reconstruction value and RS_{md}^r denotes the modified reconstruction residual. Thus, the conclusion can be drawn from Eqs. (5) and (7):

$$P_{md}^r \approx P_o \approx P_o^r \tag{8}$$

From Eq. (8), it shows that visual quality of videos generated by this kind of steganography algorithms will not be affected significantly. From Eqs. (3) and (4), conclusion can be drawn that difference among values in Eq. (8) is mainly caused by the choice of Q and QS. Thus, the degradation of visual quality will be mainly caused by the increment of QP, not increment of embedded bits.

However, according to the analysis in the above section, if the best mode is replaced with suboptimal one, coding efficiency will be reduced. From Eqs. (1) and (3), if the corresponding RD cost of current PU is increased, which means RS_{md} is larger than RS_o, the length of B_O will be increased. Thus, the total coding efficiency will be reduced.

In summary, modifying the HEVC intra coding process will cause the problem of low·coding efficiency, but the visual quality of generated video file won't be affected significantly. The degradation of visual quality is mainly caused by the increment of QP, not increment of embedded bits. Thus, it is proposed that the distortion optimization method should be applied on coding efficiency instead of visual quality. These conclusions will be proven in the experiment section.

2.3   Definition of the Proposed SCM

A SCM can represent features for steganography in the same embedding domain. Different from Secret Channel Model and Cover Channel Model, SCM focuses on features and distortion caused by the generation process of the cover, and its influence on the performance of steganography. Based on different SCMs, capacity, security and perceptibility of different steganography algorithms can be analyzed. Through analysis results, SCM can also be utilized to further improve the performance of steganography and show the advantages and disadvantages of various steganography algorithms.

Based on the above analysis, a triple is defined to denote the proposed SCM:

$$SCM = \{M_{PU}, \ H_{PU}, \ D_C\} \tag{9}$$

Where M_{PU} is the set of prediction modes of PU, which presents the cover in this model. H_{PU} is the histogram of M_{PU} and D_c is the distortion introduced by modifying M_{PU}. A mapping is built between the M_{PU} and the secret data during the embedding process, and abnormality occurs in the H_{PU}, resulting in various degrees of D_c in video file.

According to the above modeling process, the dominant distortion in D_c is coding efficiency reduction in the coding process. Steganography based on this SCM should design their algorithm based on the following equation:

$$M'_{PU} = \underset{M_{PU}}{argmin}\{F_{sm}(H_{PU}, H'_{PU}), D_c\} \tag{10}$$

Where M'_{PU} denotes the modified cover, and the output of the function F_{sm} should be inversely proportional to the similarity of the original histogram H_{PU} and modified histogram H'_{PU}.

3   The Proposed HEVC Steganography

In this section, based on the above SCM, there are two problems need to be solved: one is how to reduce the distortion D_c on coding efficiency; another is how to keep the histogram H_{PU} similar to the original during the process of embedding secret message. In our algorithm, the first one is solved by proper cost assignment of STC. The second one is solved by specific PU extraction and selection rule. The framework of the proposed algorithm is showed in Fig. 2.

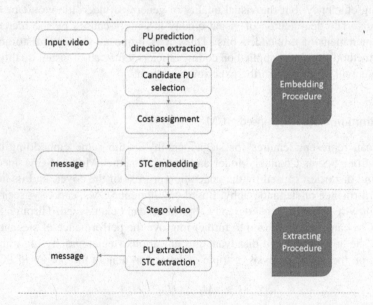

Fig. 2. Framework of the embedding algorithm and the extraction algorithm

3.1   PU Extraction and Selection Rule

According to the recursive procedure of block partition decision, large block partition tends to be applied to plain area, and small block partition tends to be applied to texture rich area. Moreover, when QP increases, the number of small blocks decreases.

Texture rich areas are more suitable for steganography. For this reason, PUs with size of 4×4 are selected as cover in our algorithm.

Observing the 35 intra prediction directions used in HEVC, it can be noticed that unlike the prediction directions in AVC, modes of HEVC have a regular pattern. In HEVC, two number-adjacent directions have similar prediction direction. The common way to modify the intra prediction mode is to replace it with a mode that is similar in prediction direction. In this case, these modes are grouped as follows:

$$\{(M_i, M_j)|2 \mid M_i = 2 \mid M_j, \quad i,j \in (0, 34)\} \tag{11}$$

Where the $|$ symbol means exact division, M_i mean the current PU prediction mode has the ith prediction direction. One element in the group denotes the bit 0, another denotes the bit 1. According to Eq. (11), the final grouping is $\{(0, 1), (2, 3)...\}$. However, this grouping method will change the histogram H_{PU} significantly. The number of mode 1 will be close to mode 0 after embedding, which will indicate the existence of secret message. Thus, the first group $(0, 1)$ is removed to keep the shape of histogram H_{PU}. Finally, all the qualified prediction modes of PUs in I frames with size of 4×4 are extracted, and taken as cover sequence.

3.2 STC and Cost Assignment Method

In order to reduce the influence on coding efficiency of the proposed algorithm. The STC method is utilized to embed the secret message into cover:

$$Hx^T = m \tag{12}$$

Where H denotes the parity check matrix generated by STC algorithm, m is the secret message and x is the modified cover sequence. Detail description and implement of STC can be found in [10]. According to the PU selection rule, one prediction mode has one candidate mode that can replace it. Thus, this is a binary STC problem. After grouping these prediction modes, the following equation is used to map them into binary sequence:

$$c_i = m_i \bmod 2 \tag{13}$$

Where c_i denotes the binary cover and m_i denotes the original cover.

As mentioned in Sect. 2, the main distortion caused for this steganography is the reduction in coding efficiency. From Eq. (1), each RD cost is calculated through estimated bitrate and distortion of each PU. Thus, difference in RD cost can represent the coding efficiency reduction caused by changing the prediction mode of the current PU. The cost of changing one PU is defined as:

$$\varphi_i = |J_i - J_j|, \; i,j \; \text{is from the same group} \tag{14}$$

Where φ_i is the cost of changing the ith PU and J_i is the RD cost of the prediction mode with the ith prediction direction. The difference of RD cost between two prediction modes is used in the same group as the cost for changing one to another. The total distortion D_c is present as:

$$D_c = \sum_{k=1}^{n} \varphi_k \tag{15}$$

Where n presents the total number of all qualified PUs in the video file. Finally, the secret data can be embedded into a video with little distortion.

4   Experiments and Analysis

4.1   Experiment Environment

The proposed steganography algorithm has been implemented in an open source software X265. HEVC is the state-of-art video codec standard, it is specially designed for high definition videos for higher coding efficiency. For this reason, twenty two YUV sequences (*aspen, blue sky, controlled burn, crowd run, ducks take off, factory, in to tree, life, old town cross, park joy, pedestrian area, red kayak, riverbed, rush field cuts, rush hour, snow mint, speed bag, station, sunflower, touchdown pass, tractor, west wind easy*) with 1080P resolution are selected in this paper. However, not all of these sequences have the same frame numbers, which will lead to difficulty in analyzing the capacity and the perceptibility. Thus, all these sequences are further divided into small sequences with 100 frames each, and 112 subsequences are generated. In these experiments, pseudo random binary sequences are generated as secret data, and all QPs are tested using different payload rates $\alpha \in \{0.25, 0.5, 0.75\}$ to produce the stego sets. Finally, a total number of 17136 modified videos are generated. The detail of experiment environment in listed in Table 2.

Table 2. Environment of experiments.

Environment	Values
Encoder	X265 (ver 2.3)
Decoder	HM16
YUV sequences number	112
Resolution of sequences	1920 × 1080
Frames to be encoded	100
GOP size	10
GOP structure	IPPP…
QP range	{1, 2, …, 51}
Payload	{0.25, 0.5, 0.75}
Total sequences number	112 × 51 × 3 = 17136

4.2 Comparison Experiment

In this section, the proposed steganography algorithm will be compared with another algorithm on a common dataset to illustrate the advantage of ours. As far as we know, Wang et al. [9] have present several steganography algorithms based on intra prediction mode. Their latest work [9] is compared with our algorithm to illustrate our advantage in this section. The experiment set and the dataset is same as it in their work [9]. The frame number is 96, and intra period is set to 16. Comparison results in capacity, BIR and difference in PSNR is showed in Table 3.

Table 3. Comparison results with other HEVC algorithm

Sequences	Algorithms	QP	Resolution	ΔPSNR (dB)	Capacity (bits)	BIR (%)	NCKR (‰)
BQ Mall	**Proposed**	22	832 × 480	**−0.02**	**30096**	**0.86**	**0.29**
	[9]	22	832 × 480	−0.06	16182	1.58	0.98
Basketball Drill	**Proposed**	22	832 × 480	**−0.02**	**37243**	**1.83**	**0.49**
	[9]	22	832 × 480	−0.06	11070	1.90	1.7
Video1	**Proposed**	22	1280 × 720	**−0.03**	**22171**	1.67	**0.75**
	[9]	22	1280 × 720	−0.04	9534	**0.76**	0.80
Video3	**Proposed**	22	1280 × 720	**−0.01**	**23096**	1.30	**0.56**
	[9]	22	1280 ×720	−0.01	8058	**0.45**	0.56
Video4	**Proposed**	22	1280 × 720	**−0.01**	**21698**	0.98	**0.45**
	[9]	22	1280 × 720	−0.03	5502	**0.46**	0.84

In Table 3, the Bit Increase Ratio (BIR) is defined as:

$$\text{BIR} = \frac{TB_{steg} - TB_{ori}}{TB_{ori}} \times 100\% \tag{16}$$

Where TB_{steg} is the total bits of original video and TB_{ori} is the total bits of modified video. BIR is normalized with 1 Kbits to show the coding efficiency reduction, named as NCKR.

$$\text{NCKR} = \text{BIR}/\text{Capacity} \tag{17}$$

From Table 3, it shows our algorithm outperforms the algorithm [9] in capacity, difference in PSNR and BIR. By setting the RD cost of candidate PUs to negative, the partition mode of CTU is flexible but the number of PUs with a certain size is preserved. The effectiveness of applying STC and the cost assignment method is well proven by BIR and difference in PSNR. Algorithm [9] designs a mapping rule between difference of intra directions and secret message. However, they do not consider the distortion and statistic character in the SCM of HEVC. With proper distortion prevention method, our algorithm can achieve higher capacity with lower bit increase ratio and difference in PSNR. PSNR is compared here because it is originally used in [9] to illustrate the perceptibility.

In Table 3, the NCKR is showed in percentage per 1 Kbits, presenting average BIR caused by embedding 1 Kbits. This index means the reduction degree of coding efficiency with certain embedding bits. Lower NCKR stands for better preserving coding efficiency. For *video1*, *video3* and *video4*, named in [9], even if BIRs of algorithm [9] are lower, our algorithm has better NCKRs, which are 0.75, 0.56, and 0.45.

It can be observed that BIR 0.86%, 1.83%, 1.67%, 1.30% and 0.98% in Table 3 is higher than average BIR 0.43% using our 1080P dataset with QP22, which is present in Fig. 5. The reason is that the resolution of the dataset used in [9] is 832 × 480, which is smaller than that in our dataset. In Fig. 5, QP22 is in the increasing area, meaning the decrement in file size is the main factor affecting BIR value. That's the reason of higher BIR for 832 × 480 videos than 1920 × 1080 videos. Combining results in Table 3 and Fig. 5, the conclusion is drawn that for QPs in range (1, 33), more bits can be embedded with lower BIR by using high resolution videos. If the QPs in range (34, 51) are used, a lower resolution video is preferred in order to lower the suspicious rate.

4.3   Performance Experiments and Analysis

In this section, the conclusion that the dominant distortion in the proposed SCM is coding efficiency reduction will be proven. Experiments on PSNR, SSIM, BIR and capacity are designed to validate the SCM described in Sect. 2. Validation is done by analyzing the performance of our steganography algorithm.

Analysis on Perceptibility
In this section, video quality and perceptibility of the proposed algorithm are tested. As explained in Sect. 2, video quality of this kind of steganography algorithm will not be affected significantly. To prove this, SSIM between original video and modified video to demonstrate the perceptibility and visual quality of the proposed HEVC algorithm. PSNR is not used here because SSIM can present visual quality better. The results are showed in Figs. 3 and 4. For each point in Fig. 3, it is the average number of SSIM from 112 videos with same QP.

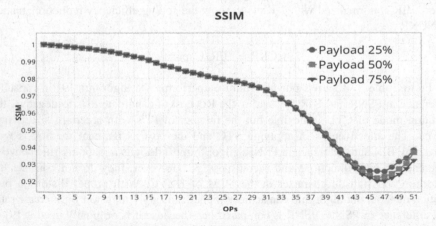

Fig. 3. SSIM of the proposed algorithm with different QPs

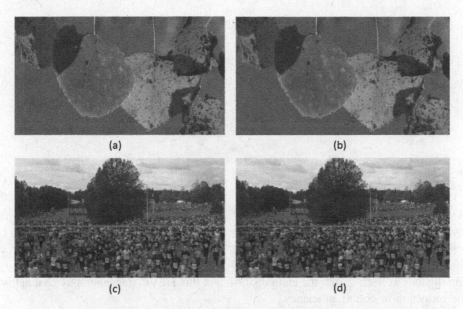

Fig. 4. Comparison between original I frames and modified I frames (a) the original I frame in *aspen*, QP = 7 (b) the modified I frame in *aspen*, QP = 7, payload = 0.5 (c) the original I frame in *crowd_run*, QP = 7 (d) the modified I frame in *crowd_run*, QP = 7, payload = 0.5

For many other steganography algorithms in other embedding channel, allocating higher embedding capacity often causes lower SSIMs. However, experiment shows that SSIMs of different embedding capacity are similar, the decreasing trend of SSIM is mainly caused by the incensement of QPs, not incensement of embedding bits. In addition, from Fig. 4, the distortion in visual quality cannot be distinguished by the human eye. These phenomena verify that the existence of secret bit will not affect the perceptibility significantly, and proves the analysis conclusion of distortion D_c in Sect. 2.

From these results, the overall SSIM value range from 0.919 to 1 and decreases with the increase of QP. QP20 to QP30 are the most commonly used coding parameters in a real application. SSIM values of these QPs are higher than 0.974, which indicates the excellent perceptibility of the proposed algorithm. There is an increasing trend in QP (46, 51) in SSIM. Combining the results in Fig. 5, the capacity decreases logarithmic with QPs. The reason for the increment of SSIM in (46, 51) is that fewer bits are embedded into videos, so the visual quality improves.

Analysis on Coding Efficiency
According to the proposed SCM, the main distortion is reduction in coding efficiency. In order to demonstrate the influence on coding efficiency of proposed algorithm and prove effective of applying STC method, BIR is calculated on the dataset. Figure 5 shows the BIR of the proposed algorithm calculated on the dataset.

Unlike the results in Fig. 3, Fig. 5 shows that with the increment of BIR, higher payload leads to higher BIR. The conclusion can be drawn that more embedded bits lead to higher distortion in video file size, which prove the correctness of the analysis

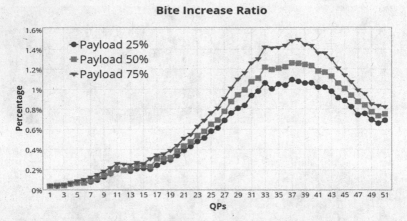

Fig. 5. BIR of the proposed algorithm with different QPs

conclusions in Sect. 2, and the main distortion in this HEVC steganography channel is the reduction in coding efficiency.

The highest BIR achieve by our algorithm is 1.498% achieved by QP38. For the most commonly used QP20 to QP30, BIR is between 0.340% and 1.162%, which will barely cause suspicion in the real world. The optimal BIR value is achieved by smaller QP and there is a decreasing trend after QP larger than 38. The reason is that decreasing speed of capacity exceeds the decreasing speed of file size in large QPs.

Analysis on Capacity of the Proposed Algorithm

In this section, capacity of the proposed algorithm is analyzed. The upper bound of embedding capacity depends on the numbers of 4×4 PUs in I frames, which is two times of the capacity using payload 0.5. The results are show in Fig. 6 and Table 4.

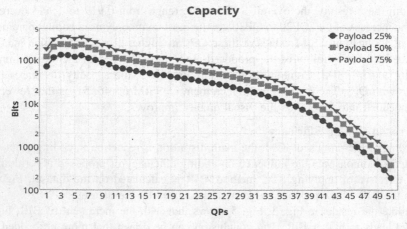

Fig. 6. Capacity of the proposed algorithm with different QPs

The vertical coordinate is logarithmic, which means the number of this kind of PU decrease logarithmically with increment of QPs. During the recursive mode decision process, RD cost is calculated by visual distortion and length of bit stream using Eq. (2). When QP increases, more reconstruction pixels will be calculated from same quantized value, which leads to a smaller RD cost for large partition mode. The sizes of PUs are exponential {4, 8, 16, 32}, meaning the larger size PUs exponentially merge the smaller size PUs during this process. This may be the reason for logarithmically decrement in capacity.

From Fig. 6 and Table 4, the higher capacity is achieved by the smaller QP, and the highest is 330 k bits achieved by QP6, the lowest is 188 bits achieved by QP51. In QP range (1, 4), capacity is increasing. This is caused by PU selection rule because prediction directions 0 and 1 are not selected in this algorithm. For the most commonly used QP20, capacity is 102758 bits. Meanwhile, proposed algorithm provides good visual quality with 0.984 SSIM and 0.439% BIR.

Table 4. Capacity (bits) of the proposed algorithm with different QPs

QP	1	2	3	4	5	6	7	8	9	10	11
25%	68004	109830	125330	123222	112796	121649	105733	95587	83138	76070	64213
50%	114869	191008	219795	216816	196813	213579	184621	165638	142703	130322	107408
75%	172303	286513	329692	325223	295220	320369	276932	248457	214055	195483	161112
QP	12	13	14	15	16	17	18	19	20	21	22
25%	61230	57069	53339	50235	47839	44270	43432	40309	38465	36437	34521
50%	102776	95610	89308	84228	80475	74368	73577	68505	65137	61836	58746
75%	154164	143414	133962	126342	120712	111553	110365	102758	97706	92755	88119
QP	23	24	25	26	27	28	29	30	31	32	33
25%	32056	30236	28530	26665	24787	22952	20974	19534	17694	15726	14093
50%	54527	51534	48733	45679	42532	39467	36138	33804	30702	27358	24613
75%	81791	77301	73100	68518	63799	59200	54207	50706	46053	41037	36920
QP	34	35	36	37	38	39	40	41	42	43	44
25%	12566	11093	9663	8366	7042	5989	4866	3887	3063	2347	1767
50%	22051	19560	17128	14930	12643	10832	8864	7133	5659	4374	3295
75%	33076	29340	25693	22395	18964	16248	13297	10700	8489	6560	4942
QP	45	46	47	48	49	50	51				
25%	1311	968	731	584	376	233	159				
50%	2466	1837	1370	1072	664	423	315				
75%	3699	2756	2056	1622	1140	611	437				

In summary, our algorithm outperforms the existing HEVC intra prediction mode algorithm with higher capacity and better perceptibility. Results prove that the main distortion in the proposed channel model is the reduction in coding efficiency, not visual quality. Thus, the distortion prevention algorithm in this channel should be mainly designed to avoid the coding efficiency reduction. STC and cost assignment method are effective in preventing coding efficient reduction. High capacity can be achieved using small QPs. Some interesting phenomenon in the experiment results is discussed, which may be helpful to improving the performance of steganography algorithm and SCM of HEVC in the future.

5 Conclusions

In this paper, a novel HEVC SCM is built. It is firstly proposed that the distortion optimization method in this SCM should be applied on coding efficiency instead of visual quality. According to this conclusion, a novel coding efficiency preserving steganography algorithm is proposed for HEVC videos. From the experiment results, the main distortion in the proposed channel model is proven to be the reduction in coding efficiency, not visual quality, and our algorithm outperforms the existing HEVC intra prediction mode algorithm with higher capacity and better perceptibility. Future work will be further investigated to the proposed channel model and adopt the algorithm to an adaptive algorithm or error propagation free algorithm.

Acknowledgement. This work was supported by the National Natural Science Foundation of China (No. 61572320, 61572321), and also supported by Zhejiang Provincial Natural Science Foundation of China (LY17F020013).

References

1. Aparna, R., Ajish, S.: A review on data hiding techniques in compressed video. Int. J. Comput. Appl. **134**(13), 1–4 (2016)
2. Juneja, M., Sandhu, P.S.: Information hiding using improved LSB steganography and feature detection technique. Int. J. Eng. Adv. Technol. (IJEAT) **2**(4), 2249–8958 (2013)
3. Hu, Y., Zhang, C., Su,Y.: Information hiding based on intra prediction modes for H.264/AVC. In: 2007 IEEE International Conference on Multimedia and Expo, pp. 1231–1234. IEEE (2007)
4. Yang, G., Li, J., He, Y.: An information hiding algorithm based on intra-prediction modes and matrix coding for H.264/AVC Video stream. Int. J. Electron. Commun. **65**(4), 331–337 (2011)
5. Bouchama, S., Hamami, L., Aliane, H.: H.264/AVC data hiding based on intra prediction modes for real-time applications. In: Proceedings of the World Congress on Engineering and Computer Science, vol. 2200(1), 655–658 (2012)
6. Zhang, L., Zhao, X.: An adaptive video steganography based on intra-prediction mode and cost assignment. In: Shi, Y.Q., Kim, H.J., Perez-Gonzalez, F., Liu, F. (eds.) IWDW 2016. LNCS, vol. 10082, pp. 518–532. Springer, Cham (2017). doi:10.1007/978-3-319-53465-7_39
7. Chang, P.C., Chung, K.L., Chen, J.J., et al.: A DCT/DST-based error propagation-free data hiding algorithm for HEVC intra-coded frames. J. Vis. Commun. Image Represent. **25**(2), 239–253 (2014)
8. Tew, Y., Wong, K.S.: Information hiding in HEVC standard using adaptive coding block size decision. In: IEEE International Conference on Image Processing, pp. 5502–5506. IEEE (2015)
9. Sheng, Q., Wang, R., Pei, A., Wang, B.: An information hiding algorithm for HEVC based on differences of intra prediction modes. Guangdianzi Jiguang/J. Optoelectron. Laser **25**(8), 1578–1585 (2016)
10. Filler, T., Judas, J., Fridrich, J.: Minimizing additive distortion in steganography using syndrome-trellis codes. IEEE Trans. Inf. Forensics Secur. **6**(3), 920–935 (2011)

A Prediction Mode-Based Information Hiding Approach for H.264/AVC Videos Minimizing the Impacts on Rate-Distortion Optimization

Yu Wang[1,2(✉)], Yun Cao[1,2], Xianfeng Zhao[1,2], and Linna Zhou[3]

[1] State Key Laboratory of Information Security, Institute of Information Engineering, Chinese Academy of Sciences, Beijing 100093, China
{wangyu9078,caoyun,zhaoxianfeng}@iie.ac.cn
[2] School of Cyber Security, University of Chinese Academy of Sciences, Beijing 100093, China
[3] School of Information Science and Technology, University of International Relations, Beijing 100091, China
zhoulinna@mail.tsinghua.edu.cn

Abstract. In this paper, with the data representation named intra prediction mode (IPM), an effective data hiding approach, called MIRO, integrated with H.264/AVC compression is proposed. The main principle is to minimize the embedding impacts on the video coding efficiency. First, a novel distortion function of individual IPM is designed reflecting its impact on Rate-Distortion Optimization. Secondly, the embedding structure based on syndrome-trellis codes (STCs) and interleaved sub-lattices are leveraged to minimize the overall embedding distortion. Comparative experimental results have demonstrated that, with similar embedding rates, the proposed method has much lower impacts on coding efficiency (both on the visual quality and compression efficiency) compared to other schemes.

Keywords: Information hiding · H.264/AVC · Intra prediction · Rate-distortion

1 Introduction

The booming of H.264/advanced video coding (AVC) [1] has created an urgent need to explore the approaches of information hiding to restrict the illegal use of digital video. This paper targets the internal dynamics of video compression, specifically the intra-prediction stage. In literature, most methods of this type perform data hiding by changing the optimal intra prediction modes (IPMs) to suboptimal ones.

In [2], a blind robust watermarking algorithm for H.264/AVC is proposed based on the idea of IPM modulation. Hu et al. [3] pointed out that the IPM of H.264/AVC is a suitable venue to hide message and proposed an algorithm by modifying intra 4×4 prediction modes (I4PMs) based on the mapping between

© Springer International Publishing AG 2017
C. Kraetzer et al. (Eds.): IWDW 2017, LNCS 10431, pp. 163–176, 2017.
DOI: 10.1007/978-3-319-64185-0_13

I4PMs and hiding bits. Since then, a considerable number of IPM-based information hiding algorithms have been proposed. Yang et al. [4] applied matrix coding to improve the embedding capacity and control the increase of bit rate. Two watermark bits are mapped to every three I4PMs and only one I4PM is changed for two watermark bits. In [5], a data hiding scheme based on inter and intra prediction modes was proposed by means of constraining the prediction modes on different block sizes so the watermark bits of "0" and "1" can be effectively hidden. Xu et al. [6] proposed that marcroblocks were selectively chosen based on a chaotic sequence and one mode can carry one bit. To enhance security, the secret message is encrypted and blocks are selected randomly. For some real-time applications, Kapotas et al. [7] exploited the IPCM encoded macroblocks during the intra prediction stage in order to hide the desired data. This scheme doesn't considerably affect either the bit rate or perceptual quality, but it has a low embedding capacity indeed. Bouchama et al. [8] presented a new approach of exploiting I4PMs to increase data hiding capacity. I4PMs are divided into four groups composed of modes of close prediction directions. The data embedding is to modify modes of the same group in order to maintain both visual quality and capacity.

Note that each IPM is a result of Rate-Distortion Optimization, any modulation will destroy its optimality. To make matters worse, because the intra-prediction is highly interlaced, arbitrary modification will affect later coding processes that cannot be controlled [9]. It has been noticed that for the existing IPM-based approaches, no effective mechanism is available to suppress the embedding impact on the coding efficiency. The main contribution of this paper is to provide a solution to solve the problem of minimizing the overall embedding impacts on both the visual quality and compressional efficiency. First, a novel distortion function of individual IPM is designed reflecting its impact on Rate-Distortion Optimization. Secondly, using STCs implemented in a Gibbs-like manner [10], messages are embedded minimizing the overall embedding distortion.

The rest of this paper is organized as following. In Sect. 2, the H.264 intra-prediction and the framework of distortion minimization are introduced. In Sect. 3, a novel distortion function reflecting the embedding impacts on Rate-Distortion Optimization is designed. And the procedure of adaptive embedding using STCs and interleaved sublattices is presented in details to show how to minimize the overall embedding impacts. In Sect. 4, comparative experiments are conducted to demonstrate the effectiveness of the proposed approach. Finally, the conclusions are given in Sect. 5.

2   Preliminaries

2.1   Intra-Prediction in H.264/AVC

In video coding standard H.264/AVC, intra-prediction is utilized to reduce the spatial redundancy and a higher compression ratio has been proved to be achieved for I-frame where all macroblocks have to be encoded in intra-modes

M	A	B	C	D	E	F	G	H
I	a	b	c	d				
J	e	f	g	h				
K	i	j	k	l				
L	m	n	o	p				

Fig. 1. The predicted and reference samples for 4×4 luminance blocks

containing 9 I4PMs and 4 intra 16×16 prediction modes (I16PMs). I4PMs are used to characterize the regions with complicated texture of a picture and suited for coding parts of significant details. In contrast with I4PM, I16PMs are more suited for coding smooth areas of a picture. In all existing IPM-based algorithms, only I4PMs are modulated to carry hidden message. As illustrated in Fig. 1, there are 16 samples $\{a - p\}$ to be predicted in current 4×4 luminance block using the neighbor samples $\{A - M\}$, after encoded and reconstructed, located in adjacent luminance blocks. To decrease the spatial redundancy, predictive coding is adopted to encode each residual of the sample. After traversal of 9 prediction modes in Fig. 2, the optimal mode (OPM) decision is performed by following R-D function

$$J(s, c, \text{IMODE} \mid QP, \lambda_{\text{IMODE}}) = SSD(s, c, \text{IMODE} \mid QP)$$
$$+ \lambda_{\text{MODE}} \cdot R(s, c, \text{IMODE} \mid QP) \tag{1}$$

where $\text{IMODE} \in \mathcal{J}$ is represented as one of IPMs in the current 4×4 luminance block. Here, $\mathcal{J} = \{0, \ldots, 8\}$ denotes the set of all 9 prediction modes for 4×4

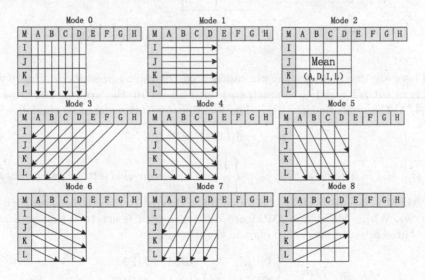

Fig. 2. The 4×4 intra prediction modes

luminance blocks. QP is the quantization parameter that is also utilized to compute the Lagrange multiplier λ_{MODE} for mode decision, approximated as

$$\lambda_{\text{MODE}} = 0.85 \times 2^{(QP-12)/3} \qquad (2)$$

R is the required number of bits to encode the luminance block, mainly containing the bits of encoding IPM and transformed coefficients. SSD is the sum of squared differences between the original sample value s and the reconstructed sample value c as followed

$$\text{SSD} = \sum_{1 \leq i,j \leq 4} |\, s(i,j) - c(i,j)\,|^2 \qquad (3)$$

Practically, the bits, required to encode the prediction mode, account for a large proportion in the total number of bits of 4×4 luminance blocks. For the current block C, as shown in Fig. 3, the most probable mode MPM_C is estimated from the spatial adjacent modes of both left block A and upper block B as followed

$$\text{MPM}_C = min\{\text{Mode}_A^{\text{left}}, \text{Mode}_B^{\text{upper}}\} \qquad (4)$$

$\text{Mode}_A^{\text{left}}$ and $\text{Mode}_B^{\text{upper}}$ are the prediction modes of previously encoded 4×4 luminance block A and B respectively. Faced with the phenomenon that either left block A or upper block B is unavailable, the corresponding value of MPM_C is set to 2(DC Mode).

Fig. 3. Current and adjacent 4×4 luminance blocks

There are two syntax elements called $pred\_intra4 \times 4\_pred\_mode\_flag(pred)$ and $rem\_intra4 \times 4\_pred\_mode(rem)$ introduced in the coding standard of H.264/AVC to encode the OPM. The identifier $pred$ is denoted as the following

$$pred = \delta(\text{OPM}, \text{MPM}_C) \qquad (5)$$

here the $\delta(,)$ is defined as $\delta(x,y) = \begin{cases} 1, & x = y \\ 0, & x \neq y \end{cases}$. If $pred$ is set to 1, which means that MPM is equal to OPM, only one bit is needed to encode $pred$ and ignore the rem. While MPM and OPM are different, $pred$ is set to 0 that indicates extra three bits are needed to encode the flag rem.

$$rem = \begin{cases} \text{OPM}, & \text{OPM} < \text{MPM}_C \\ \text{OPM} - 1, & \text{OPM} > \text{MPM}_C \end{cases} \qquad (6)$$

2.2 Framework of Distortion Minimization

For concreteness, and without loss of generality, we call a single intra-frame $\mathbb{F}$ with $m \times n$ intra-prediction modes $\mathbf{P}$ as the cover frame.

$$\mathbf{P} = \begin{pmatrix} \mathbf{p_1} \\ \vdots \\ \mathbf{p_m} \end{pmatrix} = \begin{pmatrix} p_{1,1} & p_{1,2} & \cdots & p_{1,n} \\ p_{2,1} & p_{2,2} & \cdots & p_{2,n} \\ \vdots & \vdots & \ddots & \vdots \\ p_{m,1} & p_{m,2} & \cdots & p_{m,n} \end{pmatrix} \in \mathcal{X} \triangleq \mathcal{J}^{m \times n} \tag{7}$$

is a regular lattice of 4×4 luminance block's IPM, $p_{i,j} \in \mathcal{J}, i \in \mathcal{M}, j \in \mathcal{N}, \mathcal{M} = \{1, \ldots, m\}, \mathcal{N} = \{1, \ldots, n\}$. Since the IPMs are used as the data representation, $\mathbb{F}$ can be represented by $\mathbf{P}$. With a given relative payload α, a αmn-bit message $\mathbf{m}$ is expected to be embedded by introducing modifications to IPMs in $\mathbf{P}$, and the resultant stego frame is expressed as

$$\mathbf{P}' = \begin{pmatrix} \mathbf{p_1'} \\ \vdots \\ \mathbf{p_m'} \end{pmatrix} = \begin{pmatrix} p_{1,1}' & p_{1,2}' & \cdots & p_{1,n}' \\ p_{2,1}' & p_{2,2}' & \cdots & p_{2,n}' \\ \vdots & \vdots & \ddots & \vdots \\ p_{m,1}' & p_{m,2}' & \cdots & p_{m,n}' \end{pmatrix}. \tag{8}$$

In additive framework, the modifications are assumed to be mutually independent, and let every $p_{i,j}$ be assigned a scalar $\rho_{i,j}$ expressing the distortion of replacing it with $p_{i,j}'$, the overall embedding impact can be measured by the sum of per-element distortions

$$D(\mathbf{P}, \mathbf{P}') = \sum_{i=1}^{m} \sum_{j=1}^{n} \rho_{i,j} \delta(p_{i,j}, p_{i,j}'), \tag{9}$$

In order to achieve a minimal distortion with the given payload, a flexible coding method named STCs can be leveraged to guide the embedding process. In fact, STCs are a kind of syndrome coding with which the embedding and extraction can be formulated as

$$\text{Emb}(\mathbf{P}, \mathbf{m}) = \arg \min_{\mathcal{P}(\mathbf{P}') \in \mathcal{C}(\mathbf{m})} D(\mathbf{P}, \mathbf{P}'), \tag{10}$$

$$\text{Ext}(\mathbf{P}') = \mathbb{H}\mathcal{P}(\mathbf{P}'). \tag{11}$$

Here, $\mathcal{P} : \mathcal{J} \rightarrow \{0, 1\}$ can be any parity check function, and $\mathcal{P}(\mathbf{P}) = (\mathcal{P}(\mathbf{p_1}), \ldots, \mathcal{P}(\mathbf{p_m}))^T$. $\mathbb{H}$ is a parity-check matrix of the code $\mathcal{C}$, and $\mathcal{C}(\mathbf{m})$ is the coset corresponding to syndrome $\mathbf{m}$. In more detail, $\mathbb{H} \in \{0, 1\}^{\alpha mn \times mn}$ is formed from a sub-matrix $\hat{\mathbb{H}} \in \{0, 1\}^{h \times w}$, where h (called the *constraint height*) is a design parameter that affects the algorithm speed and efficiency and w is dictated by the desired relative payload α [11].

3   The Proposed Information Hiding Approach

3.1   Interaction of Predictive Coding

For most the existing approaches, e.g., [3–6], IPMs are modified without considering the potential risk of distortion drift. Distortion drift is a typical side effect because the block-based intra prediction is highly correlated. To our best knowledge, these approaches cannot deal with interaction among embedding changes. As a result, the impacts on the coding efficiency cannot be properly controlled. To demonstrate the mutual influence, the process of how a single IPM modulation affects subsequent block codings is explained as follows.

Definition 1. *(Polluted Block).*
After changing the intra prediction mode of one 4×4 luminance block, if nothing else to be done, the latter block, whose mode cannot be decoded correctly, is defined as a polluted block.

Fig. 4. Illustration of polluted blocks

As introduced in Sect. 2, the identifier *pred* is used to indicate whether the current block's IPM is to be predicted according to the IPMs of its neighbors. if the lower block's or the right block's *pred* is set to 1, the perturbation of IPM of current block will propagate to its neighbors. As shown in Fig. 4, a 8×8 block, comprised of four adjacent 4×4 blocks, is taken from an intra-frame of H.264 stream named "*crowd_run*", with the hope of depicting the polluted blocks. The IPMs of blocks with thick red solid lines are perturbed artificially and the blocks with red dotted lines represent the polluted blocks. The numbers labeled on each blocks are the value of IPMs. What intrigues us is that these polluted blocks are induced by just the perturbation of some blocks, any of whose identifier *pred* is equal to 0. In the previous work, the blocks with the identifier $pred = 0$ are recognized as the ones causing less distortion and suitable for embedding. However, without consideration of inducing polluted blocks, the appearance of decoding incorrectly is tremendously unacceptable owing to the existence of distortion drift. It is worth mentioning that, to solve the problem, there is an easy way by setting $pred$ to 0 and re-coding the flag rem of the lower and right blocks of polluted blocks. If so, rate-distortion cost is suboptimal for not capturing the interaction among embedding changes, which requires a new distortion function with considering predictive coding.

3.2   Distortion Definition

Under the framework of described in Sect. 2.2, assuming that modification is mutually independent, the scalar $\rho_{i,j}$ assigned to every $p_{i,j} \in \mathbf{P}$ is expected to express the embedding impact. The overall embedding impact can be measured by the sum of per-element impact. It is a primary problem of designing the scalar $\rho_{i,j}$, utilized to emerge both per-element independent distortion and the interaction among elements caused by predictive coding. In order to clarify the $\rho_{i,j}$ from both aspects, we introduce two concepts "intra embedding impact" and "inter embedding impact".

Definition 2. *(Intra and Inter Embedding Impact)*.
After changing the intra prediction mode of a $4{\times}4$ luminance block, the distortion used to measure embedding impact for this block, is defined as intra embedding impact.

After changing the intra prediction modes of neighbors of a 4×4 luminance block, the distortion used to measure overall embedding impact for this block, is defined as inter embedding impact.

Putting aside inter embedding impact, in general, we can use the rate-distortion cost to describe intra embedding impact of each block. Suppose that $p_{i,j}$ in the cover $\mathbf{P}$ is flipped to be $p'_{i,j}$, $J(p_{i,j})$ and $J(p'_{i,j})$ are the R-D cost of $p_{i,j}$ and $p'_{i,j}$ respectively. Then, the scalar $\sigma_{i,j}$, used to express the intra embedding impact, is obtained as followed

$$\sigma_{i,j} = min\{J(p'_{i,j}) - J(p_{i,j}) \mid \forall p'_{i,j} \in \mathcal{J}, \mathcal{P}(p'_{i,j}) \neq \mathcal{P}(p_{i,j})\}. \qquad (12)$$

For videos of H.264/AVC, R-D cost, adopted for mode decision, is proved to be a good way of measuring both the difference, between original and reconstructed samples, and the bits of encoding residuals and modes. It ignores the mutual influence between different blocks to get a low complexity of computing. The R-D optimization cannot reach the point of global optimum in theory but get a satisfactory result with near-global optimum in practice. For this, $\sigma_{i,j}$ is introduced to represent the intra embedding impact with purpose of minimizing the perturbation of R-D cost.

To capture the mutual influence between adjacent blocks, we assign a scalar $\gamma_{i,j}$ to express the inter embedding impact, defined as the following

$$\gamma_{i,j} = \mathcal{S}(p_{i-1,j+1}, p_{i,j}, p_{i,j+1}, p_{i+1,j-1}, p_{i+1,j}). \qquad (13)$$

To illustrate the inter embedding impact, a more specific Fig. 5 is shown consisting of four subgraphs. After embedding, the extra distortion of current block $p_{i,j}$ caused by predictive coding, results from the different conditions of the lower block $p_{i+1,j}$ or the right block $p_{i,j+1}$ referring to $p_{i,j}$. For both $p_{i+1,j}$ and $p_{i,j+1}$, each is required to be either choosing $p_{i,j}$ as the reference or not. The solid arrow depicts the relationship between neighbor blocks that one uses another as the prediction mode. Having the same effect, besides, the dotted arrow can be also used to express mutual independence between neighbors. Furthermore, we can get

$$\mathcal{S}(p_{i-1,j+1}, p_{i,j}, p_{i,j+1}, p_{i+1,j-1}, p_{i+1,j}) = \delta(p_{i+1,j}^{\uparrow}, 1) + \delta(p_{i,j+1}^{\leftarrow}, 1) \tag{14}$$

$$\begin{aligned} p_{i+1,j}^{\uparrow} &= \delta(p_{i,j}, \mathrm{MPM}_{i+1,j}) \times [p_{i+1,j-1} \geq 0] \\ &= \delta(p_{i,j}, min\{p_{i,j}, p_{i+1,j-1}\}) \times [p_{i+1,j-1} \geq 0] \end{aligned} \tag{15}$$

$$\begin{aligned} p_{i,j+1}^{\leftarrow} &= \delta(p_{i,j}, \mathrm{MPM}_{i,j+1}) \times [p_{i-1,j+1} \geq 0] \\ &= \delta(p_{i,j}, min\{p_{i-1,j+1}, p_{i,j}\}) \times [p_{i-1,j+1} \geq 0]. \end{aligned} \tag{16}$$

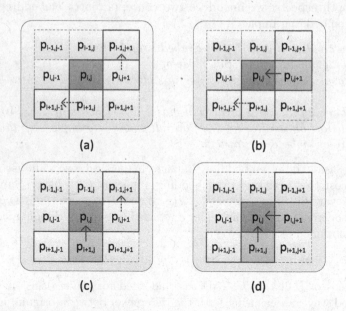

Fig. 5. Schematic diagram of measuring inter embedding impact

Here the Iverson bracket $[I]$ is defined to be 1 if the logical expression I is true and 0 otherwise. $\mathrm{MPM}_{i,j}$ is denoted as the most probable mode of $p_{i,j}$, computed by $p_{i,j-1}$ and $p_{i-1,j}$, shown in Eq. (4). To guarantee $p_{i,j-1}$ and $p_{i-1,j}$ available, used to obtain the value of $\mathrm{MPM}_{i,j}$, both $p_{i,j-1}$ and $p_{i-1,j}$ are subject to be equal or greater than zero and otherwise $\mathrm{MPM}_{i,j}$ is set to be negative resulting in $p_{i,j}^{\bullet}$ set to 0, $\bullet \in \{\uparrow, \leftarrow\}$. In this way, the scalar $\gamma_{i,j}$ can be used to reflect the importance of $p_{i,j}$, referred to by $p_{i,j-1}$ and $p_{i-1,j}$. When $p_{i,j}$ is used as the reference by more blocks, $\gamma_{i,j}$ will be assigned to be a larger value and verse vice. Since we get $\sigma_{i,j}$ and $\gamma_{i,j}$, used to measure both intra embedding impact and inter embedding impact, the distortion function $\rho_{i,j}$ can be defined as followed

$$\rho_{i,j} = \mu\sigma_{i,j} + \beta\gamma_{i,j} \tag{17}$$

where μ and β are controllable factors.

3.3   The Procedure of Embedding and Extraction

Based on the given distortion function, the practical implement of proposed method is introduced in this part. For measuring embedding impact, $\rho_{i,j}$ seems to be a favorable variable as the distortion function. However, since $\gamma_{i,j}$ has the form of a sum of locally supported potentials, if $\rho_{i,j}$ is applied for practical implement using STCs for data embedding, adjacent blocks are obviously inappropriate to be used as the cover at the same time. To resolve the problem, the embedding is implemented using Gibbs-like construction [10] on two interleaved sublattices, shown in Fig. 6. Divide the cover $\mathbf{P}$ into two parts $\mathbf{P} = \mathbf{P}_1 \cup \mathbf{P}_2$. The element of $\mathbf{P}_1$ is represented by a solid dot $\bullet$ and the element of $\mathbf{P}_2$ is represented by a hollow square $\square$. Respectively, they are defined as the following form

$$\mathbf{P}_1 = \{p_{i,j} \mid mod(i+j,2) = 0\} \tag{18}$$

$$\mathbf{P}_2 = \{p_{i,j} \mid mod(i+j,2) = 1\}. \tag{19}$$

With the support of Gibbs-like construction, two parts $\mathbf{P}_1$ and $\mathbf{P}_2$ alternate adaptive embedding for several times using STCs. Furthermore, to reduce the complexity of computing, for procedure of practical embedding, we need to rewrite it as followed

$$\rho_{i,j}^{t,l} = \mu\sigma_{i,j}^{t,l} + \beta\gamma_{i,j}^{t-1,\sim l} \tag{20}$$

where t is the meaning of $t(th)$ time for embedding, $l \in \mathcal{L} = \{1,2\}$, and $\sim l$ is the complement element of l, $\sim l \cup l = \mathcal{L}$, since $|\mathcal{L}| = 2$ is binary. The distortion $\rho_{i,j}^{t,l}$, represented by a new form, is mainly to express that the intra embedding impact $\sigma_{i,j}^{t,l}$ is obtained at the $t(th)$ time computing $\rho_{i,j}^{t,l}$ of $p_{i,j} \in \mathbf{P}_l$ but the

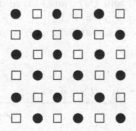

Fig. 6. Tessellation of the cover $\mathbf{P}$ into two disjoint sublattices $\mathbf{P}_1$ and $\mathbf{P}_2$

Algorithm 1. Alternate embedding with single intra-frame

Require: Input $\mathbf{P}$, ρ, α, $\hat{\mathbb{H}}$, K and $\mathbf{m}$
Ensure: Output $\mathbf{P}'$
1: Encrypt message $\mathbf{m}$ with the private key K, $\mathbf{m}' = Enc(K, \mathbf{m})$
2: Divide $\mathbf{m}'$ into two parts $\mathbf{m}_1$ and $\mathbf{m}_2$, $\mathbf{m}' = [\mathbf{m}_1\ \mathbf{m}_1]$
3: Obtain two parts of $\mathbf{P}$, $\mathbf{P}_1$ and $\mathbf{P}_2$, using (18) and (19)
4: Construct the mapping cover channel of intra prediction modes, $\mathbf{x} = \mathcal{P}(\mathbf{P}) = \{x_{i,j}\ |$
$\quad x_{i,j} = p_{i,j}\ mod\ 2, 1 \leq i \leq m, 1 \leq j \leq n\}$
5: Initial $\mathbf{y} = \mathbf{x}$, $\mathbf{y} = \mathbf{y}_1 \cup \mathbf{y}_2$, $\mathbf{y}_1 = \mathcal{P}(\mathbf{P}_1)$, $\mathbf{y}_2 = \mathcal{P}(\mathbf{P}_2)$, $t = 1$
6: Generate the STCs' parity check matrix $\mathbb{H}$ with α and $\hat{\mathbb{H}}$;
7: Compute $\gamma_{i,j}^{t-1,2}$ for all $y_{i,j} \in \mathbf{y}_1$ using all $y_{i,j} \in \mathbf{y}_2$
8: **for** $k = 1$ to *number of sweeps* **do**
9:    **for** $l = 1$ to 2 **do**
10:       Execute for all $y_{i,j} \in \mathbf{y}_l$
11:       Compute $\sigma_{i,j}^{t,l}$ for all cover $\mathbf{y}_l$ using (12), $\gamma_{i,j}^{t,l}$ for all cover $\mathbf{y}_{\sim l}$ using (14–16)
12:       Obtain $\rho_{i,j}$ for all cover $\mathbf{y}_l$ using (20)
13:       $\mathbf{y}_l = STC(\mathbf{y}_l, \rho, \mathbf{m}_l)$, and record the places of perturbation
14:       Flip all $p_{i,j} \in \mathbf{P}_l$ according to the records
15:       $t = t + 1$
16:    **end for**
17: **end for**
18: Obtain $\mathbf{P}' = \mathbf{P}_1 \cup \mathbf{P}_2$

---

inter embedding impact $\gamma_{i,j}^{t-1,\sim l}$ has been already obtained at the $t - 1(th)$ time computing the $\rho_{i,j}^{t-1,\sim l}$ of $p_{i,j} \in \mathbf{P}_{\sim l}$. The details are given in Algorithm 1.

The retrieval of hidden information is simple and fast. After decoding IPMs of an intra-frame of the H.264/AVC video, we can get a sequence of IPMs that are further processed into two parts as described in Algorithm 2. Using (11), we can extract the encrypted message and the secret message is obtained by the decryption with the key K.

Algorithm 2. Extraction with single intra-frame

Require: Input $\mathbf{P}'$, $\hat{\mathbb{H}}$, and K
Ensure: Output $\mathbf{m}$
1: Divide $\mathbf{P}'$ into two parts, $\mathbf{P}_1$ and $\mathbf{P}_2$, using (18) and (19)
2: Obtain $\mathbf{y}_1$ and $\mathbf{y}_2$, respectively, $\mathbf{y}_1 = \mathcal{P}(\mathbf{P}_1)$, $\mathbf{x}_2 = \mathcal{P}(\mathbf{P}_2)$,
3: Generate the STCs' parity check matrix $\mathbb{H}$ with α and $\hat{\mathbb{H}}$;
4: $\mathbf{m}_1 = \mathbb{H}\mathbf{y}_1$;
5: $\mathbf{m}_2 = \mathbb{H}\mathbf{y}_2$;
6: $\mathbf{m}' = [\mathbf{m}_1\ \mathbf{m}_2]$
7: Decrypt $\mathbf{m}'$ and get message $\mathbf{m} = Dec(K, \mathbf{m}')$

---

4   Experiment

4.1   Experiment Setup

The proposed information hiding approach has been implemented in the H.264/AVC JM-19.0 reference software version 19.0. The mainline profile is used in compression supporting I, P and B frames. In Fig. 7, the 14 video sequences in the 4: 2: 0 YUV (CIF, 352×288) are selected to be test sequences with an intra-period of 12 at the frame rate of 30 frame per second. The number of each frame varies from 90 to 600. To implement our proposed scheme using a good STCs listed in [11], the constraint height h is set to 7 with the relative payload $\alpha \in \{0.1, 0.25, 0.5\}$. To evaluate the effectiveness of the proposed approach, two typical IPM-based information hiding algorithms, i.e., Xu's [6] and Yang's [4] are completed to produce stego video sets, which are denoted as Alq_1 and Alq_2.

The peak signal-to-noise ratio (PSNR) and structural similarity index (SSIM) are calculated compared to the original frames of the corresponding YUV files. If PSNR or SSIM is larger, which is affected by the value of QP, the visual quality is expected to be better. When the value of SSIM is generally to be above 0.9, perceptual quality is believed to be good. Since the bit-rate increase is dependent on the embedded capacity, in order to perform a fair comparison, we define the bit-rate increase ratio (BIR) as followed

$$\text{BIR} = \frac{R_e - R_o}{R_o} \times 100\% \qquad (21)$$

where R_e denotes the bit-rate of the embedded video and R_o denotes the bit-rate of the original video.

Fig. 7. Test sequences

4.2   Performance Results and Analysis

In Table 1, the test sequences are encoded with QP = 28 and relative payload α is equal to 0.1, 0.25 and 0.5. Comparing three algorithms in terms of average PSNR, SSIM and BIR, under the same relative payload α, three methods all perform good imperceptibility since each SSIM is above 0.94 and the modification of PSNR is very small, close to each other. But MIRO shows a better performance in average BIR which means that maintaining the similar visual quality, MIRO has much lower impacts on coding efficiency, especially the compression efficiency.

With combination of Tables 1 and 2, as the same test sets being encoded with different QP, i.e., 28 and 32, we can see that, though the BIR of each method is increased, the BIR of MIRO is obviously smaller than that of Alg_1 or Alg_2. Besides, when QP is a larger value and the inter embedding impact is more significant, the BIR of Alg_1 or Alg_2 is much increased without considering the interaction between IPMs.

Table 1. Performance comparison of different information hiding methods (QP = 28, GOP Size = 12).

Method	Relative payload	PSNR(dB)	SSIM	BIR(%)
Alg_1	0.1	36.780	0.9684	0.57
	0.25	36.776	0.9677	0.71
	0.5	36.770	0.9674	0.96
Alg_2	0.1	36.783	0.9686	0.51
	0.25	36.779	0.9680	0.62
	0.5	36.773	0.9676	0.84
MIRO	0.1	36.782	0.9686	0.35
	0.25	36.780	0.9684	0.39
	0.5	36.775	0.9680	0.49

Table 2. Performance comparison of different information hiding methods(QP = 32, GOP Size = 12).

Method	Relative payload	PSNR(dB)	SSIM	BIR(%)
Alg_1	0.1	33.521	0.9486	0.83
	0.25	33.515	0.9479	1.00
	0.5	33.507	0.9469	1.41
Alg_2	0.1	33.520	0.9486	0.89
	0.25	33.514	0.9477	0.96
	0.5	33.510	0.9471	1.18
MIRO	0.1	33.523	0.9487	0.52
	0.25	33.520	0.9484	0.59
	0.5	33.515	0.9480	0.69

According to three different video sequences (*tractor, tennis* and *stockholm*), each containing 300 frames, PSNR and BIR of three methods are specifically compared in Fig. 8. With a larger value of QP, MIRO has achieved a better result for minimizing the embedding impacts. From Fig. 8(a), (b) and (c), three methods all get good visual quality and MIRO is slightly superior to others. Referring to Fig. 8(d), (e) and (f), MIRO is obviously seen with the better compression efficiency since its BIR is much lower.

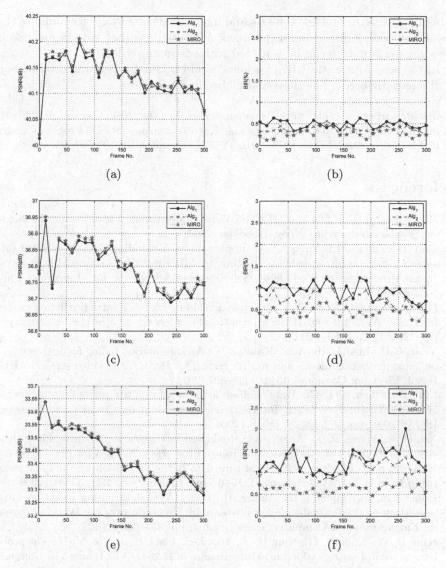

Fig. 8. Performance comparison of different information hiding methods. (a), (c), (e) the curve of PSNR with QP = 24, 28, 32. (b), (d), (f) the curve of BIR with QP = 24, 28, 32.

5   Conclusion

This paper presents a video information hiding approach tightly combined with H.264 compression, which uses the data representation called IPM to convey hidden messages. To minimize the embedding impacts on both the visual quality and compression efficiency, we define a novel distortion function of individual IPM reflecting its impact on Rate-Distortion Optimization and leverage an embedding structure based on STCs and interleaved sub-lattices to minimize the overall embedding distortion. Experimental results show that, satisfactory levels of coding performance can be achieved with adequate payloads.

In the near future, the MIRO scheme would be further optimized by testing on different distortion functions and embedding structures.

Acknowledgments. This work was supported by the NSFC under U1636102, U1536207 and U1536105, and National Key Technology R&D Program under 2014BAH41B01, 2016YFB0801003, 2016QY15Z2500 and 2016YFB0801405.

References

1. Richardson, I.E.: H.264 and MPEG-4 Video Compression: Video Coding for Next-generation Multimedia. Wiley, Hoboken (2004)
2. Cao, H., Zhou, J.L., Yu, S.S.: An implement of fast hiding data into H.264 bit-stream based on intra-prediction coding. In: MIPPR 2005 SAR and Multispectral Image Processing, pp. 60430I–60430I. International Society for Optics and Photonics (2005)
3. Hu, Y., Zhang, C.T., Su, Y.T.: Information hiding based on intra prediction modes for H.264/AVC. In: 2007 IEEE International Conference on Multimedia and Expo, pp. 1231–1234. IEEE (2007)
4. Yang, G.B., Li, J.J., He, Y.L., Kang, Z.W.: An information hiding algorithm based on intra-prediction modes and matrix coding for H.264/AVC video stream. AEU-Int. J. Electron. Commun. **65**(4), 331–337 (2011)
5. Liu, C., Chen, OT.-C.: Data hiding in inter and intra prediction modes of H.264/AVC. In: 2008 IEEE International Symposium on Circuits and Systems, ISCAS 2008, pp. 3025–3028. IEEE (2008)
6. Xu, D.W., Wang, R.D., Wang, J.C.: Prediction mode modulated data-hiding algorithm for H.264/AVC. J. Real-Time Image Proc. **7**(4), 205–214 (2012)
7. Kapotas, S.K., Skodras, A.N.: Real time data hiding by exploiting the ipcm macroblocks in H.264/AVC streams. J. Real-Time Image Proc. **4**(1), 33–41 (2009)
8. Bouchama, S., Hamami, L., Aliane, H.: H.264/AVC data hiding based on intra prediction modes for real-time applications. In: Proceedings of the World Congress on Engineering and Computer Science, vol. 1, pp. 655–658 (2012)
9. Kim, D.-W., Choi, Y.-G., Kim, H.-S., Yoo, J.-S., Choi, H.-J., Seo, Y.-H.: The problems in digital watermarking into intra-frames of H.264/AVC. Image Vis. Comput. **28**(8), 1220–1228 (2010)
10. Filler, T., Fridrich, J.: Gibbs construction in steganography. IEEE Trans. Inf. Forensics Secur. **5**(4), 705–720 (2010)
11. Filler, T., Judas, J., Fridrich, J.: Minimizing additive distortion in steganography using syndrome-trellis codes. IEEE Trans. Inf. Forensics Secur. **6**(3), 920–935 (2011)

Adaptive Audio Steganography Based on Advanced Audio Coding and Syndrome-Trellis Coding

Weiqi Luo[1,2(✉)], Yue Zhang[1,2], and Haodong Li[1,2]

[1] Guangdong Key Laboratory of Information Security and Technology,
Guangzhou, People's Republic of China
weiqi.luo@yahoo.com
[2] School of Data and Computer Science, Sun Yat-sen University,
Guangzhou, People's Republic of China

Abstract. Most existing audio steganographic methods embed secret messages according to a pseudorandom number generator, thus some auditory sensitive parts in cover audio, such as mute or near-mute segments, will be contaminated, which would lead to poor perceptual quality and may introduce some detectable artifacts for steganalysis. In this paper, we propose a novel adaptive audio steganography in the time domain based on the advanced audio coding (AAC) and the Syndrome-Trellis coding (STC). The proposed method firstly compresses a given wave signal into AAC compressed file with a high bitrate, and then obtains a residual signal by comparing the signal before and after AAC compression. According to the quantity and sign of the residual signal, ± 1 embedding costs are assigned to the audio samples. Finally, the STC is used to create the stego audio. The extensive results evaluated on 10,000 music and 10,000 speech audio clips have shown that our method can significantly outperform the conventional ± 1 LSB based steganography in terms of security and audio quality.

Keywords: Adaptive steganography · Advanced Audio Coding (AAC) · Syndrome-Trellis Codes (STC)

1 Introduction

During the past decade, most existing steganography works focused on digital image, and just a few works have been proposed for digital audio. Nowadays, lossless audio in WAV format is widely used in various real applications such as speech/music recorders. As a potential cover carrier for transmitting secret messages in the Internet, therefore, the corresponding audio steganography is worth research.

Up to now, several steganography have been proposed for digital audio in the time domain. For instance, LSB substitution, such as [1], is one of the earliest schemes for embedding data in digital audio and image. This scheme can

© Springer International Publishing AG 2017
C. Kraetzer et al. (Eds.): IWDW 2017, LNCS 10431, pp. 177–186, 2017.
DOI: 10.1007/978-3-319-64185-0_14

be applied to other transform coefficients, such as discrete wavelet coefficients, e.g., [2] and [3]. However, many existing steganalytic works have shown that the security of LSB substitution based methods is poor. LSB matching based methods can effectively remove the embedding artifacts of LSB substitution and thus have been widely used in modern steganography. Several audio steganography try to hide secret messages by combining the wavelet and Fourier transforms [4], or using discrete wavelet transform and sparse decomposition [5]. Other typical audio steganography methods, such as phase coding [6] and silence intervals [7], however, can only provide very low embedding capacities. In many previous audio steganography, the embedding capacity vs. the audio quality (or the robustness against some operations) is the chief consideration [8], while the security against advanced steganalysis is ignored. In most real applications, the security is crucial for steganography. Typically, there is a tradeoff between the security and the embedding capacity. To achieve good security, some recent steganalytic works for audio [9] and image [10] have pointed out that the embedding capacity (measured with bit per sample(bps)/bit per pixel(bpp)) should be low (e.g., less than 0.5 bps/bpp), and the modification strength should be as minor as possible. In this paper, therefore, we focus on a ± 1 based audio steganography in the time domain, and aim to improve the security and quality of conventional ± 1 LSB matching at low embedding capacity.

In most conventional LSB based audio steganography methods, the secret messages are embedded according to a pseudorandom number generator, meaning that every sample within a cover has the same probability to be selected for data embedding. In this way, some auditive sensitive parts in cover audio, such as mute or near-mute segments, will be inevitably modified after data embedding, which would lead to poorer security and quality of the resulting stegos. Up to now, some adaptive schemes, such as [3–5], have been proposed for audio steganography. Please note that most of these methods are performed in the transform domains, such as fast Fourier transform, discrete cosine transform, and discrete wavelet transform. Like image steganography (JPEG vs. Bitmap), the distortion introduced by modifying transformed coefficient with ± 1 is usually much larger than that introduced by directly modifying audio sample with ± 1. At the same embedding capacity, therefore, the stegos with these methods have lower objective quality compared to ± 1 based steganography in the time domain. Besides, empirical parameters and/or error correction coding are needed in some existing methods. Inspired by the modern adaptive methods in image steganography such as [11] and [12], we proposed a novel adaptive audio steganography. The proposed method firstly compresses the cover audio using AAC at a high bitrate, and then obtain the residual via comparing the input cover and the decompressed AAC. Due to the property of AAC, the residual can be regarded as the perceptually irrelevant components that can be removed from the cover audio. We then assign ± 1 embedding cost for each audio sample according to the residual, and finally obtain the stego via minimizing a distortion function with the STC. Our extensive experimental results have shown that the proposed scheme significantly outperforms the conventional ± 1 LSB based steganography in terms of security and audio quality.

The rest of this paper is arranged as follows. Section 2 gives a brief description of the AAC and STC. Section 3 shows the details of our adaptive steganography. Section 4 presents the results and discussions. The concluding remarks and future works will be given in Sect. 5.

2 Brief Description of AAC and STC

Advanced Audio Coding (AAC) is one of the popular standards for lossy digital audio compression. The AAC algorithm includes a set of sophisticated coding tools, such as filter bank window shape adaptation, spectral coefficient prediction, temporal noise shaping, bandwidth-/bit-rate-scalable operation, advanced noiseless coding scheme, and so on [13]. The extensive results have shown that at similar bit rates, AAC generally achieves better sound quality than MP3. Like other lossy audio compression schemes, the core of AAC is the perceptual audio encoder, which employs masking pattern of stimulus to determine the least necessary bits for each frequency sub-band so as to prevent the quantization noise from becoming audible. Usually, the more bits assigned for representing the audio, the better quality of the resulting audio. Thus it is easy to extract the perceptually irrelevant components via comparing the input audio clip and its AAC decompressed version with a high bitrate.

Another important technique used in the proposed method is the Syndrome-Trellis coding (STC)[1]. Essentially, STC is a binary linear convolutional codes represented by parity-check matrix, and it provides us a very effective way for hiding secret information without any channel code. Thus it is widely used in modern image steganography. In this paper, we also introduce such a technique in audio steganography.

3 The Proposed Adaptive Steganography

As described in Sect. 2, both AAC and STC techniques are used in the proposed scheme. Firstly, we use the AAC to obtain the perceptually irrelevant components of a cover audio clip. Based on the components, we can assign ±1 embedding costs for each cover audio sample to assure that the embedding modification is highly located at the perceptually irrelevant samples and preserve those perceptually relevant samples (such as mute/near mute parts) as they are with the help of the subsequent STC. As shown in Fig. 1, the diagram of our adaptive scheme includes the four following steps:

- **Step #1:** The input audio clip (denoted as $x(i) \in Z$, $i = 1, 2, \ldots n$, where n is the length of the audio clip) is firstly compressed with some lossy perceptual audio coding, such as AAC, at a high bitrate. In our experiments, the NeroAAC tool[2] with the "target bitrate streaming" mode and the highest bitrate (i.e., 400,000 bit per second) is used.

---

[1] The STC tool is available at: http://dde.binghamton.edu/download/syndrome.

[2] Nero AAC Codec is available at: http://nero-aac-codec.en.lo4d.com.

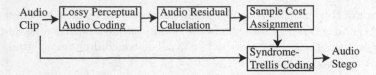

Fig. 1. The diagram of the proposed adaptive steganography

- **Step #2:** The AAC file is then decompressed into audio samples in the time domain, denoted as $x'(i) \in Z$, $i = 1, 2, \ldots n$. Then the audio residual r is calculated as

$$r(i) = x(i) - x'(i), i = 1, 2, \ldots n \tag{1}$$

- **Step #3:** Based on the residual $r(i)$ in Step #2, we define the ± 1 embedding costs for each audio sample $x(i), i = 1, 2, \ldots n$ as follows:

$$\rho_i^{+1} = \begin{cases} \dfrac{1}{|r(i)|}, & if \quad r(i) < 0 \\ \dfrac{10}{|r(i)|}, & if \quad r(i) > 0 \\ 10, & if \quad r(i) = 0 \end{cases} \tag{2}$$

$$\rho_i^{-1} = \begin{cases} \dfrac{1}{|r(i)|}, & if \quad r(i) > 0 \\ \dfrac{10}{|r(i)|}, & if \quad r(i) < 0 \\ 10, & if \quad r(i) = 0 \end{cases} \tag{3}$$

Please note that $r(i) = x(i) - x'(i)$ denotes the residual of the sample $x(i)$ after AAC compression with a high bitrate, and thus it can be wipe off from the cover $x(i)$ without introducing perceptual artifacts. It is expected that the larger value of $|r(i)|$ is, the less perceptual artifacts will be introduced after adding $+1$ or -1 (dependent on the sign of $r(i)$) to the corresponding sample $x(i)$. In the proposed method, thus, the initialization embedding cost is $\frac{1}{|r(i)|}, r(i) \neq 0$ both for $x(i)+1$ and $x(i)-1$. Please note that the since $r(i)$ is an integer, then $\frac{1}{|r(i)|} \in (0, 1], r(i) \neq 0$. Besides of the quantity of $r(i)$, the sign of $r(i)$ should also be considered. When $r(i) > 0$, it means that the sample $x(i)$ would be reduced after AAC compression. To preserve the perceptual quality well, the corresponding stego sample should also be reduced in this case. Thus, we set a relatively larger cost for $x(i) + 1$, i.e., 10 times of the initialization in our method, vice versa. When $r(i) = 0$, it means that the corresponding sample $x(i)$ located at the perceptual relevant parts since $x(i)$ is unchanged after AAC compression. Thus, we should assign a relative high cost both for $x(i) - 1$ and $x(i) + 1$, e.g., 10 in our method.

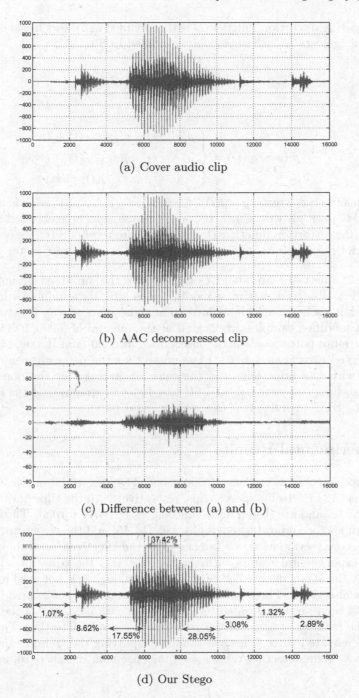

(a) Cover audio clip

(b) AAC decompressed clip

(c) Difference between (a) and (b)

(d) Our Stego

Fig. 2. An audio example with the proposed adaptive steganography. (a) Cover audio clip; (b) AAC decompressed version with 400,000 bitrate; (c) Difference between (a) and (b); (d) The Stego (0.30 bps) and the percentages of those modified samples (i.e., the number of changed samples over the number of all changed samples after data hiding) at different audio segments.

- **Step #4:** A distortion function D is then defined as follows based on the ± 1 embedding costs of each audio sample defined in Step #3,

$$D(x, y) = \sum_{i=1}^{n} \rho_i(x(i), y(i)) \tag{4}$$

where

$$\rho_i(x(i), y(i)) = \begin{cases} \rho_i^{+1}, & if \quad y(i) = x(i) + 1 \\ \rho_i^{-1}, & if \quad y(i) = x(i) - 1 \\ 0, & if \qquad y(i) = x(i) \end{cases} \tag{5}$$

and finally the stego y $(y(i) \in Z, i = 1, 2, \dots n)$ is calculated by $y = STC(m, x, \rho)$, where m is the secret message to be embedded via minimizing the distortion function D. Due to the property of STC, we can extract the secret message m correctly (error free) without the cost vector ρ.

Figure 2 illustrates an audio example with the proposed scheme. From Fig. 2(d), it is observed that most modifications after data hiding with the proposed adaptive scheme are highly located at those perceptually irrelevant parts (over 65% modified samples are located at the interval of $[6000, 10000]$), while those near mute parts (such as the intervals of $[0, 2000]$ and $[12000, 14000]$) are well preserved (less than 1.40%). Please note that the percentages at different segments with the same length is the same on average for the non-adaptive schemes, such as conventional ± 1 LSB based steganography and the steganography using STC with flat cost (see experimental part).

4   Experimental Results

In our experiments, we collect 10,000 mono 44.1 kHz 16-bit music clips and 10,000 mono 16 kHz 16-bit speech clips, respectively. All the clips have the same duration of 4 s, and are stored in the uncompressed WAV format. Three steganalytic methods for audio steganography, i.e., [14,15] and the recent work [9], are used for security evaluation. To further show the effectiveness of the proposed cost, the experimental results with the flat cost (i.e. the costs for all samples are exactly the same, denoted as "Flat Cost", although it is not used in existing works) are also given. Three embedding rates (i.e., 0.1 bit per sample (bps), 0.3 bps and 0.5 bps) are investigated respectively. In each case, half of the clips are used in the training stage, and the rest clips are used for testing. The experiments are repeated three times via randomly splitting the training and testing data. The average detection results with the ensemble classifier [16] are shown in Table 1.

Table 1. Detection accuracies (%) with different steganalytic features. The numbers with an asterisk ('*') denote the best results in the corresponding cases.

(a) For Music Audio

Embedding Rate	Steganalytic Features	Different embedding methods		
		LSB Matching	Flat Cost	Our Method
0.10 bps	"2D-Markov" [14]	53.59	52.30	51.51 *
	"D-MC" [15]	50.99	50.44	50.21 *
	Combined time & frequency [9]	59.37	56.08	55.52 *
0.30 bps	"2D-Markov" [14]	55.01	53.25	52.63 *
	"D-MC" [15]	52.14	50.84 *	50.90
	Combined time & frequency [9]	65.55	59.36	58.51 *
0.50 bps	"2D-Markov" [14]	55.38	54.78	52.55 *
	"D-MC" [15]	53.18	51.55	51.43 *
	Combined time & frequency [9]	69.62	60.47	59.96 *

(b) For Speech Audio

Embedding Rate	Steganalytic Features	Different embedding methods		
		LSB Matching	Flat Cost	Our Method
0.10 bps	"2D-Markov" [14]	50.83	50.14 *	50.16
	"D-MC" [15]	54.81	51.33	51.19 *
	Combined time & frequency [9]	63.89	53.65	53.05 *
0.30 bps	"2D-Markov" [14]	52.91	50.94	50.19 *
	"D-MC" [15]	60.97	54.52	54.02 *
	Combined time & frequency [9]	81.54	62.04	59.85 *
0.50 bps	"2D-Markov" [14]	55.33	51.77	51.22 *
	"D-MC" [15]	65.97	57.89	57.63 *
	Combined time & frequency [9]	89.84	68.54	66.09 *

From Table 1, it is observed that the security of the proposed adaptive scheme significantly outperforms the conventional ±1 LSB matching in all cases, and outperforms the "flat cost" method in most cases. Please note that for the recent steganalytic work [9], our improvements is greater especially for speech audio clips with high embedding rates. It is also observed that compared to speech audio clips, music audio clips seem more suitable for secret data hiding; and when the embedding rate is larger than 0.3 bps, the security of the conventional ±1 LSB matching is rather poor, especially for speech clips. For instance, the detection accuracy with the steganalytic work [9] is close to 90% for speech audio clips when the embedding rate is 0.5 bps. However, the proposed scheme can still achieve satisfactory results, less than 67% in this case.

Table 2. The comparative studies about modification rates and objective quality of the stego audio. The numbers with an asterisk ('*') denote the best results in the corresponding cases.

(a) For Music Audio

Embedding Rate	Modification Rate(MR) & SNR	Different embedding methods		
		LSB Matching	Flat Cost	Our Method
0.10 bps (bit per sample)	MR	5.00%	1.33% *	2.30%
	SNR	78.95dB	84.69dB *	82.33dB
0.30 bps (bit per sample)	MR	15.00%	4.93% *	8.56%
	SNR	74.18dB	79.01dB *	76.62dB
0.50 bps (bit per sample)	MR	25.00%	9.38% *	16.33%
	SNR	71.96dB	76.22dB *	73.81dB

(b) For Speech Audio

Embedding Rate	Modification Rate(MR) & SNR	Different embedding methods		
		LSB Matching	Flat Cost	Our Method
0.10 bps (bit per sample)	MR	5.00%	1.33% *	2.46%
	SNR	60.44dB	66.18dB *	63.52dB
0.30 bps (bit per sample)	MR	15.00%	4.93% *	9.03%
	SNR	55.67dB	60.50dB *	57.88dB
0.50 bps (bit per sample)	MR	25.00%	9.38% *	16.87%
	SNR	53.45dB	57.71dB *	55.16dB

Table 2 shows the modification rates (i.e., the number of changed samples after data hiding over the number of all samples) and the SNR of the corresponding stegos. It is observed that the modification rates of the proposed scheme is lower than the conventional ±1 LSB matching because of the use of STC, and thus the SNR of our stego audio clips are also higher (over 2 dB improvement on average). Both the MR and SNR of the "flat cost" method are always the best among the three steganography due to the property of STC. Please note that, however, the "flat cost" method is essentially the non-adaptive scheme, thus any audio part (including mute or near-mute parts) of an audio has the same probability to be changed as illustrated in Fig. 3, which probably leaves potential artifacts for steganalysis based on previous studies for image steganalysis and reduces the subjective quality of the resulting audio stegos at those mute/near mute segments. Please note that since the embedding rates are low (not more than 0.5 bps) and the strength of all modifications is limited in ±1, the objective quality (SNR) of all audio stegos is quite satisfactory: larger than 71 dB for music, and larger than 53 dB for speech in our experiments.

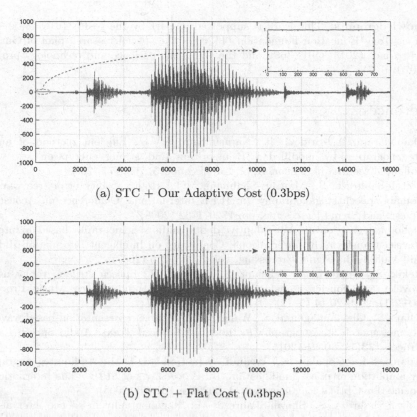

(a) STC + Our Adaptive Cost (0.3bps)

(b) STC + Flat Cost (0.3bps)

Fig. 3. The mute part within the cover audio is well preserved (see (a)) after data embedding with the proposed adaptive method, while it is contaminated (see (b)) with the flat cost.

5   Concluding Remarks

In this paper, we propose a simple yet very effective adaptive audio steganography in the time domain. The main contributions of this paper are as follows:

- We first propose to use the AAC compression to obtain the perceptually irrelevant components of cover audio for audio steganography, and design ± 1 embedding costs of samples based on the resulting components.
- We employ the STC for data hiding. Via minimizing the distortion function of embedding costs with STC, the messages can be adaptively embedded into the cover audio.
- Owing to the benefits of AAC and STC, our proposed scheme significantly outperforms the conventional ± 1 LSB based steganography in terms of security and audio quality.

In future works, we will extend the proposed adaptive scheme for other audio steganography in the frequency domain, such as MP3 and AAC.

Acknowledgments. This work is supported in part by the NSFC (61672551), the Fok Ying-Tong Education Foundation (142003), the special research plan of Guangdong Province (2015TQ01X365), and the Guangzhou science and technology project (201707010167)

References

1. Damodaram, A., Sridevi, R., Narasimham, S.V.L.: Efficient method of audio steganography by modified LSB algorithm and strong encryption key with enhanced security. J. Theor. Appl. Inf. Technol. **5**, 768–771 (2009)
2. Shirali-Shahreza, S., Manzuri-Shalmani, M.T.: High capacity error free wavelet domain speech steganography. In: IEEE International Conference on Acoustics, Speech and Signal Processing, pp. 1729–1732 (2008)
3. Delforouzi, A., Pooyan, M.: Adaptive digital audio steganography based on integer wavelet transform. In: International Conference on Intelligent Information Hiding and Multimedia Signal Processing, vol. 2, 283–286 (2007)
4. Rekik, S., Guerchi, D., Selouani, S., Hamam, H.: Speech steganography using wavelet and fourier transforms. EURASIP J. Audio Speech Music Process. **2012**(1), 20:1–20:14 (2012)
5. Ahani, S., Ghaemmaghami, S., Wang, Z.J.: A sparse representation-based wavelet domain speech steganography method. IEEE/ACM Trans. Audio Speech Lang. Process. **23**(1), 80–91 (2015)
6. Adams, S.F., Gopalan, K., Wenndt, S.J., Haddad, D.M.: Audio steganography by amplitude or phase modification. In: Proceedings of SPIE - The International Society for Optical Engineering, vol. 5020, pp. 67–76 (2003)
7. Shirali-Shahreza, S., Shirali-Shahreza, M.: Steganography in silence intervals of speech. In: International Conference on Intelligent Information Hiding and Multimedia Signal Processing, pp. 605–607 (2008)
8. Djebbar, F., Ayad, B., Meraim, K.A., Hamam, H.: Comparative study of digital audio steganography techniques. EURASIP J. Audio Speech and Music Process. **2012**(1), 25:1–25:16 (2012)
9. Luo, W., Li, H., Yan, Q., Yang, R., Huang, J.: Improved steganalytic feature and its applications in audio forensics. Technical report, Guangzhou, ER. China (2016)
10. Fridrich, J., Kodovský, J.: Rich models for steganalysis of digital images. IEEE Trans. Inf. Forensics Secur. **7**(3), 868–882 (2012)
11. Holub, V., Fridrich, J.: Designing steganographic distortion using directional filters. In: IEEE International Workshop on Information Forensics and Security, pp. 234–239 (2012)
12. Filler, T., Fridrich, J.: Gibbs construction in steganography. IEEE Trans. Inf. Forensics Secur. **5**(4), 705–720 (2010)
13. Painter, T., Spanias, A.: Perceptual coding of digital audio. Proc. IEEE **88**(4), 451–515 (2000)
14. Liu, Q., Sung, A.H., Qiao, M.: Temporal derivative-based spectrum and Mel-cepstrum audio steganalysis. IEEE Trans. Inf. Forensics Secur. **4**(3), 359–368 (2009)
15. Liu, Q., Sung, A.H., Qiao, M.: Derivative-based audio steganalysis. ACM Trans. Multimedia Comput. Commun. Appl. **7**(3), 18:1–18:19 (2011)
16. Kodovský, J., Fridrich, J., Holub, V.: Ensemble classifiers for steganalysis of digital media. IEEE Trans. Inf. Forensics Secur. **7**(2), 432–444 (2012)

Information Hiding Using CAVLC: Misconceptions and a Detection Strategy

Weike You[1,2(✉)], Yun Cao[1,2], and Xianfeng Zhao[1,2]

[1] State Key Laboratory of Information Security,
Institute of Information Engineering,
Chinese Academy of Sciences, Beijing 100093, China
{youweike,caoyun,zhaoxianfeng}@iie.ac.cn
[2] School of Cyber Security,
University of Chinese Academy of Sciences, Beijing 100093, China

Abstract. As the most commonly used entropy coding method of H.264, CAVLC (context-based adaptive variable length coding) has been widely utilized for information hiding. Various information hiding methods directly manipulate CAVLC coefficients, which are reported to be of high payload and low computational complexity. However, things are quite different in real applications. This paper addresses two misconceptions about them: (1) The CAVLC coefficients can be modified without re-encoding process. In fact, direct modifications of the number of non-zero coefficients will change the corresponding code tables for adjacent blocks and result in decoding errors. (2) CAVLC codewords can be indiscriminately substituted. Actually, it will cause serious distortion drifts. In addition, considering steganographic security, a detection strategy is proposed based on statistical analysis of some CAVLC-based methods.

Keywords: Information hiding · Steganalysis · Entropy coding · CAVLC · Trailing coefficients

1 Introduction

Currently, the concepts and methods of image information hiding are by far highly developed [3]. However, with the development of Internet services, videos can be conveniently downloaded and broadcast through the Internet such as YouTube, Facebook, and Twitter [19]. Compared to images, video files can easily achieve higher embedding capacities even with lower embedding rates [2]. As a result, information hiding using videos has caught the attention of researchers [6], and numerous methods have been developed for different situations.

Meanwhile, H.264 is the most commonly used format for the recording, compression, and distribution of video content [15]. Accordingly, a considerable portion of video information hiding methods use H.264 video objects as information carriers. Since it is a block-oriented motion-compensation-based compression standard containing a number of features, which allow it to compress videos more

© Springer International Publishing AG 2017
C. Kraetzer et al. (Eds.): IWDW 2017, LNCS 10431, pp. 187–201, 2017.
DOI: 10.1007/978-3-319-64185-0_15

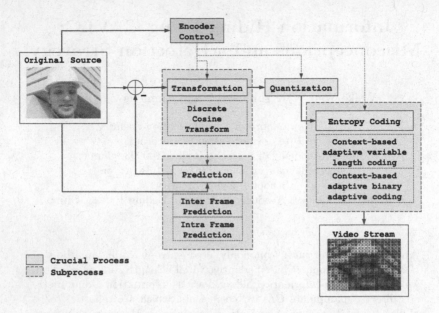

Fig. 1. The flowchart of H.264 video compression standard.

efficiently than previous standards (i.e., MPEG-2, H.263, etc.), H.264 can provide more flexibility for applications in a wide variety of network environments.

As shown in Fig. 1, H.264 consists of 4 crucial processes, i.e., prediction, transformation, quantization, and entropy coding [19].

1. Prediction: Raw video is essentially a collection of images, called frames. The frames are divided into discrete blocks, and each block is predicted based on its surrounding blocks of the same frame to reduce the spatial redundancy (Intra Frame Prediction) or blocks of neighboring frames to reduce the temporal redundancy (Inter Frame Prediction).
2. Transformation: Next, the prediction is subtracted from the original pixel block, and the residual is subjected to discrete cosine transform (DCT) to calculate its frequency components.
3. Quantization: After transformation, due to the characteristics of the HVS (human visual system), suppressing the high frequency components is allowed by dividing each DCT coefficients by a constant and rounding to the nearest integer. As a result, coefficients corresponding to high frequencies are typically rounded to zero, and others become small positive or negative integers.
4. Entropy coding: Finally, the quantized signal is coded into video streams by Entropy coding, which assigns a specific code to each symbol that occurs in the input.

Based on each process, various information hiding methods have been proposed [19], and entropy coding-based methods have been reported to be of the highest payload and the lowest embed/extract complexity [5–9, 11, 13, 14, 17, 18, 21, 22].

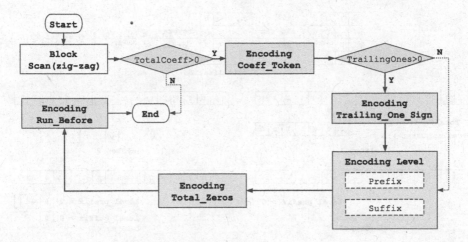

Fig. 2. Flowchart for CAVLC codec.

The idea of using entropy coding for data hiding has been generalized by [5–7,9,14,18]; Then [8,11,13,17,21,22] have proposed watermarking methods based on it. From all of these information hiding methods, novel ways for steganography can be derived like [14].

There are two entropy coding modes adopted by H.264, i.e., CABAC (context-based adaptive binary arithmetic coding) [17,21,22] and CAVLC (context-based adaptive variable length coding) [5–9,11,13,14,18]. CABAC can be used to code all syntax elements whereas CAVLC is mainly used to encode quantized transformed coefficients (i.e., quantized DCT coefficients).Compared to CABAC, CAVLC has a lower complexity and a higher coding speed. Thus, it is widely used in applications especially for portable devices and realtime communications. Moreover, CAVLC is supported in all H.264 profiles, unlike CABAC which is not supported in Baseline and Extended profiles [1].

The main contribution of this paper is summarized as follows: First, after analyzing the typical CAVLC-based information hiding methods, some fundamental errors and misconceptions are found: (1) Re-encoding process has been declared as avoidable. Actually, it is an essential part of preventing decoding errors. (2) It is implied that the codeword substitution can be indiscriminate. In fact, it will cause distortion drifts. Second, by observing the statistics of trailing coefficients of each block, a detection strategy is proposed in case the related CAVLC-based methods are used for covert communication.

This paper is organized as follows. Section 2 briefly introduces backgrounds and related works. Section 3 sets the record straight on the misconceptions contained in previous articles. In Sect. 4, a statistical based steganalysis algorithm is proposed to determine the existence of hidden information. The main contributions of this paper are summarized in Sect. 5.

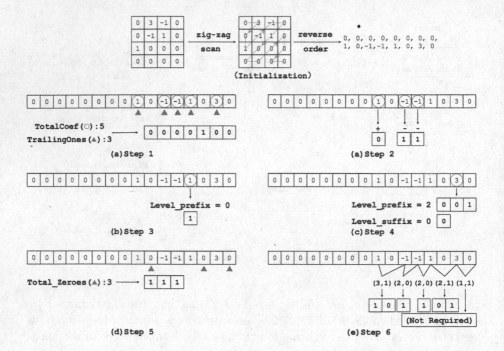

Fig. 3. An example of CAVLC encoding.

2   Backgrounds

2.1   CAVLC

As described above, CAVLC is a form of entropy coding used in H.264. It is an inherently lossless compression technique. Five data elements are used to encode transform coefficients associated with blocks of residual data in video coding processes: Coeff_Token, Trailing_One_Sign, Level, Total_Zeros, and Run_Before.

The process of CAVLC is shown as Fig. 2. More concretely, an example of CAVLC encoding of one 4×4 block is illustrated with Fig. 3 and described as follows [20]:

1. Coeff_Token is used to encode the total number of nonzero coefficients (Total-Coeff) and tailings coefficients (TrailingOnes). Since the highest frequency nonzero coefficient of each block is usually a sequence of ± 1, the last three ± 1 coefficients are marked as "Trailing ones", and others are treated as normal non-zero coefficients [16]. In this case, it is encoded as 0000100.
2. Trailing_One_Sign is used to encode the symbol bits of each TrailingOnes. In this case, it is encoded as 011.
3. Level is used to encode the value of each remaining nonzero coefficient. Level (1) is encoded as 1 (prefix); and Level (2) is encoded as 001 (prefix) and 0 (suffix).

4. Total_Zeros is used to encode the total number of zeros before the last nonzero coefficient. In this case, it is 3 and is encoded as 111.
5. Run_Before is used to encode the number of successive zeros ahead of each nonzero coefficient. In this case, it is encoded as 10-1-1-01.

After all, the resulting encoded bit stream is 0000100-011-1-001-0-111-10-1-1-01.

Note that, in CAVLC, the numbers of non-zero coefficients in adjacent blocks and their corresponding code tables are highly correlated – the number of coefficients is encoded using a look-up table, and the choice of look-up table depends on the number of non-zero coefficients in neighboring blocks [7].

2.2   Related Works

Typical CAVLC-based information hiding methods share some features in common and broadly fit into three categories according to the used embedding elements, i.e., trailing coefficient-based schemes, codeword substitution-based schemes and non-zero coefficient-based schemes:

Trailing Coefficient-Based Schemes. Trailing coefficient-based (TC-B) schemes are based on changing the number or symbols of trailing coefficients.

Along this line, S. Kim et al. [5], X. Li et al. [6] and K. Niu et al. [14] have suggested embedding message bits by mapping them to the sign bit of trailing coefficients. While K. Liao et al. [7] have utilized the number of trailing coefficients (0–3) to carry information based on their own mapping rule.

Codeword Substitution-Based Schemes. Codeword substitution-based (CS-B) schemes are based on codeword substitution.

Along this line, in YC. Lin et al.'s technique [9], a new codeword substitution approach have been developed that employs the level-suffix codewords as the hiding domain to accommodate the secret message in the compressed bitstream. G. Sherlin Shobitha et al. [18] have considered that the embedded data after video decryption must to be invisible to a human observer. Therefore, the value of Level corresponding to the substituted codeword should keep close to the value of Level corresponding to the original codeword. BG. Mobasseri et al. [13] have utilized the codeword of unused run-level pairs (i.e. those that never occurred in the video) in CAVLC to embed information.

Non-zero Coefficient-Based Schemes. Non-zero coefficient-based schemes (NC-B) are based on changing the number of non-zero coefficients.

Along this line, SD. Lin et al. [8] have proposed a method that information bits are embedded by adaptively truncating the nonzero quantized AC coefficients. The existence of truncated coefficient has least perceptual degradation and least influence on successive prediction coding. Thus, these schemes could constrain the perceptual degradation, which is caused by embedding information, within an ideal degree.

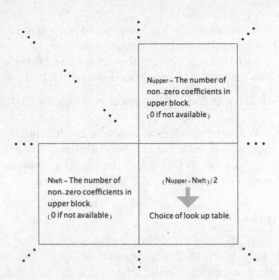

Fig. 4. The effect of neighboring blocks N_{upper} and N_{left} on encoding Coeff_Token.

3   Some Misconceptions

3.1   Misconceptions I: Re-encoding is Avoidable

The Theoretical Embedding Process. Since NC-B schemes only change the number of non-zero coefficients of each CAVLC block, they have claimed that they can not only effectively restrain the bit rate increasing but also refrain from video decoding processes [8]. In other words, these methods are time-efficient for no redundant work and able to execute in real time [19].

The Actual Embedding Performance. However, the completely re-encoding is inevitable in NC-B schemes.

As mentioned before, in CAVLC, the number of non-zero coefficients are all highly related with the code table selection of the adjacent blocks. Besides, the choice of look-up table which is used for encoding Coeff_Token, adapts depending on the number of non-zero coefficients in upper and left-hand blocks (context adaptive) N_{upper} and N_{left} [16] as Table 1, which is illustrated in Fig. 4.

Therefore, the variations of the number of non-zero coefficients in one block will affect the encoding results of all its adjacent blocks. For example, in paper [8], although it embedded message by truncating the last non-zero coefficient in the reordered series, which is before entropy encoding process and has least influence on perceptual quality, decoding errors can not be avoided. Because since it directly modifies the number of non-zero coefficients, the corresponding look-up tables of bottom and right-hand blocks is changed at the same time.

Table 1. Choice of look-up table for Coeff_Token

$(N_{upper} + N_{left})/2$	Table for Coeff_Token
0, 1	Variable-length code Table 1
2, 3	Variable-length code Table 2
4, 5, 6, 7	Variable-length code Table 3
8 or above	Fixed-length code table

3.2 Misconceptions II: Codeword Substitution Can Be Indiscriminate

The Theoretical Embedding Process. CS-B schemes claim to perform well at both hiding capacity and reconstructed visual quality [9]. For example, they force the selected pairs with similar values to represent "0" and "1" respectively, and modify the coded macro-blocks based on them [13]. The distortion from embedding is very slight, and the drift error not occurs since it is implemented in the appropriate processing point of H.264 encoder [18].

The Actual Embedding Performance. In fact, Intra-frame distortion drift and Inter-frame distortion drift are both huge problems of CS-B schemes.

While all MBs are predicted as Intra in I-frames, both intra-frame prediction and inter-frame prediction are adopted in P-frames. The encoder performs all possible combinations of modes in the case of inter modes and choose the mode combination that has the lowest RDO cost, including variable block sizes used for intra-frame spatial prediction, inter-frame motion estimation, multiple reference frames [4].

Meanwhile, since that there is a one-to-one match between each CAVLC coefficient and each quantized residual DCT coefficient (QDCT). Changing the CAVLC coefficients is actually changing the reconstructed DCT coefficients, so intra- [12] and inter-frame distortion drifts [23] are bound to happen:

The problem of intra-frame distortion drift. As illustrated in Fig. 5 (assume that current block is $B_{i,j}$), the intra-frame distortion drift in data hiding for compressed videos is provided by XJ. Ma et al. [10]. The expectation of intra-frame distortion drift is shown as follows,

$$D_{intra}(n) = p_1 \cdot E\{[\tilde{r}_n^{i-1,j-1}(3,3) - \hat{r}_n^{i-1,j-1}(3,3)]^2\} \tag{1}$$

$$+ p_2 \cdot E\{[\sum_{k=0}^{3} \tilde{r}_n^{i-1,j}(3,k) - \sum_{k=0}^{3} \hat{r}_n^{i-1,j}(3,k)]^2\}$$

$$+ p_3 \cdot E\{[\sum_{k=0}^{3} \tilde{r}_n^{i-1,j+1}(3,k) - \sum_{k=0}^{3} \hat{r}_n^{i-1,j+1}(3,k)]^2\}$$

$$+ p_4 \cdot E\{[\sum_{k=0}^{3} \tilde{r}_n^{i,j-1}(k,3) - \sum_{k=0}^{3} \hat{r}_n^{i,j-1}(k,3)]^2\}$$

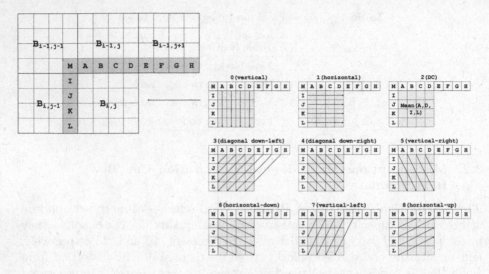

Fig. 5. The interrelationship of CAVLC blocks.

where p_i is the probability of distortion propagation in the equations. $r_n^{i,j}(x,y)$ is the residual value of the pixel x, y in the block $B_{i,j}$ of n_{th} video frame at the encoder. $\tilde{r}_n^{i,j}(x,y)$ and $\hat{r}_n^{i,j}(x,y)$ are the corresponding reconstructed values of $r_n^{i,j}(x,y)$ with and without embedding data respectively.

The problem of inter-frame distortion drift. The theoretical analysis of inter-frame distortion caused by data embedding is first presented by YZ. Yao et al. [23]. According to their achievement, the expected inter-frame distortion of CS-B schemes is

$$D_{inter}(n) = \alpha \cdot D_{inter}(n-1) + p \cdot E\{[\tilde{r}(n,i) - \hat{r}(n,i)]^2\} \tag{2}$$

where $D_{inter}(n)$ is the inter-frame distortion of the n_{th} video frame, and p is the probability of codeword substitution in n_{th} frame. α is a constant relating to the video content. $r(n,i)$ is the motion compensation residue of the pixel i in n_{th} video frame at the encoder. $\tilde{r}(n,i)$ and $\hat{r}(n,i)$ are the corresponding reconstructed values of $r(n,i)$ with and without embedding data respectively.

Obviously, undifferentiated substitution to the codewords of coefficients will cause these distortion drifts. Therefore, it would suffer from the subjective visual quality degradation due to the error propagation of the intra-prediction and the inter-prediction used in H.264. As a result, CS-B schemes cannot be regarded as desirable information hiding methods since the distortion drifts cannot be avert. Figure 6 is shown as an example.

Fig. 6. The distortion drift in CS-B schemes with high embedding quantity.

All in all, those methods which based on changing the symbols of trailing coefficients (i.e., TC-B schemes) are the only worth of video information hiding methods using CAVLC for further study.

4   A Detection Strategy for TC-B Schemes

4.1   Modeling of the Embedding Process of TC-B Schemes

For steganographic security concerns, TC-B schemes, namely the information hiding methods based on changing the symbols of CAVLC trailing coefficients are focused. It can be modeled as an additive independent signal η to Trailing_One_Sign. Therefore, Trailing_One_Sign X in the embedding process can be represented as the following equations

$$X_i = S_i + \eta_i \qquad i = 1, 2, \ldots, N \tag{3}$$

where S_i respectively are the bits of the i_{th} Trailing_One_Sign in the cover video, N is the number of trailing coefficients in whole video. The amplitude of η is 1 (flipping the bits),

$$MAX_i |X_i - S_i| = 1 \qquad i = 1, 2, \ldots, N \tag{4}$$

Note that it's similar to the simplest and most common information hiding algorithm since the hiding operation of flipping the bits of the i_{th} Trailing_One_Sign can be written mathematically in this way:

$$X = \begin{cases} X + 1 & \text{when } X \text{ is even,} \\ X - 1 & \text{when } X \text{ is odd.} \end{cases} \tag{5}$$

With the combinations of trailing coefficients, the residual blocks can be written mathematically as following equation:

$$\sum_{i=1,2,3}^{j=0,\ldots,i} Count_i^{zero=j,one=i-j} \tag{6}$$

where *zero* and *one* are the positive and negative trailing coefficient of each 4×4 block respectively, and i is the total number of trailing coefficients in one block. For example, $Count_3^{zero=0,one=3}$ represents the number of residual blocks with 3 trailing coefficients: three "-1"s and no "$+1$".

Let $\mathbf{h}[i\ j]$, $i = 1, 2, 3$, $j = 0, \ldots, i$ be the histogram of elements from the original video

$$\mathbf{h}[i\ j] = \sum_{i=1,2,3}^{j=0,\ldots,i} \delta(x[i\ j] - (i\ j)) \tag{7}$$

where δ is the Kronecker delta.

4.2   Impacts on Statistical Distribution

Assume that the hiding data is a stream of random bits, which is reasonable because the information is always encrypted [3]. Let p the payload of information hiding. Thus,

$$Pr\{X[i\ j] = (i\ j) \mid S[i\ j] = (i\ j)\} = p/2 + (1 - p) \tag{8}$$

$$Pr\{X[i\ j] \neq (i\ j) \mid S[i\ j] = (i\ j)\} = p/2 \tag{9}$$

Thus, Fig. 7 shows the effect of $Count_i^{zero=j,one=i-j}$ on histogram with hiding information.

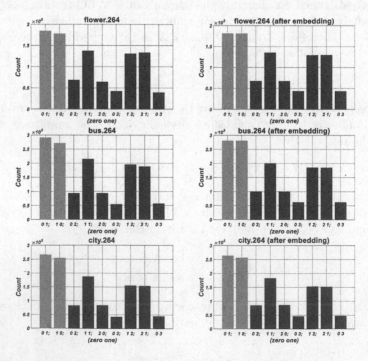

Fig. 7. Effect of $Count_i^{zero=j,one=i-j}$ on histogram.

Obviously, it has a tendency to even out the histogram within value pair $(zero = n\ one = m)$ and $(zero = m\ one = n)$, which leads to a characteristic staircase artifact and can be used as an identifying feature of hiding data and will be described in the next section.

4.3   The Steganalytic Method

A. A Statistical Characteristic of S

Based on rejecting the null hypothesis of the following hypothesis-testing problem, in original video,

$$H_0 : \mathbf{h}_p[m\ n] \sim \frac{\mathbf{h}_p[m\ n] + \mathbf{h}_p[n\ m]}{2} \tag{10}$$

$$H_1 : \mathbf{h}_p[m\ n] \not\sim \frac{\mathbf{h}_p[m\ n] + \mathbf{h}_p[n\ m]}{2} \tag{11}$$

From the point of view of axiomatic probability, the probability of observing two different combinatorial experiments is defined as follows: Let N be the number of trailing coefficients in a random block. Focus on $\mathbf{h}_p[0\ 1]$ and $\mathbf{h}_p[1\ 0]$:

$$\left.\begin{array}{c} 0 A = \varPhi \\[4pt] \dfrac{\mathbf{h}_p[0\ 1]}{\frac{\mathbf{h}_p[0\ 1] + \mathbf{h}_p[1\ 0]}{2}} A = \{O\} \\[10pt] 1 - \dfrac{\mathbf{h}_p[0\ 1]}{\frac{\mathbf{h}_p[0\ 1] + \mathbf{h}_p[1\ 0]}{2}} A = \{Z\} \\[10pt] 1 A = \{O, Z\} \end{array}\right\} P(A) \tag{12}$$

The sample space is $\{O, Z\}$. O(One) indicates there is no coefficient has a value of $+1$ and one has a value of -1, while Z(Zero) indicates there is one coefficient has a value of $+1$ and no coefficient has a value of -1.

Assuming the equal probability of O, Z sample points, the reliability of the probability will be evaluated estimate with the help of the central limit theorem.

The central limit theorem is expressed as follows: Let the random variables $X_1, X_2, \ldots X_n$ be independently identically distributed, and the mathematical expectation is μ, and the variance is $\sigma^2 \neq 0$. Then the mean $\overline{X} = \frac{1}{n} \sum_{i=1}^{n} X_i$ approximates to the normal distribution with μ and variance $\frac{\sigma}{n}$. The equivalent $\zeta = \frac{\overline{X} - \mu}{\sigma / \sqrt{n}}$ approximates the standard normal distribution.

Let the sample point O be 1 and the sample Z be 0, and if the probability is 0.5, the value of each observation will obey the zero-one distribution with $p = 0.5$.

The expected and variance of this distribution are:

$$\mu = p \times 1 + (1 - p) \times 0 = 0.5 \tag{13}$$

$$\mu^2 = (1 - \mu)^2 \times 0.5 + (1 - \mu)^2 \times 0.5 = 0.25 \tag{14}$$

In 361973 experiments, there are 184, 307 times O and 177, 666 times Z,

$$\zeta = \frac{\overline{X} - \mu}{\sigma/\sqrt{n}} = \frac{\frac{183407}{361973} - 0.5}{0.25/361972} \approx 11.04 \tag{15}$$

Typically, the level of significance is set at 5%, which means the default integral of $[-Z, Z]$ is 0.95, one side of the integral not less than 0.475. Therefore, since $Z = 1.96 \ll 11.04$, the decision is to reject the null hypothesis.

B. Detector Designing

Therefore, this statistical characteristic can be used to effectively detect steganalysis which is based on TC-B schemes. [5–7,14].

Step 1: Compute the test statistic S,

$$S = \sum \frac{(\mathbf{h}_p[m\ n] - \frac{\mathbf{h}_p[m\ n] + \mathbf{h}_p[n\ m]}{2})^2}{\frac{\mathbf{h}_p[m\ n] + \mathbf{h}_p[n\ m]}{2}} \tag{16}$$

while all trailing coefficients of videos are being traversed.

Step 2: Set a threshold η. $S > \eta$ is decided as "hiding data", and $S < \eta$ means "not hiding data". Denoting the probability density function of S as $f_S(x)$. Assume P_m is the probability of a miss:

$$P_M(\eta) = \int_\eta^\infty f_S(x)dx \tag{17}$$

Step 3: Plot and analyze data. If it is a stego-video, at first, S will nearly to value 0. Then, after traversing p (i.e., the payload of embedding), S will rise steadily. If not, the value of S rarely heads towards zero under normal circumstances.

4.4   The Steganalytic Experiments

To prove the validity of this strategy, five video sequences are encoded at frame rate 30 fps with the H.264/AVC reference software JM 19.0. The data embedding starts in the first frame in the GOP and then proceeds to subsequent frames. Then, the stego-videos are generated from them by using TC-B schemes mentioned in Sects. 2 and 3, i.e., S. Kim et al.'s [5], X. Li et al.'s [6], K. Niu et al.'s [14] and K. Liao et al.'s [7].

According to the preceding theoretical analysis, the value S is calculated while all trailing coefficients are being traversed.

The embedding rate p can be defined as the ratio of the number of actual embedded message bits to the embedding capacity. Figure 8 shows S for a sequentially information hiding with $p = 50\%$. The observation data is given as Table 2.

As can be seen, firstly, the value of S is nearly to 0. Then, after traversing the 50% information bit, S remains increasing until the end.

Thus, even though it is as naive as the histogram attack in image steganography, it can not only detect the hidden information in the video, but also estimate the embedded amount.

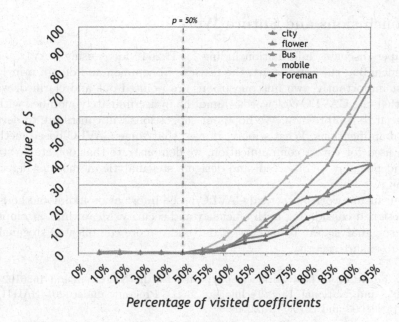

Fig. 8. The value of S for steganalytic on a sequentially information hiding with $p = 50\%$.

Table 2. The observation data of detection

	City	Flower	Bus	Mobile	Foreman
10%	0.038725	0.008444	0.562186	0.692737	0.134506
20%	0.109197	0.098954	0.144263	0.918505	0.093679
30%	0.308143	0.237939	0.152749	0.259580	0.351352
40%	0.222810	0.473226	0.062224	0.260479	0.437469
50%	0.167021	0.166318	0.082745	0.160103	0.034256
55%	0.240729	1.694671	0.263291	1.482158	0.047740
60%	1.243176	1.779992	2.966005	6.229068	2.102691
65%	7.717786	6.370842	6.040807	14.863550	4.587242
70%	11.81162	7.844273	14.512187	24.002601	5.974728
75%	20.675999	11.385219	19.764014	33.185104	8.780206
80%	24.494957	19.945367	29.503746	42.168249	15.246272
85%	25.309942	27.162142	38.774975	47.423672	17.635290
90%	29.680184	36.863571	55.986157	61.750495	23.082010
95%	39.059573	39.370593	73.692835	78.647153	25.043273

5   Conclusions and Future Work

This paper discusses information hiding for H.264 videos using CAVLC codewords, including the state-of-art, the features in common and design principles.

Most importantly, two misconceptions are pointed out and clarified, which means that the CAVLC codewords cannot be indiscriminately modified without full/partial re-compression. We hope our suggestions will contribute to develop practical applications. What's more, in case that some CAVLC-based methods may be used for covert communication, we demonstrate that detectable statistical evidence may be observed, and design a steganalytic method for detection based on it.

In our future works, practical CAVLC-based information hiding methods are to be designed considering both efficiency and security. Meanwhile, attempts of further steganalysis are to be carried out under more complicated steganalytic models to ensure security.

Acknowledgments. This work was supported by the NSFC under U1636102 and U1536105, and National Key Technology R&D Program under 2014BAH41B01, 2016YFB0801003 and 2016QY15Z2500.

References

1. Abd, M., Zekry, A.: Implementing entropy codec for H.264 video compression standard. Int. J. Comput. Appl. **129**(2), 45–53 (2015)
2. Cao, Y., Zhao, X., Feng, D.: Video steganalysis exploiting motion vector reversion-based features. IEEE Sig. Process. Lett. **19**(1), 35–38 (2012)
3. Fridrich, J.: Steganography in Digital Media: Principles, Algorithms, and Applications. Cambridge University Press, Cambridge (2009)
4. Jafari, M., Kasaei, S.: Fast intra- and inter-prediction mode decision in H.264 advanced video coding. In: IEEE Singapore International Conference on Communication Systems, pp. 1–6 (2006)
5. Kim, S., Kim, S., Hong, Y., Won, C.: Data hiding on H.264/AVC compressed video. In: Image Analysis and Recognition, pp. 698–707 (2007)
6. Li, X., Chen, H., Wang, D., Liu, T., Hou, G.: Data hiding in encoded video sequences based on H.264. In: IEEE International Conference on Computer Science and Information Technology. vol. 6, pp. 121–125. IEEE (2010)
7. Liao, K., Lian, S., Guo, Z., Wang, J.: Efficient information hiding in H.264/AVC video coding. Telecommun. Syst. **49**(2), 261–269 (2012)
8. Lin, S.D., Chuang, C.Y., Chen, M.J.: A cavlc-based video watermarking scheme for H.264/AVC codec. Int. J. Innov. Comput. Inf. Control **7**(11), 6359–6367 (2011)
9. Lin, Y.C., Hsu, I.F.: Cavlc codewords substitution for H.264/AVC video data hiding. In: IEEE International Conference on Consumer Electronics, pp. 492–493. IEEE (2014)
10. Liu, Y., Ju, L., Hu, M., Ma, X., Zhao, H.: A robust reversible data hiding scheme for H.264 without distortion drift. Neurocomputing **151**, 1053–1062 (2015)
11. Lu, C.S., Chen, J.R., Fan, K.C.: Real-time frame-dependent video watermarking in VLC domain. Sig. Process. Image Commun. **20**(7), 624–642 (2005)

12. Ma, X., Li, Z., Tu, H., Zhang, B.: A data hiding algorithm for H.264/AVC video streams without intra-frame distortion drift. IEEE Trans. Circ. Syst. Video Technol. **20**(10), 1320–1330 (2010)

13. Mobasseri, B.G., Marcinak, M.P.: Watermarking of MPEG-2 video in compressed domain using VLC mapping. In: ACM Workshop on Multimedia and Security, pp. 91–94. ACM (2005)

14. Niu, K., Zhong, W.: A video steganography scheme based on H.264 bitstreams replaced. In: IEEE International Conference on Software Engineering and Service Science, pp. 447–450. IEEE (2013)

15. Ozer, J.: Encoding for Multiple Screen Delivery. Udemy (2016)

16. Richardson, I.E.: H.264/Mpeg-4 part 10 white paper (2003)

17. Seo, Y.H., Lee, C.Y., Kim, D.W.: Low-complexity watermarking based on entropy coding in H.264/AVC. IEICE Trans. Fundam. Electron. Commun. Comput. Sci. **91**(8), 2130–2137 (2008)

18. Shobitha, G.: Implementation of cavld architecture using binary tree structures and data hiding for H.264/AVC using cavlc & exp-golomb codeword substitution. Int. J. Comput. Sci. Mob. Comput. **5**, 540–549 (2016)

19. Tew, Y., Wong, K.: An overview of information hiding in H.264/AVC compressed video. IEEE Trans. Circ. Syst. Video Technol. **24**(2), 305–319 (2014)

20. Tian, X., Le, T.M., Lian, Y.: Entropy Coders of the H.264/AVC Standard: Algorithms and VLSI Architectures. Springer, New York (2010)

21. Wang, R., Hu, L., Xu, D.: A watermarking algorithm based on the CABAC entropy coding for H.264/AVC. J. Comput. Inf. Syst. **7**(6), 2132–2141 (2011)

22. Xu, D., Wang, R.: Watermarking in H.264/AVC compressed domain using exp-golomb code words mapping. Opt. Eng. **50**(9), 097402 (2011)

23. Yao, Y., Zhang, W., Yu, N.: Inter-frame distortion drift analysis for reversible data hiding in encrypted H.264/AVC video bitstreams. Sig. Process. **128**, 531–545 (2016)

Adaptive MP3 Steganography Using Equal Length Entropy Codes Substitution

Kun Yang[1,2], Xiaowei Yi[1,2(✉)], Xianfeng Zhao[1,2], and Linna Zhou[3]

[1] State Key Laboratory of Information Security, Institute of Information
Engineering, Chinese Academy of Sciences, Beijing 100093, China
{yangkun9076,yixiaowei,zhaoxianfeng}@iie.ac.cn
[2] School of Cyber Security, University of Chinese Academy of Sciences,
Beijing 100049, China
[3] School of Information Science and Technology,
University of International Relations, Beijing 100091, China
zhoulinna@mail.tsinghua.edu.cn

Abstract. Statistical undetectability is a common problem in current
MP3 steganography. In this paper, a novel adaptive scheme of MP3
steganography is proposed for obtaining higher secure payload under the
framework of distortion minimization. To avoid disabling MP3 encoder in
the embedding process, a mapping construction algorithm using Huffman
codes of equal length is realized to hold the length of stego codestream.
Furthermore, a content-aware distortion function is designed to achieve
optimal masking effect via the psychoacoustic model (PAM). Experimental results show that our method achieves better performance than
others in terms of security and secure payload, the detection accuracy of
the proposed method is lower than 55% under 128 kbps when the relative
payload is equal to 0.25.

Keywords: MP3 steganography · Huffman code · Adaptive steganography · Distortion function · Psychoacoustic model

1 Introduction

The MP3 is becoming a kind of pervasive carrier for steganography at present,
because it is very convenient to share speech or music in almost all public plat-
form such as WeChat and YouTube. Many steganographic algorithms have been
proposed in the audio compressed domain. However, they generally have low
embedding capacity and very poor security. Conventional steganographic methods cannot satisfy security requirements, therefore adaptive MP3 steganography
is inevitable tendency in modern steganography.

Recently, several steganographic methods have been proposed for MP3 audio
files [1,5,7,8,11–15]. Wang et al. [11] presented a steganography algorithm which
changes the position of the first nonzero value within the modified discrete cosine
transform (MDCT) coefficients. In [12], according to the local signal-to-noise
ratio, the feature vector of each frame is calculated for selecting embedding

© Springer International Publishing AG 2017
C. Kraetzer et al. (Eds.): IWDW 2017, LNCS 10431, pp. 202–216, 2017.
DOI: 10.1007/978-3-319-64185-0_16

region, and then the secret massage is concealed via modifying MDCT coefficients. Liu et al. [7] proposed a steganography algorithm based on the energy of MDCT coefficients in adjacent frames. MP3Stego [8] is a well know MP3 steganographic method. The embedding operation is completed in the inner loop of MP3 encoder. The message bits are hidden based on the parity of the block length. Yan et al. [14] proposed a steganography algorithm by exploiting the rule of window switching. This algorithm establishes a mapping relationship between the secret bit and the encoding parameter, namely window type. Another algorithm proposed by Yan [13] is based on the parity of quantization step. The embedding operation is also accomplished in the inner loop of MP3 encoder. In addition, Yan [13] proposed a steganography algorithm based on the index of Huffman tables which used in MP3 encoding process. Gao et al. [5] and Yan et al. [15] respectively proposed algorithms based on Huffman codes mapping. The algorithms establish a mapping relationship between the secret bit and the Huffman code. Dong et al. [1] proposed two MP3 steganography algorithms by utilizing the Huffman codestream. Message bits are concealed within linbits or sign bits.

However, the above-mentioned steganographic methods generally have several disadvantages as follows: (1) Weak security. The detection accuracy is more than 80% with blind steganalysis [6]. (2) Low embedding capacity. For example, the maximum embedding capacity of the MP3Stego is about 154 bps (stereo, 44.1 kHz). (3) Non-adaptivity. Distortion minimization is not obeyed in existing methods. Adaptive steganography is the state-of-the-art technique to overcome the shortages [3], which is verified primely in the field of adaptive image steganography. Due to the different between the human auditory system (HAS) and the human visual system (HVS), the adaptive image steganography cannot be used directly for the audio steganography. Therefore, an adaptive MP3 steganography method is proposed in this paper, which is compatible with distortion minimization framework. In the proposed method, a mapping construction is established between Huffman codes of equal length and the binary bitstream. In addition, a distortion function is defined based on psychoacoustic model (PAM) for achieving optimized imperceptibility and security. The message bits are embedded within the binary bitstream using the syndrome-trellis codes (STCs).

The rest of this paper is organized as follows. Section 2 introduces MP3 encoding standard briefly. An adaptive steganographic scheme is proposed for the MP3 files in Sect. 3. Experimental results and discussion are shown in Sect. 4. Finally, conclusion is drawn in Sect. 5.

2   Overview of MP3 Encoder

The procedure of the MP3 encoding is shown in Fig. 1, which can be mainly divided into six steps [9]: framing, subband filter, PAM, MDCT, quantization, and Huffman encoding. The original audio is firstly partitioned into frames of 1152 samples in framing process, and each frame is further split into two granules for encoding independently. Filter bank which consists of 32 channels divides the

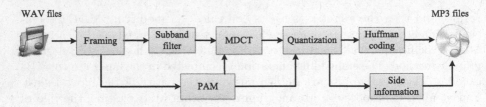

Fig. 1. The architecture of the MP3 encoder.

audio signal into 32 uniformly spaced frequency subbands. The MDCT process performs time-frequency transform. PAM process analyzes the audio signal and computes the perceptual entropy (PE). After time-frequency transform, encoder performs non-uniform quantization of the frequency lines. The quantized MDCT (QMDCT) coefficients are encoded by Huffman encoding process. Then Huffman codes and the side information are formatted into MP3 file.

The PAM is mainly based on the physical structure and the perception model of the HAS. The main purpose of PAM is to determine the window type based on the PE, which is used in the MDCT process and bit allocation. On the basis of the PAM, encoder removes the redundant information of the audio signals for efficient compressing. Including the noise, some high-frequency components of the signal are less than the auditory threshold or the masking threshold, which cannot be perceptual by human.

Quantization is the process of constraining an input from a continuous set of values to a discrete set. The key steps of quantization are realized in a three-layer iterative loop including frame loop, outer loop, and inner loop. The frame loop is designed to complete parameters initialization and to calculate remaining bits of the bit-reservoir. The outer loop calculates the quantization distortion of each scale factor band and estimates whether the distortion is under the masking threshold. Quantization is accomplished in inner loop by constantly adjusting the quantization step. Furthermore, the inner loop must meet two conditions: (1) All of QMDCT coefficients are no bigger than the theoretical maximum in the MP3 standard. (2) The length of Huffman codestream of quantized coefficients is less than the available bits.

As described in Fig. 2, a granule consist of 576 QMDCTs, which is orderly divided into three kinds of regions: big-value region, count1 region, and rzero region. Since the values of QMDCTs are equal to 0 within the rzero region, all these coefficients are no longer encoded. The values of QMDCTs in count1 region belong to $\{\pm 1, 0\}$, and quaternate coefficients are encoded by using Huffman code Table 32 and Table 33. Different with the count1 region, for the big-value region, each pair of QMDCTs are encoded using a Huffman code. The big-value region is further divided into region0, region1, and region2. Three subregions are encoded independently by utilizing the Huffman tables from Table 0 to Table 31 (Table 4 and Table 14 are unusable). If the value of a QMDCT is less than 15 then it is coded directly, otherwise the exceeding value is represented using linbits. Each nonzero coefficient possesses a sign bit, 0 indicates positive number

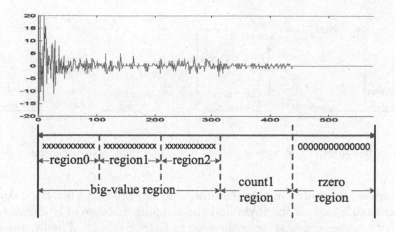

Fig. 2. Organization of QMDCTs within a granule.

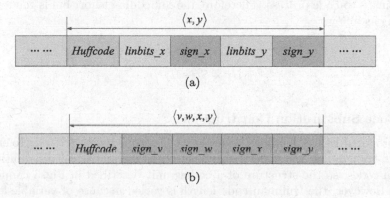

Fig. 3. Codestream structure: (a) Big-value region, and (b) Count1 region.

and 1 indicates negative number. The bitstream after Huffman coding is shown in Fig. 3. *Huffcode* denotes a Huffman code of QMDCTs, *linbits_x* denotes the linbits of the first coefficient, *sign_x* denotes the sign bit of the first coefficient, *linbits_y* denotes the linbits of the second coefficient, *sign_y* denotes the sign bit of the second coefficient. Likewise, *sign_v*, *sign_w*, *sign_x*, and *sign_y* sequentially denotes the sign bits of four QMDCTs.

3 Proposed Steganography Method

A novel adaptive steganography algorithm based on equal length entropy codes substitution (EECS) is proposed. The embedding process is located between the quantization process and the Huffman encoding process in MP3 encoder. As shown in Fig. 4, the proposed steganographic algorithm is mainly divided into four steps: code-to-binary process, distortion function computing, STCs process, binary-to-code process. First, the cover Huffman code stream H_c is transformed

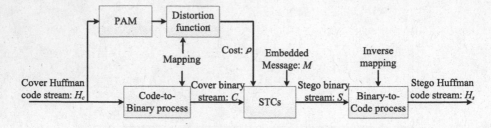

Fig. 4. A flowchart of embedding process of the proposed adaptive steganography.

into the cover binary stream C in the code-to-binary process. Then the distortion ρ is calculated based on the PAM and the mapping distance of Huffman codes. After that, message bits M are concealed in C by STCs [2]. Finally, the stego binary stream S is similarly inverse mapped to the stego Huffman code stream H_s in the binary-to-code process. Therefore, the embedding algorithm is generalized modeling as follows:

$$STC(C, M, \rho) = S, \tag{1}$$

$$H_c \times S \rightarrow H_s. \tag{2}$$

3.1   Code Substitution Construction

In the proposed EECS, Huffman codes in the big-value region are used to embed message. For holding the codestream length and the statistical distribution of Huffman codes, so the structure of a coding unit described in Fig. 3 cannot be altered. However, the Huffman code length is varied because of variable-length entropy encoding. Suppose that $h_i^{(k)}$ denotes the ith *Huffcode* within the kth Huffman table, $\langle x_i^{(k)}, y_i^{(k)} \rangle$ denotes the corresponding QMDCTs pair of $h_i^{(k)}$. Thus for $\forall i \neq j$, $h_i^{(k)}$ and $h_j^{(k)}$ is a pair of substitutable codes, which satisfies the following three conditions:

(C1) Length of Huffman codes. The length of $h_i^{(k)}$ is equal to the length of $h_j^{(k)}$,

$$L(h_i^{(k)}) = L(h_j^{(k)}). \tag{3}$$

(C2) Number of sign bits. The number of sign bits of $\langle x_i^{(k)}, y_i^{(k)} \rangle$ is equal to the number of sign bits of $\langle x_j^{(k)}, y_j^{(k)} \rangle$,

$$\Theta(\langle x_i^{(k)}, y_i^{(k)} \rangle) = \Theta(\langle x_j^{(k)}, y_j^{(k)} \rangle). \tag{4}$$

(C3) Linbits flags. The linbits flag of $x_i^{(k)}$ is consistent with the linbits flag of $x_j^{(k)}$, likewise the same as $y_i^{(k)}$ and $y_j^{(k)}$,

$$G(x_i^{(k)}) = G(x_i^{(k)}), G(y_i^{(k)}) = G(y_i^{(k)}). \tag{5}$$

According to (C3) in (5), a conservative scheme is just to use QMDCTs whose values are less than 15 in big-value region for hiding message. Based on the above-mentioned conditions in (3)–(5), a code substitution construction is described in detail as follows.

The set $\Pi^{(k)}$ contains all Huffman codes in the kth Huffman table. In the proposed algorithm, $\Pi^{(k)}$ is divided into two subsets: $\Pi_u^{(k)}$ and $\Pi_v^{(k)}$. Huffman codes in $\Pi_v^{(k)}$ are available for embedding message. $\Pi_v^{(k)}$ is generated via a iterator. $\Pi_v^{(k)}$ is initialized to $\varnothing$. After that, for $\exists h_i, h_j \in \Pi^{(k)} \backslash \Pi_v^{(k)} (i \neq j)$, if (h_i, h_j) satisfies the conditions in (3)–(5), then moving h_i and h_j to $\Pi_v^{(k)}$, otherwise moving them to $\Pi_u^{(k)}$. Repeating this process until $\Pi^{(k)} = \varnothing$.

Each Huffman code h_i in $\Pi_v^{(k)}$ is numbered according to the placement order of putting into $\Pi_v^{(k)}$. Huffman codes in $\Pi_v^{(k)}$ are divided into $\Pi_0^{(k)}$ and $\Pi_1^{(k)}$. When the placement order is odd, h_i is put into $\Pi_1^{(k)}$, otherwise it is put into $\Pi_0^{(k)}$. Huffman codes in $\Pi_0^{(k)}$ represent the bit '0'. Contrarily, Huffman codes in $\Pi_1^{(k)}$ represent the bit '1'. According to the distribution characteristics of Huffman codes length, two substitutable Huffman codes are generally more closer with zigzag scanning. As an example, the traversal of the No. 7 Huffman table is described in Fig. 5. Based on (C2) in (4), QMDCT pairs are classified into R_0, R_1, and R_2, which are sealed for independently performing search iterators. The traversal order is indicated by arrows in Fig. 5. These Huffman codes displayed with solid points are $h_{\langle 2,3 \rangle}, h_{\langle 3,2 \rangle}, h_{\langle 5,1 \rangle}, h_{\langle 4,2 \rangle}, h_{\langle 2,4 \rangle}, h_{\langle 1,5 \rangle}$. The length of these six Huffman codes is equal to eight. According to the traversal order, these six Huffman codes constitute three mapping pairs: $h_{\langle 2,3 \rangle} \longleftrightarrow h_{\langle 3,2 \rangle}, h_{\langle 5,1 \rangle} \longleftrightarrow h_{\langle 4,2 \rangle}, h_{\langle 2,4 \rangle} \longleftrightarrow h_{\langle 1,5 \rangle}$. As described in Fig. 6, $h_{\langle 2,3 \rangle}, h_{\langle 5,1 \rangle}, h_{\langle 2,4 \rangle}$ are in $\Pi_1^{(k)}$,

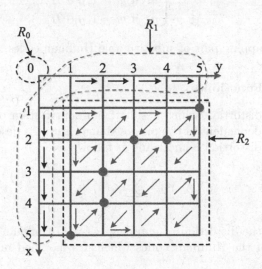

Fig. 5. Zigzag scanning of the #7 Huffman table.

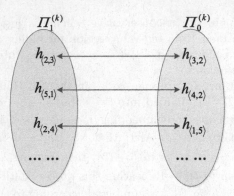

Fig. 6. An example of mapping relations of substitutable Huffman codes.

and $h_{\langle 3,2 \rangle}$, $h_{\langle 4,2 \rangle}$, $h_{\langle 1,5 \rangle}$ are in $\Pi_0^{(k)}$. Hence, in the code-to-binary process, the transfer function is defined as:

$$f_{ctb}(h) = \begin{cases} 0, & \text{if } h \in \Pi_0^{(k)}, \\ 1, & \text{if } h \in \Pi_1^{(k)}, \\ \varnothing, & \text{otherwise.} \end{cases} \tag{6}$$

Likewise, the inverse process is presented as:

$$f_{btc}(m,g) = \begin{cases} g, & \text{if } m = 0, g \in \Pi_0^{(k)}, \\ \hat{g}, & \text{if } m = 0, g \in \Pi_1^{(k)}, \\ \hat{g}, & \text{if } m = 1, g \in \Pi_0^{(k)}, \\ g, & \text{if } m = 1, g \in \Pi_1^{(k)}, \end{cases} \tag{7}$$

where $(g, \hat{g})$ is a mapping pair of substitutable Huffman codes.

3.2   Distortion Function

Suppose that the distortion which results from substitution of each Huffman code is mutually independent in the proposed algorithm. As described in Filler's work [2], the total distortion is modeling as follows:

$$D(X,Y) = \sum_{i=1}^{n} \rho_i(h_i, h_i'), \tag{8}$$

where $\rho_i(h_i, h_i')$ is the distortion of mapping between Huffman code h_i and h_i', n is the number of the Huffman codes which are modified in the embedding process.

The distortion in the proposed algorithm is mainly affected by two factors: the influence of PAM and the modified magnitude of coefficients. These two factors cause the degeneration of the audio and the change in statistical characteristics of Huffman codes.

The influence of PAM is mainly reflected as follows. The hearing frequency range of the human ear is usually between 20 Hz and 20 kHz. However, the human ear has different sensitivity to each frequency band. The sensitivity can be reflected by the absolute threshold of hearing which is obtained by large number of experiments. The absolute threshold of hearing describes how much energy a pure tone needs to be heard in a noise free environment at different frequencies. It can be approximated by the following formula:

$$T_f = 3.64 \times \left(\frac{f}{1000}\right)^{-0.8} - 6.5 \times e^{-0.6 \times (\frac{f}{1000} - 3.3)^2} + 10^{-3} \times \left(\frac{f}{1000}\right)^4, \quad (9)$$

where f is the frequency, T_f is the absolute threshold of hearing at frequency f. The smaller T_f means the higher sensitivity of human ear to audio signal. It is more likely to cause the distortion when the modification occurs in the more sensitive frequency band.

The modified magnitude of coefficients also affects the distortion. When Huffman code h_i is replaced by h_i', the QMDCT coefficients pair $\langle x_i, y_i \rangle$ becomes $\langle x_i', y_i' \rangle$ correspondingly. This change leads to the degeneration of audio. To measure the distortion, the difference between $\langle x_i, y_i \rangle$ and $\langle x_i', y_i' \rangle$ is calculated firstly. The definition of difference is given by:

$$d_i = \left| x_i' - x_i \right| + \left| y_i' - y_i \right|, \quad (10)$$

where d_i is the difference between h_i and h_i'. The greater the d_i, the larger the difference between these two Huffman codes.

From the above analysis, the distortion function is defined as:

$$\rho_i = \frac{1}{\log_2(\frac{t_{2i} + t_{2i+1}}{2} + \sigma)} \times d_i = \frac{\left| x_i' - x_i \right| + \left| y_i' - y_i \right|}{\log_2(\frac{t_{2i} + t_{2i+1}}{2} + \sigma)}, \quad (11)$$

where i is the index of h_i in the Huffman code stream, t_{2i} is the absolute threshold of hearing of the $(2i)$th frequency line, i.e. the T_f when the f is the $(2i)$th frequency line, σ is a constant to ensure that $(\frac{t_{2i} + t_{2i+1}}{2} + \sigma)$ is greater than 0, the logarithmic operation reduces the influence of some extreme values.

3.3   Embedding Procedure and Extraction Procedure

Embedding Procedure. First, the cover Huffman code stream H_c is transformed into cover binary stream C. $D_{df}(\cdot)$ is the distortion function. Then C and the distortion ρ are scrambled using the same key k. Message bits M are embedded into C by STCs. Finally, the stego binary stream S is transformed into stego Huffman code stream H_s after the inverse operation of scrambling. The pseudocode of embedding procedure is described as Algorithm 1.

Algorithm 1. The process of information embedding

Input: H_c, M, k, σ;
Output: H_s;
 1: **for** $i = 1$ to the length of H_c **do**
 2:    $C[i] = f_{ctb}(H_c[i])$
 3: **end for**
 4: $\rho = D_{df}(H_c, \sigma)$
 5: Scramble the C and ρ using the key k
 6: $S = STC(C, M, \rho)$
 7: Inverse scramble the S
 8: **for** $i = 1$ to the length of H_c **do**
 9:    $S[i] = f_{btc}(S[i], H_c[i])$
10: **end for**
11: **return** H_s

Extraction Procedure. First, the stego Huffman code stream H_s is transformed into stego binary stream S. Then S is scrambled using the same key as embedding process. Finally, secret message bits M are extracted from S by STCs. The pseudocode of extraction procedure is described as Algorithm 2.

Algorithm 2. The process of information extraction

Input: H_s, key
Output: M
 1: **for** $i = 1$ to the length of H_s **do**
 2:    $S[i] = f_{ctb}(H_s[i])$
 3: **end for**
 4: Scramble S using the same key k with embedding process
 5: Extract M from S by $STCs$
 6: **return** M

---

4   Experimental Results

The experimental settings are shown in Table 1 in detail, where w and h are the width and the height of the generated matrix in STCs, respectively. And σ is the parameter in (11). Our experiments evaluate the proposed algorithm in three aspects: embedding capacity, imperceptibility, undetectability. Meanwhile, the proposed algorithm is compared with the other three steganography algorithms. These three algorithms are MP3Stego [8], Huffman Code Mapping (HCM) [15] and Adaptive Post-Steganography (APS) [16]. The MP3Stego is the first audio steganography software for MP3. Meanwhile, it is a classical audio steganography algorithm. The HCM is a steganography algorithm which is also based on Huffman code mapping. The APS embeds message in count1 region rather than big-value region.

Table 1. The settings of experimental parameters

	Parameter	Value
Datasets	Quantity	1000
	Channel	Stereo
	Genres	Blues, classical, country, folk, pop, jazz
	Duration	10 s
	Digitalizing bit	16 bits
LAME	Version	Lame-3.99.5
	Bit rate	128 kbps, 320 kbps
	Other parameters	Default
EECS	w	2, 4, 10
	h	7
	σ	10

4.1 Embedding Capacity

The embedding capacities of these four algorithms under various bit rates and w are shown in Fig. 7.

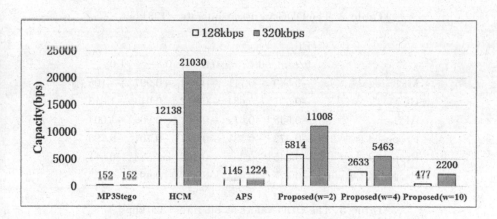

Fig. 7. Comparison of the embedding capacity.

From the Fig. 7, we can see that the embedding capacity of EECS is higher than that of MP3Stego but lower than that of HCM. That is because the payload of EECS is controlled by w and the maximum payload is 0.5 when w is equal to 2. Therefore, the embedding capacity of EECS (w is equal to 2) is roughly half that of HCM. The embedding capacity of EECS is higher than that of APS except one situation that the bit rate is 128 kbps and w is equal to 10. The greater the w, the lower the payload. This situation can be reflected in the Fig. 7

that great w results in the low embedding capacity. In addition, the embedding capacity of EECS increase with increasing the bit rate. When the bit rate is set to 320 kbps and w is equal to 2, the embedding capacity of EECS is up to 11 kbps.

4.2　Imperceptibility

Perceptual evaluation of audio quality (PEAQ) [10] is a standardized algorithm for objectively measuring perceived audio quality. The objective difference grade (ODG) is the main output parameter of this perceptual measurement method. Generally, the ODG has a range between 0 and -4. The closer the ODG value is to 0, the higher the similarity between the test audio and the reference audio. When the similarity of two audios is very high, the ODG value may be greater than 0. In this experiment, the reference audio is the WAV decompressed from cover MP3 and the test audio is the WAV decompressed from stego MP3. In addition, the imperceptibility is influenced by the embedding rate (ER). The ER here is defined as:

$$ER = \frac{n}{N},\qquad(12)$$

where N is the total number of frames of the audio file, n is the number of frames used to embed message. The results are shown in Tables 2 and 3.

Table 2. The ODG values at bit rate $= 128$ kbps

	ER				
	0.2	0.4	0.6	0.8	1.0
MP3Stego	-0.569	-0.711	-0.854	-0.997	-1.105
HCM	-0.551	-0.684	-0.812	-0.914	-1.013
APS	-0.548	-0.672	-0.801	-0.906	-1.004
Proposed (w = 2)	-0.473	-0.535	-0.627	-0.701	-0.796
Proposed (w = 4)	-0.445	-0.487	-0.536	-0.573	-0.611
Proposed (w = 10)	-0.427	-0.442	-0.479	-0.492	-0.513

Table 3. The ODG values at bit rate $= 320$ kbps

	ER				
	0.2	0.4	0.6	0.8	1.0
MP3Stego	0.043	0.028	0.014	-0.002	-0.011
HCM	0.048	0.041	0.032	0.024	0.013
APS	0.042	0.033	0.021	0.013	0.005
Proposed (w = 2)	0.051	0.042	0.038	0.030	0.022
Proposed (w = 4)	0.053	0.048	0.042	0.038	0.034
Proposed (w = 10)	0.056	0.054	0.051	0.049	0.047

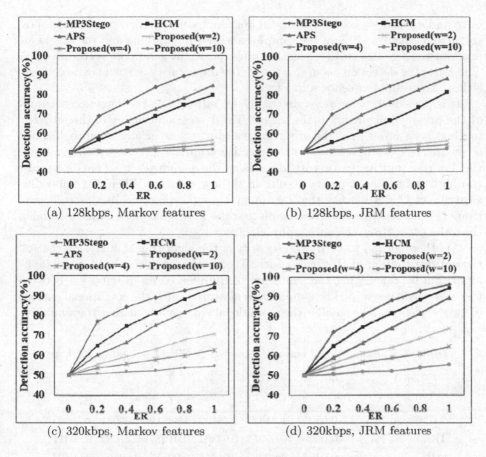

(a) 128kbps, Markov features

(b) 128kbps, JRM features

(c) 320kbps, Markov features

(d) 320kbps, JRM features

Fig. 8. Detection accuracy using Markov and JRM features

It is obvious that the ODG value of EECS is greater than that of MP3Stego HCM and APS all the time. When the bit rate is set to 128 kbps, the ODG values of these algorithms are all lower than 0. On the contrary, when the bit rate is 320 kbps, the ODG values are basically greater than 0. The ODG values decrease with increasing the ER. Besides, the ODG value of EECS increases with increasing the parameter w. Thereby it proves that the proposed algorithm has good performance on imperceptibility.

4.3 Undetectability

In the experiments, we use steganalysis algorithms which are proposed in [4,6] to detect the proposed algorithm and the other three algorithms. The steganalysis algorithm proposed in [6] is based on Markov features. Markov features are often used in audio steganalysis and achieve good results. And the algorithm proposed in [4] is based on the JPEG domain rich model (JRM). JRM features are outstanding discrete cosine transform domain features to detect steganography. In the experiments, 70% of the samples are used for training and the others are used for testing. The classifier used in our experiment is support vector machine. The lower the detection accuracy, the higher the security of steganography algorithm. The results are shown in Fig. 8.

It is obvious that for any value of the bit rate and w, the detection accuracy of the proposed algorithm is the lowest. The detection accuracy of the proposed method is far lower than the other three algorithms especially when the bit rate is set to 128 kbps. In addition, the detection accuracy increases with increasing the bit rate and increases with decreasing the parameter w. That is because the high embedding capacity results in the low security. When the embedding capacity of EECS reaches the maximum, the detection accuracy is still lower than 75%. A conclusion can be made that the EECS has better undetectability than the other three steganography algorithms.

Another method to verify the security of the algorithm is analyzing the statistical distribution of Huffman codes. This method detects the steganography algorithm by calculating the similarity of Huffman codes distribution between the cover and the stego. The similarity is measured using the conditional entropy of two sequences. The smaller the conditional entropy, the higher the similarity.

Table 4. The conditional entropy measured at ER = 1, bit rate = 128 kbps

	Table No.					
	9	12	15	24	25	26
MP3Stego	0.98254	1.31427	1.78192	1.88619	1.60931	1.16023
HCM	0.00295	0.01962	0.03302	0.01987	0.01002	0.00411
APS	0.00621	0.00932	0.01448	0.00512	0.00603	0.00404
Proposed (w = 2)	0.00169	0.00401	0.00425	0.00493	0.00311	0.00262
Proposed (w = 4)	0.00037	0.00116	0.00139	0.00174	0.00122	0.00098
Proposed (w = 10)	0.00003	0.00002	0.00011	0.00015	0.00006	0.00004

Table 5. The conditional entropy measured at ER = 1, bit rate = 320 kbps

	Table No.					
	9	12	15	24	25	26
MP3Stego	1.14861	1.36296	1.94305	1.96382	1.73284	1.28427
HCM	0.09721	0.05236	0.06326	0.03908	0.02017	0.00932
APS	0.00701	0.01039	0.01593	0.00869	0.00827	0.00502
Proposed (w = 2)	0.00425	0.00721	0.00983	0.00924	0.00615	0.00631
Proposed (w = 4)	0.00092	0.00322	0.00417	0.00472	0.00326	0.00202
Proposed (w = 10)	0.00037	0.00031	0.00084	0.00072	0.00033	0.00029

And the higher the similarity, the better the undetectability. The function of calculating the similarity is defined as follows:

$$H_p(q) = \sum_{i=1}^{n} q_i \log_2 \left(\frac{q_i}{p_i} \right), \tag{13}$$

where n is the number of bins in the distribution histogram of Huffman codes, p_i is the probability of the ith bin in the distribution histogram of Huffman codes in cover, q_i is the probability of the ith bin in the distribution histogram of Huffman codes in stego. Six Huffman tables, which have higher usage frequency than others, are used in our experiments. The other Huffman tables have similar results. The experimental results are shown in Tables 4 and 5.

From the experimental results, it is obvious that the conditional entropies of EECS are lower than other algorithms. It can be inferred that the Huffman codes distribution is kept well after embedding message in the audio. This result is consistent with the result of the steganalysis algorithms above. The smaller the change of Huffman code distribution histogram, the lower the detection accuracy. Therefore, it can be concluded that the proposed algorithm has better undetectability.

5   Conclusion and Future Work

In this paper, we propose an adaptive MP3 steganography algorithm. In the proposed algorithm, a mapping relationship between Huffman codes and binary bits is established. In addition, a content-aware distortion function based on PAM and the mapping is constructed. The message is embedded in the audio file by substituting the Huffman codes of equal length. Experimental results show that the proposed algorithm does better than the other three audio steganography algorithms in terms of security and secure payload. The detection accuracy of the proposed method is lower than 55% under 128 kbps when the relative payload is equal to 0.25.

However, a shortcoming of the proposed method is that it doesn't take into account the statistical characteristics of distribution when the cost is calculated. For example, the statistical distribution of Huffman codes isn't taken into account. Although the experiment demonstrates that the Huffman code distribution is kept well in the proposed method, it is still a weakness for the security of the proposed algorithm. In the future work, we will construct a distortion function based on other aspects of PAM or statistical characteristics of Huffman code and achieve steganography based on the multiple-base system.

Acknowledgments. This work was supported by the NSFC under U1636102, U1536207 and U1536105, and National Key Technology R&D Program under 2014BAH41B01, 2016YFB0801003, 2016QY15Z2500 and 2016QY08D1600.

References

1. Dong, Y.: Research on information hiding based on mp3. Master's thesis, Beijing University of Posts and Telecommunications (BUPT), Beijing (2015)
2. Filler, T., Judas, J., Fridrich, J.: Minimizing additive distortion in steganography using syndrome-trellis codes. IEEE Trans. Inf. Forensics Secur. 6(3), 920–935 (2011)
3. Fridrich, J.: Steganography in Digital Media: Principles, Algorithms, and Applications. Cambridge University Press, New York (2009)
4. Fridrich, J.: Steganalysis of JPEG images using rich models. In: Proceedings of SPIE - The International Society for Optical Engineering, vol. 8303, pp. 7–20 (2012)
5. Gao, H.: The mp3 steganography algorithm based on huffman coding. Acta Scientiarum Naturalium Univ. Sunyatseni 46(4), 32–35 (2007)
6. Jin, C., Wang, R., Yan, D.: Steganalysis of mp3stego with low embedding-rate using markov feature. Multimed. Tools Appl. 76(5), 6143–6158 (2017)
7. Liu, W., Wang, S., Zhang, X.: Audio watermarking based on partial mp3 encoding. Acta Scientiarum Naturalium Univ. Sunyatseni 43(S2), 26–33 (2004)
8. Petitcolas, F.A.: MP3Stego (1998)
9. Smith, J.O., Abel, J.S.: ISO/IEC 11172-3: Information Technology - Coding of Moving Pictures and Associated Audio for Digital Storage Media at Up to about 1.5 Mbit/s - Part 3: Audio (1993)
10. Thiede, T.: PEAQ-the ITU standard for objective measurement of perceived audio quality. J. Audio Eng. Soc. Audio Eng. Soc. 48(1), 3–29 (2000)
11. Wang, C., Chen, T., Chao, W.: A new audio watermarking based on modified discrete cosine transform of MPEG/audio layer III. In: Proceedings of 2004 IEEE International Conference on Networking, Sensing and Control, pp. 984–989 (2004)
12. Wu, G., Zhuang, Y., Wu, F., Pan, Y.: Adaptive audio watermarking based on snr in localized regions. J. Zhejiang Univ. Sci. A (Sci. Eng.) 6A, 53–57 (2005)
13. Yan, D.: Steganography and Steganalysis of Compressed Domain Audio. Ph.D. thesis, Ningbo University, Ningbo (2012)
14. Yan, D., Wang, R., Yu, X., Zhu, J.: Steganography for MP3 audio by exploiting the rule of window switching. Comput. Secur. 31(5), 704–716 (2012)
15. Yan, D., Wang, R., Zhang, L.: A large capacity MP3 steganography algorithm based on huffman coding. J. Sichuan Univ. (Nat. Sci. Ed.) 48(6), 1281–1286 (2011)
16. Zhang, Y., Pan, F., Shen, J., Li, N.: A post-adaptive steganography algorithm based on MP3. Comput. Sci. 43(8), 114–117 (2016)

A Steganalysis Scheme for AAC Audio Based on MDCT Difference Between Intra and Inter Frame

Yanzhen Ren[1,2(✉)], Qiaochu Xiong[2], and Lina Wang[1,2]

[1] Key Laboratory of Aerospace Information Security and Trusted Computing,
Ministry of Education, Wuhan, China
[2] School of Computer Science, Wuhan University, Wuhan, China
renyz@whu.edu.cn, xiongqiaochu_whu@163.com, lnawang@163.com

Abstract. AAC (Advanced Audio Coding), as an efficient audio codec, has been used widely in mobile internet applications. Steganographies based on AAC are emerging and bringing new challenges to information content security. In this paper, an AAC steganalysis scheme to detect the steganographies which embedded secret information by modifying MDCT coefficient is proposed. The modification of MDCT coefficient will cause the statistical characteristic of the difference between inter-frame and intra-frame changed simultaneously. Based on this ideal, we proposed a scheme to extract combination features to classify cover and stego audio. There are 16 groups of sub-features to represent the correlation characteristics between the multi-order differential coefficients of Intra and Inter frame (MDI2), each sub-feature's performance are analyzed in this paper, and an ensemble classifier is used to realize the steganalyzer. Experiment results show that the detection accuracy of the proposed scheme are above 85.34% when the relative embed rate is over 50%, this performance is obviously better than the literatures methods. Due to the similarity of the coding principle of AAC and MP3, the proposed features can be applied into MP3 steganalysis.

Keywords: MDCT · AAC · MP3 · Steganography · Steganalysis

1 Introduction

As an audio coding standard for lossy digital audio compression, AAC has been used widely in mobile internet applications. AAC is designed to be the successor of the MP3 format, and generally achieves better sound quality than MP3 at similar bit rates [1]. AAC is adopted as the default audio format for many popular applications and smart phones, such as YouTube, iPhone, Play Station, Android and BlackBerry etc., and it is also supported by manufacturers of in-dash car audio systems.

Y. Ren—This work is supported by the Natural Science Foundation of China (NSFC) under the grant No. U1536114, No. U1536204, and China Scholarship Council.

© Springer International Publishing AG 2017
C. Kraetzer et al. (Eds.): IWDW 2017, LNCS 10431, pp. 217–231, 2017.
DOI: 10.1007/978-3-319-64185-0_17

With the widely use of AAC, it has became an ideal carrier to hide secret information [2–7]. There are three main embedding domain for AAC compression parameters: MDCT coefficients [2–4], Huffman coding parameter [5,6] and quantization parameter [7]. MDCT coefficients is the mainly parameter of AAC, occupies almost 70% of the AAC coding bit stream. Slightly modifications of MDCT coefficients will not cause the declining of hearing quality. Therefore, the steganography schemes by modifying the MDCT coefficient generally have good concealment and large embedding capability. Wang [2] proposed to divide the MDCT band into different regions: Big Data Region, Small Data Region and Zero Data Region, embeds secret message into Small Data Region. Zhu [3] proposed to embed secret information by using the characteristics of the sign bits of Huffman codeword according to the structure of AAC bitstream. The coefficients which absolute value is small were changed. Zhu [5] divides the Huffman codeword into two similar groups, and embed the secret message according to the corresponding codeword groups. All schemes will cause the change of the MDCT coefficients, and have high capacity and good imperceptibility.

Up to now, there are many steganalysis methods [8–13] against MP3 steganography, but there is a fat lot of steganalysis methods for AAC. Due to the similarity between the coding principle of AAC and MP3, the methods of those MP3 steganalysis schemes can be applied into AAC steganalysis. Most of the steganalysis schemes for MP3 are designed to detect MP3Stego [14], which is an open tool to embed secret message into MP3 bitstream by controlling parity of the block length. The processing mode of MP3Stego will change the value of the MDCT coefficients. There are two types of mainstream steganalysis schemes for MP3: special scheme and general scheme. In special scheme, the features are designed based on direct change of MP3Stego. Yan [8] find that MP3Stego will change of the quantization step, so they proposed to use standard deviation of its second-order sequence as the steganalysis feature. Yan [9] found that the number of bits in the bit reservoir will be changed, they proposed to extract the statistic characters of bit reservoir and use calibration to build the steganalysis features. Yu [10] proposed to extract the statistic features of the big values in side information, used recompression to improve the features sensitivity. Those special schemes do well in MP3Stego, but failed to detect other steganography scheme of MDCT coefficients modification. In general schemes, the difference between MDCT coefficients are analyzed. Qiao [11] proposed to extract the second-order differential QMDCT (quantized MDCT) coefficients of the same sub-band, build four steganalysis feature sets: frequency-based sub-band moment statistical features, accumulative Markov transition features, accumulative neighboring joint density features and the shape parameters of generalized Gaussian; Kuriakose [12] fused Markov feature and accumulative neighboring joint density of the second-order differential QMDCT coefficients from inter-frame, and improved the performance. Based on the first-order differential QMDCT coefficients of the same sub-band, Jin [13] proposed to extract Markov features from its horizontal and vertical direction. The general schemes have good versatility.

However, The main goal of current MP3 steganalysis schemes is to detect MP3Stego. MP3Stego will change the parameters of quantization process, it will disturb the correlations of inter-frame MDCT coefficients obviously. Therefore, the current MP3 steganalysis schemes extract the features based on the correlation between adjacent MDCT coefficients in the same frame. But for AAC, the steganography schemes based on MDCT [2–4] have different influence. Those schemes modified MDCT coefficients from different domain, for example: the values of MDCT [2], the sign of MDCT [3] and the Huffman codeword [5]. The different embedding domain will cause different characters distribution. Since that the current MP3 steganalysis schemes didn't work well for AAC. To improve the generality of the AAC steganalysis, in this paper, based on the structure of AAC frame, multi-order difference between inter-frame and intra-frame are extracted, 16 sets of features are proposed to measure the influence of MDCT modification comprehensively.

The rest of the paper is organized as follows. In Sect. 2, The characters of MDCT in AAC are analyzed. In Sect. 3, our proposed AAC steganalysis scheme based on MDCT Difference between Intra and Inter Frame are introduced. In Sect. 4, the performance of each sub-features are analyzed. Experiments results are shown in Sect. 5, and conclusion is drawn in Sect. 6.

2   The Characteristics of MDCT in AAC

2.1   The Principle of AAC Coding

AAC [15] is a lossy perceptual compression standard which is based on psychoacoustic model. Its encoding principle is showed in Fig. 1. The AAC encoding process mainly includes those modules: Psychoacoustic model, Filter-bank MDCT transform, Spectral processing, MDCT coefficient quantization and Huffman coding. The core encoding process is MDCT coefficient transform and quantization.

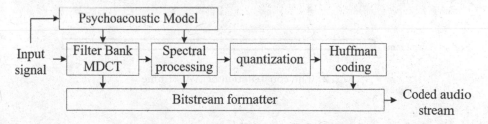

Fig. 1. Encoding procedure of AAC

The psychoacoustic model calculates the maximum distortion energy which is masked by the input signal energy, and figure up a set of signal-to-mask ratios and thresholds, labels the block type of the MDCT with long, start, stop or short types. The filter bank takes the appropriate block of time samples, modulates them by the appropriate window function, and performs the MDCT process. Each block of input samples is overlapped by 50% with the immediately preceding block and the following block. Quantization module is subdivided into three levels which are called frame iteration loop, outer iteration loop and inner iteration loop. The inner iteration loop quantizes the MDCT coefficients until they can be coded with an available number of bits. Outer iteration loop checks the distortion of each sub band, and if the allowed distortion is exceeded, attenuates the sub-band and calls the inner iteration loop again. Huffman coding is done inside the inner iteration loop, it is part of an iterative process, 1024 quantized MDCT coefficients are clipped into several sub-bands, and section coding is used. A section may include several sub-bands, each section use one codebook to encode. In each sub-band, four or two quantized MDCT coefficients are grouped and encoded as one Huffman word.

MDCT coefficients are the mainly coding parameters of AAC. According to AAC coding principle, there are two types of AAC audio frame: long frame and short frame. If the audio signal is smoothly and steadily, long frame is used, and there are 1024 MDCT coefficients in each long frame. Short frame is used when the signal is acutely. The MDCT coefficients are divided into 8 uniform short window, and each short window includes 128 MDCT coefficients. Each window is coded by MDCT transition, quantization and Huffman coding separately, which is called short frame. The structure of AAC frames is shown in Fig. 2, there are long frames and short frames, they are encoded separately.

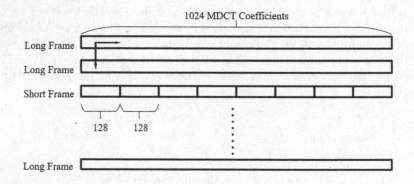

Fig. 2. The construction of AAC frame

2.2 Influences of MDCT Embedding

MDCT coefficients are the mainly coding parameter of AAC, a slightly modifications of MDCT coefficients wont bring in obviously hearing perception, so steganography schemes of AAC MDCT domain [2,3,5] usually have a good concealment and large embedding space. However, due to the short-term relationship of the audio in the time domain and frequency domain, the MDCT coefficients in

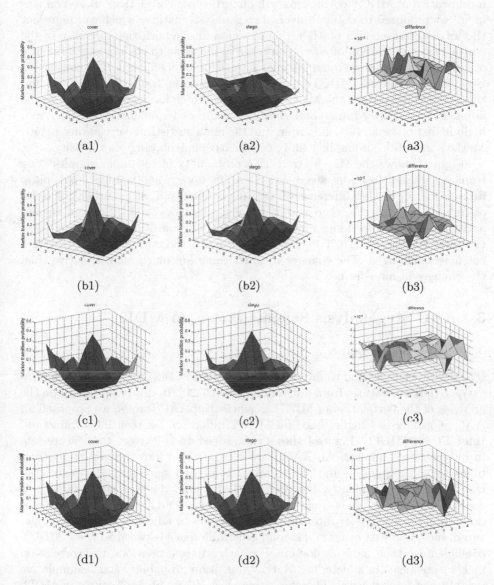

Fig. 3. Markov transition probability of first and second order differential MDCT coefficients. *a1–a3* and *b1–b3* are the first order of features distribution from intra-frame and inter-frame separately. *c1–c3* and *d1–d3* are the second order of features distribution from intra-frame and inter-frame separately. *a1, b1, c1, d1* are cover audios. *a2, b2, c2, d2* are stego audios. *a3, b3, c3, d3* are the difference between cover and stego audios.

the same frame and adjacent frames will keep certain degree of correlation. So the modification of MDCT coefficients will disturb those correlations. Based on this ideal, we proposed to design universal steganalysis features which can represent the intrinsic correlation of MDCT coefficients, distinguish the difference of the correlation distribution of cover and stego audio. Due to the obvious difference of long frame and short frame, we deal with them independently. The correlation between the adjacent MDCT coefficients in the same frame (intra-frame) and the correlation between the MDCT coefficients which has same frequency in the adjacent frame (inter-frame) and evaluated, multi-order differences are analyzed, include first order and second order, and the main statistical correlations include Markov transition probability and accumulative neighboring joint density.

Figure 3 shows the Markov transition probability of 100 audio samples' long frames, includes the cover, stego and their difference. There are four kinds data: first and second order difference of inter-frame, first and second order difference of intra-frame. All the stego audios are generated by Zhu [3], 96 kbps bitrate and the relative embedding rate (RER) is 100%. From Fig. 3 we can find that the modification of MDCT coefficients will make those correlations of MDCT coefficients changed. The changes in intra-frame are much more sensitive than the changes in inter-frame.

3   AAC Steganalysis Scheme Based on MDI2

3.1   Proposed Scheme

It is an effective method to improve the generality of the steganalysis method to extract the rich features from different angles [16–20]. In this paper, based on the analysis of the correlation of MDCT coefficient of AAC frames, we proposed an AAC steganalysis scheme based on MDCT difference between Intra-frame and Inter Frame (MDI2). Figure 4 shows the procedure to extract the feature sets in our proposed scheme. All AAC frames are divided into two groups by their block type: long frame and short frame, combined separately, and extracted the features independently. For each kind of frame, the correlation of MDCT coefficients between intra-frame and inter-frame are analyzed. In each analysis domain of intra-frame or inter-frame, two degrees of adjacent relation are measured, including first order and second order difference between adjacent MDCT coefficients in their analysis domain. For each adjacent relations, two correlation metrics are measured, including Markov transition probability and accumulative neighboring joint density. Therefore, there are 16 sets of sub-features in MDI2. Based on the analysis as follow, the range of MDCT coefficients is from -4 to 4, the number of each sub-feature is $9 * 9 = 81$, and the dimensionality of MDI2 is $16 * 81 = 1296$. Due to the good performance of ensemble classifier [21] on high dimensional features, ensemble classifier was adopted in our schemes to evaluate the classification performance of our proposed features. The key methods in this schemes are described in detail as follows.

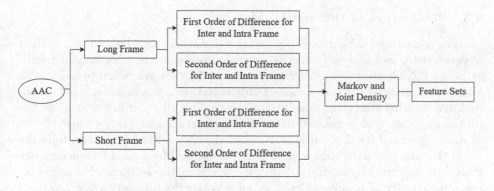

Fig. 4. Feature construction method of the proposed scheme

3.2 Differential Matrix of Inter-frame and Intra-frame

The differential operation of signal sequence can be used to distinguish the isolated point effectively. In order to get a better view of the difference between cover and stego audio, we extract features from differential MDCT coefficients. In addition, considering the limited detecting performance of independent intra-frame or inter-frame feature, we have thought of both inter-frame and intra-frame features separately.

A MDCT matrix: $M_{N*1024} = \{f_1, f_2, \cdots, f_i, \cdots, f_N\}$ is formed. N means the number of frames, f_i is consisted by 1024 MDCT coefficients of the i_{th} frame (for short frame, the number of MDCT coefficients is 128 here). Secondly, first and second order differential MDCT coefficients of intra-frame and inter-frame are calculated, which are showed in Eqs. (1) to (4). r and c are the index of MDCT matrix, so we can get four differential matrix M_{order}^{type}, in which $order$ stands for the order of differential matrix, $type$ stands for feature constructing direction, and $inter$ is inter-frame and $intra$ is intra-frame.

$$M_1^{inter} = \{x_{r,c} | x_{r,c} = M(r+1, c) - M(r, c)\} \tag{1}$$

$$M_2^{inter} = \{x_{r,c} | x_{r,c} = M(r, c) + M(r+2, c) - 2 * M(r+1, c)\} \tag{2}$$

$$M_1^{intra} = \{x_{r,c} | x_{r,c} = M(r, c+1) - M(r, c)\} \tag{3}$$

$$M_2^{intra} = \{x_{r,c} | x_{r,c} = M(r, c) + M(r, c+2) - 2 * M(r, c+1)\} \tag{4}$$

In order to reduce the computational complexity, a thresholding technique is applied to $\mathbf{D}$ ($D \in \{M_1^{inter}, M_2^{inter}, M_1^{intra}, M_2^{intra}\}$) as Eq. (5). For an arbitrary $x_{r,c}, \{x_{r,c} | x_{r,c} \in D\}$, r and c is the index of $\mathbf{D}$. If $x_{r,c}$ is either larger than a predefined threshold T or smaller than $-T$, it will be represented by T or $-T$ correspondingly. In our experiment part, T is set to 4.

$$x_{r,c} = \begin{cases} T & x_{r,c} \geqslant T \\ x_{r,c} & -T < x_{r,c} < T \\ -T & x_{r,c} \leqslant -T \end{cases} \tag{5}$$

3.3 Sub-feature of Differential Matrix

Markov transition probability is a good representation to analysis the correlation between data, and is a very effective steganalysis feature in other domains, such as image [22, 23] and videos [24, 25]. Since that, Markov transition probability is adopted to analysis the correlation of differential sequence in our scheme. Accumulative neighboring joint density is a probability distribution that gives the probability that each evaluated data falls in any particular range or discrete set of values specified for that variable, it shows the correlation of two data from the angle that the two data appear simultaneously, it will be a good complementary feature to Markov transition probability. Therefore, the accumulative neighboring joint density is also considered as an assistant feature set in our proposed scheme.

Markov transition probability of differential matrix $\mathbf{D}$ is calculated by Eq. (6). And accumulative neighboring joint density is calculated by Eq. (7). We extract features of intra-frame in horizontal direction while the features of inter-frame in vertical direction.

$$IM(m,n) = \frac{\sum \delta(x_{r,c} = m, x_{r+k_1, c+k_2} = n)}{\sum \delta(x_{r,c} = m)} \tag{6}$$

$$INJ(m,n) = \frac{\sum \delta(x_{r,c} = m, x_{r+k_1, c+k_2} = n)}{(N_r - k_1) * (N_c - k_2)} \tag{7}$$

N_r and N_c are the rows and columns of $\mathbf{D}$, and $m, n \in [-4, 4]$. $\delta(\cdot)$ is a mathematical operator, its value is set to 1 when it is agreed otherwise it is set to 0. $k_1 = 1$ and $k_2 = 0$ when inter features are constructed, otherwise, $k_1 = 0$ and $k_2 = 1$.

3.4 Sub-feature Fused Based on AAC Coding Principles

According to AAC encoding Principle, there are long and short frames in AAC audio. Long frame is used when the signal is steadily and short frame is used when the signal is acutely. AAC frames will be divided into two groups: long frame group F_l and short frame group F_s. The MDCT matrix M_l of long frames and M_s of short frames are constructed respectively. For F_l, the 1024 MDCT coefficients are put into M_l as a row, and for F_s, we divide each frame into 8 parts to form a new 8*128 sub-matrix, then the sub-matrix is put into M_s. Therefore, 16 sub-features can be obtained totally.

4 Analysis of Sub-Feature

The proposed scheme is a rich feature sets and include many kinds of features. To evaluate each sub-feature's performance, we analyzed those sub-features separately, extract each sub-feature from cover and stego audios to train the classification model, then use the model to detect the test audio samples.

In this experiment, ensemble classifier was adopted, and the metric to measure the performance of the sub-feature is AER (Average Error Rate), which means the average detecting error of the sub-feature, and is calculated as Eq. (8).

$$AER = \frac{n_1 + n_2}{n} \tag{8}$$

n is the total number of cover and stego. n_1 is the number of audios that belong to cover but wrongly classified to stego. n_2 is the number of audios that belong to stego but wrongly classified to cover. In order to describe more clearly, Those sub-features are named as the rule descried in Eq. (9):

$$name = \{frame\_type\}\,\{relation\_type\}\,\{order\}\,\{direction\} \tag{9}$$

$frame\_type$ is the type of frame: L stands for F_l while S stands for F_s. $relation\_type$ is the type of features: M stands for Markov transition probability while J stands for accumulative neighboring joint density. $order$ is the order of differential matrix: 1 stands for first-order while 2 stands for second-order. direction is the direction of feature constructing: B stands for inter-frame while I stands for intra-frame.

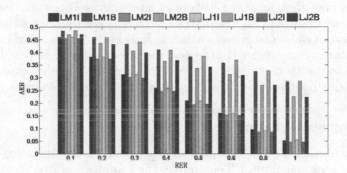

Fig. 5. sub-features' AER of F_l, 96 kbps, Zhu [3]

Figure 5 shows the sub-features' AER of F_l from stego AAC audio encoded with Zhu [3], bitrate is 96 kbps, and Fig. 6 shows the sub-features' AER of F_s from the same audio. Because of Zhu [3]'s better undetectability than Wang [2] and Zhu [5], we only give the AER analysis result of Zhu [3] as an example.

From Figs. 5 and 6 we can find that all the $AERs$ of the 16 sub-features are lower than 50% for all kind of testing RER. Especially, the AER of each sub-feature is lower than 40% when the RER is 50%, which means that all sub-features have ability to distinguish cover and stego audios, so all sub-features can be fused into our final feature sets. In addition, in both long frame and short frame, features of intra-frame outperform the features of inter-frame, it means that in AAC, the correlation between the MDCT coefficient in same frame is more tightly than in the adjacent frame. Comparing with the existed steganalysis schemes for MP3, In our scheme, the introduction of features of intra-frame is very necessary for AAC steganalysis.

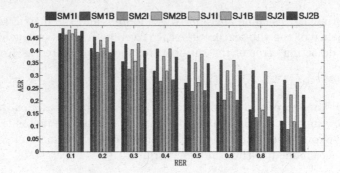

Fig. 6. sub-features' AER of F_s, 96 kbps, Zhu [3]

5   Experiments

To evaluate the performance of proposed scheme, there are two experiments are carried out. Experiment I is to test the performance of proposed scheme to analysis the contribution of the feature of inter-frame. There are two kinds of features set are evaluated: MDI and MDI2. MDI only has the intra-frame features and MDI2 is the whole feature sets which include both the feature of intra-frame and inter-frame. Experiment II is to test the universality of proposed features, and comparing with the existing steganalysis schemes. In this experiment, a mixed model is built to detect three existing steganography schemes.

5.1   Experimental Setup

Audio Database. The AAC audio database contains several types of music, such as jazz, rock and natural. The samples has a duration of 20 s, which contains 1000 frames. WAV audio set consists of 1575 44.1 kHz 16-bit quantization in uncompressed, PCM coded clips which are downloaded from network. The WAV audio set is encoded by AAC encoder [26] into M4A files with the 44.1 kHz sample ratio and bitrate of 96 kbps and 128 kbps.

Steganography Schemes. Wang [2], Zhu [3] and Zhu [5] are implemented to generate the stego AAC audios, for each encoding bitrate described as above, secret information generated by pseudo-random sequence is embedded in the WAV audio samples during the encoding process, at a RER of 30%,50%,80% and 100%.

Contrastive Steganalysis Schemes. There are three contrastive steganalysis features, which are showed in experiment result talbes as Qiao Markov [11], Qiao Joint [11] and Kuriakose [12]. The features of those three schemes are extracted from MDCT domain and used to detect MP3Stego. Qiao Markov [11] extracted Markov transition probability of second order differential QMDCT coefficients from inter-frame. Qiao Joint [11] extracted accumulative neighboring joint density of second order differential QMDCT coefficients from inter-frame. Kuriakose [12] fuses the two feature set (Qiao Markov and Qiao Joint) and obtained a combined features. In our experiment, we have implemented those three steganalysis features in AAC, and compared the performance of them with proposed scheme.

5.2 Experiments Results

To evaluate the performance of steganalysis scheme, True positive rate (TPR) and true negative rate (TNR) are used as metric. TPR stands for the proportion of stego audios correctly classified, and TNR stands for the proportion of cover audios correctly classified.

Results of Experiment I. To detect the steganography schemes: Wang [2], Zhu [3] and Zhu [5], classified model are trained separately, and the performance of MDI and MID2 are analyzed. The experiment results are showed in Table 1. We can find that the performance of MDI2 is better than MDI, it means that the feature of the inter-frame is necessary. And for different steganagraphy scheme, Wang [2] is easy to detect, for MDI2, even for the RER 30%, the TPR is bigger than 96.67%. And for Zhu [3], the detecting performance of MDI2 under RER 30% is 61.56 %, it means that this kind of steganagraphy scheme is more safer than Wang [2].

Table 1. Steganalysis performance of different scheme

Bitrate	Embedding Schemes	Feature Sets	TPR				TNR
			30%	50%	80%	100%	cover
96 kbps	Wang [2]	MDI	92.25%	96.31%	99.93%	100%	95.31%
		MDI2	96.67%	99.92%	100%	100%	99.83%
	Zhu [3]	MDI	50.33%	82.67%	94.44%	96.73%	91.21%
		MDI2	61.56%	90.33%	98.56%	100%	95.44%
	Zhu [5]	MDI	86.89%	93.01%	97.89%	98.97%	91.20%
		MDI2	92.58%	98.37%	100%	100%	94.83%
128 kbps	Wang [2]	MDI	94.37%	97.31%	99.36%	100%	96.49%
		MDI2	96.55%	99.98%	100%	100%	98.46%
	Zhu [3]	MDI	63.48%	84.67%	94.65%	98.29%	89.46%
		MDI2	71.82%	89.34%	99.67%	100%	92.37%
	Zhu [5]	MDI	85.34%	90.76%	94.14%	99.68%	91.45%
		MDI2	88.46%	92.16%	99.52%	100%	96.29%

Results of Experiment II. In this experiment, to test the universality of the proposed scheme, a mixed model of MDI2 feature is built to detect all of three steganography schemes. At the same time, the performance of existing steganalsyis schemes are compared, including Qiao Markov [11], Qiao Joint [11] and Kuriakose [12]. The experiment result is showed in Table 2. From Table 2, we can find that the proposed scheme outperforms the other three contrastive schemes under all encoding bitrate. The TNR of MDI2 is above 82% while the

Table 2. Universality of steganalysis performance with MDI2 feature sets

Bitrate	Steganalysis Schemes	Embedding Schemes	TPR 30%	50%	80%	100%	TNR cover
96 kbps	MDI2	Wang [2]	89.63%	96.54%	98.94%	100%	82.18%
		Zhu [3]	55.85%	83.78%	97.61%	100%	
		Zhu [5]	62.33%	80.32%	96.01%	97.87%	
		Average	**69.27%**	**86.88%**	**97.52%**	**99.29%**	
	Kuriakose [12]	Wang [2]	56.91%	88.83%	97.34%	98.94%	66.49%
		Zhu [3]	46.01%	55.32%	66.22%	71.54%	
		Zhu [5]	50.00%	49.47%	51.06%	53.99%	
		Average	**50.97%**	**64.54%**	**71.54%**	**74.82%**	
	Qiao Markov [11]	Wang [2]	41.76%	99.47%	100%	100%	69.68%
		Zhu [3]	47.34%	50.53%	61.70%	69.68%	
		Zhu [5]	33.51%	34.57%	35.90%	39.10%	
		Average	**40.87%**	**61.52%**	**65.87%**	**69.59%**	
	Qiao Joint [11]	Wang [2]	12.77%	96.28%	100%	100%	68.35%
		Zhu [3]	43.35%	48.67%	61.44%	61.17%	
		Zhu [5]	59.57%	62.50%	61.97%	61.17%	
		Average	**38.56%**	**69.15%**	**74.47%**	**74.11%**	
128 kbps	MDI2	Wang [2]	94.41%	99.73%	99.73%	99.47%	83.78%
		Zhu [3]	60.64%	85.64%	97.87%	99.47%	
		Zhu [5]	64.84%	84.84%	96.54%	98.67%	
		Average	**73.30%**	**90.07%**	**98.05%**	**99.20%**	
	Kuriakose [12]	Wang [2]	24.20%	88.30%	99.73%	100%	70.48%
		Zhu [3]	44.95%	52.93%	68.09%	76.33%	
		Zhu [5]	55.59%	56.91%	57.98%	59.57%	
		Average	**41.58%**	**66.05%**	**75.27%**	**78.63%**	
	Qiao Markov [11]	Wang [2]	50.53%	91.49%	99.47%	100%	60.90%
		Zhu [3]	49.73%	56.38%	65.43%	70.74%	
		Zhu [5]	41.49%	41.67%	41.67%	44.95%	
		Average	**47.25%**	**63.18%**	**68.86%**	**71.90%**	
	Qiao Joint [11]	Wang [2]	41.22%	89.36%	99.47%	100%	65.96%
		Zhu [3]	46.01%	54.79%	63.03%	69.15%	
		Zhu [5]	54.79%	55.32%	53.19%	53.99%	
		Average	**47.34%**	**66.49%**	**71.90%**	**74.38%**	

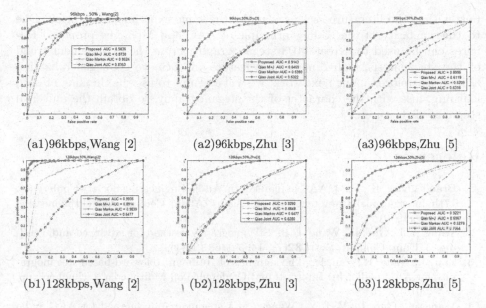

| (a1)96kbps,Wang [2] | (a2)96kbps,Zhu [3] | (a3)96kbps,Zhu [5] |

| (b1)128kbps,Wang [2] | (b2)128kbps,Zhu [3] | (b3)128kbps,Zhu [5] |

Fig. 7. ROC curve of different bitrate and steganography method from different steganalysis scheme (RER: 0.5)

compared steganalysis schemes are all below 70%. The TPR of MDI2 is above 80% when the RER is above 50%. The proposed scheme outperforms the compared stenalalysis schemes under different embedding rate obviously.

The ROC curve of the proposed scheme and the contrastive schemes are showed in Fig. 7, which shows the proposed scheme has a better detecting accuracy than the contrastive schemes. The detecting accuracy increases with the compressive bitrate increases.

6 Conclusion

In this paper, we proposed an AAC steganalysis schemes to detect the steganographies which embedded secret information by modifying MDCT coefficient. The contribution of this paper is that a rich feature sets about the MDCT correlation in audio compression stream are proposed. In this paper, we consider the intrinsic relationship of MDCT coefficient in intra-frame and inter-frame, proposed to extract the steganalysis feature sets of multi-order differential coefficients of Intra and Inter frame (MDI2). According to the structure of AAC frame, long frame and short frame are analyzed separately, and totaly there are 16 groups of sub-features are extracted. In this paper, the detecting performance of each sub-feature are analyzed, the results show that the correlation in intra-frame is more important than that of inter-frame. The comprehensive experiment results show that the detection accuracy of the proposed scheme are above 85.34% when the relative embed rate is over 50%, which is obviously better than the literatures schemes under the same experiment condition. Due to the similarity of the coding principle of AAC and Mp3, the proposed features can be used to detect MP3 steganography. From the development trend of the steganalysis, high dimensional feature will achieve good generalization ability. Therefore, in our next work, we will attempt to use the thinking of deep learning, fuse with the character of the steganography, to obtain the universal steganalysis features.

References

1. Brandenburg, K.: MP3, AAC explained. In: Audio Engineering Society Conference: 17th International Conference: High-Quality Audio Coding. Audio Engineering Society (1999)
2. Wang, Y.J., Guo, L., Wang, C.P.: Steganography method for advanced audio coding. J. Chin. Comput. Syst. **32**(7), 1465–1468 (2011)
3. Zhu, J., Wang, R., Yan, D.: The sign bits of Huffman codeword-based steganography for AAC audio. In: International Conference on Multimedia Technology, pp. 1–4 (2010)
4. Wang, Y., Guo, L., Wei, Y., Wang, C.: A steganography method for AAC audio based on escape sequences. In: International Conference on Multimedia Information NETWORKING and Security, pp. 841–845 (2010)
5. Zhu, J.: The research on information hiding in MPEG-2/4 advanced audio coding (AAC). Master's thesis, Ningbo University (2012)
6. Zhu, J., Wang, R.D., Li, J., Yan, D.Q.: A Huffman coding section-based steganography for AAC audio. Inf. Technol. J. **10**(10), 1983–1988 (2011)
7. Shuzheng, X.U., Peng, Z., Wang, P., Yang, H.: Performance analysis of data hiding in MPEG-4 AAC audio. Tsinghua Sci. Technol. **14**(1), 55–61 (2009)
8. Yan, D., Wang, R., Xianmin, Y., Zhu, J.: Steganalysis for MP3Stego using differential statistics of quantization step. Digit. Signal Proc. **23**(4), 1181–1185 (2013)
9. Yan, D., Wang, R.: Detection of MP3Stego exploiting recompression calibration-based feature. Multimed. Tools Appl. **72**(1), 865–878 (2014)
10. Yu, X., Wang, R., Yan, D.: Detecting MP3Stego using calibrated side information features. J. Softw. **8**(10), 2628–2636 (2013)
11. Qiao, M., Sung, A.H., Liu, Q.: MP3 audio steganalysis. Inf. Sci. **231**(9), 123–134 (2013)
12. Kuriakose, R., Premalatha, P.: A novel method for MP3 steganalysis. In: Jain, L.C., Patnaik, S., Ichalkaranje, N. (eds.) Intelligent Computing, Communication and Devices. AISC, vol. 308, pp. 605–611. Springer, New Delhi (2015). doi:10.1007/978-81-322-2012-1_65
13. Jin, C., Wang, R., Yan, D., Ma, P., Yang, K.: A novel detection scheme for MP3Stego with low payload. In: IEEE China Summit & International Conference on Signal and Information Processing, pp. 602–606 (2014)
14. MP3Stego. http://www.petitcolas.net/fabien/steganography/mp3stego/
15. Watkinson: Introduction to Digital Audio Coding and Standards. WatkinsonIntroduction
16. Fridrich, J., Kodovsky, J.: Rich models for steganalysis of digital images. IEEE Trans. Inf. Forensics Secur. **7**(3), 868–882 (2012)

17. Tang, W., Li, H., Luo, W., Huang, J.: Adaptive steganalysis against wow embedding algorithm. In: ACM Workshop on Information Hiding and Multimedia, Security, pp. 91–96 (2014)
18. Denemark, T., Sedighi, V., Holub, V., Cogranne, R.: Selection-channel-aware rich model for steganalysis of digital images. In: IEEE Workshop on Information Forensic and Security, pp. 48–53 (2014)
19. Tang, W., Li, H., Luo, W., Huang, J.: Adaptive steganalysis based on embedding probabilities of pixels. IEEE Trans. Inf. Forensics Secur. 11(4), 1–1 (2015)
20. Holub, V., Fridrich, J.: Phase-aware projection model for steganalysis of jpeg images. In: SPIE, Electronic Imaging, Media Watermarking, Security, and Forensics, vol. XVII, pp. 94090T–94090T-11 (2015)
21. Kodovsky, J., Fridrich, J., Holub, V.: Ensemble classifiers for steganalysis of digital media. IEEE Trans. Inf. Forensics Secur. 7(2), 432–444 (2012)
22. Pevny, T., Fridrich, J.: Merging Markov and DCT features for multi-class JPEG steganalysis. In: Proceedings of SPIE - The International Society for Optical Engineering, vol. 6505, pp. 650503–650503-13 (2007)
23. Pevn, T., Fridrich, J.: Multi-class blind steganalysis for JPEG images. In: Proceedings of SPIE - The International Society for Optical Engineering, vol. 6072, pp. 257–269 (2006)
24. Wang, K., Han, J., Wang, H.: Digital video steganalysis by subtractive prediction error adjacency matrix. Multimed. Tools Appl. 72(1), 313–330 (2014)
25. Da, T., Li, Z.T., Feng, B.: A video steganalysis algorithm for H.264/AVC based on the Markov features. In: Huang, D.-S., Jo, K.-H., Hussain, A. (eds.) ICIC 2015. LNCS, vol. 9226, pp. 47–59. Springer, Cham (2015). doi:10.1007/978-3-319-22186-1_5
26. Audiocoding.com (2011). http://www.audiocoding.com/

Emerging Threats of Criminal Use of Information Hiding: Usage Scenarios and Detection Approaches

A Prediction Model Based Approach to Open Space Steganography Detection in HTML Webpages

Iman Sedeeq[(✉)], Frans Coenen, and Alexei Lisitsa

Liverpool University, Liverpool L69 3BX, UK
{iman.sedeeq,coenen,lisitsa}@liverpool.ac.uk

Abstract. A mechanism for detecting Open Space Steganography (OSS) is described founded on the observation that the length of white space segments increases in the presence of OSS. The frequency of white space segments of different length is conceptualized in terms of an n-dimensional feature. This feature space is used to encode webpages (labelled as OSS or not OSS) so that each page is represented in terms of a feature vector. This representation was used to train a classifier which can subsequently be used to detect the presence, or otherwise, of OSS in unseen webpages. The proposed approach is evaluated using a number of different classifiers and with and without feature selection. Its operation is also compared with two existing OSS detection approaches. From the evaluation a best accuracy of 96.7% was obtained. The evaluation also demonstrated that the proposed method outperforms the two alternative techniques by a significant margin.

Keywords: Open space · Steganography · Classification

1 Introduction

Open Space Steganography (OSS) is a mechanism for hiding data in text "cover" files by utilizing white space characters. The idea was first proposed in the mid 1990s [1]. Although embedding white space characters in a text file will increase the file size, these methods offer the advantage that in any document white space characters appear frequently, more than any other character, therefore the existence of additional white space characters is unlikely to cause suspicion. In addition, and subject to how the OSS is applied and how the cover text file is viewed, in many cases the inclusion of additional white space characters will not result in any noticeable change in the look of the file from the viewer's perspective. Even where additional white space characters are visible, an observer is unlikely to pay significant attention to their presence and is unlikely consider these spaces to represent a hidden message.

WWW pages, written using HTML (Hyper-Text Markup Language) are well suited to OSS. Access to WWW pages on a daily basis will not raise any alarm. Features of HTML such as tag case-insensitivity and no bounds on attribute

C. Kraetzer et al. (Eds.): IWDW 2017, LNCS 10431, pp. 235–247, 2017.
DOI: 10.1007/978-3-319-64185-0_18

orderings do not change the way WWW browsers display webpages; similarly the inclusion of redundant space characters also do not change the way that web-pages are displayed. HTML thus provides an ideal opportunity for the steganographer. A number of HTML steganography mechanisms are available, such as: (i) attribute permutation whereby the ordering of HTML tag attributes is used to hide data [2–4] and (ii) switching HTML tag letters case as in [5–7]. An alternative is OSS, the mechanism of interest with respect to this paper. OSS uses one or more of the following to hide data: (i) inter-word spacing, spacing between two successive words; (ii) inter-sentence spacing, spacing between two successive sentences, (iii) additional spaces at the end of lines; and (iv) inter-paragraph spacing, spacing between two consecutive paragraphs. There are several steganography tools that implement data hiding using OSS methods, examples include: Spacemimic [8], wbStego4open [9], SNOW [10] and WhiteSteg [11]. Of these wbStego4open and SNOW are freely available for download and hence are used in the context of the evaluation presented later in this paper. SNOW utilizes end-of-line spacing to hide data, whilst wbStego4open makes use of both inter-word spacing and inter-sentence-spacing to embed data. Unlike SNOW, the wbStego4open tool also checks that the cover file is large enough to accommodate the desired hidden message.

In this paper an HTML OSS detection method is proposed based on the idea, first suggested in [12], that the embedding of a message using white space char-acters will affect the frequency distribution of continuous white space characters being used in sequence; an observation that holds regardless of the adopted OSS method used to hide data. The idea presented in this paper is to build a classi-fier that uses frequency distribution of continuous sequences (segments) of white space characters, of different lengths, to distinguish between normal webpages and "stego" -webpages. To the best knowledge of the authors this approach is novel. For evaluation purposes a data set of 150 well-known webpages from dif-ferent domains (news, education, shopping and business) was compiled. In the context of this set of webpages the proposed approach provided a very promis-ing steganography detection result, an average accuracy of 96.7% was obtained, significantly outperforming competitive approaches reported in [12,13].

The remainder of this paper is organized as follows. Firstly Sect. 2 presents related work, especially the work of [12,13]. Section 3 presents an analysis of the work of [12,13] and establishes the motivation for the classification-based approach presented in this paper. Section 4 then presents the proposed predic-tion model based approach. The evaluation of the proposed approach, and com-parisons with existing approaches, is then reported on in Sect. 5. The paper is concluded in Sect. 6 with a summary of the main findings and some suggested areas for future work.

2   Related Work

The main challenge of OSS detection in WWW pages is the large number of white space characters that will normally exists in a webpage regardless of whether embedding has taken place or not. Although the proposed OSS detection approach presented in this paper is unlike any other detection approaches, there has been some previous work directed at OSS detection in HTML pages. Of note with respect to the work presented in this paper is the work of [12,13].

In [12] a probabilistic model was used to detect HTML OSS. Two occurrence probability values were used for this purpose: (i) total white space character occurrence (p_{tsco}) and (ii) total white space character sequence occurrences (p_{scso}). The first is estimated using Eq. 1 where w is a webpage while the second probability is estimated using Eq. 2. These probabilities were compared with predetermined thresholds to decide whether a given webpage was a normal webpage or a stego-webpage. The thresholds in this case was identified using Zipf's and Heaps' law, and a Finite-State Model [14]. They estimated that the probability of occurrence of a white space character (p_{tsco}) in a text file was approximately 0.2 plus or minus 0.1, a threshold of 0.3 was thus proposed. Also they estimated that total white space character sequence occurrences (p_{scso}) in a text file is 0.2.

$$p_{tsco}(w) = \frac{number\ of\ white\ space\ characters\ in\ w}{total\ number\ of\ all\ characters\ in\ w} \tag{1}$$

$$p_{scso}(w) = \frac{number\ of\ all\ white\ space\ character\ sequences\ in\ w}{number\ of\ whitespace\ characters\ in\ w} \tag{2}$$

The detection approach presented in [13] used what was termed the "embedding rate" (e_{rate}). This is the number of characters in a given WWW page with white space characters removed and the number of characters without such characters being removed (Eq. 3). The authors defined the normal distribution of the embedding rate using the mean (μ) and standard deviation (δ) of the e_{rate} distribution to define a threshold with which to distinguish normal webpages from stego-webpages.

$$e_{rate}(w) = \frac{characters\ in\ w\ minus\ white\ space\ characters}{characters\ in\ w\ with\ white\ space\ characters} \tag{3}$$

In [12] the OSS mechanism which the author's adopted was not mentioned; however, in [13] the wbStego4open OSS tool for embedding hidden messages (as also used with respect to the evaluation presented later in this paper) was used. The approaches of [12,13] are both used with respect to the evaluation of the proposed OSS detection approach presented later in this paper.

3   Analysis of Existing Methods

As noted above there has been little work on OSS detection. The only work that the authors are aware of is that of [12,13]. To analyze these two approaches a collection of 150 commonly visited WWW pages was assembled, covering a variety of domains (education, news, business, shopping). OSS was applied, using both SNOW and wbStego4open (because they were publicly available), to half of the pages (75 pages) using a 83 characters English language text. In this manner two data sets were generated, D_{ws} and D_{snow}, of 150 webpages each.

Equation 1, used with respect to [12], was then applied to obtain before and after total white space character occurrence probability values (p_{tsco_e} and $p_{tsco_{\neg e}}$) with respect to webpages to which OSS had been applied. Table 1 shows the before and after p_{tsco} values obtained with respect to ten of the sample webpages in D_{ws} and D_{snow}. From the table it can clearly be seen that there is a wide variation in the range of p values obtained. A full analysis with respect to both data sets confirmed this result. A summary of this analysis, with respect to the OSS seeded WWW pages, is given in Fig. 1. The figure shows two "box plots" one for each set of OSS seeded WWW pages. Inspection of the figure confirms that the range of p values is substantial. Thus it would seem that using a p value static threshold, as proposed in [12], is unlikely to provide good OSS detection results because of this variability.

Table 1. White space character frequency in selected webpages before and after embedding

Webpage	$p_{tsco_{\neg e}}$	D_{ws}	D_{SNOW}
		p_{tsco_e}	p_{tsco_e}
www.bbc.co.uk	0.090	0.094	0.092
www.bbc.co.uk/weather	0.171	0.189	0.173
www.linkedin.com	0.032	0.078	0.046
www.cnn.com	0.046	0.053	0.048
www.microsoft.com	0.136	0.147	0.141
www.webmd.com	0.104	0.137	0.109
www.wikipedia.com	0.041	0.087	0.057
www.fda.gov	0.062	0.152	0.075

In the case of the approach proposed in [13]. Equation 3 was applied to the data sets. A summary of the er values obtained is given in Fig. 2, also using box plots. From the figure it can be seen that the application of a static er threshold for detecting OSS, as promoted in [13], is also not ideal.

4   Proposed HTML OSS Detection Method

This section presents the proposed OSS detection mechanism. The idea presented in this paper is that we use the frequency distribution of different lengths of sequences of white space characters. We use the term *segment* to describe contiguous sequences either of white space characters, or non white space characters. Table 2 shows the length of the first ten white space character segments before and after embedding for a selection of eight webpages from the data collection. The · (dot) symbol used in the table indicates the presence of character

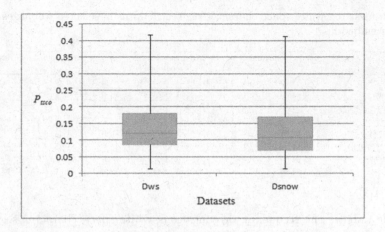

Fig. 1. Box plots for p_{tsco}

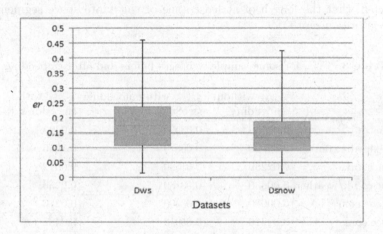

Fig. 2. Box plots for er

segments other than white space segments. From the table it can clearly be seen, as expected, that the length of at least some of the white space segments increase in the presence of OSS. Although some webpages already have space character segments of length more than 1 before any embedding has taken place (the Khan Academy and Sony webpages in the table), the idea is that we utilize this feature to detect OSS.

The frequency of a white space character segment of length l can be calculated using Eq. 4 where l is the segment length. Note that $\sum_{l=1}^{l=k} f_{cscs_l}(w) = 1.0$ (where k is the maximum size of the segments featured in w whereby w is a webpage).

$$f_{cscs_l}(w) = \frac{number\ of\ segments\ of\ length\ l\ in\ w}{total\ number\ of\ segments\ in\ w} \tag{4}$$

Table 2. First ten white space character segment lengths in selected webpages before and after embedding

Webpage	Before embedding	After embedding (wbStego4open)	After embedding (SNOW)
www.bbc.co.uk	1·1·1·1·1·1·1·1·1·1	1·1·1·1·1·1·1·8·1·1	2·6·5·3·2·3·1·1·1·1
www.dhl.com	1·1·1·1·1·1·1·1·1·1	1·3·1·1·1·1·1·5·1·1	1·1·1·1·1·1·1·7·6·7
www.ieee.org	1·1·1·1·1·1·1·1·1·1	1·1·1·1·1·1·5·1·1·1	1·1·1·1·7·6·1·1·1·1
www.google.com	1·1·1·1·1·1·1·1·1·2	2·1·1·1·1·1·7·1·1	6·1·3·3·5·1·1·1·1·1
www.sdwik.net	1·1·1·1·1·1·1·1·1·1	1·1·1·2·1·1·1·1·1·6	1·1·1·1·7·6·7·6·1·1
dailyroutines.typepad.com	1·1·1·1·1·1·1·1·1·1·2	2·1·2·1·1·1·1·5·1·1	1·1·1·1·6·1·1·1·1·3
www.khanacademy.com	1·1·1·1·1·1·1·8·1·1	4·1·1·1·1·1·4·1·1·1	7·6·7·6·5·3·1·1·1·1
www.sony.com	1·1·1·1·1·1·1·4·4·4	1·3·1·1·1·1·1·5·1·1	7·6·7·6·5·3·1·1·1·1

Table 3 shows the frequency of continuous white space character segments of length 5 (f_{cscs_5}) before and after embedding with respect to some of the webpages in the collected set of webpages. From the table it can clearly be seen, as expected, that the length of at least some of the white space segments will increase in presence of OSS.

Table 3. f_{cscs_5} for some sample webpages before and after embedding

Webpage	f_{cscs_5} without embedding	f_{cscs_5} with embedding (wbStego4open)	f_{cscs_5} with embedding (SNOW)
www.cnn.com	0.00000	0.03590	0.0399
www.wilkipedia.com	0.00000	0.06870	0.1566
www.bbc.co.uk	0.02250	0.05580	0.0612
www.bbc.co.uk/weather	0.00630	0.03180	0.0256
www.adobe.com	0.00080	0.03360	0.0216
www.cisco.com	0.02310	0.05010	0.0432
www.stackoverflow.com	0.00066	0.02999	0.0088
www.sony.com	0.00170	0.03340	0.0176
www.ipod.com	0.00200	0.04330	0.0287
www.nbc.com	0.02300	0.03500	0.0266
www.amazon.com	0.00110	0.03500	0.0152
www.expedia.com	0.00600	0.03660	0.0240

Given the above the basic idea presented in this paper is to use the frequency of white space segments, within webpages, of different length, with and without embedding, as an indicator of OSS. More specifically the idea was to build a binary prediction model (a classifier) generated using a n-dimensional feature space where n is the number of different potential white space segment lengths of interest that might be included in a webpage. The value for each dimension was then the frequency of the segment of that length occurred in a given webpage.

In this manner a webpage would be defined in terms of a feature vector $V = \{v_1, v_2, \ldots, v_n\}$. The process for generating a set of feature vectors given a set of webpages $D = \{w_1, w_2, \ldots, w_m\}$ is given by the pseudo code presented in Algorithm 1. Using the algorithm, for each webpage w_i in D, a feature vector V_i is created of length n where the elements are the frequency of white space sequences of lengths 1 to n. The process was used to generate sets of feature vectors from our evaluation data set. Note that for the experimental data set the maximum size of a space character segment was found to be 30, hence $n = 30$ was used.

Algorithm 1. Feature vector generation

1: Input: A set of webpages $D = \{w_1, w_2, \ldots, w_m\}$, and the maximum size of the
        white space segments to be considered n
2: Output: A set of feature vectors $\Phi = \{V_1, V_2, \ldots V_m\}$
3: $\Phi = \emptyset$
4: **for all** $w_i \in D$ **do**
5:     $V_i = \emptyset$
6:     s = number of white space character segments of length $>= 1$ in w_i
7:     **for** $j = 1$ **to** $j = n$ **do**
8:         t = number of segments in w_i of length j
9:         $V_i[j] = \frac{t}{s}$
10:    **end for**
11:    $\Phi = \Phi \cup V_i$
12: **end for**

There are a variety of classification models that could have been adopted, however, with respect to the evaluation presented in the following section, three well known classifiers were chosen: (i) a Multi-Layer Perceptron (MLP) Neural Network, (ii) a Support Vector Machine (SVM) and (iii) a Naive Bayes (NB) classifier, as provided within the Waikato Environment for Knowledge Analysis (WEKA) machine learning workbench [15].

5   Evaluation

In this section an evaluation of the proposed OSS detection approach, described in Sect. 4 above, is presented. Two sets of experiments were conducted, using the feature vector represented data sets generated as described above. The objectives of the evaluation were as follows:

- To determine if the proposed detection approach can be effectively applied to HTML webpage files to detect OSS using the three different classifier generation algorithms identified above.
- To determine the effect of applying a feature selection strategy to the feature vector representation prior to a classifier generation.

- To provide a comparison between the proposed detection approach and the two existing approaches to OSS detection, [12,13], as identified in Sect. 2 above.

The first two of the above objectives are considered in Subsect. 5.1, while the third is considered in Subsect. 5.2.

5.1 Effectiveness of the Proposed Detection Approach

The effectiveness of the proposed OSS detection technique was measured in terms of precision (Prec.), recall (Rec.) and accuracy (Acc.). Precision denotes the proportion of true positives detected OSS webpages out of all webpages labeled as OSS (true and false positives), recall is a ratio of a number of true positives identified OSS webpages out of the number of all actually OSS webpages (true positives and false negatives), and accuracy is a proportion of correctly identified webpages (both OSS and non-OSS). Ten cross validation was used whereby the data set was first stratified and then divided into tenths and ten classifiers generated using different nine tenths and tested on the remaining tenth. For the feature selection the "CfsubsetEval" attribute evaluation algorithm, and best first search, as provided in WEKA, was used. The idea behind attribute evaluation is to select a subset of the dimensions (recall that each dimension represents an attribute), in the feature space, that are good discriminators of class. The search method used defines how we search the feature space to identify the best attributes. Note that, unlike other feature selection mechanisms, CfsubsetEval does not select the k best dimensions (attributes) but the best performing dimensions according to some threshold. There are many different techniques that can be used for both. The advantages that are typically offered by feature selection are: (i) better accuracy than if no feature selection was undertaken (the argument being that only good discriminators are retained), (ii) prevention of overfitting (where a classifier is so precisely matched to the training data that it does not work well with other data) and (iii) better classification generation time (fewer dimensions to consider) [16].

The results are presented in Tables 4, 5, 6 and 7 (best results highlighted in bold font). Tables 4 and 5 show the results obtained without feature section, whilst Tables 6 and 7 the results obtained with feature selection. A summary is presented in Table 8. From the summary table it is clear that better results were obtained when using feature selection than without feature selection. With respect to the D_{ws} data set SVM produced consistently the best results with respect to all three metrics considered. In the case of the D_{SNOW} data set best recall and accuracy were produced using MLP, whilst best precision was produced using SVM without feature selection, and MLP with feature selection.

With respect to the feature section it is interesting to note that the selected values of l with respect to D_{ws} were $\{1, 2, 3, 4, 5, 6, 7, 8, 21\}$, the value of 21 seems odd and might simply be an "outlier". In the case of D_{SNOW} the selected values for l were $\{1, 2, 5, 7\}$.

Table 4. Effectiveness of proposed OSS detection technique using D_{ws} without feature selection

TCV	MLP			SVM			NB		
	Prec	Rec	Acc.%	Prec	Rec	Acc.%	Prec	Rec	Acc.%
1	0.88	1.00	93.33	1.00	1.00	100.00	1.00	1.00	100.00
2	1.00	1.00	100.00	0.88	1.00	93.33	0.88	1.00	93.33
3	0.78	1.00	86.67	0.88	1.00	93.33	0.64	1.00	73.33
4	1.00	1.00	100.00	1.00	1.00	100.00	1.00	1.00	100.00
5	0.88	1.00	93.33	0.88	1.00	93.33	0.86	0.86	86.67
6	0.88	0.88	86.67	0.88	0.88	86.67	0.88	0.88	86.67
7	1.00	0.88	93.33	1.00	1.00	100.00	1.00	0.75	86.67
8	1.00	1.00	100.00	1.00	1.00	100.00	0.89	1.00	93.33
9	0.80	1.00	86.67	0.89	1.00	93.33	0.75	0.75	73.33
10	0.86	0.75	80.00	1.00	0.88	93.33	0.88	0.88	86.67
Average	0.91	0.95	92.00	**0.94**	**0.97**	**95.33**	0.88	0.91	88.00
SD	0.09	0.09	6.89	0.06	0.05	4.50	0.12	0.10	9.32

Table 5. Effectiveness of proposed OSS detection technique using D_{SNOW} without feature selection

TCV	MLP			SVM			NB		
	Prec	Rec	Acc.%	Prec	Rec	Acc.%	Prec	Rec	Acc.%
1	0.86	0.86	86.67	0.78	1.00	86.67	0.83	0.71	80.00
2	1.00	1.00	100.00	1.00	1.00	100.00	0.67	0.57	66.67
3	0.75	0.86	80.00	0.86	0.86	86.67	0.56	0.71	60.00
4	0.75	0.86	80.00	1.00	0.86	93.33	1.00	0.86	93.33
5	1.00	1.00	100.00	1.00	0.86	93.33	0.86	0.86	86.67
6	1.00	0.88	93.33	0.78	0.88	80.00	0.75	0.75	73.33
7	1.00	0.88	93.33	1.00	0.63	80.00	0.80	0.50	66.67
8	0.86	0.88	86.67	1.00	0.63	80.00	0.86	0.75	80.00
9	0.78	0.88	80.00	0.80	1.00	86.67	0.67	0.75	66.67
10	0.88	0.88	86.67	0.75	0.75	73.33	0.62	0.63	60.00
Average	0.89	**0.89**	**88.67**	**0.90**	0.84	86.00	0.76	0.71	73.33
SD	0.11	0.06	7.73	0.11	0.14	7.98	0.13	0.11	11.33

5.2 Comparison with Other Detection Approaches

With respect to the second objective, comparison with existing techniques, the comparison was conducted with respect to the performance of the approaches proposed by [12,13] as described in Sect. 2. So that a fair comparison could be

Table 6. Effectiveness of proposed OSS detection technique using D_{ws} with feature selection

TCV	MLP			SVM			NB		
	Prec	Rec	Acc.%	Prec	Rec	Acc.%	Prec	Rec	Acc.%
1	0.88	1.00	93.33	1.00	1.00	100.00	1.00	1.00	100.00
2	1.00	1.00	100.00	1.00	1.00	100.00	0.88	1.00	93.33
3	0.88	1.00	93.33	0.88	1.00	93.33	0.88	1.00	93.33
4	1.00	1.00	100.00	1.00	1.00	100.00	1.00	1.00	100.00
5	0.88	1.00	93.33	0.88	1.00	93.33	1.00	1.00	100.00
6	0.88	0.88	86.67	1.00	0.88	93.33	1.00	0.88	93.33
7	1.00	0.88	93.33	1.00	1.00	100.00	1.00	0.88	93.33
8	1.00	1.00	100.00	1.00	1.00	100.00	1.00	1.00	100.00
9	0.89	1.00	93.33	0.89	1.00	93.33	0.89	1.00	93.33
10	1.00	0.75	86.67	1.00	0.88	93.33	1.00	0.75	86.67
Average	0.94	0.95	94.00	**0.96**	**0.97**	**96.67**	0.96	0.95	95.33
SD	0.06	0.09	4.92	0.06	0.05	3.51	0.06	0.09	4.5

Table 7. Effectiveness of proposed OSS detection technique using D_{SNOW} with feature selection

TVC	MLP			SVM			NB		
	Prec	Rec	Acc.%	Prec	Rec	Acc.%	Prec	Rec	Acc.%
1	0.88	1.00	93.33	0.86	0.86	86.67	0.64	1.00	73.33
2	1.00	1.00	100.00	1.00	0.71	86.67	0.64	1.00	73.33
3	0.86	0.86	86.67	0.83	0.71	80.00	0.55	0.86	69.00
4	1.00	1.00	100.00	1.00	0.86	93.33	0.88	1.00	93.33
5	1.00	1.00	100.00	1.00	1.00	100.00	1.00	1.00	100.00
6	1.00	1.00	100.00	1.00	1.00	100.00	0.72	1.00	80.00
7	0.80	1.00	86.67	1.00	0.50	73.33	0.67	1.00	73.33
8	1.00	1.00	100.00	1.00	0.63	80.00	0.67	1.00	73.33
9	0.89	1.00	93.33	0.88	0.88	86.67	0.80	1.00	86.67
10	1.00	0.88	93.33	1.00	0.88	93.33	0.64	0.88	66.67
Average	**0.94**	**0.97**	**95.33**	0.96	0.80	88.00	0.72	0.97	78.89
SD	0.08	0.06	5.49	0.07	0.16	8.78	0.14	0.06	12.19

arrived at the evaluation was again conducted using TCV, although it should be noted that the approaches proposed by [12,13] are both statistical in nature and do not require any training. The intuition here was that the evaluation would provide an unfair advantage to the proposed system if we trained on the entire data set and then tested on the same data set (it might also result in

Table 8. Summary of results presented in Tables 4, 5, 6 and 7 (best results highlighted in bold font)

Data set	Feature selection	MLP			SVM			NB		
		Prec	Rec	Acc.%	Prec	Rec	Acc.%	Prec	Rec	Acc.%
D_{ws}	No	0.91	0.95	92.00	0.94	0.97	95.33	0.88	0.91	88.00
	Yes	0.94	0.95	94.00	**0.96**	**0.97**	**96.67**	0.96	0.95	95.33
D_{SNOW}	No	0.89	0.89	88.67	0.90	0.84	86.00	0.76	0.71	73.33
	Yes	**0.94**	**0.97**	**95.33**	0.96	0.80	88.00	0.72	0.97	78.89

"overfitting"). For comparison both SVM and MLP classification with feature selection were used with respect to the proposed method, as this had been shown to produce the best performance. For the [12, 13] methods the reported threshold values were adopted. The evaluation metrics used were again precision, recall and overall accuracy.

The results are presented in Tables 9 and 10. Note that the precision, recall and accuracy values for the proposed approach have been reproduced from Tables 6 and 7 respectively. From the table it can clearly be seen that the proposed approach outperformed the previously proposed approaches by a significant margin. The proposed approach was good at identifying OSS webpages while at the the same time not miss-classifying many non-OSS webpages. Using the approach of [12] both the precision and recall were poor for both data sets, whilst using the approach proposed in [13] produced good recall values but was

Table 9. Comparison of proposed OSS detection with that proposed in [12,13] using D_{ws} (best results highlighted on bold font)

TCV	Proposed approach			[12]			[13]		
	Prec	Rec	Acc.%	Prec	Rec	Acc.%	Prec	Rec	Acc.%
1	1.00	1.00	100.00	0.50	0.57	53.00	0.50	1.00	53.33
2	1.00	1.00	100.00	0.67	0.29	60.00	0.54	1.00	60.00
3	0.88	1.00	93.33	0.50	0.29	53.33	0.38	0.71	33.33
4	1.00	1.00	100.00	1.00	0.14	60.00	0.50	1.00	53.33
5	0.88	1.00	93.33	0.25	0.14	40.00	0.47	1.00	47.00
6	1.00	0.88	93.00	0.44	0.57	47.00	0.64	1.00	73.00
7	1.00	1.00	100.00	0.33	0.14	47.00	0.38	0.71	33.33
8	1.00	1.00	100.00	0.60	0.43	60.00	0.50	1.00	53.33
9	0.89	1.00	93.33	0.50	0.43	53.33	0.47	1.00	47.00
10	1.00	0.88	100.00	0.71	0.71	73.33	0.47	1.00	47.00
Average	**0.96**	**0.97**	**96.67**	0.55	0.37	54.69	0.49	0.94	50.01
SD	0.06	0.05	3.51	0.20	0.19	8.79	0.07	0.12	11.16

Table 10. Comparison of proposed OSS detection with that proposed in [12,13] using D_{SNOW} (best results highlighted on bold font)

TCV	Proposed approach			[12]			[13]		
	Prec	Rec	Acc.%	Prec	Rec	Acc.%	Prec	Rec	Acc.%
1	0.88	1.00	93.33	0.43	0.43	46.67	0.46	0.86	46.67
2	1.00	1.00	100.00	0.50	0.14	53.33	0.53	1.00	60.00
3	0.86	0.86	86.67	0.50	0.29	53.33	0.38	0.71	33.33
4	1.00	1.00	100.00	1.00	0.14	60.00	0.50	1.00	53.33
5	1.00	1.00	100.00	0.25	0.14	40.00	0.43	0.86	40.00
6	1.00	1.00	100.00	0.38	0.43	40.00	0.64	1.00	73.33
7	0.80	1.00	86.67	0.33	0.14	46.67	0.33	0.57	26.67
8	1.00	1.00	100.00	0.60	0.43	60.00	0.50	1.00	53.33
9	0.89	1.00	93.33	0.40	0.29	46.67	0.43	0.86	40.00
10	1.00	0.88	93.33	0.67	0.57	66.67	0.47	1.00	46.67
Average	**0.94**	**0.97**	**95.33**	0.51	0.30	51.00	0.47	0.89	47.00
SD	0.08	0.06	5.49	0.20	0.15	0.08	0.08	0.14	0.13

not very precise. The later was because the approach was classifying most of the webpages as OSS webpages, hence it was correctly classifying most of the OSS webpages but also wrongly classifying most of the many webpages that did not feature OSS as OSS webpages, hence the accuracy was poor. Given that the OSS and non-OSS classes were equally distributed within the data set the accuracies obtained using [12,13] and the D_{ws} data, 54.69% and 50.01% respectively, are little better than a guess. In the case of D_{SNOW} accuraccies of 51.00% and 46.00% were obtained, the last worse than a guess.

6   Conclusion

This paper has proposed an OSS detection approach based on the observation that the length of white space segments in webpages increases in the presence of OSS and that this information can be captured in a feature vector format which can subsequently be used to build an OSS prediction (classification) model provided we have pre-labelled training data available. To evaluate the proposed mechanism a collection of 150 commonly viewed webpages was collated. This was split into two, half seeded with an embedded messages and half not. In this manner two 150 webpage test data sets were created, one using the wbStego4open OSS tool (D_{ws}) and one using the SNOW OSS tool (D_{SNOW}). The proposed approach was tested using three well known classifiers and with and without feature selection. A best average accuracy of 96.7% was obtained indicating the effectiveness of the proposed approach. The proposed approach was also evaluated by comparing its operation with the mechanisms presented in [12,13].

In this comparison, the results obtained indicated that the proposed OSS detection mechanism outperformed the two existing approaches considered by a significant margin, [12,13] achieved best accuracy of 54.7% and 50.0% for D_{ws} and 51.0% and 47.0% for D_{SNOW} respectively.While the results reported in this paper indicate viability of our approach, more work needs to be done. For future work the authors intend to examine the performance of the proposed OSS detection approach with respect larger data sets and alternative OSS tools. We plan to investigate the proposed method efficiency with respect to different embedding rates. Finally we intend to examine the approach functionality with other than white space character embeddings.

References

1. Bender, W., Gruh, D., Morimoto, N., Lu, A.: Techniques for data hiding. IBM Syst. **35**, 313–336 (1996)
2. Forrest, S.: Introduction to deogol (2006), http://www.wandership.ca/projects/deogol
3. Huang, H., Zhong, S., Sun, X.: An algorithm of webpage information hiding based on attributes permutation. In: 4th International Conference on Intelligent Information Hiding and Multimedia Signal Processing (IIH-MSP), pp. 257–260 (2008)
4. Shen, D., Zhao, H.: A novel scheme of webpage information hiding based on attributes. In: 2010 IEEE International Conference on Information Theory and Information Security (ICITIS), pp. 1147–1150 (2010)
5. Sui, X.-G., Luo, H.: A new steganography method based on hypertext. In: Proceedings of Radio Science Conference, pp. 181–184 (2004)
6. Shen, Y.: A scheme of information hiding based on html document. J. Wuhan Univ. **50**, 217–220 (2004)
7. Zhao, Q., Hongtao, L.: A PCA-based web page watermarking. Pattern Recogn. **40**, 1334–1341 (2007)
8. McKellar, D.: Space mimic (2000), http://www.spammimic.com/encodespace.shtml
9. wbStego4open (2004), http://www.wbstego.wbailer.com/
10. Kwan, M.: The snow home page (2006), http://www.darkside.com.au/snow/
11. Por, L.Y., Ang, T.F., Delina, B.: Whitesteg: a new scheme in information hiding using text steganography. WSEAS Trans. Comput. **7**, 735–745 (2008)
12. Sui, X.-G., Luo, H.: A steganalysis method based on the distribution of space characters. In: Proceedings of Communications, Circuits and Systems International Conference Guilin Guangzi, China, pp. 54–56 (2006)
13. Huang, H., Sun, X., Li, Z., Sun, G.: Detection of hidden information in webpage. In: Fourth International Conference of Fuzzy Systems and Knowledge Discovery FSKD (2007)
14. Baeza-Yates, R., Navarro, G.: Modeling text databases. Recent Advences in Applied Probablity, pp. 1–25 (2006)
15. Frank, E., Hall, M.A., Witten, I.H.: The Weka Workbench. Online Appendix for Data Mining: Practical Machine Learning Tools and Techniques, 4th edn. Morgan Kaufmann (2016)
16. Omar, N.B., Jusoh, F.B., Bin Othman, M.S., Ibrahim, R.B.: Review of feature selection for solving classification problems. J. Res. Innov. Inf. Syst., 54–60 (2013)

Towards Covert Channels in Cloud Environments: A Study of Implementations in Virtual Networks

Daniel Spiekermann[1]([⊠]) [iD], Jörg Keller[1], and Tobias Eggendorfer[2]

[1] FernUniversität in Hagen, 58084 Hagen, Germany
{daniel.spiekermann,joerg.keller}@fernuni-hagen.de
[2] HS Ravensburg-Weingarten, 88250 Weingarten, Germany
tobias.eggendorfer@hs-weingarten.de

Abstract. Cloud environments are more and more used by cyber criminals to perform their malicious activities. With the help of covert channels they hide their data transmissions and message exchange. Whereas different techniques of covert channels in common networks are well-known, the existence of covert channels in cloud environments networks is a new topic in information hiding. The virtual environments provide new ways to hide the transmission of information. These environments use virtual networks in the cloud, which separate and isolate logical networks of the different customers. In this paper we present an examination of information hiding in virtual networks. We analyzed VXLAN, STT, GENEVE and NVGRE as the most notable so-called overlay protocols and examined different ways to create covert storage channels. Furthermore, we describe a covert timing channel based on the movement of virtual machines. As a result we propose possible countermeasures of the described covert channels.

Keywords: Virtual network · Covert channel · Network steganography · Information hiding

1 Introduction

1.1 Motivation

Secure communication in networks is typically achieved by using encrypted protocols and algorithms. But the use of these techniques only protects the content of the messages. To hide the exchange of the messages itself, steganography is used. A typical usecase is malware, trying to hide itself and thus preventing its detection [5]. Spies use steganography to pass their information [29], furthermore data leakage performed by internals sometimes uses concealed communication based on steganography [2]. However steganography is not only used by criminals but might also be used by citizen of countries with political systems not allowing the freedom of speech, in order to circumvent censorship.

© Springer International Publishing AG 2017
C. Kraetzer et al. (Eds.): IWDW 2017, LNCS 10431, pp. 248–262, 2017.
DOI: 10.1007/978-3-319-64185-0_19

1.2   Background

Virtual environments provide new possibilities and techniques to create covert channels. Through cloud computing, these virtual environments including virtual machines (VM) and virtual networks became ubiquitous. A VM as an emulation of a computer system provides an operating system installed on software, which emulates the hardware functions. A virtual network is a software implementation of a physical network to interconnect VMs. Previously datacenters (DC) were unable to implement all needed requirements of these environments like flexibility, dynamic on-demand provisioning, isolation and security. Hence the development of new network protocols like *Virtual eXtensible LAN (VXLAN)* and *Generic Network Virtualization Encapsulation (GENEVE)* or new paradigms like Software-Defined-Networks try to eradicate the aforementioned limitations. Common protocols like *Virtual LAN (VLAN)* or *Multi-Protocol Label Switching (MPLS)* are limited in the number of possible logical networks and do not provide enough flexibility to interconnect globally distributed networks. Additionally these protocols are unable to handle the interconnection of hundreds or thousands online VMs, which is not uncommon in nowadays DCs.

Each of the protocols uses its own frame format, header fields and encapsulation techniques to fulfill the requirements of virtual networks. We analyzed the four protocols VXLAN, GENEVE, *Stateless Transport Tunneling (STT)* and *Network Virtualization using GRE (NVGRE)*, to identify which protocol fields facilitate the creation of covert storage channels.

The use of virtual networks increases significantly the dynamic and flexible connection of VMs. Using the migration process of VM enables a new, mostly undetectable covert channel. The movement of a VM changes various communication parameters, thus these changes might be used for information hiding.

1.3   Structure

The remainder of the paper is structured as follows. Section 2 lists related work regarding to information hiding, covert channels and virtual networks. Section 3 presents different ways to hide information in virtual environment with a focus on VMs and virtual networks, in Sect. 4 the proposed techniques are analyzed and possible countermeasures are listed. Section 5 summarizes this paper and gives an outlook to our future research.

2   Related Work

Various research has been done in the area of information hiding, virtual networks and network forensic investigation. Information hiding and steganography has been researched for more than 15 years [12]. The use of covert channels was first introduced by [13]. [18] describes the use of information hiding in communication networks. In [33] novel approaches like implementing covert channels based on protocols are presented. Covert channels in IPv6-based networks are discussed in [15].

On the other hand steganalysis is used to detect covert channels and concealed communication [10]. [11] describes possible attacks on steganography and watermarks. [8] shows several ways to identify counter forensics using covert channel.

The increase of virtual environments has lead to an additional layer in information hiding. Covert channels using shared-memory techniques are described in [20] and in [35]. [36] describes exchanging messages using the L2 cache of VMs. [4] proposes the implementation of covert channels based on the cloud service *Dropbox*. To the authors' best knowledge no work has been done yet in the field of covert channels based on virtual networks.

3   Information Hiding in Virtual Environments

The following section uses the prisoners' problem [25] as a scenario for information hiding. The prisoners, Alice and Bob are only able to exchange messages via the warden who is able to pry on the exchange. Thus a covert channel is needed, providing neither any evidence of communication nor enabling the warden to detect the exchange.

Local area networks or wide area networks have been well researched, lots of techniques, tools and research exist [18,33]. With virtual environments additional techniques to implement covert channels between Alice and Bob have become available.

The use of network protocols like VXLAN or STT creates a new logical view of the network. [1] defines this virtual network as an overlay network, which provides different isolated networks simultaneously:

With virtualization, nodes can treat an overlay as if it is the native network, and multiple overlays can simultaneously use the same underlying overlay infrastructure.

While using these overlay networks, providers are able to create per-customer networks, each under the administration of the assigned user. Each network implements a separated and isolated environment with the possibility to create an interconnection to other networks via virtual devices like virtual routers. The interconnection inside the logical network is performed with virtual switches like Open vSwitch [23]. These switches are implemented in software and work similarly to well-known network hardware switches.

Different overlay protocols coexist, each with the ability to create separated layer 2 networks on the top of an existing network infrastructure. To create a logical network, the involved network packets are encapsulated as shown in Fig. 1 and then transmitted via the underlying physical infrastructure.

Based on this, we propose two different ways of covert channels in virtual networks. Overlay protocols are used to implement covert storage channels, second we create a covert timing channel based on VM migration called VM-based covert channel. Well-known and proven methods of covert channels are extended to virtual environments.

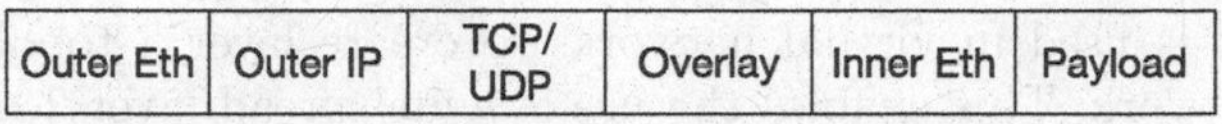

Outer Eth	Outer IP	TCP/UDP	Overlay	Inner Eth	Payload

Fig. 1. Encapsulation

3.1 Protocol-Based Covert Channels

The new network protocols implement different header fields, some of them are reserved for a future use. These fields are not defined in detail and might get used by Alice and Bob to create covert channels.

The parameters and identifiers of the virtual network are set by the physical underlay network's administrator. Since encapsulation is transparent to the user, he is unable to manipulate this information. Nevertheless a malicious administrator might use these protocols to hide his own information exchange. In addition to this, the highly customizable environment allows the user nearly every administrative change inside the own, assigned network. Alice and Bob might use nested virtualization to create their own virtual environment based on the provider's infrastructure. Inside this environment they are able to use the protocol-based covert channels to exchange their information.

VXLAN as one of the new network protocols is defined in RFC 7348 [16] and extends the VLAN protocol. The implementation of VXLAN facilitates the spreading of this subnet all over the physical infrastructure. VXLAN as shown in Fig. 2 implements a 24 bit header field named *Virtual Network Identifier (VNI)*, which provides the use of $2^{24} = 16,777,216$ different, logical isolated networks. All hosts with the same VNI belong to the same layer 2 subnet and interact as if connected to the same switch, even if the hosts/VMs are distributed over different DCs. Network packets which are sent to VMs running on other physical hosts are encapsulated by the virtual tunneling endpoint and transmitted via IP and UDP to the assigned endpoint. This system removes the VXLAN header and forwards the original network packet to the intended receiver.

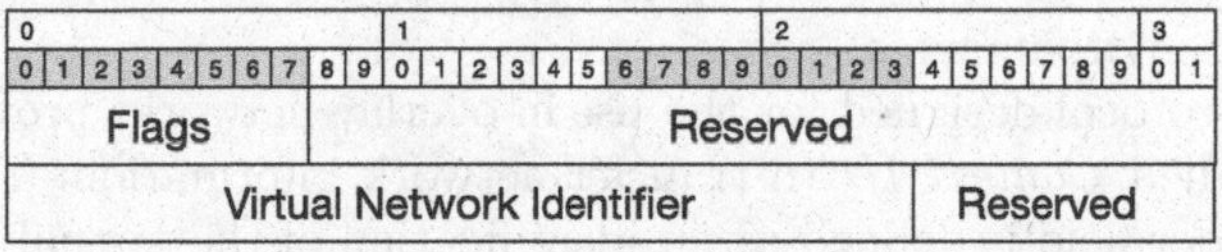

0										1										2										3	
0	1	2	3	4	5	6	7	8	9	0	1	2	3	4	5	6	7	8	9	0	1	2	3	4	5	6	7	8	9	0	1

Flags	Reserved
Virtual Network Identifier	Reserved

Fig. 2. VXLAN header

VXLAN uses flags to indicate the intented behavior. In a valid VXLAN packet, all bits but the fifth are set to 0. All reserved bits have to be set to 0, albeit being ignored by the recipient [16]. Using the flags and the reserved header fields to create a covert communication channel, an overall bandwidth of 39 bits is possible.

NVGRE [30] is used in virtual networks to create layer 2 topologies on top of a layer 3 network. This enables the use of wide spread layer 2 networks over the common borders of network·switches. Network packets are encapsulated in GRE and transmitted via IP to create the logical networks. The so-called *Virtual Subnet Identifier* separates these logical networks. Figure 3 shows the NVGRE header.

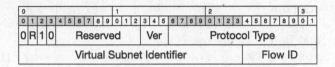

0										1										2										3	
0	1	2	3	4	5	6	7	8	9	0	1	2	3	4	5	6	7	8	9	0	1	2	3	4	5	6	7	8	9	0	1
0	R	1	0		Reserved								Ver			Protocol Type															
Virtual Subnet Identifier																							Flow ID								

Fig. 3. NVGRE header

The *Protocol Type* is set per default to 0×6558, which cannot be changed and is therefore unprofitable for the use of covert channels. Additionally the values of the first bits are pre-defined and cannot be changed. The *R-bit* on position two has no default value when using NVGRE and therefore might be used to create a covert storage channel. The reserved bits should be set to 0 by default, but there is no action defined if they are set to other values. This permits using nine bits for a covert communication channel. The *Flow ID* is used to create per-flow entropy, if this header field is not used, all bits have to be set to 0. Using this field provides a bandwidth of 8 bits.

STT tries to eradicate some limitations of other overlay protocols. One big problem of protocols like VXLAN or NVGRE is the inherent use of the internal CPU to calculate all needed checksums, perform encapsulation or transmit the packet data unit to the next layer. In common networks, network interface cards (NIC) use hardware based calculation like TCP Offload Engine or TCP Segmentation Offload to relieve the CPU from the sophisticating calculations. STT uses this to its advantage by providing a pseudo-TCP header as shown in Fig. 4 which might be analyzed by the physical NIC to profit from the optimization even in virtual environments.

STT as a protocol designed for the use in overlay networks provides a 64 bit header field called *Context ID* to transfer network information. The projected use of this header field is defined as an identification of the virtual network, but a different allocation is possible, as mentioned in [6]:

Some other encapsulations [...] use an explicit tenant network identifier or virtual network identifier. The Context Identifier can be thought of as a generalized form of virtual network identifier.

Therefore the *Context ID* is a suitable field to hide a relevant amount of bits. The flags on position 4–7 are unused and are set per default to 0, by manipulating them a covert communication channel with a bandwidth of 4 bits is possible.

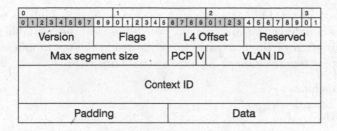

Fig. 4. STT header

Also the *L4 Offset* field might by used for covert channels, it describes the end of the STT header and the start of the layer 4 header. By increasing this value, additional information might be inserted between STT and layer 4 headers in the padding field.

The *V-flag* and *VLAN-ID* header fields are used in combination. If the *V-flag* is set, a valid VLAN identifier is transmitted. By manipulating these values an overall bandwidth of 12 bit is possible. Using these different header fields, STT provides a bandwidth of more than 80 bits.

GENEVE is described in [9] and proposes a new approach to implement flexible tunnels between cooperating devices. Figure 5 shows the GENEVE header.

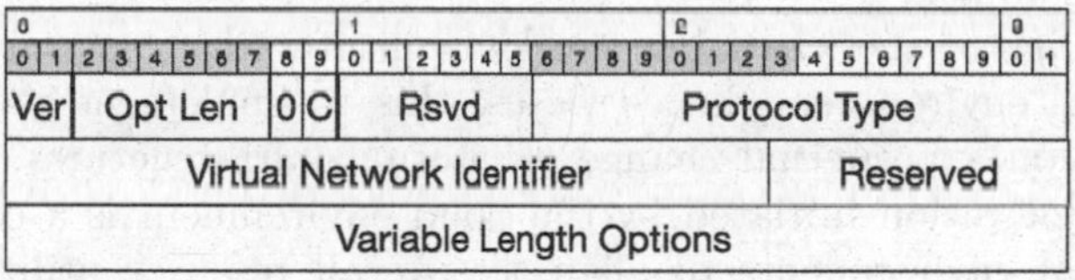

Fig. 5. GENEVE header

GENEVE provides two different reserved fields, which have to be set to 0 and are ignored by default. These values might be manipulated to create a covert storage channel with an overall bandwidth of 14 bits.

GENEVE additionally provides an header field named *Variable Length Option*. The length of this field has to be between 4 and 128, otherwise the packet is discarded silently. Therefore when creating a covert channel, the size needs to be valid.

3.2 VM-based Covert Channel

Virtual environments and virtual networks in particular provide additional ways to create covert channels. Especially the high flexibility and the possible customization of this environments increase the number of usable implementations.

The number of adjustable parts of a such an environment is high, as is the number of possible implementations evolved, which increases the available techniques or the combination of them. Nearly all parts inside the environment might be used to create a covert channel. Typical virtual entities are

- Virtual machines
- Assigned Snapshots
- Virtual networks
- Virtual storage pools
- Available subnets

Each of the following items might be used to create concealed communication, either by using covert timing or storage channels. Aspects related to the VM like snapshots, assigned storage pools, linked subnets or other parts, which might be under administration of the customer are discussed in various researches like [14] with CloudSteg or [24]. These techniques are based on the use of internal devices like shared CPUs or caches. The use of migration or customization is, to our best knowledge not under deeper research.

VM Migration Covert Channel. A hardly detectable method to create a covert channel is the use of Protocol Hopping Covert Channels [34]. These covert channels use a various number of network protocols, which are changed perpetualy [31]. This continuous change of the appointed protocol hampers an easy identification, as a result of this countermeasures like traffic normalization [32] become more complex.

The flexibility of the virtual networks facilitates the customization of the assigned logical environment, hence we use this to implement a covert timing channel based on a perpetual change of internal infrastructures, e.g. the VM location. VM migration initiated by the cloud environment is a common technique in virtual environments to align the overall resource utilization of this environment. Even users are able to migrate their VMs to change the location, e.g. to increase the availability or to improve the interconnection to other networks. Whereas the cloud environment migrates only inside a DC, customers are able to perform VM movements into other available DCs located all over world. This movement provides a fast changing infrastructure, a system might be moved from Europe to Australia within minutes or even in seconds[1].

If a VM moves to an other DC, depending of the internal interconnection of the virtual network, some values like local ip-addresses or external hostnames might be unchanged. On the other hand, different communication values like floating ip addresses[2] or internal hostnames might differ after the movement.

Depending on the used implementation, a VM Migration Covert Channel might use a proper value of one of the parameters. The use of location-based values like the round trip time (RTT) guarantees a detectable change for Alice and Bob,

---

[1] The time to migrate a VM depends heavily on the amount of data the VM uses.

[2] Floating ip addresses are used in cloud environments to assign a public ip address to a VM for a short period of time [21].

which might be used for the covert channel. The RTT is defined as the time it takes for a packet from sender to receiver plus the time it takes for the acknowledgment [22]. A migration to different DC changes the RTT in a way which enables a differentiation.

We assume a RTT of 120ms between the target VM located in an European DC used by Alice and a client used by Bob. If Alice migrates her VM to a DC in Australia, the RTT increases and might be around 210 ms. Alice and Bob define network packets with a RTT of ≥ 180 ms as '1' and a RTT of ≤ 160 ms as '0'. Packets with a RTT between 160 and 180 are ambiguous and therefore ignored. A transmission of the message '1011' is shown in Fig. 6.

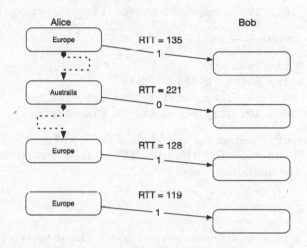

Fig. 6. VM Migration Covert Channel

The use of two different DCs limits the overall bandwidth significantly, a smaller difference in the RTT provides for the use of more different DCs, which increase the available bandwidth, although it also reduces tolerance to varying network latency.

To evaluate this covert channel, we created a virtual network inside the Amazon EC2 cloud environment. Due to the fact that Amazon EC2 does not support nested virtualization, we created our own virtual private cloud (VPC) based on three interconnected VPN gateways. These gateways act as a router for the connected VMs and reside at different locations all over the world. In detail we use DCs in London (Europe), Mumbai (Asia) and São Paulo (South America). Inside our VPC we use the private subnet 10.0.0.0/24 to address the VMs. The VM used by Alice is assigned to the ip-address 10.0.0.3, Bob's VM is assigned to 10.0.0.19.

We measured the RTT with the command *ping*. We assume the VM of Alice located statically in London, Bob creates the covert channel by moving his VM from London to Mumbai or to São Paulo.

London - London

```
alice@alice:~$ ping bob
PING bob (10.0.19) 56(84) bytes of data.
64 bytes from 10.0.19: icmp_seq=1 ttl=64 time=0.434 ms
64 bytes from 10.0.19: icmp_seq=2 ttl=64 time=0.472 ms
```

London - Mumbai

```
alice@alice:~$ ping bob PING bob
(10.0.19) 56(84) bytes of data.
64 bytes from 10.0.19: icmp_seq=1 ttl=64 time=110 ms
64 bytes from 10.0.19: icmp_seq=2 ttl=64 time=111 ms
```

London - São Paulo

```
alice@alice:~$ ping bob
PING bob (10.0.19) 56(84) bytes of data.
64 bytes from 10.0.19: icmp_seq=1 ttl=64 time=196 ms
64 bytes from 10.0.19: icmp_seq=2 ttl=64 time=197 ms
```

As a result of the VPC, neither the ip-address of Bob's VM nor the TTL changes when migrating to an other DC. Only the RTT changes and might be used as an indication of the migration.

3.3 Summary

Virtual networks provide different ways of covert channels. Whereas existing covert channels in virtual environments are based on the use of internal resources like caches or information of the hypervisor, the protocol-based covert channels work on different layers of the OSI-model [37]. Hence the protocol-based covert channels are similar to TCP- [19] or IP-based covert channels [3,15] and differ from application-specific covert channels like [4] or [17]. The VM Migration Covert Channel provides a new way to create a covert channel, but the bandwidth of the channel is constrained. Depending on the number of DCs, the number of possible destinations and therefore the differentiation of the RTT is flexible.

Table 1 summarizes the proposed techniques and lists the three main features of information hiding as defined in [7].

Robustness is defined as an amount of alteration a channel can handle without destroying the message, stealthiness defines the inability of the warden to detect the channel [18]. To rate the proposed covert channels, we classify the stealthiness of a presented channel, which is detectable with known countermeasures as *low*, otherwise as *high*. Equally we rate channels with a low amount of possible alteration as *bad*, and techniques, that provide a better robustness as *good*. The robustness of the channels is increased, if error correction codes are used, hence the rating depends heavily on the overall bandwidth.

Table 1. Steganography bandwidth of covert channels in virtual networks

Covert channel	Protocol	Header field	Bandwidth in bps	Robustness	Stealthiness
Protocol-based	VXLAN	Flags	7	good	low
	VXLAN	Reserved	32	Good	Low
	NVGRE	R-Bit	1	Good	Low
	NVGRE	Reserved	9	Good	Low
	NVGRE	Flow ID	8	Good	Low
	STT	Flags	4	Good	Low
	STT	Context ID	64	Good	Low
	STT	L4 Offset	Flexible	Good	Low
	STT	V-Flag + VLAN ID	12	Good	Medium
	GENEVE	Reserved	14	Good	Low
	GENEVE	Variable length option	4–128	Good	Medium
VM-based	Independent	-	Flexible	Medium	High

4 Countermeasures Against Covert Channels in Virtual Networks

The first step to destroy covert channels in communication systems is the identification of the channel. Depending on the intended behavior, detailed auditing, capacity limitation, elimination or interruption are possible techniques to handle an identified channel [18]. A main part of the identification is based on the capture of network traffic to determine the normal network traffic. Based on this classification a subsequent analysis might figure out possible unintended behavior, which are defined as anomalies. The knowledge of possible anomalies enables an eventual detection of unwanted network traffic.

Covert timing channels exchange the messages on a timing interval and a priori determined protocols. During the interval a single packet is sent or not from Alice to Bob. The used intervals or protocols facilitates complex implementations of covert timing channels, thereby the complete communication process might be time-consuming and a possible capture process last very long.

Whereas the capture and recording process of network traffic in common networks is well-known and mostly done without any issues, the virtual environments raise new issues [26]. Especially the capture of network traffic of a relevant VM is faced with different problems like migration, user customization and multi-tenancy. Therefore the aforementioned capture process needs to be adapted to fulfill the new requirements of highly flexible and dynamic virtual networks.

4.1 Protocols

As in traditional networks the kind of transmission has to be limited, otherwise the aggressive exchange acts as an anomaly and might be detected. To consider this trade-off between steganography bandwidth and robustness, Alice and Bob have to adjust the number of packets sent at a given time, depending on the overall network traffic. Networks with a high traffic load might detect an anomaly later as a network with a low number of transmitted packets.

All details of the protocols are described in the assigned internet standards and in public Request-for-Comments. Therefore the behavior of sender, receiver and possible middle-boxes is pre-defined and might be used for traffic normalization performed by an active warden. Although the overlay protocols do not occur in every DC yet, the necessity of these protocols is undisputed. Thus a fast implementation of available rules for traffic normalization seems to be realistic.

4.2   Migration

Whereas the communication of a solid and static VM might be intercepted and analyzed, the wiretapping of different, maybe migrating VMs is hardly feasible in modern networks. The migration of the VM might hamper the identification and therefore the capture or analysis of the network data, too. This impedes the detection of covert channels assigned to this VM. Each type of surveillance and monitoring will fail, if the used techniques are not flexible enough to identify the VM in the network and adapt the running monitoring processes.

In digital investigations the knowledge of the source of a communication is highly necessary, hence the identification of the sender is one of the first steps. After identifying the target system, capture processes, filters and monitoring systems are able to record the network packets and to analyze the transmitted data.

The identification depends on valid parameters and fingerprints marking the communication process. If these fingerprints are available, monitoring systems are able to identify the relevant streams and packets out of the flow of network information. But the identification of a system is not sufficient to detect a covert channel. Furthermore only the capture and subsequent analysis of all network data facilitates the detection of a VM Migration Covert Channel. Unfortunately the capture process inside a virtual network is complex and faced with different issues [27]. An implementation to record the network traffic of a VM inside a virtual network named ForCon is discussed in [28]. ForCon facilitates the monitoring of certain VMs in virtual networks, if needed ForCon implements a capture process of the VM even whilst this system is migrating.

5   Conclusion

This section summarizes this paper and gives an outlook of our future work.

5.1   Summary

In this paper we present different ways of implementing covert channels in virtual environments. These environments use overlay protocols like VXLAN to create virtual networks. We analyzed the four most notable implementations of overlay

protocols VXLAN, STT, GENEVE and NVGRE to identify possible implementations of covert channels. The protocols provide different header fields, which
are usable for covert storage channels. We identified 11 different covert channels
and summarized them as *Protocol-based*. The use of these covert channels differs
from other implementations like [4] which use application specific protocols. The
presented covert channels use lower layers of the OSI-model without access to
the application itself.

The aforementioned protocols create virtual networks, which on the one hand
isolate the provided VMs and, on the other hand, establish a controlled interconnection between them. Additionally the overlay protocols create virtual layer
2 networks on the top of the physical network infrastructure. Distributed VMs
appear as connected in one layer 2 network, hence a migration of a VM does not
interfere the virtual layer 2 connection. We therefore present a *VM-based* covert
channel, which uses the movement of a VM to hide the exchange of information.
As a type of covert timing channels, the VM Migration Covert Channel provides poor bandwidth, which still enables the exchange of short information like
passwords. Furthermore the detection is difficult, because of a complex capture
process and a minimum of noticeable changes.

We furthermore examined possible countermeasures of the proposed covert
channels. The protocol-based techniques provide a covert storage channel, which
are easier to detect than the VM-based technique, which acts like a covert timing
channel. On the other hand, the robustness and the overall bandwidth of the
protocol-based channels are better.

A main topic of covert channels is the relation of bandwidth, robustness
and stealthiness. To reduce the risk of identification, the amount of data sent
needs to be adjusted. If the number of extra network packets or the extent of
manipulation in packets is too high, these flows might be detected by a warden
as an anomaly and the covert channel is not concealed any more. The migration
of VMs, creation of snapshots or command and control traffic initiated by the
internal cloud controllers increase the overall number of packets in the network.
Thus, an identification is hampered by the enormous number of network flows.

We present countermeasures for both type of covert channels. Whereas the
use of traffic normalization is a proper way to attack the covert storage channel implemented by the overlay protocols, the identification of a VM Migration
Covert Channel is more complex. The migration of VMs hampers nearly all network forensic investigation in virtual networks, therefore possible countermeasures of moving VMs are hardly feasible. Any implementation of network packet
analysis requires an ongoing and adaptable capture and recording process. The
migration of a VM changes the network infrastructure of the involved systems,
so a system for monitoring and tracking is needed.

5.2   Future Work

Whereas common ways of information hiding are well-known, the wide area of
covert channels and network steganography is still under research. The evolution of modern DCs and the inherent virtualization increase the flexibility and

dynamic behavior inside these environments and facilitate new ways of covert channels. Especially the VM Migration Covert Channel provides a new technique. The overall bandwidth of these covert channel is still restricted, so our future research will be provided on improving the bandwidth and the robustness of these channels. In addition to this, the combination of the proposed techniques will be explored in our future research. The combination might use the protocol-based covert channels for the transmission of the information, whereas the VM Migration Covert Channel is used as a control protocol, which regulates the communication and commands a change of the used overlay protocol. Future work has also to be done to analyze possible countermeasures of virtual covert channels.

References

1. Anderson, T., Peterson, L., Shenker, S., Turner, J.: Overcoming the internet impasse through virtualization. Computer **38**(4), 34–41 (2005)
2. Brook, C.: Attackers hiding stolen credit card numbers in images, October 2016. https://threatpost.com/attackers-hiding-stolen-credit-card-numbers-in-images/121347/. Accessed 13 June 2017
3. Cabuk, S., Brodley, C.E., Shields, C.: IP covert timing channels: design and detection. In: Proceedings of the 11th ACM Conference on Computer and Communications Security, pp. 178–187. ACM (2004)
4. Caviglione, L., Podolski, M., Mazurczyk, W., Ianigro, M.: Covert channels in personal cloud storage services: the case of dropbox. IEEE Trans. Ind. Inf. **6**(99), 1 (2016)
5. Constantin, L.: Fileless powershell malware uses DNS as covert channel, March 2017. http://www.computerworld.com/article/3176669/security/fileless-powershell-malware-uses-dns-as-covert-channel.html. Accessed 13 June 2017
6. Davie, B., Gross, J.: A Stateless Transport Tunneling Protocol for Network Virtualization (STT). Internet-Draft draft-davie-stt-08, Internet Engineering Task Force. https://datatracker.ietf.org/doc/html/draft-davie-stt-08. Work in Progress
7. Fridrich, J.: Applications of data hiding in digital images. In: Proceedings of the Fifth International Symposium on Signal Processing and Its Applications, ISSPA 1999, vol. 1, pp. 1–9. IEEE (1999)
8. Garfinkel, S.: Anti-forensics: techniques, detection and countermeasures. In: 2nd International Conference on i-Warfare and Security, vol. 20087, pp. 77–84 (2007)
9. Gross, J., Sridhar, T., Garg, P., Wright, C., Ganga, I.: GENEVE: Generic network virtualization encapsulation. Internet Engineering Task Force, Internet Draft (2014)
10. Janicki, A., Mazurczyk, W., Szczypiorski, K.: Steganalysis of transcoding steganography. Annales des Télécommunications **69**(7–8), 449–460 (2014)
11. Johnson, N.F., Duric, Z., Jajodia, S.: Information Hiding: Steganography and Watermarking-Attacks and Countermeasures, vol. 1. Springer, New York (2001)
12. Katzenbeisser, S., Petitcolas, F.: Information Hiding Techniques for Steganography and Digital Watermarking. Artech house, Boston (2000)
13. Lampson, B.W.: A note on the confinement problem. Commun. ACM **16**(10), 613–615 (1973)

14. Lipinski, B., Mazurczyk, W., Szczypiorski, K.: Improving hard disk contention-based covert channel in cloud computing. In: Security and Privacy Workshops (SPW), 2014, pp. 100–107. IEEE (2014)
15. Lucena, N.B., Lewandowski, G., Chapin, S.J.: Covert channels in IPv6. In: Danezis, G., Martin, D. (eds.) PET 2005. LNCS, vol. 3856, pp. 147–166. Springer, Heidelberg (2006). doi:10.1007/11767831_10
16. Mahalingam, M., Dutt, D., Duda, K., Agarwal, P., Kreeger, L., Sridhar, T., Bursell, M., Wright, C.: Virtual eXtensible Local Area Network (VXLAN): A Framework for Overlaying Virtualized Layer 2 Networks over Layer 3 Networks. RFC 7348 (Informational). http://www.ietf.org/rfc/rfc7348.txt
17. Mazurczyk, W., Szczypiorski, K.: Covert channels in SIP for VoIP signalling. In: Jahankhani, H., Revett, K., Palmer-Brown, D. (eds.) ICGeS 2008. CCIS, vol. 12, pp. 65–72. Springer, Heidelberg (2008). doi:10.1007/978-3-540-69403-8_9
18. Mazurczyk, W., Wendzel, S., Zander, S., Houmansadr, A., Szczypiorski, K.: Information Hiding in Communication Networks: Fundamentals, Mechanisms, and Applications. IEEE Series on Information and Communication Networks Security. Wiley, New York (2016)
19. Murdoch, S.J., Lewis, S.: Embedding covert channels into TCP/IP. In: Barni, M., Herrera-Joancomartí, J., Katzenbeisser, S., Pérez-González, F. (eds.) IH 2005. LNCS, vol. 3727, pp. 247–261. Springer, Heidelberg (2005). doi:10.1007/11558859_19
20. Okamura, K., Oyama, Y.: Load-based covert channels between Xen virtual machines. In: Proceedings of the 2010 ACM Symposium on Applied Computing, pp. 173–180. ACM (2010)
21. OpenStack: Manage IP addresses, May 2017. https://docs.openstack.org/user-guide/cli-manage-ip-addresses.html. Accessed 13 June 2017
22. Paxson, V., Allman, M., Chu, J., Sargent, M.: Computing TCP's retransmission timer. RFC 6298, RFC Editor. http://www.rfc-editor.org/rfc/rfc6298.txt
23. Pfaff, B., Pettit, J., Koponen, T., Jackson, E.J., Zhou, A., Rajahalme, J., Gross, J., Wang, A., Stringer, J., Shelar, P., et al.: The design and implementation of open vswitch. In: 12th USENIX Symposium on Networked Systems Design and Implementation, pp. 117–130 (2015)
24. Ristenpart, T., Tromer, E., Shacham, H., Savage, S.: Hey, you, get off of my cloud: exploring information leakage in third-party compute clouds. In: Proceedings of the 16th ACM Conference on Computer and Communications Security, pp. 199–212. ACM (2009)
25. Simmons, G.J.: The prisoners' problem and the subliminal channel. In: Advances in Cryptology - CRYPTO 1983, pp. 51–67. Plenum (1984)
26. Spiekermann, D., Eggendorfer, T.: Challenges of network forensic investigation in virtual networks. J. Cyber Secur. Mobility 5(2), 15–46 (2016)
27. Spiekermann, D., Eggendorfer, T.: Towards digital investigation in virtual networks: a study of challenges and open problems. In: International Workshop of Cyber Crime, 2016 International Conference. IEEE (2016)
28. Spiekermann, D., Keller, J., Eggendorfer, T.: Network forensic investigation in openflow networks with forcon. Digital Invest. 20, 66–74 (2017)
29. Walker, S.: The day we discovered our parents were russian spies, May 2016. https://www.theguardian.com/world/2016/may/07/discovered-our-parents-were-russian-spies-tim-alex-foley. Accessed 13 June 2017
30. Wang, Y.S., Garg, P.: NVGRE: Network Virtualization Using Generic Routing Encapsulation. RFC 7637. https://rfc-editor.org/rfc/rfc7637.txt

31. Wendzel, S.: Protocol hopping covert channels. Hakin9 **8**, 20–21 (2008)
32. Wendzel, S.: The problem of traffic normalization within a covert channel's network environment learning phase. In: Suri, N., Waidner, M. (eds.) Sicherheit. LNI, vol. 195, pp. 149–161. GI (2012)
33. Wendzel, S.: Novel approaches for network covert storage channels. Ph.D. thesis, FernUniverstität Hagen (2013)
34. Wendzel, S., Keller, J.: Design and implementation of an active warden addressing protocol switching covert channels. In: Proceedings of 7th International Conference on Internet Monitoring and Protection (ICIMP 2012), pp. 1–6. IARIA (2012)
35. Wu, J., Ding, L., Wang, Y., Han, W.: Identification and evaluation of sharing memory covert timing channel in Xen virtual machines. In: 2011 IEEE International Conference on Cloud Computing (CLOUD), pp. 283–291. IEEE (2011)
36. Xu, Y., Bailey, M., Jahanian, F., Joshi, K., Hiltunen, M., Schlichting, R.: An exploration of l2 cache covert channels in virtualized environments. In: Proceedings of the 3rd ACM Workshop on Cloud Computing Security Workshop, pp. 29–40. ACM (2011)
37. Zimmermann, H.: OSI reference model – the ISO model of architecture for open systems interconnection. IEEE Trans. Commun. **28**(4), 425–432 (1980)

Steganalysis Based on Awareness
of Selection-Channel and Deep Learning

Jianhua Yang[1], Kai Liu[1], Xiangui Kang[1(✉)], Edward Wong[2],
and Yunqing Shi[3]

[1] Guangdong Key Lab of Information Security, Data and Computer Science,
Sun Yat-Sen University, Guangzhou 510006, China
isskxg@mail.sysu.edu.cn
[2] Computer Science and Engineering,
New York University, New York, NY 11201, USA
[3] Electrical and Computer Engineering,
New Jersey Institute of Technology, Newark, NJ 07102, USA

Abstract. Recently, deep learning has been used in steganalysis based on convolutional neural networks (CNN). In this work, we propose a CNN architecture (the so-called maxCNN) to use the selection channel. It is the first time that the knowledge of the selection channel has been incorporated into CNN for steganalysis. The proposed method assigns large weights to features learned from complex texture regions while assigns small weights to features learned from smooth regions. Experimental results on the well-known dataset BOSS-base have demonstrated that the proposed scheme is able to improve detection performance, especially for low embedding payloads. The results have shown that with the ensemble of maxCNN and maxSRMd2+EC, the proposed method can obtain better performance compared with the reported state-of-the-art on detecting WOW embedding algorithm.

Keywords: Adaptive steganography · Steganalysis · Convolutional neural networks (CNN) · Selection-channel

1 Introduction

Recently published content-adaptive steganography algorithms have shown a tendency to mainly execute the data embedding operations in complex texture regions of the cover image. By designing a distortion function and combining with the Syndrome-Trellis Codes (STCs) [1], the security of content-adaptive steganography has been significantly enhanced, such as steganography schemes HUGO [2], WOW [3], S-UNIWARD [4], HILL [5], and MiPOD [6].

During the development of content-adaptive steganography algorithms, some methods based on spatial rich models (SRM) [7] have been proposed to incorporate prior embedding probabilistic knowledge (the so-called probabilistic selection channel) [8–10]. Tang et al. [8] improved the original SRM by calculating the residual co-occurrences only from part of possible modified pixels with low embedding costs. Their experimental results on attacking WOW method have shown that restricting

© Springer International Publishing AG 2017
C. Kraetzer et al. (Eds.): IWDW 2017, LNCS 10431, pp. 263–272, 2017.
DOI: 10.1007/978-3-319-64185-0_20

feature extraction on suspicious regions can improve the effectiveness of steganalysis, especially for low embedding payloads. They also suggested in [9] that even if the embedding algorithm is unknown, embedding probabilities could still be estimated by using the re-embedding method. Denemark et al. [10] proposed a variant of SRM (the so-called maxSRM) to make use of the probabilistic selection channel. When computing co-occurrence matrix, the co-occurrence bin for every pixel is changed from one to the maximum of the four neighboring embedding probabilities with horizontal and vertical scans ('hv' scans). They also investigated the co-occurrence scan direction, e.g., the proposed maxSRMd2 using the 'oblique' scan could collect twice as much data for the co-occurrences, and it is always better than 'hv' scans. They suggested in [11] that incorporating knowledge of the selection channel based on three feature sets: DCT Residuals (DCTR) [12], PHase Aware Rich Model (PHARM) [13], and Gabor Filter Residuals (GFR) [14], could improve the detection performance in the JPEG domain.

The use of deep learning in the field of computer vision has marked a breakthrough and indicated the bright prospects. This technology also caught the attention of steganalysis researchers [15–20].

In late 2014, Tan and Li [15] proposed a method to utilize the CNN structure equipped with convolutional auto-encoder in the pre-training procedure. Experimental results have shown that the proposed scheme could work for attacking HUGO at 0.4 bpp, while the performance was inferior to what achieved by the SRM.

In early 2015, Qian et al. [16] proposed a CNN structure equipped with Gaussian non-linear activation. In 2016, Qian et al. [17] indicated that the difference between cover and stego are small for the embedding with low payload, so it is hard for CNN to train the model. They proposed a framework based on transfer learning, which indicated that pre-training the CNN model using high payload, then fine-tuning for low payload could improve the performance. The auxiliary information from the stego with a high payload has been used to help the task of analyzing stego with a low payload. Experimental results have shown that transfer learning can improve the performance, especially for low payloads.

In 2016, Xu et al. [18] proposed a CNN structure for steganalysis that is able to obtain comparable performance to SRM with ensemble classifier (EC) on detecting SUNIWARD and HILL. They use batch-normalization to prevent CNN training from falling into poor local minima. To prevent overfitting, they equipped the CNN structure with TanH layer at early stages and using 1×1 convolutions in deeper layers. The output probabilities from five trained CNN were averaged as the last classifying probabilities. In [19], Xu et al. further improved the structure presented in [18], then used ensemble classifiers [20] as the second-level classifier to further improve the performance.

In 2017, Sedighi et al. [21] proposed a histogram layer to simulate PSRM [22] models within the CNN framework. They select Gaussian kernel as histogram bin. Experimental results showed that the trained kernels can obtain better performance than random kernels as the PSRM used when the number of Kernels are less than 17. The proposed method indicated that it may reduce the dimensionality of the PSRM by using the kernels trained in CNN structure.

Although using deep learning for steganalysis has obtained comparable performance with SRM+EC, to the best of our knowledge, there has been no reports on applying channel selection in deep learning for steganalysis.

In this paper, we modified Xu's CNN architecture [19] to assign weights to features during the forward propagation step in the CNN architecture. The maximum value within a 9×9 neighborhood of the embedding probability matrix has been used as the weight in the CNN architecture. We name this version of CNN architecture as maxCNN in this paper. The experiments examining WOW on standard datasets have shown that the utilized channel selection can improve the detection accuracy in the CNN architecture.

The rest of this paper is organized as follows. In Sect. 2, we briefly introduce the use of channel selection in conventional steganalysis methods. In Sect. 3, we introduce the proposed maxCNN that incorporates prior probabilistic knowledge. Experiments and discussion are presented in Sect. 4. Conclusion and future work are contained in Sect. 5.

2 Steganalysis with Channel-Selection Awareness

In this section, we briefly introduce the theory of channel selection for steganalysis. Figure 1 illustrates the modification position and the embedding probabilities map for the WOW steganography method. Figure 1(b) shows the absolute value of the difference between cover and stego. It can be seen that the embedding position is concentrated on complex texture regions. Based on this observation, Tang et al. indicated that extracting residual co-occurrences only from complex texture regions can lead to better performance than extracting features from the whole image [8]. From Fig. 1(b) and (c), it can be observed that the messages were embedded into the regions where the so-called embedding probabilities are relatively larger. As was indicated in conventional steganalysis method [8–10], using embedding probabilities as weights of pixels located in different regions when extracting co-occurrence matrices can improve the detection accuracy.

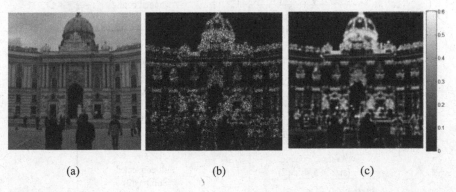

(a)   (b)   (c)

Fig. 1. Illustration of embedding modification and embedding probabilities for WOW algorithm. (a) Cover image. (b) Modification position (0.4 bpp). (c) Embedding probabilities (0.4 bpp).

The main idea here, which considers the prior embedding probabilistic knowledge (the so-called probabilistic selection channel) in feature extraction, is to assign large weights to pixels located in complex texture regions and assign small weights to pixels located in smooth regions. Based on this observation, we will explore an approach in CNN architecture that incorporates prior embedding probabilistic knowledge to improve detection performance.

3   The Proposed Scheme

In this section, we introduce the proposed scheme, maxCNN, using selection-channel awareness based on Xu et al.'s CNN architecture [19].

3.1   The Original CNN Architecture

Figure 2 illustrates the CNN architecture proposed by Xu et al. [19]. In the detailed architecture, they use a convolutional module and a classification module. In the convolutional module, they first calculate the residual through the high pass filter (HPF), and then 6 groups of layers are used to obtain the final feature vectors. Each group starts with a convolutional layer and ends with an average pooling layer.

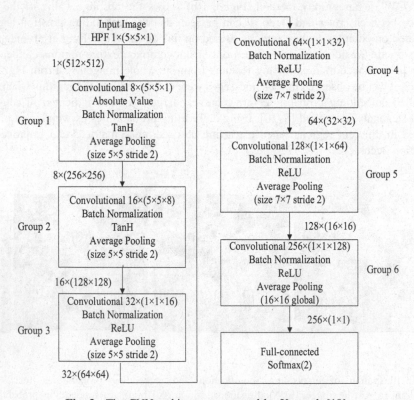

Fig. 2. The CNN architecture proposed by Xu et al. [19].

Batch normalization [23] is used in order to normalize the feature maps. Group 1 is equipped with an ABS layer to consider the sign symmetry that exists in noise residuals. In Group 1 and Group 2, TanH layers are used as nonlinear activation while other groups are equipped with ReLU for non-linear activation. In the classification module, a Softmax layer is used to obtain the final class probabilities.

3.2 The Proposed CNN Architecture Incorporating Selection-Channel Awareness

As illustrated in Fig. 3, Group 1 of the CNN architecture [19] is modified in this work. We assign weight to the feature obtained after activation function layer TanH, while the remaining groups keep the same as the original architecture. In this way, the features learned from complex texture and edge regions are assigned a larger weight, while features learned from smooth regions are assigned a smaller weight. Hence, it is expected that better detection performance may be achieved by using this strategy. The details of the modified Group1 of the CNN architecture are described as follows:

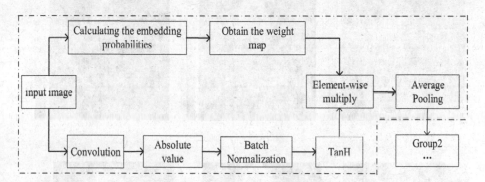

Fig. 3. The modified Group 1 in the box of dotted line.

- **Step 1: Generate the feature map.** For an input image of size 512×512, obtain 8 feature maps after the TanH layer of the modified Group 1, with cardinality of 512×512.
- **Step 2: Calculate embedding probability matrix.** For each pixel located at position (i, j) of the input image, calculate the embedding probabilities $p_{i,j}$ with optimal embedding simulator [8–10] and obtain an embedding probability matrix with cardinality of 512×512.
- **Step 3: Obtain weight map.** For each location (i, j) of the embedding probability matrix, take the maximum value within a 9×9 neighborhood and assign it as the weight $w_{i,j}$:

$$w_{i,j} = \max_{\substack{m = -4\ldots4 \\ n = -4\ldots4}} p_{i+m,j+m} \tag{1}$$

- **Step 4: Obtain the weighted feature map.** In this step, each feature map obtained in Step 1 is element-wise multiplied by the weight map generated in Step 3.

Note that Step 2 and Step 3 are not involved in back-propagation, because for a given image at certain payload, the probability matrix is fixed. Also note that the position of the weighted layer in Group 1 and the size of neighborhood 9×9 were determined after performing a number of experiments.

To provide an intuitive perception on the change before and after the feature map being weighted, let us take a look at Fig. 4. Figure 4(a) and (d) describe the feature maps after the TanH layer of Group 1 with 0.1 bpp and 0.4 bpp on detecting WOW. Figure 4(b) and (e) are the weight maps generated in Step 3. Figure 4(c) and (f) are the feature maps after being weighted. It can be seen that after multiplication with the weight map, features located in complex texture regions will be kept while features learned from smooth regions will be restrained. This phenomenon will be more obvious when the embedding payload is 0.1 bpp.

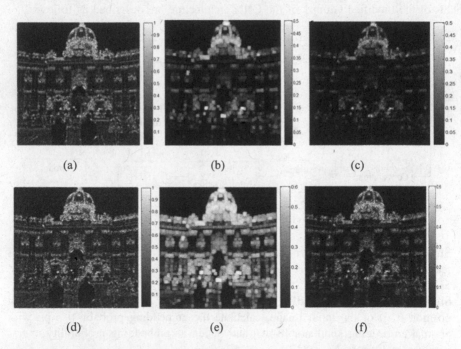

Fig. 4. Illustration of assigning weights to the feature maps on detecting WOW. (a) Before being weighted (0.1 bpp). (b) Weight map (0.1 bpp). (c) After being weighted (0.1 bpp). (d) Before being weighted (0.4 bpp). (e) Weight map (0.4 bpp). (f) After being weighted (0.4 bpp)

4   Experimental Result

4.1   Dataset and Setting

We use the standard dataset BOSSbase v1.01 [24] which contains 10,000 cover images of size 512×512 in our experiments. The Caffe toolbox [25] is used to implement the CNN. The hyper parameters remain the same as [19], except that all the CNN were trained for 200,000 iterations. The corresponding performance achieved by the CNN [19] and maxSRMd2+EC are used as references.

Before conducting the experiments, 10,000 pairs of cover/stego images are shuffled, and then 2,000 pairs of images are selected for testing. The remaining 8,000 pair of images are used in the training step.

For each experiment, we use a different seed to randomly select 7,000 pairs from the 8,000 training pairs for training the model, and the remaining 1,000 pairs are used as a validation set to select the optimal model. Every test image went through five trained CNN models and five output probabilities were averaged to make the final prediction as proposed in [18]. To ensemble the CNN models and SRM models, we use the ensemble method as proposed in [26]. For every test image, the average of the ten output predicted probabilities from the five trained maxCNN models and the five maxSRMd2+EC models is used as the final ensemble prediction probability.

4.2   Result and Discussion

We only analyzed WOW embedding algorithms with payload 0.1 bpp and 0.4 bpp due to time limitation. We initialize the network using the parameters learned from pre-trained network with 0.4 bpp as proposed in [17]. The experimental results are presented in Tables 1 and 2.

Table 1. Detection accuracy (%) on detecting WOW

Payload	maxCNN (proposed)	Xu's CNN [19]	maxSRMd2+EC [10, 20]
0.1 bpp	**66.90**	64.62	69.75
0.4 bpp	**85.08**	84.25	84.73

Table 2. Detection accuracy (%) of the ensemble method on detecting WOW

Payload	maxCNN and maxSRMd2+EC [10, 20]	maxSRMd2+EC [10, 20]
0.1 bpp	**71.52**	69.75
0.4 bpp	**87.60**	84.73

Table 1 contains results from the proposed maxCNN, CNN [19] and maxSRMd2 +EC [10, 20]. It can be seen that the improvement of the proposed maxCNN over CNN [19] are 2.28% for 0.1 bpp and 0.83% for 0.4 bpp, respectively. It can also obtain comparable performance with maxSRMd2+EC when payload is 0.4 bpp, however, it is still inferior to maxSRMd2+EC when payload is 0.1bpp.

In Table 2, the result of the ensemble method is reported. The first column refers to the ensemble of proposed maxCNN and maxSRMd2+EC. The second column refers to the accuracy of maxSRMd2+EC. It can be observed that with the ensemble of maxCNN and maxSRMd2+EC, detection accuracy can also be further improved.

To further evaluate the improved performance over CNN [19], we use ROC (receiver operating characteristic) curve and it's AUC (area under curve) value to compare with CNN [19]. Figure 5 illustrates the ROC curves on attacking WOW 0.1 and 0.4 bpp. From Fig. 5, it can be seen that the proposed maxCNN can obtain a larger AUC value than CNN [19].

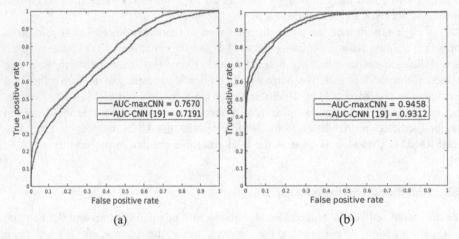

(a)   (b)

Fig. 5. ROC curves and corresponding AUC value illustrating the performance of the proposed maxCNN and CNN [19] on detecting WOW. (a) 0.1 bpp. (b) 0.4 bpp.

5   Conclusion

Modern content-adaptive steganography often embeds the changes in complex texture regions. The prior probabilistic knowledge (the so-called probabilistic selection channel) has been well-utilized in conventional steganalysis methods but still has not been utilized in deep learning method. In this paper, we have proposed a CNN architecture (the so-called maxCNN) based on CNN [19] to use the selection channel. The proposed method assigns large weights to features learned from complex texture regions while assigning small weights to features learned from smooth regions. It is the first time that embedding probabilities have been used as weights in a CNN architecture for steganalysis. Experiments on detecting WOW have shown that the proposed scheme could outperform the original CNN [19], especially for low embedding payloads such as 0.1 bpp. The ensemble of the proposed maxCNN and conventional method maxSRMd2+EC can obtain better performance compared with prior methods on detecting WOW embedding algorithm.

In the future, we will conduct research to further move this work ahead to improve performance. Furthermore, we will work on other steganographic schemes such as

S-UNIWARD, HILL, and MiPOD. We will also move the research ahead by using the selection channel to detect adaptive JPEG steganography in the CNN architecture.

Acknowledgements. This work was supported by NSFC (Grant nos. U1536204, 61379155), Special funding for basic scientific research of Sun Yat-sen University (6177060230).

References

1. Filler, T., Judas, J., Fridrich, J.: Minimizing additive distortion in steganography using syndrome-trellis codes. IEEE Trans. Inf. Forensics Secur. **6**(3), 920–935 (2011)
2. Pevný, T., Filler, T., Bas, P.: Using high-dimensional image models to perform highly undetectable steganography. In: Böhme, R., Fong, P.W.L., Safavi-Naini, R. (eds.) III 2010. LNCS, vol. 6387, pp. 161–177. Springer, Heidelberg (2010). doi:10.1007/978-3-642-16435-4_13
3. Holub, V., Fridrich, J.: Designing steganographic distortion using directional filters. In: 2012 IEEE International Workshop on Information Forensics and Security (WIFS), pp. 234–239 (2012)
4. Holub, V., Fridrich, J., Denemark, T.: Universal distortion function for steganography in an arbitrary domain. EURASIP J. Inf. Secur. **2014**(1), 1 (2014)
5. Li, B., Wang, M., Huang, J., Li, X.: A new cost function for spatial image steganography. In: Proceedings of IEEE ICIP, Paris, France, pp. 4206–4210, October 2014
6. Sedighi, V., Cogranne, R., Fridrich, J.: Content-adaptive steganography by minimizing statistical detectability. IEEE Trans. Inf. Forensics Secur. **11**(2), 221–234 (2016)
7. Fridrich, J., Kodovsky, J.: Rich models for steganalysis of digital images. IEEE Trans. Inf. Forensics Secur. **7**(3), 868–882 (2012)
8. Tang, W., Li, H., Luo, W., Huang, J.: Adaptive steganalysis against WOW embedding algorithm. In: Proceedings of ACM IH&MMSec, pp. 91–96 (2014)
9. Tang, W., Li, H., Luo, W., Huang, J.: Adaptive steganalysis based on embedding probabilities of pixels. IEEE Trans. Inf. Forensics Secur. **11**, 734–745 (2015)
10. Denemark, T., Sedighi, V., Holub, V., Cogranne, R., Fridrich, J.: Selection-channel-aware rich model for steganalysis of digital images. In: Proceedings of Information Forensics Security (WIFS), pp. 48–53, December 2014
11. Denemark, T., Boroumand, M., Fridrich, J.: Steganalysis features for content-adaptive JPEG steganography. IEEE Trans. Inf. Forensics Secur. **11**(8), 1736–1746 (2016)
12. Holub, V., Fridrich, J.: Low-complexity features for JPEG steganalysis using undecimated DCT. IEEE Trans. Inf. Forensics Secur. **10**(2), 219–228 (2015)
13. Holub, V., Fridrich, J.: Phase-aware projection model for steganalysis of JPEG images. In: Proceedings of SPIE, vol. 9409, p. 94090T, February 2015
14. Song, X., Liu, F., Yang, C., Luo, X., Zhang, Y.: Steganalysis of adaptive JPEG steganography using 2D Gabor filters. In: Proceedings of the 3rd ACM IH&MMSec. Workshop, pp. 15–23, June 2015
15. Tan, S., Li, B.: Stacked convolutional auto-encoders for steganalysis of digital images. In: Proceedings of APSIPA, pp. 1–4, December 2014
16. Qian, Y., Dong, J., Wang, W., Tan, T.: Deep learning for steganalysis via convolutional neural networks. In: Proceedings of SPIE Electronic Imaging, p. 94090J, March 2015

17. Qian, Y., Dong, J., Wang, W., Tan, T.: Learning and transferring representations for image steganalysis using convolutional neural network. In: 2016 IEEE International Conference on Image Processing (ICIP), Phoenix, AZ, pp. 2752–2756, September 2016
18. Xu, G., Wu, H., Shi, Y.: Structural design of convolutional neural networks for steganalysis. IEEE Signal Process. Lett. **23**(5), 708–712 (2016)
19. Xu, G., Wu, H.-Z., Shi, Y.Q.: Ensemble of CNNs for Steganalysis: an empirical study. In: Proceedings of the 4th ACM Workshop on Information Hiding and Multimedia Security. ACM (2016)
20. Kodovsky, J., Fridrich, J., Holub, V.: Ensemble classifiers for steganalysis of digital media. IEEE Trans. Inf. Forensics Secur. **7**(2), 432–444 (2012)
21. Sedighi, V., Fridrich, J.: Histogram layer, moving convolutional neural networks towards feature-based steganalysis. In: IS&T/SPIE Electronic Imaging, Burlingame, California, 29 January - 2 February 2017
22. Holub, V., Fridrich, J.: Random projections of residuals for digital image steganalysis. IEEE Trans. Inf. Forensics Secur. **8**(12), 1996–2006 (2013)
23. Ioffe, S., Szegedy, C.: Batch normalization: accelerating deep network training by reducing internal covariate shift, February 2015. arXiv:1502.03167
24. Bas, P., Filler, T., Pevný, T.: "Break our steganographic system": the ins and outs of organizing BOSS. In: Filler, T., Pevný, T., Craver, S., Ker, A. (eds.) IH 2011. LNCS, vol. 6958, pp. 59–70. Springer, Heidelberg (2011). doi:10.1007/978-3-642-24178-9_5
25. Jia, Y., Shelhamer, E., Donahue, J., Karayev, S., Long, J., Girshick, R., Guadarrama, S., Darrell, T.: Caffe: convolutional architecture for fast feature embedding. In: Proceedings of ACM International Conference Multimedia, pp. 675–678 (2014)
26. Liu, K., Yang, J., Kang, X.: Ensemble of CNN and rich model for steganalysis. In: 2017 IEEE International Conference on Systems, Signals and Image Processing (IWSSIP), pp. 1–5 (2017)

Watermarking

Improved Algorithms for Robust Histogram Shape-Based Image Watermarking

Bingwen Feng[1], Jian Weng[1(⊠)], and Wei Lu[2]

[1] College of Information Science and Technology,
Jinan University, Guangzhou 510632, China
`bingwfeng@gmail.com, cryptjweng@gmail.com`
[2] School of Data and Computer Science,
Guangdong Key Laboratory of Information Security Technology,
Sun Yat-sen University, Guangzhou 510006, China
`luwei3@mail.sysu.edu.cn`

Abstract. In histogram shape-based watermarking schemes, watermark bits are embedded by altering the shape of a histogram extracted from the host image. Exited embedding algorithms use a group of histogram bins to embed only one watermark bit, which results in a rather low watermark capacity. In this paper, we improve the embedding algorithm in two new ways. The first proposed algorithm performs multi-round embedding to carry more watermark bits. In each round of embedding, a specified histogram is extracted so that the embedding operation does not affect watermark bits embedded in previous rounds. The second proposed algorithm uses a group of histogram bins to embed more than one watermark bits, where the coefficient transferring is optimized to minimize the embedding distortion. These algorithms can effectively enlarge the capacity. Furthermore, a histogram preadjustment method, together with a refined coefficient transferring method, is introduced. As a result, reasonable performances on robustness and watermarked image quality are available. The proposed algorithms provide various tradeoff among capacity, robustness, and perceptibility, which supports a wide range of applications.

Keywords: Blind watermarking · Robustness · Multilevel histogram · Multiple histogram adjustment

1 Introduction

Digital image watermarking is a technique about covertly embedding messages into host images for certain security purposes. Robustness is an important property for a watermarking scheme. It calls for that the embedded messages should resist various attacks, such as common signal processing and geometric attacks. Compared with common signal processing, it is more difficult to develop effective watermarking algorithms robust to geometric attacks, since they will cause challenging synchronization problem.

© Springer International Publishing AG 2017
C. Kraetzer et al. (Eds.): IWDW 2017, LNCS 10431, pp. 275–289, 2017.
DOI: 10.1007/978-3-319-64185-0_21

Many watermarking schemes have been suggested to tackle geometric attacks. By assuming the possible space of attack parameters, some schemes embed negotiated templates and exhaustively resynchronize them in the watermarked image [1–3]. Geometrically invariant image features can also help synchronize watermark bits. Invariant feature detectors such as multiscale Harris detector [4], Harris-Laplace detector [5], scale-invariant feature transform (SIFT) [3], etc., have been used to extract local embedding areas. A concern related to these approaches is that they may suffer from expensive computational cost and high false alarm probability [6]. Some schemes exploit the geometrically invariant domain to gain the robustness against the corresponded geometric attacks. A pioneering work is the Fourier-Mellin transformation designed to be invariant to global rotation, translation, and scaling [7]. Other transformation methods such as moment invariants [8], uniform log-polar mapping [9], polar harmonic transformation [10] are also developed to create geometrically invariant domain. The complexity of these schemes is still high, which is not suitable for real-time applications.

In 2008, Xiang et al. proposed a robust watermarking scheme by utilizing the histogram shape [11]. The histogram constructed from an entire image is independent of pixel locations and thus robust to various geometric distortions. Furthermore, the corresponded watermark extraction does not require local image information, which reduces the risk of desynchronization. This histogram-based watermarking method has been further extended in [5,12,13], etc. They improve robustness by combining other robust watermarking techniques or compensating the drawback in the original design. However, the watermark embedding algorithm remains almost unchanged. In these schemes, several bins are employed to embed one watermark bit, which results in a rather low capacity. It is not satisfactory for many applications.

In this paper, two embedding algorithms are proposed to enlarge the capacity of histogram shape-based watermarking. The first one employs multilevel histogram. It embeds watermark bits via several rounds, in each of which a histogram at a specified level is extracted to carry one watermark sequence. The second one considers multiple bin adjustment. It divides the histogram into segments, into each of which a number of watermark bits can be embedded simultaneously. In the embedding procedure, a histogram preadjustment method is introduced to make the histogram extracted more suitable for embedding watermark bits. The coefficient transferring is also refined to minimize the embedding distortion. These proposed algorithms present various tradeoff between robustness and perceptibility, which enriches the application of histogram shape-based watermarking.

2   Previous Works

This section briefly describes the histogram-based watermarking method suggested in [11]. It starts by pre-filtering the host image with a Gaussian low-pass filter to gain the robustness against common signal processing. Denote the low-pass filtered image as I_{low}, which is of size $m_I \times n_I$. Then a global histogram with $\#(H)$ bins, $H = \{H(i)|1 \le i \le \#(H)\}$, is extracted from I_{low} by

$$H(i) = \sum_{x=1}^{m_I} \sum_{y=1}^{n_I} \delta\left(\left\lceil \frac{I_{\text{low}}(x,y) - b_1}{t} \right\rceil = i\right) \tag{1}$$

where $\delta(\cdot) = 1$ if and only if its argument is satisfied, otherwise $\delta(\cdot) = 0$. t denotes the histogram bin width and can be obtained as $t = (b_2 - b_1)/\#(H)$. b_1 and b_2 define the range of coefficient values used to extract the histogram. That is, H only involves $I_{\text{low}}(x,y) \in [b_1, b_2]$. This range is modeled by the mean of I_{low}.

Then each two neighboring bins form a group to embed one watermark bit. Suppose two bins $H(2i - 1)$ and $H(2i)$, $1 \le i \le \#(H)/2$, are used to embed watermark bit $M(i)$. Their population is then adjusted in order to satisfy

$$\begin{cases} \frac{H(2i-1)+n}{H(2i)-n} \ge \alpha & \text{if } M(i) = 1 \\ \frac{H(2i)-n}{H(2i-1)+n} \ge \alpha & \text{if } M(i) = 0 \end{cases} \tag{2}$$

where threshold α controls the population gap between bins, and n represents the number of coefficients that are transferred from $H(2i)$ to $H(2i - 1)$. n is negative when coefficients need to be transferred from $H(2i - 1)$ to $H(2i)$. Its value can be calculated as

$$n = \begin{cases} \max\left\{ \frac{\alpha \times H(2i) - H(2i-1)}{1+\alpha}, \; 0 \right\} & \text{if } M(i) = 1 \\ \min\left\{ \frac{\alpha \times H(2i-1) - H(2i)}{1+\alpha}, \; 0 \right\} & \text{if } M(i) = 0 \end{cases} \tag{3}$$

to minimize the number of transferred coefficients.

At the extraction phase, the histogram $\tilde{H}$ is extracted from the received image. Watermark bits are extracted according to

$$\tilde{M}(i) = \begin{cases} 1, & \text{if } \tilde{H}(2i - 1) \ge \tilde{H}(2i) \\ 0, & \text{otherwise} \end{cases} \tag{4}$$

Mean value and Gaussian kernel are searched in addition to increase the probability of watermark matching. Note that these searchings require the embedded message to be known at the receiver.

It can be observed that the maximum payload of the embedding algorithm given in Eq. (2) is $\#(M) = \lfloor (b_2 - b_1)/(2t) \rfloor$. This scheme has been extended in many approaches, e.g., [5,12,13]. However, the embedding algorithm remains similar. As a result, they suffer from the same payload limitation. In the next sections, we present two improved embedding algorithms, which can enlarge the payload effectively.

3   Improved Algorithm 1

3.1   Coefficient Transferring

The histogram shape-based embedding method requires transferring a certain number of low-frequency coefficients from one histogram bin to another.

Denote the operation of transferring n coefficients from $H(i)$ to $H(j)$ as $H(i) \xrightarrow{n} H(j)$. We propose a new transferring method to minimize the coefficient modification with respect to the Peak Signal to Noise Ratio (PSNR) index.

Take the situation $H(i) \xrightarrow{n} H(j)$, $i < j$, as an example. Since the value range of the coefficients in $H(j)$ is $[b_1 + (j-1) \times t, b_1 + j \times t)$, these coefficients can be changed to $b_1 + (j-1) \times t + 0.1$ to restrict the embedding distortion. Let $\mathcal{B} = \{(x_k, y_k) | 1 \leq k \leq n\}$ denote the set of the best n coefficients. The k-th element of $\mathcal{B}$ can be obtained as

$$(x_k, y_k) = \arg\min_{(x_p, y_p) \in \mathcal{H}'(i)} \left(b_1 + (j-1) \times t + 0.1 - I_{\text{low}}(x_p, y_p)\right)^2 \tag{5}$$

where

$$\mathcal{H}'(i) = \mathcal{H}(i) - \{(x_p, y_p) | 1 \leq p \leq k-1\} \tag{6}$$

where $(x_k, y_k) \in \mathcal{H}(i)$ holds if $I_{\text{low}}(x_k, y_k)$ belongs to $H(i)$. The situation when $i > j$ is similar, except the objective function defined in Eq. (5) now becomes

$$(x_k, y_k) = \arg\min_{(x_p, y_p) \in \mathcal{H}'(i)} \left(b_1 + j \times t - 0.1 - I_{\text{low}}(x_p, y_p)\right)^2 \tag{7}$$

3.2 Histogram Preadjustment

Occasionally some bins of the histogram extracted from the host image are thinly populated and thus not suitable to carry watermark bits. Herein we introduce a histogram preadjustment method to guarantee good population for each bin. It transfers coefficients from the other bins to those whose population is less than a threshold β. This preadjustment is detailed in Algorithm 1. The selection of β will be discussed in Sect. 5.1.

Algorithm 1. Histogram Adjustment

Require: original histogram H, threshold β.
1: **for** $i = 1$ to $\#(H) - 1$ **do**
2:    $n \leftarrow \left(\sum_{j=i}^{\#(H)} H(j)\right) - (\#(H) - i) \times \beta$.
3:    **if** $H(i) > n$ **then**
4:       $H(i) \xrightarrow{H(i)-n} H(i+1)$.
5:    **end if**
6:    $n \leftarrow \beta - H(i)$, $j \leftarrow i + 1$.
7:    **while** $n > 0$ **do**
8:       $n' \leftarrow \min\{H(j), n\}$.
9:       $H(j) \xrightarrow{n'} H(i)$.
10:      $j \leftarrow j + 1$, $n \leftarrow n - n'$.
11:    **end while**
12: **end for**
13: **return** adjusted histogram H.

3.3   Embedding Algorithm Based on Multilevel Histogram

The first embedding algorithm embeds watermark bits via several rounds. Suppose in the first embedding round, a histogram $H^{(1)}$ with $\#(H^{(1)})$ bins, which are of width $t^{(1)}$, is extracted, and the $\#(M^{(1)})$ watermark bits to be embedded are $M^{(1)} = \{M^{(1)}(i) \mid 1 \leq i \leq \#(M^{(1)})\}$. Then each two neighboring bins $H^{(1)}(2i-1)$ and $H^{(1)}(2i)$, $1 \leq i \leq \#(H^{(1)})/2$, are employed to embed watermark bit $M^{(1)}(i)$ by using Eq. (2).

In the u-th embedding round, a finer histogram $H^{(u)}$ is extracted by dividing each bin in $H^{(u-1)}$, namely $H^{(u-1)}(i)$, into two neighboring bins $H^{(u)}(2i-1)$ and $H^{(u)}(2i)$ of equal width. It can be implemented equivalently by performing Eq. (1) with bin width $t^{(u)} = t^{(u-1)}/2$. There are $\#(H^{(u)}) = 2\#(H^{(u-1)})$ bins in $H^{(u)}$. Consequently, another watermark sequence of length $\#(M^{(u)}) = 2\#(M^{(u-1)})$ can be embedded. The embedding processing is as same as that in the first round. Since it satisfies that

$$H^{(u)}(2i-1) + H^{(u)}(2i) = H^{(u-1)}(i) \tag{8}$$

reassigning coefficients between $H^{(u)}(2i-1)$ and $H^{(u)}(2i)$ does not alter the shape of $H^{(u-1)}$.

3.4   The Embedding Procedure

This section presents a watermarking scheme by using the first embedding algorithm. Suppose the number of embedding round is $\#(u)$. The procedure of embedding watermark bits with the first algorithm consists of the following steps.

1. Low-pass filter the host image I with a Gaussian filter similar to that in [11] to obtain the low-frequency component I_{low} and the high-frequency residual $I_{\text{high}} = I - I_{\text{low}}$.
2. Initialize the embedding round as $u = 1$ and the intermediate watermarked low-frequency component as $\bar{I}_{\text{low}} = I_{\text{low}}$.
3. Extract the u-th level histogram $H^{(u)}$ from $\bar{I}_{\text{low}}$ via Eq. (1) with bin width $t^{(u)}$.
4. If $u = 1$, adjust the histogram by Algorithm 1. Otherwise, adjust the histogram by using

$$\begin{cases} H(2i-1) \xrightarrow{\gamma^{(u)} - H(2i)} H(2i), & \text{if } H(2i) < \gamma^{(u)} \\ H(2i) \xrightarrow{\gamma^{(u)} - H(2i-1)} H(2i-1), & \text{if } H(2i-1) < \gamma^{(u)} \\ \text{No modification}, & \text{otherwise} \end{cases} \tag{9}$$

where $\gamma^{(u)}$ denotes the lower bound of bin population for the u-th round of embedding.
5. Embed the i-th watermark bit $M^{(u)}(i)$ into $H^{(u)}(2i-1)$ and $H^{(u)}(2i)$ by Eqs. (2) and (3) with threshold $\alpha^{(u)}$. Note that all coefficient modifications are carried out on $\bar{I}_{\text{low}}$.

6. Repeat Step 5 until all the $\#(M^{(u)})$ watermark bits have been embedded, which gives a new $\bar{I}_{\text{low}}$.
7. Increase the embedding round as $u = u + 1$. If $u \leq \#(u)$, set $t^{(u)} = t^{(u-1)}/2$ and redo the embedding procedure from Step 3 to perform the next round of embedding. Go to Step 8 otherwise.
8. Post-process the $\bar{I}_{\text{low}}$ obtained after the last round of embedding in a way similar to that in [11]. That is, for the (x, y)-th coefficient that belongs to $H^{(\#(u))}(i)$,

$$
\bar{I}_{\text{low}}(x, y) =
\begin{cases}
(i - 1) \times t^{(\#(u))} + b_1 + 0.75, & \text{if } \bar{I}_{\text{low}}(x, y) < (i - 1) \times t^{(\#(u))} + b_1 + 0.75 \\
i \times t^{(\#(u))} + b_1 - 0.75, & \text{if } \bar{I}_{\text{low}}(x, y) > i \times t^{(\#(u))} + b_1 - 0.75 \\
\bar{I}_{\text{low}}(x, y), & \text{otherwise}
\end{cases}
\tag{10}
$$

9. Reconstruct the watermarked image $\bar{I}$ by $\bar{I} = \bar{I}_{\text{low}} + I_{\text{high}}$.

In the above procedure, $\gamma^{(u)}$ and $\alpha^{(u)}$ for each round of embedding should be carefully set so that there are enough coefficients for each coefficient transferring. They will be experimentally discussed in Sect. 4.1. The embedding parameters, $b_1, b_2, t^{(1)}, \gamma^{(u)}$, and $\alpha^{(u)}$, should be prefixed. At the extraction phase, parameters b_1, b_2, and $t^{(1)}$ are required. The extraction procedure can be derived accordingly and omitted here due to limited space.

4   Improved Algorithm 2

4.1   Embedding Algorithm Based on Multiple Adjustment

The second embedding algorithm uses a group of histogram bins to embed more than one watermark bit. The histogram extracted from the host image is first divided into segments containing π neighboring bins. Then, each segment is used to embed $\pi - 1$ watermark bits.

Take the first histogram and watermark segments, denoted as $[H(1), \ldots, H(\pi)]$ and $[M(1), \ldots, M(\pi - 1)]$, respectively, as an example. Each two neighboring histogram bins in the segment, $H(j)$ and $H(j+1)$, embed one watermark bit, $M(j)$, by using the rule

$$
\begin{cases}
H(j) \geq \alpha H(j + 1) & \text{for } M(j) = 1 \\
H(j + 1) \geq \alpha H(j) & \text{for } M(j) = 0
\end{cases}
\tag{11}
$$

The desired coefficient transferring should minimize the total embedding distortion while guaranteeing the population gaps between neighboring bins and the lower bound of bin population. Still consider PSNR as the perceptual measurement. Then the best coefficient transferring can be obtained by solving

$$\arg\min_{N} \sum_{j,k} \left((j - k - 1) \times t + \delta \right)^2 |N(j,k)| \tag{12}$$

s.t. for $1 \leq \forall j, \forall k \leq \pi$:

$$H(j) - \sum_{p} N(j,p) + \sum_{q} N(q,j) \geq \gamma$$

$$\begin{cases} H(j) - \sum_{p} N(j,p) + \sum_{q} N(q,j) \geq \\ \quad \alpha \left(H(j+1) - \sum_{p} N(j+1,p) + \sum_{q} N(q,j+1) \right), \text{ if } M(j) = 1 \\ H(j+1) - \sum_{p} N(j+1,p) + \sum_{q} N(q,j+1) \geq \\ \quad \alpha \left(H(j) - \sum_{p} N(j,p) + \sum_{q} N(q,j) \right), \text{ if } M(j) = 0 \end{cases}$$

$$N(j,k) = 0, \text{ if } j > k$$

where γ represents the allowable thinnest population for each bin, and N denotes the $\pi \times \pi$ sized transferring number matrix. $N(j,k) > 0$ means we should perform $H(j) \xrightarrow{N(j,k)} H(k)$, and $N(j,k) < 0$ calls for the operation $H(k) \xrightarrow{-N(j,k)} H(j)$.

By rewriting the above l_1-norm problem to a linear program, and using, for example, the dual-simplex algorithm, we can obtain a solution, say N'. Then the histogram segment is modified according to N' by starting from the transferring with the largest distance, namely $N'(j', k')$ with

$$(j', k') = \arg\min_{j,k} |j - k| \quad \text{s.t.} \quad N'(j,k) \neq 0 \tag{13}$$

The processing of embedding the i th watermark segment into the i-th histogram segment is similar. Since the influences of modifying coefficients on PSNR are independent of each other and strictly convex, the above embedding algorithm can achieve the minimum embedding distortion with respect to PSNR.

4.2 The Embedding Procedure

A watermarking scheme using the second embedding algorithm is developed here. Note that all the coefficient transferring involved in this scheme is still performed via the method introduced in Sect. 3.1. The embedding parameters, b_1, b_2, t, π, γ, and α need to be prefixed. The procedure of embedding watermark bits with the second algorithm is as follows.

1. Obtain the low-frequency component I_{low} and the high-frequency residual I_{high} in the same way as described in Step 1 in Sect. 3.4.
2. Extract histogram H from I_{low} via Eq. (1) with bin width t. Then adjust the histogram by Algorithm 1.
3. Divide H into histogram segments of length π, and divide M into watermark segments of length $\pi - 1$.

4. Use the i-th histogram segment to embed the i-th watermark segment according to Eq. (12). Repeat this step until all the watermark segments have been embedded, which gives the watermarked low-frequency component $\bar{I}_{low}$.
5. Post-process $\bar{I}_{low}$ and reconstruct the watermarked image $\bar{I}$ via the same ways as described in Steps 8 and 9 in Sect. 3.4.

At the watermark extraction phase, parameters b_1, b_2, t, and π should be known in advance. Note that the extraction rule slightly differs from Eq. (4). Still take the the first histogram segment extracted at the receiver as an example. Suppose it is $\left[\tilde{H}(1), \ldots, \tilde{H}(\pi)\right]$. Then each two neighboring bins $\tilde{H}(j)$ and $\tilde{H}(j+1)$ are used to extract the j-th watermark bit according to

$$\tilde{M}(j) = \begin{cases} 1, & \text{if } \tilde{H}(j) \geq \tilde{H}(j+1) \\ 0, & \text{otherwise} \end{cases} \tag{14}$$

The extraction procedure can be obtained easily and still omitted here because of limited space.

5   Experimental Results

The two embedding algorithms are evaluated by testing the corresponded schemes on natural images. 50 images of size 512×512 randomly selected from the BOWS2 database [14] are employed as the test images. Some of them are illustrated in Fig. 1. The perceptual quality of watermarked images is measured by PSNR, while the robustness is measured by bit error rate (BER). The considered attacks comprise of common image processing (including JPEG compression and additive white Gaussian noise (AWGN)) and geometric attacks (including rotation, cropping, warping and random bending). These attacks are simulated by Checkmark [15].

5.1   Parameter Setting

Our experiments suggest that a suitable range of coefficient values for the histogram extraction is $[15, 240]$, that is, $b_1 = 15$ and $b_2 = 240$. This setting can effectively remove the thinly populated bins at the first and last of the histogram. In the first scheme, $\gamma^{(u)}$ can be set larger than 10 to compensate the detection error caused by thinly populated bins. However, further increasing $\gamma^{(u)}$ cannot improve robustness obviously. Note that β used in the histogram preadjustment and $\gamma^{(u)}$ used in coarser level histograms should be amplified accordingly so that $\gamma^{(u)}$ can be reached for each level histogram. The case in the second scheme is similar. The settings of β, $\gamma^{(u)}$, and γ are listed in Table 1. There are two parameters left in the first scheme, $\alpha^{(u)}$ and $\#(H^{(u)})$, and three parameters left in the second scheme, α, $\#(H)$, and π, that require to be prefixed. Herein we experimentally discuss their settings by using the test images mentioned above.

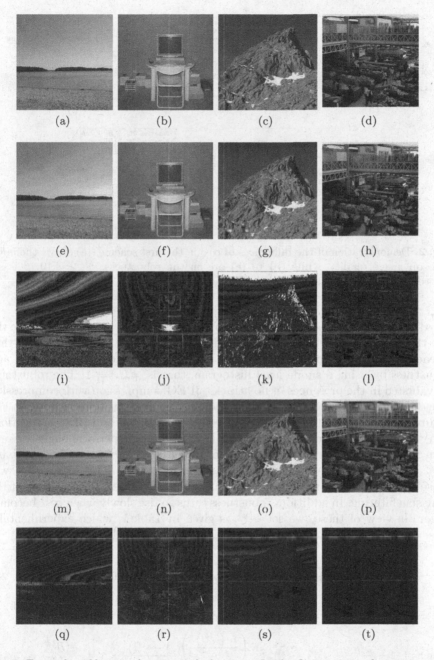

Fig. 1. Examples of host and watermarked images. In the first row are the test images: (a) "8137.pgm", (b) "7088.pgm", (c) "452.pgm", and (d) "5149.pgm". (e)–(h) are the watermarked versions obtained by Scheme I with $\#(M) = 56$. (i)–(l) are the corresponded embedding modifications, i.e., $|\bar{I} - I|$. (m)–(p) are the watermarked images obtained by Scheme II with $\#(M) = 56$, and (q)–(t) are the corresponded embedding modifications. Parameters of Schemes I and II in this case are listed in Table 2. The display range of $[0, 255]$ is employed to represent a modification value varying from 0 to 10 in (i)–(l) and (q)–(t).

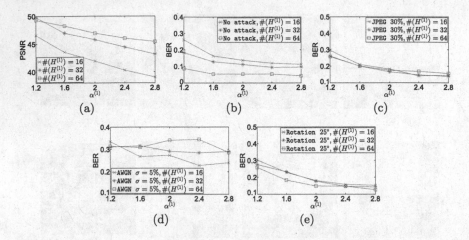

Fig. 2. Demonstration of the influences of $\alpha^{(1)}$ in the first scheme. (a) shows the influence on image quality, while (b) to (e) are on the robustness. $\gamma^{(1)} = 10$. β is set according to Table 1.

$\alpha^{(u)}$ should be set according to current $\#(H^{(u)})$ in the first scheme, since the less the bin number, the more the coefficients contained in each bin and thus in each coefficient transferring. We test their influences on image quality and robustness by using a single level histogram, that is, $\#(u) = 1$. The robustness is evaluated in the presences of no attacks, JPEG compression with compression rate 30%, AWGN with standard deviation $\sigma = 5$, and rotation with angle 25°. Figure 2 demonstrates this influence by considering PSNR and BER as functions of $\alpha^{(1)}$. It can be observed that coarser level histograms perform slightly worse than finer level histograms on both image quality and robustness when fixing $\alpha^{(1)}$. It may be because changing the shape of coarser level histograms will cause more coefficient modifications, which will aggravate the side effect of the Gaussian filtering. In addition, robustness turns to rise slowly when $\alpha^{(1)}$ becomes larger. In view of these, we set $\alpha^{(u)}$ as given in Table 1, which experimentally presents good tradeoff between robustness and perceptibility.

Table 1. Partial parameter settings in proposed schemes.

	$\alpha^{(u)}$ (or α)	$\gamma^{(u)}$ (or γ)	β	Total payload
Scheme I	$1 + \dfrac{\#(H^{(u)})}{64}$	if $u < \#(u)$: $\gamma^{(u+1)} \times \left(\dfrac{1-\left(\alpha^{(u)}\right)^2}{1-\alpha^{(u)}}\right)$ if $u = \#(u)$: 10	$\dfrac{1-\left(\alpha^{(1)}\right)^2}{2-2\alpha^{(1)}} \times \gamma^{(1)}$	$\#(H^{(\#(u))})$ $\times \left(1 - \left(\frac{1}{2}\right)^{\#(u)}\right)$
Scheme II	$1 + \dfrac{\#(H)}{64} \times \sqrt{\dfrac{2}{\pi}}$	10	$\dfrac{1-\alpha^\pi}{(1-\alpha)\times\pi} \times \gamma$	$\#(H) - \left\lceil \dfrac{\#(H)}{\pi} \right\rceil$

In the second scheme, both $\#(H)$ and π will affect the choice of α. Their influences are assessed on single level histogram with scenarios similar to those in the first scheme. Figure 3 shows the influence of varying α. It can be observed that increasing π makes watermarked image quality more sensitive to α, but affects robustness marginally. This is because increasing π will pressure some coefficients to be transferred among histogram bins with larger distance, which impairs watermarked image quality. However, disturbing one histogram bin only affects two embedded watermark bits. Therefore robustness keeps unchanged when varying π. Note that β used in the histogram preadjustment rises exponentially with π. This may also incur the rising of the BER-α curve in the case of $\pi = 12$. Therefore, α should be small enough to guarantee the success of embedding watermark bits. As a result, α is set as given in Table 1.

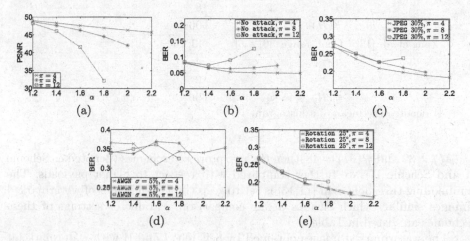

Fig. 3. Demonstration of the influences of α in the second scheme. (a) shows the influence on image quality, while (b) to (e) are on the robustness. $\#(H) = 64$. $\gamma = 10$. β is set according to Table 1.

Table 1 also lists the payloads provided by the proposed schemes. Note that the residual $\#(H) - \lfloor \#(H)/\pi \rfloor \times \pi$ bins can form an additional histogram segment to embed more watermark bits in the second scheme. It can be observed that the numbers of watermark bits that can be embedded by both schemes tend to be as same as the number of histogram bins, which is much larger than existed histogram-based embedding algorithms.

5.2   Performance Comparison

We evaluate the proposed schemes by comparing them with those suggested in [11,13]. The number of histogram bins $\#(H)$ in the compared two schemes can be increased to enlarge the payload. However, their supported payloads are still rather small. In view of this, we firstly compare all the schemes in the cases of

Table 2. Parameter settings for all the schemes.

Payload ($\#(M)$)		32	48	56	63
Scheme I	Coef. range	$[15, 240]$	$[15, 240]$	$[15, 240]$	$[15, 240]$
	$\#(u)$	1	2	3	2
	$\#(H^{(1)})$	64	32	16	42
	The other parameters are given in Table 1.				
Scheme II	Coef. range	$[15, 240]$	$[15, 240]$	$[15, 240]$	$[15, 240]$
	π	2	4	8	4
	$\#(H)$	64	64	64	84
	The other parameters are given in Table 1.				
Xiang et al. [11]	Coef. range	$[0.3A, 1.7A]$	$[0.3A, 1.7A]$	–	–
	α	2	6	–	–
	$\#(H)$	64	96	–	–
Zong et al. [13]	Coef. range	$[0, 255]$	$[0, 255]$	–	–
	α	2	4	–	–
	t	3	2	–	–
	$\#(H)$	64	96	–	–

A denotes the mean of a histogram.

$\#(M) = 32$ and $\#(M) = 48$, then the two proposed schemes (denoted as Scheme I and Scheme II) are further compared with respect to higher payloads. The embedding threshold α in [11,13] is set to keep the PSNR scores of watermarked images similar, which ensures a fair comparison. Parameter settings of these schemes are listed in Table 2.

The watermarked images obtained by Schemes I and II with watermark bit length $\#(M) = 56$ are demonstrated in Figs. 1(e)–(h) and (m)–(p), respectively, and their embedding modifications are depicted in Figs. 1(q)–(t) and (i)–(l), respectively. The corresponded PSNR scores are compared in Table 3. It can observed that Scheme I with 3 embedding rounds gives watermarked images with the worst quality. This is because embedding watermark bits in a rather coarse level histogram will cause severe distortions. Nevertheless, as shown in Figs. 1(e)–(h), this quality still seems acceptable in practice.

Table 3. Comparison of PSNRs among Different Schemes.

Payload ($\#(M)$)		32	48	56	64
Averaged PSNR	Scheme I	46.92	44.07	38.99	42.37
	Scheme II	46.92	43.69	43.40	41.67
	Xiang et al. [11]	46.85	43.97	–	–
	Zong et al. [13]	46.12	43.46	–	–

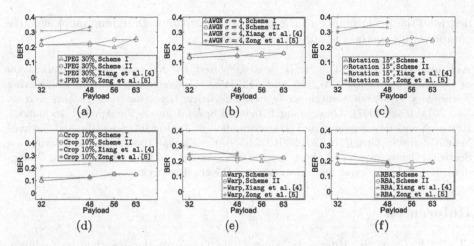

Fig. 4. Robustness performance of different schemes under: (a) JPEG compression, (b) AWGN, (c) rotation, (d) cropping, (e) warping, and (f) random bending.

We test the robustness of these schemes under common signal processing and geometric attacks. The testing results are reported in Fig. 4. It can be observed that the proposed schemes outperform the compared even in the case of small payload, which can be attributed to the coefficient transferring and histogram preadjustment methods proposed. It also shows that increasing the payload affects robustness marginally. Furthermore, the proposed two schemes perform similarly, except that Scheme I presents better robustness in the case of $\#(M) = 56$, which is at the cost of watermarked image quality. This suggests that we can choose the embedding algorithm according to practical requirements.

6 Discussion and Conclusion

In this paper, we propose two improved embedding algorithms to enlarge the capacity provided by histogram shape-based image watermarking methods. In existed approaches originally suggested in [11], each histogram bin can only embed 0.5 watermark bits at most. This value rises to almost 1 in the proposed algorithms via exploiting multilevel histogram and multiple histogram adjustment. Two new operations, namely histogram preadjustment and coefficient transferring, are developed to further enhance robustness. In the embedding procedure, we alter the embedding algorithm while retaining the other operations as given in [11], such as the low-pass filtering and post-processing, to compare different embedding algorithms. The comparison results show that the proposed algorithms can achieve good performances on both watermarked image quality and robustness. Furthermore, our algorithms present different tradeoff between robustness and perceptibility, which can support various applications. Experimentally we find that the side effect of the Gaussian filtering seriously degrades the performance of the proposed algorithms. Designing more effective compensative method is our future research.

Acknowledgements. This work was supported by National Science Foundation of China (Grant Nos. 61472165 and 61373158), Guangdong Provincial Engineering Technology Research Center on Network Security Detection and Defence (Grant No. 2014B090904067), Guangdong Provincial Special Funds for Applied Technology Research and development and Transformation of Important Scientific and Technological Achieve (Grant No. 2016B010124009), the Zhuhai Top Discipline–Information Security, Guangzhou Key Laboratory of Data Security and Privacy Preserving, Guangdong Key Laboratory of Data Security and Privacy Preserving.

References

1. Ni, J., Zhang, R., Huang, J., Wang, C., Li, Q.: A rotation-invariant secure image watermarking algorithm incorporating steerable pyramid transform. In: Shi, Y.Q., Jeon, B. (eds.) IWDW 2006. LNCS, vol. 4283, pp. 446–460. Springer, Heidelberg (2006). doi:10.1007/11922841_36
2. Dugelay, J.L., Roche, S., Rey, C., Doërr, G.: Still-image watermarking robust to local geometric distortions. IEEE Trans. Image Process. **15**(9), 2831–2842 (2006)
3. Su, P.C., Chang, Y.C., Wu, C.Y.: Geometrically resilient digital image watermarking by using interest point extraction and extended pilot signals. IEEE Trans. Inf. Forensics Secur. **8**(12), 1897–1908 (2013)
4. Gao, X., Deng, C., Li, X., Tao, D.: Geometric distortion insensitive image watermarking in affine covariant regions. IEEE Trans. Syst. Man Cybern. Part C Appl. Rev. **40**(3), 278–286 (2010)
5. Deng, C., Gao, X., Li, X., Tao, D.: Local histogram based geometric invariant image watermarking. Sig. Process. **90**(12), 3256–3264 (2010)
6. Licks, V., Jordan, R.: Geometric attacks on image watermarking systems. IEEE Multimed. **3**, 68–78 (2005)
7. Ruanaidh, J.J.O., Pun, T.: Rotation, scale and translation invariant spread spectrum digital image watermarking. Sig. Process. **66**(3), 303–317 (1998)
8. Zhang, H., Shu, H., Coatrieux, G., Zhu, J., Wu, Q.J., Zhang, Y., Zhu, H., Luo, L.: Affine legendre moment invariants for image watermarking robust to geometric distortions. IEEE Trans. Image Process. **20**(8), 2189–2199 (2011)
9. Kang, X., Huang, J., Zeng, W.: Efficient general print-scanning resilient data hiding based on uniform log-polar mapping. IEEE Trans. Inf. Forensics Secur. **5**(1), 1–12 (2010)
10. Li, L., Li, S., Abraham, A., Pan, J.S.: Geometrically invariant image watermarking using polar harmonic transforms. Inf. Sci. **199**, 1–19 (2012)
11. Xiang, S., Kim, H.J., Huang, J.: Invariant image watermarking based on statistical features in the low-frequency domain. IEEE Trans. Circuits Syst. Video Technol. **18**(6), 777–790 (2008)
12. He, X., Zhu, T., Yang, G.: A geometrical attack resistant image watermarking algorithm based on histogram modification. Multidimension. Syst. Sig. Process. **26**(1), 291–306 (2015)
13. Zong, T., Xiang, Y., Natgunanathan, I., Guo, S., Zhou, W., Beliakov, G.: Robust histogram shape-based method for image watermarking. IEEE Trans. Circuits Syst. Video Technol. **25**(5), 717–729 (2015)

14. Bas, P., Furon, T.: BOWS-2 (2007). http://bows2.gipsa-lab.inpg.fr/
15. Pereira, S., Voloshynovskiy, S., Madueno, M., Marchand-Maillet, S., Pun, T.: Second generation benchmarking and application oriented evaluation. In: Moskowitz, I.S. (ed.) IH 2001. LNCS, vol. 2137, pp. 340–353. Springer, Heidelberg (2001). doi:10.1007/3-540-45496-9_25

Image Quality Assessment in Reversible Data Hiding with Contrast Enhancement

Hao-Tian Wu[1(✉)], Shaohua Tang[1], and Yun-Qing Shi[2]

[1] School of Computer Science and Engineering,
South China University of Technology,
Guangzhou 510006, People's Republic of China
{wuht,csshtang}@scut.edu.cn
[2] Department of Electrical and Computer Engineering,
New Jersey Institute of Technology, Newark, NJ 07103, USA

Abstract. In this paper, image quality assessment (IQA) in reversible data hiding with contrast enhancement (RDH-CE) is studied. Firstly, the schemes of RDH-CE are reviewed, with which image contrast can be enhanced without any information loss. Secondly, the limitations of using the peak signal-to-noise ratio (PSNR) to indicate image quality in the scenario of RDH-CE are discussed. Subsequently, three no-reference IQA metrics and four metrics specially designed for contrast-changed images are adopted, in addition to PSNR and structural similarity (SSIM) index. By using these metrics, the evaluation results on the contrast-enhanced images generated with two RDH-CE schemes are obtained and compared. The experimental results have shown that the no-reference IQA metrics, the blind/referenceless image spatial quality evaluator (BRISQUE) for instance, are more suitable than PSNR and SSIM index for the images that have been enhanced by the RDH-CE schemes. Furthermore, how to use the suitable IQA metrics has been discussed for performance evaluation of RDH-CE schemes.

Keywords: Image quality assessment · Contrast enhancement · Reversible data hiding · Visual quality

1 Introduction

Reversible data hiding (RDH) has been extensively studied over the past two decades (e.g., [1–22]), which is initially proposed for the distortion sensitive applications such as medical and military. With the proposed RDH schemes, a piece of information can be hidden into the host signal so as to generate the signal with hidden data, from which the original signal can be completely recovered after data extraction. In the literature, most of the RDH schemes are designed for digital images (e.g., [2–18]), while the others are for audio (e.g., [19]) and video signal (e.g., [20]), as well as 3D mesh models (e.g., [21,22]). There also exists the requirement of embedding capacity, and it is preferred that the process of data hiding does not degrade the perceptual quality of host signal.

© Springer International Publishing AG 2017
C. Kraetzer et al. (Eds.): IWDW 2017, LNCS 10431, pp. 290–302, 2017.
DOI: 10.1007/978-3-319-64185-0_22

To evaluate the performance of image RDH algorithms, the hiding rate and quality of the host image after data hiding receive much attention. It has been observed that there exists a trade-off between them because increasing the hiding rate normally introduces more distortion into image content. To measure the distortion caused by data embedding, the peak signal-to-noise ratio (PSNR) between the original image and the one with hidden data is often calculated. As an objective measurement, PSNR is defined based on mean square error (MSE) and its value normally decreases when more distortions are introduced into the image content. Since it is desired to minimize the distortion at a given rate of data hiding, the curve of the PSNR value versus the hiding rate is often plotted in performance evaluation of RDH schemes, though new measures such as the structural similarity (SSIM) [23] have been proposed for image quality assessment (IQA).

Recently, significant advances have been made on RDH to keep the PSNR of host image as high as possible (e.g., [6–10]). Nevertheless, the visual quality can hardly improved by the RDH schemes by minimizing the changes made to the image content. In some circumstances, the visual quality of host image may be poor, such as the images acquired with poor illumination. In that case, preserving the PSNR high is not so important than improving the visual quality. To achieve the better visual effect, contrast enhancement [24] is often performed to improve the visibility of images with low dynamic range to bring out the interested details. For instance, contrast enhancement of medical or satellite images is meaningful to show the details for visual inspection. As shown in Fig. 1, the visibility of image details can be improved by contrast enhancement though the PSNR value of the contrast-enhanced image is rather low (which is only 17.66 dB). It can be seen that keeping PSNR high is not necessary in some applications.

To enhance the image contrast through RDH, the first scheme is proposed in [11] so that data hiding and contrast enhancement can be performed at the same time. By hiding the useful information into the contrast-enhanced image, the original image can be directly recovered after extracting the hidden data. That means the host image can be enhanced without any information loss so that reversible data hiding with contrast enhancement (RDH-CE) is achieved. Moreover, several methods have been proposed in [12–18] to achieve the effect of contrast enhancement for the natural and medical images, respectively. To measure the degree of contrast enhancement, the relative contrast error (RCE) defined in [25] is used and a RCE value greater than 0.5 indicates the enhanced contrast. However, due to the lack of using other IQA metrics, the PSNR is still used as a reference of image quality in the methods of [11–18]. Therefore, a suitable IQA evaluator is urgently needed to better evaluate the visual quality of these contrast-enhanced images generated by using the RDH-CE schemes.

Under these circumstances, three no-reference metrics and three evaluators specially designed for the contrast-changed images are adopted to compare their performances, in addition to PSNR and SSIM. By using these IQA metrics, the numerical evaluation results on the contrast-enhanced images generated with two RDH-CE schemes in [11,12] are compared with the subjective evaluations, respectively.

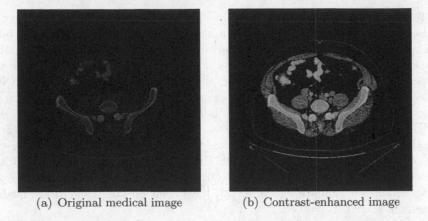

(a) Original medical image   (b) Contrast-enhanced image

Fig. 1. A medical image and its contrast-enhanced version with PSNR = 17.66 dB.

The experimental results show that the no-reference IQA metrics, the blind/referenceless image spatial quality evaluator (BRISQUE) for instance, are more suitable than PSNR and SSIM index for the image contrast has been changed with RDH-CE schemes. Furthermore, how to use the suitable IQA metrics has been discussed for performance evaluation of RDH-CE schemes.

The rest of this paper is organized as follows. In Sect. 2, we review the RDH-CE methods in [11–18] by dividing them into two categories. Then three no-reference IQA metrics and three special evaluators recently designed for the contrast-changed images are introduced in Sect. 3. With these metrics, the numerical evaluation results obtained on the contrast-enhanced images generated with the two RDH-CE schemes in [11,12] are compared with those of PSNR and SSIM, as well as the subjective evaluations. The detailed experimental results are given and analyzed in Sect. 4. Finally, some conclusive remarks are given in Sect. 5 based on the comparative study.

2   RDH Schemes for Image Contrast Enhancement

In this section, the RDH schemes proposed for image contrast enhancement are reviewed. The common feature of these RDH methods is that the image quality can be improved by contrast entrancement instead of keeping PSNR as high as possible. Instead of reviewing these schemes one by one, we divide them into two categories according to whether the pre-processing needs to be performed before histogram equalization. Interested readers may refer to [11–18] for the details.

2.1   Pre-processing Before Histogram Equalization

To perform reversible data hiding and contrast enhancement simultaneously, the first scheme is proposed in [11] by modifying the histogram of pixel values. For an 8-bit gray-level image, the histogram is calculated by counting the number of every pixel value ranging from 0 to 255. Among the non-empty bins in the obtained histogram, the two peaks (i.e. the highest two bins) are chosen, which are denoted by f_L and f_R. Then the following operation is performed:

$$f' = \begin{cases} f - 1, & \text{if } f < f_L \\ f - b_i, & \text{if } f = f_L \\ f, & \text{if } f_L < f < f_R, \\ f + b_i, & \text{if } f = f_R \\ f + 1, & \text{if } f > f_R \end{cases} \tag{1}$$

Note that f is the i-th pixel belonging to the set of $\{f_L, f_R\}$ scanned in the host image, f' is the modified pixel value, and b_i is the i-th binary value (0 or 1) in the bitstream to be hidden. After applying Eq. (1) to every pixel counted in the histogram, each of the chosen bin are split into two adjacent bins. Then the highest two bins in the *modified* histogram need to be further chosen for processing. By iteratively splitting the highest two bins in histogram by applying Eq. (1), the effect of histogram equalization can be achieved.

To avoid the overflows and underflows due to histogram shifting specified in Eq. (1), the histogram need to be pre-processed. Suppose that S pairs of histogram bins are split in total, where S is a positive integer no more than 64. The pixel values in $[0, S - 1]$ are added by S, while the pixel values in $[256 - S, 255]$ are subtracted by S in pre-processing. To memorize the locations, a binary location map with the same size as the host image is generated by assigning 1 s to the locations of those pixels modified, while 0 s are assigned to the other locations. For the recovery of the original image, the pre-computed location map is compressed by the JBIG2 standard [26], and hidden into the host image with other data. Note that the number of histogram bin pairs totally split (i.e., S) and the values of all split bins are also hidden into the contrast-enhanced image so that the original image can be blindly recovered.

To recover the original image, the values of the last two split bins are firstly used, which are denoted by f_{LL} and f_{LR}. The data hidden with them can be extracted by

$$b'_i = \begin{cases} 1, & \text{if } f' = f_{LL} - 1 \text{ or } f' = f_{LR} + 1 \\ 0, & \text{if } f' = f_{LL} \text{ or } f' = f_{LR} \\ null, & otherwise \end{cases} \tag{2}$$

Note that f' is the i-th pixel belonging to $\{f_{LL} - 1, f_{LL}, f_{LR}, f_{LR} + 1\}$ and b'_i is the i-th bit value extracted. It should also be noted that data hiding and extraction are performed in the same scanning order. Meanwhile, the histogram before splitting the bins of f_{LL} and f_{LR} can be restored by

$$f = \begin{cases} f' + 1, & \text{if } f' < f_{LL} \\ f', & \text{if } f_{LL} - 1 < f' < f_{LR} + 1. \\ f' - 1, & \text{if } f' > f_{LR} \end{cases} \tag{3}$$

By extracting the values of the other split bins, the data hidden within them can be sequentially extracted from the histogram restored by applying Eq. (2), while Eq. (3) is iteratively carried out to obtain the image after pre-processing.

To recover the original image, the pixels modified in pre-processing should be modified back according to the location map, which can be extracted from the contrast-enhanced image. Since the pixel values originally in $[0, S-1]$ are added by S in pre-processing, a pixel value within $[S, 2S-1]$ is subtracted by S if the corresponding value in location map is 1. For a pixel within $[256-2S, 255-S]$, it is added by S if the corresponding value in location map is 1. Note that the aforementioned information (including the values of the split bins, the total number of the split bins, and the location map) can be extracted from the contrast-enhanced image so that the original image can be blindly recovered. It should be noted that the RDH algorithms proposed in [12–17] also fall into this category, though different data hiding algorithms or ending conditions are used.

2.2 Histogram Equalization Without Pre-processing

In [18], an automatic contrast enhancement scheme is proposed based on RDH. Different from generating the location map before histogram equalization as in [11–17], the method generates the concurrent location map for every time of histogram shifting. At each time, the histogram is modified by expanding the highest bin for data embedding and merging the lowest bin with an adjacent one. The operation is repeated to equalize the histogram until the ever-increasing side information cannot be accommodated in the contrast-enhanced image. In this way, automatic contrast enhancement can be performed to provide convenience for the users. Although no other IQA metrics are adopted except PSNR, visual analysis shows that better visual quality can be achieved for poorly exposed images, with the similar effects of applying *histeq* (a well known global histogram equalization function in MATLAB). Meanwhile, reversible contrast enhancement is achieved to provide a recovery option for the images to be enhanced.

3 IQA Metrics

Recently, image quality assessment (IQA) has become a hot topic in the image processing community. Depending on whether and how the original image is used in quality assessment, IQA metrics can be classified into three categories: full-reference, reduced-reference and no-reference ones [32]. From Fig. 1, we know that sometimes PSNR is not a good evaluator of the visual quality, which will be further illustrated by the experimental results. But in [11–18], PSNR is still used as a reference of image quality due to the lack of an accurate image quality evaluator. In [11,12,14], the degree of contrast enhancement is evaluated by using RCE defined in [25]. But RCE itself cannot accurately indicate visual quality because the value may still be high for an enhanced image with visual distortions. Under the circumstances, the SSIM index defined in [23], three no-reference IQA metrics defined in [27–29], four IQA metric specially designed for contrast changed images are introduced, which are adopted for performance comparison with PSNR and objective evaluations.

As another popular image quality evaluator, the SSIM index is calculated between two images and equal to 1 when they are identical [23]. If one image being compared is regarded as having perfect quality, then the obtained SSIM index value can be considered as the quality measure of the other image. The obtained SSIM index between the original and contrast-enhanced images generally decreases with RCE, which has been shown in [12].

3.1 Three No-Reference IQA Metrics

To evaluate the quality of the contrast-enhanced images, the blind/referenceless image spatial quality evaluator (BRISQUE) [27], the no-reference metric called C-DIIVINE [28] and the no-reference free energy based robust metric (NFERM) [29] can be adopted.

The BRISQUE [27] is a statistic-based model to assess image visual quality in the spatial domain. It does not compute the distortion-specific features, but uses scene statistics to quantify possible losses of naturalness due to the presence of distortions. Thus no reference image is needed to calculate a BRISQUE score, which typically has a value between 0 and 100 (0 represents the best quality, while 100 represents the worst). For a smooth image, the obtained BRISQUE score can be negative and its value increases as the image quality gets worse.

The C-DIIVINE [28] is a complex extension of the distortion identification-based image verity and integrity evaluation (DIIVINE) [30], whereby distortion-induced changes in local magnitude and phase statistics are effectively captured. It blindly assesses image quality based on the complex Gaussian scale mixture model by calculating a score value, which is almost between 0 and 100. The NFERM metric [29] also calculates a score by using the free energy based brain theory and classical human visual system inspired features. For all of the three no-reference metrics, a low score indicates the good quality.

3.2 IQA Metrics Specially Designed for Contrast-Changed Images

There are several recent studies focusing on IQA of contrast distorted images, such as in [31–34]. For instance, the reduced-reference quality metric for contrast-distorted images (RIQMC) proposed in [31] achieves impressive performance by relying on partial access to the reference image without using natural image statistical models. In [32], a simple but effective method for no-reference quality assessment of contrast distorted images is proposed based on the principle of natural scene statistics (NSS), which is denoted by NFQA-NSS hereinafter. In this no-reference quality assessment method, a large scale image database is employed to build NSS models based on moment and entropy features. The quality of a contrast-distorted image is then evaluated based on its unnaturalness characterized by the degree of deviation from the NSS models.

In [33], a patch-based contrast quality index (PCQI) method is proposed by using an adaptive representation of local patch structure. Specifically, any image patch can be decomposed into its mean intensity, signal strength and signal structure components so that their perceptual distortions can be evaluated in different ways. A unique local contrast quality map can be produced to predict local quality variations over space and may be employed to guide

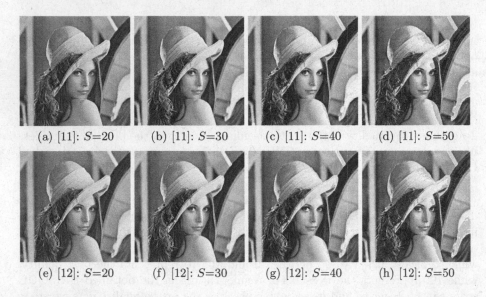

(a) [11]: $S=20$ (b) [11]: $S=30$ (c) [11]: $S=40$ (d) [11]: $S=50$

(e) [12]: $S=20$ (f) [12]: $S=30$ (g) [12]: $S=40$ (h) [12]: $S=50$

Fig. 2. The contrast-enhanced images of "Lena" generated with the RDH-CE schemes in [11,12].

contrast enhancement algorithms to provide accurate predictions on the human perception of contrast variations.

In [34], another no-reference/blind metric named NIQMC is devised for IQA· of contrast distortion. For local details, the predicted regions in an image are roughly removed while entropy of particular unpredicted areas of maximum information is computed via visual saliency. From global perspective, the image histogram is compared with the uniformly distributed histogram of maximum information via the symmetric Kullback-Leibler divergence. Consequently, an overall quality estimation of a contrast-distorted image can be generated by properly combining local and global considerations.

4   Experimental Results

In this section, the experimental results obtained with eight IQA metrics (i.e., PSNR, SSIM, BRISQUE, C-DIIVINE, NFERM, PCQI, NFQA-NSS, NIQMC) on the contrast-enhanced images generated with the RDH-CE schemes in [11,12] are reported. Then the objective evaluation results are compared with visual evaluations to find out the more suitable ones in the scenario of RDH-CE.

4.1   Image Quality Assessment of Contrast-Enhanced Images

To generate the contrast-enhanced images, integers from 1 to 64 were respectively set to S (i.e., the number of histogram bin pairs split for data hiding as defined in Sect. 2.1) in scheme [11] and scheme [12] without background segmentation.

Table 1. Evaluations on the contrast-enhanced "Lena" with eight IQA metrics

Algorithm	SSIM	BRIS-QUE	C-DII VINE	NFERM	PCQI ($\times 10^4$)	NFQA-NSS	NIQMC	PSNR (dB)	RCE	Hiding rate
[11].20p	0.947	−2.57	5.27	11.03	1.103	3.371	5.658	24.44	0.556	0.361
[11].30p	0.897	−1.25	6.84	13.52	1.099	2.994	5.858	21.26	0.582	0.492
[11].40p	0.818	5.32	10.46	22.29	1.107	2.845	5.920	19.44	0.597	0.542
[11].50p	0.653	21.22	17.54	19.49	1.099	2.904	5.900	17.87	0.597	0.720
[12].20p	0.951	−2.66	5.22	11.02	1.108	3.372	5.659	24.91	0.553	0.345
[12].30p	0.899	−1.34	6.58	13.51	1.099	2.994	5.858	21.35	0.581	0.481
[12].40p	0.824	4.09	9.54	22.28	1.107	2.845	5.920	19.38	0.599	0.540
[12].50p	0.669	19.04	16.12	19.50	1.099	2.904	5.900	18.06	0.598	0.680

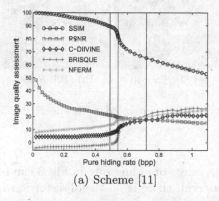

(a) Scheme [11]

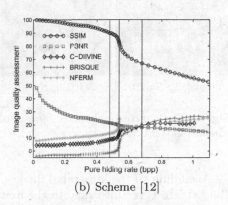

(b) Scheme [12]

Fig. 3. Five image quality evaluators subject to pure hiding rate on image "Lena" for two RDH-CE schemes.

In Fig. 2, the contrast-enhanced images of "Lena" from the test image set of [35] are shown for four different S values. The pure hiding rate (in bit per pixel, bpp for short), PSNR, SSIM, BRISQUE, C-DIIVINE, NFERM, PCQI, NFQA-NSS, NIQMC and RCE values are listed in Table 1. It can be seen from Fig. 2 that the visual quality was well preserved when $S \leq 30$ for both of the methods, while distortions were introduced into image content as more histogram bins were split for data hiding and histogram equalization.

For more comparisons, eight image quality evaluation metrics were calculated from every of 64 contrast-enhanced images generated with each RDH-CE scheme. The obtained PSNR, SSIM, BRISQUE, C-DIIVINE and NFERM values subject to the pure hiding rate are plotted in Fig. 3 by linearly scaling the range of SSIM index from [0, 1] to [0, 100]. Since no change was made on PSNR and BRISQUE score, the SSIM index, BRISQUE, C-DIIVINE and NFERM are in the same scale for the convenience of comparison. Note that for each method, three vertical lines were plotted in Fig. 3, which were respectively corresponding to three contrast-enhanced images as shown in Fig. 2 (i.e., $S = 30$, $S = 40$ and $S = 50$).

(a) [11]: S=20   (b) [11]: S=30   (c) [11]: S=40   (d) [11]: S=50

(e) [12]: S=20   (f) [12]: S=30   (g) [12]: S=40   (h) [12]: S=50

Fig. 4. The contrast-enhanced images of "Goldhill" generated with the RDH-CE schemes in [11, 12].

According to the illustrated images, the range of hiding rate in Fig. 3 can be divided into three intervals. In the first interval, there is no visual distortion in the image content. For instance, the cases to the left of the first vertical line in Fig. 3, which are corresponding to $S \leq 30$, are contained in the first interval. The second interval is called transition interval, which means slight visual distortions appear in content of the contrast-enhanced images. The second left vertical line in Fig. 3 is an example, for only a little distortions were introduced into contrast-enhanced image as shown in the case of $S = 40$ in Fig. 2. In the third interval, there are obvious artificial distortions in the image content, such as the case of $S = 50$ as shown in Fig. 2. The reason that we chose to generate the contrast-enhanced images with the two schemes in [11, 12] is to obtain the results of all cases. Similarly, the contrast-enhanced images of "Goldhill" for four different S values are shown in Fig. 4, while the corresponding pure hiding rate, PSNR, SSIM, BRISQUE, C-DIIVINE, NFERM, PCQI, NFQA-NSS, NIQMC and RCE values of the contrast-enhanced images are listed in Table 2. The more evaluation results of using PSNR, SSIM, BRISQUE, C-DIIVINE and NFERM for the contrast-enhanced images are plotted in Fig. 5, where the three vertical lines are corresponding to the cases of $S = 20$, $S = 30$ and $S = 40$ in Fig. 4.

Obviously, the first interval is most desired because no visual distortion was introduced into image content. However, the PSNR value decreased rapidly in this interval, as shown in Figs. 3 and 5. The SSIM value also decreased, but not as much as PSNR, while the BRISQUE, C-DIIVINE and NFERM values increased slowly in the first interval, despite that image contrast was enhanced. In the second interval, visual distortions began to appear in image content so that

Table 2. Evaluations on the contrast-enhanced "Goldhill" with eight IQA metrics

Algorithm	SSIM	BRIS-QUE	C-DII VINE	NFERM	PCQI ($\times 10^4$)	NFQA-NSS	NIQMC	PSNR (dB)	RCE	hiding rate
[11].20p	0.921	10.43	14.69	15.08	9.503	3.431	5.694	24.16	0.557	0.522
[11].30p	0.841	17.17	16.21	18.79	9.454	3.438	5.757	21.68	0.569	0.660
[11].40p	0.778	20.73	19.21	18.56	9.619	3.435	5.848	19.45	0.578	0.815
[11].50p	0.642	35.80	25.72	22.47	9.669	3.343	5.862	17.21	0.582	0.966
[12].20p	0.930	10.21	14.50	15.08	9.503	3.431	5.694	24.64	0.554	0.506
[12].30p	0.853	16.79	16.42	18.79	9.454	3.438	5.757	22.19	0.565	0.647
[12].40p	0.787	19.08	18.51	18.55	9.619	3.435	5.848	19.70	0.577	0.808
[12].50p	0.669	34.24	24.94	22.47	9.669	3.343	5.861	17.62	0.581	0.923

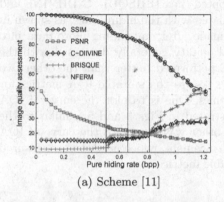

(a) Scheme [11]

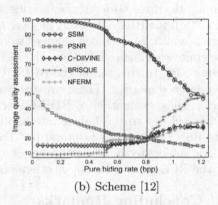

(b) Scheme [12]

Fig. 5. Five image quality evaluators subject to pure hiding rate on image "Goldhill" for two RDH-CE schemes.

the values of SSIM, BRISQUE, C-DIIVINE and NFERM dramatically changed. But there was no obvious change observed in the curves of PSNR, indicating that PSNR is insensitive to slight visual distortions. In the third interval, image quality became worse so that PSNR and SSIM values steadily decreased while the BRISQUE, C-DIIVINE and NFERM scores were raised high. As the no-reference IQA metrics and SSIM index were more sensitive to the visual distortions, the PSNR performed the worst for IQA in the scenario of RDH-CE.

4.2 No-Reference Metrics vs. SSIM Index

Although SSIM is sensitive to visual distortions, it is also sensitive to contrast enhancement because the original image needs to be used in calculation. At the hiding rate of 0.492 bpp as given in Table 1, the SSIM index dropped from 1 to 0.897 for "Lena" though quite good visual quality was obtained in Fig. 2 (b). Not surprisingly, the no-reference metrics were less affected if there was no visual distortion. Note that all of the BRISQUE, C-DIIVINE and NFERM typically have a value between 0 and 100. For the test image "Lena", the BRISQUE was only changed from -4.43 to -1.25, the C-DIIVINE was changed from 4.11 to 6.84, and the NFERM was changed from 7.22 to 13.52. For "Goldhill", the SSIM dropped from 1 to 0.921 at the hiding rate of 0.522 bpp as given in Table 2, while the BRISQUE was changed from 9.05 to 10.43, the C-DIIVINE was changed from 15.70 to 14.69 (the decrease indicates the improvement in image quality), and the NFERM was changed from 16.12 to 15.08. It can be observed that the amounts of drop in PSNR and SSIM were apparently larger than the amounts of increase in BRISQUE, C-DIIVINE and NFERM before visual distortions were introduced. So the no-reference metrics of BRISQUE, C-DIIVINE and NFERM are more suitable for quality assessment in the case of contrast enhancement.

4.3   Applying the Suitable No-Reference IQA Metrics

Among the three no-reference metrics adopted (i.e., BRISQUE, C-DIIVINE and NFERM), the BRISQUE was more correlated with the hiding rate, as shown in Figs. 3 and 5. Since more changes were made after embedding more data into the contrast-enhanced images, the visual quality generally decreased with the hiding rate. In this sense, the BRISQUE performed better than the other two no-reference metrics. There are two ways to use the suitable IQA metrics for performance evaluation of RDH-CE schemes. One is to plot the curve of IQA metric subject to the hiding rate as illustrated in Figs. 3 and 5, similar to the rate-PSNR curves in the literature. The other way is to plot the curve of IQA metric subject to the effect of contrast enhancement, which needs to be measured by the RCE defined in [25] or other suitable metrics.

5   Concluding Remarks

In this paper, we have reviewed the reversible data hiding schemes with contrast enhancement (RDH-CE) by classifying them into two categories. To evaluate the contrast-enhanced images generated with these schemes, three no-reference image quality assessment (IQA) metrics and four metrics specially designed for the contrast-changed images are adopted, in addition to PSNR and SSIM index. By generating the contrast-enhanced images with the schemes in [11,12], eight image quality assessment metrics have been calculated to compare their performances with subjective inspections. The experimental results have clearly demonstrated the advantages of using the no-reference IQA metrics, for image contrast was changed by these RDH-CE schemes. The comparative results have shown the recently proposed no-reference metrics, the blind/referenceless image spatial quality evaluator (BRISQUE) [27] for instance, are more suitable for IQA of the contrast-enhanced images than PSNR and SSIM index. Therefore, the curve of BRISQUE or other suitable IQA metrics subject to the pure hiding rate is suggested for performance evaluation of the RDH-CE schemes.

Acknowledgment. This work was supported by National Natural Science Foundation of China (No. 61632013), Natural Science Foundation of Jiangsu Province of China (No. BK20151131), Guangdong Provincial Natural Science Foundation of China (No. 2014A030308006), Guangdong Provincial Project of Science and Technology of China (No. 2016B090920081), and SCUT Fundamental Research Funds for the Central Universities of China (No. 2017MS038).

References

1. Shi, Y.Q., Li, X., Zhang, X., Wu, H., Ma, B.: Reversible data hiding: advances in the past two decades. IEEE Access **4**, 3210–3237 (2016)
2. Tian, J.: Reversible data embedding using a difference expansion. IEEE Trans. Circuits Syst. Video Technol. **13**(8), 890–896 (2003)
3. Ni, Z., Shi, Y.Q., Ansari, N., Su, W.: Reversible data hiding. IEEE Trans. Circuits Syst. Video Technol. **16**(3), 354–362 (2006)
4. Sachnev, V., Kim, H.J., Nam, J., Suresh, S., Shi, Y.Q.: Reversible watermarking algorithm using sorting and prediction. IEEE Trans. Circuits Syst. Video Technol. **19**(7), 989–999 (2009)
5. Wu, H., Huang, J.: Reversible image watermarking on prediction error by efficient histogram modification. Sig. Process. **92**(12), 3000–3009 (2012)
6. Ou, B., Li, X., Zhao, Y., Ni, R., Shi, Y.Q.: Pairwise prediction-error expansion for efficient reversible data hiding. IEEE Trans. Image Process. **22**(12), 5010–5021 (2013)
7. Dragoi, I.C., Coltuc, D.: On local prediction based reversible watermarking. IEEE Trans. Image Process. **24**(4), 1244–1246 (2015)
8. Li, X., Zhang, W., Gui, X., Yang, B.: Efficient reversible data hiding based on multiple histograms modification. IEEE Trans. Inf. Foren. Sec. **10**(9), 2016–2027 (2015)
9. Ma, B., Shi, Y.Q.: A reversible data hiding scheme based on code division multiplexing. IEEE Trans. Inf. Foren. Sec. **11**(9), 1914–1927 (2016)
10. Wang, J., Ni, J., Zhang, X., Shi, Y.Q.: Rate and distortion optimization for reversible data hiding using multiple histogram shifting. IEEE Trans. Cybern. **47**(2), 315–326 (2017)
11. Wu, H., Dugelay, J.L., Shi, Y.Q.: Reversible image data hiding with contrast enhancement. IEEE Signal Process. Lett. **22**(1), 81–85 (2015)
12. Wu, H., Huang, J., Shi, Y.Q.: A reversible data hiding method with contrast enhancement for medical images. J. Vis. Commun. Image R. **31**, 146–153 (2015)
13. Wu, H.-T., Liu, Y., Shi, Y.-Q.: Reversible data hiding by median-preserving histogram modification for image contrast enhancement. In: Shi, Y.-Q., Kim, H.J., Pérez-González, F., Yang, C.-N. (eds.) IWDW 2014. LNCS, vol. 9023, pp. 289–301. Springer, Cham (2015). doi:10.1007/978-3-319-19321-2_22
14. Gao, G., Shi, Y.Q.: Reversible data hiding using controlled contrast enhancement and integer wavelet transform. IEEE Signal Process. Lett. **22**(11), 2078–2082 (2015)
15. Yang, Y., Zhang, W., Liang, D., Yu, N.: Reversible data hiding in medical images with enhanced contrast in texture area. Digital Signal Process. **52**, 13–24 (2016)
16. Chen, H., Ni, J., Hong, W., Chen, T.S.: Reversible data hiding with contrast enhancement using adaptive histogram shifting and pixel value ordering. Signal Process. Image Commun. **46**, 1–16 (2016)
17. Gao, G., Wang, X., Yao, S., Cui, Z., Sun, X.: Reversible data hiding with contrast enhancement and tamper localization for medical images. Inf. Sci. **385–386**, 250–C265 (2017)
18. Kim, S., Lussi, R., Qu, X., Kim, H.J.: Automatic contrast enhancement using reversible data hiding. In: Proceedings of IEEE International Workshop on Information Forensics and Security, pp. 1–5 (2015)
19. Veen, M., Bruekers, F., Leest, A., Cavin, S.: High capacity reversible watermarking for audio. In: SPIE, Security, Steganography, and Watermarking of Multimedia Content, pp. 1–11 (2003)

20. Fridrich, J., Du, R.: Lossless authentication of MPEG-2 video. In: The International Conference on Image Processing, pp. 893–896 (2002)
21. Wu, H., Dugelay, J.L.: Reversible watermarking of 3D mesh models by prediction-error expansion. In: The International Workshop on Multimedia Signal Processing, pp. 797–802. (2008)
22. Wu, H., Cheung, Y.: Reversible watermarking by modulation and security enhancement. IEEE Trans. Inst. Measure. **59**(1), 221–228 (2010)
23. Wang, Z., Bovik, A.C., Sheikh, H.R., Simoncelli, E.P.: Image quality assessment: from error measurement to structural similarity. IEEE Trans. Image Process. **13**(1), 600–612 (2004)
24. Stark, J.A.: Adaptive image contrast enhancement using generalizations of histogram equalization. IEEE Trans. Image Process. **9**(5), 889–896 (2000)
25. Gao, M.Z., Wu, Z.G., Wang, L.: Comprehensive evaluation for he based contrast enhancement techniques. Adv. Intell. Syst. Appl. **2**, 331–338 (2013)
26. Howard, P.G., Kossentini, F., Martins, B., Forchhammer, S., Rucklidge, W.J.: The emerging JBIG2 standard. IEEE Trans. Circuits Syst. Video Technol. **8**(7), 838–848 (1998)
27. Mittal, A., Moorthy, A.K., Bovik, A.C.: No-reference image quality assessment in the spatial domain. IEEE Trans. Image Process. **21**(12), 4695–4708 (2012)
28. Zhang, Y., Moorthy, A.K., Chandler, D.M., Bovik, A.C.: C-DIIVINE: No-reference image quality assessment based on local magnitude and phase statistics of natural scenes. Sig. Process. Image Commun. **29**(7), 725–747 (2014)
29. Gu, K., Zhai, G., Yang, X., Zhang, W.: Using free energy principle for blind image quality assessment. IEEE Trans. Multimedia **17**(1), 50–63 (2015)
30. Moorthy, A.K., Bovik, A.C.: Blind image quality assessment: from scene statistics to perceptual quality. IEEE Trans. Image Process. **20**(12), 3350–3364 (2011)
31. Gu, K., Zhai, G., Yang, X., Zhang, W., Liu, M.: Subjective and objective quality assessment for images with contrast change. In: IEEE International Conference on Image Processing, pp. 383–387 (2013)
32. Fang, Y., Ma, K., Wang, Z., Lin, W., Fang, Z., Zhai, G.: No-reference quality assessment of contrast-distorted images based on natural scene statistics. IEEE Signal Process. Lett. **22**(7), 838–842 (2015)
33. Wang, S., Ma, K., Yeganeh, H., Wang, Z., Lin, W.: A patch-structure representation method for quality assessment of contrast changed images. IEEE Signal Process. Lett. **22**(12), 2387–2390 (2015)
34. Gu, K., Lin, W., Zhai, G., Yang, X., Zhang, W., Chen, C.W.: No-reference quality metric of contrast-distorted images based on information maximization. IEEE Trans. Cybern. (in Press)
35. The USC-SIPI Image Database, http://sipi.usc.edu/database/

Improved Reversible Visible Watermarking Based on Adaptive Block Partition

Guangyuan Yang[1], Wenfa Qi[1], Xiaolong Li[2], and Zongming Guo[1(✉)]

[1] Institute of Computer Science and Technology,
Peking University, Beijing 100871, China
{yanggy,qiwenfa,guozongming}@pku.edu.cn
[2] Institute of Information Science, Beijing Jiaotong University, Beijing 100044, China
lixl@bjtu.edu.cn

Abstract. Visible watermarking is a useful technique to perceptually protect the copyright while the reversible technique can help losslessly recover the original image. A reversible visible image watermarking scheme based on difference-expansion and adaptive block partition is presented in this paper. First, the cover image is divided into non-overlapped $k \times k$ sized blocks. Then, an adaptive visual effect factor for each block is calculated by non-watermarked blocks and estimated watermarked blocks in its neighborhood to embed the visible watermark. Since the information in watermarking region is not used, authorized users can exactly recover the original cover image without the availability of the watermark in the recovery process. Afterwards, one watermark bit is embedded into each block based on the conventional difference-expansion method. To reduce the exceeding number which denotes the pixel whose values is larger than 255 or less than 0 generated in watermark bit embedding procedure, an adaptive block partition strategy is utilized in the proposed method. Experimental results show that compared with the related work, the proposed method can greatly reduce the exceeding numbers and the visual effect is better at the same time.

Keywords: Reversible visible watermarking · Adaptive block partition · Human visual system

1 Introduction

Visible watermarking is widely used in protecting the ownership of vital images which contain the perceptual copyright information. Determined by whether the original cover image can be fully recovered, the visible watermarking techniques can be classified into two categories: *reversible and irreversible*. In traditional watermarking techniques, an imperceptible amount of host data is often sacrificed for robustness. However, in some serious scenarios, reversible watermarking is an ideal solution where the availability of original data is essential such as remote sensing, military image processing, medical image sharing, multimedia archive management, etc. [10].

© Springer International Publishing AG 2017
C. Kraetzer et al. (Eds.): IWDW 2017, LNCS 10431, pp. 303–317, 2017.
DOI: 10.1007/978-3-319-64185-0_23

Most reversible data hiding schemes concentrate on the invisible watermarking schemes [2,3,5–7,9,13,19]. Reversible data hiding technique is proposed to losslessly recover both embedded data and cover medium [1,14]. The histogram-modification-based method is firstly proposed by Ni *et al.* [12] in which the peak point of image histogram is utilized for data embedding. In [16], Tian proposes an expansion technique to use a pixel pair to embed one data bit. Afterwards, Thodi and Rodriguez [15] propose a state-of-the-art technique, prediction-error expansion (PEE), where prediction-error is firstly introduced for expansion embedding.

The visible watermark can be directly judged by human eyes and reversible techniques can be applied to allow legitimate users to remove the embedded visible watermark. In past few years, there are many researches focusing on developing efficient reversible visible image watermarking schemes. In [8], Hu and Jeon propose a scheme to replace a bit plane of the watermarking area with the watermark bits. The compressed version of the bit plane is embedded into the non-watermarked area. Liu and Tsai [11] use a deterministic one-to-one compound mappings to embed visible watermarks of arbitrary sizes on cover images. However, the watermark images are required when recovering the original cover image. In [18], Yang *et al.* propose to embed the visible watermark into the cover image based on the human visual characteristic scaling factors. After that a recovery packet, which is utilized to restore the watermarked area, is reversibly inserted into non-visibly-watermarked region. Chen *et al.* [4] design a watermarking scheme based on a conventional difference-expansion method. The cover image is partitioned into non-overlapped blocks and each watermark bit is embedded into a block. Despite the merit of [4], there may exist a large number of exceeding numbers in this approach, which affects the visual effect of the visible watermark.

In this paper, inspired by the work [4], we propose an effective reversible visible watermarking scheme based on difference-expansion method. In proposed method, an adaptive block partition strategy is adopted to decrease the exceeding numbers. Besides, an adaptive visual effect factor based on human visual system (HVS) characteristics is used to embed the visible watermark which makes the proposed method more visually satisfactory and less intrusive. In the proposed scheme, the cover image is first segmented into non-overlapped blocks which contain $k \times k$ pixels. Then the visible watermark is embedded into each block according to an adaptive visual effect factor. After finding an optimal partition of the block with the adaptive block partition strategy, the watermark bit is embedded into each block based on the conventional difference-expansion method.

The rest of the paper is organized as follows. A relevant reversible visible watermarking scheme is reviewed in Sect. 2. Then in Sect. 3, the proposed method is presented in details. The experimental results are given in Sect. 4. The final conclusions are drawn in the last section.

2   Related Work

In this section, a reversible visible image watermarking scheme [4] based on difference-expansion method is introduced. At the end of the section, a discussion of the motivation of proposed method is presented.

In [4], the cover image is partitioned into non-overlapped $k \times k$ blocks. Each block embeds one watermark bit. The parameter k determines the area of the visible watermark. For each block, the pixels are partitioned into two sets S_1, S_2 and two pixels y_1, y_2. The size of set S_1 is $\lfloor \frac{k^2-1}{2} \rfloor$ and the size of set S_2 is $\lfloor \frac{k^2-1}{2} \rfloor - 1$. An example of the partition of a block for $k = 3$ is shown in Table 1. Corresponding to the relation between the block mean b_m and the threshold T_m which is calculated according to the local mean of the watermark area, each pixel is shifted as follows,

$$x'(i,j) = \begin{cases} x(i,j) + w \cdot (B + R(i,j)), if & b_m < T_m \\ x(i,j) - w \cdot (B + R(i,j)), if & b_m \geq T_m \end{cases} \quad (1)$$

where w is the watermark bit, $x(i,j)$ and $x'(i,j)$ are the pixels in the original cover image and the watermarked image respectively. B represents the watermark strength and R is a random number generated by a seed within a small range to guarantee the security of this scheme.

Table 1. Examples of partition strategies for $k = 3$ in Chen *et al.*'s method [4].

block definition			S_1	S_2	y_1	y_2
$b_{1,1}$	$b_{1,2}$	$b_{1,3}$	$b_{1,2}, b_{2,1}, b_{3,2}, b_{2,3}$	$b_{1,3}, b_{2,2}, b_{3,1}$	$b_{1,1}$	$b_{3,3}$
$b_{2,1}$	$b_{2,2}$	$b_{2,3}$				
$b_{3,1}$	$b_{3,2}$	$b_{3,3}$				

Next, a difference-expansion based method is utilized to embed the watermark bit. The block difference d_1 and d_2 are calculated using the conventional difference-expansion method among the sum of pixel values of S_1, S_2 and the pixel y_1, y_2 respectively.

$$d_1 = \sum_{x'_1(i,j) \in S_1} x'_1(i,j) - \sum_{x'_2(i,j) \in S_2} x'_2(i,j) - y_1$$

$$d_2 = \sum_{x'_1(i,j) \in S_1} x'_1(i,j) - \sum_{x'_2(i,j) \in S_2} x'_2(i,j) - y_2. \quad (2)$$

Then the watermark bit is embedded into the pixel y_1. A new pixel value y'_1 calculated by the difference d_1 and y_1 replaces the original y_1. If the watermark bit is 1, a sign bit is embedded into the pixel y_2 by using the same way as the watermark bit to record the modification direction of the visible watermark of this block.

In the extraction procedure, the corresponding block difference $\overline{d_1}$ and $\overline{d_2}$ are first calculated and the watermark bit w and the sign bit $sign$ can be obtained by

$$w = mod(\overline{d_1}, 2), \quad sign = mod(\overline{d_2}, 2). \tag{3}$$

Then y_1 and y_2 are recovered by the watermark bit and the block difference. Finally, if the watermark bit of this block is 1, the original cover can be recovered by the watermarked pixels, the parameters $sign$, the watermark strength B and the shift number R.

Fig. 1. The details of the recovered image Lena in the area of the brim of the hat using method in [4] without recording exceeding numbers.

Although this model has achieved promising results, it has two drawbacks: On one hand, the exceeding number which denotes pixels in the watermarked image whose value is larger than 255 or smaller than 0 may occur in this approach. When y_1 or y_2 of a block is an exceeding number, all pixels in this block can not be correctly recovered that will make an unacceptable damage of the visual effect for the recovered image. Notice that in Eq. (2), d_1 is calculated by y_1 and the difference of two subsets S_1, S_2. Since the number of set S_2 is one less than the size of set S_1, d_1 is considered as a small value because of the neighborhood similarity of the natural images. However, the difference can be pretty large in some edge area (i.e., the brim of the hat in Lena as shown in Fig. 1), which causes y_1' and y_2' to be exceeding numbers. In [4], Chen et $al.$ propose to record the exceeding numbers, however, these recording pixels in the watermark can not be embedded which may lead to the consecutive loss of the watermark message when the number of the exceeding numbers are large. It causes a misread of the watermark. On the other hand, the watermark strength to be embedded in different areas of the host image is weakly depending on the underlying image content in [4]. This may lead to an obtrusive visible watermarking.

To address these two issues, we improve this model by using the following techniques: Firstly, we utilize an adaptive approach to divide the blocks which can greatly decrease the number of the exceeding numbers. Secondly, in the proposed method, an adaptive visual effect factor depending on the HVS is used to embed the visible watermark. The experimental results show that the watermarked images of proposed method have a better visual effect.

3   Proposed Method

In this section, we will introduce the proposed method in details. The embedding process mainly contains two procedures, visible watermark embedding and watermark bit embedding. We will first introduce the adaptive visual effect factor we use in the visible watermark embedding in Sect. 3.1. Then the embedding procedure will be introduced in Sect. 3.2 and the recovery algorithm will be introduced in Sect. 3.3.

3.1   Visible Watermark Embedding

Inspired by the work [17], we design a visible watermark embedding strategy using an adaptive visual effect factor based on the HVS characteristics. There are two aspects of the HVS characteristics to consider for the proposed visual effect factor.

First, considering that human eyes are more sensitive to changes in smooth areas than textured areas, we give a parameter α_i to measure the smoothness of block i,

$$\alpha_i = \frac{|k^2 - 2c_i| + \tau}{k^2 + \tau} \tag{4}$$

where k is the size of the block and τ is a parameter for avoiding α_i to be zero. Here c_i represents the number of pixels whose values are greater than the mean pixel value of the i-th block,

$$l_i = \frac{\sum_{p=1}^{k} \sum_{q=1}^{k} I(p,q)}{k^2} \tag{5}$$

where $I(p,q)$ denotes the pixel value of the block. Notice that the parameter α gets larger as the block gets smoother (more pixels values are greater or smaller than the block mean).

Secondly, the human visual is more sensitive to the changes in middle intensity regions, the luminance factor thus can be considered as

$$\beta_i = \frac{|l_i - 255/2|}{255/2} \tag{6}$$

β_i becomes larger when the pixel values of this block are in middle luminance. Thus, the visual effect factor can be derived as

$$\gamma_i = \frac{\alpha_i}{\beta_i} \tag{7}$$

In order to avoid obtrusively embedding the watermark, γ is normalized into a narrow range $[r_1, r_2]$ by

$$\tilde{\gamma}_i = \frac{r_2 - r_1}{max(\gamma) - min(\gamma)} \times (\gamma_i - min(\gamma)) + r_1. \tag{8}$$

308   G. Yang et al.

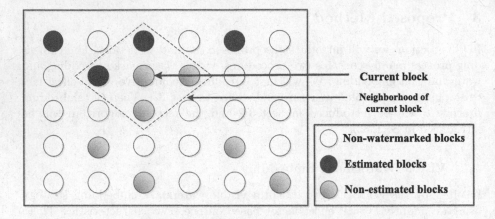

Fig. 2. The neighborhood of current block.

where $max()$ and $min()$ are maximum and minimum function respectively. Notice that the greater value of the visual effect factor is, the higher the watermark strength becomes. In order to recover the original cover image without using the watermark image in the recovery procedure, the block mean and the visual effect factor are calculated as,

$$l_i^* = \frac{1}{|O_1| + |O_2|} \left(\sum_{b_j \in O_1} l_j + \sum_{b_j \in O_2} l_j^* \right)$$

$$\tilde{\gamma}_i^* = \frac{1}{|O_1| + |O_2|} \left(\sum_{b_j \in O_1} \tilde{\gamma}_j + \sum_{b_j \in O_2} \tilde{\gamma}_j^* \right) \tag{9}$$

where the j-th block b_j belongs to the neighborhood of current block. And $O_1 = \{Non - watermarkedblocksintheneighborhoodofcurrentblock\}$, $O_2 = \{Estimatedwatermarkedblocksintheneighborhoodofcurrentblock\}$, illustrated in Fig. 2. Since the parameters of the watermarked blocks are estimated from the blocks in the original cover image and the blocks that have been estimated, they can be estimated identically in the recovery procedure without using information from the watermarking region.

Then for the i-th block, the visible watermark is embedded as follows,

$$x_i' = \begin{cases} x_i, & if \; w_i = 0 \\ (1 - \tilde{\gamma}_i^*)x_i + \tilde{\gamma}_i^* W_S - R_i, & if \; w_i = 1, l_i^* \geq 127 \\ (1 - \tilde{\gamma}_i^*)x_i + \tilde{\gamma}_i^*(255 - W_S) + R_i, & if \; w_i = 1, l_i^* < 127 \end{cases} \tag{10}$$

where x_i and x_i' are the pixels of the original cover block and the watermarked image block. W_S is the watermark strength and R_i is a set of random numbers within the range of $[0, ShiftStrength]$ generated from a seed $ShiftSeed$.

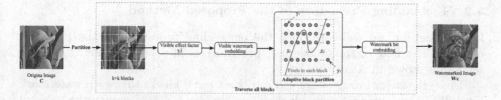

Fig. 3. Framework of proposed embedding scheme.

Algorithm 1. Embedding procedure of the proposed reversible visible watermark scheme.

Input:

The cover image $\mathbf{C}$, the watermark $\mathbf{W}$, the block size k, the watermark strength W_S, the shift sequence generator seed $ShiftSeed$, the range control parameter for the visual effect factor r_1, r_2.

Output:

Watermarked image $\mathbf{W_C}$

1: The cover image will be divided into non-overlapped $k \times k$ sized blocks, $2 \leq k < min\left\{\lfloor\frac{M_c}{M_w}\rfloor, \lfloor\frac{N_c}{N_w}\rfloor\right\}$, where M_c, N_c and M_w, N_w are the size of the original cover image and the watermark image respectively.

2: **for** Each block in the watermark region **do**

3:    Calculate the visual effect factor $\widetilde{\gamma}^*$ and the block mean l^* as shown in Eq. (9).

4:    Embed the visible watermark for each block in the watermark region using Eq. (10).

5:    All the pixels in the block denoted as S will be divided into two subsets S_1, S_2 and two pixels y_1, y_2 where $|S_1| = \lfloor\frac{k^2-1}{2}\rfloor$ and $|S_2| = \lfloor\frac{k^2-1}{2}\rfloor - 1$. Here $|\bullet|$ represents the cardinality of a set. y_1 is selected to be the top left corner pixel of the corresponding block while y_2 is the bottom right pixel of the block.

6:    **for** Every division of S_1, S_2 s.t. $S_1 \cap S_2 = \emptyset$ $S_1 \cup S_2 = S$ $[y_1, y_2]$ **do**

7:       Find S_1^* and S_2^* such that

$$S_1^*, S_2^* = \arg\min(abs(\sum_{x_i \in S_1^*} x_i - \sum_{x_j \in S_2^*} x_j - l^*)) \tag{11}$$

where $abs()$ means the absolute value.

8:    **end for**

9:    Calculate the block difference d_1 as,

$$d_1 = \sum_{x_{1,i} \in S_1^*} x_{1,i} - \sum_{x_{2,j} \in S_2^*} x_{2,j} - y_1 \tag{12}$$

10:    Then the watermark bit w is embedded into the difference d_1 and y_1 is replaced by $y_1^{'}$

$$y_1^{'} = 2d_1 + w + \left\lfloor \frac{\sum\limits_{x_i^{'} \in S_1 \cup S_2} x_i^{'}}{2\lfloor\frac{k^2-1}{2}\rfloor - 1} \right\rfloor \tag{13}$$

11: **end for**

3.2 Embedding Procedure of the Proposed Method

In this section, we will introduce the embedding procedure of the proposed method. The flow of the embedding procedure is illustrated in Fig. 3 and the scheme is shown in Algorithm 1.

First, the cover image is divided into $k \times k$ sized blocks that each watermark bit will be embedded into one block. Thus, the size k determines the watermark size in image $\mathbf{W_C}$ while the size of watermark area increases with k. In step 3 and step 4, the visible watermark is embedded into the cover image adaptively based on the visual effect factor. In Eq. (10), the block mean and the visual effect factor are calculated without using any information from the watermark area which ensures the watermark image is not needed to recover the original image. In step 5, the subset S_1 contains one more pixel than the subset S_2, thus the difference between the sum of pixels in S_1 and the sum of pixels in S_2 is nearly one pixel value. Notice that in Eq. (11), we find two subset S_1^* and S_2^* whose pixel difference is closest to the block mean which makes the absolute value of d_1 as small as possible. Thus, the $y_1^{'}$ in Eq. (13) has little possibility to be the exceeding numbers. Finally, the proposed method uses the difference-expansion method to embed the watermark bit in step 9 and step 10. The other parameters such as $W_S, k, r_1, r_2, ShiftSeed, M_w, N_w$, the position of the watermarked area and the remaining exceeding numbers' positions can be embedded into non-watermarked area by the conventional information hiding approaches.

3.3 Extraction of the Watermark and Cover Recovery

The extraction procedure and the recovery algorithm will be given out in this section. The details of the recovery algorithm is illustrated in Algorithm 2.

First, the block size k, the watermark strength W_S and some other parameters are extracted. In step 2, the watermarked image is partitioned using the same way as the embedding procedure does. Here, as some blocks may still contain exceeding numbers, the position of these blocks are recorded. In step 3, the difference $\overline{d_1}$ is calculated using y_1 and the estimated value of this block. Then the watermark bit is extracted by the difference $\overline{d_1}$. The visual effect factor and the block mean are calculated without using the information from the watermarked region. From step 9 to step 11, the subsets used in the embedding procedure are found out to recover the $y_1^{'}$. Finally, the visible watermark is removed and we obtain the recovered image.

Algorithm 2. Extraction procedure and the recovery algorithm of the proposed reversible visible watermarking scheme.

Input:

   Watermarked image $\mathbf{W_C}$

Output:

   The cover image $\mathbf{C}$, the watermark $\mathbf{W}$

1: The watermarked image is divided into non-overlapped $k \times k$ sized blocks. All the pixels in the block denoted as S will be divided into two subsets S_1, S_2 and two pixels y_1, y_2. y_1 is selected to be the top left corner pixel of the corresponding block while y_2 is the bottom right pixel of the block.

2: **for** Each block in the watermark region **do**

3:    Calculate the block difference $\overline{d_1}$ as,

$$\overline{d_1} = y_1 - \left\lfloor \frac{\sum\limits_{x_i' \in S_1 \cup S_2} x_i'}{2 \left\lfloor \dfrac{k^2 - 1}{2} \right\rfloor - 1} \right\rfloor \tag{14}$$

4:    Extract the watermark bit w and recover the original d_1 as,

$$w = mod(\overline{d_1}, 2), \quad d_1 = \lfloor \tfrac{\overline{d_1}}{2} \rfloor \tag{15}$$

5:    Calculate the visual effect factor $\widetilde{\gamma}^*$ and the block mean l^* using the non-watermarked blocks and the recovered blocks.

6:    **for** Every division of S_1, S_2 *s.t.* $S_1 \cap S_2 = \emptyset$ $S_1 \cup S_2 = S - \{y_1, y_2\}$ **do**

7:       Find S_1^* and S_2^* such that

$$S_1^*, S_2^* = \arg\min(abs(\sum_{x_i \in S_1^*} x_i - \sum_{x_j \in S_2^*} x_j - l^*)) \tag{16}$$

8:    **end for**

9:    Recover y_1' using the Eq. (17),

$$y_1' = \sum_{x_{1,i} \in S_1^*} x_{1,i} - \sum_{x_{2,j} \in S_2^*} x_{2,j} - d_1 \tag{17}$$

10:    Finally, recover all the pixels in the block using the watermark bit, the watermark strength, R and visual effect factor by Eq. (18)

$$x' = \begin{cases} x & , if \quad w = 0 \\ \dfrac{x - \widetilde{\gamma}^* W_S + R}{1 - \widetilde{\gamma}^*} & , if \quad w = 1, l^* \geq 127 \\ \dfrac{x - \widetilde{\gamma}^*(255 - W_S) - R}{1 - \widetilde{\gamma}^*} & , if \quad w = 1, l^* < 127 \end{cases} \tag{18}$$

11: **end for**

We now discuss the correctness of the proposed scheme. In the embedding procedure, the pixels in a block are first modified to embed the visible watermark. Both in the embedding and extraction procedure, since the block mean is calculated without using the information of non-estimated watermarked blocks, the same partition and S_1^*, S_2^* are used to calculate the block difference. The watermark bit is embedded into the difference among S_1, S_2 and y_1, and then y_1 is replaced by y_1' in Eq. (13). While in the extraction procedure, the new dif-

ference is firstly calculated by y_1 and $\left| \dfrac{\displaystyle\sum_{x_i' \in \{S_1 \cup S_2\}} x_i'}{2\left\lceil \dfrac{k^2-1}{2} \right\rceil - 1} \right|$ which is the same as

the estimated mean of the block in Eq. (13). Then the modified y_1 is recovered in Eq. (17). Finally, all the pixels in the block can be recovered with the visual effect factor if the watermark bit is 1. So far, all the watermark bits have been extracted and the recovered image has also been obtained.

4   Experimental Results

The experimental results are presented in this section. We will introduce the experiments from three aspects. In Sect. 4.1, the parameters used in the proposed scheme will be introduced and the security of the proposed scheme will be basically discussed. The experimental results under different block size k and watermark strength W_S will be shown in Sect. 4.2. Finally, a discussion of the exceeding numbers and the comparison between the proposed method and the related works will be shown in Sect. 4.3.

4.1   Parameter Selection and Security Discussion

Figure 4(a)–(c) show the gray-scale cover images we used for our experiments, Lena, Boat, Aerial, 512 × 512 in size while Fig. 4(d) is the binary watermark 128 × 128 in size.

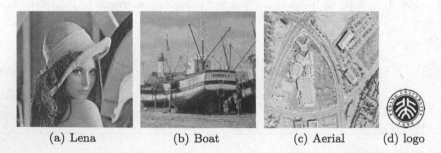

(a) Lena   (b) Boat   (c) Aerial   (d) logo

Fig. 4. (a)–(c) Three original gray scale 512 × 512 sized cover images. (d) The 128 × 128 sized binary watermark.

Table 2. The selection of the parameters of the proposed method.

k	W_S	r_1	r_2	ShiftStrength
$\{2,3\}$	$\{20,40,60,80\}$	0.3	0.5	10

We first discuss the parameters utilized in this paper. As we have described in last section, the parameters needed to be considered are listed as follows:

- The block size k.
- The watermark strength W_S.
- The normalize parameter for the visual effect factor r_1 and r_2.
- The shift number strength ShiftStrength.

The parameters used in the proposed method are described in Table 2. We use 512×512 sized cover image and 128×128 sized watermark image in our experiments. In the proposed method, each watermark bit is embedded into one block, while some parameters and extra message are embedded into the non-watermarked area. Therefore, k is supposed to be smaller than $min\left\{\lfloor \frac{M_c}{M_w} \rfloor, \lfloor \frac{N_c}{N_w} \rfloor\right\}$. For the watermark strength, we choose four different levels of strength which vary the visual effect of the watermark image. And the ShiftStrength is set up to 10 thus the shift number for each pixel is small.

There are two types of strategies to support the security of the proposed scheme. On one hand, the visible watermark is shifted by a random number. An attacker has a probability of $\frac{1}{(ShiftStrength)^{M_W \times N_W}}$ to correctly recover the original image that the completely recovery is nearly impossible. On the other hand, the wrong selection of the position of y_1 will result in a noisy recovered image. Figure 5 shows an example of the recovered image whose y_1 is wrongly selected. The watermark area of the recovered image is obviously blurred. These two strategies guarantee the security of the proposed scheme.

Fig. 5. Recovered images of Lena whose y_1 is wrongly selected. The watermark strength $W_S = 60$ and $k = 3$ (PSNR = 10.2552 dB).

4.2 Experimental Results Under Different Parameters

Figure 6 shows the results of the watermarked images under different block sizes with the same watermark strength $W_S = 60$. In Fig. 6(a)–(c), the block size

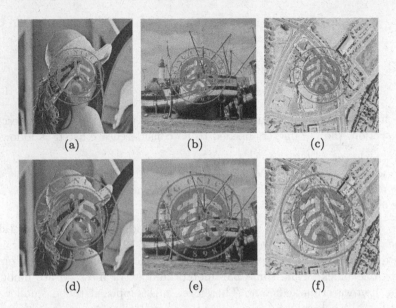

(a)   (b)   (c)

(d)   (e)   (f)

Fig. 6. Experimental results for different block size of the proposed method. (a)–(c) Three watermarked images for $k = 2$, (d)–(f) Three watermarked images for $k = 3$. The watermark strength $W_S = 60$.

$k = 2$ and in Fig. 6(d)–(f) the block size $k = 3$. Here the watermark is embedded into the center area of the cover image. The block size determines the size of the watermarked region, and a larger k leads to a larger watermark region. The size of the watermark area of Fig. 6(a)–(c) and (d)–(f) are 256×256 and 384×384 respectively. Figure 7 shows the watermarked images of different watermark strength with the same block size. Figure 7(a)–(d) show the results of cover image Lena with $W_S = 20, 40, 60, 80$, Fig. 7(e)–(h) show the results of cover image Boat with $W_S = 20, 40, 60, 80$, and Fig. 7(i)–(l) show the results of cover image Aerial with $W_S = 20, 40, 60, 80$, respectively. It can be observed that a larger parameter W_S leads to a more substantial watermark.

4.3   Discussion on Exceeding Numbers

The number of exceeding numbers of different watermarked images for proposed method and [4] are presented respectively in Fig. 8. An exceeding number denotes a pixel in the watermarked image whose value should have been larger than 255 or smaller than 0. Since the adaptive block partition strategy is used in proposed method, it can be observed that the amount of exceeding numbers of proposed method is far smaller. Otherwise, the amount of exceeding numbers increases as the watermark strength gets larger for Chen *et al.*'s method, however, it hardly changes for the proposed method. It is because the two methods use different visible watermark embedding strategies. Apparently, the amount of exceeding numbers is less influenced by HVS based embedding strategy.

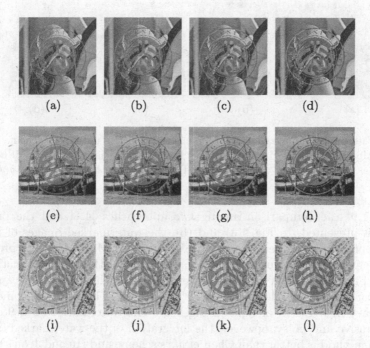

Fig. 7. Experimental results for watermark strength $W_S = 20, 40, 60, 80$ respectively. The block size $k = 3$. (a)–(d) The results of cover image Lena for $W_S = 20, 40, 60, 80$ respectively, (e)–(h) The results of cover image Boat for $W_S = 20, 40, 60, 80$ respectively, (i)–(l) The results of cover image Aerial for $W_S = 20, 40, 60, 80$ respectively.

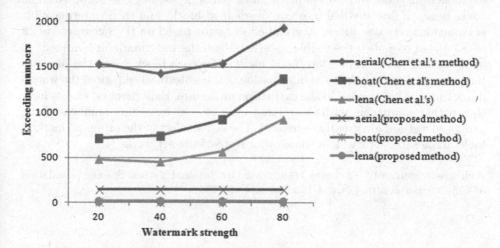

Fig. 8. Amount of exceeding numbers of different watermarked images and watermark strength.

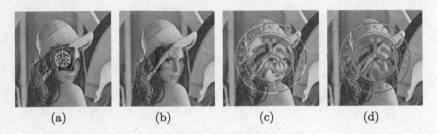

(a)   (b)   (c)   (d)

Fig. 9. Watermarked images for different schemes. (a) Hu and Jeon's scheme (Embed into the MSB plane). (b) Hu and Jeon's scheme (Embed into the third MSB plane). (c) Chen *et al.*'s scheme ($k = 3, B = 60$). (d) Proposed method ($k = 3, W_S = 60$).

In Fig. 9, the comparison among two approaches [4,8] and the proposed method is presented. In Fig. 9(a) and (b), the watermarked images of Hu and Jeon's approach embedded into the MSB and third MSB plane are presented, respectively. The results of Chen *et al.* approach and the proposed method are shown in Fig. 9(c) and (d) where the watermark strength is set up to 60 and block size is 3 for both approaches. The visible watermark of Hu and Jeon's method is either heavy in Fig. 9(a) or light in Fig. 9(b). The watermark in Fig. 9(c) looks more intrusive and noisy, however, the integration of the watermarked image of proposed method is better than Chen *et al.*' s scheme and Hu and Jeon's scheme.

5   Conclusion

In this paper, a reversible visible watermarking scheme based on difference-expansion method and an adaptive block partition strategy is proposed. The cover image is first divided into non-overlapped blocks and each watermark bit is embedded into one block. A visual effect factor based on HVS characteristics is calculated to embed the visible watermark and the watermark bit is embedded using the difference-expansion based method for each block. Since the parameters are estimated without the information of the watermarked region, the watermark image is not needed in the extraction procedure. Experimental results have shown that comparing with the related work [4], the exceeding numbers of the proposed method are greatly decreased. The visual effect of the proposed method looks more satisfactory than some other state-of-the-art works [4,8].

Acknowledgement. This work is supported by National Natural Science Foundation of China under contract Nos. U1636206 and 61572052.

References

1. Caldelli, R., Filippini, F., Becarelli, R.: Reversible watermarking techniques: an overview and a classification. EURASIP J. Inf. Secur. **2010**, 134546 (2010)
2. Celik, M.U., Sharma, G., Tekalp, A.M.: Lossless watermarking for image authentication: a new framework and an implementation. IEEE Trans. Image Process. **15**(4), 1042–1049 (2006)
3. Celik, M.U., Sharma, G., Tekalp, A.M., Saber, E.: Lossless generalized-LSB data embedding. IEEE Trans. Image Process. **14**(2), 253–266 (2005)
4. Chen, C.C., Tsai, Y.H., Yeh, H.C.: Difference-expansion based reversible and visible image watermarking scheme. Multimed. Tools Appl. **76**(6), 8497–8516 (2017)
5. Coltuc, D.: Improved embedding for prediction-based reversible watermarking. IEEE Trans. Inf. Forensics Secur. **6**(3), 873–882 (2011)
6. Fridrich, J., Goljan, M., Du, R.: Invertible authentication (2001)
7. Fridrich, J., Goljan, M., Du, R.: Lossless data embedding-new paradigm in digital watermarking. EURASIP J. Adv. Sig. Process. **2002**(2), 986842 (2002)
8. Hu, Y., Jeon, B.: Reversible visible watermarking and lossless recovery of original images. IEEE Trans. Circuits Syst. Video Technol. **16**(11), 1423–1429 (2006)
9. Li, X., Li, B., Yang, B., Zeng, T.: General framework to histogram-shifting-based reversible data hiding. IEEE Trans. Image Process. **22**(6), 2181–2191 (2013)
10. Li, X., Yang, B., Zeng, T.: Efficient reversible watermarking based on adaptive prediction-error expansion and pixel selection. IEEE Trans. Image Process. **20**(12), 3524–3533 (2011)
11. Liu, T.Y., Tsai, W.H.: Generic lossless visible watermarking - a new approach. IEEE Trans. Image Process. **19**(5), 1224–1235 (2010)
12. Ni, Z., Shi, Y.Q., Ansari, N., Su, W.: Reversible data hiding. IEEE Trans. Circuits Syst. Video Technol. **16**(3), 354–362 (2006)
13. Sachnev, V., Kim, H.J., Nam, J., Suresh, S., Shi, Y.Q.: Reversible watermarking algorithm using sorting and prediction. IEEE Trans. Circuits Syst. Video Technol. **19**(7), 989–999 (2009)
14. Shi, Y.Q., Ni, Z., Zou, D., Liang, C., Xuan, G.: Lossless data hiding: fundamentals, algorithms and applications. In: 2004 IEEE International Symposium on Circuits and Systems (IEEE Cat. No. 04CH37512), vol. 2, pp. II-33-6, May 2004
15. Thodi, D.M., Rodriguez, J.J.: Expansion embedding techniques for reversible watermarking. IEEE Trans. Image Process. **16**(3), 721–730 (2007)
16. Tian, J.: Reversible data embedding using a difference expansion. IEEE Trans. Circuits Syst. Video Technol. **13**(8), 890–896 (2003)
17. Yang, H., Yin, J.: A secure removable visible watermarking for BTC compressed images. Multimedia Tools and Applications **74**(6), 1725–1739 (2015)
18. Yang, Y., Sun, X., Yang, H., Li, C.T., Xiao, R.: A contrast-sensitive reversible visible image watermarking technique. IEEE Trans. Circuits Syst. Video Technol. **19**(5), 656–667 (2009)
19. Zhang, W., Hu, X., Li, X., Yu, N.: Recursive histogram modification: establishing equivalence between reversible data hiding and lossless data compression. IEEE Trans. Image Process. **22**(7), 2775–2785 (2013)

Robust Zero Watermarking for 3D Triangular Mesh Models Based on Spherical Integral Invariants

Chenchen Cui[1,2], Rongrong Ni[1,2(⊠)], and Yao Zhao[1,2]

[1] Institute of Information Science,
Beijing Jiaotong University, Beijing 100044, China
rrni@bjtu.edu.cn
[2] Beijing Key Laboratory of Advanced Information Science and Network
Technology, Beijing 100044, China

Abstract. At present, zero-watermarking algorithms can well resist geometric attacks and signal attacks. However, most of them are not robust to resampling attack. To solve the problem, this paper presents a robust zero-watermarking algorithm for copyright protection of 3D triangular mesh models. The watermark information is constructed by spherical integral invariants and a new computing method based on spherical crown for the invariants is proposed. CPCA(Continues Principle Component Analysis) is introduced to normalize the input mesh, while Ray-Based method is introduced to decompose the normalized mesh into ordered patches. On one hand, for the model to be protected, once the watermark is constructed, it needs to be registered in a trusted third-party IPR(Intellectual Property Rights) database together with a timestamp. On the other hand, for the model to be detected, the constructed watermark should be matched with all watermarks to recognize whether its original model is in the database. Experimental results prove that it is robust against common geometric attacks, signal processing attacks and uniform resampling attack.

Keywords: 3D triangular mesh models · Zero-watermark · Robust · Spherical integral invariants · CPCA · Ray-Based · Resampling attack

1 Introduction

With the rapid development of the Internet, more and more digital products have come into the public. Meanwhile, with the improvement of computer graphics & performance, and the maturity of 3D scanning & printing, 3D models are also faced with the problem of ownership protection. In this situation, robust watermarking is introduced for copyright protection of 3D models.

In recent years, the watermarking algorithm for 3D models has been becoming mature. Robust watermarking used for copyright protection has been the focus of the research, so does this paper. And for a wide variety of forms to 3D models, the paper only considers triangular mesh models.

General watermarking methods for 3D models modify geometry information or topology structure of meshes in spatial domain or coefficients in frequency domain to

C. Kraetzer et al. (Eds.): IWDW 2017, LNCS 10431, pp. 318–330, 2017.
DOI: 10.1007/978-3-319-64185-0_24

embed watermarks into models which will change coordinates for vertices on the model [1–5]. So they are both not suitable for models that need high precision. In order to solve the problem mentioned, zero-watermarking is introduced. It refers to use important features of models to construct watermark information, rather than modify data of models to embed watermarks. The concept of zero-watermark is put forward by Wen in the Third China Information Hiding and Multimedia Security Workshop in 2001 [6]. They researched it on 2D images firstly and defined it as a watermark that doesn't modify original data. In this algorithm, they used larger absolute value of DCT coefficients as characteristics of the image to construct watermark information and registered it in a trusted third-party IPR database together with the registration time to avoid multiple copyright statements. Later on, some other researchers also conducted a series of discussion in image zero-watermarking [7–10].

At present, the research achievements of zero-watermarking are mainly concentrated in the field of image, the study of 3D model zero-watermarking is seldom. To solve the mesh watermarking algorithm in the contradiction between robustness and transparency, Xu put forward a zero-watermarking algorithm suitable for mesh models with arbitrary topology in 2008 [11]. The algorithm through using the geometry feature in spatial domain and the secondary energy concentration in transform domain to construct watermark information. In 2011, Gao proposed a method using characters in the same two domains either [12]. Zhan put forward an algorithm based on SDF (Shape Diameter Function) in 2013 [13]. They used SDF to establish an ordered set of vertices and then together with area ratios to get a robust vertex distribution to construct watermarks.

The existing 3D model watermarking algorithms can well resist various common attacks like noise adding, simplification, smoothing, subdivision, vertex reordering, and similarity transform and so on. But most of them are based on vertices or relationships between facets on the model so that they are hard to resist resampling attack from 3D scanning and printing.

In this paper a robust 3D mesh zero-watermarking algorithm which is based on spherical integral invariants has been proposed. In the watermark construction process, the model needs to be normalized using CPCA at first to resist similarity translation attack. Then, a method named Ray-Based is used to divide the vertices on the normalized model into ordered groups. And a neighborhood sphere can be constructed in each group, meanwhile, the spherical integral invariants for each sphere can be calculated and normalized. By comparing the calculated values with a threshold (is usually 1/2), the watermark will be constructed bit by bit at last. For the model needs to be protected, the constructed watermark needs to be registered in a database together with a timestamp. And for retrieval models, the constructed watermark should be matched with all watermarks in the database. That proves we have the copyright for the retrieval model if the highest degree between two watermarks is close to 1. The outstanding contribution of the proposed method is its strong robustness against resampling attacks and simplification attacks.

Rest of this paper is organized as follows: Sect. 2 introduces the concept of integral invariants and proposes a new computing method of spherical integral invariants; Sect. 3 provides an overview of the proposed method at first and then details the watermark construction and detection procedures; Sect. 4 presents some experimental results on feasibility and robustness for the proposed method; finally, we conclude the paper and propose several directions of further research in Sect. 5.

2 Integral Invariants

2.1 The Concept of Integral Invariants

The concept of integral invariants was first put forward by Manay to research invariants for curves in a plane and one example is area integral invariant [14]. There is a point p on a curve C. We take p as the center while r as the radius of a circular $B^r(p)$. The domain D is a planar located in one side of C. Then the area of the crosshatched, which is the intersection of the circular $B^r(p)$ and domain D is defined as the invariant area $A^r(p)$ (see Fig. 1 [16]).

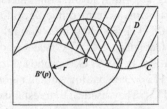

Fig. 1. Integral invariant in R^2 [16]

Pottmann generalized the concept of integral invariants from R^2 to R^3 [15]. Usually there are two kinds of integral invariants: spherical integral invariants and volume integral invariants. The proposed zero-watermarking algorithm is based on the spherical integral invariants (see Fig. 2 [16]). There is a point p on a surface S. We take p as the center while r as the radius of a sphere $B^r(p)$ and call it neighborhood sphere. The domain D is the outside space of S. Then we can define the intersected area of the neighborhood sphere with domain D as the spherical integral invariant $S^r(p)$. Now we present a new method for its computation.

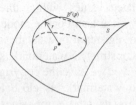

a) Neighborhood sphere   b) Spherical integral invariant

Fig. 2. Integral invariants in R^3 [16]

2.2   A New Algorithm to Compute Spherical Integral Invariants Based on Spherical Crown

To illustrate easily, we assume that the integral invariants is calculated with a neighborhood sphere $B^R(O)$ of center O and radius R and define N is the direction of the ray used in the following Ray-based section, T is a point that satisfied the equation $\overrightarrow{OT} = R \cdot N$.

For each sphere $B^R(O)$ on the model, we assume that it can intersect the surface of the model with a set of arcs on $B^R(O)$. The arcs divide the sphere's surface into two parts: inside and outside of the model. The outer part is what we want to compute. That is always worked when the model is closed and when the radius is not large enough to let $B^R(O)$ include the whole model. And we only consider simple polygon models in this paper.

The following will introduce the new method based on the assumptions above. But the value obtained by it is approximate to the true because of discrete mesh.

First, a particular situation that if the surface on the model around point O is a conical surface will be considered (see Fig. 3a)). Then the intersection between the model and the neighborhood sphere is a spherical cap. The formula for computing the area of a spherical cap is as follows:

$$S = 2\pi Rh \tag{1}$$

where, S is the area of a spherical cap, R is the radius of a neighborhood sphere and h is the height of a spherical cap.

More generally, we call it the fan spherical cap if part of the surface of model is a conical surface (see Fig. 3b)). It's a part of spherical cap.

For any case of the surface of the model, the spherical integral invariant can be approximately computed as multi-area for fan spherical caps (see Fig. 3c)).

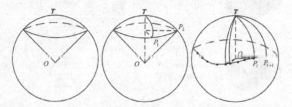

a)Surface for the cone surface   b) Surface for part of the conical surface   c) Arbitrary surface

Fig. 3. Three conditions on the surface of the model

For discrete mesh models, the intersection points P_i which are the intersections for the surface of the model and the surface of the neighborhood sphere need to be found out orderly, so as to compute the combined area for fan spherical caps. For each intersection point P_i, the area of the spherical cap can be worked out and a plane with the intersection point P_i, the center point O and the point on the surface of the sphere T can be constructed. When finally figure out all included angles α_i between plane P_iOT and plane $P_{i+1}OT$; a approximate value for the spherical integral invariant can be got. The specific formula is as follows:

$$
\begin{aligned}
S_{in\,variant} &= \sum_{i=1}^{N_{cross}} \frac{\alpha_i}{2\pi} S_i \\
&= \sum_{i=1}^{N_{cross}} \frac{\alpha_i}{2\pi} 2\pi R h_i \\
&= \sum_{i=1}^{N_{cross}} \alpha_i R h_i
\end{aligned}
\tag{2}
$$

where, N_{cross} is the total number of the intersection points, S_i is the area of the spherical cap which P_i is on it and h_i is the length of the vector from point P_i to point T in the direction of the ray. Note that the plane next to plane $P_{N_{cross}}OT$ is plane P_1OT.

3 Proposed Zero-watermarking Method

In order to protect the copyright of 3D models, this paper proposed a new zero-watermarking method. For original models, the watermark information constructed by comparing spherical integral invariants with a given threshold and needs to be registered in a IPR database. For the model to be detected, it also needs to construct watermark in the same processes. And then, the watermark should be matched with all watermarks which are in the database. Figure 4 shows the watermark construction and detection processes, which are described in detail in the following sections.

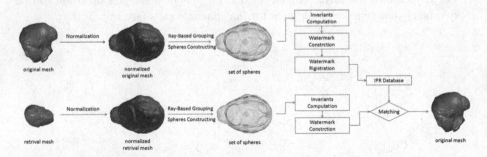

Fig. 4. The block diagram of watermark construction and detection

3.1 Model Normalization

In order to guarantee the translation, scaling, rotation invariance of model, a normalization process needs to be made on the mesh models at first. The normalization process consists of three steps, which are described in the following.

Mesh Translation. In this step, the model center will be translated to the origin of the coordinates. From a variety of computational formulas, we choose a method combined with topological relations of the model which uses areas of triangle facets as weights, in order to acquire an accurate and robust center of mass. The specific formula is as follows [17]:

$$O = \frac{1}{S_T} \sum_{i=1}^{N_f} S_i \frac{A_i + B_i + C_i}{3} \qquad (3)$$

where, N_f is the total number of facets on the model, S_i is the area of the ith triangle on the surface of the model, S_T is the total area of triangles on the model, A_i, B_i, C_i are the coordinates of three vertices on the ith triangle respectively. Assuming that $V_k = (x_k, y_k, z_k)$ and $O = (o_x, o_y, o_z)$ are the coordinates of the kth vertex on the original model and model center, the kth vertex on the translated model are computed as follows:

$$\begin{aligned} x'_k &= x_k - o_x \\ y'_k &= y_k - o_y \\ z'_k &= z_k - o_z \end{aligned} \qquad (4)$$

Mesh Uniform Scaling. This step will normalize the size of the model using a scaling factor which is calculated as the distance of two furthest points on the model. The factor is computed as follows [17]:

$$\alpha = max\left\{ x_k'^2 + y_k'^2 + z_k'^2 \right\} - min\left\{ x_k'^2 + y_k'^2 + z_k'^2 \right\}, k \in 1, 2, \ldots N_v \qquad (5)$$

where N_v is the total number of vertices on the model. The vertices of the scaled model are computed as follows:

$$x''_k = \frac{x'_k}{\alpha} \quad y''_k = \frac{y'_k}{\alpha} \quad z''_k = \frac{z'_k}{\alpha} \qquad (6)$$

Mesh Rotation. To normalize the rotation of the model, we commonly use Principle Component Analysis (PCA). But it will cause uncertainty of the normalized coordinate direction due to its nature. Therefore, a method named Continuous Principle Component Analysis (CPCA) which is usually applied to 3D model retrieval is introduced in the proposed algorithm to reduce the instability. Compared with PCA, CPCA takes advantage of areas of triangle meshes when computing the influence matrix. The model after rotating can be more stable combined with topological relations. First, the influence matrix is calculated as follows [18–20]:

$$M = \frac{1}{12S_T} \sum_{i=1}^{N_f} S_i \left[f(A_i) + f(B_i) + f(C_i) + 9f\left(\frac{A_i + B_i + C_i}{3}\right) \right] \qquad (7)$$

Here, $f(V) = VV^T$. Then, the Eigen values of M are sorted and the corresponding Eigenvectors are extracted. The Eigenvectors are normalized to Euclidean unit length. A rotation matrix R whose rows are the ordered and normalized Eigenvectors are generated. The vertices of the rotated model are computed as follows:

$$\begin{bmatrix} x_k''' \\ y_k''' \\ z_k''' \end{bmatrix} = R \times \begin{bmatrix} x_k'' \\ y_k'' \\ z_k'' \end{bmatrix} \tag{8}$$

3.2 Ray-Based Grouping

To explain conveniently, the rectangular coordinate system (x, y, z) needs to be switched to a spherical coordinate system (θ, φ, r) (see Fig. 5a)). The grouping method is to emit a series of rays evenly in an order from the model center. The direction of rays is determined by θ, φ.

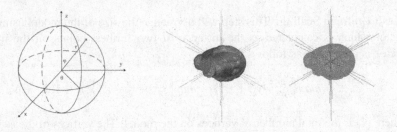

a)Ray-Based under spherical coordinate system   b)Grouping for Venus

Fig. 5. Ray-Based under spherical coordinate system

For example, at the beginning, $\theta = 0$, $\varphi = 0$, the ray is the positive axis of z axis. Then fix θ and adjust φ evenly to emit the next ray. When the ray is the positive axis of z axis once again, θ should be fixed after adjusting it evenly, and then, adjusting φ as above. Repeat the steps above until rays are full of the entire model. Figure 5b) shows the groups for Venus. Note that the number of groups is the same as the length of the watermark because one bit of watermark will be constructed from a group of model.

Combing with the previous step of normalized operations, the vertices on the model can be grouped in a fixed order. So that the watermark constructed from model after attack and the watermark constructed from original model can keep a certain synchronicity (see Fig. 6).

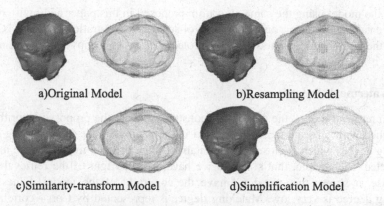

a)Original Model   b)Resampling Model

c)Similarity-transform Model   d)Simplification Model

Fig. 6. Watermark synchronization schemes

3.3 Constructing and Computing

In this step, neighborhood spheres will be constructed on the model and spherical integral invariants need to be computed for each sphere.

First, all intersection points which are the intersections between the rays emitted in Sect. 3.2 and the surface of the model should be found out. Subsequently, the shortest distance d_{min} between every two of these points needs to be calculated. To avoid vertices overlap between different spheres when calculating the integral invariants, we choose $0.4d_{min}$ as radius and the intersection point as center for each sphere. Then, the spherical integral invariants can be calculated belong to spheres using the method proposed in Sect. 2.2 and can be normalized to $(0, 1)$.

3.4 Watermark Construction

For the reason that the center of each sphere is on the surface of the model, the normalized spherical integral invariants should be floating around 0.5 in high approximation accuracy. Therefore, we choose 0.5 as a threshold to construct watermark information. The bit of watermark turns to be "1" while the spherical integral invariant is bigger than 0.5; otherwise, the bit is "0". The specific formula is as follows:

$$\begin{cases} S_{in\,variant} > 0.5, & \omega_i = 1 \\ S_{in\,variant} \le 0.5, & \omega_i = 0 \end{cases} \tag{9}$$

So, according to the features of each model, we can get different watermarks.

3.5 Watermark Registration

After constructing the watermark information of each model, it needs to be registered in a trusted IPR database with a timestamp [21] just as a record in order to give a safe, reliable and valid proof for 3D model. Even if the attacker constructed a watermark through the model using the same algorithm proposed in this paper and registered it to the IPR database, however, due to the time of attacker's registration in theory is always late for the author, this method can still protect the owner's copyright of the model.

3.6   Watermark Detection

For each retrieval model, the watermark constructed using the proposed algorithm will be matched with all watermarks registered in the database. The model of the highest matching degree which is close to 1 in database is the original model for the model to be detected. Meanwhile, that's proves we have the copyright of the retrieval model. Otherwise, it shows that we don't have the copyright of the model if the highest matching degree is very low. Matching degree is represented by Corr - correlation in this paper. It is defined as follows:

$$Corr = \frac{\sum_{i=0}^{N-1} (\omega_i^d - \bar{\omega}^d) \cdot (\omega_i^o - \bar{\omega}^o)}{\sqrt{\sum_{i=0}^{N-1} (\omega_i^d - \bar{\omega}^d)^2 \sum_{i=0}^{N-1} (\omega_i^o - \bar{\omega}^o)^2}} \tag{10}$$

where, $\bar{\omega}^d$ is the mean value of the watermark constructed from retrieval model, ω_i^d is the ith bit of it while $\bar{\omega}^o$, ω_i^o is the same meaning for the watermark constructed from original model in the IPR database.

4   Experimental Results

The experimental results when using the proposed zero-watermarking algorithm for 3D mesh models is provided in the following. The experiments address both the zero-watermark feasibility as well as robustness to various attacks. In all experiments, the length of zero-watermark is 32 bits. The proposed method was applied on several mesh models. In this paper, Fig. 7 illustrates four of them: Bunny, Venus, Rabbit and Horse. Table 1 shows the total number of vertices and facets for these models.

Table 1. The number of vertices and facets for experimental models

Models	Bunny	Venus	Rabbit	Horse
Vertices	34835	100759	70658	112642
Facets	69666	201514	141312	225280

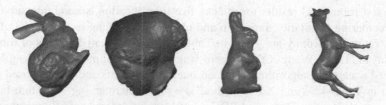

Fig. 7. Examples of experimental models

4.1 Feasibility for the Zero-watermark

Relevance evaluation index Corr - correlation value is used to evaluate the degree of similarity between two watermarks in the value range of $[-1, 1]$. The more similar two watermarks is, the Corr is closer to 1 while they are not related if the value is negative. Corr has been defined in Sect. 3.6. Table 2 shows correlation results between two watermarks of original models.

Table 2. The correlation between the watermark of each original model

Corr	Bunny	Venus	Rabbit	Horse
Bunny	1	−0.201	−0.082	−0.078
Venus	−0.201	1	0.276	0.157
Rabbit	−0.082	0.276	1	−0.078
Horse	−0.078	0.157	−0.078	1

From the table, it is obviously that the correlation between watermarks constructed through different models is not high so that the spherical invariant can be as zero-watermark for copyright protection of 3D mesh models.

4.2 Robustness Against Various Attacks

Robustness is also measured by Corr. In order to verify the robustness of the algorithm, this paper conducted a series of attacks. The parameter of smooth attack is 0.03 and the number of iterations were set to 10, 20 and 50 times; subdivision attack uses three methods: loop subdivision, midpoint subdivision and sqrt3 subdivision respectively; to simplification attack, the set of simplified strength were 30%, 50%, 70% and 90% respectively; uniform resampling attack uses the resampling method based on Marching Cube algorithm. Figure 8 shows parts of attacks to Bunny.

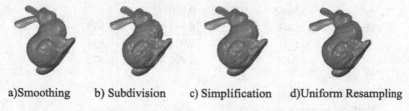

a)Smoothing   b) Subdivision   c) Simplification   d)Uniform Resampling

Fig. 8. The different attacked Bunny models

The test robustness results for attacks like simplification, smoothing, subdivision, vertex reordering, similarity transform and uniform resampling on the model of Horse, Rabbit, Venus and Bunny are given in Table 3. The comparative results of robustness for Bunny in [13] by Wang XY for a zero-watermark algorithm, [16] by Wang YP for a embedded watermark algorithm based on integral invariants and the proposed method is given in Table 4. Wang XY's method is a zero-watermarking algorithm based on SDF in spatial domain. They used SDF to establish an ordered set of vertices and then together with area ratios to get a robust vertex distribution to construct watermarks. Wang YP's method is a embedded watermark algorithm based on integral invariants in

Table 3. The robustness experimental results

Corr		Horse	Rabbit	Venus	Bunny
Smoothing	10	1	1	1	0.928
	20	1	0.923	1	0.762
	40	0.896	0.923	1	0.762
	50	0.896	0.846	1	0.762
Subdivision	loop	1	1	1	0.928
	midpoint	1	1	1	1
	Sqrt3	1	1	1	0.928
Simplification	30%	1	1	1	1
	50%	1	1	1	1
	70%	1	1	1	1
	90%	0.896	1	1	–
Reordering		1	1	1	1
Similarity transform		1	1	1	1
Uniform resampling		1	1	1	0.928

Table 4. The robustness results for compared experiments of Bunny

Corr		Proposed	Wang XY [13]	Wang YP [16]
Smoothing	10	0.928	–	0.975
	20	0.762	–	0.975
	40	0.762	–	0.963
	50	0.762	–	–
Subdivision	loop	0.928	0.970	0.987
	midpoint	1	0.938	1
	Sqrt3	0.928	0.970	1
Simplification	30%	1	0.954	0.928
	50%	1	0.938	0.914
	70%	1	0.906	0.875
Reordering		1	1	1
Similarity transform		1	1	1
Uniform resampling		0.928	–	–

spatial domain either. They embed watermarks into a model by altering coordinates of part of vetices on the model to make the integral invariants reach up to a given value.

As the tables show that the proposed algorithm has a high robustness to resist simplification attack. When the simplified degree is up to 90%, the correlation value always can be remained more than 0.85 and the reason for why Bunny cannot resist 90% simplification attack is that the number of vertices on the simplified model is too small. It also has a high robustness for uniform resampling attack and the value can keep above 0.85 either.

5 Conclusion

In this paper, a robust zero-watermarking algorithm based on spherical integral invariants for 3D triangular mesh models was proposed in the spatial domain. The algorithm uses model normalizing, grouping and a geometric invariant value called spherical integral invariants to construct watermark information and well solves the invisible digital watermarking of contradiction between the transparency and robustness. In the stage of registration, it introduces a concept of timestamp to resist refactoring watermark attack. Although the spatial domain watermarking methods usually have lower robustness than spectral domain methods, the proposed method has good robustness against various attacks, especially for uniform resampling attack and simplification attack but cannot resist cropping attack which will be the topic in the future research. And in the next step, an embedded watermarking method based on volume invariants can be integrated in the proposed method as a dual-watermarking algorithm to get a better copyright protection of 3D models. Maybe more models should be tested.

Acknowledgments. This work was supported in part by National NSF of China (61672090, 61332012). The National Key Research and Development Program of China (2016YFB0800 404), Fundamental Research Funds for the Central Universities (2015JBZ002).

References

1. Ohbuchi, R., Masuda, H., Aono, M.: Watermaking three-dimensional polygonal models. In: ACM International Conference on Multimedia 1997, vol. 16, pp. 261–272 (1997)
2. Benedens, O.: Geometry-based watermarking of 3D models. IEEE Comput. Graph. Appl. **19**(1), 46–55 (1999)
3. Cho, J., Prost, R., Jung, H.: An oblivious watermarking for 3-D polygonal meshes using distribution of vertex norms. IEEE Trans. Signal Process. **55**(1), 142–155 (2007)
4. Liu, Y., Prabhakaran, B., Guo, X.: Spectral watermarking for parameterized surfaces. IEEE Trans. Inf. Forensics Secur. **7**(5), 1459–1471 (2012)
5. Bors, A., Luo, M.: Optimized 3D watermarking for minimal surface distortion. IEEE Trans. Image Process. **22**(5), 1822–1835 (2013)

6. Wen, Q., Sun, T., Wang, S.: Based zero-watermark digital watermarking technology. In: The Third China Information Hiding and Multimedia Security Workshop (CIHW). Xidain University Press, Xi'an (2001)

7. Yang, S., Li, C.H., Sun, F., Sun, Y.: Study on the method of image non-watermark in DWT domain. J. Image Graph. **8**(1), 664–669 (2003)

8. Wang, C., Li, D.: Image zero-watermarking utilizing wavelet zerotree structure and PCA. Opto Electron. Eng. **32**(41), 75–77 (2005)

9. Lu, J., Huang, Q., Wang, M., Li, L., Dai, J., Chang, C.-C.: Zero-watermarking based on improved orb features against print-cam attack. In: Shi, Y.-Q., Kim, H.J., Pérez-González, F., Yang, C.-N. (eds.) IWDW 2014. LNCS, vol. 9023, pp. 187–198. Springer, Cham (2015). doi:10.1007/978-3-319-19321-2_14

10. Dhoka, M.S.: Robust and dynamic image zero watermarking using Hessian Laplace detector and logistic map. In: IEEE International Advance Computing Conference (IACC), Bangalore, pp. 930–935 (2015)

11. Xu, T., Zhang, Y.: Zero-watermarking technique of three-dimensional meshes. J. Jilin Univ. (Eng. Technol. Ed.) **37**(4), 901–904 (2007)

12. Gao, L.: A zero watermarking scheme for 3D meshes based on affine invariant. In: The 2011 Asia-Pacific Youth Conference of Youth Communication and Technology (2011)

13. Du, S., Zhan, Y.Z., Wang, X.Y.: A zero watermarking algorithm for 3D mesh models based on shape diameter function. J. Comput. Aided Des. Comput. Graph. **25**(5), 653–665 (2013)

14. Manay, S., Hong, B.-W., Yezzi, A.J., Soatto, S.: Integral invariant signatures. In: Pajdla, T., Matas, J. (eds.) ECCV 2004, Part IV. LNCS, vol. 3024, pp. 87–99. Springer, Heidelberg (2004). doi:10.1007/978-3-540-24673-2_8

15. Pottmann, H., Huang, Q., Yang, Y.: Integral invariants for robust geometry processing. Technical report, Vienna University of Technology (2005)

16. Wang, Y.P.: Research on 3D Model Watermark Embedding Method. Tsinghua University, Beijing (2008)

17. Molaei, A., Ebrahimnezhad, H., Sedaaghi, M.: Robust and blind 3D mesh watermarking in spatial domain based on faces categorization and sorting. 3D Res. **7**(2), 1–18 (2016)

18. Vranic, D.: 3D Model Retrieval. Universitat Leipzig, Leipzig, Germany Saxony (2003)

19. Papadakis, P., Pratikakis, I., Perantonis, S., Theoharis, T.: Efficient 3D shape matching and retrieval using a concrete radialized spherical projection representation. Pattern Recogn. **40**(9), 2437–2452 (2007)

20. Vranic, D., Saupe, D., Richter, J.: Tools for 3D-object retrieval: Karhunen-Loeve transform and spherical harmonics. In: Fourth Workshop on Multimedia Signal Processing, pp. 293–298. IEEE (2001)

21. Liu, H., Zhang, Z.H., Wen, J.: A DCT domain zero-watermark scheme based on time stamping. Comput. Technol. Dev. **19**(9), 143–145 (2009)

On the Statistical Properties of Syndrome Trellis Coding

Olaf Markus Köhler[1]([⊠]), Cecilia Pasquini[1,2], and Rainer Böhme[1,2]

[1] Department of Computer Science, Universität Innsbruck, Innsbruck, Austria
Olaf.Koehler@uibk.ac.at
[2] Department of Information Systems, Universität Münster, Münster, Germany

Abstract. Steganographic systems use Syndrome Trellis Coding (STC) to control the selection of embedding positions in a cover, subject to a set of stochastic constraints. This paper reports observations from a series of experiments on the ability of Syndrome Trellis Coding to approximate independent Bernoulli random variables. We find that approximation errors are generally small except for some outliers at boundary positions. Bivariate dependencies between embedding changes do reveal the use of the code and its parameters. While risky outliers can be hidden by permuting the cover before coding, or avoided by using the proposed "outlier corrected" variant OC-STC, the aggregate bivariate statistics are invariant to permutations and therefore constitute a potential security risk in the presence of powerful attackers.

1 Introduction

Syndrome coding is a key element of modern steganography. It allows the transmission of steganographic messages without the need to share with the recipient the location of the embedding changes in a cover. The most popular form of syndrome coding is known as Syndrome Trellis Coding (STC) [7]. STC is specifically suited for separating the concerns of *where* to embed and *how* to embed, combined with unparalleled computational efficiency and marginal coding loss. Indeed, since the introduction of STC, the research community has adopted the convention to test new embedding functions with simulated embedding rather than meaningful payloads, thereby relying on STC's ability to substitute random changes with a close to optimal encoding of payload bits [1,7,15]. In particular, the wide acceptance of and reliance on STC calls for a closer inspection of the statistical properties of the code, specifically its reference implementation [3]. That is where this paper seeks to contribute to the state of knowledge.

In a nutshell, STC takes as inputs the cover, a vector of change probabilities per cover element, and a message. It produces a vector of positions where the cover must be changed in order to embed the message. A common abstraction is that (binary) STC outputs a realization of a vector of independent Bernoulli random variables. However, the structure of the code and constraints to the solver clearly invalidate this assumption. Our objective in this research is to characterize this discrepancy with statistical means. In other words, our guiding questions

© Springer International Publishing AG 2017
C. Kraetzer et al. (Eds.): IWDW 2017, LNCS 10431, pp. 331–346, 2017.
DOI: 10.1007/978-3-319-64185-0_25

are: how close does STC come to realize the prescribed change probabilities? If there is measurable discrepancy, does it follow systematic patterns? And how do the code parameters influence the magnitude and pattern of the discrepancy?

We take an experimental approach, drawing on 150 million encodings under controlled conditions. We report observations made on the level of aggregate moments, univariate statistics, and indicators of bivariate dependency. A main finding is that the standard way STCs are presented in academic publications and reference implementations produces violates the embedding constraints at the beginning of the trellis. We propose a modified construction, called OC-STC, which avoids these outliers.

To be clear, theory predicts that some discrepancy is unavoidable. Even if characteristic patterns are statistically identifiable, we are not aware of an immediate path to mount steganalytic attacks even in the presence of outliers. This is because real-world attackers do not enjoy the same amount of control over related encodings as in our simulations. Moreover, standard constructions use a key-dependent pseudo-random permutation to shield the coding layer from the scrutiny of computationally bounded steganalysts. Nevertheless, we deem it worthwhile to explore this relevant building block of steganographic systems, with an eye on potential weaknesses in more exotic constructions, such as public key steganography [2], or as a second line of defense against side channels which reveal the stego key to the attacker [11, 13].

This paper is organized as follows. The next Sect. 2 recalls known theory. Section 3 describes the analytical approach and justifies parameter choices. The results are reported in Sect. 4, further structured in sub-sections per level of analysis, each of which includes a brief discussion. Section 5 proposes and briefly evaluates the construction of OC-STC. General observations and limitations are summarized in the concluding Sect. 6.

2   Background

Without loss of generality, we consider the spatial domain representation of natural gray scale images as communication channel. In this domain, positions are referred to as pixels. Even though images are two-dimensional, we index pixels column-wise by a single integer i.

Steganography by cover modification takes a cover image of length n, denoted as $\boldsymbol{x} = (x_i)_{i=1,\dots,n}$, and modifies it to obtain a stego image $\boldsymbol{y} = (y_i)_{i=1,\dots,n}$. The stego image contains the desired message $\boldsymbol{m} = (m_j)_{j=1,\dots,\alpha n}$, where the embedding rate α is the ratio between message and cover length. For the sake of simplicity, we assume α to be chosen such that α^{-1} is an integer. Further, let cover $\boldsymbol{x}$ be arbitrary but fixed. Slightly overloading notation, we interpret $\boldsymbol{x}$ and $\boldsymbol{y}$ as *integer* vectors when they refer to the cover and stego image, and as *binary* vectors in relation to coding. This implicitly assumes a mapping between images and their (binary) steganographic semantic. Using LSBs to carry steganographic semantic is one popular approach, but more sophisticated (and more secure) embedding operations are possible.

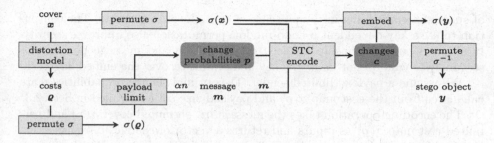

Fig. 1. System model of the embedding process.

The role of coding is to determine the position of embedding changes between the stego and cover image. It is convenient to represented the set of changes by a binary vector $c = (c_i)_{i=1,...,n} \in \{0,1\}^n$, where $c_i = 1 \Leftrightarrow x_i \neq y_i$. An objective of the coding process is to minimize the statistical distinguishability due to the embedding changes between cover and stego images. This is connected to the protection goal of "undetectability" of stego images among cover images. Quantifying this distinguishability would require full knowledge of the distribution of cover objects, which is infeasible [9, Chap. 7], so that heuristic distortion measures are used as an approximation. As a result, coding techniques generally aim at embedding the desired message and, at the same time, minimizing some kind of analytically tractable distortion measure. In our work, we study the case of Syndrome Trellis Coding (STC), a state-of-the-art technique solving the coding task while minimizing a distortion measure that is assumed to be additive over all pixels in an image.

In the rest of this section we formalize the additive distortion measure considered in the context of our system model (Sect. 2.1), present the basic concepts of STC (Sect. 2.2), and recall the calculation of the optimal change probabilities induced by the distortion model and the payload size (Sect. 2.3).

2.1 System Model

The process of embedding message m into cover x is presented in system model Fig. 1. First, the cost map $\varrho = (\varrho_i)_{i=1,...,n}$ is derived from the cover over the additive distortion model. The additive distortion model assigns each pixel with a positive scalar ϱ_i, representing the cost of changing the pixel at position i. This can be done by means of different heuristics, such as WOW [10] and HILL [12]. In the case of basic (single layer) STC [6], the following simplifications are assumed in the computation of distortion:

- Pixel i's contribution to the global distortion is given by $c_i \varrho_i$.
- The global distortion d is the sum of individual distortions: $d = \sum_{i=1}^n c_i \varrho_i$.

Both cover and cost map are permuted under the same permutation σ. The permutation can be thought of as an interleaving method which distributes messages bits over cover positions approximately equally. This increases the chance of successful embedding in the presence of dense local constraints. The convention to use a key-dependent pseudo-random permutation also improves security. It obscures the relationship between cover position and message position for steganalysts who do not know the key and cannot recover the embedding path.

We assume a payload limited sender. The optimal change probabilities p are calculated from the cost map $\sigma(\varrho)$ and payload size αn as detailed in Sect. 2.3.

The encoding operation takes the message m, permuted cover $\sigma(x)$ and permuted cost map $\sigma(\varrho)$ as inputs and returns a vector of changes c, representing the modifications that have to be applied to the permuted cover. Via the embedding operation the permuted cover $\sigma(x)$ is modified according to change vector c, returning the permuted stego object $\sigma(y)$. Before being communicated, the stego object is permuted back to the order of the cover object. To extract the message m, the recipient would permute the stego object and multiply it with the parity-check matrix.

As our main concern is to examine the encoding operation, namely STC, we observe the change vector c, which implicitly assumes knowledge of the embedding path given by permutation σ.

2.2 Syndrome Trellis Coding

We use syndrome coding for encoding. In syndrome coding, message m is derived as a syndrome via the stego object y and parity-check matrix $\mathbb{H}$, $\mathbb{H}y = m$. STC [6] is a special case of syndrome coding where the matrix $\mathbb{H}$ is constructed by concatenating and shifting a submatrix $\hat{\mathbb{H}} \in \{0,1\}^{h \times \alpha^{-1}}$ multiple times, to create a sparse and systematically constructed parity-check matrix $\mathbb{H}$,

$$
\mathbb{H} = \begin{pmatrix}
\hat{\mathbb{H}} & \begin{smallmatrix} 0...0\ 0...0 \\ 0...0 \end{smallmatrix} & & & \\
& \hat{\mathbb{H}} & & 0 & \\
\begin{smallmatrix} 0...0 \\ 0...0\ 0...0 \end{smallmatrix} & \hat{\mathbb{H}} & & \\
& & \ddots & & \\
& & & \hat{\mathbb{H}} & \begin{smallmatrix} 0...0 \quad 0...0 \\ \vdots \\ 0...0 \end{smallmatrix} \\
0 & & & \hat{\mathbb{H}} & \ddots
\end{pmatrix}, \tag{1}
$$

where constant h is called constraint length. This construction allows the use of the Viterbi algorithm [14] to efficiently find a change vector c which minimizes distortion d and implies m as syndrome, i.e., $\mathbb{H}(x \oplus c) = m$ over GF(2).

The algorithm traverses a trellis diagram of size $2^h \times n(\alpha + 1)$. Accordingly, the computational complexity is in $O(n)$ for a constant submatrix $\hat{\mathbb{H}}$ of height h. Regarding the constraint length h, the computational complexity is in $O(e^h)$. Thus, STC is only feasible for small constants h, usually $7 \leq h \leq 13$.

For a fixed cover x of length n and message m of length αn, the relevant parameter influencing the execution of the STC is the code parameter h, and more specifically, the submatrix $\hat{\mathbb{H}}$. Due to its impact on the computational complexity and the probability of finding valid stego objects, $\hat{\mathbb{H}}$ has to be chosen carefully, as described in [6, Sect. 5.2].

The strict minimization of global distortion d leads to different behavior of STC for different cost maps ϱ. For instance, embedding in a cover with only few low-distortion pixels produces embedding changes at these few pixels with a high probability, whereas for a cover with similar distortions for all pixels, such high probabilities are less likely. As we aim to include behavior under different circumstances in our experiments, variance in distortion is of interest.

2.3   Optimal Change Probabilities

As presented in [4, Sect. 2], choosing embedding changes by additive distortion minimization must follow a particular form of Gibbs distribution. This especially assumes independence between embedding changes at different pixels. For our set of assumptions presented in Sect. 2.1, the general results of [4] can be simplified. In accordance with [5, 7], we calculate the independent optimal change probabilities p_i for each pixel i with cost ϱ_i as

$$p_i = \frac{e^{-\lambda \varrho_i}}{1 + e^{-\lambda \varrho_i}}, \tag{2}$$

where λ is a scaling variable that needs to be chosen such that the overall entropy fits the length of the message, $\sum_{i=1...n} H(p_i) = n\alpha$, where (binary) entropy is defined as $H(p_i) = -p_i \log_2(p_i) - (1 - p_i) \log_2(1 - p_i)$. The scaling is based on the assumption that the message has full entropy.

By characterizing optimal embedding in terms of probability theory, let $C = (C_i)_{i=1...n}$ be the random vector of embedding changes, whose sample space is $\{0, 1\}^n$. Thus, C follows a multivariate Bernoulli distribution, which reduces to a product of univariate Bernoulli distributions due to the assumption of mutual independence of the embedding changes p_i. The pmf of C is then given by

$$P_C(c) = \prod_{i=1,...,n} (p_i)^{c_i} (1 - p_i)^{1-c_i} . \tag{3}$$

Optimal coding would produce change vectors that are indistinguishable from this distribution model. A common conjecture is that STC can approximate optimal coding the better the more computational complexity is spent on coding via the choice of the constraint length h [15].

3   Experimental Approach

The goal is to observe STC's behavior in determining the change vector with respect to the optimal embedding change distribution P_C. Supposing to embed N different messages for cover x and constraint length h, this results in N change vector samples $(c^{(1)}, \ldots, c^{(N)})$, i.e., N realizations of the random vector C. As shown in Sect. 2.3, each of these vectors is supposed to follow the distribution specified in (3). We then define the relative frequency distribution $\hat{P}_C^h : \{0, 1\}^n \to [0, 1]$, where $\hat{P}_C^h(c)$ is given by the relative frequencies of occurrence of c in the observed N change vectors.

3.1 Levels of Analysis

In principle, $\hat{P}_C^h(c)$ should be compared with $P_C(c)$. However, there are 2^n different possible realizations c of the random vector C, so that statistical observation of the whole vector would require an infeasible large sample size $N \gg 2^n$. Instead, we study different projections of the sample space with reduced dimensionality, of which we can derive theoretical distributions. In particular, we consider the following levels of analysis:

Count of Embedding Changes. First, we observe the scalar random variable A based on the count of embedding changes $A = \sum_{i=1}^n C_i$. Realizations of A are denoted by a. Under the assumption of optimal coding, A is the sum of independent Bernoulli variables with different parameters p_i, thus it should follow a Poisson binomial distribution. Deviations from this distribution lead to the conclusion that at least one of the underlying assumptions (independence among pixels or observed relative frequency equal to p_i) is violated.

We expect to observe deviations, as embedding changes are not independent due to the structured dependencies implied by parity-check matrix $\mathbb{H}$. Still, it is interesting to look at the influence of constraint length h on this statistic. We expect results closer to the optimum for larger constraint lengths h.

As a follow-up, we look into statistics that allow us to differentiate between the assumptions of empirical results fulfilling the correct individual probabilities and them being independent.

Single-Pixel Embedding Changes. Secondly, we observe the univariate random variables C_i given by the i-th components of C. Realizations of C_i are denoted by c_i. Under optimal coding, they should follow a univariate Bernoulli distribution with probability p_i.

We expect to observe slight deviations and look into the structure and distribution of deviations, as well as the influence of constraint length h.

Pair of Pixels Embedding Changes. Thirdly, we observe the bivariate random variables $C_{i,j} = (C_i, C_j)$ given by pairs of components of C. Realizations of $C_{i,j}$ are denoted by $c_{i,j} = (c_i, c_j)$. Under optimal coding, their components should be independent and we will evaluate such assumption via χ^2-tests for independence.

Computational Performance. Finally, since the statistical properties of STC depend on the choice of h, it is instructive to also evaluate the computational cost associated with this code parameter.

3.2 Selection of Distortion Profiles from Real Cover Images

In principle, STC can take arbitrary change probability vectors p as input. For better validity in the application domain of steganography, we use the probabilities produced by a typical distortion model applied to real cover images. However, to limit the computational effort, we use small patches sized 64×64 pixels.

To reflect the heterogeneity of real covers, we select covers with diverse distortion maps from a standard benchmark database used in steganography research. Therefore, we compare covers by their distortion profile, which is given by a sorted n-tuple of costs sort (ϱ) [8].

We use WOW [10] as distortion model. Since we are not interested in the security against signal-based steganalysis, this choice is not crucial for our results. The same holds for potential singularities at the patch boundaries.

We systematically select a set X of 1000 different 64×64 covers from the $10\,000$ 512×512 images in BOSSBase v1.01 [1] as follows. The $10\,000$ images are cropped at random offsets to form $10\,000$ 64×64 patches. The distortion profile for each of the $10\,000$ 64×64 patches is calculated and scaled linearly to have coinciding maxima. Scaling allows easy comparability and does not harm the profiles' information on STC's behavior, which is invariant to a linear scaling of costs. The first cover is a randomly selected patch. The set of covers is incrementally expanded by the 64×64 patch with the largest product of distances to each element of the set of covers. We define the distance of two distortion profiles as the integral of absolute difference. Figure 2 shows the first and last four 64×64 patches selected as covers by this process.

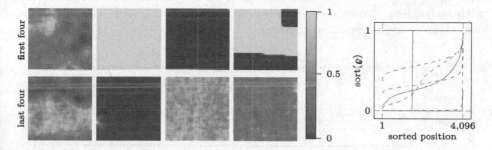

Fig. 2. WOW distortion maps (left) and profiles (right) of the first four (blue lines) and last four (red dashed lines) systematically selected covers. (Color figure online)

3.3 Experimental Setup

To gather empirical data, we use our set of covers X and fix an embedding rate of $\alpha = 0.5$. As the reference implementation of STC [3] supports submatrices for constraint lengths $h \in \{7, \ldots, 13\}$, we use the following submatrices,

$$\hat{\mathbb{H}}_7 = \begin{pmatrix} 1011011 \\ 1110001 \end{pmatrix}^T, \quad \hat{\mathbb{H}}_{10} = \begin{pmatrix} 1010011111 \\ 1100111001 \end{pmatrix}^T, \quad \hat{\mathbb{H}}_{13} = \begin{pmatrix} 1011001000101 \\ 1111101001011 \end{pmatrix}^T, \quad (4)$$

which correspond to the submatrices defined in [3] for $h \in \{7, 10, 13\}$.

For each cover $x \in X$ and $h \in \{7, 10, 13\}$, $N = 50\,000$ random messages are embedded using a fixed permutation σ. This results in a set of change vectors $Z_h = \{c^{(j)}\}_{j=1,\ldots,N}$ per cover. Recall that each c is ordered along the embedding path and thus assumes knowledge of permutation σ. We use a C implementation of the Viterbi algorithm that has been tested to be functionally equivalent to the MATLAB reference implementation in [3]. Our implementation and analysis does not support multi-layered constructions of STC [5,7].

4   Results and Discussion

We report and discuss results by level of analysis (cf. Sect. 3.1).

4.1   Count of Embedding Changes

As explained in Sect. 3.1, the count of embedding changes A under the assumption of optimal coding follows a Poisson binomial distribution [17]. Its probability mass function (pmf) is given by

$$P_A(a) = \sum_{c \in \{0,1\}^n:\ a = \sum_\iota c_\iota} \prod_{i:c_i=1} p_i \prod_{j:c_j=0} (1 - p_j). \tag{5}$$

For a fixed cover x, we choose an asymmetric 95% confidence interval $[a_{min}, a_{max}]$ such that $\sum_{a<a_{max}} P_A(a) \approx 0.975$. Then, we observe the ratio of change vectors with embedding change counts within the confidence interval. The histogram over these ratios is presented in Fig. 3.

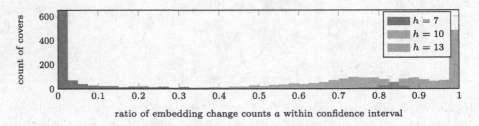

Fig. 3. Histogram of per-cover ratio of embedding change counts within the 95% confidence interval.

Discussion. We see that for larger constraint lengths h, a higher percentage of cases falls into the confidence interval. Specifically, the ratio for $h = 13$ is 92%. This comes sufficiently close to 95%, which is the expected value if the true data generating process was Poisson binomial distributed.

4.2   Single-Pixel Embedding Changes

According to (3), individual pixel changes C_i should follow a Bernoulli distribution with the pmf

$$P_{C_i}(c_i) = (p_i)^{c_i} (1 - p_i)^{1-c_i}. \tag{6}$$

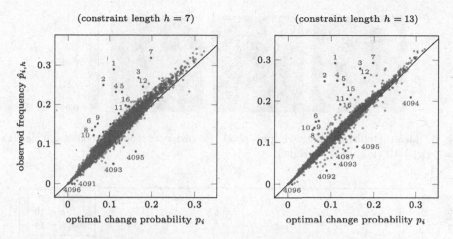

Fig. 4. Exemplary comparison of optimal change probabilities p_i and observed frequencies $\hat{p}_{i,h}$ at $h = 7$ (left) and $h = 13$ (right) for all pixels of a cover, annotated with positions during encoding. Points on the main diagonal refer to pixels with observed frequencies $\hat{p}_{i,h}$ that exactly meet the optimal change probabilities p_i. This example refers to image 5729 of the BOSSBase dataset, cropped with offset $(258, 53)$.

The optimal change probability at any pixel i is given by $P_{C_i}(1) = p_i$. For a fixed cover $\boldsymbol{x}$, let the observed frequency $\hat{p}_{i,h}$ at any pixel i with constraint length h be defined by $\hat{p}_{i,h} = \frac{1}{N} |\{c \in Z_h : c_i = 1\}|$.

The univariate Bernoulli distributions $P_{C_i}(c_i)$ and $\hat{P}^h_{C_i}(c_i)$ are compared based on their success ratios p_i and $\hat{p}_{i,h}$, as they fully define the distributions. For a fixed cover $\boldsymbol{x}$ and constraint length h and all pixels i, an exemplary visual comparison of p_i and $\hat{p}_{i,h}$ is given in Fig. 4. To quantify the divergence between p_i and $\hat{p}_{i,h}$ we calculate the Hellinger distance, $D_{\text{Hellinger}}(p_i,\ \hat{p}_{i,h}) = \sqrt{\sqrt{1-p_i}\sqrt{1-\hat{p}_{i,h}} + \sqrt{p_i}\sqrt{\hat{p}_{i,h}} + 1}$.

In Fig. 4 the pixels with the 20 highest Hellinger distances are annotated with their position during encoding (i.e., in the permuted order). We observe that most of the marked pixels are located at the beginning and the end of the change vector.

To go beyond this cover-specific observation, we look at the mean Hellinger distance per pixel over all covers. As visible in Fig. 5, the concentration at beginning and end can be observed across covers $\boldsymbol{x}$ and constraint lengths h.

Another way of looking at this result is by aggregating the difference $\hat{p}_{i,h} - p_i$ over all pixels of all covers and presenting it in a histogram, as shown in Fig. 6.

Discussion. High Hellinger distances at the borders of the change vector (as shown in Fig. 5) can be explained by the construction of the parity-check matrix $\mathbb{H}$ in (1). Consider the case of $\alpha = 0.5$: the first message bit depends only on the first 2 bits of the permuted stego object $\sigma(\boldsymbol{y})$. This means that only these two bits can be changed to embed the first message bit. Assuming that

Fig. 5. Mean Hellinger distance per pixel, in order of coding, constraint length $h = 7$ (left), 10 (middle), 13 (right).

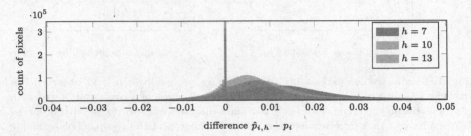

Fig. 6. Histogram of difference between observed frequency and optimal change probabilities $\hat{p}_{i,h} - p_i$ over all pixels of all covers.

(the binary representation of) x_1, x_2 and m_1 are uniformly distributed, the probability of introducing an embedding change at one of these positions is 50% even though the sum of the optimal change probabilities $p_1 + p_2$ can be much lower. A similar border effect happens, albeit to a lesser extent, at other positions $j < h$.

To recall, the calculation of optimal change probabilities p_i is based on the assumption of embedding at the entropy limit. However, STC is only able to embed as close to this limit as it is constrained by the parity-check matrix $\mathbb{H}$, specifically its constraint length h. Thus, a positive deviation of the mean of differences from zero is expected. Smaller h values impose greater restrictions on coding and thus imply higher observed frequencies, as a consequence. These expectations coincide with the findings presented in the example in Fig. 4, as well as the overall positive mean deviation (Fig. 6).

4.3 Pair of Pixels Embedding Changes

According to the distribution of optimal embedding changes P, pairwise pixel changes $C_{i,j}$ follow a bivariate Bernoulli distribution with pmf

$$P_{C_{i,j}}(c_{i,j}) = \left(p_{i,j}^{(00)}\right)^{(1-c_i)(1-c_j)} \left(p_{i,j}^{(01)}\right)^{(1-c_i)c_j} \left(p_{i,j}^{(10)}\right)^{c_i(1-c_j)} \left(p_{i,j}^{(11)}\right)^{c_i c_j}, \quad (7)$$

where the co-occurrence probabilities $p_{i,j}^{(b'b'')}$ describe the probability of the embedding changes at pixels i and j being equal to the binary values b' and

b'', respectively. Due to their pixel changes' mutual independence, (7) can be rewritten as

$$P_{C_{i,j}}(c_{i,j}) = (p_i)^{c_i} (1 - p_i)^{1-c_i} (p_j)^{c_j} (1 - p_j)^{1-c_j} \ , \tag{8}$$

consistently with (3). Similar to (7), from the observed pairwise pixel changes $c_{i,j}$ we can compute the relative co-occurrence frequencies $\hat{p}_{i,j,h}^{(b'b'')}$, determined by the ratio of observed change vectors in which the embedding changes at pixels i and j are equal to b' and b'', respectively. The empirical distribution $\hat{P}_{C_{i,j}}^h$ can then be expressed as a bivariate Bernoulli distribution with the pmf

$$\hat{P}_{C_{i,j}}^h (c_{i,j}) = \left(\hat{p}_{i,j,h}^{(00)}\right)^{(1-c_i)(1-c_j)} \left(\hat{p}_{i,j,h}^{(01)}\right)^{(1-c_i)c_j} \left(\hat{p}_{i,j,h}^{(10)}\right)^{c_i(1-c_j)} \left(\hat{p}_{i,j,h}^{(11)}\right)^{c_ic_j}. \tag{9}$$

We examine dependencies between pixels i and j under frequency distribution $\hat{P}_{C_{i,j}}^h$ by computing p-values of the χ-squared independence test on C_i and C_j.

First, we observe dependencies in relation to the first pixel $i = 1$ by collecting the p-values for all $j \neq i$. This is repeated for all covers and depicted as a mean p-value map in Fig. 7 (first row).

Then, we observe the dependencies between all pixel pairs $i \neq j$ by collecting the mean p-value for each i against all $j \neq i$. This is repeated for all covers, and depicted as a mean p-value map in Fig. 7 (second row).

To get a better understanding of the distribution of p-values, we calculate the ratio of p-values $\leq 5\%$ per cover. A ratio histogram is presented in Fig. 8.

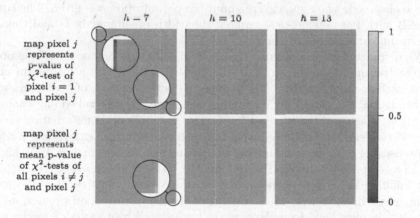

Fig. 7. Mean p-value map of chi-squared tests of first pixel against all other pixels j (first row), and of each pixel j against all other pixels (second row), j column-wise in order of coding, mean over all cover objects, $h = 7$ (left), 10 (middle), 13 (right).

Discussion. The first row of Fig. 7 indicates low p-values of the independence test between the first pixel and its neighbors, while p-values increase for more distant pixels. This can be explained by the construction of parity-check matrix $\mathbb{H}$ in (1), as it induces linear dependencies. The first $h\alpha^{-1}$ pixels are involved in

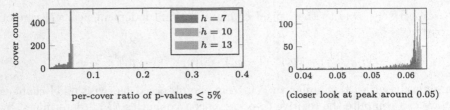

Fig. 8. Histograms of per-cover ratio of p-values $\leq 5\%$ of all ratios (left), and of ratios in the local neighborhood of the peak at around 0.05 (right).

achieving parities according to the first h message bits. These dependencies are a cascading effect, as this relation is true for any pixel. This observation is done in context of a known permutation. In case of a fixed but unknown permutation, examining such dependencies potentially allows reconstruction of the embedding path, yielding the permutation σ.

An opposite border effect in the final part of the vector is observable in both rows of Fig. 7: last pixels tend to be independent from all the other ones. Again, this can be explained as result of the parity-check matrix $\mathbb{H}$ construction in (1). The last α^{-1} stego pixels only contribute to the last message bit. The only connection to other pixels is that the previous $h\alpha^{-1}$ pixels (together with the last message bit) determine whether one of the last α^{-1} pixels has to be changed to meet the correct parity. Thus, embedding changes at these pixels have only small cascading effects on the choices at other pixels. These dependency behaviors can only be observed, when knowledge about the permutation σ is given. The count of pixels with low dependencies equals the width of submatrix $\hat{\mathbb{H}}$ and thereby contains information about the ratio α.

What matters from a security point of view is that in case of an unknown but fixed permutation, an attacker can obtain and evaluate a histogram of p-values, such as the one in Fig. 8. The expected per-cover ratio of pixel pairs with p-values below 5%, would be 5% for independently chosen embedding changes. Instead we observe ratios around 5.6%. This not only adds information to the steganalysis decision, but may reveal information about the embedding path.

Interestingly, in our experiment, the mean ratio in case of $h = 10$ is higher than in case of $h = 13$. In other words, for $h = 10$ there are on average more pixel pairs fulfilling the independence test than for $h = 13$. This can be attributed to the values in submatrix $\hat{\mathbb{H}}$ in context of the set of distortion profiles, as the submatrix implies how dependencies are formed and propagated. Clearly, such analyses should guide the choice of secure submatrices in future work.

The previous discussion focused on the analysis of STC for different constraint lengths h. Besides its impact on the achievable security, the constraint length h has exponential impact on the computational complexity of STC.

4.4   Computational Performance

The empirical measurements in this section confirm the theoretical predictions (within the tested range) and inform the tradeoff between security and performance when choosing h in practice. To give some intuition regarding the computation time, Fig. 9 presents the time per pixel of an STC run given different parameters. For each parameter setting, the values have been averaged over 2000 STC runs. The computations are done on the LEO3E HPC [16], fitted with Intel Xeon E5-2650-v3 processors. The performance is evaluated on a single core at 2.3 GHz CPU clock speed and 8 GB RAM.

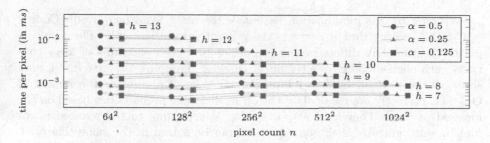

Fig. 9. STC computation time per pixel for different embedding ratios α, cover sizes n, and constraint lengths h.

Running STC, the time per pixel is mostly constant for cover sizes n and, expectedly, exponential in the constraint length h. Furthermore, the time per pixel increases slightly for increasing ratios α. These measurements fit the expected computational scaling due to the trellis size $2^h \times n(\alpha + 1)$.

5   Outlier Correction

Here we propose an improvement to STC which avoids security-critical outliers. We differentiate between outliers above and below the main diagonal in Fig. 4. Outliers above the main diagonal refer to pixels being changed with higher observed frequencies than optimal and are denoted as positive outliers. Outliers below the main diagonal are changed less than optimal and are denoted as negative outliers. Positive outliers are very risky as they might cause instances where steganalysis succeeds with certainty. Negative outliers do not impose an immediate security risk.

Positive outliers are an immediate result of the code construction, as previously discussed in Sect. 4.2. Mitigation attempts that modify the costs of the leading pixels, e.g. by windowing, are futile as this cannot overcome the restrictions imposed by the parity-check matrix. A more viable approach would be to detect risky deviations post-embedding and repeat the embedding with another cover if necessary. However, this meddles with the separation of duties, makes embedding time less predictable, and comes close to the (insecure) practice of steganography by cover selection. We do not recommend this approach.

Alternatively, we suggest to modify the code construction and use a parity-check matrix $\mathbb{H}_{OC}$ by cropping the first $h-1$ rows of $\mathbb{H}$ (1) as follows:

$$
\mathbb{H}_{OC} = \begin{pmatrix}
\ddots & \hat{\mathbb{H}} & {}^{0...0} & & \\
{}^{0...0}_{\ \ 0...0} & {}^{0...0}_{\ 0...0} & \hat{\mathbb{H}} & 0 & \\
{}^{0...0}_{\ 0...0} & {}^{0...0}_{0...0\ 0...0} & \hat{\mathbb{H}} & & \\
& & & \ddots & \\
& 0 & & {}^{0...0} & {}^{0...0} \\
& & & \hat{\mathbb{H}} & {}^{0...0}_{\ 0...0} \\
& & & \hat{\mathbb{H}} & \ddots
\end{pmatrix} . \tag{10}
$$

We refer to this modification as *outlier corrected* Syndrome Trellis Coding (OC-STC), noting that it corrects risky (positive) outliers only. The resulting parity-check matrix differs in one important property: each row of $\mathbb{H}_{OC}$ contains each element of $\hat{\mathbb{H}}$ exactly once. However, cropping the first $h-1$ rows shortens the payload by $h-1$ bits. For the sake of presenting the impact of OC-STC correctly, we recalculate the optimal change probabilities based on the lowered payload. Therefore, a new scaling λ' according to the reduced maximal message entropy is chosen. OC-STC can be solved in the same time with the same Viterbi algorithm as STC. Figure 10 demonstrates (by example) that using parity-check matrix $\mathbb{H}_{OC}$ successfully mitigates positive outliers. A more thorough investigation is left for future research.

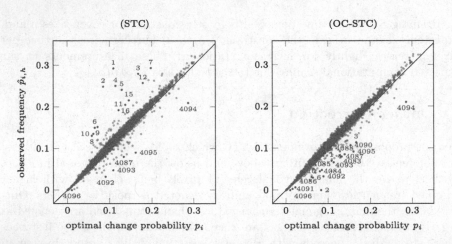

Fig. 10. Exemplary comparison of optimal change probabilities p_i and observed frequencies $\hat{p}_{i,h}$ as in Fig. 4, for default STC (left) and the proposed OC-STC (right).

6   Concluding Remarks

The results of the first (to the best of our knowledge) experimental analysis tailored to explore the statistical properties of Syndrome Trellis Coding (STC) confirms the trust it enjoys from the community: in general, STC does a good job. Even though we chose a difficult steganography setup with small covers and long messages, STC closely approximates the optimal change probabilities, as supported by the relatively small bias (coding loss) and its balanced distribution over the dimensions analyzed. Also the computational cost scales as expected.

However, it is worth noting that STC produces outliers at the boundaries of the cover vector, which seem risky in particular at the leading elements (shielded in many practical systems only by the key-dependent permutation). Using the default parity-check matrix construction, the first positions of the embedding path are prone to be changed significantly more often than optimal or intended. Our proposed modification OC-STC mitigates positive outliers by using a different construction for the parity-check matrix.

OC-STC, as STC, still produces negative outliers, in the sense of pixels being changed less frequently than prescribed by the optimal change probabilities. Negative outliers do not immediately induce a security concern, although it would be desirable to use all available pixels to their full capacity. This is an avenue for future work.

Another relevant insight gained from this work is the possibility to evaluate pairwise dependencies in the change vector. This analysis does not require knowledge of the permutation and is thus possible for attackers as soon as the permutation is fixed for sufficiently many objects. More research is needed to assess the practical security loss by using the dependency structure in the steganalysis decision directly; or by indirectly trying to recover the embedding path from the dependency structure, exploiting knowledge of the locality of pairwise dependencies as a result of message encoding with STC (and OC-STC).

Finally, the discovered non-monotonic relation between h and the ratio of independence-rejected pixels motivates to look deeper into the specifics of how the choice of submatrix $\hat{H}$ influences the measurable formation of dependencies.

In conclusion, this research has highlighted that the effect of coding on steganographic security leaves relevant open questions. It is worth recalling that the results presented here (and suggested for follow-up work) do not immediately invalidate research on steganographic security that follows the common practice of simulating change vectors and thus assumes optimal encoding. Rather, these results should be seen as upper bounds for the security of steganographic systems that replace the simulation with STC for real messages.

Acknowledgements. Alexander Schlögl helped us with implementing STC on the HPC. Pascal Schöttle and the anonymous reviewers of IWDW provided us with very valuable comments. The computational results presented have been achieved using the HPC infrastructure "LEO" of the University of Innsbruck. This research was supported by Archimedes Privatstiftung, Innsbruck, and by Deutsche Forschungsgemeinschaft (DFG) under the grant "Informationstheoretische Schranken digitaler Bildforensik".

References

1. Bas, P., Filler, T., Pevný, T.: "Break our steganographic system": the Ins and Outs of organizing BOSS. In: Filler, T., Pevný, T., Craver, S., Ker, A. (eds.) IH 2011. LNCS, vol. 6958, pp. 59–70. Springer, Heidelberg (2011). doi:10.1007/978-3-642-24178-9_5
2. Carnein, M., Schöttle, P., Böhme, R.: Predictable rain? Steganalysis of public-key steganography using wet paper codes. In: ACM Information Hiding and Multimedia Security Workshop, pp. 97–108, Salzburg, Austria (2014)
3. Filler, T., Fridrich, J., Judas, J.: Syndrome Trellis Coding, Binghamton reference implementation. http://dde.binghamton.edu/download/syndrome/. Accessed June 2017
4. Filler, T., Fridrich, J.: Gibbs construction in steganography. IEEE Trans. Inf. Forensics Secur. 5(4), 705–720 (2010)
5. Filler, T., Fridrich, J.: Minimizing additive distortion functions with non-binary embedding operation in steganography. In: IEEE International Workshop on Information Forensics and Security (WIFS), pp. 1–6, Tenerife, Spain (2010)
6. Filler, T., Judas, J., Fridrich, J.: Minimizing embedding impact in steganography using trellis-coded quantization. In: Proceedings of SPIE-IS&T Electronic Imaging: Security, Forensics, Steganography and Watermarking of Multimedia Contents X, p. 754105, San Jose, CA (2010)
7. Filler, T., Judas, J., Fridrich, J.: Minimizing additive distortion in steganography using syndrome-trellis codes. IEEE Trans. Inf. Forensics Secur. 6(3), 920–935 (2011)
8. Fridrich, J.: Minimizing the embedding impact in steganography. In: ACM Multimedia and Security Workshop, pp. 2–10, Geneva, Switzerland (2006)
9. Fridrich, J.: Steganography in Digital Media: Principles, Algorithms, and Applications. Cambridge University Press, Cambridge (2009)
10. Holub, V., Fridrich, J.: Designing steganographic distortion using directional filters. In: IEEE International Workshop on Information Forensics and Security (WIFS), pp. 234–239, Tenerife, Spain (2012)
11. Ker, A.D.: Locating steganographic payload via WS residuals. In: ACM Multimedia and Security Workshop, pp. 27–32, Oxford, UK (2008)
12. Li, B., Wang, M., Huang, J., Li, X.: A new cost function for spatial image steganography. In: IEEE International Conference on Image Processing (ICIP), pp. 4206–4210, Paris, France (2014)
13. Pevný, T., Ker, A.D.: Steganographic key leakage through payload metadata. In: ACM Information Hiding and Multimedia Security Workshop, pp. 109–114, Salzburg, Austria (2014)
14. Reed, I.S., Chen, X.: Error-Control Coding for Data Networks. Springer, New York (2012)
15. Sedighi, V., Cogranne, R., Fridrich, J.: Content-adaptive steganography by minimizing statistical detectability. IEEE Trans. Inf. Forensics Secur. 11(2), 221–234 (2016)
16. University of Innsbruck: Supercomputer LEO3E. https://www.uibk.ac.at/zid/systeme/hpc-systeme/leo3e/. Accessed June 2017
17. Wang, Y.H.: On the number of successes in independent trials. Statistica Sinica 3(2), 295–312 (1993)

A Blind Reversible Data Hiding Method for High Dynamic Range Images Taking Advantage of Sparse Histogram

Masaaki Fujiyoshi[✉] and Hitoshi Kiya[✉]

Department of Information and Communication Systems,
Tokyo Metropolitan University, 6–6 Asahigaoka, Hino-shi, Tokyo 191–0065, Japan
mfujiyoshi@ieee.org, kiya@tmu.ac.jp

Abstract. This paper proposes a method of reversible data hiding (RDH) for high dynamic range (HDR) images. An RDH method once distorts an image to hide data to the image, and the method takes data out and simultaneously recovers the original image without any distortion from the distorted image carrying hidden data. Whereas conventional RDH methods are for ordinary images whose pixel values are uniformly quantized integers, the proposed method focuses HDR images whose pixel values are non-uniformly quantized floating-point numbers. HDR images have a sparse histogram, i.e., many zero points are scattered over the tonal distribution of images, and the method modifies multiple peak and zero points of the histogram to hide data to an image. In addition, while an RDH method generally needs to memorize a set of image-dependent parameters for hidden data extraction and original image recovery, the proposed method is free from parameter memorization by introducing two mechanisms; restriction of histogram modification and a parameter hiding prior to data hiding. Moreover, keys are required to take hidden data out in the proposed method. Experimental results show the effectiveness of the proposed method.

Keywords: Digital watermarking · Steganography · Annotation

1 Introduction

Data hiding (DH) technology has been diligently studied [1–3] for non security-oriented issues [4,5] such as broadcast monitoring [6] as well as for security-related problems [4,7], in particular, intellectual property rights protection of digital contents [8]. A DH method once distorts a target signal to hide data to the signal where the signal and data are referred to as the *original* signal and the *payload*, respectively. The method takes the payload out from the distorted signal called the *marked* signal. Many of DH methods extract the hidden payload from the marked signal but they leave the marked signal as it is [9]. On the other hand, in military and medical applications, restoration of the original signal as well as extraction of the hidden payload from a marked signal are desired [10],

© Springer International Publishing AG 2017
C. Kraetzer et al. (Eds.): IWDW 2017, LNCS 10431, pp. 347–361, 2017.
DOI: 10.1007/978-3-319-64185-0_26

so *reversible* DH (RDH) methods which perfectly restores the original signal from a marked signal in addition to taking the payload out from the marked signal have been proposed [10–13].

Most of DH methods have been studied and developed for ordinary images; those images represent the limited-ranged radiance of scenes, namely, low dynamic range (LDR) images or standard dynamic range images. On the contrary, high dynamic range (HDR) images which represent radiance of scenes in much wider range are attracted in these days as real HDR image acquisition devices instead of composition of LDR images have been developed, in particular, for vehicle video recorders, astronomy, biology, and so forth [14,15]. To this end, DH for HDR images have been studied. In some irreversible methods [16–20], the hidden payload survives *tone mapping* operation where the operation is applied to a HDR image to generate its corresponding LDR image for displaying the image on non HDR-ready monitors [21]. In methods [22,23], a new concept, *distortion-free*, is introduced but the hidden payload is removed by decoding a marked image. Thus, conventional methods are not RDH methods.

This paper proposes an RDH method for HDR images so that various applications such as annotations for scientific HDR images could be realized. The proposed method hides a payload to an HDR image and completely recovers the original HDR image from the distorted HDR image with hidden payload. To the best of authors' knowledge, this is the first true RDH method for HDR images. Based on the investigation of HDR images, this paper focuses on the fact that many zero points are in the tonal distribution of HDR images. The proposed method hides a payload to an original image using multiple peak and zero points in the histogram of the image. In addition, whereas an RDH method is generally required to memorize a set of image-dependent parameters for hidden payload extraction and original image recovery, the proposed method is *blind*, viz., the method takes the payload out and recovers the original image without memorizing image-dependent parameters. Two mechanisms are introduced to the proposed method for being blind; One is restriction of histogram modification and the other is hiding a parameter before hiding a payload [24,25]. The former makes it possible that peak points are correctly identified even from the modified histogram of a marked image. The latter helps the method to distinguish peak points carrying a payload from those without the payload.

2   Preliminaries

This section briefly compares HDR and LDR images to point out what the proposed method takes into account. It also mentions the histogram modification (HM)-based RDH method for LDR images [12] to clarify the difference between it and the proposed method.

2.1   Comparison of HDR and LDR Images

Either HDR or LDR images, a color image has three color channels; red, green, and blue. A LDR image generally assigns 8 bits for a pixel in a channel where LDR images consist of uniformly quantized pixel values like $[0 .. 2^8 - 1]$, c.f., Sect. 2.2, where $[0 .. 2^8 - 1]$ indicates the interval of all integers between 0 and $2^8 - 1$. On the other hand, for HDR images in general, 16 bits are consumed in a pixel in a channel and non-uniformly quantized floating point numbers are used as pixel values [26,27]. The histogram of HDR images are sparse [28,29]; 65536 of pixel values can exist in an HDR image but a small number of pixel values form the image in practice.

Table 1. Histogram sparsity (%) of each color channel in HDR and LDR images shown in Fig. 1. LDR images are tone mapped from HDR images by photographic tone reproduction [30] where 8 and 16 bits are assigned for a pixel in a color channel.

Image	HDR			Tone mapped LDR					
	16 bits			16 bits			8 bits		
	R	G	B	R	G	B	R	G	B
Impact	94.78	94.77	94.77	23.03	27.76	27.29	4.30	4.69	0.39
AtriumMorning	97.32	97.35	97.43	20.94	10.91	10.69	7.42	7.81	7.42
AtriumNight	97.18	97.23	97.13	20.71	23.93	23.99	0	0	0
Memorial	96.76	97.11	97.76	15.95	18.15	43.01	10.55	6.25	3.52
NapaValley	97.68	98.17	98.25	14.60	28.34	36.58	8.59	17.58	23.05
LabBooth	95.34	94.62	94.64	6.57	5.87	3.55	3.13	0.39	0
LabTypewriter	96.34	94.99	94.48	10.91	7.32	4.87	6.64	1.95	0.78
LabWindow	93.53	94.26	93.40	2.69	4.23	2.54	0.39	1.95	0.39

Table 1 shows the sparsity of histograms of HDR images and those corresponding LDR images shown in Fig. 1 generated by tone mapping operation "photographic tone reproduction [30]." Here, the sparsity for a color channel with B-bit is given as

$$S = 100 \times \left(1 - \frac{N_e}{2^B}\right) [\%], \qquad (1)$$

where S is the sparsity. N_e and 2^B are the number of pixel values in a channel where a pixel value appears in the image at least once and maximum possible number of pixel values, respectively. It is obviously that HDR images have a much sparser histogram than LDR images even both images have the same content.

Table 2 summarizes this section, and Sect. 3 proposes an RDH method for HDR images based on this result.

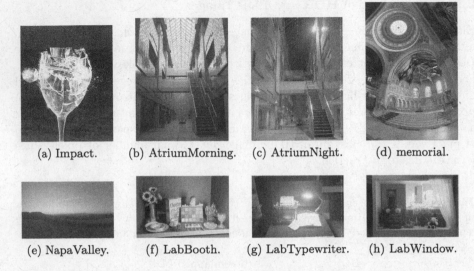

(a) Impact.   (b) AtriumMorning.   (c) AtriumNight.   (d) memorial.

(e) NapaValley.   (f) LabBooth.   (g) LabTypewriter.   (h) LabWindow.

Fig. 1. HDR image examples. Images are tone mapped to 8-bit LDR images by photographic tone reproduction [30] (Color figure online).

Table 2. Comparison of HDR and LDR images.

	HDR	LDR
Quantization bits	16	8
Pixel values	Non-uniformly quantized	Uniformly quantized
Histogram	Sparse	Dense

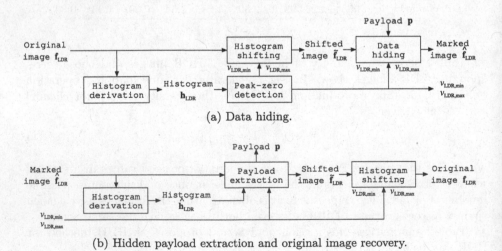

(a) Data hiding.

(b) Hidden payload extraction and original image recovery.

Fig. 2. HM-based RDH method for LDR images [12].

2.2 HM-Based RDH for LDR Images

It is assumed in this section for the simplicity, $X \times Y$-sized B-bit grayscale image $\mathbf{f}_{\mathrm{LDR}} = \{f_{\mathrm{LDR}}(x,y)\}$ is the original image, where $x = 0, 1, \ldots, X-1$, $y = 0, 1, \ldots, Y-1$, and $f_{\mathrm{LDR}}(x,y) \in [0 \,..\, 2^B - 1]$. As shown in Fig. 2(a), this HM-based RDH method for LDR images [12] firstly derives tonal distribution $\mathbf{h}_{\mathrm{LDR}} = \{h(v_{\mathrm{LDR}})\}$ from $\mathbf{f}_{\mathrm{LDR}}$, where $v_{\mathrm{LDR}} = 0, 1, \ldots, 2^B - 1$ and $h(v_{\mathrm{LDR}}) = |\{(x,y) \mid f_{\mathrm{LDR}}(x,y) = v_{\mathrm{LDR}}\}|$. This method then finds two pixel values $v_{\mathrm{LDR,min}} = \arg\min h(v_{\mathrm{LDR}})$ and $v_{\mathrm{LDR,max}} = \arg\max h(v_{\mathrm{LDR}})$, here it assumes for the simplicity that $h(v_{\mathrm{LDR,min}}) = 0$ and $v_{\mathrm{LDR,min}} < v_{\mathrm{LDR,max}}$. The method shifts a part of the histogram of $\mathbf{f}_{\mathrm{LDR}}$ toward $h(v_{\mathrm{LDR,min}})$;

$$\tilde{f}_{\mathrm{LDR}}(x,y) = \begin{cases} f(x,y)_{\mathrm{LDR}} - 1, & v_{\mathrm{LDR,min}} < f_{\mathrm{LDR}}(x,y) < v_{\mathrm{LDR,max}} \\ f(x,y)_{\mathrm{LDR}}, & \text{otherwise} \end{cases}, \quad (2)$$

where $\tilde{\mathbf{f}}_{\mathrm{LDR}} = \left\{\tilde{f}_{\mathrm{LDR}}(x,y)\right\}$ is the histogram shifted image and $\tilde{f}_{\mathrm{LDR}}(x,y) \in [0 \,..\, 2^B - 1]$. In tonal distribution $\tilde{\mathbf{h}}_{\mathrm{LDR}} = \left\{\tilde{h}_{\mathrm{LDR}}(v_{\mathrm{LDR}})\right\}$ of $\tilde{\mathbf{f}}_{\mathrm{LDR}}$, one zero point is followed by the peak point, i.e., $\tilde{h}_{\mathrm{LDR}}(v_{\mathrm{LDR,min}}) = 0$, $\tilde{h}_{\mathrm{LDR}}(v_{\mathrm{LDR,max}}) = \max \tilde{h}_{\mathrm{LDR}}(v)$, and $v_{\mathrm{LDR,min}} + 1 = v_{\mathrm{LDR,max}}$. Finally, marked image $\hat{\mathbf{f}}_{\mathrm{LDR}} = \left\{\hat{f}_{\mathrm{LDR}}(x,y)\right\}$ carrying payload $\mathbf{p} = \{p(l)\}$ is given by modifying the pixel value of a pixel with $v_{\mathrm{LDR,max}}$ in accordance with payload bit $p(l)$;

$$\hat{f}_{\mathrm{LDR}} = \begin{cases} \tilde{f}_{\mathrm{LDR}}(x,y) - 1, & (x,y) = m_l \text{ and } p(l) = 0 \\ \tilde{f}_{\mathrm{LDR}}(x,y), & \text{otherwise} \end{cases}, \quad (3)$$

where $\hat{f}_{\mathrm{LDR}}(x,y) \in [0 \,..\, 2^B - 1]$, $p(l) \in \{0,1\}$, m_l is the l-th element of set $M = \{(x,y) \mid f_{\mathrm{LDR}}(x,y) = v_{\mathrm{LDR,max}}\}$, $l = 0, 1, \ldots, L-1$, and payload size L should

(a) Original image $\mathbf{f}_{\mathrm{LDR}}$.   (b) Shifted image $\tilde{\mathbf{f}}_{\mathrm{LDR}}$.   (c) Marked image $\hat{\mathbf{f}}_{\mathrm{LDR}}$.

(d) Original histogram $\mathbf{h}_{\mathrm{LDR}}$. (e) Shifted histogram $\tilde{\mathbf{h}}_{\mathrm{LDR}}$. (f) Marked histogram $\hat{\mathbf{h}}_{\mathrm{LDR}}$.

Fig. 3. An example of HM-based RDH method for LDR images [12] ($B = 3$, $X = Y = 4$, $\mathbf{p} = \{1,0,1,1,0\}$, and $L = 5$).

be less than or equal to *maximum conveyable payload size* $|M| = h(v_{\text{LDR,max}})$. A tangible example is given as Fig. 3.

It is noted that the maximum distortion per pixel introduced by DH, i.e., by Eq. (3), is always one regardless of pixel values in this method because of uniform pixel values. So, this method uses pixels with $v_{\text{LDR,max}}$ for DH among any arbitrary pixel values to maximize maximum conveyable payload size $|M|$.

As shown in Fig. 2(b), with pixel values $(v_{\text{LDR,max}} - 1)$ and $v_{\text{LDR,max}}$, $\mathbf{p}$ is extracted by tracing pixels with $(v_{\text{LDR,max}} - 1)$ and $v_{\text{LDR,max}}$. Increasing the pixel value of pixels with $(v_{\text{LDR,max}} - 1)$ by one gives $\tilde{\mathbf{f}}_{\text{LDR}}$, and then the inverse shifting is applied to $\tilde{\mathbf{f}}_{\text{LDR}}$ to restore $\mathbf{f}_{\text{LDR}}$. It is noted that this method requires to memorize a pair of pixel values $v_{\text{LDR,max}}$ and $v_{\text{LDR,min}}$ to take out $\mathbf{p}$ and recover $\mathbf{f}_{\text{LDR}}$ from $\hat{\mathbf{f}}_{\text{LDR}}$ whereas descendent methods overcome this disadvantage [31].

Further increase of the maximum conveyable payload size could be achieved by employing multiple peak and zero points for DH, but the number of pixel value pairs to be memorized are also increased. In addition, the number of zero points are so small in LDR images because of the dense histogram, so pixel values and pixel positions corresponding to several smallest points should be memorized, in addition to pixel value pairs, to make zero points by modifying pixel values of several smallest points.

3   Proposed Method

This section proposes an RDH method for HDR images. The method is developed based on the observation results given in the previous section, namely,

(i)   HDR images practically have a sparse histogram and
(ii) HDR images consist of non-uniformly quantized pixel values.

3.1   Strategies

Strategies of the proposed method are described here. The sparse histogram of HDR images has many zero points, so

(A) a payload is hidden to an HDR image based on HM,
(B) no preprocessing is needed to place a zero point next to a peak point in the histogram, and
(C) multiple pairs of peak and zero points are used for DH.

HDR images have non-uniformly quantized floating-point pixel values, and the maximum distortion per pixel by DH for HDR images fluctuates depending on the direction of pixel value modification. Based on several formats for HDR images [26, 27] and the metric for HDR images [32], it is desired that

(D) only decreasing pixel values is used in the proposed method to reduce the distortion by DH.

In addition, strategies below are introduced to the proposed method for being a blind method;

(E) partial pixels belonging to a peak bin are remained as they are to identify original peak points even from the histogram of the marked image and

(F) the number of peak points used for DH is also hidden to the image to distinguish marked peak points and unprocessed peak points.

For strategy E, two sub-strategies are simultaneously satisfied, c.f., Fig. 4;

(E-1) The remained peak must be higher than the next peak, c.f., the upper row of Fig. 4 and

(E-2) the remained peak must be higher than its split, c.f., the lower row of Fig. 4.

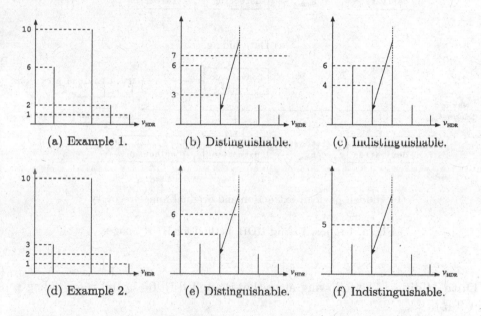

(a) Example 1.   (b) Distinguishable.   (c) Indistinguishable.

(d) Example 2.   (e) Distinguishable.   (f) Indistinguishable.

Fig. 4. Restriction of histogram modification. In both rows, a part of the center bar is moved on its left for data hiding and the other part is remained, where the moved part consists of pixels randomly selected from pixels belonging to the center bar; (b) three of ten pixels are randomly selected and moved, (c) four of ten pixels are randomly selected and moved, (e) four of ten pixels are randomly selected and moved, and (f) five of ten pixels are randomly selected and moved. For the histogram shown in (a), the center bar is identified as the peak even in (b), i.e., only one peak is *distinguishable* from other bars, but the center and the leftmost bars are recognized as peaks in (c), viz., only one peak is *indistinguishable* from other bars. For the histogram shown in (a) of the lower row, the center bar is identified as the peak even in (b) but the center and its split bars are recognized as peaks in (c). So, proposed method modifies the histogram of images as (b) and (c) to guarantee only one peak is distinguishable from other bars even in marked images.

3.2   Algorithm

An implementation example of the above mentioned strategies is given in this section. The block diagram of algorithms are shown in Fig. 5. It is assumed here that L-length binary payload $\mathbf{p} = \{p(l)\}$ is hidden to a B-bit color channel, $\mathbf{f}_{\mathrm{HDR}} = \{f_{\mathrm{HDR}}(x,y)\}$, of a $X \times Y$-sized HDR image for its simplicity, where $p(l) \in \{0,1\}$, $l = 0,1,\ldots,L-1$, $x = 0,1,\ldots,X-1$, and $y = 0,1,\ldots,Y-1$.

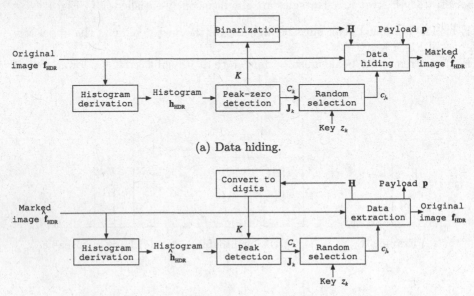

(a) Data hiding.

(b) Hidden payload extraction and original image recovery.

Fig. 5. Proposed blind RDH method for HDR images.

Data Hiding. The following algorithm is applied to $\mathbf{f}_{\mathrm{HDR}}$ and $\mathbf{p}$ for hiding $\mathbf{p}$ to $\mathbf{f}_{\mathrm{HDR}}$.

1. **Histogram derivation and usable peak-zero pairs detection**
   Derive tonal distribution $\mathbf{h}_{\mathrm{HDR}} = \{h(v_{\mathrm{HDR}})\}$ from $\mathbf{f}_{\mathrm{HDR}}$ where $h(v_{\mathrm{HDR}}) = |\{(x,y) \mid f_{\mathrm{HDR}}(x,y) = v_{\mathrm{HDR}}\}|$ and v_{HDR}'s are format-dependent non-uniformly quantized pixel values with floating point numbers [26,27]. To follow strategy C, find peak-zero pairs from $\mathbf{h}_{\mathrm{HDR}}$ where pairs simultaneously satisfy two criteria and let the number of pairs K;
   - A zero point followed by a peak point (from strategies B and D) and
   - the k-th peak is greater than the $(k+1)$-th peak + 1 (from strategy E-1), i.e., $h(v_{\mathrm{HDR},k}) > h(v_{\mathrm{HDR},(k+1)}) + 1$ where $k = 0,1,\ldots,K-1$, $v_{\mathrm{HDR},0} = \arg\max h(v_{\mathrm{HDR}})$, and $h(v_{\mathrm{HDR},k}) > h(v_{\mathrm{HDR},(k+1)})$, $\forall k$.

   It is noted K fluctuates image by image and $0 \leq K \leq 2^B$.

2. **Determination of movable amount of pixels**
   For K peak-zero pairs, the movable amount of pixels is determined as

$$C_k = \min\left(h\left(v_{\mathrm{HDR},k}\right) - h\left(v_{\mathrm{HDR},(k+1)}\right), \left\lfloor \frac{h\left(v_{\mathrm{HDR},k}\right) - 1}{2} \right\rfloor\right) \tag{4}$$

   where C_k is the movable amount of pixels for the k-th peak (from sub-strategies E-1 and E-2). It is noted maximum conveyable payload size C is $\left(\sum_{k=0}^{K-1} C_k\right) - B$ [bits] (from strategy F).

3. **Pixel selection and data hiding**
   For the k-th peak, C_k pixels are randomly selected from $h\left(v_{\mathrm{HDR},k}\right)$ pixels belonging to the k-th peak, based on a pseudo random number generator and k-th key z_k which is fed to the generator. Marked image $\hat{\mathbf{f}}_{\mathrm{HDR}} = \left\{\hat{f}_{\mathrm{HDR}}(x, y)\right\}$ is given by

$$\hat{f}_{\mathrm{HDR}}(x, y) = \begin{cases} f_{\mathrm{HDR}}(x, y) - \alpha_k, & (x, y) = c_{j_k} \text{ and } d(\lambda) = 0 \\ f_{\mathrm{HDR}}(x, y), & \text{otherwise} \end{cases}, \tag{5}$$

   where α_k is the difference between $v_{\mathrm{HDR},k}$ and its smaller one pixel value, c_{j_k} is the j_k-th random selected element of set $\mathbf{J}_k = \{(x, y) \mid f_{\mathrm{HDR}}(x, y) = v_{\mathrm{HDR},k}\}$, $\lambda = j_k + \sum_{n=0}^{k-1} C_n$, $j_k = 0, 1, \ldots, C_k - 1$, $d(\lambda)$ is the λ-th element of $\mathbf{d}$, $\mathbf{d}$ is concatenation of $\mathbf{H}$ and $\mathbf{p}$, and $\mathbf{H}$ is the B-length binary representation of K (from strategy F).

Payload Extraction and Original Image Recovery. The following algorithm is applied to $\hat{\mathbf{h}}_{\mathrm{HDR}}$ for taking out hidden payload $\mathbf{p}$ and recovering original HDR image $\mathbf{f}_{\mathrm{HDR}}$.

1. **Histogram derivation**
   Derive tonal distribution $\hat{\mathbf{h}}_{\mathrm{HDR}} = \left\{\hat{h}\left(v_{\mathrm{HDR}}\right)\right\}$ from $\hat{\mathbf{f}}_{\mathrm{HDR}}$ where $\hat{h}\left(v_{\mathrm{HDR}}\right) = \left|\left\{(x, y) \mid \hat{f}(x, y) = v_{\mathrm{HDR}}\right\}\right|$.

2. **Peaks detection and determination of the movable amount of pixels**
   Set $\chi := 2$ and find χ peaks $\hat{h}\left(v_{\mathrm{HDR},k}\right), \ldots, \hat{h}\left(v_{\mathrm{HDR},(k+\chi-1)}\right)$ from $\hat{\mathbf{h}}_{\mathrm{HDR}}$. Computer C_k by Eq. (4) where

$$h\left(v_{\mathrm{HDR},k}\right) = \hat{h}\left(v_{\mathrm{HDR},k}\right) + \hat{h}\left(v_{\mathrm{HDR},k} - \alpha_k\right) \tag{6}$$

$$h\left(v_{\mathrm{HDR},(k+\chi-1)}\right) = \hat{h}\left(v_{\mathrm{HDR},(k+\chi-1)}\right) + \hat{h}\left(v_{\mathrm{HDR},(k+\chi-1)} - \alpha_{(k+\chi-1)}\right). \tag{7}$$

   Calculate $H_\chi = \sum_{n=0}^{\chi-1} C_n$ and repeat this step with $\chi := \chi + 1$ until $H_\chi \geq B$.

3. **Determination of usable peak-zero pairs**
   Take $\mathbf{H} = \{H(g) \mid H(g) \in \{0, 1\}\}$ out from $\hat{\mathbf{f}}_{\mathrm{HDR}}$ by

$$H(g) = \begin{cases} 0, & \hat{f}_{\mathrm{HDR}}(x, y) = v_{\mathrm{HDR},k} - \alpha_k \text{ and } (x, y) = c_{j_k} \\ 1, & \hat{f}_{\mathrm{HDR}}(x, y) = v_{\mathrm{HDR},k} \text{ and } (x, y) = c_{j_k} \end{cases}, \tag{8}$$

where $g = 0, 1, \ldots, B - 1$ and c_{j_k} is the j_k-th randomly selected element of set $\mathbf{J}_k$ based on the pseudo random number generator with key z_k. Convert B-length binary string $\mathbf{H}$ to decimal integer K. Find K peaks from $\hat{\mathbf{h}}_{\text{HDR}}$.

4. **Hidden payload extraction**
Take $\mathbf{p}$ out from $\hat{\mathbf{f}}_{\text{HDR}}$ as

$$p(l) = \begin{cases} 0, & \hat{f}_{\text{HDR}}(x, y) = v_{\text{HDR},k} - \alpha_k \text{ and } (x, y) = c_{j_k} \\ 1, & \hat{f}_{\text{HDR}}(x, y) = v_{\text{HDR},k} \text{ and } (x, y) = c_{j_k} \end{cases} \quad (9)$$

where $l = j_k + \left(\sum_{n=0}^{k-1} C_n \right) - B$.

5. **Original image recovery**
Original image $\mathbf{f}_{\text{HDR}}$ is recovered by

$$f_{\text{HDR}}(x, y) = \begin{cases} \hat{f}_{\text{HDR}}(x, y), & \hat{f}_{\text{HDR}}(x, y) = v_{\text{HDR},k} \text{ and } (x, y) = c_{j_k} \\ \hat{f}_{\text{HDR}}(x, y), & \text{otherwise} \end{cases} . \quad (10)$$

3.3 Features

This section summarizes the main features of the proposed method, i.e., HDR image-compliant, reversible, and blind.

HDR Image-Compliant. The proposed method is for HDR images where the images are compound of non-uniformly quantized floating-point numbers. Assumptions for LDR images with uniformly quantized integers do not hold for HDR images and new strategies are needed based on the actual observation results. This paper investigated HDR images as described in Sect. 2.1 and it was found that the histogram of HDR images is sparse. Four strategies are developed for reversible data hiding for HDR images as listed in Sect. 3.1 and algorithms are implemented following the strategies as developed in Sect. 3.2. In addition, the proposed method subtracts floating-point number value α_k from the floating-point number pixel value to hide an element of $\mathbf{d}$ in Eq. (5) where the value of α_k depends on the pixel value to be modified. Consequently, the proposed method is suitable for HDR images.

Reversible. The proposed method guarantees to completely recover the original image from marked images, i.e., RDH, whereas near-lossless methods [33], visually lossless methods [34], and so to say best effort RDH methods which do not always recover the original image [35, 36] do not guarantee to recover the original image. The latter three type methods can hide a payload much larger sized than RDH methods to an image in exchange for not guaranteeing to recover the original image. The proposed method chooses the reversibility over the payload size. It is noted that RDH can be applied to images consisting of floating-point number pixel values. B-bit floating-point numbers form a finite subset consisting of 2^B real values. For HM-based RDH methods, telling 2^B values apart is important where HM-based RDH methods tell 2^B integer pixel values apart. Thus, the proposed method is an RDH method.

Blind. The proposed method is a blind RDH method for HDR images. To take out the hidden payload from the given marked image, non-blind RDH methods mainly for LDR images have to identify the marked image among all possible images to retrieve the corresponding parameters. If the marked image is not identified correctly, the parameters are wrongly retrieved, and the hidden payload cannot be taken out or is taken out with errors. In addition, the original HDR image cannot be recovered. Strategy E helps the proposed method to identify peaks as shown in Fig. 4 and Strategy F stops the proposed method needless digging of the hidden payload. Thus, the proposed method is a blind method. It is noted that wrong $\mathbf{H}$ is taken out from a marked image with wrong z_k's, so wrong $\mathbf{p}$ is taken out from the marked image and the original image is not recovered because of wrong $\mathbf{H}$.

4   Experimental Results

HDR images stored with the OpenEXR format [27] including images shown in Fig. 1 are used for evaluation here. The OpenEXR format uses binary16 of IEEE standard 754-2008 [37] which consumes 16-bit for a pixel in a color channel; one sign bit, five exponent bits, and 10 significand precision bits. So, 65536 non-uniformly quantized floating-point values from -65504 to 65504 become pixel values of HDR images.

Here, the proposed method hides a payload consisting of equiprobable binary data to images as much as possible, i.e., it hides a maximum conveyable sized payload to an image. The quality of marked images are evaluated with well-known metrics for HDR images; HDR-VDP-2 [32] and perceptually uniform encoding [38] +MSSSIM [39]. The former could be a positive and negative real value up to 100 and 100 represents the best[1], and the latter could be a real value from zero to one and one represents the best.

Table 3 shows the evaluation results. The proposed method achieves not so much maximum conveyable payload size in exchange of blindness. It was found from the table that HM-based data hiding in the proposed method slightly degrades the image quality by DH and that maximum conveyable payload size C does not depend on image size XY similarly to LDR images.

Figure 6 shows the tone mapped LDR images of memorial where the left is the original and the right is a marked. The tone map operator is the photographic tone reproduction [30]. It was confirmed that it is hard to distinguish them. It was also confirmed that the proposed method perfectly recovers the original HDR image from marked HDR images.

---

[1] The HDR-VDP-2 consists of five metrics; a pixel-by-pixel noticeable probability map, a summarized noticeable probability value, a contrast threshold scaling map, and the maximum threshold scaling factor, and the whole image quality. Values in Table 3 are the last metrics.

Table 3. Performance evaluation. The averaged values over 100 trials with different pattern payload **p**'s and key z_k's are presented for the HDR-VDP-2 [32] and PU encoding [38] +MSSSIM [39], respectively. The hiding rate is given as L/XY [bits/pixel] where L is different for different images but is fixed for an image. The maximum conveyable sized payload is hidden to an image ($L = C$).

Image	Image size	hiding rate [bits/pixel]			HDR-VDP -2 [32]	PU encoding [38] +MSSSIM [39]
		R	G	B		
Impact	554 × 699	0.07	0.05	0.17	93.16	1.00
AtriumMorning	760 × 1016	0.00009	0.00009	0.00011	99.99	1.00
AtriumNight	760 × 1016	0.0007	0.0022	0.0026	99.99	1.00
memorial	512 × 768	0.0008	00017	0.020	99.98	1.00
NapaValley	853 × 520	0.00015	0.00046	0.00018	99.99	1.00
LabBooth	3070 × 2039	0.0004	0.0002	0.0024	99.99	1.00
LabTypewriter	3071 × 2040	0.001	0.0011	0.0005	99.99	1.00
LabWindow	3072 × 2040	0.0079	0.0062	0.0054	95.28	1.00

(a) Original.   (b) Marked (PSNR: 87.32 dB, SSIM: 1.00).

Fig. 6. Tone mapped original and marked LDR images example.

5 Conclusions

This paper has proposed a true RDH for HDR images. Utilizing the character-istics of HDR images, viz., the sparse histogram, the proposed method hides a payload to an HDR image based on histogram modification. Since the method is a blind method, it is not required to memorize a set of image-dependent para-meters. By introducing keys for being blind, the hidden payload is not taken out without keys and the original image cannot be recovered without keys.

Further works include the extension of the proposed method with generalized histogram modification technique [13].

Acknowledgment. This work has been partly supported by JSPS KAKENHI Grant Number JP15K00156.

References

1. Wu, M., Liu, B.: Multimedia Data Hiding. Springer, New York (2003)
2. Cox, I.J., Miller, M.L., Bloom, J.A., Fridrich, J., Kalker, T.: Digital Watermarking and Steganography, 2nd edn. Morgan Kaufmann Publishers, San Francisco (2008)
3. Fridrich, J.: Steganography in Digital Media. Cambridge University Press, Cambridge (2010)
4. Langelaar, G.C., Setyawan, I., Lagendijk, R.L.: Watermarking digital image and video data. IEEE Signal Process. Mag. **17**(5), 20–46 (2000)
5. Barni, M.: What is the future for watermarking? (part II). IEEE Signal Process. Mag. **20**(6), 53–59 (2003)
6. Tachibana, T., Fujiyoshi, M., Kiya, H.: A removable watermarking scheme retain-ing the desired image quality. In: Proceedings of IEEE International Symposium on Intelligent Signal Processing and Communication Systems, pp. 538–542, December 2003
7. Barni, M.: What is the future for watermarking? (part I). IEEE Signal Process. Mag. **20**(5), 55–59 (2003)
8. Kuo, C.-C.J., Kalker, T., Zhou, W. (eds.): Digital rights management. IEEE Signal Process. Mag. **21**(2) 11–117 (2004)
9. Sae-Tang, W., Liu, S., Fujiyoshi, M., Kiya, H.: A copyright-and privacy-protected image trading system using fingerprinting in discrete wavelet domain with JPEG 2000. IEICE Trans. Fundam. **E97-A**(11), 2107–2113 (2014)
10. Caldelli, R., Filippini, F., Becarelli, R.: Reversible watermarking techniques: an overview and a classification. EURASIP J. Inf. Secur., Article ID 134546 (2010)
11. Shi, Y.Q., Li, X., Zhang, X., Wu, H.T., Ma, B.: Reversible data hiding: advances in the past two decades. IEEE Access **4**, 3210–3237 (2016)
12. Ni, Z., Shi, Y.Q., Ansari, N., Su, W.: Reversible data hiding. IEEE Trans. Circ. Syst. Video Technol. **16**(3), 354–362 (2006)
13. Fujiyoshi, M.: Generalized histogram shifting-based blind reversible data hiding with balanced and guarded double side modification. In: Shi, Y.Q., Kim, H.-J., Pérez-González, F. (eds.) IWDW 2013. LNCS, vol. 8389, pp. 488–502. Springer, Heidelberg (2014). doi:10.1007/978-3-662-43886-2_35
14. Reinhard, E., Heidrich, W., Debevec, P., Pattanaik, S., Ward, G., Myszkowski, K.: High Dynamic Range Imaging: Acquisition, Display, and Image-Based Lighting, 2nd edn. Morgan Kaufmann, June 2010

15. Dufaux, F., Le Callet, P., Mantiu, R., Mrak, M. (eds.): High Dynamic Range Video: From Acquisition to Display and Applications. Academic Press, April 2016

16. Guerrini, F., Okuda, M., Adami, N., Leonardi, R.: High dynamic range image watermarking robust against tone-mapping operators. IEEE Trans. Inf. Forensics Secur. 6(2), 283–295 (2011)

17. Wu, J.L.: Robust watermarking framework for high dynamic range images against tone-mapping attacks. In: Gupta, M.D. (ed.) Watermarking, vol. 2, 229–242. InTech, May 2012

18. Autrusseau, F., Goudia, D.: Non linear hybrid watermarking for high dynamic range images. In: Proceedings of IEEE International Conference on Image Processing, September 2013

19. Maiorana, E., Campisi, P.: High-capacity watermarking of high dynamic range images. EURASIP J. Image Video Process., January 2016

20. Lin, Y.T., Wang, C.M., Chen, W.S., Lin, F.P., Lin, W.: A novel data hiding algorithm for high dynamic range images. IEEE Trans. Multimedia 19(1), 163–196 (2017)

21. Murofushi, T., Iwahashi, M., Kiya, H.: An integer tone mapping operation for HDR images expressed in floating point data. In: Proceedings of IEEE International Conference on Acoustics, Speech and Signal Processing, pp. 2479–2483, May 2013

22. Yu, C.M., Wu, K.C., Wang, C.M.: A distortion-free data hiding scheme for high dynamic range images. Displays 32(5), 225–236 (2011)

23. Chang, C.C., Nguyen, T.S., Lin, C.C.: A new distortion-free data embedding scheme for high-dynamic range images. Multimedia Tools Appl. 75(1), 145–163 (2016)

24. Hwang, J.H., Kim, J.W., Choi, J.U.: A reversible watermarking based on histogram shifting. In: Shi, Y.Q., Jeon, B. (eds.) IWDW 2006. LNCS, vol. 4283, pp. 348–361. Springer, Heidelberg (2006). doi:10.1007/11922841_28

25. Kuo, W.-C., Jiang, D.-J., Huang, Y.-C.: Reversible data hiding based on histogram. In: Huang, D.-S., Heutte, L., Loog, M. (eds.) ICIC 2007. LNCS, vol. 4682, pp. 1152–1161. Springer, Heidelberg (2007). doi:10.1007/978-3-540-74205-0_119

26. Ward, G.: Real pixels. In: Arvo, J. (ed.) Graphics Gems II. Graphics Gems, pp. 80–83. Academic Press (1991)

27. Kainz, F., Bogart, R., Hess, D.: The OpenEXR image file format. In: Proceedings of ACM SIGGRAPH, July 2003

28. Iwahashi, M., Kobayashi, H., Kiya, H.: Lossy compression of sparse histogram images. In: Proceedings of IEEE International Conference on Acoustics, Speech and Signal Processing, pp. 1361–1364, March 2012

29. Odaka, T., Sae-Tang, W., Fujiyoshi, M., Kobayashi, H., Iwahashi, M., Kiya, H.: An efficient lossless compression method using histogram packing for HDR images in OpenEXR format. IEICE Trans. Fundam. E97-A(11), 2181–2183 (2014)

30. Reinhard, E., Stark, M., Shirley, P., Ferwerda, J.: Photographic tone reproduction for digital images. ACM Trans. Graph. 21(3), 267–276 (2002)

31. Fujiyoshi, M.: A histogram shifting-based blind reversible data hiding method with a histogram peak estimator. In: Proceedings of IEEE International Symposium on Communications and Information Technologies, pp. 318–323, October 2012

32. Mantiuk, R., Kim, K.J., Rempel, A.G., Heidrich, W.: HDR-VDP-2: a calibrated visual metric for visibility and quality predictions in all luminance conditions. ACM Trans. Graph. 30(4), July 2011

33. Fujiyoshi, M.: A near-lossless data hiding method with an improved quantizer. In: Proceedings of IEEE International Symposium on Circuits and Systems, pp. 2289–2292, June 2014

34. Fujiyoshi, M., Kiya, H.: A visually-lossless data hiding method based on histogram modification. In: Proceedings of IEEE International Symposium on Circuits and Systems, pp. 1692–1695, May 2012
35. Zhang, X.: Reversible data hiding in encrypted image. IEEE Signal Process. Lett. **18**(4), 255–258 (2011)
36. Hong, W., Chen, T.S., Wu, H.Y.: An improved reversible data hiding in encrypted images using side match. IEEE Signal Process. Lett. **19**(4), 199–202 (2012)
37. IEEE Standard for Floating-Point Arithmetic, 754–2008 (2008)
38. Aydın, T.O., Mantiuk, R., Seidel, H.P.: Extending quality metrics to full dynamic range images. In: Proceedings of SPIE Human Vision and Electronic Imaging XIII, San Jose, USA, vol. 6806, 10 January 2008
39. Wang, Z., Simoncelli, E.P., Bovik, A.C.: Multi-scale structural similarity for image quality assessment. In: Proceedings of IEEE Asilomar Conference on Signals, Systems and Computers, November 2003

Other Topics

A Novel Visual Cryptography
Scheme with Different Importance of Shadows

Peng Li[(⊠)] and Zuquan Liu

Department of Mathematics and Physics,
North China Electric Power University, Baoding 071003, Hebei, China
lphit@163.com, 1538940899@qq.com

Abstract. Traditional (k, n) visual cryptography scheme (VCS) encrypts a secret image into n shadows. Any k or more shadows can be printed on transparences and stacked together to reveal the secret image, while any $k-1$ or less shadows cannot get any information about the secret image. Most of the previous VCSs do not distinguish the importance of shadows. In this paper, we propose a novel (t, s, k, n) essential and non-essential visual cryptography scheme (ENVCS) with different importance of participants. According to the concept of constructing VCS from smaller schemes, we construct the basis matrices for (t, s, k, n)-ENVCS by concatenating the basis matrices of these smaller schemes. The constructed (t, s, k, n)-ENVCS is also progressive VCS. Experiments and analyses are conducted to verify the security and efficiency of the proposed method.

Keywords: Visual cryptography · Access structure · Essential participants · Image secret sharing

1 Introduction

Visual cryptography scheme (*VCS*) is a category of secret image sharing (SIS) schemes. In a (k, n)-VCS, where $k \leq n$, a secret image is encrypted into n noise-like shadows (shares) by expanding a secret pixel into m subpixels of each shadow. The value of m is referred to as the pixel expansion. There is no difference between the pixel and the subpixel except that the pixel denotes the secret pixel located in the secret image, and the subpixel is the pixel located in shadows. They have the equal size and the shadow size is expanded m times compared with the size of secret image. The superposition of any k or more shadows can reconstruct the secret image by the human visual system (HVS) without any cryptography knowledge and complex computation, while $k-1$ or less shadows cannot recover the secret image. The first threshold-based VCS encrypting a binary secret image into shadows was proposed by Naor and Shamir [1]. VCS [2] can be applied not only in information hiding [3–5], but also in transmitting passwords, watermarking [6, 7], etc. However, Naor and Shamir's VCS also suffers from the pixel expansion problem [2], and the pixel expansion will increase storage and transmission bandwidth. Because the visual quality of the reconstructed image is degraded by a large pixel expansion, most studies try to reduce the pixel expansion [8–11]. Some schemes even have a non-expandable shadow size,

© Springer International Publishing AG 2017
C. Kraetzer et al. (Eds.): IWDW 2017, LNCS 10431, pp. 365–377, 2017.
DOI: 10.1007/978-3-319-64185-0_27

and they are known as the probabilistic VCS [8–11]. Besides, random grid (RG)-based VCS firstly proposed by Kafri and Keren [12] maybe an alternative method to overcome the drawbacks of traditional VCS [12–14], since RG-based VCS has no pixel expansion and require no codebook design.

All above schemes consider each participant has the same importance in reconstruction. However, there are many examples that some participants are accorded special privileges due to their status or importance, e.g., heads of government, managers of company... and etc. Researchers proposed essential secret image sharing (ESIS) schemes [15–18] to generate shadows including essential and non-essential ones. Since two kinds of shadows meet the requirement of participants with different privileges, the essential secret image sharing problem merits our study. A (t, s, k, n)-ESIS shares the secret image among n shadow images, classified into s essential shadows and n-s non-essential shadows. In the revealing process, it needs at least k shadows, which should include at least t essential shadows.

In 2012, Arumugam et al. [19] proposed a (k, n)-VCS with one essential participant. Afterward, Guo et al. [20] extended Arumugam et al.'s idea and proposed a (k, n)-VCS with t essential participants, say (t, k, n)-VCS for brevity. In the study of ESIS, Li et al. first proposed the concept of (t, s, k, n)-ESIS [15]. Yang et al. [16] then, modified Li et al.'s scheme [15] to reduce total size of shared shadows. In 2016, Chen adopted two SIS with different thresholds to share a secret image among essential and non-essential shadow images [17]. However, Chen's scheme [17] exhibits a threshold fulfillment problem that satisfying only one threshold requirement partially recovers the secret image. In order to solve the threshold fulfillment problem, Chen et al. [18] proposed a two-layered scheme to improve Chen's scheme [17]. Unfortunately, the all above (t, s, k, n)-ESIS schemes are designed based on the Lagrange interpolation polynomial, they have no property of stacking-to-see in the recovery phase and suffer from more complicated computations and known order of shadows for decoding. In 2014, for the first time essential and non-essential VCS (ENVCS) is introduced based on pre-existed (k, n)-VCS [22]. But the scheme in [22] has a serious problem that when collecting $(t + 1)$ essential shadows unsatisfied with the threshold condition, that is $t + 1 < k$, the secret image can still be recovered. In this paper, in order to solve the problem mentioned above, we propose a novel (t, s, k, n) essential and non-essential visual cryptography scheme $((t, s, k, n)$-ENVCS). Our proposed scheme not only satisfies the two threshold requirements but also possess the property of stacking to see the secret image in reconstruction.

This paper is organized as follows. Section 2 briefly introduces some related works. The proposed (t, s, k, n)-ENVCS is introduced in Sect. 3. Experimental results and comparisons are given in Sects. 4 and 5 is conclusion.

2   Related Works

2.1   Visual Cryptography Schemes

Let $P = \{1, 2, ..., n\}$ be a set of elements called participants, and let 2^P denote the set of all subsets of P. let $\Gamma_{Qual} \subseteq 2^P$ and $\Gamma_{Forb} \subseteq 2^P$, where $\Gamma_{Qual} \cap \Gamma_{Forb} = \emptyset$.

We refer to the members of Γ_{Qual} as qualified sets and the members of Γ_{Forb} as forbidden sets. The pair $(\Gamma_{Qual}, \Gamma_{Forb})$ is called the access structure of the scheme. Let Γ_0 be the set of all the minimal qualified sets, and it can be defined as follows.

$$\Gamma_0 = \{Q \in \Gamma_{Qual} | \, Q' \notin \Gamma_{Qual} \text{ for all } Q' \subseteq Q, Q' \neq Q\}.$$

In the case where Γ_{Qual} is monotone increasing, Γ_{Forb} is monotone decreasing, and $\Gamma_{Qual} \cup \Gamma_{Forb} = 2^P$, the access structure is said to be strong, and Γ_0 is the basis. In a strong access structure, $\Gamma_{Qual} = \{Q \subseteq P | \, Q' \subseteq Q \text{ for some } Q' \in \Gamma_0\}$ and we say that Γ_{Qual} is the closure of Γ_0 (denoted by $cl(\Gamma_{Qual})$).

Usually, a binary secret image is shared into n shadows. When sharing each secret pixel, each shadow will receive an m-pixel block. The sharing structure can be described by an $n \times m$ Boolean matrix $S = [s_{ij}]$ where $s_{ij} = 1$ if the jth sub-pixel in the ith shadow is black. Therefore, the grey level of combined share, obtained by stacking the transparencies, is proportional to the Hamming weight of the m-vector $V = OR(r_{i1}, r_{i2}, ..., r_{is})$ where $r_{i1}, r_{i2}, ..., r_{is}$ are the rows of S associated with the transparency we stack. This grey level is interpreted by the visual system of the users as black or as white in according with some rule of contrast. We recall the formal definition of VCS proposed in [21], which is an extension of [1].

Definition 1 [21]. Let $(\Gamma_{Qual}, \Gamma_{Forb})$ be an access structure on a set of n participants. Two collections of $n \times m$ Boolean matrices C_0 and C_1 constitute a visual cryptography scheme $(\Gamma_{Qual}, \Gamma_{Forb}, m)$-VCS if there exist the value $\alpha(m)$ and the set $\{(X, t_X)\}_{X \in \Gamma_{Qual}}$ satisfying:

1. Any (qualified) set $X = \{i_1, i_2, ..., i_p\} \in \Gamma_{Qual}$ can recover the shared image by stacking their transparencies.
   Formally, for any $M \in C_0$, the "OR" V of rows $i_1, i_2, ..., i_p$ satisfies $W_H(V) \leq t_X - \alpha(m) \cdot m$; Whereas, for any $M \in C_1$ it results that $W_H(V) \geq t_X$.
2. Any (forbidden) set $X = \{i_1, i_2, ..., i_p\} \in \Gamma_{Forb}$ has no information on the shared image.

Formally, the two collections of $p \times m$ matrices D_t, with $t \in \{0, 1\}$, obtained by restricting each $n \times m$ matrix in D_t to rows $i_1, i_2, ..., i_p$ are indistinguishable in the sense that they contain the same matrices with the same frequencies.

To share a white (black, resp.) pixel, the dealer randomly chooses one of the matrices in C_0 (C_1, resp.), and distributes the i-th row to the i-th participant. The chosen matrix defines the m sub-pixels in each of the n transparencies. It should be noted that the size of the collection C_0 and C_1 does not need to be the same.

The first property is related to the contrast of the image. It states that when a qualified set of users stack their transparencies they can correctly recover the secret image. The value $\alpha(m)$ is called relative contrast and the value $\alpha(m) \cdot m$ is referred to as the contrast of the revealed image. We want the contrast to be as large as possible and at least one, that is, $\alpha(m) \geq 1/m$. The second property is called security condition. It implies that, even by inspecting all their shares, a forbidden set of participants cannot gain any information in deciding whether the shared pixel was white or black.

2.2   Constructing VCS from Smaller Schemes

In this section we present a construction for visual cryptography schemes using small schemes as building blocks in the construction of larger schemes.

Let $(\Gamma'_{Qual}, \Gamma'_{Forb})$ and $(\Gamma''_{Qual}, \Gamma''_{Forb})$ be two access structures on a set of n participants P. Suppose there exists a $(\Gamma'_{Qual}, \Gamma'_{Forb}, m')$-VCS and a $(\Gamma''_{Qual}, \Gamma''_{Forb}, m'')$-VCS with basis matrices R^0, R^1 and T^0, T^1, respectively. We will show how to construct a VCS for the access structure $(\Gamma_{Qual}, \Gamma_{Forb}) = (\Gamma'_{Qual} \cup \Gamma''_{Qual}, \Gamma'_{Forb} \cap \Gamma''_{Forb})$. From the matrices R^0, R^1, T^0 and T^1 we construct two pairs of matrices, $(\hat{R}^0, \hat{R}^1)$ and $(\hat{T}^0, \hat{T}^1)$ as follows. Let us first show how to construct $\hat{R}^0$. For $i = 1, ..., n$, the i-th row of $\hat{R}^0$ has all zeros as entries if the participant i is not a participant of $(\Gamma'_{Qual}, \Gamma'_{Forb})$; otherwise, it is the row of R^0 corresponding to participant i. The matrices $\hat{R}^1, \hat{T}^0$, and $\hat{T}^1$ are constructed similarly. Finally, the basis matrices S^0 (S^1, resp.) for $(\Gamma_{Qual}, \Gamma_{Forb})$ will be realized by concatenating the matrices $\hat{R}^0$ and $\hat{T}^0$ ($\hat{R}^1$ and $\hat{T}^1$, resp.). That is, $S^0 = \hat{R}^0 \circ \hat{T}^0$ and $S^1 = \hat{R}^1 \circ \hat{T}^1$, where $\circ$ denotes the operator "concatenation" of two matrices.

Theorem 1 [21]. Let $(\Gamma'_{Qual}, \Gamma'_{Forb})$ and $(\Gamma''_{Qual}, \Gamma''_{Forb})$ be two access structures on a set of n participants P. Suppose there exists a $(\Gamma'_{Qual}, \Gamma'_{Forb}, m')$-VCS and a $(\Gamma''_{Qual}, \Gamma''_{Forb}, m'')$-VCS with basis matrices R^0, R^1 and T^0, T^1, respectively. Then the previous construction yields a $(\Gamma'_{Qual} \cup \Gamma''_{Qual}, \Gamma'_{Forb} \cap \Gamma''_{Forb}, m' + m'')$-VCS. If the original access structures are both strong, then so is the resulting access structure.

The next corollary is an immediate consequence of Theorem 1.

Corollary 1 [21]. Let $(\Gamma_{Qual}, \Gamma_{Forb})$ be an access structure. If $\Gamma_{Qual} = \bigcup_{i=1}^{w} \Gamma_{(i,Qual)}$, and $\Gamma_{Forb} = \bigcap_{i=1}^{w} \Gamma_{(i,Forb)}$ for $i = 1, ..., w$, there exists a $(\Gamma_{(i, Qual)}, \Gamma_{(i, Forb)}, m_i)$-VCS constructed using basis matrices, where $m = \sum_{i=1}^{w} m_i$. If the m original access structures are strong, then so is the resulting access structure.

2.3   Guo's (t, k, n)-VCS

In this part, we mainly introduce Guo's construction method of a VCS for the strong access structure specified by the set Γ_0 of all minimal qualified sets, where $\Gamma_0 = \{S: S \subseteq P, \{1, 2, ..., t\} \subseteq S \text{ and } |S| = k\}$. Any VCS for this strong access structure is call a (t, k, n)-VCS. Let $\Gamma = (Q, F)$ be an access structure on a set P of n participants, and let $\Gamma^* = (Q^*, F^*)$ also be an access structure on a set P_t, where $P_t = \{t + 1, t + 2, ..., n\}$, $Q = Q^* \cup \{1, 2, ..., t\}$, and $F = \{2^{P_t} \cup T: T \not\subseteq \{1, 2, ..., t\}\} \cup \{X \cup \{1, 2, ..., t\}: X \in F^*\}$. In such a case, the elements of the set $\{1, 2, ..., t\}$ are specified to be essential, since the absence of any of them will make the secret image be unavailable, no matter how many participants are at the scene.

M^0 and M^1 denote the basis matrices for the optimal (t, t)-VCS [1], Where M^0 is a matrix composed of all possible column vectors with even Hamming weight exactly once, and M^1 is a matrix composed of all possible column vectors with odd Hamming weight exactly once.

Let $\hat{S}^0$ and $\hat{S}^1$ be the basis matrices for a Γ-VCS with pixel expansion m, where $\hat{S}^0$ is the white basis matrix and $\hat{S}^1$ is the black basis matrix.

Let $X = \{1, 2, ..., t\}$, then $M^0[X][i]$ denotes the i-th column vector of $M^0[X]$, where $M^0[X]$ denotes the $|X| \times m$ matrix obtained from M^0 by considering only the rows corresponding to the elements in M^0, and $1 \leq i \leq 2^{t-1}$. Let $mM^0[X][i] =$

$$\underbrace{M^0[X][i] \circ \cdots \circ M^0[X][i]}_{m}$$ denote a matrix by concatenating m copies of column vector

$M^0[X][i]$. We now define two basis matrices S^0 and S^1 for the Γ-VCS as follows:

$$S^0 = \begin{bmatrix} mM^0[X][1] & \cdots & mM^0[X][2^{t-1}] & mM^1[X][1] & \cdots & mM^1[X][2^{t-1}] \\ \hat{S}^0 & \cdots & \hat{S}^0 & \hat{S}^1 & \cdots & \hat{S}^1 \end{bmatrix}$$
$$S^1 = \begin{bmatrix} mM^0[X][1] & \cdots & mM^0[X][2^{t-1}] & mM^1[X][1] & \cdots & mM^1[X][2^{t-1}] \\ \hat{S}^1 & \cdots & \hat{S}^1 & \hat{S}^0 & \cdots & \hat{S}^0 \end{bmatrix}$$

$$(2.1)$$

Remark: Arumugam et al.' scheme [4] can be regarded as a special case of this scheme, when $t = 1$.

3 The Proposed (t, s, k, n)-ENVCS

3.1 (t, s, k, n)-ENVCS

In a (t, s, k, n)-ENVCS, s out of n shadows are essential. A (t, s, k, n)-ENVCS has not only the threshold property (i.e. at least k shadows should be involved in reconstruction) but also the essentiality property (i.e. the k involved shadows include at least t essential shadows). For example, the secret image cannot be recovered by superimposing k shadows including $(t-1)$ essential shadows and $(k-t+1)$ non-essential shadows, due to the essentiality property unsatisfied. Another example of k shadows including t essential shadows and $(k-t)$ non-essential shadows satisfies the conditions of the threshold and the essentiality simultaneously, and it can reconstruct the secret image. We do not consider the case $t = k$ in (t, s, k, n)-ENVCS, since $t = k$ implies that the non-essential shadows have no contributions in reconstruction, and (t, s, k, n)-ENVCS can be reduced to (t, s)-VCS. Obviously, a (t, s, k, n)-ENVCS is reduced to a traditional (k, n)-VCS for $s = n$. A (t, s, k, n)-ENVCS also can be reduced to an (n, n)-VCS for $k = n$. From the definition of threshold secret sharing scheme, k should be an integer lager than 1. Otherwise, $k = 1$ implies each shadow can reveal the secret image. Therefore, we have $t < s < n$, and $t < k < n$, where t, s, k and n are integers. In addition, the number of non-essential shadows in any qualified set should be no more than the whole number of non-essential shadows. Hence we have $k-t \leq n-s$. But when $k-t = n-s$, although the k shadows including all $(k-t)$ non-essential shadows is selected for reconstructing the secret image, it also have t essential shadows, thus in this condition, a (t, s, k, n)-ENVCS can be reduced to a (k, n)-VCS. To sum up, the relationship between four parameters t, s, k and n are shown as follows.

$$\begin{cases} t < k < n \\ t < s < n \\ k + s < n + t \\ t, s, k \text{ and } n \text{ are integers.} \end{cases}$$

The threshold of reconstructing a secret image in (t, s, k, n)-ENVCS is k, which is the same as that of the conventional (k, n)-VCS. Let P be the set of all participants and Q be the set of participants involved in reconstruction, $Q \subseteq P$. And, let EP and NEP be the sets of essential participants and non-participants, respectively, where $P = EP \cup NEP$. Participants in EP and NEP have the different importance of shadows, and the cardinalities of EP and NEP are $|EP| = s$ and $|NEP| = (n-s)$. Let $(Q \backslash NEP)$ denote the set having elements in Q but not in NEP. A qualified subset of participants in (t, s, k, n)-ENVCS should satisfy the threshold condition: $|Q| \geq k$. Meanwhile, the set $(Q \backslash NEP)$, has at least t essential participants due to the essentiality condition. Both conditions allow any k participants including at least t essential participants can recover the secret. The threshold condition and the essentiality condition of (t, s, k, n)-ENVCS are formally defined as follows.

$$\begin{cases} (i) \text{ Threshold condition} : |Q| \geq k, \\ (ii) \text{ Essentiality condition} : |Q \backslash NEP| \geq t. \end{cases}$$

3.2   The Proposed Scheme

In this paper, we mainly design two basis matrices to construct a (t, s, k, n)-ENVCS. In previous schemes [1, 8, 9], the authors design the basis matrices directly. However, in our proposed scheme, we utilize the method that constructing VCSs from smaller schemes to realize the construction of a (t, s, k, n)-ENVCS. We firstly decompose the (t, s, k, n)-ENVCS into some smaller schemes, and then we design the basis matrices for these smaller schemes. Finally, we construct the basis matrices of the (t, s, k, n)-ENVCS by concatenating the basis matrices of these smaller schemes.

Here, we describe the specific implementation process in detail. Without loss of generality, suppose that the first s participants, namely, $1, 2, \ldots, s$ are the essential participants. If X is a set of t participants taken from the s essential participants, thus EP has altogether C_s^t such subsets. Base on the lexicographic ordering we arrange the subsets as follows: $E_1, E_2, \ldots, E_c$ where $c = C_s^t$. For example, if $EP = \{1, 2, 3\}$, $t = 2$ and $s = 3$ then $E_1 = \{1, 2\}$, $E_2 = \{1, 3\}$ and $E_3 = \{2, 3\}$. According to the concept of constructing VCS from smaller schemes, we first decompose the original (t, s, k, n)-ENVCS into c (t, k, n_i)-VCSs on the set P_i with basis matrices $M_{(i, 0)}$ and $M_{(i, 1)}$ constructed using the method in [20], respectively, where $n_i = n + t - M(E_i)$, $P_i = E_i \cup \{P - \{1, 2, \ldots, M(E_i)\}\}$ and $1 \leq i \leq c$. And then we obtain c pairs of matrices $(\hat{M}_{(i,0)}, \hat{M}_{(i,1)})$ as described in Algorithm 2. Finally we construct the two basis matrices M_0 and M_1 for the (t, s, k, n)-ENVCS by concatenating the c pairs of matrices $(\hat{M}_{(,0)}, \hat{M}_{(i,1)})$, that is,

$M_0 = \hat{M}_{(1,0)} \circ \cdots \circ \hat{M}_{(c,0)}$ and $M_1 = \hat{M}_{(1,1)} \circ \cdots \circ \hat{M}_{(c,1)}$, where $\circ$ denotes the operator "concatenation" of c matrices. If there exist the common columns between the two matrices M_0 and M_1, we will delete the common columns until there are no identical columns. The reduced basis matrices still satisfy the conditions of the contrast and the security referred to [24]. Finally, we use the two reduced basis matrices M_0 and M_1 to share the secret image in accordance with the sharing rule of the traditional (k, n)-VCS. The formal decomposition process and construction of basis matrices are shown in Algorithms 1 and 2, respectively. Notations used in our algorithms are defined below.

Notation	Description
P	The set of all participants.
EP	The set of all essential participants.
NEP	The set of all non-essential participants.
C_n^m	The number of all combinations of taking m elements from n different elements.
E_i	A set of t elements taken from s different elements, where $i = 1, 2, ..., c$.
$M(A)$	The maximal value of the elements in the set A.
$|A|$	The number of elements in the set A.
$M[X]$	The vector obtained by applying the Boolean OR operation to the rows of M corresponding to the elements in X, where $X \subseteq P$.
$H(M[X])$	$H(M[X])$ The Hamming weight of the row vector $M[X]$, which is the number of ones in the vector $M[X]$.

Algorithm 1. The decomposition of the (t, s, k, n)-access structure

Input: a (t, s, k, n)-access structure and a parameter c, where $c = C_s^t$.

Output: c access structures $\Gamma_i = (\Gamma_{(i, Qual)}, \Gamma_{(i, Forb)})$, where $1 \leq i \leq c$.

Step1: Distribute the set EP into c subsets E_i, each of them consists of t elements taken from the set EP, where $i = 1, 2, ..., c$;

Step2: Let P_i denotes the set of participants involved in the i-th Γ_i-acess structure, where $P_i = E_i \cup \{P - \{1, 2, ..., M(E_i)\}\}$ and $1 \leq i \leq c$.

Step3: For $i = 1, 2, ..., c$, let $\Gamma_{(i, 0)} = \{Q \subseteq P_i | E_i \subseteq Q$ and $|Q| = k\}$ be the set of all minimal qualified subsets of P_i;

Step4: Generate the c Γ_i-access structures with the basis $\Gamma_{(i, 0)}$, $i = 1, 2, ..., c$;

According to the Step 3 of Algorithm 1, we can see that the threshold of each Γ_i-access structure is k, and only the set E_i is included in all qualified subsets for Γ_i-access structure, where $i = 1, 2, .., c$. And because of $|E_i| = t$, thus, the Γ_i-access structure is actually a (t, k, n_i)-VCS on the participants of set P_i, where $P_i = E_i \cup \{P - \{1, 2, ..., M(E_i)\}\}$, $n_i = |P_i|$ and $1 \leq i \leq c$. Let X be a subset of all participants, and X_i be the set having elements in X but not in $EP \backslash E_i$, that is, $X_i \subseteq P_i$, and Y_i be the complementary set of X_i, where $i = 1, 2, ..., c$. According to the Step 1 of Algorithm 2, if the element $p \in EP \backslash E_i$, the p-th row of $\hat{M}_{(i,0)}$ (resp. $\hat{M}_{(i,1)}$) has all zeros as entries. Therefore we

Algorithm 2. Constructing the basis matrices of the (t, s, k, n)-ENVCS.

Input: c access structures Γ_i with basis matrices $M_{(i,\ 0)}$ and $M_{(i,\ 1)}$, where $i=1,2,...,c$.

Output: The basis matrices M_0 and M_1 of the (t, s, k, n)-ENVCS.

Step1: For any element $p \in P$, the i-th row of $\hat{M}_{(i,\ 0)}$ (resp. $\hat{M}_{(i,\ 1)}$) has all zeros as entries if the participant p is not the element of the set P_i; otherwise, it is the row of $M_{(i,\ 0)}$ (resp. $M_{(i,\ 1)}$) corresponding to participant p;

Step2: Repeat Step1 until all elements of the set P have been selected;

Step3: The basis matrices M_0 (resp. M_1) can be realized by concatenating c matrices $\hat{M}_{(i,\ 0)}$ (resp. $\hat{M}_{(i,\ 1)}$), that is, $M_0 = \hat{M}_{(1,0)} \circ \cdots \circ \hat{M}_{(c,0)}$ and $M_1 = \hat{M}_{(1,1)} \circ \cdots \circ \hat{M}_{(c,1)}$, where $\circ$ denotes the operator "concatenation" of c matrices;

Step4: Deleting the common columns if there exist common columns between M_0 and M_1, else go to Step 5.

Step5: Obtain two basis matrices M_0 and M_1.

have $\hat{M}_{(i,0)}[Y_i] = \mathbf{0}$ ("$\mathbf{0}$" is a zero vector) and $\hat{M}_{(i,0)}[X_i] = M_{(i,0)}[X_i]$, then we have H $(\hat{M}_{(i,0)}[X]) = H(M_{(i,0)}[X_i])$ and $H(\hat{M}_{(i,1)}[X]) = H(M_{(i,1)}[X_i])$ for each Γ_i-access structure, where $1 \leq i \leq c$.

In order to prove that the matrices M_0 and M_1 constructed by Algorithm 2 are the basis matrices of a (t, s, k, n)-ENVCS, we have to prove if and only if the matrices M_0 and M_1 satisfy the contrast condition and the security condition. Suppose that p shadows involved in reconstruction are denoted by $X = \{i_1, i_2, ..., i_p\}$, and that there are t_1 essential shadows and t_2 non-essential shadows, where $p = t_1 + t_2$. Firstly, we prove the contrast condition. When both the threshold condition and the essentiality condition are satisfied, we have $t_1 \geq t$ and $p \geq k$. According to the definition of E_i, there exists at least one integer g satisfying $E_g \subseteq X$, and the set X is a qualified subset for Γ_g-access structure, where $g \in \{1, 2..., c\}$, thus we have $H(\hat{M}_{(g,1)}[X]) > H(\hat{M}_{(g,0)}[X])$. Then we have $H(\hat{M}_{(i,1)}[X]) \geq H(\hat{M}_{(i,0)}[X])$ for other $i \in \{1, 2..., c\}/\{g\}$, because the set X may be the qualified subset for Γ_i-access structure. Therefore we have $H(M_1[X]) > H$ $(M_0[X])$, the contrast condition is satisfied. Next, we will prove the security condition. Case (i): If the threshold condition is unsatisfied, that is $p < k$. We can know that the threshold for each Γ_i-access structures is k from Step 3 of Algorithm 1, so the set X belongs to forbidden subset for Γ_i-access structures, and then $H(\hat{M}_{(i,0)}[X]) = H$ $(\hat{M}_{(i,1)}[X])$, where $i = 1, 2, ..., c$. Thus, according to Step 3 of Algorithm 2, we have H $(M_1[X]) = H(M_0[X])$. Case (ii): if the essentiality condition is unsatisfied, that is $t_1 < t$, then the set X is forbidden subset for each Γ_i-access structures which is a (t, k, n_i)-VCS, where $i = 1, 2, ..., c$. Then we obtain $H(\hat{M}_{(i,0)}[X]) = H(\hat{M}_{(i,1)}[X])$ where $i = 1, 2, ..., c$. Thus, we have $H(M_1[X]) = H(M_0[X])$, the essentiality condition is satisfied.

To Further Illustrate the Proposed Scheme, We Give the Following Example of $(1, 2, 2, 4)$-ENVCS.

Example 1. For a $(1, 2, 2, 4)$-ENVCS, the secret image is shared into 4 shadows, including 2 essential shadows and 2 non-essential shadows. Let $\Gamma_0 = \{\{1,2\},\{1,3\},$

$\{1,4\},\{2,3\},\{2,4\}\}$ be the set of all minimal qualified subsets. According to Algorithm 1, we can construct a visual cryptography scheme for the strong access structure (Γ_{Qual}, Γ_{Forb}) having basis Γ_0 by using VCS for the strong access structures with bases $\Gamma_{(1,0)} = \{\{1,2\},\{1,3\},\{1,4\}\}$ and $\Gamma_{(2,0)} = \{\{2,3\},\{2,4\}\}$, respectively. According to Lemma 1, the two pair of basis matrices are constructed using the method proposed in Guo's scheme [20].

$$M_{(1,0)} = \begin{bmatrix} 10 \\ 01 \\ 01 \\ 01 \end{bmatrix}, M_{(1,1)} = \begin{bmatrix} 10 \\ 10 \\ 10 \\ 10 \end{bmatrix} \text{ and } M_{(2,0)} = \begin{bmatrix} 10 \\ 01 \\ 01 \end{bmatrix}, M_{(2,1)} = \begin{bmatrix} 10 \\ 10 \\ 10 \end{bmatrix}.$$

From Algorithm 2 and the above matrices we obtain the matrices $\hat{M}_{(1,0)}$, $\hat{M}_{(1,1)}$, $\hat{M}_{(2,0)}$ and $\hat{M}_{(2,1)}$.

$$\hat{M}_{(1,0)} = \begin{bmatrix} 10 \\ 01 \\ 01 \\ 01 \end{bmatrix}, \hat{M}_{(1,1)} = \begin{bmatrix} 10 \\ 10 \\ 10 \\ 10 \end{bmatrix} \text{ and } \hat{M}_{(2,0)} = \begin{bmatrix} 00 \\ 10 \\ 01 \\ 01 \end{bmatrix}, \hat{M}_{(2,1)} = \begin{bmatrix} 00 \\ 10 \\ 10 \\ 10 \end{bmatrix}.$$

Concatenating the matrix $\hat{M}_{(1,0)}$ with $\hat{M}_{(2,0)}$ and the matrix $\hat{M}_{(1,1)}$ with $\hat{M}_{(2,1)}$, we obtain the following basis matrices M_0 and M_1 for a visual cryptography scheme for the strong access structure with basis Γ_0:

$$M_0 = \begin{bmatrix} 1000 \\ 0110 \\ 0101 \\ 0101 \end{bmatrix} M_1 = \begin{bmatrix} 1000 \\ 1010 \\ 1010 \\ 1010 \end{bmatrix}.$$

Then, we can see that there exists one common column between M_0 and M_1. Thus, the final basis matrices M_0 and M_1 can be achieved by deleting the common column. The result is shown below:

$$M_0 = \begin{bmatrix} 100 \\ 010 \\ 001 \\ 001 \end{bmatrix} M_1 = \begin{bmatrix} 100 \\ 100 \\ 100 \\ 100 \end{bmatrix}.$$

4 Experiments and Discussions

In this section, we conduct two experiments to test the effectiveness of the proposed (t, s, k, n)-ENVCS. In our experiments, two binary secret images with the size of 200×100 are used as shown in Fig. 1(a) and Fig. 2(a), respectively. In addition, we make the comparisons between the proposed scheme and the relative schemes.

4.1 Experimental Results

In our experiments, (2, 3, 3, 5)-ENVCS is conducted with the secret image 1 as shown in Fig. 1(a). Figure 1(b) shows the three essential shadows S_1, S_2 and S_3, which are randomly noise-like. Figure 1(c) shows the two non-essential random noise-like shadows S_4 and S_5. When superimposing two essentials (see Fig. 1(d–1)), we cannot obtain any information from the result because the threshold condition cannot be satisfied. As shown in Fig. 1(d–2), although the threshold condition is satisfied, we also have no information about the secret image due to the essentiality condition unsatisfied. However, when both the threshold condition and the essentiality condition are satisfied, the secret image can be reconstructed as shown in Fig. 1(e). The visual quality of recovered secret image by $k = 4$ shadows is better than that by $k = 3$ shadows.

From the results shown in above experiments, we have:

(1) The shadows are randomly noise-like, hence the proposed (t, s, k, n)-ENVCS has no cross interference of secret image in the shadows.
(2) The progressive visual quality of the recovered secret can be gained by the proposed (t, s, k, n)-ENVCS.
(3) When the threshold condition or the essentiality condition unsatisfied, no information of the secret image could be recognized, which shows the security of the proposed (t, s, k, n)-ENVCS.

4.2 Comparisons

In this subsection, we mainly discuss the properties of relative contrast and pixel expansion among the proposed scheme and some related scheme especially [19–22]. When $t = s$ and $s < k$, the proposed scheme is reduced to the (t, k, n)-VCS [20]. And it can further be reduced to the beginning scheme [19] for $s = 1$. Due to some existed problem in [22], thus we should only compare the proposed (t, s, k, n)-ENVCS with the related method introduced in [21]. Since the (t, s, k, n)-ENVCS is a strong access structure, which is also a special case of general access structure. As shown in Table 1, the pixel expansion of both the method in [21] and the proposed scheme is identical. With the number of the stacking shadows increasing, the relative contrast of the proposed scheme will become larger, but the relative contrast in [21] maintains an unchangeable value as described in Table 1. In a word, the proposed scheme is also a progressive scheme.

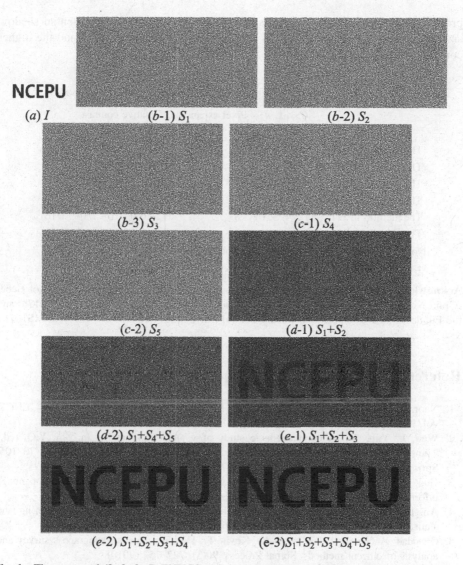

Fig. 1. The proposed (2, 3, 3, 5)-ENVCS: (a) the secret image of 200 × 100 pixels (b) three essential shadows of 600 × 300 pixels (c) two non-essential shadows of 600 × 300 pixels (d-1) superimposition of shares S_1, S_2 (d-2) superimposition of shares S_1, S_4, S_5 (e-1) superimposition of shares S_1, S_2, S_3 (e-2) superimposition of shares S_1, S_2, S_3, S_4 (e-3) superimposition of all shares.

5 Conclusion

In this paper, we propose a (t, s, k, n)-ENVCS, where essential shadows are more important than non-essential shadows. A qualified subset of shadows Q should satisfy the threshold condition ($|Q| \geq k$) and the essentiality condition ($|Q\backslash EP| \geq t$). In our proposed scheme, the non-essential shadow size is the same as the essential shadow size. Designing a (t, s, k, n)-ENVCS with the smaller pixel expansion and the higher contrast requires further study.

Table 1. Comparison of properties between the method in [21] and the proposed scheme.

	(t, s, k, n)	Pixel expansion	Relative contrast*			
		m	$l = 3$	$l = 4$	$l = 5$	$l = 6$
The method in [21]	(1, 2, 3, 5)	13	1/13	1/13	1/13	
The proposed scheme		13	1/13	3/13	5/13	
The method in [21]	(2, 3, 3, 5)	9	1/9	1/9	1/9	
The proposed scheme		9	1/9	3/9	3/9	
The method in [21]	(2, 4, 3, 6)	16	1/16	1/16	1/16	1/16
The proposed scheme		16	1/16	3/16	6/16	6/16

Note. * denotes the maximal relative contrast.

Acknowledgments. This work was partially supported by the Natural Science Funds of Hebei (Grant No. F2015502014), National Natural Science Foundation of China (No. 61602173) and the Fundamental Research Funds for the Central Universities (No. 16MS131, No. 13MS107).

References

1. Naor, M., Shamir, A.: Visual cryptography. In: Santis, A. (ed.) EUROCRYPT 1994. LNCS, vol. 950, pp. 1–12. Springer, Heidelberg (1995). doi:10.1007/BFb0053419
2. Weir, J., Yan, W.: A comprehensive study of visual cryptography. In: Shi, Y.Q. (ed.) Transactions on Data Hiding and Multimedia Security V. LNCS, vol. 6010, pp. 70–105. Springer, Heidelberg (2010). doi:10.1007/978-3-642-14298-7_5
3. Gao, X., Deng, C., Li, X., Tao, D.: Local feature based geometric-resistant image information hiding. Cogn. Comput. 2(2), 68–77 (2010)
4. An, L., Gao, X., Yuan, Y., Tao, D.: Robust lossless data hiding using clustering and statistical quantity histogram. Neurocomputing 77(1), 1–11 (2012)
5. Cheddad, A., Condell, J., Curran, K., Kevitt, P.: Digital image steganography: survey and analysis of current methods. Signal Process. 90(3), 727–752 (2010)
6. An, L., Gao, X., Li, X., Tao, D., Deng, C., Li, J.: Robust reversible watermarking via clustering and enhanced pixel-wise masking. IEEE Trans. Image Process. 21(8), 3598–3611 (2012)
7. Deng, C., Gao, X., Li, X., Tao, D.: Local histogram based geometric invariant image watermarking. Signal Process. 90(12), 3256–3264 (2010)
8. Kuwakado, H., Tanaka, H.: Size-reduced visual secret sharing scheme. IEICE Trans. Fundam. Electron. E87-A(5), 1193–1197 (2004)
9. Yang, C.N., Chen, T.S.: New size-reduced visual secret sharing schemes with half reduction of shadow size. IEICE Trans. Fundam. Electron. E89-A(2), 620–625 (2006)
10. Yang, C.N.: New visual secret sharing schemes using probabilistic method. Pattern Recogn. Lett. 25(4), 481–494 (2004)

11. Cimato, S., Prisco, R., Santis, A.: Probabilistic visual cryptography schemes. Comput. J. **49** (1), 97–107 (2006)
12. Kafri, O., Keren, E.: Encryption of pictures and shapes by random grids. Opt. Lett. **12**(6), 377–379 (1987)
13. Chen, T.H., Tsao, K.H.: Visual secret sharing by random grids revisited. Pattern Recogn. **42** (9), 2203–2217 (2009)
14. Chen, T.H., Tsao, K.H.: Threshold visual secret sharing by random grids. J. Syst. Softw. **84** (7), 1197–1208 (2011)
15. Li, P., Yang, C.N., Wu, C.C., Kong, Q., Ma, Y.: Essential secret image sharing scheme with different importance of shadows. J. Vis. Commun. Image R **24**(7), 1106–1114 (2013)
16. Yang, C.N., Li, P., Wu, C.C., Cai, S.R.: Reducing shadow size in essential secret image sharing by conjunctive hierarchical approach. Signal Process. Image Commun. **31**(1), 1–9 (2015)
17. Chen, S.K.: Essential secret image sharing with increasable shadows. Opt. Eng. **55**, 013103 (2016)
18. Chen, C.C., Chen, S.C.: Two-layered structure for optimally essential secret image sharing scheme. J. Vis. Commun. Image Represent. **38**, 595–601 (2016)
19. Arumugam, S., Lakshmanan, R., Nagar, A.K.: On (k, n)*-Visual Cryptography Scheme. Des. Codes Crypt. **71**(1), 153–162 (2014)
20. Guo, T., Liu, F., Wu, C., Ren, Y., Wang, W.: On (k, n) visual cryptography scheme with t essential parties. In: Padró, C. (ed.) ICITS 2013. LNCS, vol. 8317, pp. 56–68. Springer, Cham (2014). doi:10.1007/978-3-319-04268-8_4
21. Ateniese, G., Blundo, C., Santis, A., Stinson, D.R.: Visual cryptography for general access structures. Inf. Comput. **129**(2), 86–106 (1996)
22. Yan, X., Wang, S., Niu, X., Yang, C.-N.: Essential visual cryptographic scheme with different importance of shares. In: Loo, C.K., Yap, K.S., Wong, K.W., Beng Jin, A.T., Huang, K. (eds.) ICONIP 2014, Part III. LNCS, vol. 8836, pp. 636–643. Springer, Cham (2014). doi:10.1007/978-3-319-12643-2_77
23. Blundo, C., De Santis, A., Stinson, D.R.: On the contrast in visual cryptography schemes. J. Crypt. **12**(4), 261–289 (1999)

A Novel Image Classification Method with CNN-XGBoost Model

Xudie Ren, Haonan Guo, Shenghong Li$^{(\boxtimes)}$, Shilin Wang,
and Jianhua Li

School of Cyber Space Security, Shanghai Jiao Tong University,
800 Dong Chuan Road, Shanghai 200240, China
{renxudie,haonan2012,shli,wsl,lijh888}@sjtu.edu.cn

Abstract. Image classification problem is one of most important research directions in image processing and has become the focus of research in many years due to its diversity and complexity of image information. In view of the existing image classification models' failure to fully utilize the information of images, this paper proposes a novel image classification method of combining the Convolutional Neural Network (CNN) and eXtreme Gradient Boosting (XGBoost), which are two outstanding classifiers. The presented CNN-XGBoost model provides more precise output by integrating CNN as a trainable feature extractor to automatically obtain features from input and XGBoost as a recognizer in the top level of the network to produce results. Experiments are implemented on the well-known MNIST and CIFAR-10 databases. The results prove that the new method performs better compared with other methods on the same databases, which verify the effectiveness of the proposed method in image classification problem.

Keywords: Convolutional Neural Network · eXtreme Gradient Boosting · Image classification

1 Introduction

Image classification problem is one of the key research objectives in the field of image processing, and has a wide range of applications in object recognition, content understanding as well as image matching and so on. Over the years, although there have been substantial research results, classification problem is still the focus of researches due to the complexity and diversity of image information. This task worth researching for it can be wildly applied in the fields of pattern recognition and computer vision. Image classification methods vary from numerous aspects including Support Vector Machine (SVM), Nearest Neighbor (NN), Gradient Boosting (GB), Convolutional Neural Network (CNN), etc. These machine learning and data-driven algorithms are able to efficiently classify images and have indicated their reliability and validity. Nevertheless, most of the existing methods on the application of image classification do not sufficiently utilize image information as well as establish robust features for recognizing, thus leaving the space for improve the recognition rate through providing reliable high-level features.

© Springer International Publishing AG 2017
C. Kraetzer et al. (Eds.): IWDW 2017, LNCS 10431, pp. 378–390, 2017.
DOI: 10.1007/978-3-319-64185-0_28

In the aspect of intelligent image classification methods, the model based on neural network is one of the important research directions. Deep neural networks can theoretically approximate any complex function and effectively solve the problems of image feature extraction and classification. However, due to the model complexity, training difficulty and high cost, this kind of structure can hardly obtain very effective application. Recently, the latest research on neural network- Deep Learning techniques have obtained continuous breakthroughs and developments in many fields, including image classification [1, 2], object detection [3, 4] and face recognition [5–7], etc. Deep architectures have been successfully applied to large-scale image processing system and achieved the state of the art performance, which showing an optimistic prospect to solve the classification task.

Feature extraction is the most important process in an automatic image classification system. The feature quality can directly influence the recognition performance which leads to a time-consuming feature engineering in traditional image classification task. CNN is an efficient Deep Learning model with hierarchical structure to learn high quality features at each layer. Since the model can reduce the complexity of network structure and the number of parameters through local receptive fields, weight sharing and pooling operation, it has been widely used in image classification problem and achieved excellent results. It also can directly input raw images in automatic classification system, which contributes to save more image information for the following feature extraction.

On the other hand, classification is another significant process in an automatic image classification system. CNN has been recognized as the most powerful and effective mechanism for feature extraction, but traditional classifiers connected to CNN do not fully understand the extracted features. Therefore showing a promising direction for proposing new solution to the image classification problem. eXtreme Gradient Boosting (XGBoost) [9] is an integrated learning algorithm based on GB, the principle of which is to achieve accurate classification results through iterative computation of weak classifiers. XGBoost is widely applied in many domains [7, 8, 10] because of its high efficiency and accuracy.

Motivated by the above facts, this paper explores the incorporation of CNN model and XGBoost algorithm since both CNN and XGBoost have already perform excellently in image classification problem. A novel image classification method with CNN-XGBoost model is proposed to improve the performance of image classification problem. The proposed CNN-XGBoost model provides more precise output by integrating CNN as a trainable feature extractor to automatically obtain features from input and XGBoost as a recognizer in the top level of the network to produce results. Such unique two-stage model guarantees the high reliability feature extraction and classification.

The rest of the paper is organized as follows: Sect. 2 introduces the basic concepts of CNN and XGBoost respectively. Then the CNN-XGBoost model is also described in this section. Experimental results on the well-known MNIST and CIFAR-10 databases are presented and discussed in Sect. 3. Finally, Sect. 4 concludes the paper.

2   The Novel CNN-XGBoost Model

In this paper, we propose a novel image classification method with CNN-XGBoost model to improve the classification performance. By integrating CNN as a trainable feature extractor to automatically obtain features from input and XGBoost as a recognizer in the top level of the network to produce results, our method can guarantee the high reliability feature extraction and classification. In the following section, we will briefly describe the two brilliant classifiers respectively and introduce the novel CNN-XGBoost model at last.

2.1   Convolutional Neural Network

Convolutional neural network (CNN) was first proposed by Professor Yann LeCun and his colleagues at the University of Toronto in Canada and used for recognition and classification of handwriting digital images [11]. CNN takes advantage of the concepts of receptive fields, weight sharing and sub-sampling (pooling) to reduce the complexity of the network structure and the number of parameters. "Receptive field" is equivalent to constructing a number of spatially localized filters which can obtain some salient features of the input. While "weight sharing" can reduce the number of parameters which needs to be trained. "Pooling" can simplify the model and prevent it from over-fitting.

A typical CNN is consisted of alternating convolution and sub-sampling layers, then turns into fully connected layers when approaching to the last output layer. It usually adjusts all the filter kernels (convolution kernels) by back-propagation algorithm [12], which is based on stochastic gradient descent algorithm, to reduce the gap between the network output and the training labels. Overall, the convolution layer (C layer) obtains the local features by connected with local receptive fields. The sub-sampling layer (S layer) is a mapping feature layer which is used for pooling operation and completing the secondary extraction calculations. Each C layer is followed by an S layer, and the special twice feature extraction structure makes convolutional neural network have strong distortion tolerance on the input images.

LeNet-5 [11] is a classic convolutional neural network architecture for handwritten digit recognition proposed by Yann LeCun et al. The structure consists of 8 layers: an input layer, two C layers, two S layers and three fully connected layers and an output layer. In order to reduce the computational complexity, the specific structure of CNN for image classification in this paper is a simplified version of LeNet-5, which includes an input layer (Input), two C layers (C1, C2), two S layers (S1, S2), fully connected layers and an output layer (Output). Figure 1 demonstrates the specific structure of CNN for image classification. Since a convolution kernel of the convolution layer can only extract one characteristic of input feature maps, it requires multiple convolution kernels to extract different features.

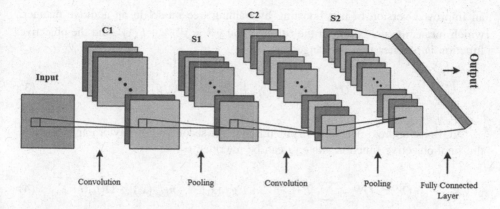

Fig. 1. The Specific structure of CNN for image classification

2.2 eXtreme Gradient Boosting

XGBoost has been widely used in many fields to achieve state-of-the-art results on many data challenges, which is a high effective scalable machine learning system for tree boosting. Developed by Tianqi Chen et al. the scalability in all scenarios of XGBoost is due to several important systems and algorithmic optimizations, which includes a novel tree learning algorithm, a theoretically justified weighted quantile sketch procedure as well as parallel and distributed computing [13].

Tree boosting is a very effective ensemble learning algorithm, which can transform several weak classifiers into a strong classifier for better classification performance. Let $D = \{(x_i, y_i)\}(|D| = n, x_l \in \mathbb{R}^m, y_l \subset \mathbb{R}^n)$ represents a database with n examples and m features. A tree boosting model output $\hat{y}_i$ with K trees is defined as follows:

$$\hat{y}_i = \sum_{k=1}^{K} f_k(x_i), f_k \in F \tag{1}$$

where $F = \{f(x) = \omega_q(x)\}(q : \mathbb{R}^m \to T, \omega \in \mathbb{R}^T)$ is the space of regression or classification trees (also known as CART). Each f_k divides a tree into structure part q and leaf weights part ω. Here T denotes the number of leaves in the tree.

The set of function f_k in the tree model can be learned by minimizing the following objective function:

$$O = \sum_{i} l(\hat{y}_i, y_i) + \sum_{k} \Omega(f_k) \tag{2}$$

The first term l in Eq. (2) is a training loss function which measures the distance between the prediction $\hat{y}_i$ and the object y_i. The second term Ω in Eq. (2) represents the penalty term of the tree model complexity.

Tree boosting model whose objective function is Eq. (2) cannot be optimized through traditional optimization methods in Euclidean space. Gradient Tree Boosting is an improved version of tree boosting by training tree model in an additive manner, which means the prediction of the t-th iteration $\hat{y}^{(t)} = \hat{y}^{(t-1)} + f_t(x)$. And the objective function in t-th iteration is changed as:

$$O^{(t)} = \sum_{i=1}^{n} l(y_i, \hat{y}_i^{(t-1)} + f_t(x_i)) + \Omega(f_t) \tag{3}$$

XGBoost approximates Eq. (3) by utilizing the second order Taylor expansion and the final objective function at step t can be rewritten as:

$$O^{(t)} \simeq \tilde{O}^{(t)} = \sum_{i=1}^{n} [l(y_i, \hat{y}_i^{(t-1)}) + g_i f_t(x_i) + \frac{1}{2} h_i f_t^2(x_i)] + \Omega(f_t) \tag{4}$$

where g_i and h_i are first and second order gradient statistics on the loss function, and $\Omega(f) = \gamma T + \frac{1}{2}\lambda\|\omega\|^2$ in XGBoost.

Denote $I_j = \{i|q(x_i) = j\}$ as the instance set of leaf j, after removing the constant terms and expanding Ω, Eq. (4) can be simplified as:

$$\tilde{O}^{(t)} = \sum_{j=1}^{T} [(\sum_{i\in I_j} g_i)\omega_j + \frac{1}{2}(\sum_{i\in I_j} h_i + \lambda)\omega_j^2] + \gamma T \tag{5}$$

The solution weight ω_j^* of leaf j for a fixed tree structure $q(x)$ can be obtained by applying the following equation:

$$\omega_j^* = -\frac{\sum_{i\in I_j} g_i}{\sum_{i\in I_j} h_i + \lambda} \tag{6}$$

After substituting ω_j^* into Eq. (5), there exists:

$$\tilde{O}(q) = -\frac{1}{2}\sum_{j=1}^{T} \frac{(\sum_{i\in I_j} g_i)^2}{\sum_{i\in I_j} h_i + \lambda} + \gamma T \tag{7}$$

Define Eq. (7) as a scoring function to evaluate the tree structure $q(x)$ and find the optimal tree structures for classification. However, it is impossible to search the whole possible tree structures q in practice. [13] describes a greedy algorithm that starts from a single leaf and iteratively adds branches to grow the tree structure. Whether adding a split to the existing tree structure can be decided by the following function:

$$O_{split} = \frac{1}{2}\left[\frac{(\sum_{i\in I_L} g_i)^2}{\sum_{i\in I_L} h_i + \lambda} + \frac{(\sum_{i\in I_R} g_i)^2}{\sum_{i\in I_R} h_i + \lambda} - \frac{(\sum_{i\in I} g_i)^2}{\sum_{i\in I} h_i + \lambda}\right] - \gamma \tag{8}$$

where I_L and I_R are the instance sets of left and right nodes after the split and $I = I_L \cup I_R$.

XGBoost is a fast implementation of GB algorithm, which has the advantages of fast speed and high accuracy. This XGBoost classifier is added to the top level of the CNN to produce results for image classification in our paper.

2.3 CNN-XGBoost Model

In this paper, the specific structure of the CNN-XGBoost model for image classification is shown in Fig. 2. First, the input image data is normalized and transfer to the input layer of CNN. After training CNN by BP algorithm for several epochs to obtain a proper structure for image classification, XGBoost replaces the output layer, a soft-max classifier, of CNN and utilizes the trainable features from CNN for training. Finally, the CNN-XGBoost model gets the new classification results of testing images. Our CNN-XGBoost model can automatically obtain features from input and provides more precise classification results combining the two outstanding classifiers.

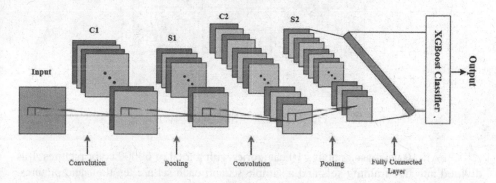

Fig. 2. The Specific structure of CNN-XGBoost model for image classification

3 Experimental Results

In order to verify the improvement and validity of the above mentioned method, we compare it with the classical ones by carrying out experiments on different databases respectively. We also compare the classification results of different methods on the same databases to evaluate the effectiveness of CNN-XGBoost model. The databases, parameter settings and classification results are shown in the following.

3.1 Database

The two selected databases in this paper are two commonly databases used in image classification problems. They are MNIST handwritten digital database and CIFAR-10 color image database. The two databases are universal, which means it is convenient to compare to other methods.

MNIST handwritten digital database is a subset of NIST dataset, which is composed of SD-1 and SD-3 dataset. It has a total number of sixty thousand training pictures and ten thousand test images, all of which are handwritten 0-9 grayscale image.

Sixty thousand training samples are handwritten digits from about 250 individuals, part of the dataset is displayed in Fig. 3.

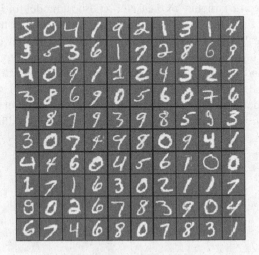

Fig. 3. Part of MNIST database

CIFAR-10 database contains 10 categories with a total of 60000 color pictures. It is divided into five training sets and a sample set and each set are ten thousand pictures. Figure 4 is the results for random selection of 10 picture results.

Fig. 4. Random selection of Cifar-10 database

3.2   Parameter Settings

To determine the parameters of CNN based on PCA initialization for image classification, we use 5 iterations as standard and calculate average classification accuracy rates of 5 times for diverse numbers of convolution kernels of the two C layers on the two databases. Finding the numbers of feature maps corresponding to maximum accuracy rate as parameters.

Considering the complexity and run-time of the network structure, we have the numbers of the first C layer feature maps tuned in the range from 3 to 12 with step size of 1, and the numbers of the second C layer feature maps in the range from 3 to 21 with step size of 3 for MNIST database. Similarly, we experiencedly have the numbers of the first C layer feature maps tuned in the range from 22 to 40 with step size of 2, and the numbers of the second C layer feature maps in the range from 24 to 72 with step size of 8 for CIFAR-10 database. Then we calculate the CNN classification accuracy rates respectively for each different feature maps. As it is shown in Figs. 5 and 6, the numbers of the feature maps in MNIST database are chose as 10 and 21, while CIFAR-10 database are 38 and 72.

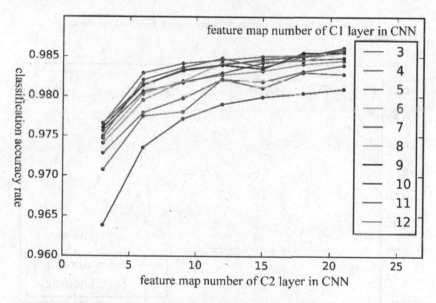

Fig. 5. Feature map number selection on MNIST database

Taking into account that the image sizes of MNIST and CIFAR-10 datasets are 28×28 and 32×32 respectively, the size of convolution kernels and sampling area are set on the basis of LeNet-5 [11] as 5×5 and 2×2.

When training the CNN on the above two databases, we take 128 pictures as a batch and whole pictures as an iteration to calculate the classification accuracy for 100 iterations after determining the feature map numbers. The classification accuracy rates on train and test sets of the two databases are displayed in Figs. 7 and 8 respectively.

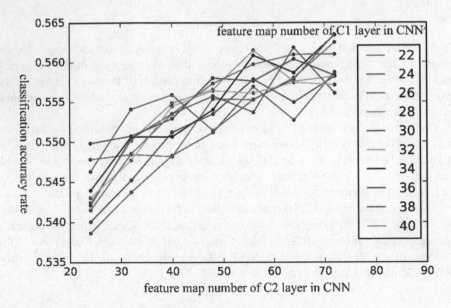

Fig. 6. Feature map number selection on CIFAR-10 database

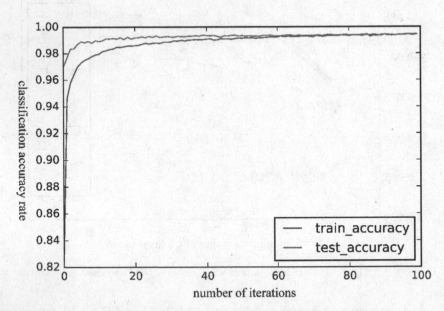

Fig. 7. Classification accuracy rates of MNIST database

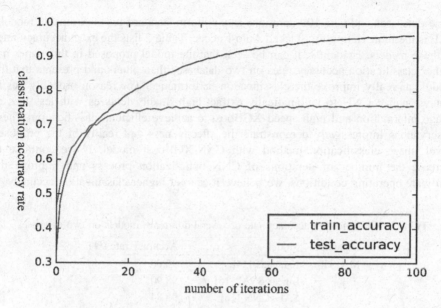

Fig. 8. Classification accuracy rates of Cifar-10 database

For the selection of parameters in XGBoost classifier, it can be determined by testing the final classification accuracy rate under different iterations, maximum tree depths and shrinkage steps. In this paper, we choose five iteration values of 100, 200, 300, 400, 500, five maximum tree depth values of 4, 6, 8, 10, 12 and five shrinkage step values of 0.005, 0.01, 0.05, 0.1, 0.2 to enumerate the classification accuracy rates in different XGBoost parameter settings and the final details of CNN-XGBoost model parameter settings are described in Table 1.

Table 1. Parameters in CNN-XGBoost model

	Parameter		MNIST	CIFAR-10
CNN	Learning rate		0.01	
	Kernel size		5	
	Pooling size		2	
	Feature map numbers	C1 Layer	10	38
		C2 Layer	21	72
XGBoost	Iterations		400	300
	Maximum tree depth		12	12
	Shrinkage step		0.05	0.01

3.3 Results and Analysis

To test the effectiveness and reality of the proposed model in this paper for image classification, we evaluate it on the above two database. In addition, we compare the classification accuracy rate with several different intelligent classification models on the same databases and take 100 iterations as a uniform standard for the trainable models. SAE is the abbreviation for Stacked Auto-Encode. Table 2 lists the exact accuracy rates of these models. Evidently, it can be seen that the model proposed in this paper has higher classification accuracy rates on two databases than others and presents that the model can really improve the classification performance. The reason probably lies in that we utilize CNN to automatically extract high quality features with less loss of image information and high speed XGBoost to achieve efficient classification. These observations impressively demonstrate the effectiveness and reality of the proposed novel image classification method with CNN-XGBoost model. If we continue to increase the number of iterations of CNN optimization process and improve the hardware operating conditions, we believe it can get higher classification accuracy.

Table 2. Classification accuracy rate of several difference models on two databases

Database	Model	Accuracy rate (%)
MNIST	K-means [14]	95.00
	Linear SVM [15]	98.90
	SAE+CNN [16]	98.84
	CNN	98.80
	CNN-SVM [17]	99.15
	CNN-XGBoost	99.22
CIFAR-10	LR on Raw Pixels [18]	37.32
	Linear SVM [18]	42.30
	SAE+CNN [16]	62.74
	CNN	76.28
	CNN-SVM [17]	78.06
	CNN-XGBoost	80.77

4   Conclusion

In order to further enhance the classification performance of a typical Deep Learning framework – CNN, which owns outstanding performance in the image classification problem, this paper proposes novel image classification method with CNN-XGBoost model. By combining the CNN and XGBoost classifiers, this model provides more precise output by integrating CNN as a trainable feature extractor to automatically obtain features from input and XGBoost as a recognizer in the top level of the network to produce results. Experiments are implemented on the well-known MNIST and CIFAR-10 databases to examine the performance and the results demonstrate that the new method performs better compared with other methods on the same databases, which verify the effectiveness and reality of the proposed method in image classification problem.

Further work will be focus on adjusting the CNN structure to further extract higher quality features and speeding up the convergence of the cost function by changing the optimization techniques to promote the classification result and training effect.

Acknowledgement. This research work is funded by the National Key Research and Development Project of China (2016YFB0801003), the Key Laboratory for Shanghai Integrated Information Security Management Technology Research.

References

1. Hinton, G.E., Osindero, S., Teh, Y.W.: A fast learning algorithm for deep belief nets. Neural Comput. **18**(7), 1527–1554 (2006)
2. Krizhevsky, A., Sutskever, I., Hinton, G.E.: Imagenet classification with deep convolutional neural networks. In: Advances in Neural Information Processing Systems, vol. 25(2), pp. 1097–1105 (2012)
3. Erhan, D., Szegedy, C., Toshev, A., et al.: Scalable object detection using deep neural networks. In: Proceedings of the IEEE Conference on Computer Vision and Pattern Recognition, pp. 2147–2154 (2014)
4. Diao, W., Sun, X., Zheng, X., et al.: Efficient saliency-based object detection in remote sensing images using deep belief networks. IEEE Geosci. Remote Sens. Lett. **13**(2), 137–141 (2016)
5. Li, C., Wei, W., Wang, J., Tang, W., Zhao, S.: Face recognition based on deep belief network combined with center-symmetric local binary pattern. In: Park, J., Jin, H., Jeong, Y. S., Khan, M. (eds.) Advanced Multimedia and Ubiquitous Engineering. LNEE, vol. 393, pp. 277–283. Springer, Singapore (2016). doi:10.1007/978-981-10-1536-6_37
6. Taigman, Y., Yang, M., Ranzato, M.A., et al.: Deepface: closing the gap to human-level performance in face verification. In: Proceedings of the IEEE Conference on Computer Vision and Pattern Recognition, pp. 1701–1708 (2014)
7. Schroff, F., Kalenichenko, D., Philbin, J.: Facenet: a unified embedding for face recognition and clustering. In: Proceedings of the IEEE Conference on Computer Vision and Pattern Recognition, pp. 815–823 (2015)
8. Song, R., Chen, S., Deng, B., Li, L.: eXtreme gradient boosting for identifying individual users across different digital devices. In: Cui, B., Zhang, N., Xu, J., Lian, X., Liu, D. (eds.) WAIM 2016, Part I. LNCS, vol. 9658, pp. 43–54. Springer, Cham (2016). doi:10.1007/978-3-319-39937-9_4
9. Mackey, L., Bryan, J., Mo, M.Y.: Weighted classification cascades for optimizing discovery significance in the HIGGSML challenge. In: NIPS 2014 Workshop on High-energy Physics and Machine Learning, pp. 129–134 (2015)
10. Bekkerman, R.: The present and the future of the KDD cup competition: an outsider's perspective
11. Lecun, Y., Boser, B., Denker, J.S., et al.: Handwritten digit recognition with a back-propagation network. In: Advances in Neural Information Processing Systems, pp. 396–404 (1990)
12. Zipser, D., Andersen, R.A.: A back-propagation programmed network that simulates response properties of a subset of posterior parietal neurons. Nature **331**(6158), 679–684 (1988)
13. Chen, T., Guestrin, C.: Xgboost: a scalable tree boosting system. In: Proceedings of the 22nd ACM SIGKDD International Conference on Knowledge Discovery and Data Mining, pp. 785–794. ACM (2016)
14. Lecun, Y., Bottou, L., Bengio, Y., Haffner, P.: Gradient-based learning applied to document recognition. Proc. IEEE **86**(11), 2278–2324 (1998)

15. Chan, T.H., Jia, K., Gao, S., et al.: Pcanet: a simple deep learning baseline for image classification. IEEE Trans. Image Process. **24**(12), 5017–5032 (2015)
16. Ao, D.: Integration of Unsupervised Feature Learning and Neural Networks Applied to Image Recognition, pp. 19–37. South China University of Technology (2014)
17. Elleuch, M., Maalej, R., Kherallah, M.: A new design based-SVM of the CNN classifier architecture with dropout for offline arabic handwritten recognition. Procedia Comput. Sci. **80**, 1712–1723 (2016)
18. Le, Q., Sarlós, T., Smola, A.: Fastfood-approximating kernel expansions in loglinear time. In: Proceedings of the International Conference on Machine Learning (2013)
19. Hinton, G.E., Salakhutdinov, R.R.: Reducing the dimensionality of data with neural networks. Science **313**(5786), 504–507 (2006)
20. Krizhevsky, A.: Learning multiple layers of features from tiny images. Master's thesis, pp. 30–35. University of Toronto (2009)

Improvement and Evaluation of Time-Spread Echo Hiding Technology for Long-Distance Voice Evacuation Systems

Akira Nishimura[✉]

Department of Informatics, Faculty of Informatics,
Tokyo University of Information Sciences,
4–1 Onaridai, Wakaba, Chiba, Chiba 265-8501, Japan
akira@rsch.tuis.ac.jp

Abstract. Several improvements to the time-spread echo hiding method are proposed for an aerial audio data hiding in which speech signals are broadcast by the outdoor loudspeakers of a voice evacuation and mass notification system. Evaluations of the data hiding system for speech signals were conducted using computer simulations including several disturbances caused by the long-distance (from 70 to 800 m) aerial transmission of sounds. The frequency response of a distant horn-array loudspeaker system, the absorption of sound by the atmosphere, reverberation and a single long-path echo, a constant frequency shift that mimics a small Doppler shift and a mismatch of sampling frequencies between sending and receiving devices, and additive background noise are simulated as disturbances. A background noise recorded outdoors was mixed to simulate a loud outdoor space in a city at signal-to-noise ratios of −5, 0, and 5 dB. The computer simulation results showed that the suppression of high- and low-frequency regions in the logarithmic spectral domain in the decoding process was significantly effective for the decoding performance. A novel hiding method of the alternating sign of echoes was moderately effective under relatively high SNR (0 and 5 dB) conditions.

Keywords: Bilateral symmetric time-spread echo · Frequency response · Absorption by the atmosphere · Reverberation · Long-path echo

1 Introduction

This paper aims to improve the time-spread echo hiding method for speech signals broadcast by the outdoor loudspeakers of a voice evacuation and mass notification system. Evaluations of the data hiding system for speech signals are conducted by computer simulations including several disturbances caused by the long-distance (several hundreds of meters) aerial transmission of sounds.

Large-scale disasters such as earthquakes, tsunamis, terrorism, and firing of ballistic missiles occasionally threaten our lives and society. Voice evacuation

© Springer International Publishing AG 2017
C. Kraetzer et al. (Eds.): IWDW 2017, LNCS 10431, pp. 391–405, 2017.
DOI: 10.1007/978-3-319-64185-0_29

and mass notification systems that use outdoor loudspeaker systems play an important role in propagating emergency information in Japan. However, there is a severe problem of informing the hearing impaired and the elderly who have difficulty in hearing as well as informing tourists and foreigners who do not understand the Japanese language. Therefore, aerial data transmission combined with voice evacuation messages should be realized with the aid of information hiding technology.

The payload data embedded in the speech signal, which is coded in small numbers of information bits, is information for refugees from disasters. Therefore, the raw bit rate of the payload is from 3 to 10 bps (bits per seconds), and the actual bit rate of the information after error-correction coding is considered to be 1 to 2 bps. The received and decoded information is displayed on a digital terminal such as a smartphone.

In recent years, a number of audio data hiding technologies that embed some information into aerial sounds and utilize the decoded information at the smartphones of users have been proposed. These technologies can be classified into three categories: digital watermarking technologies that embed information by modulating the host speech and/or music signals [1,9,11,13], acoustic modem technologies that modulate one or more carrier wave signals to encode digital information for aerial transmission [10,12], and hybrid technologies that replace components of the cover signal above 16 kHz, which are nearly inaudible for adults, with the modem signal.

The acoustic modem technologies are not suitable for mass notification systems because nobody obtains information without a decoding device. The hybrid technologies are also not suitable because the general long-range horn-array loudspeakers for voice evacuation and mass notification systems are not able to radiate sounds above 6–7 kHz [3].

Audio watermarking technologies combined with mass notification systems are promising systems that can transmit both hidden information and voice messages via speech sounds emitted from a loudspeaker. However, it is unclear whether the audio data hiding technologies that have been previously proposed can be used for aerial long-distance transmission and low (approximately 0 dB) signal-to-noise ratio (SNR) conditions in an outdoor environment.

Some of the aerial audio watermarking technologies were intended for use in an evacuation and mass notification system [10,16,17]; however, their evaluation of the proposed system was not based on outdoor long-distance transmissions. They did not take into account the background noises and their relative intensities, the frequency response of outdoor horn loudspeakers, and the absorption of sound by the atmosphere. These disturbances are crucial for aerial long-distance audio data hiding, as shown in Sect. 5.

Other studies on audio data hiding for aerial transmission [1,9,13] conducted experiments in actual space. However, they tested only indoor environments, where the transmission distance was below 10 m, and the power of the background noise was not strictly controlled [1,9].

The following section proposes several improvements to the time-spread echo hiding method [2,7,8] to enhance its effectiveness under outdoor long-distance aerial transmissions. The succeeding section then describes a realistic simulated environment that takes the typical disturbances in the long-distance aerial transmission of sounds emitted from outdoor loudspeakers of voice evacuation and mass notification systems into account [14]. The computer simulation results for long-distance aerial transmission show the effectiveness of the improvements on the time-spread echo hiding.

2   Time-Spread Echo Hiding

2.1   Conventional Time-Spread Echo Hiding [8]

The embedding process segments the host signal $s(n)$ into $F + T_r$ samples with an overlap of T_r samples. The stego signal $r(n)$ is obtained by the convolution of the framed host signal $s(n)$ with the impulse response $k(n)$, consisting of the Dirac delta function $\delta(n)$ and an echo kernel $P(n)$ of length L and a delay time of $d0$.

$$k(n) = \delta(n) + \alpha P(n - d0), \tag{1}$$

$$r(n) = s(n) * k(n), \tag{2}$$

where $*$ means convolution and α is the echo gain, which is maximized to $\alpha = 1/\sqrt{L}$. Subsequently, the framed stego signals are concatenated with initial and final overlaps of $T_r/2$ samples each. The payload data are embedded in every segmented frame signal. The top panel of Fig. 1 shows an impulse response of the time-spread echo.

The original echo hiding [4] represents a binary bit by switching the delay time between $d0$ and $d1$. The current hiding scheme circularly shifts $P(n)$ to obtain $P'(n)$ depending on the integer value m encoded by payload bits, as follows:

$$P'(n) = \begin{cases} P(n + L - m) & (1 \leq n \leq m), \\ P(n - m) & (m + 1 \leq n \leq L). \end{cases} \tag{3}$$

m is quantized by m' steps, in other words, $m \in \{0, m', 2m', ..., \lfloor L/m' \rfloor m'\}$, to be robust against frequency shifts of the stego signal. Consequently, the amount of payload is $\log_2(\lfloor L/m' \rfloor + 1)$ per segmented frame.

In the detection process, the real cepstrum transform˜of the stego signal $r(n)$ is calculated using the absolute spectrum obtained from DFT (discrete Fourier transform). $\tilde{r}(n) = \mathrm{Re}(\mathrm{IDFT}(\log(\mathrm{abs}(\mathrm{DFT}(r(n))))))$, where IDFT represents the inverse DFT and Re extracts the real part of it. Equation (4) is the real cepstrum transform of Eq. (2). The cross-correlation (xcorr) of $\tilde{r}(n)$ and $P(n)$ exhibits a peak at the amount of circular shifting m.

$$\tilde{r}(n) = \tilde{s}(n) + \tilde{k}(n), \tag{4}$$

$$x(n) = \mathrm{xcorr}(\tilde{r}(n), P(n)). \tag{5}$$

Table 1 shows the parameter values of the time-spread echo hidings tested in this study.

Table 1. Parameter values of the time-spread echo hidings.

Parameter	Values			
Sampling freq. [Hz]	16,000			
Delay time ($d0$)	80 samples (5 ms)			
Frame overlap ($T_r/2$)	50 samples			
Frame length (F)	16,384		32,768	
Length of PN series (L)	1,023	2,047	1,023	2,047
Payload bits per frame	8	9	8	9
Bit rate [bps]	7.8	8.8	3.9	4.4

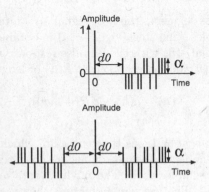

Fig. 1. The top panel shows an example of the impulse response of time-spread echo hiding, and the bottom panel shows that of bilateral echo kernel.

2.2 Bilateral Symmetric Time-Spread Echo Kernel

A bilateral symmetric echo kernel was first proposed by Kim and Choi [7]. Chou and Hsieh [2] applied the bilateral symmetric echo kernel technique to the time-spread echo kernel. The bottom panel of Fig. 1 presents an example of the impulse response of the bilateral symmetric time-spread echo kernel, which is henceforth called the bilateral method. The detection gain, which represents a gain in the peak of the cross-correlation (Eq. 5), exhibits a maximum value when the echo gain $\alpha = 1/(2\sqrt{L})$. It achieves approximately 1.7 times greater detection gain than that of the conventional unilateral condition, thereby resulting in better performance [2,14]. A drawback of the bilateral echo kernel is the degradation of imperceptibility; however, it is less important for broadcasting voice messages in this study.

2.3 Frame Synchronization

Previous works on echo hiding technologies have not addressed the frame synchronization because a detection frame that is shorter than the size of the embedded frame F can extract the payload data. To maximize the detection performance, the following method is proposed and used for frame synchronization [14].

During the detection process, payload detection is conducted to shift the frame of the stego signal by every $F/8$ samples. The probability of correct detection is maximized when the stego frame is synchronized to the embedded frame, and the same payload can be extracted from before and after the synchronized frame. Therefore, differentiation of the extracted payload exhibits one or more zeros in every eight frames. The period of eight frames can be detected by Fourier analysis of the differentiated payload data. The correct payload can be detected from the zero-phase frame of the period.

3   Improvements to Time-Spread Echo Hiding

This section proposes several improvements to the time-spread echo hiding for aerial long-distance transmissions under low SNR conditions in terms of encoding, emitting from loudspeakers, and decoding.

3.1   Alternating Signs of Echoes Between Sub-frames

If a strong low-frequency and periodic background noise, such as noises of fans and engines, or a strong short echo are continuously recorded at a decoder, then the cepstrum of such sounds exhibits a peak at a delay time corresponding to its period or delay. It interferes with the cross-correlation calculation in the decoding of the time-spread echo hiding.

To cancel such background noises, a new embedding method that alternates the sign of echoes is developed. This method is realized by inverting the amplitude of the echo kernel α between two successive sub-frames of which the length is $F/2$ samples for embedding. It is combined with the bilateral method and is henceforth called the alternating sign method.

In the decoding process, the cepstrum obtained from the latter sub-frame is subtracted from that obtained from the former sub-frame. Consequently, the common components between the cepstrums of the two sub-frames are canceled. If there is no common component between the cepstrums of the sub-frames, as often holds true in most of the background noise, the subtraction described above simply doubles the amplitude of the echo kernel in the cepstrum domain, whereas the amplitudes of the other components are $\sqrt{2}$ times.

Figure 2 shows the outcomes of the cancellations in the cepstrum domain. The top lines are the cepstrum obtained from the recorded signal of the former sub-frame, the middle lines are that obtained from the latter sub-frame, and the bottom lines are the subtracted cepstrum. The left panel shows the results from a speech signal mixed with a 50-Hz periodic noise at an SNR of −5 dB. The peaks at quefrencies (delay time) of 20 ms and 40 ms, which can be seen in the top and the middle, are canceled as a result of the subtraction. The right panel shows the results from a speech signal and a 45.3-ms-delayed −6 dB signal mixed with a background noise at an SNR of 5 dB. The strong peaks at a quefrency of 45.3 ms are canceled in the subtracted cepstrum.

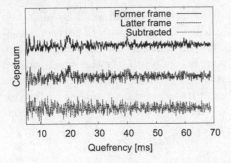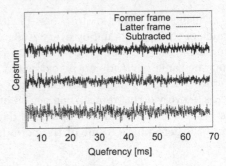

Fig. 2. Cancellations in the cepstrum domain. The left panel shows the results from a speech signal mixed with a 50-Hz periodic noise at an SNR of −5 dB. The right panel shows the results from a speech signal and a 45.3-ms-delayed −6 dB signal mixed with a background noise at an SNR of 5 dB.

A sophisticated frame synchronization can be realized by observing the maximum amplitude of the cross-correlation function. The recorded sound is segmented to the sub-frame signal of which the length is $F/2$ samples. Then, cross-correlation functions are calculated by shifting the frame location by $F/16$. The decoded data from the frame that exhibits the maximum peak in the cross-correlation function obtained over 16 frames is the most reliable data to be decoded because if the frame signal to be decoded spreads over the different sub-frame pairs, then the peak of the cross-correlation function is attenuated by the cancellation in the cepstrum domain.

A similar canceling method, in which a host signal is divided into even and odd samples, has been proposed [19]. The divided signals are convolved to the time-spread echo kernels that have inverse amplitudes. In the decoding process, the stego signal is divided into even- and odd-sampled signals. The cepstrums obtained from the odd-sampled signal is subtracted from that obtained from the even-sampled signal to cancel the common components between the cepstrum of the two signals. However, this cancellation mechanism does not work properly in the current scenario because a slight frequency shift, which is shown in Sect. 4.1, induces misalignment between the odd and even samples of the recorded stego signal.

3.2   Boosting High-Frequency Sounds Before Reproduction

Boosting a high-frequency region of the speech sound reproduced by the loudspeaker system may improve the performance of the aerial data hiding because the high-frequency region is attenuated in long-distance aerial transmissions by the absorption of sound by the atmosphere. Moreover, the frequency response of the horn-array loudspeaker system, which is shown in Fig. 4, shows that the cutoff frequency of the lowpass characteristics of the system is approximately 2 kHz. Another advantage of boosting the high-frequency region is an improvement in the clarity of speech sounds. However, a drawback of boosting in an actual audio system is amplitude clipping of the speech sound at the output of the amplifier. It causes degradation in the clarity of the speech sounds by distortion.

To simulate clipping prevention at the output of the amplifier, the maximum amplitude of the speech signal after boosting a high-frequency region is limited to the maximum amplitude of the speech prior to boosting. The boosting is realized by a parametric equalizer whose center frequency is 3 kHz and Q-factor is unity. The gain of the parametric equalizer is +6 dB. The frequency response of boosting is also shown in Fig. 4.

3.3   Suppression of High- and Low-Frequency Logarithmic Spectrum

For speech signals, frequency regions that have relatively strong power are the middle frequency region (200 Hz–3 kHz), where the first and second formants exist. This frequency region maintains spectral peaks and dips of the speech signals, which are generated by the echo kernel, while other frequency regions do not. Therefore, under low SNR conditions, suppressing low- and high-frequency regions in the logarithmic spectrum domain is effective for decoding.

The suppression of low- and high-frequency regions is realized by multiplying the logarithmic magnitude spectrum below the low-cutoff frequency and above the high-cutoff frequency by 0.1. Several cutoff frequencies are tested in Sect. 5.

4   Simulation of Long-Distance Aerial Sound Transmission

4.1   Conditions of disturbance

Figure 3 shows a block diagram of the simulated environment of long-distance aerial transmissions. The frequency response of a distant horn-array loudspeaker system, absorption of sound by the atmosphere, reverberation and a single long-path echo, a constant frequency shift, and an additive background noise are simulated. Modeling and implementations of the signal processing for each disturbance are described in detail in the literature [14]. Table 2 shows the disturbances and their simulated parameters for implementation. All signal processing units are connected in series.

Figure 4 shows the estimated spectral envelope and the frequency response of the IIR filter that simulates the loudspeaker system, including the frequency characteristics of 70-m absorption by the atmosphere.

Figure 5 presents the frequency attenuation characteristics per 100 m calculated using the ISO 9613-1 method under typical temperature, relative humidity, and air pressure of the atmosphere.

The frequency of the received sound is slightly fluctuated or shifted compared with the emitted sound due to changes in speed and wind direction, a Doppler shift caused by movement of the receiver, and a mismatch of sampling frequencies between sending and receiving devices. The following simulation introduces a +0.1% constant frequency shift before mixing of the background noise.

'STRAFFIC/ch01.wav', which was recorded at a busy traffic intersection; 'SPSQUARE/ch01.wav', which was recorded at a public town square with

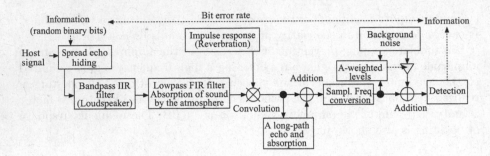

Fig. 3. A block diagram of the simulated environment.

Table 2. Disturbances and their simulated parameters for long-distance aerial sound transmission.

Disturbance	Implementation	Parameters
Loudspeaker characteristics including 70-m absorption	Bandpass IIR filter	Highpass: 3rd-ord. Butterworth, 300 Hz Lowpass: 2nd-ord. Butterworth, 2 kHz
Absorption of sound by the atmosphere	Lowpass FIR filter	ISO-9613-1, Temp: 15 °C Humidity: 60%, Pressure: 1013 hPa
Reverberation	Synthesized impulse response using Gaussian noise with Exp. decay	Reverberation time: 1 s, Direct to reverberant ratio: 4 dB, Speech transmission index [15]: 0.6
A long-path echo	A single delay with reverberation and absorption	−6 dB, delay time is randomly chosen from 0.1–1.0 s
Frequency shift caused by Doppler shift	Re-sampling	+0.1%
Background noise	DEMAND database	A-weighted SNR: 5, 0, −5 dB

many tourists; and 'SCAFE/ch01.wav', which was recorded from the terrace of a cafe in a public square, are selected from DEMAND (Diverse Environments Multichannel Acoustic Noise Database) [18] as background noises. These noises are sampled at 16-kHz, 16-bit quantization, and single channel. A randomly selected segment is mixed with the stego speech signal at several SNRs. In this study, the SNR is calculated based on the A-weighted sound pressure levels defined by the international standard IEC 61672:2003, which is commonly used for measuring environmental noise. The SNR is expressed in Eq. (6), where $r_a(t)$ is an A-weighted filtered signal after simulating long-distance transmission, $g_a(t)$

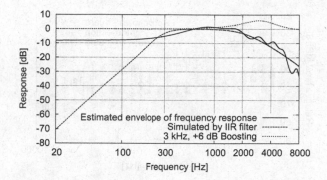

Fig. 4. Estimated spectral envelope of the loudspeaker system at a distance of 70 m, including the frequency characteristics of absorption by the atmosphere and frequency response of the IIR filter that simulates the loudspeaker system [14]. In addition, a frequency response of 3 kHz and +6 dB boosting (see Sect. 3.2) is shown.

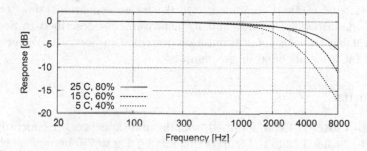

Fig. 5. Frequency attenuation characteristics per 100 m calculated using the ISO 9613-1 method under typical temperature and relative humidity of the atmosphere at a pressure of 1013 hPa.

is an A-weighted filtered noise, and $t \in \{0, 1, 2, ..., N-1\}$ is a time series with a segmental length of N.

$$\text{SNR} = 10 \log_{10} \frac{\sum_{t=0}^{N-1} s_a(t)^2}{\sum_{t=0}^{N-1} g_a(t)^2} \qquad (6)$$

The average 1/3-octave band levels of the background noises relative to the full-scale sinusoidal wave of 16-bit quantization are shown in Fig. 6.

4.2 Simulation conditions

A total of 753 speech files spoken by 10 male speakers, where two speech files are concatenated, and 903 speech files spoken by 12 female speakers serve as cover data. These files are recorded in the Continuous Speech Database for Research (Vol. 1) published by the Acoustical Society of Japan. All speech files are sampled at 16 kHz and 16-bit quantization.

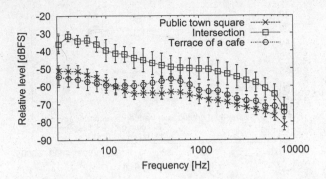

Fig. 6. Average 1/3-octave band levels of three background noises measured for every 1 s. Error bars show ± 1 standard deviation. The power levels are scaled to dBFS, where 0 dBFS is defined as the maximum sinusoidal amplitude of 16-bit quantization.

The bilateral method combined with the frame synchronization technique, which are described in Sect. 2, and its improvements described in Sect. 3 are evaluated using the computer simulation described in Sect. 4.1. Watermarks of a random bit are embedded in the samples.

5   Results

The bit error rates (BERs) obtained from the male speakers are generally better than those obtained from the female speakers by 1% to 7% because of the lower fundamental frequencies of the male speakers. The average BERs obtained from the background noise SCAFE are the worst among the three noise files; they are larger than those obtained from STRAFFIC by 6% to 10% under −5 dB SNR conditions because the sound of SCAFE mainly consists of human speech noises, where the spectrum is overlapped with that of the stego message voice. To investigate the effectiveness of speech watermarking in the worst outdoor conditions, the following results show data obtained from the female speakers and the background noise SCAFE.

5.1   Suppression of High- and Low-Frequency Logarithmic Spectrum

Figure 7 shows the median BERs obtained from the bilateral method with suppression of the logarithmic spectrum in the decoding process. Suppression of the high-frequency band, particularly that above 3 kHz, is the most effective. Therefore, the simulation hereafter always includes suppression below 200 Hz and above 3 kHz.

5.2   Boosting High-Frequency Sounds Before Reproduction

Figure 8 compares the BERs obtained from no boosting and 3 kHz, +6 dB boosting conditions at the simulated loudspeaker distances of 70 m, 400 m, and 800 m.

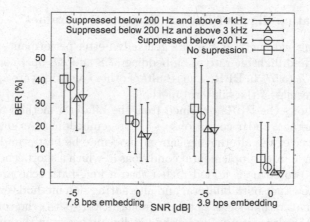

Fig. 7. The effects of the frequency-band suppression on BERs obtained from the bilateral method. Each point represents the median BERs. Error bars represent the 10th and 90th percentiles.

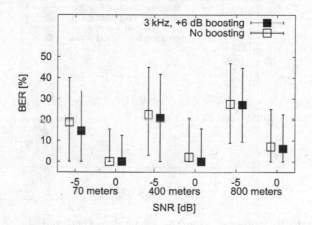

Fig. 8. Effects of boosting 3 kHz and +6 dB on the median BERs obtained from the simulated loudspeaker distances of 70, 400, and 800 m. The embedding bit rate is 3.9 bps.

In contrast to our expectations, the results show that little improvement of 3-kHz boosting is observed at the loudspeaker distance of 800 m. Slight improvements of the boosting are observed at the loudspeaker distances of 70 and 400 m. These results may be caused by an amplitude attenuation by the clipping prevention mechanism, which is required in an actual amplifier. A drawback of the clipping prevention is diminishing the relative power of the emitted sounds below 3 kHz, which is the dominant frequency region of speech sounds.

5.3   Alternating Signs of Echoes Between Sub-frames

The alternating sign method exhibits generally better performance at high SNR (5 and 0 dB) and high bit rate of embedding (7.8 and 8.8 bps) conditions. The advantage is 1% to 5% in BER. The results of other conditions are approximately equal to the results of the bilateral method.

Figure 9 shows the BERs obtained from the bilateral method and the alternating sign method under conditions of 8.8 bps embedding. As shown in Fig. 2, the performance of the alternating sign method may be better under short echo conditions. Therefore, supplemental conditions in which a short echo delayed randomly from 10 to 60 ms is added rather than a long-path echo are also tested. The results show that both bilateral and alternating sign methods exhibit slightly better performance than those obtained from the long-path echo conditions. The advantage of the alternating sign method is slightly larger in the short echo conditions compared with the long-path echo conditions.

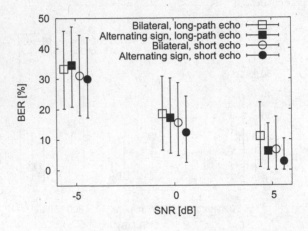

Fig. 9. Median BERs obtained from the bilateral method and the alternating sign method. Error bars represent the 10th and 90th percentiles. The embedding bit rate is 8.8 bps.

Some extended simulation conditions revealed that the alternating sign method under higher SNR (above 10 dB) and higher bit rate of embedding (above 16 bps) conditions exhibits considerably better performance than the bilateral method.

6   Discussion

The computer simulation results depend on the type of background noise. The average 1/3-octave band levels of the three background noises show different spectral shapes in Fig. 6. The difference in the spectral shape of the background noise causes differences in the effects of suppression of the logarithmic spectrum in the decoding process, particularly the cutoff frequencies. However, suppression outside of the speech frequency band, below 200 Hz and above 3 kHz, is efficient in most of the background noise environments.

The strong periodic noise and strong short echo shown in Sect. 3.1 can be removed by signal processing posterior to the receiving from the device. However, some noise reduction algorithms might collapse the hidden data expressed by the echo kernel. The alternating sign method can decrease the disturbance caused by the background noise in relatively high SNR conditions without deteriorating the performance, as shown in Fig. 9.

The benefit of the time-spread echo hiding is that the timbre formed by the echo kernel is similar to that formed by random reflections observed in indoor and outdoor environments; thus, the quality and clarity of the stego speech are not severely degraded. The current study did not confirm the subjective quality and clarity of the stego speech signal, and the quality of the stego speech is less important. Moreover, improvements in the clarity of speech sounds due to boosting the 3-kHz band in long-distance aerial transmissions are not clear. These topics are some of the research interests for further work.

Several studies that improve the detection performance of the time-spread echo hiding have been reported [5,6,20]. Hua et al. [5] proposed a joint detection that combines both the real part and imaginary part of a cepstrum to further suppress the interference. The current study utilizes the real part of the cepstrum, and further studies on the joint detection under low SNR conditions are required.

An optimization-based finite-impulse-response filter design is utilized to obtain the optimal echo filter coefficients that concentrate the frequency response of the echo kernel to the perceptually insignificant frequency region [6,20]. In contrast to such studies, designing an optimal echo filter that concentrates the effects of the echo kernel to the speech frequencies is worth addressing.

7 Summary

Several improvements to the time-spread echo hiding method are proposed for an aerial audio data hiding where speech signals are broadcast by the outdoor loudspeakers of voice evacuation and mass notification systems. Evaluations of the data hiding system for speech signals were conducted by computer simulations that include several disturbances caused by long-distance (from 70 to 800 m) aerial transmissions of sounds. A background noise recorded outdoors was mixed to simulate a loud outdoor space in a city at SNRs of −5, 0, and 5 dB. The computer simulation result showed that suppression of high- and low-frequency regions in the logarithmic spectral domain in the decoding process was significantly effective on decoding performance. A novel hiding method of the alternating sign of echoes was moderately effective under relatively high SNR (0 and 5 dB) conditions. In addition, +6 dB boosting of a frequency band centered at 3 kHz showed a slight improvement in performance.

Acknowledgment. This study was partially supported by TOA Corporation. The author thanks the anonymous reviewers for their helpful comments and suggestions on this manuscript.

References

1. Cho, K., Choi, J., Jin, Y.G., Kim, N.S.: Quality enhancement of audio watermarking for data transmission in aerial space based on segmental SNR adjustment. In: Proceedings of IIHMSP 2012, pp. 122–125 (2012)
2. Chou, S.A., Hsieh, S.F.: An echo-hiding watermarking technique based on bilateral symmetric time spread kernel. In: Proceedings of ICASSP 2006 III, pp. 1100–1103 (2006)
3. TOA Corp.: TOA horn array speaker HA-450H (2014). http://www.toaelectronics.com/media/specs/ha450h_sale.pdf
4. Gruhl, Daniel, Lu, Anthony, Bender, Walter: Echo hiding. In: Anderson, Ross (ed.) IH 1996. LNCS, vol. 1174, pp. 295–315. Springer, Heidelberg (1996). doi:10.1007/3-540-61996-8_48
5. Hua, G., Goh, J., Thing, V.L.L.: Cepstral analysis for the application of echo-based audio watermark detection. IEEE Trans. Inf. Forensics Secur. **10**(9), 1850–1861 (2015)
6. Hua, G., Goh, J., Thing, V.L.L.: Time-spread echo-based audio watermarking with optimized imperceptibility and robustness. IEEE/ACM Trans. Audio Speech Lang. Process. **23**(2), 227–239 (2015)
7. Kim, H.J., Choi, Y.H.: A novel echo-hiding scheme with backward and forward kernels. IEEE Trans. Circ. Syst. Video Technol. **13**(8), 885–889 (2003)
8. Ko, B.S., Nishimura, R., Suzuki, Y.: Time-spread echo method for digital audio watermarking. IEEE Trans. Multimedia **7**, 212–221 (2005)
9. Matsuoka, H., Nakashima, Y., Yoshimura, T.: Acoustic OFDM system and performance analysis. IEICE Trans. Fundam. **E91-A**(7), 1652–1658 (2008)
10. Munekata, T., Yamatuchi, T., Handa, H., Nishimura, R., Suzuki, Y.: A portable acoustic caption decoder using IH technique for enhancing lives of the people who are deaf or hard-of-hearing – system configuration and robustness for airborne sound. In: Proceedings of IIHMSP 2007, pp. 406–409 (2007)
11. Nishimura, A.: Presentation of information synchronized with the audio signal reproduced by loudspeakers using an AM-based watermark. In: Proceedings of the 3rd International Conference on Intelligent Information Hiding and Multimedia Signal Processing, vol. 2, pp. 275–278. IEEE (2007)
12. Nishimura, A.: Aerial acoustic modem that is suitable to decode using a CELP-based speech encoder. In: Proceedings of IIHMSP 2010, pp. 514–517 (2010)
13. Nishimura, A.: Audio data hiding that is robust with respect to aerial transmission and speech codecs. Int. J. Innov. Comput. Inf. Control **6**(3), 1389–1400 (2010)
14. Nishimura, A.: Simulation of long-distance aerial transmissions for robust audio data hiding. In: Proceedings of the 13th International Conference on Intelligent Information Hiding and Multimedia Signal Processing. Springer, Heidelberg (2017, in press)
15. Schroeder, M.R.: Modulation transfer functions: definition and measurement. Acustica **49**, 179–182 (1981)
16. Tetsuya, K., Akihiro, O., Udaya, P.: Properties of an emergency broadcasting system based on audio data hiding. In: Proceedings of IIHMSP 2015, pp. 142–145 (2015)

17. Tetsuya, K., Kan, K., Udaya, P.: A disaster prevention broadcasting based on audio data hiding technology. In: Proceedings of Joint 8th International Conference on Soft Computing and Intelligent Systems and 17th International Symposium on Advanced Intelligent Systems, pp. 373–376 (2016)

18. Thiemann, J., Ito, N., Vincent, E.: DEMAND: diverse environments multichannel acoustic noise database (2013). http://parole.loria.fr/DEMAND/

19. Xiang, Y., Natgunanathan, I., Peng, D., Zhou, W.: A dual-channel time-spread echo method for audio watermarking. IEEE Trans. Inf. Forensics Secur. **7**(2), 383–392 (2012)

20. Xiang, Y., Peng, D., Natgunanathan, I., Zhou, W.: Effective pseudonoise sequence and decoding function for imperceptibility and robustness enhancement in time-spread echo-based audio watermarking. IEEE Trans. Multimedia **13**(1), 2–13 (2011)

Temporal Integration Based Visual Cryptography Scheme and Its Application

Wen Wang[1,2]($\boxtimes$), Feng Liu[1,2], Teng Guo[3], and Yawei Ren[4]

[1] State Key Laboratory of Information Security,
Institute of Information Engineering, Chinese Academy of Sciences, Beijing, China
wangwen@iie.ac.cn
[2] School of Cyber Security,
University of Chinese Academy of Sciences, Beijing, China
[3] School of Information Science and Technology,
University of International Relations, Beijing, China
[4] School of Information Management,
Beijing Information Science and Technology University, Beijing 100192, China

Abstract. Visual cryptography scheme (VCS) is an image secret sharing method which exploits the spatial responds characteristics of Human visual system (HVS). Applications of traditional OR and XOR based VCSs are seriously limited by the implementation carrier in practice. In this paper, we proposed a new kind of VCS which is implemented on modern display terminal of high refresh rates. Our approach exploits the temporal responds characteristics of HVS that light signals are temporal integrated into a single steady continuous one if the frequency exceeds critical fusion frequency (CFF). Furthermore, basing on the proposed VCS, we implement an information security display technology that can prevent unauthorized photography. Only authorized viewers can recover the secret information with the help of synchronized glass. While unauthorized viewers with naked eye or camera get nothing about the secret information. Experimental results show the effectiveness of proposed temporal integration based VCS and information security display technology.

Keywords: Visual cryptography scheme · Human visual system · Critical fusion frequency · Information security display

1 Introduction

Visual cryptography scheme (VCS) was first proposed by Naor and Shamir [12] to share secret image among public. A (k, n) visual cryptography scheme $((k, n)$-VCS) encrypts a secret image into n share images that consist of random looking distributed black and white pixels. In decoding phase, we can visually recover the secret information by simply overlapping any amount of share images that no less than k. But if the amount of overlapped share images is less than k, we get nothing about the secret information. Visual cryptography exploits the spatial frequency response characteristics of human visual system (HVS) that spatial

© Springer International Publishing AG 2017
C. Kraetzer et al. (Eds.): IWDW 2017, LNCS 10431, pp. 406–419, 2017.
DOI: 10.1007/978-3-319-64185-0_30

adjacent pixels are integrated by retina of our eyes and perceived as a single pixel of mixed color. Since the decryption of VCS does not need complicated mathematical computation, VCS has attracted much attention during the past twenty years. More comprehensive knowledge can be found in publication [11].

The decryption of VCS only requires to overlap the share images together where the method of overlapping is called "stacking model" of VCS. According to the former researches, there are two kinds of "stacking model" in construction of VCS, OR-based [1,4,10,17,18,25] and XOR-based VCS [3,9,16,21,22,28]. OR-based VCS is the primary scheme proposed by Naor and Shamir [12] where the share images are printed on transparencies. Figure 1 shows the principle of OR-based stacking model. Share images are usually expressed by binary matrix where black pixel is denoted as "1" while white pixel is denoted as "0". Light through the transparencies will be blocked by black pixels which is abstracted into "OR" mathematical operations: $1 + 1 = 1$, $0 + 1 = 1$, $1 + 0 = 1$, $0 + 0 = 0$. Though most researches of VCS are based on OR stacking model, the transparency carrier does has some deficiencies in practice which seriously limit the application of VCS. For example, the transparency is physically inconvenient to carry with, and the alignment is really a challenge for ordinary users. XOR-based VCS is proposed to improve the contrast of recovered secret information. The stack of XOR-based share images is usually implemented by polarizer or liquid crystal display (LCD) with multi-layer that can rotate the polarization direction of light. Figure 2 shows an example of XOR-based stacking model with two-layer liquid crystal. In the model, backlights go through a polarizer are transformed into polarized light. States of pixels of share images are converted into electrical signals which decide the rotation of polarization direction of the light. See from Fig. 2, pixels with state of "1" rotates the polarization direction of the light by 90° while "0" keeps its original state. Thus, after passing through two layer of liquid crystal, the polarization direction of the light is as shown in liquid crystal layer 2. At last, the lights go through another polarizer which blocks the light with orthogonal directions. The stacking model of multi-layer LCD based VCS is abstracted into "XOR" mathematical operations: $1 + 1 = 0$, $0 + 0 = 0$, $1 + 0 = 1$, $0 + 1 = 1$. Compared with OR-based VCS, XOR based VCS improves the visual quality to a large extent. But the drawback of XOR-based VCS also lies in its carrier of implementation. For carrier of polarizer, it is similar to the transparency used by OR-based VCS which has same deficiencies in practice. For carrier of multi-layer LCD, increasing the liquid crystal layer is costly in economy and hard to be implemented technically since the color management of such display is very complicated. Thus, the implementation carrier of VCS confines its application in public.

In recent years, display technologies have got substantial development. Stereoscopic display that works at high refresh rates is widely used among public. Information security display technology [6,24] is a direct application of such kinds of displays. In this paper, we investigate the temporal response characteristics of HVS and extend the current OR and XOR based VCS to temporal

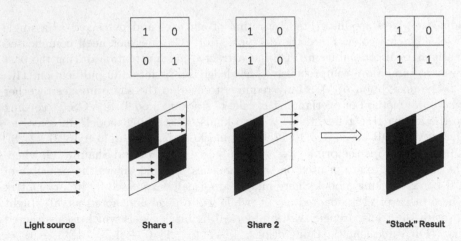

Fig. 1. Principle of OR-based stacking model

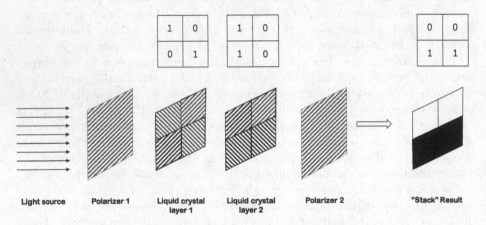

Fig. 2. Principle of XOR-based stacking model

integration based VCS which utilizes the high refresh rates of modern display system to implement VCS. Then basing on the proposed implementation method of VCS, we propose a new construction approach of information security display method that can prevent unauthorized photography.

The rest of this paper is organized as follows. In Sect. 2, we will introduce some preliminaries of the proposed temporal integration based VCS. In Sect. 3, we present the design of temporal integration based VCS which makes use of high refresh rates display system. In Sect. 4, we show a new construction approach of information security display technology basing on proposed VCS. In Sect. 5, we will shows the experimental results of our proposed temporal integration based VCS and information security display technology. Finally, we conclude and indicate some future work in Sect. 6.

2   Preliminaries

In this section, we introduce some related works on temporal responds characteristics of HVS and VCS.

2.1   Temporal Responds Characteristics: "Persistence of Vision"

According to the psychophysical researches on characteristics of HVS [7]. The luminance perception of VCS always falls behind the changes of light signals which is also know as "persistence of vision". It is an optical illusion that our sensation of light lasts much longer since the light disappears. Since it takes some time for our eye to process the light signals. When the frequency of light signals beyonds the capability of our HVS that can process, the light signals are temporally integrated by retina of our eyes and perceived as a smooth perfectly steady signal. The limitation of the frequency of our HVS is called is called the critical fusion frequency (CFF). Generally, CFF is influenced by many factors. Researches have found that CFF is closely related with the luminance of light signals where there is a famous law indicates the relation.

Ferry-Porter Law [14, 15]

$$f_c = a \lg L_m + b \tag{1}$$

f_c denotes the value of CFF. L_m is the luminance of light signals. a and b are two constant numbers which are usually set as 9.6 and 26.6. According to Ferry Porter law, when the brightness L_m is about 800 cd/m², the CFF of our HVS is about 54 Hz. Hence, the refresh rate of traditional cathode ray tube display is always set to 60 Hz which guarantees the steady of screen signals.

When the frequency of light signals exceeds the CFF of our HVS, the light signals are temporal integrated into a single one with mixing color. Talbot-Plateau Law indicates the relation between the displayed light signals and integrated one.

Talbot-Plateau Law [5, 20]

$$L_m = \frac{1}{T} \int_0^T L(t) \, dt. \tag{2}$$

In Talbot-Plateau Law, T is the period of time where the light signals is perceived as single one. $L(t)$ is the real time-varying luminance taken over one period T. L_m denotes the luminance of integrated signal perceived by HVS in this period.

According to Ferry-Porter Law, the CFF of our HVS is about 54 Hz. For modern stereoscopic display, the refresh rate of is 120 Hz. So it allows two images displayed on screen to be perceived by our HVS without any flicker. If L_1 and L_2 are two light signals of one period T, which last $T/2$ respectively. L_m is the luminance value perceived by our HVS in period T. The relation between L_m and the two light signals is as follows:

$$L_m = \frac{1}{T}(\int_0^{\frac{T}{2}} L_1 \, dt + \int_{\frac{T}{2}}^T L_2 \, dt) = \frac{L_1 + L_2}{2}. \tag{3}$$

Generally, the grayscale space of an image and the luminance space of display are not linear correlated [8,13,23]. When the grayscale value is displayed on screen, the luminance value perceived by our visual system is usually exponential correlated with it. The correlation coefficient which represents the relationship between luminance space and grayscale space of a display is called the Gamma value [26,27].

Denote G_n as the normalized grayscale space, and L_n as the normalized luminance space of a screen. γ is the Gamma value of the screen. Then the luminance space can be derived from grayscale space as follows,

$$L_n = (G_n)^\gamma \tag{4}$$

According to the relationship between luminance space and grayscale space of display, we can easily transform a image from its grayscale view to luminance view and vice versa. If we denote V_G as the grayscale view of a image and V_L as its corresponding luminance view. Both of them are in the range of $[0, 255]$, then the luminance view of the image can be derived as:

$$V_L = 255 \times (\frac{V_G}{255})^\gamma. \tag{5}$$

2.2 Definition of Visual Cryptography Scheme

(k, n)-VCS encrypts a secret image into n shares which are distributed to n participants. Any k out of n participants can recover the secret information. Generally, a (k, n)-VCS is constructed by two collections of $n \times m$ binary share matrices C_0 and C_1. A white (resp. black) pixel is shared by randomly choosing one matrix in C_0 (resp. C_1) and distributing the rows to n participants. Here, we give a formal definition of VCS.

Definition 1 ([12]). For a vector $v \in GF^m(2)$, $w(v)$ denotes its the Hamming weight. Two collections of $n \times m$ Boolean matrices C_0 and C_1 constitute a (k, n)-VCS if the following contrast and security conditions are satisfied:

1. (Contrast) For any matrix S in C_0 (resp. C_1), the vector v derived from the OR (or XOR) operation of any k out of n rows satisfies $w(v) \leq l$ (resp. $w(v) \geq h$), where $0 \leq l < h \leq m$.
2. (Security) For any subset $\{i_1, i_2, \ldots, i_t\} \subset \{1, 2, \ldots, n\}$ with $t < k$, the two collections of $t \times m$ matrices, obtained by restricting each $n \times m$ matrix in C_0 and C_1 to the rows $\{i_1, i_2, \ldots, i_t\}$, contain the same matrices with the same frequencies.

Note: in the above definition, m is called the pixel expansion of VCS. It means each pixel in the secret image is represented as an m-pixel block in the share images.

Due to the spatial responds characteristics of HVS, m-pixel block is perceived by retina of our eye as a single one with mixed grayscale color. $\alpha = \frac{h-l}{m}$ is defined as the contrast of VCS which is recognized as a measurement of visual quality. Larger contrast usually means better visual quality of recovered secret image. Particularly, the collections C_0 and C_1 are able to be constructed from the column permutation of a pair of basis matrices B_0 and B_1.

3 Temporal Integration Based VCS

3.1 Design

Traditional VCS makes uses of the spatial responds characteristics of HVS that our retina integrates spatial adjacent pixels into a single one with mixed color. But the implementation carrier of VCS has limited its application. In this section, we propose a new kind of VCS which utilizes the temporal responds characteristics of HVS. Light signals with frequency exceeds CFF of HVS are integrated by retina and perceived as a single continuous signal. The proposed VCS exploits the refresh rates redundancy of modern display terminal. By alternatively displaying the share images of VCS on a screen with high frequency, we can visually recover the secret information from the screen. Figure 3 shows the principle of temporal integration based VCS.

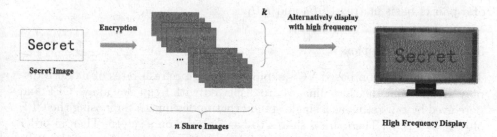

Fig. 3. Principle of Temporal Integration based VCS

The stacking model of our scheme is different from tradition OR and XOR model. Pixels stacking under "persistence of vision" follows Talbot-Plateau Law in the former section which states the color mixing rule of luminance space. Thus, in temporal integration based VCS, pixels of sharing matrix should be based on luminance space which is called *luminance share matrix*. By converting pixels to normalized luminance space, white pixel is denoted as "1" while black pixel is denoted as "0" in luminance share matrix. Supposing there are m pixels (where the amount of white pixels is n) to be temporal integrated by retina, according to the Talbot-Plateau Law, the luminance of perceived pixel is calculated as $\frac{n}{m}$.

Basing on the statements, we give a formal definition of temporal integration based VCS as follows:

Definition 2. Supposing vector v is in the field of rationals. $\sigma^2(v)$ denotes the variance of v. Then the two collections of $n \times m$ Boolean matrices LC_0 and LC_1 constitute a (k, n) temporal integration based VCS if the following contrast and security conditions are satisfied:

1. (Contrast) For any matrix S in LC_0 (resp. LC_1), vector v_0 (resp. v_1) is the temporal integration result of any k out of n rows. Then, relation $\sigma^2(v_0) > \sigma^2(v_1)$ should be satisfied.
2. (Security) For any subset $\{i_1, i_2, \ldots, i_t\} \subset \{1, 2, \ldots, n\}$ with $t < k$, the two collections of $t \times m$ matrices, obtained by restricting each $n \times m$ matrix in LC_0 and LC_1 to the rows $\{i_1, i_2, \ldots, i_t\}$, contain the same matrices with the same frequencies.

Note: The above definition of temporal integration based VCS is similar to Definition 1. But the difference lies in the contrast condition which uses the variance between v_0 and v_1 to distinguish recovered black and white pixels. Actually, the total luminance of vector v_0 is same as v_1. The utilization of variance is due to the fact that our HVS can perceive the luminance variance of the recovered m-pixel block. Thus, $\alpha = \dfrac{\sigma^2(v_0) - \sigma^2(v_1)}{\sigma^2(v_0) + \sigma^2(v_1)}$ can be defined as the contrast of temporal integration based VCS. Larger contrast generally means more apparent difference between recover black and white pixels. Similarly, the collections LC_0 and LC_1 are able to be constructed from the column permutation of a pair of basis matrices LB_0 and LB_1.

3.2   Implementation

Temporal integration based VCS exploits the high refresh rates of modern display system that the share images are displayed with frequency above CFF and perceived by our retina as a single steady continuous image. Supposing the CFF of our HVS is f_c. There are n shares to be displayed on a screen. Then in order to visually recover a steady integrated secret information with no flicker, the frequency of share images displayed on screen should satisfy

$$f_s = n \times f_c. \tag{6}$$

Thus, when implementing temporal integration based VCS, we should select proper display terminal that supports as high refresh rates as f_s. For example, according to Talbot-Plateau Law, our CFF is about 54 Hz. A stereoscopic display with refresh rates of 120 Hz will support 2 out of n temporal integration based VCS in practice. Basing on the analysis above, we give a full construction of the proposed VCS.

Construction 1. Supposing S is the secret image to be shared by participants. f_c is the CFF of our HVS. f_d is the maximum refresh rates of a display system which satisfies $f_d \geq k \times f_c$. Then a k out of n temporal integration based VCS can be implemented as follows:

1. Selecting proper collections of luminance matrices LC_0 and LC_1 that satisfy the conditions of Definition 2.
2. Encrypting S into n share images $s_1,...,s_n$ by collections LC_0 and LC_1.
3. Randomly selecting t share images $s_1,...,s_t$, where $k \leqslant t \leqslant min(\frac{f_d}{f_c}, n)$.
4. Displaying images $s_1,...,s_t$ on the screen alternately at the refresh rate of $t \times f_c$ Hz.
5. Visually recover the secret image S from screen.

4 Application of Temporal Integration Based VCS

Information security display technology [6,24] is proposed to protect screen privacy from unauthorized peeping which also exploits the temporal responds characteristics of HVS and frequency redundancy of modern display. Authorized viewers can get secret information from display terminal with the help of synchronized glasses, while unauthorized viewers only see a uniform grayscale or meaningful image which functions as a mask of secret information. The technology is confirmed to solve the visible space problem of display terminal completely since unauthorized viewers get nothing from any position while the visible space of authorized ones is not affected. However, the technology can't prevent unauthorized photography in practice because of there are only two images alternatively displayed on screen. The sensor of camera samples the optical signals periodically which captures the secret information and makes it visible for unauthorized viewers.

In this section, we propose a new approach of information security display technology that can prevent unauthorized photography by encrypting the secret information with temporal integration based VCS. Figure 4 shows the principle of our approach. For a secret information, we first invert its the luminance and get an auxiliary image. Then we encrypt the secret and auxiliary images by temporal integration based VCS and generate corresponding share images which will be integrated as a randomly looking image on high frequency display terminal. In order to prevent information disclosure caused by the unauthorized photography, we can mix the sequence of shares images generated by secret and auxiliary images. Thus, even if the sensor of camera can sample the share images periodically, the secret information is secure if the sequence of shares generated by secret image is safe. Only authorized viewers can visually recover the secret information by active shutter glasses which is synchronized with the sequence of shares generated by secret image. More precisely, we give a formal construction of our proposed information security technology in detail.

Construction 2. Supposing S is the secret information prepared for authorized viewers. Then the information security display system that can prevent unauthorized photography is constructed as follows:

1. Generating an auxiliary image A by inverting the luminance of secret image S.
2. Encrypting S by temporal integration based VCS and generating n share images $(s_1,...,s_n)$.

414   W. Wang et al.

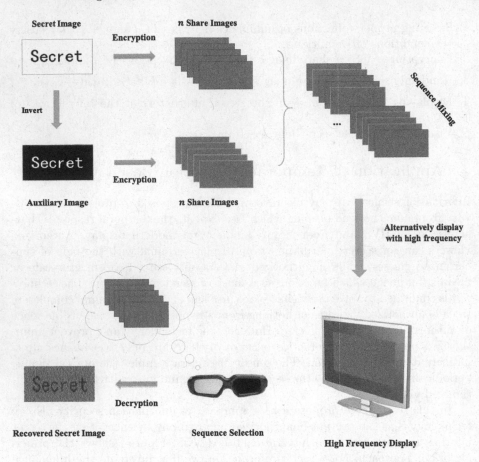

Fig. 4. An information security display technology basing on temporal integration VCS.

3. Encrypting A by temporal integration based VCS and generating n share images $(a_1, ..., a_n)$.
4. Mixing the sequence of share images $(s_1, ..., s_n, a_1, ..., a_n)$ where position of $(s_1, ..., s_n)$ are set to $(p_1, ..., p_n)$.
5. Displaying the share images on screen alternately with the mixed sequence of former step at high refresh rates.
6. Programing the state of active shutter glasses to allow the through of light at position $(p_1, ..., p_n)$ which synchronize with the shares generated by secret information.
7. Visually recover the secret image S from screen with the help of synchronized glasses.

5   Experimental Results

In this section, we implement and show experimental results of temporal integration based VCS and the constructed information security display system to evaluate the effectiveness of our work. Here, we use $NEC^{®}L102W+$ projector as the display system which works at the refresh rate of 120 Hz. Besides, we use mobile phone Huawei P9 to capture the experimental results which is confirmed to simulate the characteristics of HVS well.

5.1   Experiment on Construction 1

In this experiment, we construct an 2 out of 2 temporal integration based VCS and implement the scheme on $NEC^{®}L102W+$ projector to show the effectiveness.

First, we construct two collections of 2×2 luminance share matrices LC_0 and LC_1 by permuting the columns of a pair of luminance basis matrices $LB_0 = \begin{pmatrix} 1 & 1 & 0 & 0 \\ 1 & 1 & 0 & 0 \end{pmatrix}$ and $LB_1 = \begin{pmatrix} 1 & 1 & 0 & 0 \\ 0 & 0 & 1 & 1 \end{pmatrix}$. According to Talbot-Plateau Law, the temporal integration results of two rows of LB_0 and LB_1 are $(1,1,0,0)$ and $(\frac{1}{2}, \frac{1}{2}, \frac{1}{2}, \frac{1}{2})$. Variance of the results are $\frac{1}{4}$ and 0. Thus, LC_0 and LC_1 are effective temporal integration based VCS since the contrast and security conditions are satisfied. Then we encrypt the secret image with LC_0 and LC_1. Figure 5 shows the results of constructed 2 out of 2 temporal integration based VCS. (a) is the secret image to be shared by public; (c) and (d) are generated share images; (b) is the recovered secret image implemented by alternatively displaying share images (c) and (d) at refresh rates of 120 Hz which is captured by Huawei P9 with exposure time $\frac{1}{30}$ s.

5.2   Experiment on Construction 2

In this experiment, we implement the proposed information security display technology by exploiting the constructed 2 out of 2 temporal integration VCS in former experiment. Secret image and luminance inverted auxiliary image are encrypted into share images (s_1, s_2) and (a_1, a_2) respectively. The four share images are displayed with sequence (s_1, a_1, s_2, a_2). The synchronized glasses can split the share images (s_1, s_2) and (a_1, a_2) precisely. Figure 6 shows the experimental results of *Construction 2* in detail. (a) is the secret image to be hided on screen; (b) is the generated auxiliary image; (c) is the photography effect captured by Huawei P9 with exposure time $\frac{1}{100}$ s; (d) is the visually recovered secret image with synchronized glasses.

(a) Secret image

(b) Recovered secret image

(c) Share image 1

(d) Share image 2

Fig. 5. Results of temporal integration based VCS.

(a) Secret image

(b) Auxiliary image

(c) Photography effect

(d) Recovered secret information

Fig. 6. Results of proposed information security display technology.

6   Conclusion and Future Work

In this paper, we proposed a new kind of VCS which is implemented on the modern display terminal of high refresh rates. The proposed VCS makes use of the temporal responds characteristics of HVS that light signals are temporal integrated into a single steady continuous one if the frequency exceeds our CFF. Applications of traditional OR and XOR based VCS are seriously limited by the implementation carrier in practice. But our method breaks through the limitation since it can be easily implemented on modern display terminals which is widely used in public nowadays. Besides, we further implement an information security display technology basing on the proposed temporal integration based VCS. The sequence of share images generated by secret image is actually a key to the secret. Only authorized viewers can recover the secret information with the help of synchronized glass. Unauthorized viewers with naked eye or camera get nothing about the secret information since they can't extract the shares of secret image precisely. Thus, our approach can effectively prevent unauthorized photography.

The current implementations of temporal integration based VCS and information security display system are prototypes that we designed to demonstrate the effectiveness. As such, there are still some evident deficiencies in practice. First, the implementations have relatively high requirement on the refresh rates of display terminal. Generally, a stereoscopic display of 120 Hz only supports two images to be integrated by retina without any flicker. But recent years, display technologies have got substantial development with the progress of optoelectronic technique. The refresh rates of display terminal may be improved to 480 Hz which allows the temporal integration of eight secret images. Thus the limitation of refresh rates may be alleviated. Second, the proposed information security display technology encrypts the secret image into several share images. The active shutter glasses are required to synchronize with the share images that have particular sequence. Generally for most glasses in market, the requirement is hard to achieve. But recently, programmable active shutter glasses are already available in public applications [2,19] which help to solve the synchronization problem in the future. We believe that, as future work, various implementations can be developed to solve the deficiencies in temporal integration based VCS and information security display technology.

Acknowledgments. Many thanks to the anonymous reviewers for their valuable comments to improve our work. This work was supported by the National Key R&D Program of China with No. 2016YFB0800100, NSFC No. 61671448 and the Scientific Research Project of Beijing Municipal Educational Committee Grant No. 71E1610972.

References

1. Ateniese, G., Blundo, C., De Santis, A., Stinson, D.R.: Visual cryptography for general access structures. Inf. Comput. **129**(2), 86–106 (1996)
2. BenEzra, O., Herzog, R., Cohen, E., Karshai, I., BenEzra, D.: Liquid crystal glasses: feasibility and safety of a new modality for treating amblyopia. Arch. Ophthalmol. **125**(4), 580–581 (2007)
3. Biham, E., Itzkovitz, A.: Visual cryptography with polarization (1998)
4. Blundo, C., De Santis, A., Stinson, D.R.: On the contrast in visual cryptography schemes. J. Cryptol. **12**(4), 261–289 (1999)
5. Galifret, Y.: Visual persistence and cinema? Comptes Rendus Biologies **329**(5), 369–385 (2006)
6. Gao, Z., Zhai, G., Min, X.: Information security display system based on temporal psychovisual modulation. In: 2014 IEEE International Symposium on Circuits and Systems (ISCAS), pp. 449–452. IEEE (2014)
7. Kalloniatis, M., Luu, C.: Temporal resolution. www.webvision.med.utah.edu/temporal.html
8. Lee, P.-M., Chen, H.-Y.: Adjustable gamma correction circuit for TFT LCD. In: 2005 IEEE International Symposium on Circuits and Systems, pp. 780–783. IEEE (2005)
9. Liu, F., Wu, C.: Optimal XOR based (2, n)-visual cryptography schemes. In: International Workshop on Digital Watermarking, pp. 333–349. Springer, Heidelberg (2014)
10. Liu, F., Wu, C., Qian, L., et al.: Improving the visual quality of size invariant visual cryptography scheme. J. Vis. Commun. Image Representation **23**(2), 331–342 (2012)
11. Liu, F., Yan, W.Q.: Visual Cryptography for Image Processing and Security, vol. 2. Springer, New York (2014)
12. Naor, M., Shamir, A.: Visual cryptography. In: Santis, A. (ed.) EUROCRYPT 1994. LNCS, vol. 950, pp. 1–12. Springer, Heidelberg (1995). doi:10.1007/BFb0053419
13. Parraga, C.A., Roca-Vila, J., Karatzas, D., Wuerger, S.M.: Limitations of visual gamma corrections in LCD displays. Displays **35**(5), 227–239 (2014)
14. Porter, T.: Contributions to the study of flicker, paper iii. Proc. R. Soc. London Ser. A Containing Papers Math. Phys. Charact. **86**(590), 495–513 (1912)
15. Porter, T.C.: Contributions to the study of flicker. Paper ii. Proc. R. Soc. London **70**(459–466), 313–329 (1902)
16. Shi, L., Yu, B.: Optimization of XOR visual cryptography scheme. In: 2011 International Conference on Computer Science and Network Technology (ICCSNT), vol. 1, pp. 297–301. IEEE (2011)
17. Shyu, S.J., Chen, M.C.: Optimum pixel expansions for threshold visual secret sharing schemes. IEEE Trans. Inf. Forensics Secur. **6**(3), 960–969 (2011)
18. Shyu, S.J., Jiang, H.-W.: General constructions for threshold multiple-secret visual cryptographic schemes. IEEE Trans. Inf. Forensics Secur. **8**(5), 733–743 (2013)
19. Spierer, A., Raz, J., BenEzra, O., Herzog, R., Cohen, E., Karshai, I., BenEzra, D.: Treating amblyopia with liquid crystal glasses: a pilot study. Invest. Ophthalmol. Vis. Sci. **51**(7), 3395–3398 (2010)
20. Talbot, H.F.: Experiments on light. Lond. Edinb. Philos. Mag. J. Sci. **5**(29), 321–334 (1834)

21. Tuyls, P., Hollmann, H., Lint, H., Tolhuizen, L.: A polarisation based visual crypto system and its secret sharing schemes (2002)
22. Tuyls, P., Hollmann, H.D., Lint, J.V., Tolhuizen, L.: XOR-based visual cryptography schemes. Des. Codes Crypt. **37**(1), 169–186 (2005)
23. Walton, H.G., Brownlow, M., Lock, J., Rahal, M., Zebedee, P.: LCD gamma correction by nonlinear digital-to-analogue converter. In: Electronic Imaging 2003, pp. 170–178. International Society for Optics and Photonics (2003)
24. Wang, W., Liu, F., Guo, T., Ren, Y., Shen, G.: Information security display technology with multi-view effect. In: Shi, Y.Q., Kim, H.J., Perez-Gonzalez, F., Liu, F. (eds.) IWDW 2016. LNCS, vol. 10082, pp. 198–208. Springer, Cham (2017). doi:10.1007/978-3-319-53465-7_15
25. Wang, W., Liu, F., Yan, W., Shen, G., Guo, T.: An improved aspect ratio invariant visual cryptography scheme with flexible pixel expansion. In: Shi, Y.-Q., Kim, H.J., Pérez-González, F., Echizen, I. (eds.) IWDW 2015. LNCS, vol. 9569, pp. 418–432. Springer, Cham (2016). doi:10.1007/978-3-319-31960-5_34
26. Woo, J.-H., Lee, J.-G., Jun, Y.-H., Kong, B.-S.: Accurate quadruple-gamma-curve correction for line inversion-based mobile tft-lcd driver ics. IEEE Transactions on Consumer Electronics **59**(3), 443–451 (2013)
27. Xiao, K., Fu, C., Karatzas, D., Wuerger, S.: Visual gamma correction for LCD displays. Displays **32**(1), 17–23 (2011)
28. Yang, C.-N., Wang, D.-S.: Property analysis of XOR-based visual cryptography. IEEE Trans. Circ. Syst. Video Technol. **24**(2), 189–197 (2014)

Author Index

Printed in the United States
By Bookmasters